The Ultimate Challenge:

Coping with Death, Dying, and Bereavement

The Ultimate Challenge:
Coping with Death, Dying, and Bereavement

Marilyn Hadad

Ryerson University

NELSON EDUCATION

NELSON / EDUCATION

The Ultimate Challenge: Coping with Death, Dying, and Bereavement

Marilyn Hadad

Associate Vice President, Editorial Director:
Evelyn Veitch

Editor-in-Chief, Higher Education:
Anne Williams

Executive Editor:
Cara Yarzab

Marketing Manager:
Lenore Taylor-Atkins

Developmental Editor:
Sandy Matos

Permissions Coordinator:
Sheila Hall

Content Production Manager:
Susan Wong

Production Service:
ICC Macmillan Inc.

Copy Editor:
Dawn Hunter

Proofreader:
Dianne Fowlie

Indexer:
Maura Brown

Manufacturing Coordinator:
Loretta Lee

Design Director:
Ken Phipps

Managing Designer:
Katherine Strain

Interior Design:
Tammy Gay

Cover Design:
Dianna Little

Cover Image:
"Relatives" by Roy Thomas, acrylic on canvas. "The water spirits inspire us to visit our relatives and also to meet other people from different ways of life." — © Roy Thomas
http://www.ahnisnabae-art.com

Compositor:
ICC Macmillan Inc.

Printer:
Edwards Brothers

Library and Archives Canada Cataloguing in Publication Data

Hadad, Marilyn, 1950- The ultimate challenge : coping with death, dying and bereavement / Marilyn Hadad. — 1st ed.

Includes bibliographical references and indexes.

ISBN 978-0-17-610433-7

1. Death—Social aspects. 2. Bereavement. I. Title.

HQ1073.H33 2009 306.9
C2007-903812-3

10-digit: 0-17-610433-X
13-digit: 978-0-17-610433-7

I have been singularly fortunate in my life to have been given the gift of close friends. In particular, the female friends I have made over the years have graced me with their humour, support, compassion, and wisdom. It is to these luminous women that I dedicate this book. In alphabetical order,

Julia Brandwin-Glait

Wendy Cole

Patricia Comley

Milana Drobner

Cate Elliott

Susan Keen

Maureen Reed

Dana Williams

and, as always, my treasured cousin, Kathleen Bryant

CONTENTS

CHAPTER 3 RELIGIOUS AND CROSS-CULTURAL ATTITUDES TOWARD DEATH 25

For many years Western society engaged in a denial of death, fuelled by the miracles of modern medicine and fuelled by society's desire to ignore the negative and unpleasant details of life. In the past few decades, however, greater awareness has emerged of the pain confronted by all individuals when they or one of their loved ones receives a diagnosis of a potentially life-ending disease and when a loved one dies. This change has many possible explanations, but what is important is the effect that this change has had. Today, books are written that deal with these topics, and college and university courses have been created to impart greater understanding of the impact of this "ultimate challenge" on all of us.

The academic courses that are delivered today serve several purposes: they exist to educate those who have not confronted the possibility of death in themselves or others; they serve to allow those who have been touched by death and bereavement to understand and deal with their emotions and the practical changes in their lives more effectively; and they act as guides for both laypeople and professionals in their interactions with those who are dying or who face bereavement. Today, among the many academic textbooks in the area, the most widely used ones are effective and insightful. Although they differ from one another in many respects, they all serve their function admirably. From a Canadian academic perspective, however, these books also share one glaring problem: they are all based on the American experience.

Of course, commonality exists across cultures regarding the pain felt by impending death and bereavement, but the definite cultural differences should not be ignored. The Canadian experience, although similar in many ways to the American experience, has certain differences that need to be addressed when presenting this material to a Canadian audience. For example, the recent massacre of students and others at Virginia Polytechnic Institute on April 16, 2007, reminded Canadians of the similar massacre at Montreal's École Polytechnique on December 6, 1989, but Canadians were also aware that the number of innocent people killed in the American calamity far exceeded those in Canada (14 in Canada, 32 in the United States). The tragedy of the destruction of the World Trade Center in New York in 2001 brought shock and sorrow to the world; however, the Canadian reaction (like that of many other nations) also contained a little relief that the United States was the target, not Canada. Newspapers in Canada ran the headline "Could It Happen Here?" This reaction was distinctly different from the American one, where headlines said, "It *Did* Happen Here." Random death from violence is becoming of greater concern in Canada, but it has not yet reached the high levels of many American cities. Violent death by nature also plays a larger role in the American consciousness than it does in Canada, as was seen in the devastation of the American southern coast by Hurricanes Katrina and Wilma.

Another example of the difference between Canada and the United States is the case of suicide, especially among the young. Canada has been confronted with the heartbreak of a rash of suicides among children in the Native community of Davis Inlet, a situation that has brought concern and even shame to our national awareness. A further illustration of differences can be derived from the different cultural mix in Canada and the United States: although American texts are (rightly) concerned with the African-American and Hispanic-American experiences of death, dying, and bereavement, these cultural divisions have far less meaning in Canada. Canada, as the proudly pluralistic mosaic, recognizes cultural differences on a less generalized level. Thus, in Canada, an examination of the cross-cultural differences needs to inspect the belief systems of different religions and different cultures on a smaller scale (e.g., the African-Canadian and the Caribbean-Canadian experiences differ from each other and cannot be examined together under one heading).

This book, *The Ultimate Challenge: Coping with Death, Dying, and Bereavement,* presents the topic from a Canadian perspective. Thus, some of the material is in common with the existing textbooks when this material reflects phenomena common to all peoples. Other material presents the experience of death, dying, and bereavement within the Canadian context, including Canadian demographics and examples taken from events within Canada. The balance of theoretical, empirical, and practical material makes the book appropriate for students who want a basic knowledge of the area and for students who are training in mental health or medical areas in which such knowledge will have immediate applications. The area of death, dying, and bereavement is multi-disciplinary, and this book draws on material from the different disciplines: psychology, sociology, anthropology, economics, history, political science, literature, and the arts. Issues and concepts are illustrated with newspaper items and case studies, increasing the immediate relevance of the material presented.

It would have been easy to write a book on the topic of death, dying, and bereavement that was more than seven hundred pages long, but such a book would be far too long to be appropriate for courses that are generally only one semester long, so decisions had to be made about what to include and what to exclude in *The Ultimate Challenge*. The decisions were often difficult, and they reflect my own preferences and experiences in teaching such a course. I hope that students and instructors will be motivated by what I have included to further explore other aspects of the end-of-life experience. Below is an outline of what the chapters of this book contain.

CHAPTER 1: THE CHALLENGE OF DEATH

Chapter 1 discusses the history of the way death has been regarded and portrayed, from ancient times to the present. Included is a brief history of palliative care and the need for education in this area. The Leming Fear of Death Scale is also included in this chapter in order for readers to gauge their own attitudes toward end-of-life issues before going on to read the rest of the book.

CHAPTER 2: CONTEMPORARY ATTITUDES TOWARD DEATH

Chapter 2 focuses on contemporary Canadian attitudes toward end-of-life issues, including the way attitudes are formed and the role of the media in shaping attitudes. A discussion of how grief and bereavement are handled in the workplace serves as an example of the prevailing attitudes and expectations surrounding death, dying, and bereavement.

CHAPTER 3: RELIGIOUS AND CROSS-CULTURAL ATTITUDES TOWARD DEATH

In Chapter 3, the beliefs of several religions are discussed, focusing on these religions' views of death and the afterlife. Several cross-cultural attitudes regarding death and bereavement are described, highlighting the need for cultural sensitivity in this multi-cultural country.

CHAPTER 4: END-OF-LIFE RITUALS

Following the description of different religious and cultural beliefs about death, dying, and bereavement in Chapter 3, Chapter 4 describes how these views are manifested in end-of-life rituals. Included in this discussion are the functions of funerals and an evaluation of their effectiveness in comforting people who are bereaved.

CHAPTER 5: GRIEF AND BEREAVEMENT

Chapter 5 describes the common emotional, cognitive, and behavioural manifestations of grief. Several theoretical frameworks for understanding these reactions are presented, with an eye to recognizing the complexity of reaction to loss and the complementary nature of different models of grief and bereavement.

CHAPTER 6: DEATH AND THE CHILD

In Chapter 6, the ways children of different ages conceive of death are described, along with a description of how children at various ages manifest their grief. Special attention is paid to the responses of children who have lost a parent or sibling. Additionally, Chapter 6 contains information about the feelings of dying children.

CHAPTER 7: DEATH AND THE ADULT

Chapter 7 examines some of the common experiences of adults, through loss of a spouse, a child, a sibling, or a parent, as well as the grief felt in cases of miscarriage, still-birth, and abortion. Also discussed are the responses of adults when they are given the diagnosis of a terminal illness.

CHAPTER 8: DEATH AND THE SENIOR ADULT

Chapter 8 concentrates on the reactions of seniors to the loss of a loved one. An integral part of this chapter is a discussion of older people's attitudes toward death and what they say they need and want as their own end of life approaches.

CHAPTER 9: SUICIDE

Chapter 9 contains an exploration of what leads people to takes their own lives, what the risk factors are, and the theoretical models of suicide that can shed some light on this tragedy. Particular attention is paid to suicides among seniors, adolescents, and Canadian Native Peoples.

CHAPTER 10: DEATH AND TRAUMA: WHEN MOURNING IS MORE DIFFICULT

Chapter 10 discusses the various types of complicated grief, noting the special problems of trying to deal with the loss of a loved one who has died through traumatic circumstances, such as homicide. In addition, disenfranchised grief is discussed, noting the difficulty of coping with a loss when society is less supportive that is warranted.

CHAPTER 11: END-OF-LIFE CARE

Chapter 11 describes the experience of death in such settings as home, hospital, and hospice. It also discusses how decisions are made regarding where a person will die and what kind of care he or she will receive. Special attention is paid to the stress felt by people involved in the care of dying patients and the stress felt by dying people themselves.

CHAPTER 12: HOW TO HELP

Chapter 12 is a practical chapter that suggests ways for the individual, the institution, and society to help people of various ages cope with their bereavement or their imminent deaths.

CHAPTER 13: MAKING MEANING

One important way that dying people have of coping with their impending deaths, and one important way of dealing with the death of a loved one, is in finding meaning for the individual's life and the end of life. Chapter 13 reviews the role of making meaning in coping with loss and discusses various ways of making meaning, such as storytelling. The important role of religion in this endeavour is also discussed.

CHAPTER 14: ETHICAL AND LEGAL ISSUES AT THE END OF LIFE

Chapter 14 discusses the controversial issues of the definition of death, advance directives, organ donation, euthanasia, and physician-assisted suicide. Arguments on both sides of the debates are presented, as is the present state of the law in Canada on these issues.

CHAPTER 15: THE FUTURE

The final chapter in this book outlines the various issues surrounding end-of-life care that need to be addressed in Canada. Special attention is paid to the increasing need for palliative care resources in the future.

On a personal note, I have spent a year immersed in the writing of this book on death, dying, and bereavement, an endeavour that many friends and colleagues found a "depressing" way to spend a sabbatical. But there is a difference between sadness and depression. Listening to stories of bereavement and reading the literature in this area often saddened me, and the process has not always been easy. I have come to the conclusion that writing such a book as this and, I think, reading a book like this changes us. I know I have been changed—my own issues have been confronted and my understanding and compassion have deepened, as have my profound admiration for those people who work in the field of end-of-life care and my respect for you who have the courage to deal with your own loss and to learn more about the losses that others bear. I hope this book helps.

ACKNOWLEDGMENTS

The Ultimate Challenge was born out of my frustration with teaching a course about death, dying, and bereavement in a Canadian university without having Canadian material in available textbooks. My frustration was voiced to part of the dynamic Nelson team and before I knew it, a contract was signed and I took a sabbatical from my position as associate professor in the psychology department at Ryerson University in Toronto to begin work. At Nelson, the associate vice-president and editorial director, and amazing human being, Evelyn Veitch, headed and inspired the team that worked with me: managing developmental editor Alwynn Pinard; executive editor Cara Yarzab (who selected the wonderful cover for this book); developmental editor Sandy Matos, who held my hand and smoothed the way for my work with support and humour on a continual basis; and Dawn Hunter, copy editor, who became a rich and inspiring source of ideas and information in addition to her copy editing. To these people, as well as to the rest of the Nelson team, I extend my profoundest thanks. No author was ever more fortunate than I have been in my work with Nelson, because of the professionalism, passion, and caring of this wonderful group of people.

A special note of thanks must go to my friend and colleague Julia Brandwin-Glait who, despite her busy schedule as an instructor at Nova Scotia Community College, read every word I wrote and made insightful and incredibly useful comments all along the way. Her tireless work, her support, and her front porch made spending a year immersed in a difficult topic possible.

Finally, I have been blessed with reviewers of the drafts of this book who were unfailingly constructive and helpful. In many ways, I feel that they have been partners in this enterprise, and I extend to them my deepest appreciation:

Brenda Bennett, *George Brown College*

Anne Marie Dalton, *Saint Mary's University*

Jennifer Dimoff, *Mount Saint Vincent University*

Andrew Feron, M.S.W., R.S.W., *Parkwood Hospital/St. Joseph's Health Care London*

Dr. Mary Theresa Howard, *University of Ottawa*

Darcy Nichols, *University of Western Ontario*

ABOUT THE AUTHOR

Marilyn Hadad is an associate professor at Ryerson University, specializing in issues surrounding death, dying, and bereavement; personal growth; and other areas of adjustment. She received her B.Sc. from the University of Toronto and her M.A. and Ph.D. from Queen's University in Kingston, Ontario. She is the coauthor, with Ryerson Professor William Glassman, of the one-semester introductory psychology textbook *Approaches to Psychology*, fourth edition, Open University Press, and is presently working on the fifth edition of that textbook. She is also coauthor, with Ryerson Associate Professor Maureen Reed, of the textbook *The Post-Secondary Learning Experience*, published by Nelson, to help students handle, enjoy, and prosper in their postsecondary education. In addition, she has authored the custom publication manuscript *Models of Personal Growth* for her popular and dynamic course of the same name. When not teaching, conducting research, serving on committees, writing, or reviewing textbooks and articles, Marilyn enjoys Canada's art scene and her calico cat, Peaches.

ABOUT THE ARTIST

ROY THOMAS 1949–2004

WOODLAND OJIBWA ARTIST

Born in 1949, Roy Thomas was an Ahnisnabae-born Ojibwa artist who devoted himself to learning the history and teachings of his people. Thomas's paintings have a quality that commands attention without overwhelming the viewer. His oeuvre reveals an illuminating simplicity—the stroke of his paintbrush was comparable to a conversation with Roy. Roy's work transcends the Ojibwa Woodland style of his predecessors. His paintings incorporate elements of Ojibwa traditions, legends, and realistic depictions of Native life. Roy often worked with artistically gifted people of various backgrounds and his paintings reflect the ideas he drew from these experiences.

Roy devoted a great deal of time to learning about the ways of his people, their teachings, and the ways of nature. Although he was basically a self-taught artist, Roy was guided by the memories of his grandparents, who had taught him what to paint. At an early age Roy could see the stories his grandparents told him. His grandparents recognized his talent and encouraged him to draw what he seen through their stories.

The first time he drew, Roy used his finger and drew on his grandmother's back as she told him stories. Eventually, Roy used a stick on the ground, in the sand, in the snow banks, and in the dark with the end lit. Roy would tell his grandparents at the time that these drawings would disappear. His grandparents told him, "One day, my grandson, these drawings will come back to you; what is yours is never gone away forever." This was the beginning of Roy Thomas the Ahnisnabae artist.

Roy was a painter in the Ojibwa Woodland style. This style uses symbolisms and imagery inspired by the pictographs that Roy had also seen as a child. The presence of the pictographs and other artists also inspired Roy. The spirit of art and his elders taught him what to paint. He painted the visions of the teachings of his people for his family, for the community, and for his nation.

During his 35-plus years of painting, Roy presented his art in numerous one-man shows in Canada and the United States. He participated in a number of group shows nationally and internationally. His work is found in many national and international collections, including the Art Gallery of Ontario, Toronto, Ontario; Esso Resources, Edmonton, Alberta; Foreign Affairs and International Trade (Canada); McMichael Canadian Art Collection, Kleinburg, Ontario; the Royal Ontario Museum, Toronto, Ontario; the National Museum of Man, Ottawa, Ontario; Thunder Bay Art Gallery, Thunder Bay, Ontario; Inuit Gallery, Mannheim, Germany; and the National Gallery of Ethnology, Osaka, Japan.

The Challenge of Death

Dawson College

▶ At 12:41 p.m. on September 13, 2006, Kimveer Gill, dressed in a black military trench coat, entered Dawson College in Montreal. He shot and killed 1 student, 18-year-old Anastasia De Sousa, and injured 19 others, 8 critically, in a rampage that extended outside the school. After being shot in the arm by police, Gill committed suicide by shooting himself in the head. A note found on Gill said that the shootings and his suicide were premeditated. Students and faculty who had been evacuated from Dawson College were given emergency trauma support by the Dawson Student Union, with the aid of the Concordia University Student Union. Classes were cancelled until September 17, and the school administrators invited all students to an open house on September 18 to meet with staff and faculty for information and support. That day, a shrine of flowers and notes surrounded the entrance that Gill had used. Students waited until 12:41 p.m. to enter the school by this entrance. Few spoke; onlookers cheered and applauded. Many students wore pink, Anastasia De Sousa's favourite colour.

Death is always with us. Wherever we turn, we see the cycle of life. Even our own bodies give us signs of death, if we choose to interpret them in that way. For example, our skin sloughs off in tiny flakes all the time (scratch your arm and see what is underneath your fingernail). We can see this process as part of the renewal of our bodies, or we can regard it as the death of organic matter. So too can we see the final death of our bodies as part of the cycle of life, leading to a renewal in an afterlife, or, at the other extreme, as the final end of what has never been more than biological material. However we choose to regard it, death is a part of us—yet it is a part that is often avoided as if it did not exist. "Don't be so morbid," some people say when the topic of death arises, as if by not talking about it, it will never come.

Historically, interest in the area of death, dying, and bereavement, called **thanatology,** has been sporadic. Some ages and societies have made death a cultural centrepiece, while others have regarded it as a taboo topic. This book examines this universal phenomenon to provide you with more understanding. To begin, it is useful to know how those who came before us portrayed death.

A HISTORY OF THE PORTRAYAL OF DEATH

The Ancient Perspective

Early literature suggested that death is not a natural outcome of life, but a curse imposed on humankind by a vengeful power in retribution for humankind's wrongdoing. In the Bible's Book of Genesis, Chapter 3 (King James Version), the story of the first man and woman, Adam and Eve, is told to explain the origins of death and suffering. God gave Adam and Eve a perfect place to live, the Garden of Eden. It had but one stricture imposed on it: they should not eat the fruit of the Tree of Knowledge. Eve was tempted by the Devil to break this one restriction; she ate the fruit and then induced Adam to do the same. God discovered their transgression and, in anger and disappointment, punished them by driving them out of the garden into a world where they would be masters, but they would know toil, pain, and, finally, death.

Other early myths portray death more as an accident than as a punishment. Davies (2005) reviewed the work of Sir James Frazer in his classification of early myths. Sir James found four categories that the majority of death-origin myths fit into:

1. *The two messengers.* In this type of tale, prevalent in Africa, God sends two animal messengers to humankind. The first is charged with God's message that human beings will not die. The second must deliver the message that human beings will die. Unfortunately for humankind, the second messenger is swifter than the first, so the only message received, and the one that humankind must endure, is that human beings will eventually die.

2. *The waxing and waning moon.* In these tales, all people lived, died, and then lived again in cycles, like the waxing and waning of the moon. But in some way (the details vary among cultures) human beings lost this ability, leaving only the moon to remind them of their former abilities. The Hindu beliefs in the rebirth of the soul fit into this category: the Yogic spiritual tradition of the Vedas, the earliest dating back to 2500 B.C.E., tells of the death of the body but the rebirth of the soul in a new body (Eliade, 1969; Frager & Fadiman, 1998).

3. *The serpent and his cast skin.* The third category is typified by a Melanesian myth in which God, who hated snakes, sent a messenger to tell people to shed their skins in renewal and so live eternally. The messenger was also directed to tell snakes to shed their skins and die. The messenger, however, made an error and reversed the messages so that fate was sealed: snakes live "forever" and human beings die.

4. *The banana tree.* In this category, people ask God for something other than what has been given to them. In the version told in the Celebes, the people ask for a change from the food that God has been giving them, and God lets down a stone on a rope. The people protest, and God next lets down a banana on a rope, which the people receive gladly. But God tells them that, presumably in punishment for their demands, they will henceforth be like the banana tree and die after they have produced their own fruit, children.

Box 1.1 illustrates the accidental origin of death that Frazer discusses by telling a traditional Aboriginal story.

That death occasions pain and suffering for those left behind is inherent in the myths and is shown particularly clearly in the earliest literature in existence, the ancient Babylonian epic of Gilgamesh, found in the library of a seventh-century B.C.E. king and probably going back, in oral form, to the third millennium B.C.E. Gilgamesh, who is part god, and his friend Enkidu conquered and killed many people and animals. The gods decreed that for their conquests, one of them must die. Enkidu was chosen to die, and Gilgamesh mourned bitterly, adding he had developed a fear of death. He

The traditional story of the origin of death among the Blackfoot of Alberta, Saskatchewan, and the Great Plains in the northern part of the United States refers to the Creator, Old Man, who fashioned the first woman and child out of clay. When they began to move, he took them to the river, where they asked him what this walking, breathing, eating state was.

"It is life," he answered. "Before you were lumps of clay and now you are alive."

"When we were lumps of clay, were we not alive?" they asked.

"No," he responded. "You were dead; when you are not alive you are dead."

Then they asked, "Will we always be alive or will we go back to being dead someday?"

The Old Man thought for a while and finally answered, "I hadn't thought about that. Let's see—we'll take this buffalo chip and throw it in the water. If it floats, then people will die, but they will come back to life in four days."

The woman, who was too new to have any knowledge of the world, said no. "The buffalo chip will dissolve in the water. Throw in a stone that won't dissolve. If it floats, we will live forever, but if it sinks, then we'll die." So she threw the stone in the water where it promptly sank.

The Old Man sighed and said, "It was your choice. Now people will die."

Source: Adapted from Ortiz and Erdoes (1996).

then begins a journey in search of someone who can tell him how to live eternally (Davies, 2005).

Conviction of an afterlife was evident in the belief system of ancient Egypt (circa 2500 B.C.E.). The individual was thought to have at least four types of soul, which would live on in various ways after the death of the body. The great tombs of Egypt, the Pyramids, stand as a tribute to the Egyptian belief in immortality, providing a dwelling and a place to store items (including murdered servants) needed for life after death. The rulers and the wealthy also had their bodies mummified, preserved from decay, underscoring this belief (Taylor, 2002). Death was not an end but a transition to another plane of existence.

The ancient Greeks regarded death as a passage into an afterlife as well, but that afterlife was not pleasant, at least according to Homer in *The Odyssey* (Homer, trans. 1967), a story dating from perhaps 1000 B.C.E.: Odysseus travels to the land of the dead where he meets dead heroes and friends and relatives, who wish for the joys of an earthly existence. Plato paints a picture in *The Republic* (about 370 B.C.E.; trans. 2003) of an afterlife with two degrees of hell and two degrees of heaven. After spending a thousand years in one of these realms, the individual may choose to be reborn in human or animal form.

The ancient Israelites, before about 600 B.C.E., regarded death as a transition to a shadowy underworld where life went on in a limited fashion. After 600 B.C.E, when the belief in monotheism developed, the belief in the underworld, Sheol, continued. Here existence was marginal and the dead were isolated from living people and from God. From the Babylonian captivity (586 B.C.E.) to about the fourth century B.C.E., the concept of the afterlife was refined: death still meant a transition to Sheol, but now, people who had been good and faithful were expected to be resurrected to live for another five hundred years. Then they died again and remained dead for eternity. Since death presaged an unpleasant condition, virtuous people were thought to live very long lives (e.g., Methuselah) and have many children.

After the invasion of Palestine by Alexander the Great in 332 B.C.E., the belief changed to the idea that all the dead will be judged by God and sent to an eternal reward or an eternal punishment (Robinson, 2004). As time went on, these beliefs became a less important part of Judaism as emphasis was placed on the present rather than the future and on the importance of living a virtuous life, although support remains for various levels of belief in an afterlife.

The advent of Christianity in the first century C.E. brought about a strong belief in death leading to an afterlife to be determined by the individual's deeds and beliefs while living. This belief was shared by Islam, which is generally considered to have begun in 622 C.E. Both Christianity and Islam see death as the ending of only life on earth; life eternal after death is a cornerstone in the belief systems of both these religions.

The Classification of Philippe Ariès

Thus far, we examined conceptions of death in terms of the prevalent religious beliefs of the time and culture, because, until quite recently, there was little separation of church and state; that is, religious life was dominant in the ruling of a culture, with leaders often functioning in both secular and religious domains. Social historian Philippe Ariès (2004) examined the history of Western culture's view of death from a more psychological perspective. He concluded that a society's view of death

The word *Halloween* is a contraction of All Hallows Eve, the Catholic Church's All Saints Day. Celebration of All Hallows Eve began with the Celts in Ireland, the United Kingdom, and the north of France around the fifth century B.C.E. At that time, in that culture, the year ended on October 31, and the new year was celebrated as the feast of Samhain (pronounced *sow-en*). On this night, it was believed that the borders between life and death became thin. The dead would return in search of live bodies to possess for the upcoming year and to make trouble, such as by destroying crops. The living guarded against the dead by dressing up in outlandish costumes, lighting bonfires, and making a great deal of noise to keep the spirits at bay. The custom was later adopted by the Romans, and, eventually, presumably in an effort to Christianize the culturally embedded festival, Pope Boniface IV in the 800s C.E. renamed the festival and declared that it would honour and commemorate the sacrifices of the saints and martyrs. The day may be nominally religious, but the traditions of costumes, bonfires, and general mischief making remain.

Source: "History of Halloween," The History Channel, http://www.historychannel.com.

was organized around individuals' self-awareness, the defence of society against the uncontrollability of nature, the belief in an afterlife, and the belief in the existence of evil. From these themes, Ariès derived five models of death, which we will now discuss in detail.

The Tame Death

Death is considered an uncontrolled and evil phenomenon, often imposed by malevolent outside forces, that must be tamed or controlled in some way. Society's aim is to tame death through ceremonies and rules in the belief system. In this view, the individual is inextricably connected to his or her society. When an individual dies, all society is affected and weakened. Naturally, the society feels insecure and anxious in the face of this weakening, less able to defend itself against the vagaries of nature. Elaborate rituals are performed at the time of a death to express this apprehension. In most cases, the final ceremony is one of celebration, as the society rejoices in its ability to absorb the death and to reaffirm the continuity of the society.

The afterlife is considered a place of repose, where the dead wait for final judgment. The dead who have been virtuous may sleep blissfully, but those who have not led an honourable life may be troubled and cannot rest; they may even return and haunt the living. Ariès contends that to tame this aspect of death, society makes rules that the dead can return only on certain days and under certain conditions (e.g., All Hallows Eve or Halloween; see Box 1.2), when society can guard itself against the effects of the dead's return. Other ceremonies keep the dead asleep so that they will not return to menace the living. Prayers and special rituals are offered for the souls of the dead, perhaps in the sincere wish that the dead loved ones rest in peace, but also to ensure that the loved ones will not haunt the living.

The Death of the Self

In larger or more affluent societies, the concept of individualism predominates. Death is still regarded as an evil against which society must be defended, and the concept of an afterlife remains but in a somewhat changed form. A person is no longer regarded as inextricably interwoven with the rest of society and is now seen as a distinct and discrete being whose destiny lies apart from those of other people. Defending society against an individual's death is easier, with ceremonies becoming more formal and elaborate. In many societies, the individual and his or her death were concealed, with a ceremonial covering of the dead person's face and removal of the body to a casket, which often remained closed. The death mask, or the physical features of the dead person with its attendant decomposition, which had been in prominent view during death rituals, was now hidden.

At death, the individual, who had been so distinct in life, was expected to continue being distinct. As such, wills came into more prominence. The dead could exert control and indicate their wishes from beyond the grave. They could reward or punish anyone in their post-death instructions by bequeathing or withholding goods and properties. Rather than lying in reposeful sleep awaiting final judgment, the dead were seen as still asserting their individual identities, both through their wills and through the idea that the afterlife was more than just a sleep, however sweet. The dead were thought to be "living" in some fashion in the afterlife, in a Heaven with streets paved with gold, a Hell of flames and torment, or

BOX 1.3   What is Heaven Like?

According to John Bunyan (1678/2005) in the seventeenth century, Heaven is a very beautiful city:

Now I saw in my dream, that these two men went in at the gate; and lo! As they entered, they were transfigured; and they had raiment put on, that shone like gold.... I looked in after them, and behold, the City shone like the sun; the streets also were paved with gold: and in them walked many with crowns on their heads, palms in their hands, and golden harps.... There were also of them that had wings, and they answered one another without intermission, saying, "Holy, holy, holy is the Lord!" And after that they shut up the gates, which then I had seen, I wished myself among them. (p. 94)

Ernest Hemingway, in a letter to F. Scott Fitzgerald, described Heaven in a different way:

To me heaven would be a big bull ring with me holding two barrera seats and a trout stream outside that no one else was allowed to fish in and two lovely houses in the town; one where I would have my wife and children and be monogamous and love them truly and well and the other where I would have my nine beautiful mistresses on nine different floors. (Gilley, 2000)

Bunyan and Hemingway were clearly individuals with very different personalities. Contrast these Western conceptions of a concrete location of the afterlife with a Hindu view of a spiritual union with All or Brahman for the person who has attained enlightenment:

This is the Eternal in man, O Arjuna. Reaching him all delusion is gone. Even in the last hour of his life upon earth, man can reach the Nirvana of Brahman—man can find peace in the peace of his God. (*Bhagavad Gita*, trans. 1962, 2.72, p. 55)

a vague Limbo that was remote from the presence of God without being torturous in any other way. Different conceptions of Heaven are described in Box 1.3.

Remote and Imminent Death

According to Ariès, before the sixteenth century, death had been tamed by the ceremony and belief system surrounding it. Then a barely perceptible change took place: death started to be seen as violent and wild and passionate. By the eighteenth century, the Western world had experienced technological advances and the work of science. The Age of Reason, with its emphasis on rationale and the triumph of reason over emotion, was now in full sway, yet death was increasingly portrayed in savage, even sexual, terms. Pain and pleasure were intermixed; death throes and the throes of orgasm were combined. The very ceremonies that had tamed death and removed it from common experience also titillated the imagination, and death was imbued with an erotic tinge felt by the individual (hence the term "remote" in its removal from common experience, and "imminent" in its closeness to the human sexual experience). Death was not purely evil any more.

Belief in the afterlife persisted, but a new fear developed: the fear of being buried alive. During this time, the first mechanisms for alerting people that the corpse was, in fact, still alive were invented. For example, a string was placed in the coffin and connected to a bell above the ground. If the buried individual awoke, he or she could pull the string that was placed close to or in the hand and ring the bell so that those above could disinter the person. Men were hired to spend the whole night in graveyards listening for the ringing of these bells—giving rise to the expressions "graveyard shift" and "saved by the bell." This fear is graphically illustrated in the prose of Edgar Allan Poe in Box 1.4.

BOX 1.4   Edgar Allan Poe

A writer of poems, stories, and essays, Edgar Allan Poe (1809–1849) is noted for his themes of death. He was reputed to be particularly terrified by the possibility of premature burial, consistent with his cultural milieu. This is seen clearly in the following excerpt from one of his most famous stories, *The Fall of the House of Usher*:

We have put her living in the tomb! Said I not that my senses were acute? I *now* tell you that I heard her first feeble movements in the hollow coffin . . . the rending of her coffin and the grating of the iron hinges of her prison, and her struggles within the coppered archway of the vault!

. . . without those doors there DID stand the lofty and enshrouded figure of the lady Madeline of Usher. There was blood upon her white robes, and the evidence of some bitter struggle upon every portion of her emaciated frame. (Mabbott, 1951, p. 130)

The Death of the Other

The nineteenth century, with its advances in agriculture and industry, ushered in a strengthened sense of family. No longer was the individual seen as an inextricably interwoven part of the community at large, but neither was the individual discrete from all others. Now the individual was seen as part of a family, a unit smaller than society yet greater than an individual. The anxiety engendered by the thought of death was now not only for the death of the self but also for the death of the other, a loved one. The rituals surrounding death no longer contained the feelings that arose at the death of a loved one, as survivors mourned the agonizing separation. On the contrary, the emotional last words were glorified and the deathbed scene was romanticized. In consequence, a person's own death was no longer seen as an evil but as a state to be desired, as it meant reunion with the deceased loved ones.

Death was seen neither as wild and savage nor as remote. It was seen as a force of nature, uncontrolled and beautiful, not something to preserve society from. The whole concept of evil was changing in people's view as well: conceptions of Hell diminished and the idea of Purgatory, or a waiting and purifying place for the less than virtuous, predominated, especially among Catholics. Heaven was conceived of more as a place for reunification with departed loved ones than as a place of unification with God. Some did not believe in an afterlife; for them, the dead were preserved only in memories. The memory of the dead became glorified and a "cult of the dead" (Ariès, 2004, p. 46) emerged. Both believer and nonbeliever had a romantic notion of what follows death: "They all have built the same castle, in the image of earthly homes, where they will be reunited—in dreams or in reality, who knows?—with those whom they have never ceased to love" (Ariès, 2004, p. 46). This romanticism is illustrated in a poem by Christina Rossetti in Box 1.5.

The Invisible Death

Until the twentieth century, death had been a visible part of life, with the family and community responsible for grieving and for sending the dead to the next life. In the twentieth century, however, Western society became dominated by the concept of success. Death represented the failure of medical science. To cope with this universal ultimate failure, the pathos of the deathbed scene was removed; compassion was shown by denying to a dying person that death was imminent. The dying person, although knowing better, went along with the charade. No final deathbed utterances to loved ones were made to maintain the fiction that death would not occur. The scene itself shifted from the family home and familiar bedside to the sterility of a hospital in which medical science prolonged life to the point of ugliness, says Ariès. Death became foul, with the decay of terminal illnesses and with the attendant caretaking. The medical profession, becoming so skilled in prolonging life, took over death and sanitized it with white coats and medicinal smells. The emotional concomitants of death were removed to make way for scientific efficiency. The individual no longer had the identity of his or her own death.

Society was no longer involved in the death of one person because this death did not threaten the existence of the community in any way. Nature was tamed by science to a great extent, so death was no longer wild or passionate. Physical illness was not malevolent, as pain was minimized by painkillers. Only death remained, not as an evil but as a defeat, a slap in the face of success. And so, death engendered shame, and shame engendered silence. This change did not eradicate the fear of death, it altered it; the fear is now of becoming a patient in hospital, riddled with tubes and machinery, being ministered to by distant, impersonal, and nameless medical personnel, and often dying alone, unseen by others.

BOX 1.5 Christina Rossetti

The poet Christina Rossetti (1830–1894) wrote several poems about death and remembrance. Her short poem "Remember" clearly shows the romanticism of death and what Ariès means by "the cult of the dead."

Remember me when I am gone away,
Gone far away into the silent land;
When you can no longer hold me by the hand,
Nor I half turn to go yet turning stay.
Remember me when no more day by day

You tell me of our future that you planned:
Only remember me: you understand
It will be too late to counsel then or pray.
Yet if you should forget me for a while
And afterwards remember, do not grieve:
For if the darkness and corruption leave
A vestige of the thoughts that once I had,
Better by far that you should forget and smile
Than that you should remember and be sad.
(Eastman, 1970, p. 410)

Box 1.6 illustrates the coldness and sterility that engenders this fear.

A Contemporary View

The last decades of the twentieth century and the beginning of the twenty-first have seen more changes in the way death was viewed. In 1969, a book for professionals

In his highly acclaimed book *Cancer Ward*, first published in 1969, Alexander Solzhenitsyn gives a vivid description of the impersonality and coldness of the medical system in the former Soviet Union. Patients were not told their diagnoses, except that "it's not cancer," when, in fact, it was. Deprived of support and visits from family and friends, they were not consulted on their treatment and were expected to blindly follow physicians' directions and not trouble anyone.

> And already she was rushing off. An unpleasant feature of all public hospitals is that nobody stops for a moment to exchange a few words.
>
> The doors into the ward were always kept wide open, but still as he crossed the threshold Pavel Nikolayevich was conscious of a close, moist, partly medicinal odor. For someone as sensitive to smells as he, it was sheer torment.
>
> The beds stood in serried ranks, with their heads to the wall and narrow spaces between them no wider than a bedside table, while the passageway down the middle of the ward was just wide enough for two people to pass.
>
> . . . There was a constant line of applicants for admission sitting in the waiting room, sometimes for days on end, and requests were always coming in from provincial cancer clinics asking permission to send patients... Nizamutdin Bahramovich insisted too on discharging those who were doomed. So far as possible, their deaths should occur outside the clinic. This would increase the turnover of beds, it would also be less depressing for those who remained and it would help the statistics, because the patients discharged would be listed not as "deaths" but as "deteriorations." (pp. 7–8, 57–58)

and laypeople came out that sparked immediate controversy and interest: *On Death and Dying* by Elisabeth Kübler-Ross. This innovative and courageous physician talked to people who were dying and their families about death as it pertained to them, and she asked how they felt about their situations. This discourse was regarded as almost scandalous at the time, and people wondered whether Kübler-Ross was doing more harm than good in her frank discussions with terminally ill patients. Yet people were also very drawn to her book, and it was quickly followed by *Questions and Answers on Death and Dying* in 1974. Since that time, death has ceased to be invisible in Western society, for the most part. Many researchers have followed Kübler-Ross in exploring the emotions and reactions of the dying and the bereaved, sometimes agreeing with her original ideas, sometimes disagreeing, sometimes building on what she found, sometimes explicating her findings. The major point is that people were talking about death.

Although Canada is a country of widely diverse views, for many people, in the model of Ariès (2004), death is no longer perceived as a great evil, but the process of dying now is. With medical advances, people live longer and have a better quality of life, but sometimes, medical interventions prolong life after the quality has irrevocably deteriorated. To many people, the view of the abandoned and isolated patient who dies alone in a hospital hooked up to frightening-looking machines is more horrific than is death itself. When Kübler-Ross revealed the emotional needs of the dying and that they were not being met, Western society found it necessary to defend itself against the psychological pain of death that the concept of the invisible death had imposed. People, inevitably aging, began to think more of what they want for their own ending. Medical science recognized, for purely practical reasons, that as the aging population grew, the previous method of care for the terminally ill was not sustainable, or morally or ethically right.

On the academic front, 1970 saw the publication of the first volume of the peer-reviewed journal *Omega: The Journal of Death and Dying*. The journal *Death Studies* followed in 1976, and as specialized care for the dying became popular and more desired, in 1984 *The American Journal of Hospice & Palliative Care* and the *Journal of Palliative Care* began. Many other respected and popular journals have followed, and books about the care of the dying and coping with grief can be found in the self-help section of any major bookstore. Books have even been published for children to help them cope with death—their own or the death of others. Lists of books, videos, and movies pertaining to death are in the Appendix, along with websites and further resources.

The Dorothy Ley Hospice Organization (2006) offers the following statistics:

- More than 220 000 Canadians die each year.
- Approximately 160 000 Canadians are in need of hospice palliative care.
- Less than 15 percent of these people have access to hospice palliative care.
- Seventy-five percent of the Canadians who die each year die in a hospital or long-term care residence.
- More than 86 percent of Canadians would like to die at home.

- Home care for the terminally ill in Canada is cheaper than hospital or residential care by 25 percent to 60 percent.
- Only 6 percent of Canadians believe that, in their final days, they can be properly cared for by a loved one.
- The kind of care that 90 percent of Canadians want at the end of their lives is the kind of care that hospice palliative care provides.
- Only 53 percent of Canadians have heard of hospice palliative care.

In addition to the literature, new methods of caring for the dying and for their families have been instituted. Care for the dying aimed at relieving symptoms to improve the quality of the time remaining, and not directly intended to prolong life or to bring about a cure, is called **palliative care** (a term coined by Dr. Balfour Mount, one of Canada's most noted innovators in the area). Palliative care can take place in the patient's home, in a hospital, or in a setting devoted to the care of terminally ill patients, traditionally known as a **hospice.** Today, the term *hospice palliative care* is widely used in Canada to denote terminal care that is given in a variety of settings. The important part of this care is the focus on maintaining quality of life rather than on curing or preserving it at any cost.

THE HISTORY OF HOSPICE PALLIATIVE CARE

Hospices were instituted and maintained by Christian religious orders in the Middle Ages as shelters for the poor, ill, and homeless. In more modern times, Madame Jeanne Garnier in Lyon, France, in 1842, founded the Dames de Calvaire, a hospice for the terminally ill, and in Dublin, Ireland, in 1879, the Irish Sisters of Charity opened Our Lady's Hospice for needy and sick seniors. The Irish Sisters expanded their work to London's East End in 1905, opening St. Joseph's Hospice to care for the victims of tuberculosis, which was almost inevitably fatal at that time. Dame Cicely Saunders, a British physician, opened St. Christopher's Hospice in 1967, which has become the preeminent model for hospice care throughout the world (Auger, 2003).

The palliative care movement started in Canada in 1974 with the formation of specialized units or designated beds within hospitals. The first palliative care unit opened at St. Boniface General Hospital in Winnipeg, shortly followed by the palliative care unit at the Royal Victoria Hospital in Montreal in 1976 (Auger, 2003). Palliative care programs proliferated in conjunction with hospitals and other agencies and now, according to the Canadian Hospice Palliative Care Association (2006), Canada has about 500 palliative care agencies and services. These programs include all services to improve the quality of life for the terminally ill or senior patient and his or her family. The services provided range from pain and symptom control to psychological and spiritual counselling. Not all services are obtainable in all locations in Canada, and across the country the demand still far exceeds the availability (see Box 1.7). Palliative care programs are covered more extensively in Chapter 11.

EDUCATION IN DEATH, DYING, AND BEREAVEMENT

Today, most colleges and universities that teach medicine, social work, gerontology, psychology, sociology, and a variety of other disciplines have courses in death, dying, and bereavement. Less formal courses are given in this area in many hospitals to patients, families of patients, and medical personnel. Although the taboos against discussing death have lifted to a great extent, people who work in hospice palliative care or who take a course in death, dying, and bereavement report that many people they meet respond with "Oh no, that's so depressing!"

when the work or the course is mentioned. This reaction is unfortunate because this topic is important for everyone; after all, everyone will be exposed to it in some form, probably multiple times, during his or her life.

The question has been raised that people managed to cope with death, dying, and bereavement without being educated in it, so why is there a need for this education now? For several reasons: First, in the past, people living in Western society were exposed to the realities of life and death far more than they are today. Now, hospitals, residential placements, and funeral directors carry out the chores previously performed in the family home. So today we, in fact, know less about death and dying than our ancestors did. Second, because modern medicine and nutrition have increased the life span and prolonged life in the face of terminal illness, we are more frequently exposed to a longer period of dying than in the past. Finally, education in death, dying, and bereavement can help us deal with what we will face ourselves, and it can help us help others who are facing the ultimate challenge.

Corr, Nabe, and Corr (2006) discussed six goals of education in thanatology, goals which we want this book to meet.

1. *Personal enrichment.* Most people cope better with life's vicissitudes when they have information about the situation they are facing. Knowing about death makes life richer. Only when individuals can face the fact that life is a terminal condition can they appreciate their own lives in the present moment and become aware more fully of their own strengths.
2. *Plans for the future.* People need to know what decisions they will need to make and the resources that will be available to them for their own death and the death of their loved ones. The study of thanatology relates that information and helps people make informed choices.
3. *Participation in society.* Decisions about end-of-life issues need to be made on a broader basis than just at the individual level. Municipal, provincial or territorial, and federal policy decisions about the resources available to people at the end of life must be governed by the will of the citizenry. By studying thanatology, the individual can make informed

choices in directing governing powers to allocate resources and to provide guidelines for the administration of these resources.

4. *Professional and vocational training.* Many people taking courses in death, dying, and bereavement need the information provided to do their work effectively. For example, medical personnel need to know about the psychological, social, emotional, and spiritual needs of terminally ill patients to give them the best possible care in their final days and to help their families cope. Social workers need to know about these issues to help their clients deal with the circumstances they are facing and to help them access resources. Teachers are better able to help and to teach bereaved children in their classes if they are aware of the way children respond to bereavement.
5. *Communication.* Death, dying, and bereavement are often difficult to discuss. Education in this area makes communication with others about death easier. For example, it becomes easier to discuss end-of-life issues, our own wishes, and the wishes of significant people in our lives without trepidation when we are accustomed to the subject. Also, people who want to do and say the "right" things when dealing with a bereaved person have a better idea of what the right things are with an education in thanatology.
6. *Understanding of the continuing effects of bereavement.* By studying death, dying, and bereavement, people can understand the different feelings and reactions to death throughout the life span and how issues faced at one developmental point may need to be addressed and worked through at other developmental points. The person who has studied thanatology knows that the question of how long it takes to get over the death of a loved one often depends on what is meant by "get over." In some ways, we never get over it.

In the chapters that follow, different aspects of death, dying, and bereavement will be discussed by using the most recent evidence available. First, however, take the test in Box 1.8 to find out your own feelings about death.

BOX 1.8   The Leming Fear of Death Scale

Read the following 26 statements. Decide whether you strongly agree (SA), agree (A), tend to agree (TA), tend to disagree (TD), disagree (D), or strongly disagree (SD) with each statement. Give your first impression. There are no right or wrong answers. In any given subscale, a score of 3.5 or higher means slightly fearful of death.

I. Fear of Dependency

   1. I expect people to care for me while I die.
      SA A TA TD D SD
      1   2   3   4   5   6

   2. I am fearful of becoming dependent on others for my physical needs.
      SA A TA TD D SD
      6   5   4   3   2   1

   3. While dying, I dread the possibility of being a financial burden.
      SA A TA TD D SD
      6   5   4   3   2   1

   4. Losing my independence due to a fatal illness makes me apprehensive.
      SA A TA TD D SD
      6   5   4   3   2   1

   Total of 4 scores _____ divided by 4 = _____

II. Fear of Pain

   5. I fear dying a painful death.
      SA A TA TD D SD
      6   5   4   3   2   1

   6. I am afraid of a long, slow death.
      SA A TA TD D SD
      6   5   4   3   2   1

   Total of 2 scores _____ divided by 2 = _____

III. Fear of Indignity

   7. The loss of physical attractiveness that accompanies dying is distressing to me.
      SA A TA TD D SD
      6   5   4   3   2   1

   8. I dread the helplessness of dying.
      SA A TA TD D SD
      6   5   4   3   2   1

   Total of 2 scores _____ divided by 2 = _____

IV. Fear of Isolation/Separation/Loneliness

   9. The isolation of death does not concern me.
      SA A TA TD D SD
      1   2   3   4   5   6

   10. I do not have any qualms about being alone after I die.
      SA A TA TD D SD
      1   2   3   4   5   6

   11. Being separated from my loved ones at death makes me anxious.
      SA A TA TD D SD
      6   5   4   3   2   1

   Total of 3 scores _____ divided by 3 = _____

V. Fear of Afterlife Concerns

   12. Not knowing what it feels like to be dead makes me uneasy.
      SA A TA TD D SD
      6   5   4   3   2   1

   13. The subject of life after death troubles me.
      SA A TA TD D SD
      6   5   4   3   2   1

   14. Thoughts of punishment after death are a source of apprehension to me.
      SA A TA TD D SD
      6   5   4   3   2   1

   Total of 3 scores _____ divided by 3 = _____

VI. Fear of the Finality of Death

   15. The idea of never thinking after I die frightens me.
      SA A TA TD D SD
      6   5   4   3   2   1

   16. I have misgivings about the fact that I might die before achieving my goals.
      SA A TA TD D SD
      6   5   4   3   2   1

   17. I am often distressed by the way time flies so rapidly.
      SA A TA TD D SD
      6   5   4   3   2   1

   18. The idea that I might die young does not bother me.
      SA A TA TD D SD
      1   2   3   4   5   6

Continued on next page

BOX 1.8   The Leming Fear of Death Scale ...Continued

19. The loss of my identity at death alarms me.
    SA   A   TA   TD   D   SD
    6   5   4   3   2   1

Total of 5 scores _____ divided by 5 = _____

VII. Fear of Leaving Loved Ones

20. The effect of my death on others does not trouble me.
    SA   A   TA   TD   D   SD
    1   2   3   4   5   6

21. I am afraid that my loved ones are emotionally unprepared to accept my death.
    SA   A   TA   TD   D   SD
    6   5   4   3   2   1

22. It worries me to think of the financial situation of my survivors.
    SA   A   TA   TD   D   SD
    6   5   4   3   2   1

Total of 3 scores _____ divided by 3 = _____

VIII. Fear of the Fate of the Body

23. The thought of my own body decomposing does not bother me.
    SA   A   TA   TD   D   SD
    1   2   3   4   5   6

24. The sight of a dead body makes me uneasy.
    SA   A   TA   TD   D   SD
    6   5   4   3   2   1

25. I am not bothered by the idea that I may be placed in a casket when I die.
    SA   A   TA   TD   D   SD
    1   2   3   4   5   6

26. The idea of being buried frightens me.
    SA   A   TA   TD   D   SD
    6   5   4   3   2   1

Total of 4 scores _____ divided by 4 = _____

Source: From *Understanding Dying, Death and Bereavement*, 6th edition by Leming/Dickinson. 2007. Reprinted by permission of Wadsworth, a division of Thomson Learning: http://www.thomsonrights.com. Fax 800-730-2215.

SUMMARY

- Societies throughout history have differed in how they regard death, ranging from making it the centrepiece of their culture to making it a taboo topic.
- Death origin myths are exemplified by the themes of punishment for transgression (the banana tree theme, Adam and Eve), a mistake (the two messengers and the snake casting off its skin), or a reflection of the natural world (the waxing and waning moon).
- Mythology about death also reflects the grief that the survivors feel at the death of an important person in their lives.
- The ancient Egyptians, Greeks, and Hebrews, followed by Christians and Muslims, incorporated belief in an afterlife into their religions, although the quality of life after death varied according to the religion, the historical period, and the type of life lived by the deceased individual.
- Social historian Philippe Ariès concluded that over the past one thousand years, each society's view of death was organized around the themes of the individual's self-awareness, the defence of society against the uncontrollability of nature, the belief in an afterlife, and the belief in the existence of evil.
- Using these themes, Ariès described five dominant patterns in the attitudes of Western societies toward death: (1) the tame death, in which death is seen as an uncontrolled force that threatens society and that society must defend itself against; (2) the death of the self, in which the identity of the individual remained distinct after death, and the dead were seen as still living on in an afterlife and controlling their descendants through the dictates of their wills; (3) remote and imminent death, in which death was viewed with a mixture of horror and fascination as pain and pleasure intermingled; (4) the death of the other, in which the focus is on the pain of separation

from the dead loved one, as well as a longing for death, which will bring reunion; and (5) the invisible death, in which death is sanitized, put in the hands of medical personnel, and removed from the general viewing of the public.

- The past 30 years has seen a surge of interest and study in the area of death, dying, and bereavement, with the emergence of research, books, journals, and courses on this topic.

- Most notable in the contemporary view of death is the hospice palliative care movement in which the terminally ill patient and family are assisted in making the end of life as good as possible, instead of pursuing fruitless treatments. The aim is for quality of life rather than cure.

- Today, Canada has about 500 palliative care agencies and services, with services ranging from pain and symptom control to psychological and spiritual counselling.

- The goals of education in thanatology include (1) personal enrichment, (2) plans for the future, (3) participation in society, (4) professional and vocational training, (5) communication, and (6) understanding of the continuing effects of bereavement.

KEY TERMS

hospice   palliative care   thanatology

INDIVIDUAL ACTIVITIES

1. What category of death origin myth does the story in Box 1.1 fall into? Make up a story for each of the remaining three categories. Do any of your own cultural traditions include stories that can be categorized according to Frazer?

2. Think about the way you were raised in your own family. Which conception of death that Ariès describes do you think your family adheres to?

3. Start thinking about what you want for yourself and your loved ones at the end of life. Hospice palliative care will be more fully described in Chapter 11, but for now, think about what kind of palliative care you would request. Your results on the Leming Fear of Death Scale may help you.

GROUP ACTIVITIES

1. In groups of four or five, research the anthropological literature on death myths of different cultures. Can you find examples of the types of myths that Sir James Frazer described? Do any of your own cultural traditions have stories that fit Frazer's categories?

2. As a group, make a list of movies that have portrayed attitudes toward death and classify them according to Ariès descriptions. For example, some horror movies might use the idea of a tame death for dramatic purposes (e.g., *The Masque of the Red Death*), while some romances might use the death of the other (e.g., *Love Story*). If you have time, watch one or two of these movies and discuss the way death is portrayed.

3. Compare answers to the Leming Fear of Death Scale in a small group. Are there commonalities that might reflect the historical time you are living in? Are there variations that might indicate cultural, religious, or personality differences?

In this chapter, we will discuss

- how North American society in general views death-related issues

- the portrayal of death in the media (i.e., literature, music, movies)

- the results of media portrayal of death

- how the media influence attitudes toward death and dying

- how grief is handled in the workplace

Contemporary Attitudes toward Death

You Are Doing What?!

▶
- "You're taking a course on death?!"
- "You're reading a book on death?!"
- "You're using your sabbatical to write a book on dying and bereavement?!"
- "Stop talking about that stuff!"
- "Only depressed people talk about death. Are you depressed?"
- "Don't you get depressed writing and reading that stuff?"

These reactions are all heard by the author when a course or a book on death, dying, and bereavement is mentioned. Fortunately, other responses were made too:

- "That's so fascinating!"
- "Can I read your work when you're done with it?"
- "My grandfather died last month. Tell me what you know about grief. Am I normal?"
- "It's about time somebody talked about this stuff openly."

These negative and positive reactions are all consistent with the general attitudes toward death-related matters in Canada. If you are reading this book, you must be willing to discuss death, at least in an objective sense. But what about your personal views about death, death that may touch you? For example, have you made a will, or told anyone how you would like your last days to end? Have you listened to others tell you about their final wishes? Have your loved ones given you any direction regarding what their last wishes would be? Did you feel comfortable listening to this?

In Chapter 1, you were asked to fill out the Leming Fear of Death Scale. Now, before you read this chapter, find out what your attitudes toward death are by answering the questions in Box 2.1.

CANADIAN ATTITUDES ABOUT DEATH

An **attitude** is a belief or feeling that gives us the tendency to respond in particular ways to certain objects, events, and people. So, if we have an attitude of tolerance for other religions, for example, it means that we tend to respect the beliefs of others and act courteously when other people talk about their beliefs. The attitudes we have about death and end-of-life issues determine to a great extent whether we talk about these issues and think about our wishes for our own final days. They also influence how we deal with our own grief and with other people who are mourning. Attitudes toward death and end-of-life issues vary greatly in Canada, with its diverse population. Canada's traditional culture has predominantly English roots, and although this is becoming less so, the English-based outlook on death forms the basis for what might be considered a Canadian cultural view.

In Chapter 1, the historical view of death according to Philippe Ariès (2004) was briefly discussed. He suggested that today, the Western world views death as ugly and has made it invisible, with people dying in institutions rather than in their homes. This has sanitized death by its removal from people's day-to-day lives by putting it in the hands of medical personnel and funeral directors who take care of the unpleasant details that accompany the end of life. The process of death is more of a mystery now than it was when the family and community took care of the dying person and disposed of the body. Today, the family and community are involved in trying to prolong life, with death seen as a sort of failure to be banished from awareness in daily life. As a result, many people have little personal experience with death. Ariès contends that what individuals know of death is riddled with images of hospital rooms and machinery connected to a helpless and usually barely conscious patient. Unsurprisingly, the fear of death now centres on the process of dying rather than on death itself.

Ariès has likely overstated his case in calling death "invisible." In fact, death is very much in the public eye today. The emphasis on healthy eating and exercising, the importance of benefit packages in the workplace that include medical and life insurance and pensions, and the attention paid to fundraising for medical research all indicate that as a society, we are very much aware of the potential imminence of death and we try to avoid it. We are exposed to death in an impersonal way every day, through newspapers, books, magazines, television programs portraying both fictional and real events, and movies.

It is not surprising that many people report having **death anxiety,** a fear of death, often demonstrated by a refusal to talk about death and avoidance of anything related to it. A great deal of research has been done on the topic of death anxiety. For example, it is often found that females show more death anxiety than males do, and younger people report more death anxiety than do seniors. Additionally, people who are more religious generally have less death anxiety than do those who have little religious belief (e.g., see DePaola, Griffin, Young, & Neimeyer, 2003, for a review of some of the literature on gender, age and religiosity differences; Harding, Flannelly, Weaver, & Costa, 2005). However, these results are controversial for several reasons. For example, measures of death anxiety rely on self-reports, or what people say about themselves. Females may be no more anxious about death than are males, but females may be more willing to admit it than males are. Similarly, seniors, socialized in a generation less accustomed to revealing its innermost thoughts and feelings than today's generation, may have been less candid in their answers. Death anxiety also is multifaceted (DePaola et al., 2003). You may have seen this when you took the Leming Fear of Death Scale in Chapter 1. This scale partitioned some components of death anxiety into smaller subscales, and you may have found that you scored higher on some subscales than on others. Does this mean you have death anxiety? Or is it more likely that people find some aspects of death more anxiety provoking than others? Research on death anxiety today tends to regard it as made up of many individual and sometimes unrelated factors rather than as a single concept.

In general, in a young and multicultural society, such as Canada's, cultural beliefs about end-of-life issues are both affected by and derived from personal and impersonal experiences. Canadian attitudes toward death reflect the lack of personal experience that most people have had with death and dying. This lack leaves impersonal understanding, obtained through second-hand observations of other people's experiences and through the media to dictate much of the Canadian view of death. These impersonal experiences also predominate in Great Britain and the United States. As will we discuss in upcoming chapters, though, Canadian attitudes on specific end-of-life issues, such as suicide and mercy killing (euthanasia), vary widely and differ from those in other countries.

BOX 2.1   Attitudes Toward Death Survey

Indicate whether you agree or disagree with the following statements. There are no right or wrong answers and you may feel that some statements only partly reflect your feelings. Indicate that as well. This survey is for your own information only, to make your attitudes clearer to you.

1. I don't like to talk about my own death.
   Yes   No   Sometimes   Not sure
   Comments: _____

2. I worry about the death of my loved ones more than my own death.
   Yes   No   Sometimes   Not sure
   Comments: _____

3. I don't like it when my loved ones try to talk to me about what they want for their final days.
   Yes   No   Sometimes   Not sure
   Comments: _____

4. Death and end-of-life issues were never discussed in my home when I was growing up.
   Yes   No   Sometimes   Not sure
   Comments: _____

5. I would want to know if I had a terminal illness.
   Yes   No   Sometimes   Not sure
   Comments: _____

6. If I had a terminal illness, I would use any means possible to prevent my death or prolong my life.
   Yes   No   Sometimes   Not sure
   Comments: _____

7. I believe that suicide is wrong.
   Yes   No   Sometimes   Not sure
   Comments: _____

8. I believe in life after death.
   Yes   No   Sometimes   Not sure
   Comments: _____

9. When it's time for a person to die, there's nothing he or she can do about it.
   Yes   No   Sometimes   Not sure
   Comments: _____

10. I want to plan my own funeral.
    Yes   No   Sometimes   Not sure
    Comments: _____

11. My loved ones know what I want done if I die or am in a medical state where I can't make my own decisions.
    Yes   No   Sometimes   Not sure
    Comments: _____

12. I think "passed away" is a better term than "died."
    Yes   No   Sometimes   Not sure
    Comments: _____

13. I would rather die young than live to be old.
    Yes   No   Sometimes   Not sure
    Comments: _____

14. Children should be sheltered from the deaths of other people.
    Yes   No   Sometimes   Not sure
    Comments: _____

15. People usually get over the death of a loved one within a year.
    Yes   No   Sometimes   Not sure
    Comments: _____

16. The best way to deal with grief is to put the past behind you and move on.
    Yes   No   Sometimes   Not sure
    Comments: _____

17. Having a miscarriage is too bad, but it doesn't really involve grief.
    Yes   No   Sometimes   Not sure
    Comments: _____

18. You can tell when people have stopped grieving because they are able to cope with day-to-day life and they can laugh again.
    Yes   No   Sometimes   Not sure
    Comments: _____

19. The most important thing to remember about the end of life is that people want to die with dignity.
    Yes   No   Sometimes   Not sure
    Comments: _____

20. I want my loved ones to be able to die in their own homes.
    Yes   No   Sometimes   Not sure
    Comments: _____

Keep the answers to this survey and take it again when you have finished reading this textbook. Note whether some of your attitudes have changed or whether they have become stronger in light of what you have learned.

SOURCES OF ATTITUDES

Specifically, where do attitudes come from? People often assume that their attitudes about various issues are the result of considered thinking about the issues. Sometimes people recognize that they have never thought about the issues at all, or only minimally, and they assume that their attitudes reflect "what everybody knows." In fact, attitudes come from a variety of sources, some more influential than others, but all having an impact.

The Family

Attitudes begin to form in childhood, with the family as the first and primary source of attitudes. What parents say to a child and in his or her presence helps the child to form a view of what the world is and what life is all about. Equally important and influential are the topics parents do *not* discuss in front of the child. Death, in particular, is a topic that parents may want to shelter their children from, so they avoid talking about it in front of the child. The oft-heard excuse is that the child is "too young to understand death anyway." As will be discussed in Chapter 6, children do, in fact, understand death and react to it in their own fashion; without parental discussion, they may form some erroneous and problematic beliefs. Children's attitudes toward death, then, are very much coloured by whether their parents have discussed death with them, how their parents handle death within the family, and whether the end of life has remained a hidden subject. If it has been hidden, children may believe there is something wrong with discussing end-of-life issues; death can seem more frightening than it does to children whose parents talk about death and the issues surrounding the end of life. These children typically grow up feeling more comfortable about the topic and their attitudes indicate less fear.

The behaviour of parents at end-of-life events also has an impact on the child apart from any verbal discussions. For example, parents often quickly replace a pet after one dies, which may communicate to the child that a lost loved one should be replaced and life should go on as quickly as possible. The child, grieving for the lost pet, may believe his or her emotions are inappropriate in some way and retain this idea in some fashion into adulthood. Similarly, if the child witnesses a grieving parent behaving stoically and showing little emotion when a loved one dies, the message communicated is that emotions should not be displayed, no matter what pain is felt. The child may then retain into adulthood the idea that public displays of grief are not acceptable and that the difficulty a grieving person may have in dealing with daily life is a sign of weakness or psychological disorder.

However, if the child witnesses family members showing their grief, the message received is that grief is acceptable and expected.

Peers

Although the immediate family is the primary socializing agent of the child and is responsible for many attitudes that the child develops and carries into adulthood, the impact of other socializing sources are important. Especially as a child grows older, the influence of the peer group becomes greater. Children are exposed to other children's and families' attitudes regarding death and may begin to question their own and their families' attitudes, or more likely, assume that their peers are "wrong" in their attitudes and reactions.

When a peer dies, the reactions of the school administrators become important as well. In most schools, policies are in place for dealing with the death of a child, with counselling available for both children and staff. If the school simply carries on as usual despite the death, children may feel confused and even resentful that such a monumental occurrence has been ignored and may develop an attitude that grief and attention should be minimal when a friend dies.

Religion and Culture

If a child has been inculcated into a religious belief, it plays a large part in determining attitudes toward death, especially if the family reinforces that belief in the home. In Chapter 3, religious beliefs in the afterlife and views of death will be examined in more detail. These particular attitudes and beliefs may be strongly indoctrinated into children through religious training at places of worship or in schools as well as in the home. Depending on the beliefs, they may form an attitude of calm acceptance of death or a fear of final judgment. Religious training also affects attitudes toward specific issues surrounding the end of life, such as whether abortion is acceptable or whether particular medical treatments (e.g., blood transfusions) may be used to save a life.

Cultural background also influences a family's attitudes and its practices in many issues, including those that arise at the end of life. Superstitions abound in all cultures; for example, the author recalls her Irish great-grandmother saying that no relatives would die that night because the banshee (a witch whose shrieks foretell death) had not been heard. The dominant culture of Canada, the English-based culture, reflects a stoical acceptance of death with a minimum of emotional display, but Canada is increasingly made up of many diverse cultures, so it is probably inaccurate to contend that there is a "Canadian cultural view" of end-of-life issues.

Instead, throughout this textbook, different cultural attitudes and beliefs will be discussed, with the reminder that all these attitudes and beliefs are "Canadian."

Language

Western society has many euphemisms for death. **Euphemisms** are generally vague or mild substitutions for terms, which help to distance people from the harsh reality of the real terms. In many cases, euphemisms for death devalue and make light of it; in others, they communicate a deeper meaning in a religious or cultural sense. Thus, the common euphemism *croaked* invokes a life-like activity that implies a minimalization and even a vulgarization of death. *Passed on* suggests that the essence of the human being resides in another world or dimension after death. Children, hearing these terms on a regular basis, may use the implications of the terms in forming their own attitudes as well. Box 2.2 lists more common euphemisms used in Western society.

Euphemisms are a shorthand way of communicating thoughts as well. Sometimes the shorthand also creates distance between people and particularly painful episodes. For example, the two towers of the World Trade Center in New York City were destroyed and almost three thousand people killed in September 2001.

BOX 2.2   Euphemisms for Death

The following words and phrases are common euphemisms for death and dying:

bit the dust

cashed in

checked out

croaked

departed

ended it all

expired

gave up the ghost

kicked the bucket

left this world

left us

lost

met his or her maker

no longer with us

offed himself or herself

passed away

passed on

went to his or her reward

That day and its events are referred to as *9/11*, a euphemism that stands for all that occurred that day and its immediate aftermath. No painful description of that day is needed, and people can avoid remembering the terrible images of the tragedy by using this shorthand. Similarly, the killing of 14 women at Montreal's École Polytechnique on December 6, 1989, is known as *the Montreal Massacre,* and the shooting of students and a teacher at Columbine High School in Colorado on April 20, 1999, is known simply as *Columbine.* The shootings at Dawson College in Montreal on September 13, 2006, will likely become known as *Dawson College,* and the April 16, 2007, shooting at Virginia Polytechnic Institute, in which 33 people died and many more were injured, may become known as *Virginia Tech.* The intense pain and tragedy of all these, and many more events, are not conveyed to a child who hears only "Montreal Massacre" or "9/11," especially because these events may not be in the child's memory.

Literature and the Arts

The societal view of death is revealed in literature as well. Fairy tales are replete with deaths, although more recent versions have sanitized these to a great extent. The original *Little Red Riding Hood* described the deaths of a grandmother and a wolf; *Hansel and Gretel* includes the attempted murder of the two children and the subsequent death of the witch; *Snow White and the Seven Dwarves* describes the attempted murder of Snow White. In film, the theme continues: *Bambi II* begins with the death of Bambi's mother and *The Lion King* begins with the death of Simba's father. The Disney film *Old Yeller* ends with the death of the dog. In cartoons (e.g., Coyote and Roadrunner episodes, some Japanese cartoons) the deaths of villains abound, although they often return to life quickly.

These are only a few examples of the death imagery that literature and film bring to children, but perhaps the most pointed appear in the child's game of Ring Around the Rosy and the rhyme that accompanies it: "Ring around the rosy, / Pocket full of posies, / Hush-a, hush-a, / We all fall down." Many people believe that this rhyme, originating in England hundreds of years ago, describes the outbreak of a plague: "rosy" refers to the red rash that appeared on plague victims; "posies" refer to the belief at the time that carrying sweet-smelling flowers would stave off contagion; and "We all fall down" refers to death from the plague itself. The rhyme may reflect the ever-present reality of death to the children who created it and played it in early England and may have served to distance children from it by turning it into a game. Today's children know only the fun they have playing it.

To be fair, however, many fine books for children have been written recently to explain death and to help them cope with the pain of losing a loved one. Examples of these are in the Appendix.

In literature for adults, Shakespearean tragedies, such as *Macbeth, King Lear, Hamlet,* and *Othello,* are based on deaths and murders. Such books as *The Stone Angel* by Margaret Laurence, *Moby Dick* by Herman Melville, *Death in Venice* by Thomas Mann, and the myriad detective novels that line the shelves of bookstores and libraries reveal a literary preoccupation with death. Art and music also show this preoccupation. For example, one of the most famous pieces of sculpture in the world is the *Pietà* by Michelangelo showing the grieving Virgin Mary holding the body of her dead son, Jesus. In music, funeral dirges, requiem mass music, and many religious hymns reflect views of death, as does more modern music (e.g., Kansas's "Dust in the Wind"). Consider the death, dying, and bereavement themes in the following:

- *Opera:* death is the endpoint of many operas, such as *Carmen* and *Madama Butterfly*
- *Classic pop:* Elvis Presley's performance of *In the Ghetto,* for example, describes the death of a young man and his mother's subsequent grief; *Abraham, Martin and John,* performed by Dion (DiMucci), mourns the assassinations of great American political leaders; Eric Clapton's heart-rending rendition of *Tears in Heaven* shows his grief at the death of his son.
- *Rap, heavy metal, and hip-hop:* these genres use death imagery to great effect in such songs as Coolio's *Gangsta Paradise* and Metallica's *Fight Fire With Fire.*
- *Country music:* such songs as *One Night A Day,* performed by Garth Brooks, or *The Man Comes Around* by Johnny Cash, have treated the theme of death and bereavement.
- *Folk:* in the 1960s, many folk song lyrics deplored the deaths that happened in the Vietnam War. For example, *Where Have All the Flowers Gone?* and *Blowin' In The Wind* became anthems for a generation of young people.
- *Blues:* blues singers, such as Muddy Waters and Blind Lemon Jefferson, have described the pain of death, the longing for death, and the desire to be remembered in *I Feel Like Going Home* and *See That My Grave Is Kept Clean.*
- *Classical:* one of the best-known examples of classical music about death is Mozart's *Requiem,* which reflects the Catholic Requiem Mass (the Mass for the Dead). Many other composers (e.g., Berlioz, Verdi) have also composed music of the Requiem Mass, but Mozart's has been the most popular, played often in commemoration of great tragedies, such as the terrorist destruction of the World Trade Center on September 11, 2001.

Given the abundance of views of death in the media, special attention must be paid to the media as sources of attitudes about end-of-life issues.

THE ROLE OF THE MEDIA IN SHAPING ATTITUDES TOWARD DEATH

Today, the media play a bigger role in transmitting information than ever. No longer does news of a death spread by word of mouth alone through a community; today, deaths are announced on television, on the Internet, and in newspapers, and are discussed at greater length in magazine articles. Because death is removed from people's daily experience, the media have become most people's main (or single) source of information about how it occurs and what emotions and behaviours are expected from mourners. A closer examination of how death is portrayed in the media is therefore well warranted.

Death is covered extensively by the media. Newspapers report, often in detail, the deaths of noted people and descriptions of crime or accident scenes, murders, and warfare, and many reports are accompanied by very graphic photographs. Reactions of loved ones to a death are related fully, again often with accompanying photographs of the mourners in the midst of their grief. Occasionally, the public complains that the photographs and depictions of death are too graphic, and the people controlling media content may choose not to display or are prevented from displaying the most graphic illustrations (Walter, Littlewood, & Pickering, 1995). Sometimes choices of what is shown and how it is shown are made by an editor; sometimes choices are dictated by censorship regulations; and sometimes showing the images is merely postponed to later in the evening in the assumption that children, who could be upset by these images, will not be awake to view them.

The News Media

Newspapers and newsmagazines have the responsibility of informing the public of local and world events. Their reporting may provide valuable information, such as in the case of wartime events or the assassination of a world leader. Oftentimes, however, the amount of detail and the accompanying photographs seem to go beyond what can be considered purely informational. For example, Nicole Brown and her friend Ron Goldman were brutally murdered outside Brown's home on June 12, 1994. Her ex-husband, former professional football star and actor O. J. Simpson, was accused of the crime and stood trial in 1995. The attention paid to the murders and the subsequent televised trial of Simpson (in which he was acquitted) appeared excessive to many people. Although some people were riveted to their television sets during the trial, others were quickly bored. Therein lies the danger of overexposure to an event: the public's sensitivity to the very real tragedies that have occurred may be decreased (Comstock & Strasberger, 1993). Families of murder victims, for example, often claim that media coverage paints the victim in unrealistic and unflattering ways, with the emphasis on the perpetrator rather than on the tragedy (see Chapter 10 for more discussion of this).

The depictions of real tragedies lead to another problem: the victims and their families may feel further victimized by the intrusiveness of the media. Photographs of a heartbroken mother on the front page of a newspaper may draw in readers, but the mother may feel even more violated by having her grief publicly exposed. A more concrete example comes from the recent publicity surrounding the case of a serial murderer in British Columbia who buried many bodies on his pig farm. The media published the photographs of the identified women, with suggestions that they may have been involved in prostitution. Although the families of these women, many of whom had been missing for a long time, may have found some comfort in having the bodies discovered and a suspect arrested, the details of their loved ones' lives (which may not be completely factual or are, at least, very incomplete) being exposed surely causes them embarrassment and even more grief.

The Entertainment Media

In the entertainment media, DeSpelder and Strickland (2005) report that an examination of *TV Guide* for one week revealed that about two-thirds of the programs listed describe plots that involve death or dying in some way. One estimate indicates that by the time children graduate from elementary school, they will have witnessed at least eight thousand murders on television alone (as cited by Corr, Nabe, & Corr, 2006). Most of this programming depicts violent, unrealistic death occurring almost immediately after the victim is shot or stabbed. The reality of the visible and auditory changes in the body are overlooked, as is the fact that in the case of such violence, death may result hours, days, or even months after the event. Adults often report that when they first witnessed a death, usually of a family member, they were amazed that death was so unlike anything they had seen on television, so much so that they had a difficult time believing that their relative was really dead.

Some television depictions of death, of course, are very different from those found in the more common detective or forensic science fiction on television and in the movies. Notable exceptions are some documentaries, such as *Dying at Grace* (2003) by Canadian filmmaker Allan King and the PBS series *On Our Own Terms* (2000) hosted by Bill Moyers, which examined end-of-life experiences and bereavement in a moving and accurate manner.

Another type of portrayal of death is seen in the television programs *Six Feet Under* and *Dead Like Me*. *Six Feet Under* is an award-winning dramatic series portraying the funeral industry and the lives of funeral directors and their families. Depictions of death and bereavement are very brief but thought provoking. *Dead Like Me* is a dark comedy about the fate of some dead people who continue a sort of life as Grim Reapers, helping to take the souls of those who are about to die. This program minimizes the complexity of death for the most part, but in its depiction of the family (especially the sister) of the narrator, George, the effects of bereavement can be seen quite poignantly.

Movies portray death in the most graphic ways of all. Blood and gore abound in horror movies, such as *Texas Chainsaw Massacre* and the *Halloween* and *Friday the 13th* series. But other movies, such as *The Death House, The Son's Room, Life as a House,* and *Ordinary People* show dying, and especially bereavement, with sensitivity and attention to the complexity of end-of-life experiences.

The Media as a Reflection of the Public's Attitudes

The way that the media portray any topic presumably reflects the way its consumers see the world and their place in it, yet the relationship is reciprocal; while the media reflect the conceptual framework of society, society's framework is also shaped by the media. For example, if a particular medium feels that its audience wants to avoid unpleasant descriptions of a death, then that medium will presumably exclude these descriptions from its content when reporting a death, giving instead a more sanitized version of the event. By so doing, however, the audience becomes further removed from the reality of the dying process and public attitudes about an "invisible death," in Ariès's (2004) terms, are strengthened. In Canada, the depiction of end-of-life issues in many magazines seems to be enhancing society's removal from the real suffering that death brings (see Box 2.3).

The media also influence and reinforce attitudes concerning the circumstances surrounding deaths. In August 1997, Princess Diana and Dodi Al Fayed were killed in a car accident in Paris, along with their driver. Much was made of the fact that the driver of the car was trying to escape the pursuit of media photographers,

BOX 2.3   The Portrayal of Death in Canadian Magazines

Clarke (2005–2006) at Wilfrid Laurier University in Waterloo, Ontario, reviewed a number of English-language magazines published in either Canada or the United States and available in Canada. She found that the prevailing theme in articles from 1991, 1996, and 2001 was the need for control of death by the individual. Many articles, she states, discussed the experiences of people who take control of their own deaths through suicide or through euthanasia (ending their own lives through a deliberate lack of attention to medical treatments or being killed by others), with discussions of the "right to die" movement. Other articles focused on dramatic murders, in which someone else has clearly taken control of the life and death of another person, or new medical techniques and technologies designed to help people prolong their lives. Very few articles discussed the experience of grief or the need for society to reduce the suffering that accompanies death, in Canada or in the rest of the world. The attitude that death is controllable for the individual is maintained, with a lack of emphasis on the role or the responsibility of society to become involved.

who were always eager to get new photographs of the princess. Several investigations concluded that the crash was caused by the driver's alcohol consumption, but many people still have questions and suspicions about the responsibility of media photographers. Some people are convinced that the tragedy involves conspiracies and cover-ups, and formal investigations continue 10 years after the accident. The unprecedented media coverage of the accident investigations and of the funeral of Princess Diana brought her death closer to the public.

Often, the media seem to push the envelope on public reactions; that is, if the audience might, in fact, want to be exposed to a particular level of death images, then the media often present a level just a little higher. The audience then becomes accustomed to this higher level and demands it. Consequently, the media push a little further, and present a higher level still. A tolerance for graphic depictions builds in the audience. Take the example of Alfred Hitchcock's 1960 black-and-white film *Psycho*. Many viewers do not realize it, but the murder of a woman in a shower is actually not shown; all that is shown is blood (in shades of gray) mixed with water flowing down a bathtub drain. In the 1950s, this was considered sufficiently graphic and the movie scene is considered a classic of terror. Would moviegoers today find this scene as terrifying as did moviegoers of the 1960s? Contrast this to the extreme explicitness of *Texas Chainsaw Massacre*.

The major point is that the media are instrumental in shaping public attitudes toward death, dying, and bereavement, just as the public is instrumental in shaping what the media present. That the media have this power is seen in research, such as that of King and Hayslip (2001–2002). These researchers asked 147 American college students about their perceptions of death in relation to their personal experiences and their exposure to media reporting of deaths. The students overestimated the number of murders that are committed in the United States, a finding that the researchers attribute to the overrepresentation of murder in media messages. Furthermore, exposure to media reports of death was found to increase students' fears of death, especially when the reports concerned the deaths of a group of people, such as the Columbine shootings, the shuttlecraft *Challenger* explosion, the O. J. Simpson murder case, or the AIDS crisis in Kenya.

Similar results were found by Schiappa, Gregg, and Hewes (2004). These researchers measured death-related attitudes of college students, exposed them to 10 episodes of the television program *Six Feet Under*, and measured their attitudes again. Students became slightly more afraid of death after watching the 10 episodes but less afraid of what would happen to their bodies after death. The question then becomes, why does the public want to see and read about death if it increases fear? Why does a large proportion of the public wants to see depictions of death and, for many, the bloodier and gorier, the better? These questions have been asked by many theorists.

In early psychology, Carl Jung (1967) suggested that seeing horror acts as a release for the horror within each of us, contained in what he called the "shadow." Such catharsis allows people to keep more control over emotions and to alleviate fear. For many people, this answer is not sufficient. They suggest that by surviving the visual impact of such messages, we can reassure ourselves that we are still safe and are able to withstand the fear that death and dying raises, thus lessening it. Yet King and Hayslip's (2001–2002) research indicating that fear increases, not decreases, with exposure to media messages about death does not support this notion. It is beyond the scope of this book to investigate why some people are so drawn to horrifying images and reports. Perhaps for now, the best answer is the one that horror film enthusiasts give: they like it because it excites them. The feeling of excitement is heady indeed, and so is the relief that comes afterward. It means that the viewers have survived where others (the actors) have not, and it makes death almost a farce—the depictions are so extreme that it removes death from reality.

Contemporary theorists (e.g., Walter et al., 1995) suggest a very different explanation for people's interest in death-related issues (those that are depicted in a less gory fashion): in a fast-changing and multicultural society, we have become removed from death in our daily lives, so we are particularly interested in death for informational purposes. When we see death portrayed in the media, we feel that we gain information about what will befall us and those we love (even if the depiction is inaccurate). Further, when we see the reactions of the mourners, we gain information regarding how to behave when we are confronted with end-of-life issues. The media, then, provide guidelines as to what is expected of us and what to expect for ourselves, a framework for understanding and handling a critical part of our world (Altheide, 2002). The norms of society are thereby perpetuated by the media to a great extent, and attitudes are shaped or modified by this exposure.

AN EXAMPLE OF ATTITUDES: GRIEF IN THE WORKPLACE

In the privacy of their own homes, people can behave in ways of their choosing. In the public domain, however, societal expectations of how to behave are more strictly enforced. Society sets rules indicating how, where, and when to mourn; for how long; and for whom (Doka, 2002). Nowhere, perhaps, is this more clearly seen than in the workplace. The workplace is based on productivity, with employees expected to contribute competently and efficiently. Professional concerns are paramount, and personal concerns are expected to be left at home, a reflection of the predominant Anglo attitudes in Canada and the United States.

When a member of an employee's immediate family dies, he or she is given time off work. Part III of the *Canada Labour Code* stipulates that all employees must be allowed this time off work, and if the employee has been continuously employed by the workplace for three months, this leave must be paid. The maximum amount of time allowed by the code is three days, but this does not mean working days. Therefore, if the death occurs on a Friday and the worker generally has the weekend off, only Monday is granted as bereavement leave. The *Canada Labour Code* specifies that leave applies only when members of the immediate family die. The immediate family include a spouse or common-law partner (providing the employee and the partner have been cohabiting for at least one year); parents or stepparents of the employee, employee's spouse, or common-law partner; children of the employee or the employee's spouse or common-law partner; the employee's grandchildren, siblings, or grandparents; or any relative with whom the employee lives. Time off is not legally required to be given for the death of an aunt or uncle, a cousin, or a friend, even if the relationship is meaningful to the employee (Human Resources and Social Development Canada, 2005).

In some cases, employers offer more than is legally required through collective agreements or company policy. Time off is then usually determined by the relationship the employee had with the deceased. A week may be given for the death of a spouse, child, or parent; less time is given for the death of a sibling or grandparent; no time off may be given for more remote kin or for friends, even if the loss felt is greater.

In most cases, a bereaved employee returns to work as quickly as possible, sometimes for the perceived need to keep busy and more often for financial reasons (Eyetsemitan, 1998). After a bereavement, a worker is expected to return to work and carry on as if nothing happened. In fact, many people see a return to work as soon as possible as being therapeutic for bereaved individuals, a distraction to take their minds off their loss (Lattanzi-Licht, 2002). The expectation is that the employee will function well in the job, with little disruption to the workplace. Grief, in the workplace, must be contained and ignored (Eyetsemitan, 1998), which may be extremely difficult for someone whose emotions are in upheaval because of a bereavement. The return to work may have as much to do with society's discomfort in dealing with death and the desire for everything to get back to normal as with the financial concerns of the workplace. As we will see in Chapter 5, people who have been recently bereaved experience pain, anger, depression, loss of energy, decreased efficiency in thinking, as well as many other characteristics of grief, which reduce worker effectiveness. Most of those who work in the field of bereavement agree that although distraction and keeping busy are often helpful to the bereaved person, trying to ignore the emotions accompanying grief is maladaptive and perhaps impossible (e.g., Rando, 1993; Stroebe & Schut, 1999; Worden, 2002). Box 2.4 describes some of the experiences of bereaved people in the workplace.

Many people experience bereavement while they are employed, and several workplaces recognize this, providing extra leave time and support services for employees who have lost loved ones. This support is not only more humane to the employees, but it is also financially beneficial for the workplace: workers who feel supported and have high morale function better and are more productive. Box 2.5 gives recommendations

BOX 2.4   Experiences of the Bereaved in the Workplace

Eyetsemitan (1998) surveyed 145 Americans who had been bereaved while employed to find out about their experiences at work following the bereavement. Some of his findings follow:

- Eighty-four percent reported that on returning to work, they resumed the full responsibilities of their jobs.
- Sixty-four percent of people who picked up their normal work responsibilities reported that they received no support for their bereavement from the workplace.
- Fourteen percent of these people reported receiving informal support from coworkers.

- Nineteen percent of these people indicated that their workplaces provided formal bereavement support through the services of clergy or psychologists.

These results indicate a lack of sensitivity to the emotional state of bereaved employees and clearly suggest that both formally in the workplace's policies and informally through coworkers, little attention is paid to a person's grief. For this reason, Eyetsemitan contended, grief becomes "stifled."

BOX 2.5   Recommendations for Employers

Lattanzi-Licht (2002) makes the following recommendations for employers in dealing with bereaved employees:

1. *Create services that are based on the value of respect and support for employees.* She points out that wages are not always the most important factor that potential employees consider; just as important are benefits packages. These packages should include reasonable paid leave at the time of a death and follow-up support for the bereaved employee.
2. *Solicit employees' opinions about desired services.* The needs of employees vary considerably following a death, given their differing backgrounds and existent support systems. Their requests and expectations of an employer are usually relatively modest at this time, often including only referrals to support services and an extra day or two off. Lattanzi-Licht suggests general services that include support, counselling, and education will probably meet the needs of both the employees and the employers.
3. *Help bereaved employees fulfill job responsibilities.* Because the recently bereaved, in particular, may have difficulty in sustaining their usual work efficiency, it would be advisable to check in with the employee frequently and adjust work hours and priorities as needed. The employee wants to do the job, and assistance through flexibility or even by reassign-

ing some of the workload to another worker can relieve the extra pressure the employee feels and enhance a feeling of support.
4. *Train managers and supervisors in understanding the experience of grief.* Managers and supervisors are usually in constant contact with employees and so may be the first to notice a bereaved employee's obvious distress or a disruption in work. Many people are uncomfortable in dealing with the grief of another, so educating managers and supervisors in this area will help ensure that the bereaved employee is supported and can be referred for more help, while it also sends the message that the workplace cares. For a bereaved person, the simple knowledge that someone cares about his or her distress is extremely helpful.
5. *Become aware of the burdens the employees are carrying.* Many employees are involved in caring for ill or dying relatives. By becoming aware of the stresses on employees, the workplace can help to reduce some of them, especially those that work brings, as well as be prepared for changes in the situation (e.g., the sick mother's health worsens and she dies). Once more, management's concern for the workers helps them to cope with stresses while allowing them to feel less alone. The workplace is then in a position to handle a worker's absence or less-than-customary work.

for employers in dealing with bereaved employees; but these recommendations require a systemic change in prevailing attitudes about end-of-life issues and greater comfort in facing them.

The English-based Canadian attitude toward death is one that often shows distaste for and a general lack of knowledge and understanding about what termi-nally ill people and their families and friends confront during this critical time and after a death. This attitude is often revealed through a lack of sensitivity to what people are undergoing. With knowledge and under-standing, some of the aversion to the topic of death, dying, and bereavement may be removed and, it is hoped, society's sensitivity will increase.

SUMMARY

- An attitude is a belief or feeling that gives us the tendency to respond in particular ways to certain objects, events, and people.

- Ariès (2004) suggested that in contemporary times, the Western world has viewed death as ugly and has made it invisible, with people dying in institutions rather than in their homes. This has sanitized death, removing it from people's day-to-day lives and putting it in the hands of medical personnel and funeral directors, who take care of the unpleasant details that may accompany the end of life.

- Canadian attitudes toward death reflect the lack of personal experience that most people have had with death and dying, leaving impersonal experiences, obtained through secondhand observation of other people's experiences and through the media, to dictate much of the Canadian view of death, similar to the situation in Great Britain and the United States.

- Attitudes are derived from a variety of sources: the family, peers, the school, religion and culture, language, literature, and the arts.

- The Anglo outlook on death, with a stoical acceptance of death and a minimum of emotional display, forms the basis for what might be considered a Canadian cultural view of end-of-life issues.

- Insofar as death is removed from people's daily experience today, the media have be-come most people's main (or single) source of information about how it occurs and what emotions and behaviours are expected from mourners.

- When news media report a death frequently, the public's sensitivity to the very real tragedies that have occurred may be decreased. The victims and their families may feel further victimized by the intrusiveness of the media.

- One estimate indicates that by the time children graduate from elementary school, they will have witnessed at least eight thousand murders on television alone. Most of the deaths on television and in the movies are portrayed very unrealistically.

- Death is a recurring theme in almost every form of music.

- As much as the media reflect the conceptual framework or norms of society, society's framework is also shaped by the media. The media are instrumental in shaping pub-lic attitudes toward death, dying, and bereavement, just as the public is instrumental in shaping what the media present.

- The media often provide guidelines as to what is expected of us and what to expect for ourselves, supplying a framework for understanding and handling end-of-life issues.

- The norms of society are most clearly seen in the workplace where, after a bereave-ment, a worker is expected to return to work and carry on as if nothing happened. The expectation is that the employee will function well, with little disruption to the workplace. In the workplace, grief must therefore be contained and ignored.

KEY TERMS

attitude	death anxiety	euphemisms

INDIVIDUAL ACTIVITIES

1. Think about how your family handled the topic of death when you were a child. Were there discussions of end-of-life issues? What kind of language was used? What terms were used for "dead" or "died"? Was there an openness about the topic? Or was the topic of death hidden? How do you think this has affected your current views and attitudes?

2. From your religious or cultural background, what are the expectations of behaviour for someone who has been bereaved?

3. Use a television guide to count the number of prime-time television shows in one evening that contain death. Do you watch any of these shows? Is the issue of death integral or tangential to your enjoyment of the show?

4. Grief in schools at a postsecondary level is often stifled as much as in the workplace. If you were to lose a loved one in the middle of a semester, what would you hope and expect the school would do for you?

GROUP ACTIVITIES

1. In groups of four or five, discuss the different terms for death and dying that you have come across. Add these to the list of euphemisms in Box 2.2. Discuss which terms the group finds most and least acceptable.

2. Survey the class to find out how many people enjoy watching horror movies. In a nonchallenging atmosphere, ask individuals why they enjoy these movies.

3. In groups of four or five, or in a class, ask each individual to survey some working people for the bereavement leaves and support in the organizations for which they work. Compare these differences in class. Are there wide differences? Do these differences depend on the size of the organization?

4. In groups of four or five, research how your school handles student bereavement. Does the group find the measures adequate? Design a better policy if necessary and consider submitting it to the counselling centre at your school.

Religious and Cross-Cultural Attitudes toward Death

When the Time Comes

The airplane was about to crash. In the minutes before their seemingly unavoidable deaths, passengers reflected on their beliefs of what would follow.

"God is good and I will be resurrected to meet with my loved ones again because I have lived a righteous life," thought the Jew.

"I believe in Jesus Christ so I am going to have life eternal in Heaven," thought the Christian.

"There is no God but Allah, and Muhammad is his prophet. May Allah the just and compassionate bring my soul to Paradise," thought the Muslim.

"God, bring my soul to another life in which I may end my circle of karma," thought the Hindu.

"I am at peace and ready to begin my journey through the bardos to another life in which I may end the cycle of karma," thought the Buddhist.

"God, God, God," thought the Sikh.

"I believe I have lived a good life. My journey continues in its progress to the light of God," thought the Bahá'í believer.

"My spirit goes to the Creator," thought the Native Canadian.

"Who knows what comes next, if anything. I guess I won't be disappointed, though," thought the agnostic.

"I'm lost," thought the atheist.

But the skilled pilot reversed the spin of the airplane and landed safely. All passengers felt a renewed appreciation for life, and some reflected on how to live their lives in closer accordance with their beliefs.

Many people have brushes with death, and everyone who lives past childhood experiences the deaths of those they hold dear. As in all times of crisis, we tend to reflect on what we believe. For many, religion forms the basis of belief about this world and what is to come, and it is a comfort in crises. For others, belief centres on a feeling of spirituality that does not necessarily include belief in an organized religion's tenets or even the existence of a deity. This feeling of spirituality encompasses the sense that there is something more to the human being than the physical body and something more to the universe than what can be seen. Spirituality and religious faith often coexist, but they need not. Some people have no belief in any divine presence or plan of the universe and take their beliefs from the teachings of science alone; nonetheless, they too reflect on what their lives mean and sometimes wish they had lived their lives differently.

Because religion can play such a large part in how people think about death and dying, and in how they face their own deaths, a valid study of thanatology must examine religious beliefs. Canada, while predominantly Christian (Statistics Canada, 2003), hosts a plethora of beliefs, all of which merit respect and consideration. We will look at some of these religious belief systems, paying special attention to the system's views of death and belief in an afterlife. Within any religion, individuals may differ from one another in their beliefs, and many religions evolve over time, now regarding some elements in a more metaphorical light than had been the case historically. This chapter focuses mainly on the traditional beliefs of each religion. In Chapter 4, we will examine each religion's traditions and rituals surrounding death.

HOW DIFFERENT RELIGIONS VIEW DEATH

Judaism

The Basic Beliefs

Judaism is one of the oldest religions and one of the first religions to embrace the concept of a single, all-powerful God. The Jews are often referred to and consider themselves to be the chosen people. This phrase has been misinterpreted as one of arrogance; it means that, in a covenant that their progenitor, Abraham, made with God, Jews were chosen to receive the teachings of the **Torah,** the first five books of Moses. This gift did not make them superior to other groups; it meant simply that they had more responsibilities in life and were

---

BOX 3.1   The Thirteen Principles of Maimonides

In the Middle Ages, Rabbi Moshe ben Maimon outlined 13 principles of the Jewish faith:

1. God exists.
2. God is one and unique.
3. God is incorporeal.
4. God is eternal.
5. Prayer is to be directed to God and to no other.
6. The prophets' words are true.
7. Moses was the greatest of the prophets and his words are true.
8. The written Torah was given to Moses, as were other oral teachings now included in the Talmud.
9. There will be no other Torah.
10. God knows the thoughts and deeds of people.
11. The good will be rewarded and the wicked punished by God.
12. The Messiah will come.
13. The dead will be resurrected.

Source: Adapted from Robinson (2005).

---

given harsher punishments for failure. The tale is told of Rabbi Hillel, a first-century rabbi, who, when asked by a non-Jew to explain the Torah while standing on one foot, responded, "What is hateful to you, don't do unto your neighbour. Now, go and study." Many writings explicating points of the Torah have been collected in the **Talmud,** often referred to as the Oral Torah. In medieval times, Rabbi Moshe ben Maimon, more commonly known as Maimonides, outlined 13 principles of the Jewish faith (see Box 3.1). These principles have been generally accepted by Jews since then, although some more liberal groups of Judaism dispute some of them.

In Judaism, the emphasis is placed on living ethically. The Ten Commandments in Exodus 20:1-17 and Deuteronomy 5:6-21 prescribe laws, which mandate devotion to a single deity, ethical living, and respect for all persons (see Box 3.2). The basic nature of humankind is good, as is all creation because it was made by God. Like other religions, Judaism prescribes certain ceremonies and rituals during life (for an example, see the format of the Jewish funeral in Chapter 4), but the fundamental belief is in the human being's direct connection to God in everyday life. For this reason, a special person, such as a priest, is not necessary to intercede with God for the individual; therefore, the leaders of religious groups are termed **rabbis,** who are teachers well versed in Judaic law and customs.

The Ten Commandments, given in Exodus 20:1-17 and Deuteronomy 5:6-21, prescribe laws for living ethically:

1. Thou shalt have no other gods before Me.
2. Thou shalt not make unto thee a graven image.
3. Thou shalt not take the name of the Lord thy God in vain.
4. Remember the Sabbath day, to keep it holy.
5. Honour thy father and thy mother.
6. Thou shalt not murder.
7. Thou shalt not commit adultery.
8. Thou shalt not steal.
9. Thou shalt not bear false witness against thy neighbour.
10. Thou shalt not covet thy neighbour's possessions.

Source: Adapted from Mechon Mamre (2002).

The Afterlife

Although early Judaism did not include a belief in the afterlife, it is a fundamental concept of Judaism today, with this world seen as a preparation and a gestation period for the birth of the immortal soul into a new world. Exactly what that afterlife will be like is unclear, as is the way the soul will enter the afterlife. Jews are instructed by Maimonides not to concern themselves with wondering what will happen to them after death, but to trust in the justice and mercy of an ethical God who created them and be assured that it will be a state of bliss. Just as colours cannot be conceived of by someone born blind, he continues, neither can the afterlife be understood by living beings.

The dead will be resurrected, according to Judaism, in the Messianic Age. The Messiah, a great leader (human, not divine), will arrive on earth to rehabilitate the Jews and regenerate all humankind. A time of peace and paradise on Earth will begin; those who have been righteous in life will come back to life, and the wicked will go to Gehenna or Sheol, a place of punishment and purification. What happens to the dead until this time is unclear, but some, especially those adhering to the more mystical traditions of Judaism, believe that the souls of good people may be reborn several times to continue the task of perfecting the world in anticipation of the arrival of the Messiah.

For more information on Jewish beliefs on death and the afterlife, see Lamm (1969) or visit http://www.religioustolerance.org/jud_desc.htm or http://www.jewfaq.org.

View of Death

According to Judaism, death should not be feared because life is a transitory state to the true life to come. Judaism is conceived of as more than just a religion: it is a culture, a tradition, a way of life. If one has lived a good life, trying to abide by God's commandments, then death is only a pause. Survivors of the deceased will, of course, mourn, but their mourning will be for the person's absence, with the consolation that they will be reunited one day.

Christianity
The Basic Beliefs

Christianity is the largest religion today, claiming more than one billion adherents throughout the Americas, Europe, the Philippine Islands and Oceania, also having many adherents in parts of Africa. Christianity is rooted in Judaism, with the Torah regarded as the first five books of the Old Testament. It maintains a belief in a unitary, omnipotent, omnipresent God and in the Ten Commandments, but it diverged from Judaism with the teachings of a Jewish man known as Jesus. He preached that God is infinitely merciful and humans could be redeemed from sins through belief. His followers, the apostles, took this message further, and subsequent followers extended the Torah to include the New Testament of the Bible (King James Version), which describes the life and message of Jesus.

Christians believe that Jesus was the Son of God, the embodiment of God in physical form, and the Messiah. His prescription for life was to love God and love one another. By doing this, people could attain life everlasting. According to the statement of faith, the Apostles' Creed, Jesus made the ultimate sacrifice in allowing himself to be tortured, killed, and sent to Hell for three days in atonement for the sins of all humankind. Belief in Jesus is the bedrock of all Christian faiths; through his suffering and sacrifice, the souls of people are offered the chance of salvation and entrance into the presence of God after their deaths. It is common today for the Apostles' Creed to be modified to exclude the mention of Jesus' descent into Hell because, for many groups, the emphasis is placed on the sacrifice and the resurrection as the fundamental elements of the faith.

The Afterlife

Christianity is divided into many different groups, which have somewhat different beliefs about what happens after death. All groups believe in the immortality of the soul, with the idea that the body is nothing but a receptacle for it. Those who have lived a life of belief and compassion toward others are rewarded with entrance into Heaven. Just what Heaven is differs across groups and individuals. For some, Heaven is a physical place of great beauty and peace. For others, Heaven is an abstract state characterized by unification with God.

Traditionally, the Roman Catholic Church believed that the soul enters Purgatory, a place of purification, to wait until the final Day of Judgment, when all the righteous will be allowed into Heaven and the presence of God. Today, the concept of Purgatory is mainly bypassed, with the emphasis placed on the soul's admittance into the presence of God on confession of and repentance for sins at the time of death. Protestant Churches do not believe in Purgatory but believe that judgment will come immediately on death. Many Protestant denominations believe that all people who repent their lifetime sins will be admitted to God's presence because of God's mercy and forgiveness. Christadelphians believe that there is no consciousness after death until the Day of Judgment, when only those people who have heard the Gospel will be resurrected and judged, while the rest will remain unconscious for eternity. For Jehovah's Witnesses and Seventh-day Adventists, Hell does not exist; those who have not been saved through their faith will simply cease to exist. Mormons believe in three levels of Heaven, with the righteous dead going to the level appropriate to his or her lifetime faith and good acts.

In many Christian churches, the belief system has evolved in recent times to stress the need for a good life that is a reward in itself and that will also be rewarded by admittance to the presence of God after death. If a person does not live a moral life or repent of an immoral life, most denominations today believe that God will forgive the sinner and admit him or her to the divine presence. Note, however, that the more recent emphasis on universal forgiveness does not preclude the beliefs of many individual Christians in the existence of Hell. Whether they conceive of Hell as an absence of God or an actual place of physical and spiritual suffering depends on which church they attend, as differences exist even within a denomination, and on their own belief systems as created by their families and religious leaders.

View of Death

For many Christians, death is a time of judgment. At some point, depending on the beliefs of the particular denomination, the righteous will be allowed into Heaven and the presence of God. The fate of the wicked is not as clear, with some people believing that the wicked will go to a place of eternal damnation, or Hell, which comprises eternal suffering in the absence of God, or will cease to exist forever. Fear of death is not uncommon because some Christians do not know whether God will judge their life works and beliefs as being sufficient for immediate entry into Heaven. Those who have led a good life and have repented for their sins have little to fear because, through the sacrifices of Jesus, death means eternal bliss in the presence of God.

Box 3.3 presents another view—that of Unitarian Universalism. It is often included as a Christian faith, but it has some differences.

BOX 3.3   Unitarian Universalism

Unitarian Universalism is a religion with very diverse beliefs. Many groups of Unitarians believe in Christianity, while others revere Jesus but not as the Messiah or the Son of God. Most Unitarians believe that the Bible should be understood metaphorically and that science and natural processes account for the origins of the cosmos and everything in it. Similarly, Heaven and Hell are regarded as symbols, with many Unitarians believing that these are states of consciousness within life or continuing after death. Others believe in reincarnation, while still others believe that there that is no afterlife or what comes after death is unknown and unimportant because the focus should be on the actions in life. People are inherently good but have free will, and an imperfect nature can lead an individual to make choices in life that result in immoral behaviour. For many Unitarians, salvation of the soul after death is the result of the sacrifices of Jesus, while others believe that ultimately everyone will be saved through God's mercy and compassion. Unitarians who believe in reincarnation feel that people must go through several lifetimes to learn the lessons of selflessness and compassion, thereby achieving salvation eventually. For still others, salvation and enlightenment are relatively irrelevant terms and may even be disbelieved.

Some Unitarians do not believe or are skeptical about the existence of a divinity, but all believe in people's responsibility to one another in terms of guarding their civil rights and working to promote peace, end poverty, and protect the environment. The Unitarian Universalist associations attract people with liberal views and feelings of spirituality; tolerance of diversity is a hallmark of this group.

For more information about Christianity, go to the website of the Ontario Consultants on Religious Tolerance at http://www.religioustolerance.org.

Islam

The Basic Beliefs

Islam is one of the fastest-growing religions in the world, with 20 percent of the world's population adhering to this faith. Islam, like Judaism and Christianity, traces its roots to the patriarch Abraham. The belief is in one omnipotent and omniscient God (Allah), who is the source of all creation and who communicates with human beings through the inspiration of the prophets. There have been many prophets, including Moses and Jesus, but the greatest is the prophet Muhammad, who lived in the seventh century. The Muslim holy book, the **Koran (Qur'an)** contains the words and teachings of Muhammad, discussing both spiritual devotion and the way to live a virtuous life.

Islam has two denominations, the Shi'i and the Sunni. Both hold to the same beliefs, but they differ in whom they believe to be the divinely appointed successor to Muhammad.

The message sent by Allah through all the prophets is to love God and obey all commandments in order to attain peace in the world. To Muslims, all people are born without sin and can maintain their spiritual purity through constant devotion, prayer, and virtuous living. The responsibility of the individual includes working to make the world just and reflective of Allah. People cannot take on responsibility for the sins of others. Allah, the all-compassionate, however, is always forgiving of those who repent their sins sincerely. See Box 3.4 for more description of Muslim beliefs, the Five Pillars of Islam.

The Afterlife

Muslims believe that this earthly existence is a preparation for a life to come. There will be a day of judgment, at which time the souls of all humans will be judged as to whether they have shown devotion to Allah and have lived according to the injunctions laid on them. If they are judged to be worthy, the souls are sent to Heaven, which is described in the Koran as a place of great

---

BOX 3.4   The Five Pillars of Islam

The Five Pillars of Islam are fundamental to Islamic belief:

1. *Bearing witness.* The pinnacle of Islam is the conscious assertion that Allah is the only God and that Muhammad is the chosen prophet, servant, and messenger. Muslims recite in prayer, "There is no god but Allah, and Muhammad is His prophet."

2. *Daily prayer.* Muslims are required to pray at five set times daily while facing toward Mecca, the site of Muhammad's revelations and the holiest shrine in Islam. This interruption of daily life serves to reorient the Muslim to Allah and the moral and religious injunctions set forth. The prayers also indicate the equality of all human beings: none are exempt from the requirement and all come together to pray, regardless of their socioeconomic status.

3. *Fasting.* During the Muslim month of Ramadan, believers refrain from food, sex, and any impure thoughts or actions from dawn until dusk. This practice, though difficult, reminds Muslims of the conflict that is inherently present between the spirit and the flesh and serves to strengthen the will and resolve to overcome the baser desires.

4. *Charity.* All things belong to Allah; human beings are merely temporary custodians of wealth. To be a good custodian, ethical business procedures must be followed and some of this wealth must be returned to the Muslim community. Muslims are therefore asked to donate 2.5 percent of their accumulated wealth to the poor at the end of Ramadan.

5. *Pilgrimage to Mecca.* In the city of Mecca, Saudi Arabia, lies the Kaaba, the holiest Islamic shrine. Mecca was the city in which Allah revealed the word to Muhammad, and the shrine was dedicated to Allah by him. Muslims are enjoined to make a pilgrimage to this shrine at least once in their lifetimes. There are set religious observances and a specified time of the year in which this pilgrimage occurs. The most fundamental purpose of this pilgrimage is to heighten Muslims' devotion to Allah and Allah's will, but it also serves to remind Muslims of the equality of all human beings because all pilgrims wear the same clothes and follow the same rituals.

Sources: Frager and Fadiman (1998); Smith (1986).

CHAPTER 3 Religious and Cross-Cultural Attitudes toward Death

delight and beauty. The greatest joy is being in the presence of God:

> And their Lord has accepted of them, and answered them: "Never will I suffer to be lost the work of any of you, be he male or female: you are members, one of another: those who have left their homes, or been driven out therefrom, or suffered harm in My Cause, or fought or been slain,—verily, I will blot out from them their iniquities, and admit them into Gardens with rivers flowing beneath;— a reward from the presence of Allah, and from His Presence is the best of rewards." (Koran, Surah 3, 195)

If the souls are deemed unworthy of entry into Heaven, they will arrive in Hell, a dreadful place of perpetual torment and the absence of Allah.

View of Death

Death, to the righteous Muslim, is not to be feared. Dying with Allah's name on their lips, Muslims who have lived according to their faith look forward to being reunited with their loved ones and an afterlife of bliss in the presence of God. Muslims who have been faithless in life, however, unless they repent sincerely, see death as fearsome and the future life as terrifying. Crying is an acceptable response to a death but not wailing because this would indicate a lack of faith in the goodness and mercy of Allah.

  For more information on Islam, go to http://www .al-islam.org or http://www.islam-guide.com.

Hinduism
The Basic Beliefs

The term "Hinduism" refers to a wide collection of beliefs originating in India. The oldest literature in any Indo-European language is the *Rig-Veda*, a series of 1028 hymns written in ancient Sanskrit around 1500 B.C.E. The term *Rig-Veda* means "knowledge of praise." These hymns were written by poets who had visionary experiences through meditation, and they describe the revealed wisdom of these experiences. The messages of this work provide the basis for Hinduism, but these messages had already been in existence for some time, certainly more than one thousand years, conveyed to people by an oral tradition. Other literary works came much later. The *Upanishads* are a collection of revelations obtained through mystical experience that were written beginning about 900 B.C.E. and continuing into the twentieth century. The most well known work, and

probably the best loved, of yoga literature is the *Bhagavad Gita*, composed about 350 B.C.E. The *Bhagavad Gita* is a long poem about Prince Arjuna and his conversations with his god/teacher/mentor Krishna. Arjuna is in the difficult position of having to go to war against friends and family in order to restore justice. He shudders at having to kill those he has loved, but part of what Krishna teaches him is that he must do his worldly duty without abandoning the path of spirituality. Krishna teaches Arjuna yoga. To many Westerners, yoga is a set of physical fitness exercises; however, these exercises are a part of only one school of yoga, hatha yoga. Yoga is the entire body of philosophy and understanding that Hinduism is based on, as well as a means of devotion.

Based on these traditions, Hinduism developed as a belief system that does not fit into any recognized definition of an organized religion. A basic tenet of Hinduism is that God (Brahman) has given each person free will and so each individual must pursue truth in his or her own way. There is neither a mandated pathway to follow, nor the proselytizing of others to Hinduism. Brahman lies within each individual, and realization of this may be pursued by many paths. Nonetheless, most Hindus adhere to certain beliefs, as summarized in Box 3.5.

The Afterlife

Unless the individual has achieved enlightenment and becomes one with Brahman, the Hindu belief is that when a person dies, his or her soul, or the essence of Brahman within the individual, and some residual consciousness leave the mortal body, go to another world, and are then reborn into a new body. The process of reincarnation is in keeping with the individual's karma; for example, having lived a righteous life, the individual may expect to be born into the world again, to fulfill karma and evolve to a higher level of enlightenment. Before rebirth, however, the spirit leaves the body and enters another world. What world this is depends on several factors. For example, if the individual's last thoughts are of his or her family, the spirit will likely go to the world of the ancestors before being born into the same family again. As another example, if the individual has lived a good life, the spirit will enter a pleasant world, whereas those who have committed wicked deeds will enter a much less pleasant, lower world. These are the Hindu versions of Heaven and Hell, but in Hindu belief, the purpose of Heaven and Hell are not reward and punishment. Rather, the function of both is to remind individuals of the true purpose of existence, thereby giving them some guidance in how to conduct their future lives. Heaven and its delights remind the

BOX 3.5   Basic Beliefs of Hinduism

Although realization of Brahman can be pursued through many paths, most Hindus adhere to certain beliefs.

1. There is one active and dynamic God, but there can be many physical incarnations of this God who aim to relieve earthly suffering and restore world order. There will be eventual unification of the incarnations as the One.
2. People are divine in nature, with the basic purpose of life being the recognition of this divinity.
3. All beings share in spiritual existence and are all equally important in creation. All beings, including humans, are evolving to reach the liberation of the earth and achieve Oneness. The Oneness is referred to as *Brahman*. Brahman is everything. It is every object, every person, every event. It is every molecule, every atom, and every space between every particle. Just as the whole scope of numbers includes zero, so too, Brahman, being everything, includes being nothing.
4. The world is an illusion, temporary and insubstantial. Transcendence of ego involves

recognizing this and the single reality of the One.

5. Ego is the basis of all earthly suffering. Ego is attached to the material world and events within it. Transcendence of ego and identification as being the limitless One is achieved through recognizing the illusory nature of the world and so abjuring from attachment to it.
6. Hinduism gave rise to the concept of **karma**. Karma is the moral law of cause and effect that is inherent in everything, that is, in Brahman. All actions have consequences that have effects on individual lives and so, on Brahman.
7. The effects of karma can be seen in the present lifetime or in a future lifetime, because Hinduism believes in reincarnation or the rebirth of spirit into new bodies. Similarly, the events of the present lifetime may reflect the karma of a past lifetime. The aim of reincarnation is to allow the individual to further evolve and so become liberated from the cycle of karma and rebirth, to eventually achieve the recognition that individuality is an illusion and there is only Brahman.

righteous person that the pleasures of life are temporary and insubstantial, and future lifetimes should be spent with this in mind. Hell and its torments alert the wicked individual to the pain he or she has caused in past lifetimes, with the reminder to make the next lifetimes more virtuous. Many of these lessons may be forgotten, however, when the reborn person encounters the earthly world of illusion again.

View of Death

Since Hindus believe in the reincarnation of the spirit, which is the essence of Brahman within the individual, death is not considered to be a tragedy but only a temporary cessation of physical being:

> Death is therefore not a great calamity, not an end at all, but a natural process in the existence of soul as a separate entity, by which it reassembles its resources, adjusts its course and returns again to the earth to continue its journey. In Hinduism death is a temporary cessation of physical activity, a necessary means of recycling the resources and energy and an opportunity for the jiva

(that part which incarnates) to review its programs and policies. (Jayaram, 2006)

For more information on Hinduism, visit http://www.hinduwebsite.com.

Buddhism
The Basic Beliefs

Based on his life experiences (see Box 3.6), Buddha preached a belief system that was not, in the strictest sense, any kind of belief system at all. On the contrary, he saw no purpose in tradition, ritual, or orthodoxy. He did not even see himself as an authority of any kind. Rather, he said, each individual must learn for himself or herself. The only way to come to enlightenment is to experience it. Many may suggest methods to encourage people or to prepare for this experience, but these are only suggestions. The truth is within the individual and can only be reached by individual experience. Nonetheless, at the urgings of his followers, Buddha put into words his deepest convictions about the nature of life. These have been called the Four Noble Truths.

BOX 3.6   The Life of Buddha

In the middle of the sixth century B.C.E., a prince was born in northern India to the Gautama family. They named him Siddhartha. His father, the ruler of an Indian kingdom, called on sages to foretell the baby's future. They told of greatness: if Siddhartha remained with the world, he would become a great king and conqueror, the unifier of all India. But if he forsook the world, he would become the world redeemer. Siddhartha's father, a worldly man, determined that his child would become the great king, and so he spared no effort and no expense to give Siddhartha a worldly education and experience. The child grew up in luxury. He wore only the finest garments, ate only the finest foods, and was given every material pleasure. His days were spent mainly in the confines of his father's expansive palaces, where no element of sadness or pain or ugliness would ever touch him. At the age of 16, Siddhartha married a princess of great beauty and they quickly had a son.

In spite of this idyllic existence, Siddhartha became discontented in his 20s, asking, "Is this all there is?" Although his father had enlisted runners to clear his son's path when he went riding, some say that the gods intervened to give Siddhartha experiences that would change him forever. On one ride, he encountered an old, decrepit man, and so he learned of the inevitability of old age. On the next ride, he encountered a man riddled with illness, and so he learned of disease. A corpse was in his path on the next ride, teaching him about death. And on the fourth ride, he met a monk with a shaven head, possessing only a robe and a bowl, and so he learned that withdrawal from the world was possible. After these lessons, Siddhartha could not return to the luxury of his father's palaces. One night, when he was 28 years old, he silently stole away from his home

and his family, exchanged clothes with a poor person, shaved his head, and entered the forest, seeking enlightenment.

First, he sought two renowned yogis, who taught him the philosophy and practices of raja yoga. But enlightenment did not come. Then he joined a band of ascetics, who believed that attachment to the body was the impediment to enlightenment. Siddhartha adhered to their teachings, fasting, exposing himself to the elements, not sleeping, and not washing. Instead of reaching enlightenment, though, he almost died. Severe asceticism was not the route to enlightenment, he decided, any more than the indulgence in luxury in his father's house had been.

Tired, fighting despair, he sat beneath a fig tree, determined to remain there in meditation until enlightenment came to him. Despite temptations from a jealous demon, and challenges to his right to claim enlightenment, Siddhartha persevered. And it happened. The veils of the material world lifted, the whole of existence and nonexistence was revealed. Siddhartha was now Buddha, the Enlightened One. The fig tree has been known ever since as the Bo tree, short for Bodhi, or enlightenment. The temptation to remain where he was, in the bliss of enlightenment, was great, but Buddha committed himself to telling others what he had found and how he had found it. His mission was to help others achieve the enlightenment that he had found. He followed this mission for 45 years, until he died at the age of 80 after accidentally eating some poisoned mushrooms. Even on his deathbed, he sought to relieve the cook of any guilt for serving the mushrooms and conveyed the message that he was grateful for the meal that finally released him to Nirvana, or ultimate bliss.

The first noble truth is that life consists of suffering. No matter how much pleasure people might derive from the joys of the earth, the reality of life is that people are born in pain and fall ill, bodies fail with aging, and death is inevitable and feared. In between birth and death, people may be tied to situations that they would rather avoid, and they may be separated from that which they love. The reason for this lies in the second noble truth.

The second noble truth reveals the cause of the suffering in life. People believe that the life they see before them is the ultimate reality, and they are attached to this reality. The true reality of the universe goes

beyond the sense organs, though. If people could see beyond, as Buddha did in his enlightenment, they would know that there is only One, that each individual person and object are all One. As an example of this concept, the second noble truth says there really is no boundary between this page and the person reading it. Such ignorance of what is real leads people to desire those elements of life that enhance their egos, what they think will make them feel fulfilled and satisfied. The more they concentrate on this, the less likely they are to feel satisfied and fulfilled because concrete objects and experiences are temporary and insubstantial.

The third noble truth states that suffering can be eliminated and people can overcome the self-absorbed craving that has made them so dissatisfied and frustrated. The fourth noble truth was Buddha's advice on how to remove the cause of suffering in our lives, called the Eightfold Path. The Eightfold Path is a prescription for living a moderate and righteous life, which includes refraining from activities, words, or thoughts that do not reflect reverence and respect for all creation, and having the determination to remain unattached to the material side of life.

After his death, Buddha's followers found several issues that Buddha had remained silent on and other issues that he did speak about, and different followers interpreted what he said in different ways. Divisions appeared. The Theravada school remained a somewhat fundamentalist division, while the Mahayana school was more interpretive and open to more divisions within itself. The Mahayana school is the more popular division, winning more adherents throughout Mongolia, Tibet, China, Korea, and Japan, where it gave rise to Zen Buddhism. The more rigorous Theravada school remains confined for the most part to Sri Lanka, Burma, Thailand, and Cambodia.

The Afterlife

Like Hinduism, Buddhism believes in karma and reincarnation, with the ultimate aim of release from this cycle into a total merging into the All (**Nirvana**). Whether individual consciousness of the self remains in this merging is debated among the various schools of Buddhism. Buddha himself was silent on this topic.

Tibetan Buddhism (led by the Dalai Lama) has the most detailed description of the stages or **bardos** the soul experiences after it leaves the body at death. The first bardo lasts from half a day to four days. In this time, the deceased realizes that his or her physical body has died and sees a clear light. The more enlightened the individual, the longer and clearer he or she will see the light and the higher the level of reality he or she will enter. In the second bardo, the deceased meets apparitions of the people and events of life resulting from the individual's karma. The third bardo is the process of rebirth into another body or into Nirvana. The entire process is said to take 49 days (Goss & Klass, 1997; Sogyal Rinpoche, 1993).

View of Death

According to Buddhism, there is no death because life has only been an illusion. Death brings an end to the illusion of a material life, with an extinction of all desire and attachment through merging with the All, or a rebirth into another physical body and the renewed

opportunity to become enlightened enough to escape the cycle of karma and reincarnation. There is no fear of death because of this, and those who practise Buddhism faithfully are said to die happily. An emphasis on life and the present moment often precludes worry about physical death, which is seen as part of the natural cycle.

For more information about Buddhist beliefs, go to http://www.buddhanet.net or http://www.shambhala.org. For more information in a Westernized context, see *When Things Fall Apart: Heart Advice For Difficult Times,* a book written by Pema Chödrön (2005), a Buddhist nun who is the spiritual leader of Gampo Abbey in Pleasant Bay, Nova Scotia.

Sikhism
The Basic Beliefs

Sikhism was founded by Guru Nanak Dev at the beginning of the sixteenth century in Northern India. Today, it is the fifth-largest organized religion in the world, with more than 23 million adherents, most living in the Indian state of Punjab. Nanak was a Hindu who had a strong desire to explore the spiritual world more fully and left home. When he was seen again, he kept repeating "There is no Hindu, there is no Muslim, so whose path shall I follow? I shall follow the path of God."

The fundamental belief of Sikhism is that there is one God, *Vāhigurū,* who is omnipresent and seen everywhere in all creation by those who are spiritually awakened. The less awakened see *māyā,* a human perception of reality that is actually an illusion. The path to spiritual awakening is through inward devotion and meditation, a difficult path that leads to salvation through a spiritual union with God. The path is so difficult because the illusory world is tempting, fraught with many social conflicts and many ultimately unsatisfying distractions from an inner pursuit of devotion. In particular, Sikhism speaks of people being susceptible to the effects of the Five Evils (ego, anger, greed, attachment, and lust), which separate them from God in a belief that the world as they perceive it is the only world and represents the ultimate reality. Only through constant devotion and meditation can these evils be transcended so that the true nature of God is seen in all creation. In everyday life, Nanak stressed the importance of a balance of work, devotion, and charity, with special attention to sharing, truthful living, and service to the community, especially in the defence of all living creatures. Outward observances, rituals, and services are of much less importance, although there are religious observances and Sikhs are required to wear five items of faith at all times (see Box 3.7). Blind rituals carried out through rote and superstition are denounced. Nanak prescribed the

CHAPTER 3 Religious and Cross-Cultural Attitudes toward Death

The 10th guru, Guru Gobind Singh, of Sikhism ordered his followers to wear the Five Ks to remind them of the difference their devotion could make to their own lives and the lives of others. The five Ks are as follows:

1. *Kesh* (hair). Sikhs never cut their hair (for men, this includes the beard) to indicate the perfection of what God has created.
2. *Kanga* (a small wooden comb). Sikhs wear this comb in their hair at all times and use it twice a day to keep their hair neat and clean. As well as emphasizing cleanliness, this practice reminds Sikhs that their lives should be tidy and organized as well.
3. *Kara* (link). This is an iron bracelet worn on the dominant wrist to indicate the constant link between Sikhs and God and between fellow Sikhs. The circular nature of the bracelet also is a symbol to the Sikh of the need to control feelings and behaviours so that each action and thought may reflect God.
4. *Kaccha* (knee-length shorts). These shorts may be worn on their own or under other clothing, and they symbolize the high moral nature of the life Sikhs are expected to live.
5. *Kirpan* (dagger). The *kirpan* is not primarily a weapon, although it may be used in self-defence or in the defence of others. It is never to be used in anger or with malice. Its primary significance is to symbolize power and freedom of spirit to Sikhs.

repetition of the name of God or a sacred syllable as an internal way of keeping God's presence as a constant part of the individual's life, because union with God is reached only through the internal devotion and remembrance of the heart.

Nanak was followed by nine other leaders or gurus, who enshrined the teachings of Sikhism in the holy book, the *Sr Gūrū Granth Sāhib*, which includes selected works of many writers of varied socioeconomic and religious backgrounds.

The Afterlife

In common with Hinduism and Buddhism, Sikhism believes in karma and reincarnation. The cycle of reincarnation can be broken only by unstinting devotion to God and righteous living. When, by God's grace, the cycle is broken, the Sikh can then live with God forever. The afterlife in Sikhism is not a place but a spiritual union with and absorption into God. There is no Heaven but this, and there is no Hell or place of punishment or purification, except through successive incarnations.

View of Death

In Sikhism, death is a part of God's will and a natural process, nothing more than the ending of the bodily receptacle for the soul. Death brings the chance of being reincarnated into a life closer to a union with the divine. Thus, mourning is discouraged, as are elaborate funerals or memorials (see Chapter 4).

For more information on Sikhism, go to http://www.sikhs.org.

Bahá'í
The Basic Beliefs

Bahá'í believes in one transcendent God who created the universe and who sends prophets to humankind to reveal His will. These prophets include some of those of other religions, such as Abraham, Moses, Krishna, Zoroaster, Buddha, Jesus, and Muhammad. All religions, then, spring from the same spiritual source. Two great prophets are particular to Bahá'í, however: the Bab and Baha'u'llah, both prophesizing in the nineteenth century. The Bahá'í scriptures include the writings of these two prophets, and the faith claims several holy books.

The core beliefs of Bahá'í are the existence of God and the unity of humankind. Humankind is believed to have gone through a long and turbulent growth period, but now maturity has been reached and it is capable of forming a just and peaceful society. It is the responsibility of a believer to further this civilization by both personal devotion and actions, and by working in the service of humanity. There is neither sacrament in the Bahá'í religion, nor clergy or rituals. Rather, the believer lives a life of honesty, chastity, and high moral principles. Believers are urged to pray each day, recognizing that their work is a form of worship. They believe in avoiding detrimental practices, such as gambling, drinking, partisan politics, and excessive materialism, and they are enjoined to seek truth independently while maintaining fellowship with followers of all religions. The social principles espoused by Bahá'í are listed in Box 3.8.

The Afterlife

Bahá'í's believe that every human being has an immortal soul that is rational and grows and develops through the individual's relationship with God. On death, the soul is free to travel through spirit worlds, which are timeless and coexistent with the earthly world (i.e., not in a remote place). The soul of an individual who has lived according to ethical and moral principles progresses through these planes of existence, coming ever closer to the presence of God. This is the Bahá'í conception of Heaven. If the soul has not developed through devotion and work in the service of humanity, it remains in planes of spirit that are distant from God. Such would be the Bahá'í idea of Hell. Heaven and Hell, then, are regarded as descriptions of the individual soul's proximity and spiritual progress to God, but the exact nature of the spirit planes are a mystery.

View of Death

Death is a natural event in which only the body decomposes, according to Bahá'í. It is a rebirth into a spiritual level that allows the unencumbered soul to reach God, depending on the way the individual has developed spiritual qualities in life. For the person who has lived a good life, death may bring great joy as he or she will enter a plane of being that is close to God. For the person whose life has been less exemplary, death will bring no torment but remoteness from God that causes its own anguish.

For more information on Bahá'í beliefs, go to http://www.bahai.org or http://www.bahai.us.

Native Peoples
The Basic Beliefs

Many Native Peoples have embraced Christianity as a religion, but Native beliefs and traditions are often incorporated into these beliefs. Native Peoples are very heterogeneous, so not surprisingly, Native groups differ in their traditional beliefs, but commonalities can be extrapolated, such as the belief that the spirit world is completely connected with the physical world. No single word in any of the Native Peoples' languages means "religion" (Deloria, 1994, 1999; McGaa, 1990; Renault & Freke, 1996), because there is no separation between religion and other parts of life. All acts are spiritual acts and spirituality is part of everything. For example, picking a blueberry and eating it must be accompanied by appreciation and a message of thanks for the gift of the berry, the elements of nature that have helped the berry to grow, the spirits that have directed the elements of nature, and the Creator who started the whole process by giving the gift of the world and all its contents. In a way, all day-to-day life for Native Peoples is a prayer, and blasphemy is just as possible when brushing your teeth if the act is not appreciated as it is when showing disregard for ceremonies. Natives Peoples, then, live and breathe in an atmosphere of the spirit as much as in a literal biosphere.

This connection does not mean that ceremonies or religious rituals are any less important for Native Peoples; it means that ceremonies and rituals are not the only expressions of spirituality. And one thoughtless act does not upset the harmony of life; the forces of life are stronger than that. But a continued disregard—a series of many thoughtless acts—will have ramifications, and then restoring the harmony may be more difficult.

The spirituality of life is an ongoing process. The revelations and insights of spirituality are just as likely to occur today, in the Native view, as they were thousands of years ago, which provides another reason that spirituality must be seen as a vital component of everyday life.

Change is seen as a normal component of life, another commonality of belief among Native groups. Although respect is given to the insights of ancestors, and guidance is sought from them, the prime focus is on the experiences of the individual in the present. What the individual experiences may give him or her a new, fresh, or deepened understanding of the web of life. This "truth" is deeply personal; what one person experiences is not preached to others on the understanding that if the spirits or ancestors had wanted to reveal this insight to others, they would have done so. If an individual does relate a meaningful experience, the person does not discuss his or her interpretation of that experience. Rather, the tale is told and the listeners are left to form their own meaning (or not) from the tale. From this, they may decide whether or not to incorporate the message into their own belief framework.

The Afterlife

Among Native Peoples, there is no precise belief about what happens to the individual after death. In many cases, a number of beliefs may be combined. These beliefs include the idea of reincarnation, in which an individual may be reborn in human or animal form, or in the return of the spirit to the earthly world as a ghost. Another belief is that the individual's spirit goes to another world, which may or may not be pleasant. For example, among the Algonquian Peoples of Canada and the United States, when a person who has followed the Path of Life with reverence for creation dies, his or her soul is thought to remain with the living in a specially built spirit house. A plate of food is offered to feed the spirit while it prepares to depart for the Land of Souls, where it will be greeted with a feast and happiness. See Box 3.9 for a description of the Inuit view of the soul.

Many Native Canadians' belief in the afterlife mirrors that of the Christian denomination to which they belong. Others feel that what happens after death is one of the great unknowns of the universe.

View of Death

From the Native Peoples' perspective, death is part of the cycle of life, a change in being that is expected and further indicates the inseparability of the concrete world from the spirit world.

 For more information on Native beliefs, go to http://www.religioustolerance.org or http://www.answers.com/topic/religion-in-canada.

HOW CULTURES VIEW DEATH

Many countries have a dominant religion, one that forms or has formed the basis of government. For example, Iran makes no separation between church and state insofar as Islam is a fundamental part of the governing structure. In the past, for example, Italy and Spain were ruled by monarchs whose devotion to Catholicism formed a basic structure for their reigns.

Other countries, such as Canada and the United States, have a clear division between religion and government. Although the Queen of England and Canada is still known as "Defender of the Faith," the faith being Anglicanism, this title was retained in Canada with the explanation by the prime minister that it didn't refer to a particular faith. Recently, Prince Charles suggested it be changed to "Defender of Faith." Candidates for public office in many countries use their religious beliefs or affiliations to promote their campaigns and their governmental proposals. The separation of church and state allows for more diversity in the religions of the citizens and in the belief systems they follow (or choose not to follow).

Canada and the United States are highly diverse not only in terms of the religions practised but also in the cultural makeup of their inhabitants.

> *Culture* is a unified set of values, ideas, beliefs, and standards of behavior shared by a group of people; it is the way a person accepts, orders, interprets, and understands experiences throughout the life course. Most important, culture is transmitted on an unconscious level from generation to generation, influencing day-to-day behavior and ensuring a people's survival. (Thomas, 2001, p. 40)

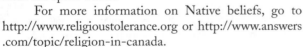

BOX 3.9 The Inuit View of the Soul

Although most Inuit of the northern part of Canada adhere to Christianity, some retain a more traditional view of the soul. In the traditional Inuit account, human beings have more than one soul. Some have three souls: one that leaves the body and enters a spirit world at death, after remaining near the dead body for a time; one that ceases to exist at death; and one that resides in the individual's name, persisting after death and coming to rest again in a newborn baby who is named for the deceased. Thus, an essential part of the person is reincarnated in a new generation. This part is thought to strengthen the baby, allowing it to survive infancy, and provides the baby with a guardian spirit throughout life. Both human and nonhuman beings are believed to have souls, which can change form, into demonic spirits, for example. Souls can enter the body of a shaman, who is an intermediary between the physical world and the spirit world, bringing messages and guidance. Like other Native Peoples' groups, then, the spirit world and the physical world are not truly separated, and spirituality continues to be a part of daily life.

Source: Hirschfelder and Molin (1992).

Canada, in particular, has chosen to celebrate its cultural diversity, with emphasis in schools and governmental policies on multiculturalism. Diversity refers to the mixture of people within a group. Although diversity is usually regarded as differences in cultures, an individual need not be from a different culture to be part of the diversity of the society. Besides religion and culture of origin, differences among people come from many different sources, including race, sex or gender, age, education, abilities, values, sexual orientation, and habitual practices. In this chapter, diversity of cultures will be highlighted, while recognizing that not all individuals within a cultural background hold to its traditions and beliefs. In embracing diversity is recognition of the richness and broadness of perspective that different cultures bring to a country. On an individual level, exposure to and knowledge of different cultures enhance understanding of the world and its inhabitants, and provide a basis for reflection on our own beliefs.

The society or culture from which a person derives and with which a person identifies has a marked influence on his or her attitudes toward life and on how he or she views death. Even when people have strong belief in a religion and live by its principles, the culture they identify with often modifies and adds to their views of death and the way in which they grieve. For this reason, it is necessary to develop **cultural sensitivity,** that is, an awareness and willingness to acknowledge that people of different cultures and subcultures act in different ways and have different norms and values (Hadad & Reed, 2007). This cultural sensitivity also needs to include an awareness that cultures and traditions evolve and are modified, especially when individuals from different cultures have been exposed for long periods to Western influences (e.g., a third-generation Canadian of Chinese descent).

Anthropologists, such as Straus (1978), Evans-Pritchard (1968), Radcliffe-Brown (1964), and Conklin (1995), as well as many others, have studied different cultures and published detailed accounts of their death and dying practices. Yet little unifies these accounts in terms of models or theoretical conceptions within the anthropological literature (Palgi & Abramovitch, 1984). A notable exception is in the work of Rosenblatt, Walsh, and Jackson (1976), who examined the anthropological descriptions of mourning patterns in 78 societies and found that nearly universally, death is associated with extreme negative emotionality, crying being the most typical behavioural expression of grief. Anger was also found to be present in most societies, and the researchers suggest that it may be present almost universally as well, but the expression of anger may be concealed, given societal norms. They conclude that most societies have developed mechanisms, rituals, and practices to control and channel this anger. It would seem, then, that for the most part, grief is experienced in much the same way in all peoples in all cultures; only the expression of grief and the practices surrounding death and dying differ.

Within the Western world, several studies have examined differences in reactions to grief, although few of these have focused on the Canadian experience. Some information may be gleaned from studies originating in the United States, however. For example, Catlin (1993) compared the reactions of American students and Spanish students to the death of a loved one. He found that Spaniards experience more lowering of self-esteem when a loved one dies but an increase in liking and trust of others as compared with Americans. He attributes this to the greater role of family and community in Spain, as opposed to the United States, which has a cultural value of independence. Thus, when a loved one dies in the United States, people experience a greater cultural prescription to deal with grief alone and not rely on the support of others. In contrast, in such countries as Spain, where interpersonal ties are central to the individual's identity, loss of a loved one diminishes that identity, leading to lowered self-esteem, and increases the individual's reliance on social support, which is more readily given, resulting in greater trust and affiliation with others. The intensity of grief was no different between the groups, only the personal and interpersonal effects.

Thomas (2001) reports that among many Asian groups, as well as among some Native groups, is a belief that talking about death will make it happen. Therefore, these groups may have a reluctance to inform a patient of a terminal condition or to discuss end-of-life care, including advance directives, such as do-not-resuscitate orders or organ donation. Lobar, Youngblut, and Brooten (2006) cite research that indicates that Hispanics believe that it is harmful to the patient to know the seriousness of his or her illness, so the patient's family has the duty to be decision makers for the patient. When death occurs, women may cry and wail loudly but men are restricted by the belief in the machismo, that men must be strong and stoical, a belief shared by Polish men.

When comparing Mexican-American college students with Anglo-American college students, Oltjenbruns (1998) found stronger outward expressions of grief among the Hispanic students, along with more physiological reactions. But all Hispanics do not necessarily react the same way to grief: Grabowsky and Frantz (1992), for example, found that people from Puerto Rico experienced a higher intensity of grief when confronted with an unexpected death than did those from other Hispanic backgrounds. These results support the existence of differences within groups, that is, subgroups within a culture may have very different norms and behaviours.

CHAPTER 3 Religious and Cross-Cultural Attitudes toward Death

BOX 3.10 Focus Group Reports of Cross-Cultural Practices

Although Lobar et al. (2006) caution that their results may not be indicative of any culture as a whole, some of the answers given by nursing students are worth noting. All the students indicated that belief in a supreme being and an afterlife was dominant in their families, and events surrounding dying and death reflected this. However, the students found it difficult to distinguish which practices reflected religion and which reflected culture, thereby indicating the strength and influence of religion on end-of-life practices. Some of the practices they discussed follow:

- Asian students said that their families avoid having an ill loved one in a room with the number four in it, because this number is associated with death. Furthermore, these families preferred that the loved one's feet not be facing the door, because a dead body is removed from a room feet first.
- An East Indian student revealed that some people in her culture believe that there is a good and a bad time to die. A Hindu priest is required to check a special book to determine if the time of death is good or not. If it is good, then the usual Hindu end-of-life ceremonies proceed. But if it is not, special rituals must be performed to ward off evil and protect the living. Neglect of this may cause more deaths.
- African-American, Jamaican, and Baptist students stated that children and pregnant women should not attend funerals.
- A Nicaraguan student said that in her native culture, sick people would not attend funerals because of the "toxins around the body of the deceased" (p. 48).
- In the Jamaican culture, it was reported, parents did not go to the funerals of their children because parents should not have to bury their child.

- An East Indian student reported that widows are not allowed to attend their husbands' funerals in her culture.
- African-American students discussed the importance of showing respect and caring for the deceased by having a large and lavish funeral.
- Hispanic and Guyanan students reported the belief that if food falls during a ceremony, it must be picked up immediately and the spirit of the deceased must be told to go back and rest or the deceased's soul will be troubled. Similarly, the deceased's spirit will be troubled if the deceased is discussed. Hispanic students said that the deceased may be discussed, but only if the words "God rest the dead" are also spoken.
- African-American, Thai, and Filipino students noted that loud wailing is a sign of respect and love for the deceased, and the Filipino nurse reported that in the Philippines, wailers may be hired, with the wailing accompanied by music. The louder the volume, the greater the respect and importance of the deceased. Fainting, she said, was also common at Filipino funerals.
- A Buddhist nurse said that "no red or flashy" (p. 49) clothing should be worn at any of the end-of-life ceremonies.
- Asian nurses reported that male Hindu relatives and Buddhist sons shaved their heads for some time after the death of a relative.
- Hindu and Filipino nurses reported the custom of turning on a light each day at 6 p.m. for some time after the death of a loved one.
- Hispanic nurses noted that carnations are worn on Mother's Day if a mother has died.

In some cases, the nurses did not know the purpose of the customs or the history of them. Although they sometimes regarded them as oddities or old-fashioned, they practised them in respect of their cultures and of their families.

Another example of the cultural influence on beliefs can be seen in the descriptive study done by Braun and Nichols (1997). They found that although Japanese Americans and Vietnamese Americans are usually Buddhist, there are differences in the practices surrounding death. As an illustration, Japanese Americans preferred cremation to burial, while Vietnamese Americans preferred burial, sometimes including coffee or tea and a piece of rice or gold in the casket.

Lawson (1990) notes that among Asian groups, mental illness or emotional lack of control is considered shameful. Therefore, crying is acceptable, but intense grief is more likely to be expressed by somatic complaints, such as digestive problems or muscular pain. Yick and Gupta (2002) noted the evolving nature of culture over time and asked Chinese Americans to describe the prevalent beliefs and behaviours surrounding death in their milieus. Among Chinese Americans, traditional beliefs, such as saving face, were still evident. Crying was permitted, to show the esteem in which the deceased was held, especially if many people cried. The more people who cried at someone's death, the more the person was revered and loved; thus, the crying enhances the esteem accorded to the deceased.

Lobar et al. (2006) interviewed 14 nurses from a variety of ethnic backgrounds who were working toward a master's degree, asking them about the practices surrounding dying, death, and bereavement in their families. Some of their answers are given in Box 3.10.

It is clearly beyond the scope of this chapter to describe all the cultural differences concerning the end of life. In a widely multicultural country, such as Canada, large differences exist in every province and territory. In general, two main guidelines for cultural sensitivity in this area are applicable to all cultures:

1. Treat the dying individual and his or her family and mourners with respect and courtesy, no matter what culture, religion, ethnicity, or other aspects of diversity you encounter.
2. Listen nonjudgmentally to the individual and the family. Ask what their expectations and wishes are and what traditions need to be followed. Comply with these as much as possible. The recognition that *all* people are facing the pain of grief and loss at the time of a death or diagnosis of a terminal illness of a loved one should naturally lead each of us to respond with the sensitivity that we would want to be shown.

In the next chapter, we will discuss many of the rituals and traditions of death in the religious and cultural systems described in this chapter.

SUMMARY

- Most people have a religious faith or a sense of spirituality that they reflect on in times of crisis.
- Modern Judaism believes in an afterlife and resurrection of the dead after the Messiah comes. Death should not be feared because life is only a transitory state to the true life to come. If a person has lived a good life, trying to abide by the commandments of God, then death is only a pause.
- Christianity, in general, believes that death is a time of judgment when the righteous will be allowed into Heaven and the presence of God. The fate of the wicked is less clear, with some people believing that the wicked will go to a place of eternal damnation, or Hell, which comprises eternal suffering in the absence of God, or will cease to exist forever.
- In Islam, death for the righteous is not to be feared. Dying with the name of Allah on their lips, Muslims who have lived according to their faith look forward to being reunited with their loved ones one day and an afterlife of bliss in the presence of God. To the Muslim who has been faithless in life, however, unless he or she repents sincerely, death is fearsome and the future life is terrifying.
- Hinduism believes in the reincarnation of souls, so death is not considered to be a tragedy, only a temporary cessation of physical being.
- According to Buddhism, there is no death because life is only an illusion. Death brings an end to the illusion of a material life, with an extinction of all desire and attachment through merging with the All; or it brings a rebirth into another physical body, with the renewed opportunity to become enlightened enough to escape the cycle of karma and reincarnation.
- In Sikhism, death is a part of God's will and a natural process, nothing more than the ending of the bodily receptacle for the soul. Death brings the chance to be reincarnated into a life closer to a union with the divine.
- According to the Bahá'í faith, death is a natural event in which only the body decomposes. It is a rebirth into a spiritual level that allows the unencumbered soul to

CHAPTER 3 Religious and Cross-Cultural Attitudes toward Death

reach the light of God, depending on the way the individual has developed spiritual qualities in life.

- From the Native Peoples' perspective, death is part of the cycle of life, a change in being that is expected and further indicates the inseparability of the concrete world from the spirit world.

- Canada and the United States are highly diverse not only in terms of the religions practised but also in the cultural makeup of their inhabitants. Even when people have a strong belief in a religion and live by its principles, the culture they identify with often modifies and adds to their views of death and the way in which they grieve.

- For the most part, grief is experienced in much the same way, as a negative emotional event, in all peoples in all cultures. Only the expression of grief and the practices surrounding death and dying differ.

- The general guidelines for showing cultural sensitivity to peoples of all cultures are (1) to treat the dying individual and his or her family and mourners with respect and courtesy, no matter what culture, religion, ethnicity, or other aspects of diversity are encountered; and (2) to listen nonjudgmentally to the individual and the family. Ask what their expectations and wishes are and what traditions need to be followed. Comply with these are far as possible.

KEY TERMS

bardos	Koran (Qur'an)	rabbis
cultural sensitivity	*māyā*	Talmud
karma	Nirvana	Torah

INDIVIDUAL ACTIVITIES

1. What cultural or religious group do you belong to, if any? What traditions or practices accompany the end of life in your tradition? Do you find these traditions satisfying? Why or why not?

2. Have you ever known anyone from a different cultural background who practised different traditions? What were they? Did they seem strange to you? What was the strangest part?

3. Ask someone of a different cultural background about his or her traditions regarding death, dying, and bereavement.

4. Knowing about the multiplicity of different traditions, do you find any particularly attractive and would like to include in your own views and behaviours concerning the end of life?

GROUP ACTIVITIES

1. In class or in groups made up of a variety of people, discuss the different traditions that you and your family have concerning the end of life.

2. Apart from religion and culture, are there differences in regional practices or traditions among you and your classmates? For example, are there differences in the practices of people living in urban centres as opposed to rural centres? Are there idiosyncratic family practices that differ among you?

3. In groups of four or five, research other religious or cultural beliefs and practices concerning the end of life. For example, you might look at Quakerism, Jainism, or Zoroastrianism, or at specific African or Native Canadian beliefs and practices. One place to start is the Ontario Consultants on Religious Tolerance at http://www.religioustolerance.org or at http://www.answers.com/topic/religion-in-canada.

4. Imagine the following scenario and discuss this within a group of four or five. You are working in a hospital when a man arrives who is clearly dying. You have been given the responsibility of determining his care until he dies. You have unlimited resources at your disposal, but there is no chance of identifying the man or of finding his family or friends. There are no clues regarding his culture or religion. What would you do?

End-of-Life Rituals

"Attention Must Be Paid"

► When the epidemic was over, 22 people had died. These people were of different races, religions, and ethnic backgrounds. Their socioeconomic statuses differed, their occupations were varied, and their lifestyles were dissimilar. But they all had one thing in common: they left behind people who loved them and wanted to memorialize their lives and their deaths. Some of these people had been deprived of a chance to say goodbye because of the speed of the illness or because of the strict quarantine that the city had undergone. All these people believed, as Arthur Miller once wrote, that "Attention must be paid." Family members and friends began to prepare the rituals that would allow them to honour and pay tribute to their dead loved ones. These rituals would bring them together with others who cared for the deceased and would give them memories and, perhaps, the solace of shared grief.

Throughout life we encounter transitions or changes that transform much of our existence. In fact, some people have described life as a series of changes or transitions (see, for example, Sheehy's book, 1976, *Passages*). For example, we might measure our lives in the following terms:

- We are born.
- We may be accepted into a religion.
- We start school.
- We finish school.
- We buy our first car.
- We get our first full-time job.
- We get married.
- We buy our first house.
- We have children of our own.
- We send our first child off to the first day of school.
- We watch our children graduate from school, marry, and leave home.
- We become grandparents.
- We are recognized as "senior citizens."
- We die.

Clearly, the changes differ from individual to individual; in the above list, for example, some people may or may not marry or have children. For some, the list of significant transitions will include different life events, depending on their culture, religion, ethnic background, and what they find personally meaningful. Two of the transition events are universal, though: we are born and we die.

Most societies mark births. Sometimes a person may not be considered a member of society until formally accepted into it (which is a special transition marking in itself) or life expectancy may be so short that little is invested in a child until it is demonstrated that he or she will live to become a member of society. These societies, and several others, have special ways of marking the transition from pregnant woman to mother in giving birth, sometimes with a purification ceremony after the painful and bloody experience of childbirth.

All societies, however, mark death to some extent. The extent may be large, as in the case of a community leader, or small, as in the case of an infant who dies shortly after birth (and in many societies, a stillborn child is not considered to have lived). The extent of marking is determined by the deceased's family and friends to some degree, but the cultural/religious traditions of the deceased tend to dominate the event. The cultural milieu and the religion of the deceased prescribe rituals that are performed at this and other major transition points of life. In this chapter, we will examine the purpose of these rituals and the form that they take within several cultural and religious groups.

THE PURPOSES OF RITUALS

For hygienic reasons, there must be some mechanism for disposing of a dead body. But this can occur in many ways, and simple disposal of decaying waste does not mandate an elaborate ritual. Yet some of the most intricate rituals in many societies are those involved in this procedure. Anthropologists have given us detailed descriptions of several of these rituals in many different cultures and the importance of these rituals to the society is noteworthy.

Anthropologist Arnold van Gennep (1960) discussed what he named **liminality,** the state of being in transition. The deceased person can be viewed as making the transition from living in this world, to passing from it, and, in some belief systems, to living in another world. The mourners are also in transition from their roles in life associated with their relationship to the deceased. Thus, for example, a wife makes a transition into widowhood. To mark these transitions, societies have **rites of passage.** Simply put, rites of passage are rituals or ceremonies which note and sometimes facilitate the change from one state to another. **Rituals** are patterned responses to a situation that are usually symbolic and give expression to the emotions of the individual or group (Rando, 1985).

Van Gennep (1960) divided rites of passage into three parts:

1. **Rites of separation.** The end of life means a separation of the dying individual from society and a separation of the mourners from the presence and the roles of the deceased.
2. **Rites of transition.** At the end of life, several belief systems (e.g., some Indonesian groups, as described by Hertz, 2004) believe that the spirit of the deceased remains around the home or place of death before moving into a spirit world. In some cultures, special rituals acknowledge this state of the deceased. In more contemporary Western terms, Froggatt (1997) suggested that an individual's time in hospice care, waiting for death, constitutes a time of transition. For the mourners, the time of mourning and the rituals accompanying it (e.g., the wake, the visitation at a funeral home, sitting shivah) is a time when society places fewer demands on the mourner to fulfill his or her normal social roles. The mourners, then, are in a transitional state, not dead but not fully functioning in society.
3. **Rites of incorporation or integration.** In belief systems that include an afterlife, these rites usher the deceased into the spirit world. For the mourners, special ceremonies (e.g., memorial service or

unveiling of a headstone at the end of a year) may mark the societally acknowledged mourning period. At this point, the mourners are accepted back (reintegrated) into society, with all the usual expectations placed on them.

Some anthropologists suggest that end-of-life rituals developed because of a fear of the dead (see Irion, 1990–1991; Kastenbaum, 2004). Although this cause cannot be established with certainty, the purpose that people put on the rituals can. Romanoff and Terenzio (1998) reviewed the literature on end-of-life rituals and compiled a substantial number of purposes that these rituals serve:

- *Preservation of social order.* When a member of society dies, a gap is left in the constellation of roles and duties that were fulfilled by that individual, often leaving confusion, unpredictability, or even chaos among those who relied on the deceased. With end-of-life or funerary rituals, which are patterned and predictable, society attempts to re-establish order. The change in society's network is noted while providing stability and order to the group. In this regard, Turner (1969) noted that during the transition period, the individual is in a state of confusion and disorder while the old identity is reshaped to prepare the individual for a new identity with different demands and expectations.
- *Expression and containment of strong emotions.* The death of an individual brings pain and anxiety to those left behind. Most societies try to find ways of dealing with strong emotions because their free expression might endanger the functioning of the group. For example, among several North American Aboriginal groups is a cultural norm to control strong emotions (Bopp, Bopp, Brown, & Lane, 1984). If a person gives way to the expression of grief (or anger, joy, etc.), there is little chance that the individual will be able to perform the duties that the group relies on for survival (refer, for example, to the traditional Cree and Ojibwa, as discussed by Ross, 1992, 1996). The strong emotion might be overwhelming and certainly is energy sapping. Anxiety is often paralyzing. Nonetheless, these emotions exist and need an outlet for the healthy functioning of the individual and the group. Funerary practices can provide such an outlet, in a controlled and contained space in which the needs of the group are not disrupted and are more fully met. The predictable nature of the ritual is helpful in dealing with the anxiety engendered by the individual and the group unpredictability left through death. Thus, end-of-life rituals may have a healing function.
- *Mediation of transitions.* As van Gennep (1960) has pointed out, death is a transition for the individual, for the mourners, and for the society. End-of-life rituals mark these transitions, such as from wife to widow, or parented child to orphan, making clear the new social status of at least some mourners and the new expectations and roles that this status confers on them. At the same time, the continuity of the society, even in the absence of the deceased, is reaffirmed by drawing together individuals with the common goal of the end-of-life rites.
- *Affirmation of the deceased's place in, and value to, the group.* With a formal ritual, the life of the deceased, including his or her relationship to the group, the functions served within the group, and the significance of the role the deceased played in the group are noted and honoured.
- *Social support.* As noted by Grimes (2000), the funerary rites provide the mourners with more social support at the time of their greatest grief, anxiety, and confusion. The ritual also serves as an acknowledgment that the world is not the same as it was before the death. This provides additional assurance to the mourners that their loved one was important, and it assures the living that when they die, their importance to the group will be noted as well. "A good funeral is one that celebrates a life, comforts the bereaved, and facilitates working through grief," says Grimes (p. 230).

Kastenbaum (2004) points out two other highly significant functions of end-of-life rituals:

- *Taking care of the dead.* Many societies and belief systems considered it necessary for the living to perform behaviours to ease the passage of the dead into the next life. Thus, many cultures buried their dead along with tools, instruments, and food for use in the afterlife (e.g., ancient Egyptians). Even today, in some belief systems (e.g., Catholicism, Buddhism), prayers for the dead are said to speed the deceased on his or her journey to the next life, be it in Paradise or in a new earthly incarnation.
- *Facing the reality of death.* One of the prime issues that mourners must face is the reality that someone they love has died. Until that has been assimilated, it is extremely difficult for the living to reformulate their societal networks and move on in the healthy functioning of life. Especially in the case of unanticipated death, people may experience a great deal of shock or denial that the death has truly occurred. Rituals that are specific to the end of life help the mourners, and the rest of the community, to acknowledge that the death really happened.

In modern Western society, end-of-life rituals have often become remote, artificially formalized, one-time events that are devoid of personal meaning to a great extent. The larger society that the individual functioned in may not be involved to any degree, thus robbing the rituals of much of the meaning that they once held for a community. This does not have to be the case: think of the millions of people who watched the funerals of former prime minister Pierre Trudeau or Princess Diana on television. In these cases, the larger society was involved in a way that is unlikely to occur when the deceased is not famous. But even when the deceased is not famous, we have ways to make the end-of-life rituals more meaningful. People are increasingly arranging for more personalized and less rigidly stylized rituals to mark the end of life (Emke, 2002; Kastenbaum, 2004; Parsons, 2003; Vandendorpe, 2000). These rituals will be discussed more later and Box 4.4 gives some examples.

In some cases, rituals are prescribed or created for the individual before the death. Box 4.1 discusses some of these. In other cases, the only rituals follow the death. Almost all religious traditions allow for some flexibility in what occurs at the rituals, as long as the basic prescribed one is followed as well. Let us turn to a brief examination of the basic structure of the religious traditions discussed in Chapter 3 in their end-of-life rituals, noting that within general belief systems are varieties of specific beliefs that are reflected in rituals. So, for example, within the Christian tradition, a Catholic funeral will be different from a Protestant funeral. Note too that different cultural milieus may add to or even modify some rituals; thus, an Italian Catholic funeral will not look the same as a Filipino Catholic funeral.

BOX 4.1   Pre-Death Rituals

Several religious traditions include special rituals for the individual who is at the threshold of death (e.g., reading of Psalm 23 or 139 in Judaism, confession of sins and asking for forgiveness in the presence of family in Islam, last rites or anointing of the sick in Roman Catholicism). These rituals mark the beginning of the separation of the individual from this life. They are also designed to give comfort to the dying person and to facilitate the movement of his or her soul from this life into the afterlife.

A new pre-death ceremony is gaining popularity in Japan. Japan has been noted for its cultural respect for seniors, but this has been declining in recent years, perhaps because, with modern medicine, a long life is becoming very common. With a declining reproductive rate in Japan comes the very real fear that there will not be sufficient younger workers to pay for pensions and medical care for an expanding older population. To address this and the very impersonal funeral service that typically exists in Japan, a new ceremony, the pre-funeral (*seizensô*), emerged in the early 1990s to celebrate the senior individual's independence and self-sufficiency. The ceremony is planned and executed by the older individual in a very idiosyncratic way; the individual combines whatever elements he or she wants and may or may not stipulate that this ceremony take the place of a traditional post-death funeral. The event typically includes feasting, music, and speeches resembling eulogies, and the person says thank you and

goodbye to those attending, usually from a seat on a flower-decked altar. No religious authority is involved in this ceremony.

The pre-funeral is reminiscent of more traditional Japanese rituals surrounding the attainment of old age, but the traditional rituals celebrate growing older as a desirable state and are planned by the younger generation. The pre-funeral emphasizes the elements of parting from the social community more than a traditional funeral does, allowing the celebrant to communicate with those he or she will part from eventually. The mood is festive rather than sombre, and the event often signifies a transition for the individual from one state into another. The individual is not considered socially dead, but the usual social expectations are no longer binding. For example, the individual may no longer take part in the socially important tradition of sending New Year's cards. Thus, the cultural interdependence that has been part of the Japanese senior person's life is loosened: the individual may now live with more thought to his or her own wants than to the welfare of the community. This event is a concrete way of taking charge of life and so combines death and rebirth in a unique way; it also has the benefit of acting as a preparatory ritual for the future mourners.

Source: Adapted from "Pre-funerals in contemporary Japan: The making of a new ceremony of later life among aging Japanese" by Kawano, S. (2004). Reprinted with permission of Ethnology.

END-OF-LIFE RITUALS

The Judaic Ritual

Several schools of Judaism exist, but the most formal and detailed end-of-life rituals are found among Orthodox Jews (Lamm, 1969). In the Judaic tradition, it is important that the dying person be attended by family and friends at all times. When the individual dies, a son or close relative closes the deceased's eyes and mouth, binding the lower jaw. The family places the corpse on the floor, covered with a sheet, with a lighted candle at the head. The body is washed in a ritual fashion by the family or specially designated community members. The body is covered in a white shroud and placed in a plain wooden coffin with no metal nails or screws, indicating that in the eyes of God, all people are equal and all that is buried will return to the ashes and dust from which it was created. Embalming is forbidden, and the body should be buried (not cremated, except occasionally among Reform Jews) within 24 hours of death, if possible. The casket is always closed during funeral services. Flowers are not considered appropriate (except in a minor way among Reform Jews); contributions to charity are considered to be a more fitting memorial to the deceased. In a service that uses little decoration or ostentation, mourners tear a portion of an outer garment or wear a torn ribbon to symbolize their grief and their disregard of superficialities. The funeral service itself is marked by the reading of prayers and psalms and the recitation of the *El Molai Rachamim* prayer and sometimes the **Kaddish** prayer, a prayer for the dead that is delivered in an Aramaic dialect. A eulogy may be given by a rabbi as well. Whether or not the Kaddish is recited at the funeral, it is recited often by the mourners afterward.

The casket is carried slowly to the graveyard, with several pauses along the way. After prayers and the *El Molai Rachamim* have been said, each person participates by placing one shovelful of earth into the grave. The family then leaves by passing between two rows of those who have accompanied them to the gravesite.

A primary mourning period of seven days follows the funeral for Orthodox Jews (usually three days for Reform Jews), which is known as sitting **shivah.** During this time, the mourners sit on low stools, do no work, including anything but the minimal amount of personal grooming (e.g., the men do not shave), and avoid wearing leather. In addition, mirrors are covered. All of this is to indicate the mourners' lack of interest in superficialities at this time. A special memorial candle is burned for the seven days, and the community visits, bringing food for the mourners, who do not cook, either. The next period of mourning is known as *shloshim* (meaning 30, because it lasts until the 30th day after burial). Traditionally, during that period, the mourners do not attend parties or celebrations, do not shave or cut their hair, and do not listen to music.

A third mourning period of one year consists of the Kaddish being recited by mourners and a **minyan** (group of at least 10 males above the age of 13) attending every service in the synagogue if the deceased was a parent. The grave is properly demarcated as soon as possible with a simple tombstone, but the unveiling of the tombstone typically takes place near the end of the mourning year, with prayers, including the Kaddish, and often a eulogy. Each year, on the anniversary of the death, the deceased's name is read in the synagogue and the family lights a candle, which burns for 24 hours.

The Christian Ritual

The Christian tradition has hundreds of permutations, each with its own funerary practices. The most elaborate are those of Roman Catholicism. These traditions have become more flexible in recent years; however, the format of the funeral service is basically the same. The body of the deceased is usually prepared (embalmed or not) by the funeral director. The casket containing the corpse is lodged in the funeral home, or in some cases the deceased's home, for visitation, the time when family and friends come together to view the body (if the casket is open) and to reminisce, give eulogies, and lend support to the chief mourners. Sometimes mourners eat and drink as they celebrate the life of the deceased (a **wake**).

After one or two days, the casket is closed and transported to a Catholic church. A funeral **Mass,** the Mass of the Resurrection, that blesses the dead, relating his or her life and death to the life of Christ, and commends his or her soul to God's mercy is performed by a priest in the church. The prayers for the dead are to speed the deceased on the journey through Purgatory to Heaven (see Chapter 3). In a Catholic funeral, attendants partake of Holy Communion (ingesting bread and wine that have been transmuted into the body and blood of Christ). Candles, incense, and holy water are used in the service, but other secular symbols, such as flags, are not allowed to be near the casket during the service. No eulogies are given at this time. The casket is then transported to a cemetery, hallowed ground that has been blessed by a priest, or to a crematorium. Prayers are said at the graveside or at the crematorium, and the casket is lowered into the ground or pushed through a curtain, where it is taken to a furnace if it is to be cremated. If the deceased is cremated, the ashes must be interred. There

BOX 4.2   The Day of the Dead in Mexico

The celebration of the Day of the Dead in Mexico serves as a good example of how a religious tradition and a cultural tradition have come together. Mexico is a highly Catholicized country and has been for several centuries. However, before the arrival of Catholic missionaries, the Mexican culture (Aztec) was highly developed, with its own rituals. At the end of July and the beginning of August, Aztec rituals celebrated children and the dead. Finding that these rituals were impossible to abolish, Catholic missionaries sought to "Christianize" them by moving them to the Christian holy day of All Hallows Eve at the beginning of November.

Today, the celebrations combine Christian and Aztec features. Although the practices of the Day of the Dead differ across communities, in general,

this is the time when families visit the graves of their close kin, tending to the graves and decorating them with flowers and religious Catholic amulets. This is a very social time, with families having sumptuous picnics in the graveyard and interacting with other families. Stories are told about the dead, not in a morbid fashion, but in a festive way that celebrates the lives of the deceased. On November 2, the Day of the Dead feast is held, with special confections in the shape of skulls and skeletons, and gifts with a death motif are given as well. A gift with a skull or skeleton emblazoned with one's name is particularly prized. The presence of death within life is acknowledged and life is celebrated in this context.

Source: Salvador (2003).

are no specific ceremonies that are analogous to sitting shivah, but Masses may be said for the dead for many years after the death. (See Box 4.2 for an example of the continuing rituals for the dead in the Mexican culture.)

The Eastern Orthodox Church includes a vigil over the body of the deceased. This is a time of contemplation on death. Chants, hymns, prayers, and Bible readings are included in the funeral service. The body is typically buried, although cremation is acceptable in those countries whose law demands it.

Protestant churches have their own specific funeral services, but these tend to be much more flexible. A Protestant funeral may consist of prayers and Bible readings alongside readings of literature, singing, eulogies, and so on. These may occur either in a church or in the funeral home. In either venue, fewer symbols are present (e.g., no incense or holy water), although Anglican and Lutheran funerals may also include Holy Communion for the attendants. Both burial and cremation are acceptable; if the body is buried, some traditions (e.g., Lutheran) allow mourners to throw handfuls of dirt on the casket when it has been lowered into the grave. **Cremains** (the ashes left from cremation) may be interred, scattered, or kept in any location, depending on the wishes of the family. No particular after-funeral services are prescribed.

Because of the flexibility of the Protestant tradition, funerals are more easily and more likely to be personalized. For example, Jamaican funerals include brightly coloured clothing for the mourners, singing, dancing, and eating. Attendance at what is perceived as a

social occasion may be huge, with everyone welcome (Hopwood, 2003).

The Islamic Ritual

In the Islamic tradition, when the time of death approaches, friends, family, or a religious authority give comfort to the dying person, reading verses from the Koran and reminding the individual of the love and mercy of Allah. If possible, the dying person is encouraged to say, as his or her last words, a declaration of faith: "I bear witness that there is no god but Allah." At the time of death, the attendants at the death say, "To Allah we belong and to Him is our return."

After death, the eyes of the dead person are closed, and the body is washed in a ceremonial fashion in scented water and covered with special pieces of white cloth. The body may be clothed in the cloth that was worn when the deceased went on a pilgrimage or *hajj.* Male deceased are ministered to by other males, and female deceased by other females, but otherwise everyone is treated in the same manner, to indicate that all are equal in the eyes of Allah. Embalming is not permitted (unless required by law), and the body is placed in a simple wooden coffin for the funeral, which takes place as soon as possible after death, preferably within 24 hours. The body is taken to an outdoor location, usually a cemetery, where prayers are said. Both males and females are allowed to participate to this point, but when the body is taken to the gravesite for burial (not cremation), the final rituals are performed by men only.

The body is removed from the coffin (if permitted by law) and the deceased is laid in the grave on his or her right side, facing Mecca. By tradition, the corpse is surrounded by stones and a wooden plank is laid on top of the body before the grave is filled with earth. Also, strictly speaking, detailed tombstones, markers, and flowers or other objects are not encouraged on the grave, although some Islamic gravesites are quite elaborate (e.g., the Taj Mahal). Generally only simple markers, with the deceased's name and date of death are erected, and the family may give money to the poor instead of spending it on an intricate memorial stone. Mourners are permitted to cry, but they are discouraged from showing any other signs of grief (such as wailing or screaming), though in some Muslim countries, the women engage in stylized wailing and lamentation. It is preferred that the mourners think of Allah and mercy, and pray for the dead person.

Mourners observe a three-day mourning period, at which time visitors may offer condolences and attend a feast to commemorate the deceased. Mourners refrain from wearing jewellery or decorative clothing. Relatives visit the gravesite and recite passages from the Koran on the third day. A widow's mourning period is 4 months and 10 days long, during which she may not wear jewellery or decorative clothing, move from her home, or remarry.

The Hindu Ritual

Before death, in the Hindu tradition, the dying person is placed on the floor ("earth to earth") to facilitate the journey of the soul from the body. The family and a priest recite readings from sacred texts and remind the dying person that the soul cannot die. A basil leaf is dipped into the water of the sacred river, the Ganges, and some of this water is placed on the tongue of the dying person. The windows are kept open to allow for the easy departure of the soul (Laungani, 2005).

After death, the family washes the dead body and clothes it in a shroud decorated with sandalwood paste and garlands of flowers. The face of the deceased is clearly in view. The body is cremated, usually the same day as the death occurs, with the belief that this will release the person's essence so that his or her soul can leave the area and continue its journey to the next incarnation. The body is carried to the funeral pyre by the family on an open wooden bier and is carried around the pyre three times counterclockwise. The nearest male relative lights the fire and walks around the burning body three times while reciting sacred Hindu verses. Three days after the body has been burned, someone (not usually the chief mourner) collects the ashes and temporarily buries them. On the 10th day after the crematory ceremony, relatives

of the deceased scatter the ashes in a sacred river, preferably the Ganges. Another funeral ceremony is held within 31 days of the cremation. An important part of this service is for the deceased's son to recite prayers and invoke the beneficence of the ancestors. If the deceased had no son, another male relative can take this duty, but the effect is not considered as beneficial (which is one reason that Hindus traditionally have desired to have a son). In Western countries, these practices have been modified somewhat, in accordance with the law (see Box 4.3).

After the cremation, mourners return home to eat and offer prayers, but before entering the house, they wash and change their clothes. During the days of mourning, mourners are considered impure, so they cover all religious pictures in the house and do not engage in any religious activity, such as festivals or marriages. Usually, a priest will visit to purify the house with incense and spices, and visitors come for 13 days to convey their condolences to the mourners. A photograph of the deceased, decorated with a garland of dried or artificial flowers, is usually on display.

On the first anniversary of the death, food is given to the poor in memory of the deceased and a priest offers prayers. This ritual continues for one month, during which time the family does not buy new clothes or attend parties. Some families continue this tradition on every anniversary of the death. The responsibility for this rests with the eldest son.

Before 1829, when the ruling British outlawed the practice, it was common for widows to willingly allow themselves to be cremated along with their dead husband (*suttee*). This practice still occasionally occurs in very rural areas of India.

The Buddhist Ritual

No specific dogma dictates what should compose a Buddhist funeral. The different schools of Buddhism typically combine with the culture of the country to form a funeral rite. Thus, Chinese Buddhist funeral traditions are different from Tibetan, Japanese, Thai, and so on, Buddhist funeral traditions. In all traditions, however, the body of the deceased is available for mourners to view. By Buddhist beliefs, viewing the body is a valuable reminder of the impermanence of life. Thus, even the dead body teaches a Buddhist lesson.

As an example of the Buddhist rituals, we will examine rituals in China. The Chinese form of Buddhism is in the Mahayana school, which has a flexible, community emphasis. In China, Buddhism combines with Confucianism and Taoism, and with folk customs, in the formation of a belief system and funeral rites. On the death of a father, the eldest son becomes head of the family. If the eldest son is also dead, his son assumes the

BOX 4.3   Hindu Funerals in Western Societies

Canada and Britain have large Hindu populations. Many of the traditions of a Hindu funeral cannot be followed, given Canadian and British law and physical considerations, but funeral directors try to accommodate requests whenever possible. Laungani (2005) discussed the differences between Hindu funerals in Britain and more traditional funerals in India:

- In Britain arrangements are made by funeral directors, not by the family, who often do not participate in the washing and clothing of the body.
- In Britain cremations are more likely to be 4 to 6 days after the death rather than within 24 hours.
- In Britain the body is transported in a closed coffin rather than an open bier, meaning that the face of the deceased is not seen during the transportation. This can cause significant distress to mourners. On April 13, 2006, mourners in India rioted at the funeral procession of film star Raj Kumar because, contrary to India's norms, they were unable to see his face.
- In Britain funeral directors are usually dressed in black, and black is the colour of most funeral cars. The Hindu colour of mourning is white.
- In Britain a funeral pyre is replaced by a crematorium. Instead of the body being placed on a pyre, the body is slid into the furnace. There is no opportunity for the highly significant rituals of walking in a circle around the funeral pyre

and setting a torch to the pyre. The eldest son hits a switch to start the cremation instead.

Hindu tradition considers the family's duty to the dead to be of paramount importance. Thus, depriving the family of the chance to perform the rituals is greatly disturbing to many. Although the reasons for not having a funeral pyre are clear, less clear are the reasons for not allowing the family to participate in the washing and laying out of the body. (Some more enlightened funeral directors offer families the opportunity to do this, but it is far from universal.) The deceased must be transported in a closed coffin because of environmental laws in Britain, but Laungani (2005) points out that both funeral directors and Hindu families would welcome such an innovation as coffins with transparent tops to honour both the Hindu traditions and the British law.

The amendments made to conform to British law do violate some of the precepts of Hinduism. For example, Hinduism teaches that for the soul of the deceased to be successfully reincarnated, the cremation of the body should take place in open air. *The Toronto Star* reported on July 22, 2006, ("Funeral pyre," 2006) that the first open air cremation in Britain had taken place in violation of the law. Rajpal Mehat's remains were cremated in a field rented for the occasion by the Anglo-Asian Friendship Society. They did this, they explained, because Mehat's remains were unfit for transport back to India, as is often done to avoid the "catastrophic consequences to the departed soul" (p. L11).

---

leadership position, that is, the head of the family status does not go to the second-eldest son. The role of the head of the family is replete with duty and responsibilities toward the ancestors.

In the Chinese tradition are two major rituals concerning the dead. First, a funeral ceremony traditionally lasts for 49 days, with the first 7 days being the most important. If the family can afford it (daughters usually bear the expenses), priests and monks hold a prayer ceremony, with drums and trumpets, as well as the chanting of prayers taken from sacred Buddhist writings (*sutras*) every day for seven days. The prayers are to help the deceased on the journey to rebirth and to redeem the soul from the possibility of an unpleasant next life. The head of the family should be present for the first, and at least the second, ceremony and for the burial or cremation. If the family (daughters) does not have enough money, the intense period of the funeral is three days

instead of seven. The head of the family should also be present for the burial or the cremation.

Second, a prayer ceremony is held every 10 days, the first quickly following the death, and then at three succeeding periods of 10 days. At the end of this, the deceased is buried or cremated. An optional component is a final prayer ceremony at the end of one hundred days, but this is not considered as important.

In the ceremonies, paper money and household objects made of paper may be burned so that the deceased can have the use of these objects in the next life. The favourite foods of the dead person are placed in the funeral hall or funeral parlour, and *feng shui,* which optimally positions furniture and other objects in space, is practised to balance the influences of earth, water, and air. The aim is to create a harmony among the dead, the living, and the cosmos (Martinson, Chao, & Chung, 2005). White is traditionally worn by the mourners, at least in the form of a paper flower; red is eschewed. The deceased may be viewed in a casket, with wreaths placed nearby. Neither burial nor cremation is preferred in the Mahayana tradition, but whether the deceased or his or her ashes are buried, a tablet or tombstone is erected, often inscribed with not only the deceased's date of birth and death but also the names of other family members (Wu, 2005).

In the Mahayana tradition, the belief is that a transition period occurs between death and reincarnation. During this period, the deceased's rebirth may be affected by the prayers and remembrance ceremonies performed by the family: if the ceremonies and prayers are omitted, the deceased may not have a favourable rebirth. Some Chinese believe that in this case, the deceased's ghost may come back to trouble the neglectful family.

Other countries have somewhat different Buddhist funeral traditions. In Japan, for example, the funeral ceremony may resemble a Christian ceremony, with prayers and eulogies at a funeral home. In Cambodia, Sri Lanka, and Thailand, up to three ceremonies may take place: the first is typically in the home of the deceased within two days of the death, conducted by Buddhist monks. The second, which occurs in a funeral home, is within two to five days of the death, at which time the burial or cremation takes place. The third, which may be in a funeral home or a Buddhist temple, is held seven days after the burial or cremation. This last ceremony, called a **merit transference,** is led by monks, with prayers to send positive energy and goodwill toward the deceased for his or her next incarnation. After a death has occurred and every year following, Buddhists give food and money to monks and to the poor.

The Sikh Ritual

Because Sikhs believe that death is only a transition point of life and signifies a meeting with God, a showing of grief or mourning is not considered appropriate when someone dies. At this time, everyone is treated alike, reflecting the fact that all are equal in the Sikh tradition. As someone is dying and at the death, the body is not immediately moved, but the family and friends who are present say prayers acknowledging death as being part of the will of God.

The body is then prepared for cremation by being bathed in yogurt while prayers are said and then being dressed in new clothing. The symbols of Sikhism (the *kirpan,* the *kara,* the *kachera,* the *kanga,* and *kesh;* see Chapter 3) are included with the body in a coffin.

The body is usually brought to the deceased's home or to a funeral home, where a brief service of prayers and readings is conducted, which may or may not be led by a minister. The men wear black headscarves and the women wear light-coloured or white headscarves.

Sometimes a second ceremony is held in a Sikh place of worship, but this is optional. Hymns may be sung as the body is transported to a crematorium. These hymns are designed to induce detachment and help the family not to display their natural grief. At the crematorium, prayers of blessing for the deceased are said and a family member lights the funeral pyre (or activates the switch that makes the casket disappear and starts the crematory furnace). The ashes of the deceased are collected, and although they may be scattered anywhere that was meaningful to the deceased, they are more likely scattered in a body of flowing water.

The guests at the funeral go the family's home after the cremation for more hymn singing and prayers, and the community undertakes to make a sizable meal for the chief mourners. Everyone who has attended the funeral must bathe as soon as they get home to cleanse themselves, and the home of the deceased is cleansed by the burning of a sweet-smelling candle made from clarified butter (*ghee*) and cotton.

The period of major mourning is between two and five weeks. One year after the death, special prayers are said and a meal is shared by the family as a remembrance and celebration of the life of the deceased.

The Bahá'í Ritual

In accordance with the Bahá'í belief in the immortality of the soul, death is regarded positively, and the disposal of the body is not accompanied by many rituals. No particular last rites are given, although if the person is sick or dying, members of the community may gather with him or her for healing prayers.

When death occurs, the body may be autopsied and organs (or the whole body) may be donated, but when the body is released, it must be treated with respect and the few burial laws that exist must be followed. For Bahá'í in Middle Eastern countries, the body is washed and clothed in a plain white cotton or silk shroud. A burial ring is placed on the deceased's finger and he or she is put in a casket of fine hardwood. The body is not embalmed (unless required by law), and the casket may be closed or open for viewing. The deceased is buried with the feet pointing toward the Holy Land. These regulations are not obligatory for Bahá'í followers from other countries.

The place of burial should be in a cemetery within one hour's travel time of the place of death because the faith teaches that the whole world is a person's home and no one should favour any particular geographical location. The funeral service itself is simple, the only requirement being that the Prayer of the Dead be said. Other readings, prayers, eulogies, and music are at the family's discretion. The service may be in a place of worship or at the graveside and is conducted by a family member or a member of the community because this tradition has no clergy.

No mourning rituals are prescribed, but many Baha'i families choose to have memorial services with more readings and prayers. The grave is usually marked with a headstone, but any engraving on it is the family's preference.

The Native Peoples' Rituals

As discussed in Chapter 3, the majority of the Native Peoples are Christian, yet many are either returning to traditional Native beliefs or incorporating these beliefs into their lives to better satisfy their spiritual needs. The different bands have many differing beliefs in their approach to the end of life, although a similar core exists. We will examine only a few of the specific rituals that different bands use at the time of death.

The Algonquian People of the Great Lakes and Ohio Valley regions may bury a body or wrap a body in animal skins, place it on a scaffold until the flesh has decayed, and then bury the bones. Personal possessions, such as the person's medicine bag, pipe, and tobacco, plus a bowl containing some corn and a spoon, are buried with the body so that the deceased can join in feasting in the Land of Souls, the afterlife. Family and community members keep a fire burning on the grave mound for four days, the time it takes the soul to reach the Land of Souls. Traditionally, the time of mourning for the family is one year (Carmody & Carmody, 1993).

The Iroquois, also of the Great Lakes area, are provided with guidelines for the funerary ritual by the Great Law of Peace: the deceased is buried and told to go to the Creator. Mourners can grieve but should be restrained in their grief and avoid engaging in idle behaviour and gossip. Strict mourning practices are observed for 10 days after the burial, at which time the mourners are brought together for a feast to thank them for their participation and to release them from their mourning. Although the strict mourning is over in 10 days, the family is considered to be in a lesser mourning for one year.

The Lakota Sioux of the Great Plains (southern parts of Saskatchewan, Manitoba, and Alberta; and Montana, North and South Dakota, and Wyoming in the United States) have a ritual called the **keeping of the soul** for death rites (Brown, 1989). This ritual is for purification of the soul so that it may move on to the afterlife and not wander the earth disconsolately. The body of a dead person is placed on a scaffold and left exposed to the elements, symbolically giving the body back to its source. The bones are kept in a sacred bundle until the keeping of the soul ritual, which occurs when the family has accumulated the necessary accoutrements

(such as special purified food), usually in one year. Then the formal ceremony is performed. This includes ritualized smoking of the pipe, chanting, and praying. It is seen as acceptable and appropriate to express grief at this point, in recognition of the community's loss and the power of God. The special purified food is offered to the soul and is ritually consumed by some members of the community. Prayers are then offered directing the soul to leave the sacred bundle and journey to the afterlife. This is followed by joyful feasting and the giving of charity to the poor.

The Kwatkiutl of British Columbia, as well as the Bella Coola, Haida, Tlingit, and Salish of the Pacific Northwest Coast, honour the dead by holding a **potlatch**, a ceremony of gift giving, typically on a lavish scale. The body of the deceased is usually cremated and then the attendees feast and gifts are given to all. The extent of gift giving used to be an indication of the status of the deceased and his or her family, and it often served prestige functions directly, but the prime function is to honour and as tribute to the deceased. In many Pacific Northwest Coast tribes, a second potlatch is held as a memorial one year after the death (Beck, 1993).

ARE FUNERALS EFFECTIVE IN COMFORTING THE BEREAVED?

Whether funerals are effective in providing comfort depends on many things. Anecdotally, it is common to hear people state that they hate funerals. The purposes that an end-of-life ritual is supposed to serve are clearly not served for them. The reason may be the lack of meaningfulness of the ritual for a particular individual. In general, as long as a ritual has personal significance for an individual, it may comfort him or her and be regarded as an appropriate closure to the deceased's life. For example, Quartier, Hermans, and Scheer (2004) found that even devout Catholics regarded the personal and biographical elements of a funeral to be more important than the liturgical, ritualized elements of a funeral Mass. Perhaps the formal ritual of the Mass has less meaning for the grieving person than do the personal memorial tributes to the dead loved one, although it is clear that for some people, the formality and structure of the ritual is in itself a comfort, perhaps as it signifies continuity of a community or belief system. The issue of meaningfulness, whether it pertains to funerals, death, the process of dying, or, indeed, to life itself, is of paramount importance and, as such, will be discussed in detail in Chapter 13.

Personalizing funerals has become much more common and can be viewed as the mourners' attempt to make individual meaning of the final rituals for the deceased. In some cases, people plan their own funerals and pay for them ahead of time, so that when they die, the funeral directors or religious authorities can follow the instructions without having to involve the family or friends. In other cases, people give specific instructions for their funerals to their families and friends, perhaps within a special document or perhaps simply verbally. In all these cases, the need to inject personal characteristics of the deceased and the mourners becomes apparent. Only in this way can these people find meaning in the end-of-life ceremonies. See Box 4.4 for examples of personalized funerals.

People, especially those who hate funerals, often have a particular animosity toward funeral directors (Parsons, 2003). Some people regard them as morbid associates of death while others regard them as mercenary and insincere. Much of this hostility is a result of the natural anger that accompanies bereavement and some of it is due to the inherent role difficulties of the funeral director. Parsons (2003) outlines some of the conflicts and misunderstandings:

- *Economics of the funeral.* The funeral industry is often seen as mercenary and profiting at the expense of the bereaved. This has especially occurred since the advent of Jessica Mitford's book *The American Way of Death* (1963), which suggested that the funeral industry profiteers from the grief of others (see also Prothero,

---

BOX 4.4 Personalized Funerals

The only limit to what can be requested at an end-of-life ceremony is the imagination. Whether the request will be acceded to depends on the flexibility of the funeral director and the religious officiant and whether it contradicts the law of the community (e.g., in Belgium, cremains can only be scattered in designated "memorial gardens" or at sea; Vandendorpe, 2000). Below are some of the requests that have been made. You may find them strange or poignant, but the critical issue is that acceding to these requests made the end-of-life rituals more personal and meaningful for the mourners:

- playing favourite music, even a theme song from a soap opera
- having a parade of all-terrain vehicles to the graveyard (Emke, 2002)
- placing special objects, such as a prized hunting rifle or a crochet hook, in the casket
- asking mourners to wear bright-coloured clothing instead of the more traditional black
- reading from personally meaningful, secular literature, such as poetry, *Tuesdays with Morrie* (by Mitch Albom), even children's books
- passing out bubble gum to participants at a memorial service

Sofka (2004) described one memorial service that was arranged by the deceased before her death. She asked that participants eat her favourite food, chocolate, and blow bubbles while listening to stories. Also, because she had been active in animal rescue, she asked that this be commemorated by participants bringing stuffed animals, which would be put in small wagons and pulled down the church aisle by children she had specifically invited in what she called a "Critter Parade," while her veterinarian sang *All God's Critters.*

In planning her own funeral, nurse Brianne Koning, one of the author's students, provided the following directions for her funeral and her wake:

> I am definitely having a funeral. It will be a Catholic one, but it will be tailored to my own likings. My readings will be meaningful, the songs will be joyful, not sad. Nobody will sing *Amazing Grace.* The songs might not even be hymns. I will make them country music songs and people will end up tapping their toes to the beat. They won't be sad I'm dead, they'll be happy because of how I lived! My life is/will be awesome and they'll be a part of it.
>
> After the funeral, there will be a big party! Huge! People will play euchre and there will be a huge cake with my face on it. There will be a big bonfire in the field at the end of the night and everyone will sit around it telling hilarious stories and memories from my life with them. Each story will be personalized to their memory of me and how I was in their life. Celebrators (not mourners) will be able to camp out in tents or go home for the night.

Another innovation that reflects society's greater concern with the environment is the Bio Urn: cremains are placed in the urn, along with a seed that germinates on burial. The idea is that one day, forests will arise from graveyards ("Recommended," 2006).

In yet another attempt at personalization, a book entitled *Fancy Coffins to Make Yourself* was featured in an article in *The Toronto Star* on May 27, 2006 (Patch, 2006).

CHAPTER 4 End-of-Life Rituals

2001, for a discussion of cremation in this regard). This sentiment is exacerbated by the fact that most people are neither in a position to do without the funeral industry's services nor able to "shop around" for a good buy. Much of the resentment comes from the hidden costs of a funeral: the funeral itself may take less than two hours, but the preparations for it, that the mourners do not see, may take 40 work hours. In many areas, funeral directors are required to give a financial breakdown of their services to the person who pays for the funeral, but even so, the real complexity of funeral arrangement is unclear to almost everyone who is not in the industry. For example, *embalming* is one simple word, but the actual process is complex and can only be performed by a trained professional. Also, although it is certainly true that an unscrupulous person can take advantage of people who are in the extremes of grief and are therefore not thinking clearly, some people spend more than they can afford on after-death services as a means of resolving their own feelings of guilt about the deceased. In general, funeral directors, like other businesspeople, depend on the goodwill of the client to return and to recommend these services to others. Sacrificing this goodwill by taking advantage of clients is simply not a good business practice and is ethically repugnant.

- *Conflict within the family.* Who makes the funeral arrangements? There is no formal mechanism to establish this, so in most cases, one family member or a small family group steps forward to make the arrangements and pay the costs. In most cases, the funeral director must simply assume that the person or group who steps forward is, in fact, ethically entitled to do so and, on a more practical note, will pay the bill (or remainder if a deposit has been required). Sometimes, however, the situation is not simple: sometimes conflict exists within the family, which is often increased in the highly emotionally charged environment of a fresh bereavement, and the funeral director hears conflicting instructions about the arrangements. Certainly, the funeral director is required to follow the instructions (where possible) of the paying client, but other friends and family members may be resentful of this, feel excluded from the process, and believe that they have better ideas about how the end-of-life ceremonies should be conducted than does the paying client. Take the example of the estranged mother of a deceased man who is paying for the funeral of her son, excluding his common-law wife of 10 years from the process. The wife must allow this since she does not have the money to pay for the funeral, but her wishes and her knowledge of what the deceased wanted as an end-of-life ritual are ignored. The funeral director may receive the brunt of the wife's anger but be unable to follow her wishes.

- *Control of the proceedings.* In many cases, funeral directors take almost complete control of the end-of-life services: they take possession of the corpse and are responsible for the treatment of it; they make the arrangements for the rituals accompanying the disposition of the body; they take charge of the interment or cremation of the body. Although most family members are glad to have someone to take over on these matters (Emke, 2002), they also may feel shut out and placed in the role of passive observers. Parsons (2003, citing Paul) suggests that this makes mourners feel like victims at a time when they already feel victimized by the death of a loved one. Feelings of victimization often lead to anger, which, coupled with the normal anger accompanying grief, is aimed at the funeral director.

- *Post-funeral regret.* When a death occurs, unless a funeral has been preplanned, important decisions must be made quickly. These decisions may be irrevocable: for example, if cremation is selected, the body cannot afterward be buried. It is common for people to rush when making the arrangements for a funeral, wanting to get it out of the way as quickly as possible, and later regret the decisions that they made. For example, the family may want a "simple" service but later feel that the simplicity was cold or impersonal. The regret they feel is often transmuted into anger against the funeral director, whom they regard as the person who arranged for the service to lack personalization.

This list does not include the anger-arousing problems that arise in planning any major event, such as delay of the service because the officiant is late, traffic congestion on the way to an interment, refusal of the officiant to honour mourners' requests, and so on. In all these cases, the anger of the mourners is often aimed at the funeral director. As people insist on more personalized end-of-life services, the funeral director's job will undoubtedly become more complex, resulting in more areas in which the mourners may find reasons to be angry, justly or not.

All cultures engage in end-of-life rituals. The form of these rituals varies greatly, but all show respect for the dead, remembrance of the life that has ended, and hope and solace for the bereaved individuals and the whole community. In these ways, we share grief and our own humanity.

SUMMARY

- All cultures have end-of-life rituals. These rituals may be divided into rites of separation, rites of transition, and rites of integration.

- The purposes of end-of-life rituals include (1) preserving social order; (2) expressing and containing strong emotions; (3) mediating personal and social transitions; (4) affirming the value of the deceased's life; (5) giving social support to mourners; (6) taking care of the dead; and (7) facing the reality of death.

- Some religious systems and cultural systems include pre-death rituals to mark the beginning of the separation of the dying person from the community, to give comfort to the dying, and to facilitate the movement of the soul to an afterlife. These may also help the future mourners to prepare for their bereavement.

- Descriptions are given of Judaic, Christian, Islamic, Hindu, Buddhist, Sikh, and Bahá'í religious traditions following death. Many people in Native Canadian groups, while adhering to the Christian faith, include elements of their traditional ceremonies along with a religious service.

- Funerals are of comfort to the bereaved when they have meaning for the individual. Today, more funerals are being personalized or have personal elements included in more traditional services to increase the meaningfulness.

- Sometimes the funeral does not satisfy the needs of the mourners, and often anger is directed toward the funeral director. Part of this is a deflection of the mourner's natural anger at the death of a loved one, and part is a function of the role of the funeral director. Areas of potential conflict include the financial aspects of the funeral, disagreement among the mourners as to what elements the funeral should contain, and the inherent control over the deceased's body and the arrangements that the funeral director has. Another area of potential conflict is the fact that the mourners must quickly make irrevocable decisions about the funeral; sometimes they later regret their choices, blaming the funeral director for them.

- Although cultural and religious differences among end-of-life rituals are large, all cultures show respect for the dead and concern for living.

KEY TERMS

cremains	merit transference	rituals
feng shui	*minyan*	shivah
hajj	potlatch	*sutras*
Kaddish	rites of incorporation or integration	*suttee*
keeping of the soul	rites of passage	wake
liminality	rites of separation	
Mass	rites of transition	

INDIVIDUAL ACTIVITIES

1. What are the transition points in your life? Make a list of the transitions you have already encountered, then speculate on what future changes may be turning points for you.

2. What losses have you experienced? Make a list, recognizing that every loss engenders grief. For which of these losses are there societally recognized rituals? For

which are there no rituals? Would a ritual have helped you to deal with some of these losses? Create a ritual for yourself for a specific loss.

3. Plan a very personalized funeral. This could be for you, for someone you know, even for a fictional character.

GROUP ACTIVITIES

1. In groups of four or five, compare your answers to the first question in the individual activities. How much commonality is there among you in what changes you have found significant and what changes you expect to find significant in the future? Is there a difference between males and females? Is there a difference depending on religious, ethnic, or cultural background? Having heard the significant transitions of others, would you modify your own list in any way?

2. In groups of four or five, compare your answers to the third question in the individual activities. What different personal elements do people include? After hearing a variety of personal elements, are there changes you would make in your personalized funeral?

3. In groups of four or five, plan a personalized funeral for a fictional character that is known to all group members. Is there accord or disagreement on what elements should be included?

4. Have each member in a group of four or five contact a funeral director and ask what he or she finds the easiest and the most difficult parts of the job. What is the most memorable funeral element the funeral director can remember? Bring the answers back to share with the group.

Grief and Bereavement

Bereavement Reactions

Student nurses and social workers who had never experienced a personal bereavement were asked how they thought they would react if the person closest to them suddenly died. Here are some of their answers:

- "I would scream and yell and cry and get hysterical."

- "I would be in a total state of shock. I might never come out of it."

- "I would be furious! I would hate everybody who was still alive."

- "I'd probably kill myself."

- "I'd wither away and die."

- "I'd be so confused I wouldn't be able to make sense out of anything that was happening."

- "I'd go into a deep, deep depression."

All of these statements are normal reactions to bereavement.

BOX 5.1   The Case of Edgar Bevins

Edgar Bevins had been happily married to Samantha for 14 years. They had no children, but they didn't mind too much because they said they were enough for each other. On a bright winter's morning, while she was driving to work, Samantha's car was hit by a truck that skidded on ice and she was fatally injured. Edgar, already at work, picked up the phone and heard someone tell him what had happened and to come to the hospital right away if he wanted to say goodbye to his wife. He hung up the phone in a daze. "This must be some sick prank," he thought, quickly dialling his wife's cell phone number. When she didn't answer, he said to himself, "She forgot to turn it on again. How many times have I told her?"

One of his coworkers, seeing him behaving in an uncustomary fashion, asked him what was wrong, and Edgar told her. The coworker became alarmed and phoned the police, only to find that the call had not been a prank at all. She took Edgar's arm gently and told him she would drive him to the hospital. He angrily resisted, claiming he had no need to go to the hospital; his wife was fine. The coworker finally prevailed and took Edgar to the emergency entrance of the local hospital, where they were met by police officers and a physician who hurriedly ushered Edgar, still protesting, into a small cubicle. There Samantha lay dying. Edgar fell to his knees on seeing her and demanded that the doctors "do something." The emergency ward physician informed him that nothing could be done, that Samantha's injuries would soon prove fatal. Within an hour, Samantha died. The medical personnel let Edgar stay with her body for as long as he wanted, but within the hour, Edgar's sister, notified by the coworker, arrived and led Edgar away.

The next few days passed with Edgar scarcely aware of them. He was conscious of having gone to the funeral parlour to arrange Samantha's funeral and of people coming back and forth to his home. He couldn't remember eating or sleeping, but he supposed he must have. The only thought in his mind that he was aware of was getting through the funeral in as calm a manner as possible for Samantha's sake. After taking a week off work (he was allowed five days by his employer), he returned to work and the sympathy of his coworkers. His concentration was faulty at work, though, and he made mistakes on simple procedures that he knew well. The employer was understanding and asked little

of him for the first month after Samantha's death. After that, however, the sympathy started to fade; after all, the company needed to make money, not carry someone who couldn't do the job. Edgar's coworkers also began to get frustrated at having to do so much of his work for him. But Edgar noticed little of this. He still felt like a man in a trance.

Edgar's sleep was haunted by nightmares of Samantha's accident and he woke screaming and crying. His thoughts went to her final moments constantly, and he felt great rage at the doctors who had, in his opinion, not done what they could to save his wife's life. His rage also extended to the truck driver, whom he referred to as "a murderer" (even though the police contended that the truck driver was not at fault), and to the city officials who had not ensured that the roads were properly salted to free them of ice. Occasionally, with feelings of great guilt, he felt angry with Samantha, thinking that she shouldn't have driven to work that day or that she must have been inattentive to driving conditions. He also reproached himself for not having driven her to work himself that day and he felt that he should have found a way to make the car she was driving safer. He found himself resenting the way other people continued on with their lives, as if nothing had happened. In addition to this, Edgar usually forgot to eat because he had no appetite and food was tasteless to him anyway. Sometimes he had frightening heart palpitations and feelings of choking, but these passed after a few dreadful minutes, so he didn't consult a physician, thinking he should "tough it out like a man."

After six months, Edgar's anger started to fade and he began to feel nothing but despondent. He didn't admit to anyone that he spent hours in the evening looking at pictures of his life with Samantha and holding a sweater that she had loved. Sometimes he fell into his fitful sleep holding the sweater to his face. Every blonde woman on the street made his heart jump, as he thought, "It's Sam!" only to lead to his profound disappointment and dejection as he realized it wasn't her and it never would be. At every meaningful day that he and Samantha had celebrated, such as Victoria Day, when they had always watched a display of fireworks, Edgar felt the grief again as if the death had just occurred.

A year after Samantha's death, people were starting to say to him that it was time to move

BOX 5.1   The Case of Edgar Bevins

on and perhaps even start dating again. After all, they pointed out, he still hadn't managed to teach himself how to cook or to keep a home the way Samantha had. Perhaps a new woman would be helpful to him. This type of conversation left Edgar feeling incredulous: didn't they understand? The idea of dating another woman, of forgetting Samantha and replacing her, was abhorrent to him, and he felt that he would never love again. But maybe people were right: he *did* have to learn how to cook and do laundry properly. When his sister gave him some lessons in basic cooking and housekeeping, Edgar found, to his astonishment, that it wasn't so difficult and that he might even become a good cook. He felt some self-satisfaction at this and said silently, "See, Sam? I'm doing it. Not bad, eh?"

The year after Samantha's death had been one of almost unremitting pain for Edgar, and every holiday, every anniversary, seemed to pierce him anew. But at least he could concentrate a little better now and he was doing much better at work. His sleep was a little better, too, with fewer nightmares. He had avoided the cemetery where she was buried, but at the first anniversary of her death, he wanted to go to her grave to place some flowers. Standing over her grave, Edgar found it impossible to believe that a year had passed and that he had survived. There had been the proverbial three steps forward and two steps

back all along; some days had been not too terrible and some days had been almost unbearable. But he could honestly say that, as time progressed, he had fewer bad days and more good days. Maybe, just maybe, he could see light at the end of the tunnel, even though neither he nor life would ever be the same.

On the second anniversary of Samantha's death, Edgar put away most of his photographs of her, keeping the one he liked the most on display in his bedroom. He thought that perhaps it was time to cook dinner for a few people who had been particularly helpful and supportive to him, so he called his sister and his coworker who had taken him to the hospital that terrible day, inviting them and their families to dinner the following week. Edgar enjoyed planning and cooking the dinner, and almost amazingly to him, the dinner was a great success, with good food and good conversation. They talked about how the last two years had gone by with difficulty, and they laughed about how Samantha would be so surprised at Edgar's newfound cooking prowess. Sharing memories of Samantha brought smiles to Edgar's face, and he suggested to his coworker, with whom he and Samantha had played bridge, that perhaps she could help him find a new bridge partner. "She doesn't have to play the same way Sam did," he said. "I'll learn to figure out her way."

In this and other chapters, we will use terms that must be understood as being different from each other. **Loss** refers to the removal of someone or something that we hold valuable, precious, and meaningful. Thus, for example, loss occurs when the individual has a limb amputated, when a relationship ends, when a loved one dies. **Bereavement** is the state the individual is left in when a loss occurs. This state is usually one that includes **grief**, emotional, physical, and spiritual reactions to the loss. **Mourning** is the way in which this grief is expressed by the individual. Depending on the individual's experiences with loss and seeing others reacting to their losses, mourning can be expressed in many ways. The society and culture in which a person lives influence mourning greatly, as do religious beliefs. For example, in some cultures and religions, bereaved people are expected to follow specific rituals. Less formally, among some groups of people, loud expressions of grief are permitted and expected, while among other groups, such a demonstra-

tion is considered inappropriate and unacceptable. In this chapter, we will examine reactions to bereavement, paying closest attention to the reactions that people have to grief. Remember, however, that the way these reactions manifest, or the style of mourning, will differ among individuals and among groups of people.

In the rather lengthy case study in Box 5.1, we see Edgar experiencing a typical and normal grieving process. Not everyone will experience grief in this way and progress through the grieving process is not as straightforward as the description of Edgar's journey. In this case study, Edgar's grieving, while perhaps never completely over, is resolved to a great extent after two years. This is a realistic time frame for some people, but others take much longer. The oft-asked question "How long does normal grieving take?" has no answer; it takes as long as it takes. Grieving for less than a year is unlikely in most cases (but not all!), but two to six years of primary grief is not uncommon. Even after that, grief may still be felt,

BOX 5.2	Grief Reactions	
EMOTIONAL REACTIONS	COGNITIVE REACTIONS*	BEHAVIOURAL/PHYSICAL REACTIONS

sadness, sorrow
anger, hostility
longing, yearning, pining
loneliness
guilt, reproach
hopelessness
despair
fear
anxiety
ambivalence
relief
jealousy of others not
    suffering loss
	confusion
	disbelief
	distractibility
	decrease in attention, concentration
	inability to make decisions
	pessimism
	rumination about the deceased
	apprehension
	decreased motivation
	feelings of unreality
	search for meaning of the loss, of life,
	    of work, of it all
	cynicism
	feelings of alienation
	hypervigilance
		sighing
		sleep disturbances
		eating disturbances
		crying
		social withdrawal
		uncharacteristic increased or
		    decreased activity level
		substance use and abuse
		avoidance of stimuli associated with
		    the deceased
		lack of energy
		fatigue
		self-destructive behaviour (e.g., high-
		    speed driving)
		lethargy
		trembling
		headache
		heart palpitations
		digestive problems
		sweating
		hot flashes or chills
		shortness of breath
		physical signs of nervousness

Source: Kübler-Ross (1969, 1974, 1981); Parkes (1996); Rando (1993); Worden (2002).

Note that some of these cognitive components also have emotions attached to them.

especially on meaningful days, such as holidays and anniversaries. It is more useful, then, to describe the grieving process without putting time constraints on it. Box 5.2 summarizes some of the different grief reactions, but other reactions are possible. Note that any given individual may experience some or all of these reactions: no two individuals will have the same experience, and the same individual may not react in the same way to two different losses.

It is also normal for some aspects of a grief reaction to continue for many years after the death has occurred, including the occurrence of **subsequent temporary upsurges of grief (STUGs).** These are brief periods in which the grief for the deceased is experienced afresh, as if the bereavement had occurred very recently. These episodes happen during the initial grieving period and may crop up for many years thereafter. They are usually triggered by something that stimulates the memory about the deceased and emphasizes the absence of the loved one. This trigger could be a cue, such as a significant date or holiday; an event, such as a wedding or graduation; a meaningful piece of music; even a smell ("whenever

I smell gingerbread, I feel like Grandma died just yesterday").

As can be seen from the partial list of possible manifestations of grief, an incredibly wide variety of potential reactions exists. In fact, it is such a wide variety that the area seems confused and chaotic. Many people who have worked with dying and bereaved people, however, have noted general patterns of response, and some models of dying and bereavement have since been developed to impose some order on the chaos and to enhance our understanding of the process. In some cases, the models are very detailed; in others, only general suggestions are made in forming a framework of understanding. For the most part, these models are not mutually exclusive; indeed, most of the developers of the models have no real argument with other models, their aim being simply to examine the bereavement process from a different perspective or to expand on the work done by others. In this chapter, we will examine several of the models, recognizing that all have merit and all add to our comprehension of grief.

ELISABETH KÜBLER-ROSS'S STAGE MODEL

In the late 1960s, a psychiatrist named Elisabeth Kübler-Ross began publishing the results of her interviews with hundreds of people who were dying. Very little attention had been directed to the area of the reactions of the dying, probably because of the discomfort that Western society has shown in this area (see Chapter 2). Kübler-Ross's work was groundbreaking in opening up the discussions of death in modern Western society and in her attempts at providing a structure for understanding what had seemed to be chaotic and disorganized reactions to the crisis that a patient with a terminal diagnosis was facing. In her observations, she derived what she termed "stages" in the process of dying. These stages have been misunderstood by some laypeople as being inviolate and progressive in a step-wise fashion, whereas Kübler-Ross meant to indicate only a very general guide to the emotional trajectory of dying. Nonetheless, her work has spawned a great deal of research that has, in several ways, validated many of her observations and has extended our understanding of the psychological reactions that an individual may show when confronted with the diagnosis of a terminal illness. Her stages have also been found to be applicable to the reactions of the bereaved. Because of this, it is worthwhile examining the stages of dying that she proposed (Kübler-Ross, 1969, 1974, 1981).

1. *Denial and isolation.* When first given the diagnosis of a terminal condition, patients report reacting with shock and denial. One of the most common responses to the diagnosis is, "No, the tests must be wrong. This can't be happening to me," especially if the diagnosis is unexpected. Patients may look for a second and even a third opinion to confirm the facts. Kübler-Ross saw the denial as a chance for patients to collect their thoughts and to assimilate the news. The initial denial is usually temporary, although patients may still experience disbelief in periods until death. When experiencing denial, patients also feel isolated and very alone: they cannot talk freely about what is happening to them because they have not yet come to grips with their new reality.

2. *Anger.* The second stage that Kübler-Ross discussed was characterized by the patient's anger. The anger is certainly at the new reality that the patient is dealt, but it often manifests in other ways. Many patients direct anger at their physicians, nurses, other medical staff, friends, and family members. In these cases, criticisms might be levelled at physicians for not making the diagnosis faster or for not being sufficiently caring; other medical personnel might be charged with being inattentive, cold, and uncaring; while everyone in the patient's environment might be accused of lacking understanding and empathy. The specific reasons that patients give for their anger at these people vary, plainly showing that with this reaction, others cannot mollify patients or change the situation. Sometimes patients showed anger at more abstract targets, such as drug companies, or governmental agencies that might not be giving adequate funding for medical research. In some cases no target was clear but rather patients seemed to be generally angry at everything, showing a lack of patience and tolerance that was not customary for them. Patients' anger is very difficult to cope with for those around them, but understanding that the anger is being displaced from its true source, the terminal diagnosis and all that this entails, is helpful. Kübler-Ross also notes that sometimes patients' anger is rational: some people around patients *are* insensitive, and medical regulations and regimes often seem unnecessary and even punitive to patients. For example, can dying patients be blamed for being angry at a nurse who wakes them from their first sound sleep in days to take a blood pressure reading?

3. *Bargaining.* It is a natural response to want to avoid death in some way, and most people have had the experience, at least as children, of having been granted what they wanted or having been rewarded for "good" behaviour. Kübler-Ross observed dying patients to be using the same childhood techniques to attain their ends. For example, patients might say, "If I follow through on this medical regimen, I will live longer." This is tantamount to saying, "I'll make a bargain with you: I'll follow the medical regime if you will let me live longer." Also commonly heard are such comments as, "I just want to live to see my daughter graduate," or "I want to celebrate Passover/see spring/go skiing just one more time." Implicit in these comments is the bargain, "If I keep fighting and do what the physicians say, you'll let me live long enough to see or do what I want." For some people, the "you" who will grant the bargain is God; for others, it is the physician; for still others, it is some nameless, faceless force of destiny; and for some, it is a combination of many targets. In bargaining, patients are not only trying to gain more time to live (or even a remission of the terminal condition) but also

attempting to take back some control of their lives. This is especially important to people who have had control in their lives and who now feel that fate and medical personnel are in charge. Much of the time, these bargains are not broadcast to the world and are confided only to a primary physician, chaplain, or other person who is intimately involved with the patient, if the patient confides in anyone. Sometimes the bargain is very explicit and dramatic: "If God lets me live, I swear I'll become a priest"; sometimes the bargain is more vague: "If you let me live, I'll become a better person." The implication in all these bargains is that if the patients are granted the bargain, they will never ask for anything else again. This, Kübler-Ross found, was rarely the case: if patients did live to see their daughter graduate, for example, they might then say, "But I have another daughter in school too!" with the idea that another bargain might then be struck.

4. *Depression.* The next stage that Kübler-Ross described is the very natural and expected response of depression. She contended that as the patient becomes progressively debilitated, the anger and bargaining give way to a sense of profound loss and hopelessness. The depression may be centred on one or many sources. It may reflect the impending loss of life and separation from all one has known and loved, as well as the anxiety of entering into an unknown state. It may reflect remorse or guilt for past misdeeds, regret for deeds undone, or omissions that may or may not be too late to rectify. It may centre on the present pain, weakness, possible disfigurement, and removal from customary life and sense of control that patients are undergoing. Some of this depression may be alleviated: for example, if patients want to, they may have time to make amends and redress for past misdeeds, to do what was left undone in the past. With perceptive modern medical and social care, patients may be made free from most pain and given more control and strength in the last portion of life. But part of the depression is perfectly reasonable: Kübler-Ross saw part of the depression as being preparatory for the leaving of this life and saw attempts at alleviating this depression as being both fruitless and insensitive.

5. *Acceptance.* As patients progress toward the end of life, anger, bargaining, and depression tend to decrease as patients enter a calmer state in which they understand that life will soon be over, and they have made peace with this. The acceptance that Kübler-Ross described is not a joyful state; it is a state in which individuals no longer fight the inevitable and, compounded with a typically seriously debilitated physical condition, withdraw from the world, sleeping more, and feeling little. At this point, patients may have resolved the emotional issues of the end of life to the best of their ability, said goodbye to the people closest to them, and are ready for the end to come. This is often misunderstood and found to be disturbing to people around the patient, including medical personnel. Often it is assumed that patients are just giving up when more fighting would keep them alive for a little longer. Family and friends may feel rejected and abandoned because the person no longer wants to fight or sometimes even to talk to or to see them. It is important to understand that the "giving up" is not a product of depression at this point but a product of having accepted that death cannot be avoided. Not all patients experience this stage: sometimes death intervenes before this stage is reached, sometimes patients have not had appropriate responses to earlier reactions and so have not been able to work through their emotions, and sometimes patients' own personalities are such that they keep raging and fighting to the end. This stage is a desirable final stage to Kübler-Ross, who suggested that in some cases, terminally ill patients may need counselling to reach acceptance.

Kübler-Ross recognized that elements of each stage could be found at every point in patients' trajectory toward death (e.g., soon after the diagnosis, they may display signs of acceptance, and near the end they may show anger), so she did not insist that the responses of each stage necessarily follow sequentially and in isolation from other responses. However, this is often misunderstood: for example, on hearing of the death of a long-term patient, a young nurse exclaimed, "She can't be dead! She hasn't reached acceptance yet!"

Kübler-Ross extended the stages of grief that patients feel on receiving a terminal diagnosis to apply to the family of the patient as well. She saw families as going through much the same process as they journey with dying patients to the end of life, and she saw the same process occurring after the death as well. Thus, on hearing that someone has died, mourners may first react with denial ("I can't believe he's gone!"), then anger ("Damn it, why didn't someone catch the cancer sooner?"), bargaining ("I'll wake up and this will just be a dream"), depression ("I miss him so much; I'd give anything to just talk to him once more; how can I go on?"), and finally acceptance ("I'll always love him and miss him, but I'm going on with life with his memory in my heart"). Kübler-Ross's work has been criticized as being too general and as not taking into account the individual

BOX 5.3   Edgar's Case in Kübler-Ross's Framework

Kübler-Ross would point out that Edgar showed great shock and denial when he first heard of his wife's death: he refused to believe that the initial phone call was anything but a prank, he concocted the unlikely explanation that his wife was not answering her cell phone because she had forgotten to turn it on, and so on. Finally, a coworker had to intervene to break through Edgar's denial. But in his resistance to acknowledge his wife's accident, Kübler-Ross might also suggest that he was showing bargaining: "As long as I don't go to the hospital, Samantha is alive." His anger became very apparent in his reaction to the medical personnel, the truck driver, and to the rest of the world who insisted on going on with life. Within a short time, Edgar became depressed, as manifested in his sleeping and eating disturbances and his feelings of hopelessness. Finally, Edgar reached some acceptance and began to move on with his life, to the point of considering finding a new bridge partner.

differences that exist in regards to the death (e.g., mode of death, social support, degree of attachment), and colleagues and subsequent researchers have broadened and refined her work, but with the acknowledgment that, despite the limitations, they stand on her shoulders.

Box 5.3 describes how Edgar's responses fit Kübler-Ross's stage model.

COLIN MURRAY PARKES'S PHASE MODEL

Based on work with widows, Colin Parkes (1996) amended Kübler-Ross's bereavement stage model somewhat. He regarded bereavement as having much in common with receiving a physical injury. He continued the biological approach by recognizing a physical component of the stress response and noted that physical stress reactions occur throughout the bereavement period. Parkes believed that if complications arose, as with an injury, the result may be fatal. The phases he suggested are as follows:

1. *Numbness.* A blunting of emotions occurs immediately or shortly after hearing of the death. This blunting is adaptive in allowing the bereaved to make final arrangements and to carry out end-of-life rituals before being more debilitated by the force of the emotions.
2. *Searching and pining.* In the second phase, Parkes described the "pangs" of grief, the episodes of anxiety and pain felt by the bereaved. At this time, all interest in the outside world is curtailed and the individual thinks only of the lost loved one. Some anger may be felt in this and the next phase, but unlike Kübler-Ross, Parkes believed that anger can often be considered a sign

that complications in the grieving process are arising.
3. *Depression.* When the pangs diminish and the individual recognizes the inability to regain the lost loved one, he or she experiences despair and profound sadness. During this phase, Parkes felt, the individual first recognizes the necessity of changing his or her world view and making changes in the way he or she has dealt with life.
4. *Recovery.* The bereaved person makes the adjustments in world view and in ways of thinking about himself or herself and roles in life.

These phases are more general and flexible than those posited by Kübler-Ross. Parkes called his divisions "phases" instead of stages because he wanted to avoid the implication that the progression from one step to the next is inviolate, and he felt that the term "phases" implies an overlap and a movement backward and forward, with a general projective trajectory that moves toward recovery.

Box 5.4 describes how Edgar's responses fit Parkes's phase model.

JOHN BOWLBY'S ATTACHMENT MODEL

John Bowlby (1980) is best known for his work on **attachment** theory, that is, the bonds that tie children to their primary caretakers early in life. He used this theory as the basis for a formulation of loss, with the inclusion of the concept of **defensive exclusion.** This refers to the cognitive tendency to block the processing of information that is perceived to be threatening or painful. By incorporating these concepts and recognizing that

BOX 5.4   Edgar's Case in Parkes's Framework

Parkes would interpret Edgar's initial reactions to the news of his wife's fatal car accident as reflecting numbness: Edgar, he might say, is buffering himself from the intense shock of the situation and in his denial is experiencing a general lack of emotion. This can also be seen in the way that Edgar goes through the funeral on "automatic pilot," devoid of any feeling except that he must be strong for the sake of Samantha's memory. This numbness continues at work, where he goes through his work day in a fog. He pines for Samantha, having nightmares about her accident and finding consolation in holding her sweater as a way of recapturing her. He is despondent in realizing that she cannot be recaptured and he

feels that he can never love again. He experiences physical symptoms that are characteristic of stress responses, such as sleep disturbances, heart palpitations, and feelings of choking. He begins to recognize, however, that he needs to make adjustments in his life to continue functioning, so he learns to cook. Finally, he finds some enjoyment in the tasks of living and he begins to see himself in a different light: no longer is he a man who will never have another pleasant social moment; now he is a man who can entertain on his own and might even find a new bridge partner. In all, he has coped with the intense stress and the injury done to him, and his healing may have left scar tissue, but it is complete.

attachment can occur between adults, Bowlby described bereavement by the following phases:

1. *Numbness.* When news of the death is first given to the individual, the predominant feeling is that of being stunned and unable to fully comprehend what has happened.
2. *Yearning and searching.* As the blunting of emotions decreases, the bereaved experienced **separation anxiety,** the fear and trepidation experienced with the loss of an attachment figure. At the same time, the individual uses defensive exclusion to block out the information that reunion with the attachment figure will not occur. The bereaved person yearns for the deceased and finds only frustration in his or her seeking for reunion.
3. *Disorganization and despair.* The bereaved feels his or her life has been completely uprooted and is in a state of confusion, and experiences sadness and intense grief.
4. *Reorganization.* As time passes, the individual shapes a new concept of the world and his or her identity, learning new roles and new skills in the absence of the deceased.

Although Bowlby gave little further description of his third or fourth stages, his greatest contributions to the understanding of bereavement came from his relating of the process of grief to separation anxiety, and his explanation of the interplay of belief that the loved one is gone with periods of disbelief. His model can be extended to animals because of the attachment behaviours young animals show toward their attachment figure (usually the mother). When separation from the attachment figure

occurs, young animals, as well as human babies, cry and search for the attachment figure. This behaviour is often successful in retrieving the attachment figure and so has an adaptive value to it. The reaction to the death of a loved one is, then, another example of this behaviour; as such, Bowlby believed, it has a biological and evolutionary basis that transcends species and culture. The exact form of this behaviour may be affected by the species and environmental factors, such as culture, but the basics remain unchanged. His formulation of the process of bereavement, then, is further-reaching and more encompassing than many other formulations.

Box 5.5 describes how Edgar's responses fit Bowlby's attachment model.

DENNIS KLASS'S MODEL OF CONTINUING BONDS

Dennis Klass (1996, 1999) concentrated on what he saw as the root of grief: attachment. He believed, with Bowlby, that grief is a reflection of having lost someone to whom we were attached, in childhood or in adulthood. The depth and intensity of the grief depends on the attachment that had been formed, and the way the grief manifests is dependent on environmental factors as well as on the personality of the bereaved. He emphasized that the resolution of grief does not mean a severing of the attachment but a reformulation of it, suggesting that the bonds to the deceased continue past death. This, he believed, is a universal finding: in all cultures and throughout history, in one way or another, the connection to the dead is present in religions, customs, and belief systems.

BOX 5.5   Edgar's Case in Bowlby's Framework

Bowlby would first note the deep attachment that Edgar has to his wife: as a couple they have been sufficient unto themselves for more than 14 years. When confronted with the news of Samantha's accident, Edgar uses defensive exclusion in blocking the information that is so painful to him. He is numb and denies that anything bad has happened to his beloved wife. He later shows separation anxiety, yearning for Samantha and seeing her in every blonde woman on the street, only to be met with frustration and despair when the woman turns out not to be his wife. He continues to use defensive exclusion because he cannot as yet face the fact that Samantha is gone forever. Edgar's life is in turmoil, he has problems concentrating, and his sleeping and eating are disturbed. Finally, he recognizes that he must restructure his life and take on new tasks and new roles.

As evidence, he pointed to the still-extant Japanese custom of having a shrine to dead ancestors, who are available for communication and consultation for 35 to 50 years after death (Klass, 1996; Klass & Goss, 1999). He and Goss (2002, 2003) also cited the examples of the Spiritualism movement in the United States in the nineteenth century in which the bereaved sought out mediums who would communicate messages to and from the dead, and more modern examples in Islam and Christianity, in which prayers for the dead and to the dead are part of the religious rituals. In essence, he stated that all bereavement can be examined in terms of how the bereaved keep their bonds with their deceased loved ones. By examining such cross-cultural and historical evidence, as well as contemporary data, he hoped that a truly universal model of grief could be designed. Klass did not formulate a model beyond this, but his hope that an all-inclusive model would one day emerge from cross-cultural studies is clear.

Box 5.6 describes how Edgar's responses fit Klass's model of continuing bonds.

CATHERINE SANDERS'S INTEGRATIVE MODEL

Catherine Sanders (1999) built on the existing phase models to develop what she has called an integrative model, which includes both a biological and a motivational aspect to account for the bereaved's progress through different phases of grief. According to her model, when a death occurs, bereaved individuals have both an emotional reaction to their loss and a physiological reaction to the stress they incur. In examining the stress response, she drew on the work of stress researchers, such as Hans Selye (1976), much of which has recent empirical validation. Her formulation is as follows:

1. *Shock.* As described by such theorists as Kübler-Ross (1969), when first presented with the news of a death, the individual reacts with shock and disbelief. Sanders noted that this is the first presentation of a highly stressful event, and so the individual's sympathetic nervous system reacts with the stress response of "fight or flight," which includes an attendant increased flow of adrenalin and other homeostatic changes that prepare the person for action. The adrenalin keeps the individual in an aroused state, which allows the bereaved to get through the initial difficult period of assimilating the painful news and carrying out the practical arrangements that cannot be delayed. The price of this, however, is a numbness of feeling and a disorientation and confusion of the mind, as well as a weakening of the immune system.

2. *Awareness of loss.* As time progresses, the parasympathetic nervous system responds to decrease the fight or flight response, bringing the person's physiological balance close to a normal level. Adrenalin decreases and, with it, the blunting of the emotions decreases as well. Now the dreadful reality of the loved one's death is fully experienced and the individual undergoes the pain and yearning, as well as the guilt, anger, shame, and so on, typically found when a death occurs. Because the stress on the individual has not abated, the individual's body

BOX 5.6   Edgar's Case in Klass's Framework

Klass might emphasize that in resolving his grief, Edgar does not replace his tie to Samantha: part of his resolution is in keeping her picture on display and in visiting her grave. In his decision to resume his social life, Klass might note the signifi- cance of Edgar's recognition that he cannot find a new bridge partner who will play the same way that Samantha did, but he is willing to be flexible enough to adapt to a new partner's method of play.

is at an above-normal resting level, and the emotional energy expended in dealing with this phase creates more stress for the individual. The result is a further flagging of the immune system.

3. *Conservation-withdrawal.* This phase is a reformulation of stages described by other theorists and was added as a result of the observations that Sanders herself, as well as others, made of people who are bereaved. In this phase, the exhausted individual pulls away from the social network and feels despair that he or she can never recapture the life of old with the deceased. Other theorists (e.g., Kübler-Ross, 1969) identified this as depression, but Sanders disagreed, while admitting that it looks much like depression. Sanders saw this phase as having a redemptive value insofar as it provides the necessary rest for the individual to cognitively begin to cope with a world without the deceased and for his or her immune system, which has been badly compromised, to recuperate, returning to a more normal level. Near the end of this phase, Sanders believed that a turning point comes for the individual as he or she makes the decision whether to (1) move forward in life, (2) act as if nothing has happened (status quo), or (3) give up. As strength is regained in the conservation-withdrawal phase, the individual usually finds the strength and motivation to choose the first option and face the changed future. In this phase, Sanders emphasized the active process of mourning: the individual is not a passive pawn of his or her grief but actively chooses how to cope with the pain.

4. *Healing.* Once the usually unconscious decision to move forward in life has been made, the gradual process of assuming control and forming a new role and identity takes place. Sanders contended that in this phase "forgiving and forgetting" also occur. Forgiving refers to self-forgiveness, in that the bereaved learns to handle the guilt and anger surrounding the death, no longer feeling extreme remorse for sins of omission or commission toward the deceased or the rage at having been abandoned by the deceased. In describing forgetting, Sanders emphasized that she does not mean that all memories of the deceased are banished, but rather the bereaved places the memory of the deceased on the backburner of the mind, in that special place for memories, no longer conflicting with the possibility of taking on new roles and new relationships. The individual now experiences some hope for the future and conceives of a life in which a new identity can be formed and even enjoyed.

5. *Renewal.* In this, the final phase, the pain of the bereavement has mostly subsided. The individual still, and will always, remember the deceased and may always have pain at anniversaries or other significant dates, but now the individual re-engages in life and acts on the hope that began in the previous phase. New roles, responsibilities, and relationships are tried, sometimes with success and sometimes not. Each success brings about greater vitality and a sense of competence, and the individual, while forever changed by the bereavement, feels the strength and joy in continuing life.

In her model, Sanders recognized that the individual's own personality, age, gender, attachment level to the deceased, support system, manner of the deceased's death, socioeconomic status, and so on, can all play a part in how he or she will progress. The phases do not necessarily progress in an invariant order, and they do not exist in isolation from one another. What Sanders proposed is a free-flowing progression as the bereaved moves on, with portions of one phase overlapping the next, with stops and starts and occasional regressions. The process has no fixed or optimal time, and Sanders emphasized that some (such as the final stage) may be very long.

At the time of her death in 2002, Sanders had been developing the idea of a sixth phase, one that sometimes follows the phase of renewal (Doka, 2005–2006). She tentatively called this phase *fulfillment* because of the reports she received from several people that although they would never wish that their loved one had died, they grew from their bereavement in ways that would not have occurred had they not been bereaved. For example, one mother whose child was killed in an accident reported that because of her bereavement, she had become more involved in community affairs, helping to get legislation passed that would prevent the kinds of accidents that had killed her child. She would always grieve for her child, but she could no longer conceive of herself as she was before the death. Some good can come from awful events, if we choose to make it so, the mother stated.

Box 5.7 describes how Edgar's responses fit Sanders's integrative model.

SIMON SHIMSON RUBIN'S TWO-TRACK MODEL OF BEREAVEMENT

Simon Rubin (1999; Rubin, Malkinson, & Witztum, 2003) formulated what he called the two-track model of bereavement. Contending that previous models of bereavement have not considered the complexity of

Sanders would note the presence of an alarm reaction in Edgar when he first receives the news of Samantha's accident. He actively responds with a call to her cell phone and resistance to his coworker's suggestions. His emotions become blunted as he arranges and goes through her funeral. His cognitive processes are impaired in the months following Samantha's death, as seen in his inability to function normally at work. Edgar's stress response abates somewhat, bringing emotions of longing and sadness as he experiences sleep and eating disturbances, continued physiological stress responses, and a lack of interest in anything but his lost love. Edgar is receiving less social support as time goes on, and by the time six months have passed, his social life seems to consist only of work experiences and evenings reminding himself of Samantha. His withdrawal from the social realm lessens as he makes the decision to learn to cook and do housekeeping to move on with his life. Edgar is not as angry anymore, and he stops berating himself for his imagined complicity in his wife's death. In having a small dinner party, he re-engages in the social realm, and he now indicates to his coworker that he is ready to enjoy more social interaction. Edgar is becoming renewed as a somewhat changed person, and although never severing his connection to Samantha, he is willing to try a new relationship, at least in playing bridge, seeming more open to the possibility of a pleasant life before him. A full entry into such a new life may take time, though.

bereavement, his model noted that with bereavement (1) people lose the ability to control their lives, and functioning on a day-to-day basis is impaired, and (2) people still have their connections with significant others who are deceased.

The first track is reflective of the effects of the stress of the bereavement and as such examines the ability to function under this extreme stress. This track includes critical areas of functioning, such as how the individual perceives the meaning of life events, interpersonal relationships with others, and emotional investment in life's tasks, all of which are disrupted by the stress of bereavement. It is in this arena that most research and examination of bereavement has been done.

The second track examines the relationship to the deceased in terms of the types of memories the mourner has of the deceased (e.g., positive, negative, idealized, conflicted), the degree of preoccupation with the deceased, and memorialization of the deceased. This track has been largely overlooked in determining how well a mourner has adapted to his or her loss.

Information about these two tracks leads to a greater understanding of the way that people process grief and move through mourning. Rubin contended that this is beneficial both in a theoretical sense of understanding and in the applied sense of clinically aiding those in mourning.

In support of the usefulness of his model, Rubin cited his research on mothers of babies who died of sudden infant death syndrome (SIDS), either recently or five years previously, and mothers of sons killed in Israeli wars. The research indicated that progress along Track I and Track II might not be the same: for example,

mothers tended to progress better on Track I (although they still had difficulties) than on Track II. Mothers, then, were more likely to get back to their day-to-day lives over time, but their relationships with their dead children remained strong. This type of information is typically obscured when research examines an overall picture of progress through bereavement and suggests that portions of the bereavement experience are perhaps never ameliorated. Furthermore, additional research indicated that people regard difficulties in Track I as more problematic than difficulties in Track II. Rubin interpreted this to mean that in regards to mourners, other people in the environment are missing some of the real distress that mourners are experiencing, and this insensitivity is likely making the mourning process even more difficult.

Other research is consistent with this: Rubin described research done by Prigerson and colleagues (1995) that demonstrated that symptoms related to the relationship with the deceased were distinct from symptoms of depression, and these are the symptoms that are most related to the development of complicated grief or bereavement-related difficulties (see Chapter 10).

Rubin, Malkinson, and Witztum (2003) also pointed out the usefulness of the two-track model in understanding complicated grief. Although all bereavement is traumatic, some bereavement has been classified as leading to serious bereavement-related difficulties (see Chapter 10). Typically, mental health professionals have regarded deaths that are sudden, unexpected, or violent, or involve a death threat to the mourner as being more likely to lead to complicated grief responses. But Rubin

BOX 5.8   Edgar's Case in Rubin's Framework

Rubin would note that on Track I, Edgar is showing the effects of the trauma of his wife's unexpected and violent death: his ability to concentrate and function cognitively is impaired, as seen in his work difficulties; he has sleeping and eating disturbances; he withdraws from social interaction, spending his evenings alone with his memories; and he has physical manifestations of stress. Only gradually does his work performance improve and he comes to realize that he has to learn basic cooking and housekeeping skills to maintain his life. On Track I, Edgar has shown the reactions to the stress of bereavement and has learned how to function on a day-to-day basis.

On Track II, however, Edgar has a little more difficulty coming to terms with his loss. His attachment to his wife was strong, and it took him a year to be able to visit her grave and two years to put away all but one of the photographs of her. By the time of Edgar's dinner party, two years after Samantha's death, he seems to have come a long way in resolving his Track II grief: he can share memories of Samantha with others and smile, and he can contemplate getting a new bridge partner, not as a replacement for Samantha but as a way of reentering a pastime he formerly enjoyed in a new way.

contended that this representation looks only at trauma from the standpoint of Track I processes, that is, externally imposed trauma. He emphasized the need to look at Track II processes as well in determining the mourner's trauma. A death may be quiet, expected, and even a relief in cases of intractable pain, but they may still contain trauma if the death brings about an unexpected and unwelcome revelation that affects the relationship the mourner has with the deceased (Track II). Examples that Rubin, Malkinson, and Witztum gave include finding that the deceased was a war criminal, a child molester, or a habitual criminal, or had a second bigamous family. Any revelation that suggests that the relationship with the deceased before death was based on inaccurate or incomplete information can trigger severe trauma in the mourner; not only does the mourner have to establish a new relationship with the deceased, but the prior relationship must also be re-evaluated and reinterpreted, and it cannot be used as a basis for a new relationship given its erroneous nature.

Resolution of grief, complicated or not, according to Rubin, must examine both tracks, with the recognition that although a mourner may appear to function well (Track I), he or she may still have issues on Track II that provide distress or suggest that complete resolution has not occurred. For example, Rubin noted a respondent in one of his studies idealizing her son, dead for 14 years, at the expense of her other children. Superficially, her functioning may seem to indicate grief resolution, but this may not really be the case. For Rubin, only when Track I functioning is demonstrated and Track II reactions indicate a realistic, balanced, and calm recollection of the deceased and impact of these memories on the mourner, can anyone speak of resolution of grief.

Box 5.8 describes how Edgar's responses fit Rubin's two-track model of bereavement.

WILLIAM WORDEN'S TASK MODEL

William Worden (2002) did not disagree with the conception of the bereavement process as progressing in phases, but as a clinician, he saw a conceptualization of tasks of bereavement as more useful. Bereavement, as a process not a state, is a matter of adaptation to a new reality, he averred, and as such it is more beneficial to mourners to see the tasks that they are actively performing in their adaptation. The tasks he outlined are as follows:

1. *To accept the reality of the loss.* Worden emphasized that the tasks are not an invariant series and may be returned to repeatedly. Nonetheless, it is difficult to comprehend how the remaining tasks can be accomplished without the mourner first accepting the reality of the loss on both an intellectual and an emotional level. Worden noted that typically the mourner has a cognitive grasp of the new reality before he or she has an emotional grasp of it. The mourner needs to adjust to the fact that reunion with the deceased will not be possible, at least in this lifetime. This is often denied in a very overt manner with the mourner saying simply, "I can't believe it," or by distorting the situation in keeping up hope after all hope is gone (e.g., by insisting that the deceased was not really on the airplane that crashed with no survivors but is

wandering around somewhere with amnesia). More subtle forms of denial are seen when the bereaved denies the full meaning of the loss. For instance, Worden pointed to those mourners who contend that they will not really miss the deceased because "He wasn't a good father," or "We weren't really close." Denial is also seen in cases in which parts of the deceased's character and behaviour are "forgotten" or altered while other parts are remembered accurately.

2. *To work through the pain of grief.* Worden believed that some degree of pain is a universal experience when a loved one dies. The type and intensity of the pain can be moderated by such factors as the cultural milieu, the support system available, the character of the mourner, the depth of the relationship with the deceased, and so on. This second task is a difficult one, necessitating a direct confrontation with the pain. Many people try to avoid this through various forms of distraction or by inhibiting their own thinking about the event, but the emotions of sadness, anger, frustration, helplessness, guilt, and loneliness must be acknowledged as valid and worked through in this task.

3. *To adjust to an environment in which the deceased is missing.* Worden discussed three areas in which the bereaved must make adjustments to the new reality. In the first area, external adjustments, the mourner has to take on the duties and roles previously fulfilled by the deceased. The mourner is often quite surprised to see the magnitude of the practical void left by the deceased: the full scope and complexity of the roles that the deceased had filled may not be fully apprehended until some months after the death. The second area, internal adjustments, refers to the need for the mourner to adjust his or her own sense of self in view of the loss. The death of a person who is meaningful in our lives typically has a profound effect on our sense of self and our identity, beyond that of simply "married person" or "widow/widower" for example. In some cases, a sense of identity may have been built around the deceased ("Mrs. John Doe"), and in other cases, the mourner may have depended on the deceased for self-esteem and feelings of self-efficacy, or a sense of control and the ability to handle life in a competent manner. In the third domain of adjustment, the spiritual adjustments, Worden referred to the need to adjust the world view and change the assumptions about life and the world the mourner had before the death. The most common assumptions challenged by the death of a loved one are (1) the world is a benevolent place, (2) the world makes sense, and (3) the mourner is a worthy person who will encounter only positive experiences.

4. *To emotionally relocate the deceased and move on with life.* In Worden's earlier formulations of the tasks of mourning, he saw the last task as removing emotional energy from the deceased and investing it in a new relationship. With the continued research in the field of bereavement, however, he reformulated this idea, recognizing that in most cases, the bonds with the deceased are never relinquished but are changed in such a way as to reflect the new reality with positive memories. This is accomplished in Task 4 with the bereaved finding ways of maintaining the bonds while not permitting them to interfere with going on with life and new relationships. Worden (2002) gave the poignant example of the young woman who, two years after her father died, wrote to her mother, "There are other people to be loved . . . and it doesn't mean that I love Dad any less," (p. 37).

Box 5.9 describes how Edgar's responses fit Worden's task model.

BOX 5.9   Edgar's Case in Worden's Framework

Edgar had a great deal of initial difficulty in accomplishing Worden's first task, to accept the reality of his loss. He fought hard to deny that Samantha had really been in an accident, and even much later, his emotional denial was still evident as he searched for Samantha, seeing her in every blonde woman on the street. Eventually Edgar accepted the reality of the loss of Samantha, at least in part, and he was then met with extreme pain. In dealing with Worden's second task, to work through the pain of grief, Edgar had to allow himself to feel the anguish, anger, and the frustration. In learning how to cook and do basic housework, Edgar was trying to accomplish the third task of adjusting to an environment in which Samantha was missing. Edgar now took on tasks that Samantha had fulfilled and began to see himself as someone who could handle life on his own. It is likely that Edgar found himself being more cautious and less trusting of the world, for now he knew it as a place where the innocent may be killed for no apparent reason. Finally, Edgar begins work on Task 4, to emotionally relocate Samantha and move on with life, as he puts away her photographs, leaving out only his favourite in the bedroom, and asking his coworker to help him find a new bridge partner, one who would not replace Samantha, but would help Edgar resume a formerly pleasant activity.

THERÈSE RANDO'S SIX Rs MODEL

Thérèse Rando (1992–1993, 1993) has worked extensively in the area of **complicated mourning,** the problematic responses following some losses (see Chapter 10). To understand what can go awry with the bereavement process, she was first compelled to understand the process of mourning that more commonly occurs. She broke the mourning process into three broad phases. Her descriptions of each phase are very general, not directly pertaining to any one individual but reflecting the totality of reactions that have been reported by many people.

1. *The avoidance phase.* In the avoidance phase, the person is first confronted by the news of a death. The initial reaction is shock and often a feeling of being overwhelmed, confused, dazed, and emotionally numb. The individual finds it difficult to think rationally or to make sense of his or her feelings. Behaviour may be erratic and ill-thought-out as well. The person then cannot believe what has happened. Rando contended that this denial and avoidance of the reality are therapeutic because they allow the person to absorb the painful news more gradually. At this point, the person's reactions are quite idiosyncratic: some people rage against the injustice of the death, others experience intense sorrow, some cope with their disbelief by questioning why this death has happened, still others feel disconnected and emotionally flat. In some cases, people put their feelings to the side while they cope with other critical events, such as arranging a funeral, handling children, or recovering their own health.

2. *The confrontation phase.* The confrontation phase is the most intense and dramatic phase of the mourning process. At this time, the individual is left with the reality of his or her loss and must cope with what this means in his or her life. The anguish of pining is experienced at this time, with the person yearning for the presence of the dead loved one. It may seem to the individual that every stimulus in the day is a poignant reminder of the loss that has occurred, and the grief is felt afresh with each small or large cue. Rando believed that each occurrence is a learning experience that drives home the reality of the death to the mourner. Each experience is accompanied by extreme sadness, anger, and frustration. In many cases, guilt, whether justifiable or not, is also experienced.

These emotions are spelled by periods of denial and numbness, leaving the mourner at the mercy of wildly fluctuating feelings. This causes even more confusion and turmoil for the already burdened mourner, and many people at this point wonder whether they are going crazy. To further tax the mourner, he or she often has physical symptoms, such as energy loss, tension, agitation, nausea, headache, and insomnia. The emotions are mainly responsible for the physical symptoms, and the physical symptoms exacerbate the emotional symptoms, conveying the individual into a difficult and downward spiral.

3. *The accommodation phase.* The accommodation phase sees a decline in the intensity of emotions and a re-establishment of social relationships and responsibilities. By this time, the mourner has had to learn a new set of responses and often has an entirely new set of roles to fulfill. The deceased loved one is recognized as irrevocably gone, and a new relationship with the deceased is being formed. The mourner may be reentering everyday life, but it would be a mistake to assume that he or she is "over" the grief. Rando stressed that aspects of the grief may be with mourners for the rest of their lives. Portions of the confrontation phase may still spill over into the accommodation phase, but gradually the mourner learns to accept the fact that the loved one is dead and the world will never be the same. The mourner recognizes that he or she will never be the same either, but the individual that emerges, while bearing scars, can emotionally re-invest in life and the living, integrating the past life with it. Understandably, the individual's world view, or the assumptions he or she makes about how the world works and what people in general are like, changes with the experience of grief. In the accommodation phase, the mourner decides (consciously or not) what the new individual will be like: deepened and sensitized? embittered and cynical? hopeless or hopeful? In the accommodation phase, mourners create the new meaning for their lives. Such organizations as Mothers Against Drunk Driving (MADD) and Parents of Murdered Children (PMC) were formed by parents whose children were killed arbitrarily and who, in the accommodation phase, decided that caring, social, and political action would be the appropriate way to give their lives and their dead children's lives meaning.

Within this broad framework, Rando concentrated on the tasks that a mourner must do to resolve grief and successfully reenter life. The tasks begin in the avoidance phase and continue throughout to the accommodation phase. She called the tasks the Six R processes.

A) Avoidance phase
1) *Recognize the loss.*
  (a) The mourner must understand that the death has occurred, at least on the intellectual level if not the emotional level. The mourner will find *acknowledging the death* to be more difficult in those cases in which a body cannot be recovered or is mutilated to the point of being unrecognizable; because the individual does not want the loved one to be dead, it is easier to contend that the loved one is, in fact, alive if there is no body or other identifying confirmatory element to view.
  (b) In recognizing the death, it is helpful for the mourner to *understand how and why the death occurred* to make it a cognitive reality to him or her. Such cosmic questions as "Why did he have to die?" might not have answers, but answers are usually available about the mechanics of the death, what led up to it, and the circumstances around it. Because the mourner is in a confused state in which his or her world has been turned upside down, knowing the facts surrounding the death helps to put it into a more relevant and meaningful context, one that can be more readily assimilated and handled. Rando noted that it is not necessary to know the truth about the death: she pointed to cases in which mourners may insist that the loved one died as the result of an accident rather than admitting that the death was a suicide. The truth may be denied, but the mourners are aided in satisfying their need to make sense of what has happened. Rando also pointed out that this understanding is typically denied to parents of children who die of SIDS: the cause of the death is labelled but not understood.
B) Confrontation phase
2) *React to the separation.*
  (a) The mourner must actively *feel the pain* of the loss, without repressing or shying away from it. This is obviously difficult to do because it is a natural want to avoid pain. But in mourning the pain cannot be avoided, except for very short-lived respites and distractions. Attempts to avoid cues about the death or thinking about the death are only temporarily effective and briefly useful because concentrating on the pain all the time would be too debilitating. In the long run, however, the mourner must mourn, and feeling the pain is the main component of this.
  (b) The mourner must also *examine his or her feelings about the loss, identifying, accepting, and giving some expression* to these feelings. Most societies give their members a list of "shoulds" in terms of how to react and how to behave in given circumstances (see Chapters 2 and 3). The individual mourner, however, may not feel the way that the list prescribes. For example, in some cultures and some religions, mourners are told, "Be happy that your loved one has gone to be with God." No matter how great the mourner's faith, however, happiness is not what is usually felt at this time. Rando contended that it is important for the mourner to confront and accept what he or she really feels and find a way to express it, rather than inhibiting these reactions in favour of the socially or religiously mandated response. Unacknowledged emotions are typically impossible to control or to handle; only by facing the real emotions can the mourner take some control and deal with the problems that are arising in learning to live without the loved one.
  (c) Besides dealing with the primary loss of the loved one, the mourner must also *acknowledge, identify, and mourn the secondary losses* that occur as a result of the death. When a person dies, not only is the physical presence lost, but the social and occupational networks are also disrupted. In losing a loved one, the mourner has lost the companionship, support, love, and stimulation that the deceased provided. Other losses are also often present: financial losses; validation and reinforcement losses; the loss of hopes, dreams, and envisioned future; and the customary world view. The mourner needs to recognize and acknowledge the myriad effects that the death of one person brings about.
3) *Recollect and re-experience the deceased and the relationship.*
  (a) Rando recognized that death does not sever a relationship with the deceased but brings about an altered relationship. To form such a new relationship, the mourner must first *remember the deceased accurately and realistically.* After a death mourners often talk about the deceased as if he or she were a saint or a devil. Such canonizing or demonizing

obscures the real relationship that the mourner had with the deceased, and so impedes the understanding of feelings about the loss and the formation of a new relationship. The mourner can only evaluate his or her emotions accurately in the context of the person and the relationship as they really existed; viewing the positive, negative, and neutral elements of the deceased and the relationship is of great importance. Sometimes viewing all elements of the deceased and the relationship leads to unpleasant emotions, such as anger, guilt, and remorse for the mourner. It is understandable that people would want to avoid these emotions, but doing so means that the feelings continue to fester rather than being resolved.

(b) During the relationship before the loved one died, feelings of attachment deepened and the loved one became tied to countless hopes, dreams, plans, memories, and so on. The closer and more meaningful the relationship was, the stronger and more numerous are the attachment ties. Each tie must be *revived and the feelings surrounding them must be re-experienced* during the mourning process. The reason for this, asserted Rando, is that to progress, each tie must be undone so that the energy put into the attachment ties can be released to form new ties of attachment. The mourner, then, must not only recall the deceased and the relationship realistically, but he or she must also feel everything that the deceased meant in his or her life again. As the mourner does this repeatedly, the bonds become loosened a little each time as the mourner becomes accustomed to this process. It is important to realize that this does not mean that the deceased is abandoned or forgotten: it merely reflects the fact that the deceased can no longer be an active part of the bond.

4) *Relinquish the old attachments to the deceased and the old assumptive world.*

(a) Having revived and re-experienced the attachment ties of the relationship with the deceased, the mourner must now give them up. Perhaps even more difficult is giving up the beliefs that were formerly held regarding the way the world operates and life progresses (i.e., the assumptive world). The mourner typically begins to realize what sorts of assumptions he or she had been living under up until the loss. Assumptions might include such personal cognitions as "He'll always be there for me," or "My child will be there to take care of me when I'm old," or, more globally, "If you take care of your health, you'll live to be old," or "God will take care of you if you're good." Depending on the relationship, the manner of death, and the personality of the mourner, many assumptions will have been shattered by the death of a loved one: "He won't be there—he's dead," "My child will not grow up," "Even if you take care of your health, you may be hit by a car," "Sometimes God doesn't seem to be watching." Simply put, through a death, the mourner often discovers that he or she has not been realistic regarding the world.

C) Accommodation phase

5) *Readjust to move adaptively into the new world without forgetting the old.*

(a) Because the old assumptive world has been shattered, the mourner must now *develop a new assumptive world*: if the old ideas are false, what is true? Sometimes the development of new ideas comes suddenly, especially if the death has been abrupt and unexpected, and sometimes this happens without the mourner even being aware. Depending on many factors, the development of a new assumptive world may be lengthy and difficult, or relatively easy. In many cases, parts of the old assumptions are retained. For example, instead of thinking, "He'll always be there for me," a revised idea might be "He'll be watching over me from Heaven while I take care of myself," or "Taking good care of your health is important but you can't control outside forces that may end your life." Sometimes mourners see the changes in their assumptive world as lessons they have learned and part of the growth they have achieved through their bereavement.

(b) Now the mourner must take all the new thoughts and new realities, and *develop a new relationship with the deceased*. Clearly the old relationship cannot be maintained, but the relationship should not be severed either. The deceased was loved and made a substantial difference in the mourner's life, which cannot be dismissed. The mourner cannot think that any part of him or her is not affected by the relationship with the deceased. Maintaining some sort of relationship with the deceased is not pathological, claimed Rando, although uninformed—albeit well-meaning—people often think it is ("Get over it, move on, let the past go"). The relevant question is, What form will the new relationship take? For some people, it may be a belief that the deceased is watching over them. For others, it may be thinking about how the deceased would react to certain situations that arise in the mourner's life. Perhaps, for some, traditions that were shared with the deceased are maintained as a memorial (e.g., decorating the garden with some of the deceased's favourite flowers). The list of possibilities is limited only by the imagination. As long as the new relationship has the clear understanding and acceptance of the death of the loved one and it does not prohibit the mourner from engaging in new relationships, the relationship with the deceased can be continued in a new and meaningful way.

(c) Part of the accommodation phase includes the mourner *taking on new ways of being in the world*. The mourner cannot continue with life as if no change had occurred. In some instances practical changes must be made, for example, the mourner must now be a sole breadwinner or parent; the mourner no longer needs to make child- or elder-care provisions; the mourner must learn to cook, sew, do laundry, maintain the family car, and so on. More subtle changes usually occur as well: for example, the mourner may have to learn to provide his or her own moral support and encouragement or learn how to deal with not having a companion and the loneliness that this might entail. It may be necessary for the mourner to take on new roles and new behaviours, to learn new skills, especially if the deceased was an intimate part of the mourner's day-to-day life. It may be necessary to modify and expand old roles (e.g., becoming a worker in addition to being a parent). These challenges may be very daunting, but most people come through this phase with an increased sense of competence.

(d) With all the changes engendered by the death of a loved one, the mourner in the accommodation phase is *forming a new identity*, one that reflects the changes but also retains many of the components of the pre-loss identity. Thus, a wife may become a widow. She is different from the woman she was, but her relationship with her deceased husband has not been ignored. She is a woman who can remarry but remains one who has been married. The child becomes an orphan, a reflection of the fact that a child (of any age) who loses his or her parents is different from one whose parents are alive and available for love, nurturance, and support. Yet, the love, nurturance, and support that had been the child's are never completely lost; the deceased parents helped form the child's personality. The new identity of the mourner also includes scars that had not been present before; the wound will heal but may always have a vulnerability and a tenderness that was not present before.

6) *Reinvest*.

(a) The final task of the accommodation phase is to take the vigour that had been poured into the relationship with the deceased and place it in new relationships with people or with activities, beliefs, or objects. The new relationships are ones that will give reinforcement and pleasure to the mourner, not replacing the deceased but finding a new outlet for emotional energy. This requires that the mourner re-engage in life, with hopes and dreams and plans that are compatible with the new existence in the world.

Rando stressed that no timetable exists for accomplishing the Six R processes. If the mourner is making progress, even though it is very slow, Rando believed that the forward progress precludes a judgment that there is anything pathological about the mourner's reactions. In her therapeutic work with mourners, she used the Six R processes to gauge how the mourner was progressing.

Box 5.10 describes how Edgar's responses fit Rando's Six Rs model.

MARGARET STROEBE'S DUAL PROCESS MODEL OF COPING WITH BEREAVEMENT

Margaret Stroebe and Henk Schut (1998, 1999) took exception to the truism that a mourner must "work through" grief. This notion was born with Freud (1984), who first used the term "grief work" to indicate that, in his view, resolution of grief does not come about automatically with the passage of time, but rather needs the active labour of the bereaved to resolve his or her pain. This assumption has continued, especially with those theorists who have described tasks that mourners must

BOX 5.10   Edgar's Case in Rando's Framework

Edgar tried very hard not to acknowledge that Samantha was dead, even to the point of not wanting to go to the hospital where she was dying. He finally intellectually acknowledged that she was injured, but he could not understand why, or why the physicians could not do more to save her (R1: Recognize the loss). Emotionally, the task of acknowledging his loss was much more difficult as he saw Samantha in every blonde woman he met. He confronted his pain at the separation from her, and he gave expression to his pain by spending his evenings thinking of her and holding her sweater. The secondary losses he experienced were of little importance to him in the beginning: housework meant nothing to him, and cooking was irrelevant because he had no appetite anyway. He saw himself as changed as well, from a man rich with love to a man who, he felt, would never experience such love again (R2: React to the separation). In thinking about Samantha, Edgar, as he began to learn how to cook, recognized that she would probably be incredulous at his new ability, and he felt satisfaction in "surprising" her. He could re-experience her as if she were alive in his silent conversation with her, gloating a little at his success (R3: Recollect and re-experience the deceased and the relationship). Edgar's bonds with Samantha changed as he realized that he had survived the first terrible year without her and he started to think that maybe he could have a meaningful life without her. In putting away all mementoes of her except his favourite photograph, Edgar indicated that he was giving up the idea that his only happiness lay with her (R4: Relinquish the old attachments to the deceased and the old assumptive world) and he began to fulfill more of her roles such as that of host (R5: Readjust to move adaptively into the new world without forgetting the old). His suggestion that he find a new bridge partner implies that he now sees himself as a man without a partner (R6: Reinvest), although the memory of his former partner remains precious to him.

accomplish (Rando, 1993; Worden, 2002). However, not everyone copes with grief in this way, as shown in the literature if studied carefully across history and across cultures. Stroebe pointed to an analysis by Rosenblatt (1983) indicating that people in the nineteenth century experienced grief in much the same way as people did in the twentieth century, but they did not attempt to detach themselves from the deceased; that is, they did not attempt much of what is considered "grief work" today. Yet there is no indication of a greater degree of difficulty in coping with grief in the nineteenth century. Also, the cross-cultural literature suggests that some non-Western cultures would consider the "working through" of grief to be detrimental (Wikan, 1990), and they have devised other ways of dealing with grief, such as tearing or cutting hair or mutilating parts of the body (Stroebe & Stroebe, 1987). Stroebe and Schut (1999) also noted that within Western culture, gender differences in coping with grief often exist, with males showing less overt expression than females.

Stroebe and her colleagues also stated that existing models of bereavement discuss what must be done to cope with grief, not how it can be done; that is, content, not process is emphasized. Finding both bereavement and general stress management models to be lacking, Stroebe and her colleagues devised the dual-process model, to examine what people actually do to cope with their grief.

First, the theorists specified the stressors of bereavement: (1) the need to cope with the practical aspects of bereavement and (2) the personal loss. In this, Stroebe and her colleagues are very much in line with Rubin's (1999) Track I and Track II, respectively. Loss orientation refers to grief over the loss of the person and the yearning for this person. It includes the necessity of formulating a new relationship with the deceased. Restoration-orientation refers to the pragmatic tasks and roles that the deceased undertook and that must now be absorbed by the mourner.

Next, the theorists emphasized that in the course of mourning, individuals switch between loss-orientation and restoration-orientation. This is a dynamic process, reflecting the fact that sometimes mourners need distraction from their grief, so they switch from concentration on their loss to more practical matters, from loss-orientation to restoration-orientation. This may be a necessity as well: as much as grief may be felt, bills still must be paid and the children must be fed. When the mourner has a respite from practical matters, or when a cue in the environment is presented, or perhaps for no discernable reason, the individual switches from restoration-orientation to loss-orientation. In this way,

BOX 5.11   Edgar's Case in Stroebe's Framework

In Stroebe's view, Edgar, being a Western male, has mainly a restoration-orientation and so he found resuming his work easier than coping with his loss. Indeed, after an initial period of inefficiency at work, his work skills seemed to return more quickly than his ability to function in his wife's previous roles or to cope with the strong emotions he experienced at her loss. In fact, when he showed physical symptoms of stress, he did not consult a physician but preferred to "tough it out like a man." Admitting to the severity of the physical symptoms might have made him concentrate on his emotional loss more than he was ready to do. The loss-orientation was more onerous for Edgar than the restoration-orientation, and it is not unreasonable to assume that taking refuge in restoration and using work as a distraction was less difficult and even a relief for him.

the mourner moves between confronting the loss and avoiding the loss. In support of this, Stroebe and her colleagues noted that stress literature is consistent with the idea that mourners cannot confront their loss unremittingly without harm to their health.

This formulation of the grief response accounts for why some people have particular problems in dealing with grief: they do not switch between the two orientations sufficiently to become habituated with the grief responses. Also, it accounts for the gender difference, indicating that males may maintain more restoration-orientation and females may maintain more loss-orientation. This provides an explanation for the oft-found familial discord after a child dies: mother and father are grieving differently and do not recognize or understand the grief that the other is experiencing. Similarly, other cultures may concentrate on one orientation more than the other. Thus, Wikan's (1988) findings are explained a little more clearly: the Muslim community in Bali is restoration oriented and discourages expressions of grief when someone dies. The Muslim community in Egypt, however, expresses grief openly, being a loss-oriented community.

Box 5.11 describes how Edgar's responses fit Stroebe's dual-process model of coping with bereavement.

IN CONCLUSION

Table 5.1 presents a summary of the models covered in this chapter.

The models of bereavement that have been examined in this chapter do not necessarily contradict one another; rather, they highlight different perspectives of examining the grief process. Other models exist (e.g., Gamino, Sewell, and Easterling's, 2000, adaptive model

of grief; Moos's, 1995, integrative model of grief), and they too examine slightly different aspects of the grieving process. It is not profitable to try to determine which model is "right" and which is "wrong": they complement one another in many cases, and they appeal to different individuals trying to understand this confusing and agonizing experience.

However, Esther Shapiro (1994, 1996) cogently pointed out that the models described in this chapter, and those others that are usually discussed, all refer to the reactions of the individual to a bereavement. She noted that families are also bereaved, and a family is more than just a collection of individuals. "Grief is a family developmental crisis that becomes interwoven with family history and current developmental moment and radically redirects the future course of shared family development" (Shapiro, 1994, p. 17). She proposed a model of family grief that highlights the disruption of the family identity and stability. In her model, she noted that when a family member dies, no matter what the culture, relationships within the family are changed and with them the identity of the individuals and the equilibrium of the entire family. For example, when an only child dies, the parents no longer have the role of "parents"; when an older sibling dies, the next-oldest child becomes the oldest; when parents die, a child becomes an orphan.

Thus, not only the individual who has been bereaved but also the whole family must learn to adjust to the loss by restructuring the network of relationships and the roles played by the remaining family members. Part of the mourning process, then, includes the reorganization of the family and the attempt to gain a new harmony and equilibrium within the family. In the upcoming chapters, we will pay attention to both the grief of the individuals and the disruption of the family as a whole.

TABLE 5.1 Summary of Models

STAGE/PHASE THEORISTS	TASK THEORISTS	OTHER THEORISTS
Kübler-Ross 1. denial 2. anger 3. bargaining 4. depression 5. acceptance	**Worden** 1. accept the reality of the loss 2. work through the grief and pain 3. adjust to a new environment 4. relocate the deceased and move on	**Klass: continuing bonds**
Parkes 1. numbness 2. searching and pining 3. depression 4. recovery	**Rando** R1. recognize the loss R2. react to the separation R3. re-experience the deceased and the relationship R4. relinquish the old attachments to deceased and the old assumptive world R5. readjust to the new world without forgetting the old R6. reinvest	**Rubin: two-track model**
Bowlby 1. numbness 2. yearning and searching 3. disorganization and despair 4. reorganization		**Stroebe: dual-process model**
Sanders 1. shock 2. awareness of loss 3. conservation-withdrawal 4. healing 5. renewal		

SUMMARY

- The symptoms of grief are wide and varied, being seen in the domains of the emotions, the cognitions, the physical, and the behavioural. These symptoms include sadness; lethargy; anger; and stress reactions, such as heart palpitations, fear, anxiety, numbness, fatigue, and sleeping and eating disturbances.

- Several researchers have proposed models to describe the grieving process. These models are not necessarily mutually exclusive, but each highlights a different facet or perspective on grief and, as such, increases overall understanding.

- Elisabeth Kübler-Ross formulated a stage model of dying and bereavement in which the individual follows a general trajectory from denial to anger to bargaining to depression, and finally to acceptance.

- Colin Parkes's phase model noted the role of stress in bereavement and regards the trajectory as progressing from numbness to searching and pining to depression, and finally recovery.

- John Bowlby's attachment model suggested that grief is an emotion experienced by many different species because of their attachment to a primary caretaker. He emphasized the bonds that tie the bereaved to the deceased and postulated that the intensity of grief is determined, at least partially, by the strength of the attachment that had existed between the bereaved and the deceased. He suggested that the bereaved progress from numbness to yearning and searching to disorganization and despair, and at last to reorganization.

- Dennis Klass's model of continuing bonds strove to provide the basis for a cross-cultural model of grief in noting the correctness of Bowlby's assertion that attachment is the pivotal factor in grief. Klass encouraged the formulation of a model that takes into account the fact that the bereaved do not sever their ties with the deceased but find new ways to be connected, and those ways do not interfere with the formation of new relationships and bonds to others.

- Catherine Sanders's integrative model emphasized the role of stress in the grief response and she asserted that both the physiological and the emotional components must be examined to understand bereavement. She suggested the following phases of a grief trajectory: shock, awareness of loss, conservation-withdrawal, healing, and finally renewal. She also emphasized the active role the mourner plays in progressing through the grief trajectory.

- Simon Rubin's two-track model also emphasized the multifaceted nature of the bereavement experience. On Track I is the emotional, cognitive, and behavioural reaction to the stress of bereavement, and on Track II is the social reaction of the mourner's relationship with the deceased. Rubin pointed to the idea that resolution of grief must come on both tracks, and the progress on one track does not necessarily reflect progress on the other.

- William Worden felt that a task model is more useful in a clinical sense. He posited that the bereaved must accomplish the following tasks: (1) accept the reality of the loss, (2) work through the pain of grief, (3) adjust to an environment in which the deceased is missing, and (4) emotionally relocate the deceased and move on with life.

- Thérèse Rando combined phases and tasks in her view of the bereavement process. In the first phase, avoidance, the individual must (R1) recognize the loss. In the second phase, confrontation, the second task is (R2) react to the separation and then (R3) recollect and re-experience the deceased and the relationship, followed by (R4) relinquish the old attachments to the deceased and the old assumptive world. In the last, the accommodation phase, the mourner must (R5) readjust to move adaptively into the new world without forgetting the old, and finally (R6) reinvest energy into life, new understandings, and new relationships.

- Margaret Stroebe's dual-process model regarded bereavement as comprising loss-orientation (reacting to the loss of the loved one) and restoration-orientation (coping with the practical aspects of the loss of the loved one). The bereaved moves between one orientation and the other, restoration-orientation serving as a relief and distraction from coping with emotional loss, and loss-orientation allowing the mourner to recognize the loss and experience the grief. Different individuals and different cultures may emphasize one orientation at the expense of the other.

- Esther Shapiro noted that families as a whole, as well as individuals, face grief when a family member dies, and reorganization and restructuring of the bereaved family is part of their mourning process.

KEY TERMS

attachment	defensive exclusion	mourning
bereavement	grief	separation anxiety
complicated mourning	loss	subsequent temporary upsurges of grief (STUGs)

CHAPTER 5 Grief and Bereavement

INDIVIDUAL ACTIVITIES

1. Which model appeals to you the most? Why? If you have been bereaved, does this model fit your own experience best?

2. If you have witnessed someone who was bereaved, which model did he or she most seem to follow immediately after the death? Which model did he or she most seem to follow later? If they were different models, provide an explanation why you think this was so.

GROUP ACTIVITIES

1. In groups of four or five, compare your answers to the first individual activity above. What differences and similarities do you note?

2. In groups of four or five, create a "blended" model that you feel best suits your group. Why were these items chosen? Why were others discarded?

Death and the Child

Children and Grief

Eliot Jackson died in a car accident on June 14, 2004. He left behind his wife, Anna, and their three children: Trevor, aged 14 years; Belinda, aged 9 years; and Morgan, aged 4 years. Anna is completely distraught: she has been a stay-at-home mother who devoted herself to her husband and children. Now, however, she will have to find a job to support the children, and she will have to move the family to a new, less expensive home in another neighbourhood. Besides worrying about practical matters, such as these, and being in a state of extreme grief, she wants to help her children cope with the death of their father.

At first, she had confidence that Trevor was dealing with the situation well; as the new "man of the house," he expressed little grief and tried to be a source of strength to his mother, who depended on him and confided in him. After a few months, however, Anna began receiving reports from Trevor's new school that he was acting aggressively toward his peers and the school counsellor wondered if he might be involved with drug abuse. Anna had noticed that Trevor did not make new friends after the move, and he did not interact with his old friends very much anymore; instead, he spent more and more time alone in his room, wearing his father's shirts constantly. Anna assumed that this was a typical teenage phase.

Morgan, the youngest child, had commanded more of her attention, with her constant questions of "When is Daddy coming home?" and "How will Daddy find the new house?" even though Anna had explained to her that Daddy was in Heaven. Morgan was also showing babyish behaviour, such as returning to bedwetting and baby talk. Anna did not worry overly about Morgan though because she seemed to have only brief periods of sadness and then went back to playing and drawing.

Belinda, the nine-year-old, was the greatest source of worry to her mother because she seemed to have a great deal of anger and plagued herself with the thoughts of being responsible for her father's death, despite reassurance to the contrary. She seemed to swing between being solicitous to her mother, if somewhat overconcerned about her mother's well-being, and being resentful of the move to a new neighbourhood and new school. She also has a great deal of difficulty in understanding why she had to give up her ballet and tennis lessons, even though her mother tried to carefully explain to her the need to be very frugal because the family did not have the same amount of money anymore. Belinda spoke little of her father's death, but she kept one of her father's photographs under her pillow and fell asleep every night touching it.

Anna, though a loving and concerned parent, had very little physical or emotional energy left to expend on her children, and she only hoped that they will work through their grief on their own.

As demonstrated in Box 6.1, there are many misconceptions about children and grief. For example, it is often assumed that children do not understand death and therefore do not mourn. This is a mistake, perhaps born of adults' desire that children not experience pain, of adults' difficulty in dealing with children's pain, and of their own discomfort with the subject. In fact, from a very early age, children mourn the death of someone they hold dear, whether or not they have a mature and sophisticated understanding of what death is; however, they may not show their grief in the same way that adults do, again leading to the adult error of believing that children do not grieve.

In 2003 in Canada, 3561 children under the age of 19 years died, many of them after long terminal illnesses (Statistics Canada, 2006). This number has been relatively constant since 1998. In addition, 16 053 adults between the ages of 20 and 49 years died in that year. It is likely that many of these adults were parents, leaving children under the age of 21. These numbers mean that a very large number of children are affected by death and dying every year in Canada. In fact, Ens and Bond (2005) surveyed 226 adolescents between the ages of 11 and 18 in private schools in Manitoba and found that more than 60 percent of them had already experienced the death of a close family member, usually a grandparent. In this chapter, we will examine children's understanding of

death and their short- and long-term reactions to the death of a loved one and to their own impending death.

FIRST CHILDHOOD EXPERIENCES OF DEATH

What do children perceive and feel when they first encounter death? Dickinson (1992) asked that question of 440 college students, who reflected on their first exposure to death. For just more than half the respondents, the first encounter with death involved the death of a relative; for a further 28 percent, the first encounter was with the death of a pet; and the remainder experienced death for the first time when another person (not a relative) died. On the average, the respondents were just less than eight years old at the time. They recalled their first responses to the death vividly and reported them as including such diverse reactions as fear, anxiety, confusion, anger, happiness, and relief. In this, little difference between adults' and children's responses is noted.

But a large difference is found in later responses to the death, mainly depending on how adults in the child's environment dealt with the child. For example, many children were given explanations of the death that served to confuse them or to give them a false impression of what had occurred. Using some euphemisms, such as "passed away" or "went to sleep," often conveyed the message that the dead person or pet would return to life, or that going to sleep meant that a person would die, a terrifying thought. Other euphemistic explanations, such as "was too sick to live" or "was called home by God" served to frighten the children that the same thing might happen to them or their loved ones in the near future. Similarly, lack of adequate information about funerals led to confusion and often anxiety as well ("If Grandpa is asleep, they can't close the lid on that box!" "When are you going to dig him up?").

CHILDREN'S CONCEPTIONS OF DEATH

Several researchers over the past 70 years have studied how children conceive of death. Some general patterns have emerged, although the data are often inconsistent and not all studies are directly comparable.

Maria Nagy's Research

One of the earliest and best-known studies of children's conceptions of death was done by Maria Nagy (1948) in

---

BOX 6.1   True or False?

Are the following statements true or false?

- Young children do not grieve because they have no understanding of death.
- Bereaved children should be protected from the pain and suffering of bereavement because they are too young to cope with death.
- Bereaved children are able to resolve their grief quickly and readily go on with life in the absence of the deceased.
- Adolescents are too self-absorbed to really mourn the loss of another person.
- The best way for children to cope with the death of someone close is to forget about the deceased and to be given a replacement for that person.
- Children should not attend funerals.
- A child who loses a parent early in life is psychologically scarred forever.
- Unless they are specifically told, dying children do not know that they are dying.

Answers: All of these statements are false.

Hungary during World War II. She asked children aged 3 to 10 years, "What is death?" engaging them in conversation and having them draw pictures. From this research, she concluded that children pass through three stages of understanding.

In the first stage, from three to about five years of age, children are curious about death and regard it as much like life but in a diminished form: dead people are similar to living people, but their lives are severely restricted insofar as they do not need much food or water and they do not possess the ability to interact with others. They are conceived of as living "somewhere else" in this diminished form.

In the second stage, from about five or six years until about eight or nine years of age, children recognize the finality of death and they personify it as, for example, the Grim Reaper, a skeleton, or an angel. If they are clever, they indicated, they might elude this personification of death. The idea of death coming to everyone did not seem fully fixed in these Stage 2 children's minds.

In the final stage, children from about nine or ten years of age understand death as adults do, as final, inescapable, and an event that will happen to everyone.

Speece and Brent's Research

Building on Nagy's work, more recent researchers refined their understanding of how children conceive of death. Noting that death is a very complex concept, Speece and Brent (1984, 1992) examined the relevant literature to analyze the major components of the concept of death and stated that the understanding of each component may proceed independently of understanding of the other components. Speece and Brent's five components discussed are as follows:

1. **Irreversibility.** Once death has occurred, it cannot be reversed; the dead will not come back to life.
2. **Nonfunctionality.** When death occurs, all life-sustaining functions, such as breathing, cease.
3. **Universality.** Death comes to every living thing.
4. **Causality.** What causes death? Why do living things die?
5. **Personal mortality.** Related to universality, this is an understanding that the individual himself or herself will die.

The discussion of other research on children's understanding of the concept of death is illuminated by this breakdown of the different components of the concept.

Other Research
Infancy (Birth to Three Years Old)

The child from birth to about three years of age has limited cognitive skills; however, he or she has emotional responses to the death of a familiar person. John Bowlby (1980) points to the fact that infants less than one year of age become attached to certain people in their environments and show outrage, confusion, despair, and depression when those people disappear. Although these very young children may not have an understanding of the components of death discussed by Speece and Brent (1984, 1992), they do recognize that a familiar person is gone, and this causes them pain (Norris-Shortle, Young, & Williams, 1993). These children may be responding to the emotional states of those around them, but because of their lack of communicative ability, it is difficult to be sure of exactly what they understand.

Early Childhood (Three to Five Years Old)

By the age of three years, children have some conception of death, although it is limited and inaccurate (Stambrook & Parker, 1987). Until children are about five years old, they typically do not understand death as comprising the components discussed by Speece and Brent (1984, 1992). That is, they show **magical thinking** that somehow the death will be nullified. Thus, like Morgan in the opening vignette, they believe it is possible for the deceased to come home, and they may continue to question when the deceased will return, although they have been told of the death. This is because they do not see death as being final or irreversible (Christ, 2000). They may dig up a dead pet to see if it has come to life again. Similarly, they believe that dead people can still see and hear although they are confined to a coffin because their "lives" are now circumscribed by death. Because of this, children are sometimes very disturbed by the closing and sealing of a casket, as well as by burial and cremation. Also, they believe that death will not come to everyone, and certainly not to them, if they are clever and careful.

Middle Childhood (Five to Ten Years Old)

At around the age of five, children typically begin to come to a clearer understanding of the irreversibility, finality, and nonfunctionality of death, although their understanding is not yet complete regarding all components until about nine or ten years of age (Speece & Brent, 1984). From age five to nine or ten, the component of universality develops first, followed by irreversibility, and then nonfunctionality, with causality following later, independently (Lazar & Torney-Purta, 1991; Speece & Brent, 1992).

Interestingly, children comprehend the death of humans before they comprehend the death of animals (Lazar & Torney-Purta, 1991; Orbach, Gross, Glaubman, & Berman, 1985), a phenomenon that may be related to children's identification with animals and their need for a defence against their personal mortality. For example, because children identify with a pet hamster or a teddy bear or a dog seen in a television show more than they identify with adults, the death of an animal feels closer to them than the death of an older human being. Because they feel that "if it happened to Lassie, it could happen to me," they block the personally threatening understanding of death that is near to them, while gaining an understanding of death that is more remote and thus less threatening. Another explanation may be that children's understanding that the concept of death can be generalized to different forms of life is incomplete.

Maare Tamm and Anna Granqvist (1995) asked Swedish children to draw pictures of their conceptions of death and to verbally comment on them. They found that, as Nagy (1948) suggested, death is very often drawn as a person, such as a Grim Reaper or a skeleton. Their results, however, indicated that even older children (12 to 18 years of age) often personified death, and boys were more likely to do this than girls were. Children between the ages of 9 and 12 years were found to represent death in mainly biological terms; that is, they concentrated on the physical means of death and results of death. In addition, boys' drawings were more often of a violent means of death (e.g., murder, war, explosions) while girls were more likely to represent death more peacefully (e.g., death in bed, after an illness). Tamm and Granqvist suggested that this finding is consistent with the tendency to greater aggressiveness in boys and their interest in television programs involving violent death, as seen in their games (e.g., cops and robbers).

Adolescence (Ten to Sixteen Years)

By the age of 10 years, the majority of children have acquired an understanding of the individual components of death. With adolescence (10 or 11 years to about 16 years), a more sophisticated understanding emerges as these young people now think in more complex, abstract ways. Tamm and Granqvist (1995) found that Swedish children in general showed an increase in the representation of death in mystical as opposed to biological terms. Specifically, as opposed to younger children, adolescents were more likely to draw death as a mystery (e.g., candles

shining in blackness, swords, bleeding heart), and they were much more likely to draw representations of emptiness in their conceptions of death (e.g., black or grey fields). These adolescents used fewer traditional Christian symbols to represent death (e.g., cross, crucifix) and more spiritual (e.g., candlelight) or existential (e.g., black field), reflecting both their own more sophisticated understanding and, perhaps, the mainly secular society of Sweden.

The understanding of death can be seen in the questions that children ask. Box 6.2 gives some of the questions that arise when children are given the opportunity to question physicians (Thompson & Payne, 2000).

Factors Affecting the Development of the Concept of Death

In a recent review of the literature, Brenda Kenyon (2001) of the University of Guelph examined factors thought to have an impact on children's acquisition of the various components of death. Although she found that age is a strong and reliable predictor of the acquisition of the death concept—with an understanding of death as a changed state by the age of three years and full understanding of the various components by ages nine or ten years—her other findings may seem rather surprising.

1. *Cognitive ability.* Although it has been assumed that the child's understanding of death proceeds along with his or her general cognitive development, studies examining this have yielded inconsistent results. Some indication exists that verbal ability enhances the organization of understanding death and communication of this understanding. It might be, then, that studies that use an interview method are obscuring the demonstration of understanding by less verbally facile younger children.
2. *Gender and socioeconomic status.* Neither gender nor socioeconomic status has much affect on the acquisition of the concept of death.
3. *Cultural/religious effects.* Cross-culturally, children are more similar than different in their acquisition of the concept of death; however, the differences that are found are noteworthy. Children who have been exposed to death stimuli (e.g., Israeli children) understand irreversibility and nonfunctionality sooner than other children, although universality and causality are relatively unaffected.

BOX 6.2   The Questions Bereaved Children Ask a Physician

Francesca Thompson and Sheila Payne (2000) reported the questions to a physician that were posed by more than one hundred children from 5 to 14 years of age who had lost a family member from three months to three years previously. The setting was a camp for bereaved children in the United Kingdom, and all the children were sent by their parent(s), suggesting that these children all had parents who were interested in informing and supporting their children regarding death of a loved one. By far the largest category of questions concerned the causes of death, followed by questions about life span, doctors and their roles, dead bodies, and finally, the emotions of grieving. The ages of the questioners are not all reported, but those that are reported are indicated in parentheses below.

- Is it my fault that my dad died? (5 years)
- Is cancer caused by germs? (5–7 years)
- Why do people get heart disease and why does it sometimes cause them to die? (8–10 years)
- Why do heart attacks happen suddenly? (9–11 years)
- Does having asthma mean that you're more likely to die? (9–11 years)
- How do people get cancer? (9–11 years)
- If people can't find anything wrong after people die, why can't they find anything? (12 years)
- Can you put someone in a coffin and bury them, but they can still be alive? (12 years)
- When somebody says that someone dies instantly without pain, how do I know if they are telling the truth? (13 years)

- Why do people catch cancer?
- Why can't doctors make everyone better?
- What causes suicide?
- Why did my dad die so slowly?
- What happens to your brain when you die?
- Why do people die? It always seems that nice people die and horrible people live until they are old.
- Why are the doctors always wrong? Why don't they notice sooner?
- Why didn't the doctor tell our family he had cancer?
- How long does it take to rot away when you're dead?
- If people go to Heaven, can they see you all the time?
- When people die and you see everything, why do you get pictures in your head and they don't go away?
- Why do some people cry and some not when they both knew the dead person?

Also noteworthy is the report of almost all the children that they are teased at school for having lost a loved one. The researchers stress the need for teachers and parents to be aware of this prevalent phenomenon, which exacerbates the bereaved child's already existent feelings of isolation and being different.

Source: Thompson and Payne (2000).

More research will undoubtedly follow the violent and tragic events in Lebanon and Israel that took place in the last half of 2006: will these children, exposed both to war that targets even noncombatants and to the sudden death of those around them, have a different understanding of what death means?

The effects of religion depend on the belief in an afterlife; children raised with a belief in an afterlife (e.g., Baptist) are later in understanding irreversibility than are children raised without a belief in an afterlife (e.g., Unitarian). Note, however, that children raised with belief systems that include an afterlife may not be referring to a physical return from the dead when they say that death is reversible; on the contrary, they may be referring to a spiritual continuation of the soul while fully knowing that the corporeal body will not reanimate.

4. *Experience.* Sadly, some children have been exposed to family deaths or to their own life-threatening illnesses. This kind of experience, as expected, hastens a child's understanding of the concept of death. These children understand the causes of death and their personal mortality better than other children, and some studies found an advanced understanding of nonfunctionality and physical irreversibility as well. The effects of some types of experience on children will be discussed in greater detail later in the chapter.

5. *Social-emotional factors.* Highly anxious children aged 6 to 11 years have more trouble understanding the component of universality than do less anxious children. Perhaps also reflecting the effects of anxiety, children in this age group who are asked about the death of a hypothetical relative show less understanding of the concept of death than when

they are asked about the death of a stranger. Kenyon noted, however, that an effect of the anxiety may be to lessen the communicative ability of these children rather than genuinely impairing their understanding of the concept of death.

HOW DO CHILDREN SHOW THEIR GRIEF?

William Worden's Research

William Worden (1996), with the help of co-researcher Phyllis Silverman, designed the Child Bereavement Study, which consisted of intensive interviews with 125 American children between the ages of 6 and 17 years at four months, one year, and two years after the death of a parent. Worden was careful to note that the death of a parent involved more than just the loss of that one person for the child; it also meant a great disruption in the child's life in terms of the changed family constellation and the amount of care and attention given to the child. After the death of a parent, that parent's interactions with the child (e.g., putting the child to bed, partaking of special activities with the child) ended and the surviving parent, being deeply in mourning as well, was often unable to fill in or to provide attention and comfort for the child. Other changes often came with the death of a parent as well, for example, family finances, working and child-care arrangements, even the location of the family home, as in the case of the Jackson family in the opening vignette. All of these changes bring about high levels of stress and are potential factors in the child's reactions to the death.

For the most part in the Child Bereavement Study, the reactions of the children are all reported together, with little detail concerning the ages at which certain responses are more likely to occur. Nonetheless, the information obtained is extremely illuminating. The predominant reactions that Worden (1996) and his colleagues found were expressions of sadness, anger, guilt, and anxiety. How these emotions were expressed often differed from child to child, but common expressions included apprehension that something would happen to the surviving parent or to himself or herself, remorse for misbehaviour or for not having said "I love you" to the deceased parent, frequent crying, and occasionally acting out behaviours. The general findings are summarized here:

- Anxiety rose over the first year of bereavement and was expressed more by girls than boys. The children who expressed the most anxiety were generally those who had experienced the most disruption in their daily lives and who felt that they had little control over their circumstances.
- Crying was found less in adolescent boys than in any other age group. This might reflect the greater social sanctions against boys' crying, sanctions that play heavily in the life of an adolescent boy trying to assert his masculine identity (Lenhardt & McCourt, 2000). In all children, crying became less frequent over time.
- Anger was more evident in bereaved children at the interview one year after the parent's death than at any other time. These children displayed more anger than did nonbereaved control children.
- During the first year after the death of a parent, the children (especially the girls) showed more physical reactions and illnesses than nonbereaved children. Children have more accidents during this time as well, with boys showing the highest incidence.
- Psychologically, bereaved children felt less in control of the circumstances of their lives than did nonbereaved children at the one-year and two-year interviews. At the two-year interview, bereaved children rated themselves as having lower self-esteem than did nonbereaved children. Boys and adolescents of both genders, however, felt that the bereavement had increased their maturity.

Other Research

Several other researchers have examined the reactions of children to bereavement. John Bowlby (1960) analyzed the reactions of infants who are separated from their attachment figures for a long period. He described their reactions as grief that manifests in three steps. First, the child protests the separation, showing both anger and pain. Next, when the attachment figure still does not return, the child shows despair as he or she gives up hope for reunion. Finally, the child detaches himself or herself from people in general, often developing what may be a permanent inability to trust or bond with others.

In a review of the literature, Hames (2003) noted that infants who experience long-term loss of a primary caregiver have been found to cry more and show sleep, eating, and elimination disturbances. Bereaved toddlers show regressive behaviours, such as using baby talk and losing toilet-training skills, as well as displaying increased anxiety and decreased independence. They also adapt to change poorly and may be prone to episodes of agitation and anger more often than nonbereaved toddlers.

Grace Christ (2000) reported the results of interviews with 157 American children between the ages of 3 and 17 years who had lost a parent to cancer. The interviews occurred shortly following the death, 8 months after the death, and 14 months following the death. Her interest was mainly in how to help the children cope with their loss, and her analysis reflected this in its emphasis on the different reactions of children of different ages. Children from the ages of three to about five years feel the separation anxiety when a loved one dies and they struggle to comprehend what it means. Christ found that major problems for children in this age range were their confusion in understanding what had happened and their being overwhelmed by the grief of their surviving parent, which is sometimes not realized by adults.

Adults often fail to examine the nature of the children's play and drawing and so jump to the conclusion that the children are unaffected by the death, because they seem to be playing and behaving normally. However, children's expressions of grief and confusion are seen in their play and in their drawings, both because of their lack of facility in verbal communication and because they cannot deal with intense emotions for prolonged periods (Geis, Whittlesey, McDonald, Smith, & Pfefferbaum, 1998). For example, the children may use only dark colours in their drawing or portray themselves as small and abandoned. Or they may hide under tables more in their play, or throw a doll away because "she's dead." Because children at this age do not have a full comprehension of the components of the death concept, like Morgan in the opening vignette, they often ask repetitively when the deceased person is coming home. Sometimes they show more infantile behaviour than has been their habit (e.g., clinging and whining) and in some cases, they develop symptoms like those of the deceased. For example, Christ (2000) describes Amanda, aged four years, who complained of stomach pains and sat in her father's chair with blankets wrapped around her after her father's death from cancer. Similarly, Worden (1996) quotes a child whose father died from cancer as saying. "I had his symptoms. I have myself convinced that I probably had the same thing" (p. 65).

Children from six to eight years old have a greater understanding of the concept of death and show sadness and upset when learning of the death of a loved one (Christ, 2000). These children have brief spells of sadness and anger, and also have sleeping disturbances and fearfulness. They tend to speak openly about the deceased and to him or her, saying that they wish they could be with him or her (although the children are not suicidal). They also describe pleasant memories very joyfully and like to have photographs of the deceased and objects belonging to the deceased.

Nine- to 11-year-old children avoid their own strong emotions and those of others (Christ, 2000). Control is paramount to them. They want detailed, factual information about the death to gain more control. Because of their inhibitions about expressing their grief, children in this age group often manifest their pain indirectly by increased aggressiveness, acting out behaviours, messiness, withdrawal, argumentativeness, and anger.

These children, like younger children, desire objects belonging to the deceased (**transitional or linking objects**) and enjoy looking at photographs to maintain a connection with the deceased (Normand, Silverman, & Nickman, 1996); however, they are more private and less emotionally expressive in this than are the younger children.

Bereavement in adolescence is even more complicated than it is in younger ages (Balk, 1996; Schoen, Burgoyne, & Schoen, 2004). Twelve- to 14-year-olds are still more reluctant to show emotions than are younger children, even wanting to avoid information about the final illness of the deceased. The only emotional expressions they tend to show publicly are anger and disdain (Christ, 2000). But alone, they experience the pain that adults feel, often more intensely than adults (Christ, Siegel, & Christ, 2002), writing fiction and poetry and in diaries and crying into pillows. These adolescents were more open about wanting objects belonging to the deceased, wearing clothing, for example, that had belonged to the deceased.

Adolescents between the ages of 15 and 17 experience the same reactions as adults (e.g., loss of pleasure in day-to-day activities, longing, despair, sadness), but they may also show such behaviours as argumentativeness, drinking bouts, anger, and limit-testing by avoiding chores and staying away from home. Kirwin and Hamrin (2005) noted that teenagers are also going through a developmental stage of separating from their families and gaining their own independent identities. This is often a time of discord in the family. When a family member dies, considerable guilt may be experienced by teenagers because of the stress they may have caused to the deceased. Because their bodies often look adult-like, it may be the case that adults in their environment assume that their emotions and their coping abilities are also adult-like, leading to an expectation that these children need no help in the grieving process. This may have been the case for Trevor, in the opening vignette: his mother may have assumed that he had more maturity than was true.

Lenhardt and McCourt (2000) discussed the tendency of adolescents to use **affective denial** in reacting to their grief. Affective denial refers to an inhibition of an appropriate emotional response, even though the death is cognitively recognized and accepted. Lenhardt and McCourt believed that adolescents use affective denial, especially when confronting the death of a parent, for several reasons:

1. They feel a pressure to conform to their peers, most of whom have not lost a parent. Overt expressions of grief would set them apart from their peers, an outcome they want to avoid.

2. They are striving to appear adult-like and may perceive grieving as child-like behaviour.
3. The surviving parent, in his or her grief, may unwittingly encourage the adolescent to suppress grief so that the stoical child can then assist the parent and provide no extra worry for the parent.

The affective denial that many adolescents show may impede the process of dealing with grief by effectively disenfranchising it (Rowling, 2002), leading to a lack of the support that the adolescent may need so badly (see Chapter 10 for a discussion of disenfranchised grief).

Notable, and troubling in some instances, is the adolescent's tendency to engage in risky behaviour, such as drinking alcohol, driving at high speeds, and using drugs. These behaviours may be seen in bereaved adolescents as a reaction to their grief, say Noppe and Noppe (2004) because although adolescents may have an adult-like intellectual understanding of death, they do not yet have the life experience and wisdom to emotionally understand death. Physical risk provides a means of coping with the stress of a bereavement while testing the limits of mortality, "cheating" death, and providing the positive social outcome of gaining peer acceptance and regaining a feel of personal control and mastery that had been diminished by the death of a loved one.

Another description of the developmental progression in the understanding of death is given in Table 6.1. Included are some reactions to death that children may show. Some have been discussed and some

TABLE 6.1 Overview of Children's Understanding of and Reactions to Death

AGE	CONCEPTS	NORMAL BEHAVIOUR
Less than 3 years	little understanding of death sense of separation or abandonment	increased crying fussiness clinginess regression change in sleep, eating, and elimination behaviours resistance to change
3–6 years	death is seen as temporary or reversible magical thinking	sadness aggression magical thinking regression nightmares bladder/bowel problems noncompliance
6–9 years	gradual comprehension that death is final some magical thinking personification of death	guilt compulsive caregiving phobias possessiveness aggression regression difficulty expressing grief difficulty concentrating psychosomatic symptoms
9–12 years	cognitive awareness of death and its finality difficulty conceiving of their own death or that of a loved one concrete reasoning about how and why death occurs	defiance phobias possessiveness aggression psychosomatic symptoms
More than 12 years	death is irreversible, universal, and inevitable abstract and philosophical reasoning understand all people and self must die, but believe death is in distant future	anger defiance risk taking increased sexual activity substance abuse aggression possessiveness psychosomatic symptoms suicidal ideation

Source: Busch and Kimble (2001), Hames (2003), Kirwin and Hamrin (2005), Schoen, Burgoyne, and Schoen (2004).

have not been specifically discussed because they tend to occur less frequently. Although acting-out behaviours are normal, they should not be ignored. For example, substance abuse in an adolescent should never be overlooked. In particular, though, an acceleration of any of these behaviours suggests problems that might call for professional intervention.

FACTORS AFFECTING CHILDREN WHO LOSE A PARENT

Worden (1996) found that the following factors had effects on the grieving of the American children in the Child Bereavement Study who had lost a parent to death:

- The loss of a mother is generally harder for children to cope with than the loss of a father. Worden suggests that this may be because mothers are typically more involved in the day-to-day lives of their children, and so their loss provides greater disruption and more changes for the child than the loss of a father does. Lenhardt and McCourt (2000) agreed and added that the father, usually taking a traditional male role, deals with grief in a problem-solving, instrumental fashion and may therefore not encourage expressions of grief in his children; mothers, taking a traditional female role, encourage emotional expressiveness. Children who have lost a mother may therefore not seem to be as affected as children who have lost a father because of the differential encouragement of emotional expressiveness. But being able to talk about the loss and their feelings about this loss is helpful in coping with bereavement, so it is not surprising that loss of a mother may be more difficult for children to actually cope with than loss of a father. Worden's next finding supports this idea.
- The most powerful predictor of a child's subsequent adjustment to parental loss is the adjustment of the surviving parent. In Worden's group, the children whose surviving parent coped with the loss in adaptive ways were more likely to cope adaptively themselves. This was especially true if the surviving parent accurately perceived and responded to the child's needs and administered consistent and predictable discipline.
- Although engagement or remarriage after one year was associated with decreased anxiety among the bereaved children, the surviving parent's dating during the first year of bereavement was associated with withdrawal, acting-out behaviour, and physical complaints in bereaved children.
- Bereaved children who have siblings or large families have fewer problems in coping with their bereavement. Worden suggested this was probably because the addi-

tional sources of support for the child can compensate for the surviving parent, who may not be functioning well in the midst of his or her own grief.
- A not-surprising finding is that cohesive families are beneficial for coping in bereaved children, as are families who use active rather than passive means of dealing with stress and families who have no additional sources of stress. Children from such families show less acting out and higher self-esteem, as well as fewer emotional problems in general.

Worden (1996), as well as Silverman (2002) and Hames (2003), also notes that children re-experience and reprocess grief anew at each stage of their growth. Thus, for example, the little girl who mourns that her mommy is no longer alive to cuddle her, mourns again later for having no mother to join her at the Girl Guide mother-daughter banquet, once more later for the lack of a mother to go shopping with, and yet again at a later date for not having a mother to watch her graduate from high school, and so on. At each developmental level, the lack of the loved one brings a renewed sense of bereavement and a new understanding and meaning of the loss: the small child mourns what the deceased meant to the small child and years later, the child, now an adolescent, mourns what the deceased would have meant to the adolescent.

Surprisingly, Worden (1996) and his colleagues found that bereaved children did not have a clearer or more advanced understanding of death than did their nonbereaved counterparts. However, this finding is not commonly found, as seen in Kenyon's (2001) review.

Buxbaum and Brant (2001) also noted that special problems may arise when a parent dies from cancer. Usually, for a long period before death, the parent is clearly very ill and may be incapable of fulfilling the child's needs. This long phase may be a time of **anticipatory grief** for adults, a time in which the impending survivors may resolve old conflicts, make new memories, say their goodbyes, and, in general, prepare themselves for the loss to come. This time is generally considered to be helpful in the grief process. But this may not be the case for children. Too young and inexperienced in dealing with stress, this long anxious period may be overwhelming. In their inexperience with death and their inability to project accurately into the future, and with an all-too-common lack of communication from adults, children may not realize that this is a period of anticipatory mourning; that is, if they do not recognize the inevitably of the death, they will not get the benefit of recognizing how precious this time is, and so they miss the opportunity to resolve relationships and say goodbye. Conversely, children who do understand that death is an inevitable outcome of this period may experience more anticipatory mourning than adults do and may show enhanced acting out and distress reactions, including a greater fear of illness, which, because of to their current experience, suggests that death will always follow.

HOW CHILDREN REACT TO THE LOSS OF A SIBLING

Most of the research done in the area of children's grief is in the context of losing a parent. The loss of a sibling is not an area that has been researched as extensively as the loss of a parent, yet the effects on children who lose a sibling are often quite profound. When a child dies, the devastation that the parents feel cannot be underestimated (see Chapter 7 for a more detailed discussion of this loss). In this tragedy, the parents are often too enmeshed in their own grief to be able to parent surviving children in ways that are optimal for the children. In many cases, no well-functioning adult is available to help children deal with their own grief and to deal with the daily tasks of growing up. Because children do not always demonstrate their grief in ways that are immediately comprehensible to adults, the grief of children who lose a sibling is often overlooked. In addition, the family disruption and obvious extreme distress of the grieving parents provide more reasons that children who have lost a sibling may show severe effects of grief and stress, such as problems in school work, personal relationships, and later adult development (Kemp, 1999), and increased incidence of aggression, withdrawal, bedwetting, and nightmares (Pantke & Slade, 2006).

Schwab (1997) has outlined four areas of potential problems for children who have lost a sibling:

1. *Cognitive distortions.* As has been discussed, because of their developmental level, young children may form incorrect ideas about death and what has happened in their families. This problem is exacerbated when parents (or other close adult) do not give children sufficient information about what has happened, either because of a misguided protectiveness of surviving children or because talking to the surviving child about the death of a sibling is simply too painful. It is not uncommon for children to use their imaginations and form distorted ideas about the sibling's death, often feeling responsible and guilty about the death, especially if they had wished the sibling dead in a moment of anger.

   In reviewing the literature, Schwab notes that children are aware of perinatal deaths as well; that is, even though parents may assume that children are not keenly aware of a stillbirth, neonatal death, or miscarriage of a sibling because the child had no contact with the deceased, children are still affected by these deaths. For example, they may feel that they caused the miscarriage because they bumped into their pregnant mother or expressed a preference against having a sibling. Or they may mistakenly assume that the parents are somehow guilty of the murder of the deceased child. As Schwab says, "Such cognitive distortions on the part of children naturally lead to their being angry, fearful, and mistrustful of their parents" (p. 260).

2. *Reactions to parental distress.* As has been noted, the climate of the family in which a child has died is usually full of sorrow, disruption, and often neglect of any surviving children. Surviving children are not only disturbed in their own tasks of growing up, but their parents' distress is also very obvious and very troubling to them. They typically show great concern for their parents' comings and goings as well as for their parents' general welfare, not only because they fear another family death, but also because of their love for and loyalty to their parents. Consequently, they may hide their own grief, not wanting to burden their parents further at this time of distress, and they may become very protective of their parents in other ways. A heart-rending example given by Schwab concerns a six-year-old boy who was hit by a car six months after his older brother's death. To avoid upsetting his parents, he insisted on walking home and saying nothing about his pain so that they did not know he was hurt; his broken arms were only incidentally discovered by his mother later that night.

   The effects of parental distress is also sometimes seen in the parents becoming overprotective of the surviving children and not wanting to discipline them or to allow them normal activities that would promote their autonomy. Both departures from normal parenting are detrimental to the surviving children, undermining their developmental progress.

   Finally, the parents' preoccupation with their grief over a prolonged period may leave surviving children feeling neglected and insignificant, feelings that may have long-term ramifications for children's sense of self-worth and the establishment of meaningful relationships later.

3. *Being a replacement child.* It is not uncommon for surviving children to be compared with a deceased sibling in terms of appearance, abilities, and personalities. But sometimes the deceased child is idealized, remembered as being more accomplished and more attractive than was the true case. When the surviving children are measured according to these standards, approval and acceptance may be impossible, and, at the very least, the situation is not

conducive to children's development of a sense of identity and self-worth. In some (thankfully rare) cases, parents may have another child to deliberately replace the one who was lost, sometimes even giving the newborn the name of the deceased child.

Obviously, children are not coffee mugs that can be replaced when one is lost, but many children feel that they are replacements for the dead sibling, if only in the context of the changed family constellation. Thus, the second child becomes the oldest when an older sibling dies; the middle child may become the "baby" when a younger child dies. Parental and other people's expectations of surviving children may be in the framework of these new roles rather than in terms of children's former identities. Not surprisingly, many children who have lost a sibling report that they feel the responsibility to accomplish more, be better behaved and, in general, to "compensate" their parents for the loss of their child. Sadly, as Schwab notes, both children and parents lose in this situation: children lose a chance to develop and be valued for their unique selves, and parents lose the opportunity to watch the uniqueness of their children emerge.

4. *Parental failure to cope with grief.* Finally, Schwab discusses the case of parents who cannot resolve the grief they feel at the loss of their child. Although attention has been mainly paid to the agony felt by these parents, their surviving children are suffering too. Not only are they deprived of support in dealing with their own grief, but they are deprived of the guidance they need to grow and develop in their own lives. When parental grief is so all-consuming and unresolved, the surviving children may also develop psychological problems, such as depression and the inability to form lasting relationships. This may particularly be the case for children born after the parents have experienced the death of a child (sometimes perinatally or when one twin dies) and have not yet had sufficient time to deal with their grief; the newborn may not enjoy the full measure of attachment to the parents because of their preoccupation with their grief and perhaps their fear of becoming attached to another child who may die as well.

In adolescence, losing a sibling can have important effects on the development of children's social relationships and sense of identity. Although it is normal for adolescents to be highly involved in social activities with their peers, adolescents who have lost a sibling may feel different from peers and see their activities as uninteresting and trivial. Withdrawal from these activities is a common consequence; this withdrawal, however, may be very detrimental to the adolescents' formation of identity, which relies to a high degree on peer interaction

---

BOX 6.3 Losing a Twin

People tend to be fascinated by twins, especially identical twins: two human beings, unique and yet identical. Many anecdotal reports exist of the special bond that twins feel with each other, and so it is reasonable to wonder whether twins are more profoundly affected when one of them dies. Withrow and Schwiebert (2005) reviewed research that demonstrates that when one twin dies, it is an especially difficult challenge for parents to raise the surviving twin. In many cases, the parents become very overprotective of the surviving twin, impeding the child's development of autonomy; in other cases, the parents withdraw because the surviving twin reminds them so much of the child who died, or they expect the child to fulfill the roles of two children. For the child, the loss of a twin is usually even more painful than the loss of another sibling: twins are often regarded as exceptional because of their twinship. When one twin is lost, the other may experience a severe disruption of identity as a twin, the loss of a role that can never be regained.

For twins, very often the attachment to each other is more intense than any other attachment. The loss of this attachment figure, the loss of the companionship and support that the twin brought, may be devastating for the survivor. Withrow & Schwiebert (2005) also report that feelings of guilt in the surviving twin may be intense, especially if the deceased twin committed suicide or had a disability. The surviving twin often feels that he or she could have done more to help the deceased twin, or should have seen the possibility of suicide and acted to prevent it, especially given the twins' strong bond. Fear for his or her own survival is also prevalent when one twin dies of a genetic disease, especially for monozygotic twins, who share 100 percent of their genes. In adolescence, reports Macdonald (2002), twins often define themselves and form their identities in regard to each other (e.g., "I'm the quiet one," or "We're like one person"). Therefore, the loss of a twin disrupts the burgeoning identity of the adolescent. Not surprisingly, many bereft twins say they feel that they have lost half of themselves.

(Kemp, 1999; Withrow & Schwiebert, 2005). Although many adolescents report feelings of isolation, responsibility for the sibling's death, being overprotected by parents, and, in some cases, even depression to the point of suicidal ideation (Wilson, 1995), many also report enhanced autonomy and maturity, as well as increased appreciation of the present and loved ones and compassion toward others (Kemp, 1999; Withrow & Schwiebert, 2005). As adults, those who lost a sibling as children report that they perceive their mothers (but not their fathers) as having been overprotective and controlling of them following the death, but they did not believe that their general parental care had been affected by the sibling death (Pantke & Slade, 2006).

Losing a twin is a special case with additional sources of grief and problems for the surviving twin, as discussed in Box 6.3. The tasks that children face in handling the death of any sibling are discussed in Box 6.4.

BOX 6.4 Children's Tasks of Grieving

Some researchers in the area of bereavement regard the process of grieving as comprising a series of tasks. For example, Worden (1996) outlined four tasks that he believes everyone, child and adult, must accomplish (see Chapter 5 for a full discussion of Worden's tasks). Baker, Sedney, and Gross (1992), however, see childhood grief as comprising several, more specific steps.

In the first, early phase of grief, when the bereaved are in a state of shock and numbness, the child must

1. comprehend that a person has died and the implications of this death
2. concentrate on protecting themselves and their families

The middle phase of grief is a time of pain and suffering. Anger and guilt may also be present. Now the child's tasks are to

1. accept the reality of the loss and emotionally acknowledge it
2. investigate the lost relationship with the deceased and re-evaluate what it meant
3. face and experience the pain of bereavement

In the last, late phase of grief, the child must adapt to a life without the deceased loved one. Specifically, the child's tasks are to

1. develop new relationships with others
2. develop and maintain a new relationship with the deceased that will last over time
3. return to normal activities and developmental processes
4. re-experience and reprocess the grief at different significant developmental periods

For example, Belinda, the nine-year-old described in the opening vignette, must first comprehend that her father has been killed and that she and her family will have to accommodate themselves to a new life without him. She must deal with her feelings of insecurity engendered by her father's death by assuring herself that her remaining parent and her siblings, as well as she, will not meet a similar sudden end, that the death of her father does not presage the death of anyone else in the family.

Then Belinda will have to face her own pain and anger at losing her father. She must think of the relationship she had with her dad, remembering the good times and the bad times, and what it meant to her. She may think of the support he gave her, the fun they had, the times he lost patience with her, the love he felt for her. In doing this, she must fully comprehend and experience what she has lost with this death.

Then Belinda needs to find the courage in herself to love again, investing her emotions in others, perhaps new people in her life, or perhaps in her existing relationships in a new way. For instance, Belinda may learn to love and trust an aunt whom she was previously unfamiliar with but who has given her nurturance during the crisis; she may become more nurturant herself in her relationship with Morgan, her younger sister; or she may ask her older brother to partake in activities that she had formerly engaged in with her father. As well, Belinda must find a new relationship with her father; that is, her goal is not to replace or forget him but to have a new sort of relationship with him. Perhaps she will feel that he is watching over her, like a guardian angel; perhaps she will talk to him internally or at his grave, apprising him of her joys and sorrows; or perhaps she will plant a garden that she dedicates to him, remembering him every time she waters a plant. The possibilities are endless, and only she can decide what form the new relationship will take. She must then go back to being a developing nine-year-old girl, going to school, playing with friends, finding satisfaction in her day-to-day life. Finally, as she grows, she must face the increasingly mature sorrow of losing her father again when the milestones of her life arise: her first date, her graduation from school, and so on.

CHAPTER 6 Death and the Child

CHILDREN'S LONG-TERM REACTIONS TO THE LOSS OF A PARENT

It is common and even reasonable to believe that the loss of a parent in childhood must be more traumatic and have a larger and longer-term effect than the death of another person in the child's environment. After all, in most families, a parent is a primary caretaker of the child, one who provides physical, emotional, and spiritual care for the child. Loss of such a person would therefore disorder the child's whole world, both in the physical environment and in psychosocial development. Understandably, then, it has been assumed that the child who loses a parent will be more prone to psychological disturbances (mainly depression and anxiety disorders) later in life, especially in the case of the death of a mother, and some studies have indeed found this to be true (e.g., Dowdney et al., 1999). However, other research finds that this is an overstated and simplistic conclusion (e.g., Tremblay & Israel, 1998; Worden, 1996); parental death, it is contended, is not necessarily the direct causation of later problems when they occur.

One way of examining the possible effects of parental death on the child is through the psychosocial theory of Erik Erikson (1963). He contended that children pass through stages of psychosocial development in which they must resolve certain characteristic issues. Theoretically, what would parental loss during these stages potentially mean for the children's development?

In infancy, said Erikson, children learn trust or mistrust of the world. If children's caretakers are consistent, attentive, and sensitive to the children's needs, the children learn trust. Clearly, in the case of parental death, this attentive and sensitive care may be disrupted and in theory would lead to the development of mistrust for the world. Similarly, in the toddler years, Erikson believed that children learn to separate from parents, exploring the world with more autonomy while having a safe home base with a parent. With parental death, this process also may be disrupted, which would then lead to the children's perhaps long-term decreased independence and sense of competence.

At about age four, according to Erikson, if parents encourage their children, the children will form plans and carry them out independently, becoming individuals with initiative who enjoy challenges. The death of a parent, and the grief of the remaining parent, may find the children overlooked and lacking in the needed encouragement, however, which theoretically may lead the children to feel fearful of attempting something on their own and to lack assertiveness.

Middle childhood finds children moving away from parents into the world of school and peers. Success at academic work and the formation of satisfying relationships with peers leaves children with a feeling of confidence, industry, and ability. Many children, though, need parental help with academic work and encouragement in socialization. Without these, children may develop a feeling of being inferior to others.

In adolescence, said Erikson, identity formation is the major task. Making decisions about who they are and what they will become occupies a great deal of the adolescents' thinking. Developing a strong sense of self grounds adolescents in a secure base so that satisfying long-term plans can be made and carried out. Without the successful accomplishment of prior tasks and without the guidance and role models of parents, accomplishing this task will be difficult for adolescents, leaving them feeling aimless and adrift, without a stable role or identity.

The question now is whether empirical evidence substantiates these theoretical formulations. Several researchers have certainly found the short-term problems with trust and independence in infancy and toddlerhood that Erikson's theory suggested (e.g., Bowlby, 1960; Davies, 1999; Silverman, 2000). However, the long-term effects of parental death appear to be mediated by factors other than the psychosocial stage of the child at the time of parental death and these are much more potent in predicting the degree of later-life difficulty children will have after losing a parent. In particular, Tremblay and Israel (1998) focused on the quality of parental care following the loss of a parent. When a parent dies, in most cases the surviving parent is in such grief and the family is in such disruption that children in the family are often overlooked and even neglected. As Shapiro (1994) noted, the entire family is bereaved and the network of relationships is disordered. The family members' normal roles within the family must be altered and a new equilibrium must be attained at the same time that the family members are grieving. Adults, as we have discussed, may assume that children do not understand death and do not grieve as deeply as adults, and so need less help in dealing with their grief. Children, as well, often hide their feelings from the surviving parent so as not to cause the parent additional distress and further family disruption. Not surprisingly, people who recall feeling neglected or that they must be the ones to provide support for a surviving parent show the most vulnerability to psychiatric problems and problems in forming peer relationships. Several studies confirm that when the loss of a parent is followed by emotional support for the children and an atmosphere in which they can feel secure and taken care of, they are far less likely to have any long-term problems in adjusting to parental death.

One of the most critical aspects of emotional support for the child is communication about the facts of the parental death and the feelings engendered by it. Also important is the ease with which the family is restructured to compensate for the roles the deceased parent played, thereby minimizing the disruption and insecurity children feel (Shapiro, 1994). Children's prior relationship with the deceased parent is an important factor in their subsequent adjustment as well: children whose relationships with the deceased parent were strong and marked by high nurturance show fewer problems subsequent to the parent's death. But children whose attachment to the deceased parent had been weak or incomplete (sometimes because of the parent's inability to function because of their illness) were more likely to have long-term problems. Tremblay and Israel (1998) conclude that

> Parental death, then, is best understood as creating a vulnerability, rather than inflicting a crippling injury by itself: Children appear to be at risk for concurrent and later difficulties *primarily to the extent that* they suffer a higher probability of inadequate parental functioning or other environmental support before, as well as after, the loss of a parent. (p. 431)

This conclusion is in line with Worden's (1996) finding that the most powerful predictor of children's subsequent adjustment to parental loss is the adjustment of the surviving parent, presumably because of the support that the surviving parent is able to give.

Further substantiation of this conclusion was found by Lin, Sandler, Ayers, Wolchik, and Luecken (2004). They, too, approached the understanding of the effects of parental death on children by regarding the bereavement experience as a process rather than as one discrete event. They supported the research indicating that the environmental changes and the surviving parent's ability to cope with disruption and the degree to which they can function as emotional support for the children are predictive of psychological health in the child. They related this to the considerable evidence indicating that the surviving parent's own psychological health predicts the adjustment and psychological health of the children: that is, being widowed predicts psychological problems, which then result in a decreased ability to parent children adequately.

Lin and his colleagues tested 179 American children between the ages of 8 and 16 to find the short- and long-term effects of parental death on these children. All had lost a parent between 4 and 30 months before their first testing. In this research (as well as in that of Kwok et al., 2005, and prior research), it was found that the ability of the surviving parent to provide warmth and consistent discipline was related to children's adjustment, and the surviving parent's own psychological problems predicted impaired adjustment in the children. In addition, children's characteristics also affected their adjustment: children who adjusted well (resilient children) did not perceive negative events in their environment to be threatening to their well-being. They also felt more capable of dealing with the stress of negative events. It is possible that these resilient children were less threatened and more able to cope with stress because their surviving parent coped with stress better, thus providing both a support and a role model for the children. It is also possible that the children who did not cope with stress well had more psychological problems because of their inability to handle stress rather than because of their parent's death per se. Nonetheless, Lin and his colleagues have provided information that may be very helpful in designing programs to help children cope with parental death (see Chapter 12).

A question that is often asked is whether children should be allowed or expected to attend funerals, especially those of their parents. Is this helpful or harmful to them? Research on this question is discussed in Box 6.5.

THE DYING CHILD

Much less research is done on the concepts and feelings of children with terminal illnesses than on bereaved children, for several reasons. First, it is difficult to get permission from parents of terminally ill children to talk to the children about their feelings regarding death. Parents themselves are often in denial of the fact that their child will die, and the idea of talking to the child about death is abhorrent to them. Second, many researchers consider asking parents of terminally ill children and the children themselves to be part of a study that will not benefit them to be unethical and unduly burdensome for the children and family. Finally, and perhaps most importantly, no one wants any child to die. Besides being a heart-breaking event, the death of children makes adults feel guilty, powerless, and cheated (Sahler, Frager, Levetown, Cohn, & Lipson, 2000; Stillion & Papadatou, 2002). If it is easier for adults to pretend that *bereaved* children do not understand death and therefore will not be hurt by it, how much more so do adults not want to believe that children understand the seriousness of their illness and contemplate their *own* death? As has been discussed, children do understand death much more than adults have assumed. Additionally, like Aidan in Box 6.6, terminally ill children do know that they are dying, but they may not indicate it because they are shielding adults who they can see are very upset.

John Holland (2004) attempted to find an answer to the question of whether children should be allowed or expected to attend a parental funeral in his doctoral study in the United Kingdom. He asked 70 adults who had experienced the death of a parent when they were children to recollect the event and the feelings they had around the funeral. None of the children younger than 8 attended their parent's funeral, and percentages increased with age: 44 percent of 8- to 11-year-olds attended, as did 63 percent of 12- to 15-year-olds, and 100 percent of those 16 years old and older. However, this represented only 47 percent of the sample. Of the 53 percent who did not attend their parent's funeral, 24 percent were forbidden to attend and 11 percent were "distracted" from attending by being sent to school or to stay with relatives or neighbours; the rest chose to stay away. Most noteworthy is that none of the adults who attended their parent's funeral as children reported having had any negative experiences from this. In fact, two-thirds of them reported feeling that attendance at the funeral had helped them in coping with their grief. When Holland asked the adults who had not attended their parent's funeral as children how they felt looking back on this, more than three-quarters of them reported that they wished they had attended. The greatest number of these people reported feeling regret, while others felt anger, hurt, and frustration in what they perceived as isolation and exclusion from the family at this time.

Holland's results and his suggestions tally well with the observations and suggestions made by Daniel Schaefer (2004). Schaefer, a funeral director with many years of experience, found that adults do not communicate sufficiently with children about death and, in particular, do not adequately explain what happens at a funeral. For example, he cited the commonly held belief of children that the lower portion of the deceased's body has been cut off because it is not seen in a traditional casket with the bottom half closed. His position, like that of Holland, is that children should be well prepared for the funeral by being given complete and explicit information about what will occur so that they can make an informed decision themselves about whether they want to attend. Indeed, Worden (1996) found that children who had not been adequately prepared for the funeral were more likely to show lower self-esteem and self-efficacy as well as disturbed behaviour two years later. This is most likely reflective of a state of high disruption and parental distress; that is, the surviving parent's distress probably led to both the subsequent adjustment problems for the child and the lack of satisfactory preparation for the funeral.

Both Holland (2004) and Worden (1996) found that children responded well when they were allowed some control over the preparations or the conduction of the funeral, by selecting music to be played, choosing burial clothes, reading a poem, and so on. These results highlight the need for children to feel included in the event.

Especially in the case of younger children, it is advisable to have children accompanied by a familiar, caring adult who is not a major mourner and who is completely available for the children's support and welfare. As children make a decision about whether to attend the funeral, it is important for them to know that they will be constantly upheld by this adult, who will take the children out of the funeral area whenever the children want.

I've been really sick for a long time. At first, I thought I was going to get better. That's what everybody told me. Now I don't think so. They still tell me that but I don't think it's true. I think it's just what Mom and Dad want to believe. They look so sad when they think I'm not watching them, so I try to smile a lot and act like I'm feeling OK. My friends used to visit me, but they can't come anymore because they all live back home in Ignace and now I'm in Toronto. That's OK. I understand that I have to be in the Hospital for Sick Children. But it's kind of hard being away from home for so long.

I wish my Gran could come and visit me. I really miss her. When I was home she used to smudge for me and I really liked the smell of the sage. Dad used to laugh at her for it, but Mom said it was part of her Cree tradition. I made some new friends in the hospital, though. We talk a lot because we can't play too much. We talk about what it would be like to die. We're all kind of scared of dying. Is it going to hurt? What happens after I die? What I'm really worried about is how Mom and Dad will be. I know they'll be sad, but how sad? I'm trying my best to hang on and be well, but sometimes I get so tired. I don't let Mom and Dad know how tired I am because I know that scares them. They call me a real trouper. I'm very tired of being a trouper.

Elisabeth Kübler-Ross (1983; Elliott, 1981, Furth, 1981; Kramer, 2004–05) did not shy away from talking to terminally ill children about their feelings regarding their illnesses. Her discoveries were revealing for many. According to her, if children have fear and anxiety about death, it comes mainly from the people in their environment who leave them confused by not interacting with them, indicating to the children that there is something to be upset about. That is, Kübler-Ross believed that children have an inherent wisdom that makes them accept death as part of life rather than as something to be feared. Adults make children feel that they must be wrong about this because the adults refuse to talk about death and dying.

Children with terminal illnesses have a more advanced understanding of the concept of death than their age-mates do, particularly in the areas of irreversibility and finality (Faulkner, 1997; O'Halloran & Altmaier, 1996; Stillion & Papadatou, 2002). Stillion and Papadatou (2002) reviewed the literature on terminally ill children and concluded that those aged three to six years have more death-related fantasies and seem to have more negative outlooks on their lives, including loneliness and body intrusion, indicating an awareness of illness and death not typically seen in healthier children. Similarly, terminally ill children aged six to ten years, they reported, have more anxieties with thoughts of loneliness and body mutilation, even when they are not informed of their disease. Adolescents who are dying have a more adult-like reaction to their condition, but they may have trouble believing that death will really occur to *them*, making enforcement of sometimes unpleasant medical regimens difficult.

Stillion and Papadatou (2002) also noted seriously, perhaps terminally, ill children's problems in progressing through the psychosocial tasks suggested by Erikson (1963). Thus, infants, whose task it is to gain trust in the world may be impeded in this given the separations from parents and the unpleasantness that medical procedures may bring. Toddlers may not be able to develop a sense of autonomy when their physical mobility is limited by illness and when parents and health-care workers are overprotective. School-age children, whose tasks include gaining a sense of competency and social facility, may find that limited energy, medical regimens, and side effects (e.g., baldness) may militate against their successful achievement of these tasks, resulting in a less adequate sense of self-worth. Similarly, adolescents, who are struggling with gaining a sense of identity and developing intimacy with another person, may be forestalled in these endeavours, because their bodies may be too weak to function well and their own futures may be in doubt. The changes in a terminally ill child's self-identity with the progress of the illness are discussed further in Box 6.7.

Although little empirical evidence exists on the feelings of dying children and adolescents, much clinical experience indicates that these children mourn for the loss of their abilities and their future, and they worry about potential pain and leaving their families to grieve for them (Hinds, Schum, Baker, & Wolfe, 2005). Hinds and her colleagues (2005) speculated that in some cases the children may be depressed, but they noted that it is very rare for anyone to assess these children for depression. A major problem for children is the lack of information they are given about their medical condition and what to expect; therefore, although they know how very ill they are, they may feel insecure and mistrusting because of adults' refusal to give them accurate and detailed information (Freeman, O'Dell, & Meola, 2003; Ishibashi, 2001).

BOX 6.7   Terminally Ill Children's Self-Identity

Children's sense of identity is also affected by illness. Bluebond-Langner (1977) worked with children who had leukemia and found that the information the children gathered about their illnesses translated into their self-images.

1. Children first understand that they are ill and that their illness is serious. They see themselves as individuals who lack the health they previously had.
2. In receiving medical intervention, the children learn about drugs and their direct and indirect side effects. If the intervention works, bringing about a remission of symptoms, the children see themselves as in a temporary state of ill-health, which will be corrected, and they will return to their previously healthy state.
3. As time progresses, the remission ends and the symptoms of the disease return. The children, now fully acquainted with the medical regimes, start to suspect that the illness will always be present, but life will go with more medical treatment.
4. Still later, the children become accustomed to the cycle of remissions and relapses and start to see themselves as people who will always have to live with the unpredictability of the disease.
5. Finally, terminally ill children see that eventually all treatments will fail and they will die.

Adolescents who are trying to form their own identities and become adults at this developmental point often have increased conflict with their families (see Ishibashi, 2001, for a review of the literature). This may be due to the increased time spent with parents, who tend to be overprotective, leading to more conflicts. Another explanation, not mutually exclusive to the first, may be that these adolescents have increased needs for independence, perhaps to "spite" their illness. Although adolescents perceive parents as being supportive, they perceive less support and interaction with healthy friends, probably because healthy adolescents are unsure how to interact with a terminally ill friend, not because of the stigma of a terminal illness. This isolation is most likely exacerbated by the adolescents' own self-consciousness about being different from their peers and by the existence of any physical indications of the disease (e.g., baldness, weakness, pallor, disfigurement). Whatever the causes, this leaves dying adolescents feeling lonely and wishing for more interaction with healthy friends.

Children can rarely be shielded from the diagnosis of their illness and the poor prognosis, and trying to shield children with lies or half-truths only disrupts the relationships that children have with adults (Nitsche et al., 2000; Stillion & Papadatou, 2002). Children who ask about their medical condition feel isolated and abandoned if they are not given an honest answer. They also feel insecure because they have no one they can trust to tell them the truth (Sahler et al., 2000). Although it is undeniable that the adults want to help, they seem to be doing the wrong things in many cases. How to help those who are dying and those who are bereaved is the topic of Chapter 12.

SUMMARY

- Children's first experiences with death are often fraught with misinformation and confusion because of the lack of adequate information given to them by adults.

- The understanding of the concept of death is not an all-or-none phenomenon. Rather, it is understood in terms of irreversibility (whether it is reversible), nonfunctionality (the nonfunctioning of all living parts and activities), universality (that death comes to every living thing), causality (the reasons that death occurs), and personal mortality (that eventually the individual himself or herself will one day die).

- Under the age of three, children react mainly to the separation from a loved one and the general distress and disruption of the household at the time of a death.

- From three years to about five years of age, children do not understand the irreversibility of death and think that somehow the dead person is still living a life (albeit diminished) and may return home.

- At around age five years, children start to form an understanding of irreversibility, finality, and nonfunctionality of death, but clear understanding is not achieved until about age nine or ten years. At that time, the understanding of the universality of death is comprehended, followed by a clear understanding of irreversibility and nonfunctionality.

- By adolescence, children have a full understanding of the various components of the concept of death.

- Factors affecting children's understanding of the concept of death include their age, their experience with death and death stimuli, and their social-emotional characteristics, such as presence of anxiety.

- A death in the family causes disruption because of the grief of family members, the redistribution of roles that the deceased played, and often a change in overall family circumstance. All these factors, as well as the actual death, are stressful for children and affect their reactions to the death of a loved one.

- Young children may show separation anxiety and regressive behaviours, such as clinginess and bed-wetting. In middle childhood, children react to the death of a loved one with sadness, anger, anxiety, and guilt. After about the age of nine, children try to control their emotions publicly but may act out or become withdrawn from family and friends. Adolescents experiencing bereavement may find their task of identity formation disrupted and they may engage in risk-taking behaviour.

- The most powerful predictor of children's adjustment to parental loss is the adjustment of the surviving parent. Surviving parents who are consumed with their own grief may not attend sufficiently or be sensitive enough to their children's grief to give them the help they need. As well, seeing their surviving parent in such distress is upsetting and confusing for children who, depending on their age, may feel insecure or feel the need to appear stoical and strong for the surviving parent.

- Children must reprocess and re-grieve at each developmental milestone they achieve. The bereavement is perceived to mean something new to them at each new point on their growth trajectory.

- Children who lose a sibling are also profoundly affected by their parents' ability to put their own grief aside and attend to the grieving children. Many surviving children feel that they are "replacement" children in some sense, that they must take the place of their deceased sibling and will be compared with him or her. Adolescents who lose a sibling may also feel estranged enough from their nonbereaved peers that their identity formation is compromised.

- When the loss of a parent is followed by emotional support for children and an atmosphere in which they can feel secure and taken care of, they are far less likely to have any long-term problems in adjusting to parental death. Additionally, children whose relationships with the deceased parent were strong and marked by high nurturance show fewer problems subsequent to the parent's death.

- Terminally ill children generally do know that they are dying, but they may not indicate it because they are shielding adults, who they can see are very upset. Children who ask about their medical condition feel isolated and abandoned if they are not given an honest answer. They feel insecure because they have no one they can trust to tell them the truth.

- Children with terminal illnesses have a more sophisticated understanding of the concept of death than their age-mates do, particularly in the areas of irreversibility and finality.

KEY TERMS

affective denial
anticipatory grief
causality

irreversibility
magical thinking
nonfunctionality

personal mortality
transitional or linking objects
universality

INDIVIDUAL ACTIVITIES

1. What was your first experience with death? How did you feel about the death? What did you think death was?

2. Did you ever attend a funeral as a child? Whose was it? How did you feel about it? If you were prevented from attending the funeral of a loved one as a child, how do you feel about that now?

3. If you have children whom you are close to, ask them about what death is (try to keep it light-hearted!). What age-related differences do you see?

4. With the permission of the health-care workers, visit a pediatric cancer ward and talk to the children about anything they want to talk about. *Do not lead the discussion!* What forms do their conversations take? Consider becoming a volunteer on a ward such as this.

GROUP ACTIVITIES

1. Share your first experience of death with others in your group or class. How have their experiences differed and been similar? Are there differences that reflect gender, culture, or religion?

2. In groups of four or five, have each person talk to a child to whom he or she is close and ask, "What is death?" The answers may be in drawings rather than verbal. Then bring all the answers back to the group and compile a trajectory of understanding of the concept of death based on the ages and answers of the children.

3. If possible, in a small group, interview a person who lost a sibling in childhood. What were the experiences of bereavement for this person? What (if any) long-term effects does this person feel that the bereavement brought to him or her and to his or her family?

4. In a group of five or six, select a movie or television program that deals with a seriously ill or dying child or teenager, or one that is bereaved, and rent the movie or program to view (suggestions: *21 Jump Street, Degrassi Junior High, Ordinary People, Harry Potter and the Philosopher's Stone*). As a group discuss whether the writers, actors, and director of the movie or program captured the reactions of the characters in what seems to be an accurate way. What would you change if you were the director?

Death and the Adult

Adults Facing Grief

▶
- Shelby and Phil Newinski's seven-year-old daughter died after a boating accident.
- Ellen Forsythe's husband of 27 years died of heart complications from diabetes.
- Douglas Steadman's mother died at the age of 75.
- Sudhir Patel's brother died of an unknown viral infection at the age of 32.
- Davina Raymond had an abortion of a deformed fetus in her fourth month of pregnancy.
- Richard Cartwright has been diagnosed with lung cancer.

Each of these adults is facing a critical point in their lives and facing great loss. In many ways, their reactions to their grief bear remarkable similarities; in other ways, the differences cannot be underestimated. In this chapter, we will learn more about these people and their reactions to the crises.

In 2003 in Canada 226 169 people died out of a population of more than 31.6 million (Statistics Canada, 2006). The vast majority of the people who died left behind adults who mourn them. Adulthood brings the potential for many types of bereavement. In general, the closer the relationship with the deceased, the more distress an individual will feel in bereavement. But there are particular differences found among bereavements given the relationship. For example, the death of a child and the death of a parent both occasion pain, but adults typically have different reactions and responses to this grief. In this chapter, we will examine different relationships, noting the particular problems and issues that may arise when one member of the relationship dies.

THE DEATH OF A CHILD

In 2003, according to Statistics Canada (2006), 3561 children aged 19 years or younger died in Canada. That means that roughly 7122 parents were bereaved, which does not account for stepparents or cases in which a parent is also deceased or missing or unknown. Other adult family members add to the number of adults directly affected by the death of a child. The death of their child is surely the worst devastation that adults can experience. Not only is the child much beloved by the parents, but he or she has also fulfilled other roles within the family:

- *The biological continuation of the line.* Children are the future; they assure the parents' immortality through their existence and their having children of their own. Birth children are also part of their parents' bodies, especially in the case of a mother, who carried the child inside her own body for nine months and who experienced the physical strain of childbirth.
- *The fulfillment of parental hopes and dreams.* Some people experience their own lives vicariously through their children, wanting their own dreams to be fulfilled by the children. Even when this is not the case, parents want for their children everything that they never had, a better life than they had, to be better than they ever were.
- *The couple's bond.* Children bond parents together in a sharing that is unequalled. Both their gene pools are continued in children, both of them are required to provide for the children and care for them, and, most importantly, both parents share a love for the children that is unrivalled by any other attachment.
- *The parents' social life.* Parents very commonly base their own social lives on the activities of their children, making friends with the parents of their children's friends, interacting with adults in the context of the shared activities of their children, and finding more in

common with other parents than with adults who are childfree.

When a child dies, parents can be expected to undergo the most severe grief imaginable. Parents' reactions to their child's death include the following (Sanders, 1999; Schwab, 1997):

- *Despair.* No matter how old their child or the manner of death, parents experience the death of their child as untimely and unjustifiable. The world seems irrational, threatening, and unfamiliar to them; their view of the world as a generally good and benign place, with life unfolding in an ordered fashion, has been challenged to the point of annihilation. They feel vulnerable and defenceless in the face of the tragedy.
- *Confusion.* Although confusion is an expected reaction in the early days of grief, Sanders reports that it is more pronounced in the case of parental bereavement. Concentration, attention, and decision making are all impaired as parents think about a jumble of memories of the child and the death itself.
- *Guilt.* Parents are supposed to protect their children; even most other species of mammals take care of their offspring. The death of their child represents the most profound failure of this responsibility, even when the parents did all that they could for the child or when the death was inevitable. Reason does not count with parents: no matter how much they know that they could not have prevented their child's death, parents feel deeply responsible. They feel that they did not give the child adequate care as a parent should, that they were not the type of parents they should have been, or that they and their dead child are being punished for some sin the parents committed.
- *Anger.* Anger is often a severe reaction to the death of a child. Parents have anger against the universe, against a deity, or against other people who might have been involved in the child's death, which they regard as unjust and unfair. It is not uncommon for bereaved parents to proclaim a loss of religious faith at this time, or to rail against medical or police personnel, who they believe could have, should have, done more to save their child or who conveyed the news of the child's death without showing compassion. Not the least of their anger is directed against themselves for their failure to save their child. Enhancing this anger is their feeling of helplessness: while the child was alive, they could take measures to solve problems concerning the child and to protect the child, but now death has robbed them of the ability to care for the child.
- *Stress responses.* The death of a child obviously is a highly stressful, traumatic event. It is not unexpected, then, that bereaved parents show typical physical responses to stress, such as sleeping and eating

difficulties, digestive problems, lethargy, heart palpitations, and headaches.

- *Marital problems.* Sanders reported that an estimated 75 percent to 90 percent of couples experience problems in their relationships after the death of their children. Many of these problems stem from each partner's expectation that each grieves in the same way, whereas in reality, each person grieves differently. Thus, for example, it is common that one parent is experiencing tearful lethargy while the other is lashing out in anger. Without understanding that grief takes different forms, sometimes even from minute to minute, for each person, the potential for problems between the parents escalates. Each assumes both should be experiencing the same emotions at the same time.

Gender roles are changing in society, and it is no longer possible to say that males and females typically fit any one pattern of behaviour. However, traditional gender roles, which indicate that males are strong, unemotional, and action oriented, while females are emotional, nurturant, and emotion oriented, still commonly exist in Canada. The following discussion reflects the traditional gender roles of males and females, but it is vital to note that individuals behave differently, regardless of their gender, and that families can comprise widely disparate elements. Thus, mothers are neither necessarily the primary caretakers, nor are they necessarily the more emotionally oriented parent. Similarly, fathers do not always take the role of active problem solver in an unemotional fashion. Also, families can contain two mothers or two fathers, or one parent. With these cautions in mind, let us discover what research has found about parents' reactions to the death of their children.

Fathers and mothers react differently, although it cannot be said that one grieves more than the other. Fathers, like mothers, react to grief in their own idiosyncratic ways, but they have a certain pressure to behave in keeping with the traditional male gender role. Consequently, men are expected to appear calm, logical, unemotional, and strong. Their role is that of protector and problem solver of the family. The death of a child, then, attacks a man at the basic level of his identity: he has failed in the male role; he may even believe that he has failed as a man. In attempting to fulfill the male role as much as he can, he may inhibit his emotions, appearing to be uncaring, while going back to work as soon as possible to continue to fulfill the role he has left, that of family provider. Mothers, conversely, can grieve openly because being emotional is part of the traditional female gender role. For women, though, a major part of the gender role is to be the nurturer, the one to keep the family together. In this, a bereaved mother has failed, she may

believe, and the structure of the family is broken with the death of the child. Her role, like the father's, has been shattered. She may find it very difficult to function without her main role in the family.

Notice the conflict that is likely to arise between husband and wife: the man is being uncommunicative in his attempt to control his grief while the woman is unable to function in day-to-day life. Neither one can understand the other's manner of grieving. This would seem to be what has happened to Shelby and Phil Newinski, the case presented in Box 7.1. They do not understand each other's expressions of grief, and each

BOX 7.1 Shelby and Phil Newinski

Shelby and Phil Newinski's only child, their daughter, Deborah, was seven years old when she drowned in a boating accident at her grandparents' cottage. Deborah ran off with her friend who, contrary to parental instruction, took an inflatable canoe into the water. The boat leaked, running out of air before the children could reach shore. The other child was a strong swimmer and managed to stay afloat until rescued, but Deborah could only swim a little and drowned before rescue arrived. Attempts to resuscitate her on shore failed.

Shelby and Phil are shocked and heartbroken, and they blame themselves and each other for what has happened. Phil went back to work two weeks after the death, but he has trouble concentrating, and he finds it unbearable when strangers ask him whether he has any children, not knowing how to answer. Shelby can barely get herself out of bed in the morning. Deciding whether or not to have breakfast seems like a huge problem to her, but then, as far as she is concerned, life has no meaning anyway. Deciding on whether or not to have breakfast is only a trivial part of her day. The couple argues more than they ever did before Deborah's death and not just about blame; every little thing seems to set them off and their interactions are consumed by, at best, bickering and, at worst, shouting matches. Shelby resents the way Phil scarcely talks about Deborah and shows a lack of emotional display, except for anger at every little frustration in life. Either he's in denial or he didn't really love Debbie, she thinks. Phil is frustrated with Shelby's constant crying and reminiscing. She's wallowing in grief, he thinks, while she needs to get up and do things to take her mind off it. Divorce may be in the offing for the couple.

CHAPTER 7 Death and the Adult

assumes that the other is functioning in a maladaptive way. Shelby believes that Phil's stoicism indicates denial or a lack of caring. Phil believes that Shelby is allowing herself to be overcome and that she can pull herself out of her obvious pain and confusion if she only tries hard enough. He is locked into the role of male and she is locked into the role of female, with neither of them comprehending the other's role and both of them misinterpreting the other's feelings.

The loss of a child leaves parents in intense pain for many years. Other children in the family, especially those born subsequent to the death, may find that their parents become more controlling and protective of them (Pantke & Slade, 2006). This change in parental behaviour is undoubtedly part of the parents' attempts to make sure that they never lose another child. In the next chapter, the grief of senior parents for a child lost many years before will be discussed. The child is never gone from the parents' thoughts, and very few parents ever regard the death as anything but unfair and tragic (Murphy, Johnson, & Lohan, 2003; Sanders, 1999).

DEATH OF A SPOUSE OR LIFE PARTNER

Statistics Canada (2006) reports that in 2003 in Canada, 47 018 people between the ages of 20 and 64 died. Most of these people had spouses or life partners, suggesting that perhaps close to the same number of people were left without their companion. (Bereavement in the senior years is discussed in Chapter 8.) Although comparisons are odious, it can probably be fairly said that losing a spouse is next in pain to losing a child, especially if the relationship had been a happy one. Western society often seems to be based on the notion that people should be part of a couple. Invitations are extended to "Mr. Jones and guest," travel accommodations in tours are advertised as being "for double occupancy," and even food is packaged with the assumption that the quantity needed will be enough for two or more. For some people, a large part of their identity has derived from their position in a couple relationship; in particular, women have been known by their husband's last name, sometimes even as "Mrs. John Smith," instead of "Jane Smith." For Ellen Forsythe, the case described in Box 7.2, the loss of her husband has meant a significant loss in her identity: her friends used to joke that the couple was "FredandEllen," one word, indicating the inseparability and devotion of the couple. Now she is only Ellen.

In losing a life partner, whether the union is legalized through a marriage ceremony or not, heterosexual or homosexual, the stress placed on the surviving partner is twofold: first is the emotional devastation of having to go on in life without the person counted on to be there forever, and second is the practical stress of having to take on roles and tasks for which the person may be unaccustomed. The emotional stress is, of course, multifaceted in itself and is reflected in the general reactions to grief, as discussed in Chapter 5. Added on to this are the problems and stresses of day-to-day life that were formerly shared but must now be shouldered alone. The majority of relationships have a division of labour, often breaking into traditional gender roles. For example, in traditional relationships, the widow may not be accustomed to dealing with finances or household repair problems. These had been taken care of by her husband and she may feel overwhelmed in having to deal with insurance matters, bill paying, plumbing repairs, or knowing how to use the lawn mower to mow the grass.

The widower, conversely, may have no idea about meal planning and preparation, laundry, housecleaning, or even how to select clothing for himself. In addition, the bereaved man may realize after his wife's death that she had been the one to manage and organize their social life: it often falls to the female partner to keep in touch with the family, select gifts (even for in-laws), and organize social events with family and friends. Consequently, the husband often finds himself somewhat socially isolated unless others take the initiative to extend invitations and help him in this regard.

If the couple had children, the bereaved has the additional stress of becoming a single parent, raising the children, and dealing with their grief at losing a parent. Most bereaved people learn the practicalities of the tasks they have never before undertaken, but the problems of learning these tasks may be magnified by the lack of concentration and attention usually found in bereaved people, along with their emotional responses of resentment at the injustice of being forced to learn these tasks by an unfair world that has taken their partner from them.

Sanders (1999) reports that specific practical hardships occur for the bereaved spouse or life partner. Disposing of the deceased partner's clothing is often particularly difficult, and although it is usually accomplished gradually, the deceased partner's wallet is often kept. The wallet, being used every day and containing the elements of daily life, seems to be especially difficult to part with: the driver's licence, the health card, the pictures of the family, and so on, represent some meaningful parts of the deceased loved one's life and provide a link for the surviving spouse to the lost partner. Eating alone is another practical stress for both widows and widowers. Mealtime is often considered to be a family-sharing time, with dinner, above all, a time when couples come together to share their daily experiences and to discuss many topics. It is a renewal of the bonds within the family. When the family circle is broken by the death of a spouse, the

Ellen Forsythe had been married to Fred for 27 years when he died of heart complications from diabetes. Fred was only 56 when he died, and Ellen is 54. He had been her only real love, her soul mate. She thought they would be together for all eternity. Of course, she knew that Fred was ill, but she convinced herself that the diabetes was well under control and Fred would live to a ripe old age with care. They had made such plans for retirement! With the children grown and on their own, they could travel to exotic places and try activities that they had only heard about. Fred particularly had wanted to learn photography so that he could document their travels with more professional tools than they had had for taking pictures when the children were growing up. But retirement was still several years off. *What am I supposed to do now?* she wonders. Her most meaningful roles in life had been that of wife and mother, but now she feels that she has lost both roles. The children are both grown up and living their own independent lives—Fred was so proud of them!—and her job as a sales clerk is one to which she feels little commitment. No husband, no children needing her, no significant career, no point in living, she thinks.

The children were wonderful in the first months after Fred's death, putting their own grief aside while they called and visited her often, making sure that she had no needs that they could fulfill. Friends and neighbours were wonderful too, bringing casseroles and cakes that she didn't eat. But now, nine months later, she sees a difference. The children call and visit less often, and the friends and neighbours seem uncomfortable around her. No one mentions Fred's name anymore, as if he never existed. Ellen understands this: people don't know what to say to her, so they never mention Fred. *Do they think that if they don't mention him, I won't be reminded that he's gone?* she wonders. *As if I ever forget!* Some people even suggest that Ellen start dating again. That infuriates Ellen. As far as she's concerned, she's a married woman and no one could ever take Fred's place anyway. Besides, she feels that Fred is still there; sometimes she thinks she catches sight of him out of the corner of her eye. Her children say that this is just a manifestation of her unwillingness to let him go, but how do they know? Doesn't anyone understand how empty the house is, how empty her life is, how much this hurts? And it will be this way until she dies and joins Fred again, she thinks. What a horrible future to contemplate!

empty chair may seem like an open wound to the surviving spouse. Often the surviving spouse, especially if without children, stops preparing regular meals and eating. Widows report commonly that they find meal preparation and eating without their husbands to be distasteful and painful. Because grief often brings a diminution of their appetites, it is all too easy to simply go without food.

Both men and women whose life partner has died have a higher likelihood of physical health problems and death following their bereavement (Parkes, 1996). This is especially the case for men, particularly in the first year or so after the bereavement. Men's mental health suffers from a spousal bereavement more than women's does as well, and widowed men show an increase in alcohol consumption as compared with married men, although this increase is not found in widows as compared with married women (Cramer, 1993). In a critical review of the literature concerning bereavement and gender, Stroebe, Stroebe, and Schut (2001) concluded that men suffer more distress from losing a life partner than women do. The common explanation for this is that women have a stronger social network to support them in their bereavement than men do (Stroebe & Stroebe, 1983), but Stroebe, Stroebe, and Schut suggested a more complex explanation. They noted the fact that given traditional gender roles, men have become accustomed to coping with their stress by inhibiting their emotions and using practical approaches, problem solving, and diversion (the "strong, active, logical, unemotional man"), whereas women use more emotionally based tactics, such as crying, talking to others, and ruminating (the "emotional, social, passive woman"). When the stress is loss of a life partner, the practical approaches of men, along with their avoidance of emotion, may not serve them well: Although they may learn to deal with the practical problems their bereavement has brought them, the loss in itself is emotionally based, and avoiding the myriad emotions involved in grief may result in further problems for the man. Women, conversely, are more likely to be given help with the practical responsibilities that their husbands had assumed and are more likely to confront the painful emotions, thereby eventually coping with them more effectively.

By far, the greatest effect of losing a life partner is the intense loneliness that the survivor feels. This is the case in both heterosexual and homosexual relationships (Forrest & Austin, 2002). Ellen Forsythe is finding this to be the worst possible life for her and she despairs of ever feeling any differently. Sanders (1999) cited research that indicates that it may take four or five years for those who have lost a life partner to move on in a new life. This is particularly true for people who have been dependent on their partners, practically or emotionally. Those people who are widowed when they are young find it easier to be optimistic about a future, but for older people, like Ellen, the likelihood of a new, bright future seems remote. Seniors who are bereaved, knowing their own lives to have limited days, rarely contemplate the possibility of a new life.

Homosexual, or same-sex, life partners who have been bereaved may face an even more difficult burden because they may not be given the same support from society as heterosexual life partners are given for their loss. In Chapter 10 we will discuss the way in which this grief is often disenfranchised and so may become harder to bear.

DEATH OF A PARENT

In the cycle of life, it is expected that people will experience the death of their parents. Thanks to modern technology and knowledge in medicine, nutrition, and safety standards in the Western world, this usually occurs when the parents are elderly and the surviving children are in middle age. But knowing that this will happen in the normal course of events provides very little comfort in most cases. The bond between parent and child is the first and most important bond in most people's lives. The period of dependency on a parent is very long in the human species, much longer than in other species, so the bond is strengthened through the memories and experiences of many years. The breaking of this bond in life cannot come without resultant emotional reactions. In addition, parents are the people who knew us first, from the day of birth throughout the life span. The death of these people, then, severs the tie to the past: often no one is left who knew the individual from the beginning in such great detail. There may be no one left to share early memories with or to tell the story of the family (Sanders, 1999).

Petersen and Rafuls (1998) interviewed six women who had a parent die approximately two years before the interview. In free-ranging discussion, they found common themes emerging in these women's reactions. The first reaction they found was surprise that the parent had died. Even in cases in which the parent had been ill for some time, the daughters did not expect the death to come at that time. Most of these women indicated that they had not allowed themselves to contemplate the reality of a parent's death, although they knew such deaths were inevitable. This is not surprising: just as parents tend to see even their adult children as their "child," it is unlikely that children can see parents completely as aging and no longer the dominant source of security and love in their lives. For the women in Petersen and Rafuls's study, however, the shock and denial of grief was quickly put aside when practical matters, such as arranging a funeral and caring for a surviving parent, took predominance.

As time passed, the women reported less intense emotional reactions and more quiet pensiveness and reflection. Many women described the aftermath of their loss as being transformative: the death of a parent spurred them to withdraw from their immediate families somewhat and to reflect on the meanings of their lives and the priorities they had set in their lives. Connections to their remaining family members became more important to them, and the women felt a sense of responsibility to carry on in their deceased parent's stead, "receiving the scepter," as Petersen and Rafuls (1998) termed it. The women felt that they now had the responsibility of "doing the right thing" (p. 514). This meant caring for ill or distressed surviving parents and managing the practicalities of the funerals or memorial services, as well as taking on the obligations of a new role in a changed family constellation. For example, the woman might now become the oldest woman in the family, with the perceived obligation to provide guidance for the younger family members and a strong connective link to keep the family together, a role previously held by her mother. The women strongly indicated that "doing the right thing" had additional meaning in their lives as they regarded their futures. Doing the right thing meant doing what the deceased parent might have wanted for them (e.g., ending an extramarital affair, not drinking alcohol) and doing what would be beneficial for their remaining family (e.g., spending more time with family members, making sure that their children would feel supported and have good memories of their mothers). Women who had had a conflicted relationship with the deceased parent felt a freedom from the role of criticized daughter or of having to witness and deal with the aftermath of a deceased parent's self-destructive behaviour. Yet the emotional intensity of grief was greater for these women, perhaps because of the knowledge that they would now have no time to repair the damaged relationships and, in some cases, perhaps because of guilt for hurtful things that had been said and done.

The role of the partners of these women was noteworthy: both heterosexual and homosexual partners remained quietly supportive while these women withdrew from them in their grief. After a time, the partner was usually the one to suggest gently a resumption of normal life and to remind the woman of the needs of her remaining family. This invitation to end the withdrawal and resume family relationships was welcomed by the women, who said that their partners had been instrumental in their reflections on their own lives and their plans for the future.

In the case presented in Box 7.3, Douglas Steadman shares many of the feelings that the women in the Petersen and Rafuls's (1998) study expressed: he too did not feel prepared for his mother's death although he knew her health had been failing consistently. Although his mother had been dependent on him for help for some time, he clearly still felt an emotional dependency on her. He was powerless to stop her health from failing, but he had the power to help her in her daily functioning. Unlike most men following the death of a parent, Douglas will probably not experience much guilt over not spending much time with his mother or caring for her enough; he was clearly a very present and devoted son (Moss, Resch, & Moss, 1997). Yet, the mutually dependent relationship, and one of the longest relationships of his life, is gone, leaving a large gap in his life. Douglas's relationship with his father will change now too. His father is his last surviving parent and is himself now grieving and aging. Douglas will most likely feel the need and the responsibility to watch over his father even more than he has up to now. His own grief will be increased by the additional sorrow that he feels for his father in losing his life's companion, but he may feel that he needs to suppress it, given his father's increased reliance on him and his own feeling that he must be strong for his father. By being a strong support to his father, Douglas may feel that he is doing what his mother would have wanted, and this may be a comfort to him (Marshall, 2004). Similar to the women in Petersen and Rafuls's (1998) study, Douglas too is reflecting on his life, wondering whether he has chosen the right course and whether his priorities have really been the ones he wants. It is hoped that Douglas's wife, Althea, will take on the quietly supportive role that the women's partners in the study did, which will help him to resume normal functioning after a time. Family support will be needed because Douglas is unlikely to receive much support at work: the death of a parent when a person is in midlife is considered "normal"; coworkers and superiors often underestimate the upheaval and pain that this loss entails (Marshall, 2004).

Douglas will experience more grief in his future: one day his father will die too. How will Douglas respond then? Marshall (2004) specifically examined the feelings of people who had lost both parents. The primary focus was the transition made from being someone's child to being an orphan. This emotion was strong in the people that Marshall interviewed. Even if the remaining parent had been old and death had been timely, the surviving children tended to perceive the death as "unfair" (p. 363). A sense of extreme loneliness was experienced as the adult children recognized that they were now parentless and they too would one day die. The recognition of their personal mortality had come to them when the first parent died ("Parents really do die and I will too one day"), but the death of the remaining parent leaves the adult children with the additional recognition that they are now among the family elders and, in the normal course of events, they will be the next generation to die. Furthermore, the death of a second parent brought renewed grief for the first parent. The grief that is often suppressed at the death of the first parent because of the perceived need to be strong for the remaining parent is now released: they have no one left for whom to be strong, the grief is wholly their own, and no one is left to remind them of the secure parental base and unconditional love experienced in childhood.

The death of a parent brings sorrow, often guilt and remorse, and usually feelings of additional responsibility for caring for remaining family and for living well. The relationship with the deceased parent is continued in

BOX 7.3 Douglas Steadman

Douglas Steadman was 48 years old when his 75-year-old mother, Serena, died of heart failure. She had not been very well for some years, and Douglas, who lives nearby, and his father, Fred, provided the extra help that she had needed to function normally. Serena appreciated their efforts and lived happily despite her limitations. Douglas has a wife, Althea, and two children who are in their mid-teenage years. Douglas makes a good living and enjoys his job as a computer programmer. But his mother's death has thrown him. He never really believed that she would die, for some reason. Oh yes, he knew it intellectually, especially as her health started to fail, but emotionally, he wasn't ready for it. Somehow, she wasn't supposed to die *today*, someday maybe, but not *today*. Suddenly, Douglas, who has lived independently of his parents since his graduation from university, feels bereft and isn't sure how he can continue his life without his mother. He isn't even sure that his life is following the course he wants. But first things first: he feels the responsibility to make sure that his mother's funeral is just as she would have wanted it and that his father is cared for and supported.

acting on the new responsibilities, thereby giving meaning to the future and more purpose to life. As painful and difficult as it is to adjust to the new autonomy, new family constellation, and new life and identity, many people experience a transformation in their lives, with renewed dedication to living according to the priorities they really want and new appreciation for the life they have and their remaining family. It is not uncommon to find a transcendence of purely personal concerns in the bereaved adult children as they find a heightened sensitivity to others and their needs following a parental death (Pope, 2005). In growing and developing as human beings as a result of the death, bereaved adult children also have the comfort of the continuing relationship with the deceased parent as they live their lives by "doing it right."

DEATH OF A SIBLING

Although much attention has been paid to the bereavement responses of children and adolescents when they lose a sibling, a marked lack of attention has been paid to the reactions of a similarly bereaved adult. The implication is that society considers the sibling bond to be a weakened one in adulthood because siblings typically form their own lives, often very much separated from their nuclear family. Indeed, it is not uncommon to hear people refer to friends as their family, indicating that they feel closer to a friend in some cases than to their actual relatives ("He's like a brother to me"). Even if siblings have led very separate lives, with little contact, the bond of siblings remains markedly different from that of friends: siblings share genetic makeup, earliest experiences, knowledge of each other in very intimate ways, and roles in the total family constellation. Friends are chosen and relatives are not. Although the pain of losing a close friend must not be minimized, the pain of losing a sibling can be qualitatively different and more complicated.

Among seniors, some studies have found that the death of a sibling can be more distressing than the death of a spouse (Cleiren, 1991; Hays, Gold, & Peiper, 1997), while some have found no difference (e.g., Zisook & Lyons, as cited by Eaves, McQuiston, & Miles, 2005). Although these results tell us little about the specific grief reactions that losing a sibling brings, they do suggest that the magnitude of the grief is great. This research also suggests that women whose brother had died were more distressed than were women who lost a sister, and men who lost a sibling felt that their physical health was worse than women who lost a sibling and worse than men who had lost a wife or a friend. Again, the indication is that loss of a sibling brings a great deal of grief, with men showing more physical complaints and women showing more psychological upset (Hays, Gold, & Peiper, 1997).

The reactions of Sudhir Patel to the death of his brother, the case presented in Box 7.4, reflect a great deal of grief, especially because the brothers were close. Sudhir must not only accommodate himself to the loss of his best friend but also take over the role of oldest son in the family, with all the responsibilities that entails. He is now not the second or the youngest child; he is the only child, a position that is new in his family's structure and one that will require him to adjust his own view of himself and his family. The psychological burdens of an only

---

BOX 7.4 Sudhir Patel

Sudhir Patel is the second of two children born two years apart to Aruna and Anand Patel. Sudhir and his brother, Bhanu, were both born in Canada, but their Indian heritage has been a respected part of their lives, although their parents think that they have become very "Westernized." Sudhir and Bhanu have been very close throughout their lives, living close to each other and to their parents in adulthood and socializing with each other often. In fact, the brothers considered themselves to be best friends. When Sudhir's brother died suddenly of an unknown viral infection at the age of 32, the whole family was shocked and in a state of disbelief.

Aruna and Anand are devastated at the loss of their firstborn son and are discussing returning to India rather than face the continuing reminders of Bhanu's life and death. They look to Sudhir for strength and comfort. Traditionally, in his parents' culture, the responsibility of caring for his parents as they aged would have fallen to Bhanu. The brothers always agreed that they would share the responsibilities when the time came, although they thought that the day was far off. Sudhir now recognizes that the burden of responsibility is entirely his, and his parents' needs are clear as they face the greatest grief of their lives. Sudhir feels that he must put his own grief aside to care for them, but he is very worried. If his parents return to India, he wonders whether he must follow them in order to fulfill his filial obligations. This prospect is not pleasant to him because he is Canadian, and while he loves India, his life, including his friends, his girlfriend, and his career, is in Canada. Increasing his distress is the fact that he feels he has no one with whom to discuss this or other matters because his brother, his best friend, and perhaps the only one who could fully understand the situation, is gone.

child will now be present for him, as well as the caretaking responsibilities. For example, if his parents are to have grandchildren, he must be the one to produce them. All parental hopes and expectations now fall on him, with no one to compensate for any laxity or failure from him. As well, given his parents' position, Sudhir might have to face an even greater upheaval in his life in a move to another country, even one that he loves and whose culture is familiar to him. This undoubtedly adds to his grief. As the only surviving son, it is not surprising that Sudhir feels that he must suppress his own grief at the loss of Bhanu in order to provide a reliable source of strength for his parents. This is common among children who have lost a sibling, and it must be supposed that this feeling is even more prevalent in adults (Robinson & Mahon, 1997). Because Sudhir is a grown man, it is unlikely that he will receive very much support at work or from friends; the supposition that adults can bear the loss of a sibling relatively well will decrease the sensitivity that Sudhir needs and deserves.

STILLBIRTH, ABORTION, MISCARRIAGE

Stillbirth

Statistics Canada (2005a) reported that 3234 stillbirths occurred in Canada in 2004. Stillbirth is not a very common event, but it is emotionally devastating. The emotions of parents who experience the birth of a child who never takes a breath (**stillbirth**) resemble most closely the grief of parents whose child has lived for a significant time and then died. Parents face shattering disappointment at the death of plans and dreams for the child and entire family, and feel a loss of meaning in life: why was the child even conceived, let alone born, if he or she was to die without ever living? Mothers tend to feel guilt, as if they were in some way to blame for the death, and inadequacy in their abilities to carry and give birth to a live baby, examining their every behaviour during the pregnancy for clues to what they may have done wrong (Hsu, Tseng, Banks, & Kuo, 2004). Furthermore, about one-fifth of the bereaved mothers have prolonged depression in their grief, and about one-fifth have post-traumatic stress disorder in a subsequent pregnancy. After a stillbirth, mothers often become overly anxious for their other or subsequent children, likely because of unresolved mourning, which may have an adverse effect on their parenting of these children and the children's emotional development (Hughes, Turton, Hopper, & Evans, 2002).

Abortion

Canada is one of the few countries in the world that assert a woman's right to abort a fetus without legal impediments. In 2002, Canadian women obtained 105 154 **abortions** (induced terminations of pregnancies), a rate of 32.1 per 100 live births recorded in that year, with 52 percent of these abortions obtained by women in their twenties (Statistics Canada, 2005b). For many women, however, abortion is not an option because of their moral or religious convictions that it is wrong.

Several reports indicate that after an **elective abortion,** the induced termination of a pregnancy, usually at the request of the mother for personal reasons, in the first trimester of pregnancy, women generally experience few negative emotions and greater relief and happiness (e.g., Adler, David, Major, Roth, Russo, & Wyatt, 1990, 1992). In fact, in 1989 the then surgeon general of the United States, C. Everett Koop, testified before Congress that the potential for psychological problems in the aftermath of an elective abortion was minimal, although he admitted that for some women, the effects can be severe. But McAll and Wilson (as cited by Tentoni, 1995) reported that between 7 percent and 14 percent of women who undergo an abortion report having significant emotional distress after the procedure: guilt, doubt, anger, regret, depression, and fear of disapproval (Tentoni, 1995). These occur especially among women who are highly religious and report themselves to be disapproving of abortion. Many of these women presumably have a double burden: they carry the guilt of having violated their own moral or religious code, and they feel that they have taken a life. The psychological and the spiritual grief for them are enhanced.

Although data from the past 10 years on the aftermath of abortion are lacking, it is still to be expected that some women will experience distress after having had an abortion. More telling is the experience of a woman in the situation of Davina Raymond in Box 7.5. Davina chose to abort her pregnancy because of the nonviability of the fetus. This was a highly desired pregnancy for her, and, as it is for many other women, the choice to abort was made with much grief. The decision she and others have made is one that cannot be escaped, and it carries with it the connotation of the woman "killing her own child." In addition, by the time the diagnosis of extreme fetal deformity or nonviability is made, the mother is typically far enough along in her pregnancy that the abortion must be done by induced labour and childbirth. For some women, the child has died before birth but has not spontaneously aborted. For them, the choice is removed, but certainly not the pain. It can only be imagined how difficult it must be for a woman to wait for the

BOX 7.5   Davina Raymond

Davina Raymond is 36 years old and her husband Ned is 40 years old. They have been trying to have a child for the past seven years, and, finally, with medical help, Davina became pregnant. The couple and their families were ecstatic and planned eagerly for their child, furnishing a nursery and buying baby clothes and toys. But an ultrasound test at the end of Davina's fourth month of pregnancy revealed that the fetus was badly deformed, with little chance of surviving. Broken-hearted, Davina and Ned decided to abort the fetus. Their families were concerned about this choice, feeling strongly that the fetus should be given a chance to develop. They avoid Davina and Ned now, not knowing what to say to them or how to react around them.

Davina and Ned are grief-stricken, feeling guilty and anxious about whether they made the right choice. Davina is also feeling despair: the deformity, she thinks, must be her fault and she must be inadequate as a woman, given her inability to conceive readily and to carry a healthy baby. Ned feels lost and has spent a great deal of time quizzing the doctors about how this tragedy could have happened. He is adamant, though, that he will stay strong for Davina's sake, so he hides his tears most of the time and tries to put on an optimistic front for her, but he wishes he had a brother or male cousin or friend to talk to.

procedure to begin, for the contractions to start, and then to deliver a dead child. In the aftermath of such a trauma, the woman generally feels a grief that has the potential to become pathological in anxiety and depression (Kersting et al., 2004).

Fathers too feel intense grief when a child dies before birth, often reporting that their entire view of life was challenged by the tragedy. The death of the child is generally perceived as a waste of life and a violation of the natural order of life. Ned, like most men, tries to remain strong for his partner, Davina, and he seeks to understand how this terrible event could have occurred. Again, like many other men, he wishes he had another man with whom he could feel comfortable talking (Samuelsson, Rådestad, & Segesten, 2001).

Miscarriage

When a fetus is spontaneously aborted before about 16 to 20 weeks gestation, a **miscarriage** is said to have occurred. About 12 percent to 24 percent of pregnancies terminate in a miscarriage, most of these occurring in the first trimester (Brier, 2004; Klier, Geller, & Ritsher, 2002; Maker & Ogden, 2003). These figures may be low because many women miscarry so early in their pregnancies that they may have been unaware that they were pregnant. Clearly, miscarriage is a relatively common phenomenon. As such, it is often regarded as an unfortunate, but hardly dramatic, event, marked by no ritual. Consequently, parents who have miscarried are rarely given more support than a cursory, "Oh, that's too bad" (Renner, Verdekal, Brier, & Falucca, 2000). However, the effects of miscarriage are more far-reaching than is often acknowledged.

If the pregnancy was unwanted, a miscarriage may come as a relief to a woman, but in other cases, research has demonstrated that following a miscarriage, a woman is likely to experience depression, anxiety, and a yearning for the lost child. In addition, similar to the death of a child, the woman often feels the need to find a meaning in the experience and a desire to talk to others about what happened. The woman may also question her adequacy given the "failure" that she has experienced, particularly if this was not her first miscarriage and she has no other children. She may also use the experience as a trigger for reexamining her life and her priorities (Maker & Ogden, 2003).

Klier, Geller, and Ritsher (2002) noted that studies examining the degree of distress that a woman feels after a miscarriage as related to length of gestation have been inconsistent: that is, some studies indicate that the later in the pregnancy that the miscarriage occurs, the greater the grief of the mother, while other studies have found no difference in distress level despite the length of the pregnancy. Klier and her colleagues suggest that further research needs to be done in this area, especially because parents are able to visualize and begin bonding with their child earlier today than previously, by using ultrasound technology. It would be expected that the lengthier the pregnancy and the more ultrasound viewings, the greater the distress, as the child became more "real" to the parents. Countering this, however, are two research results: first is the finding that women visualize, talk to, and dream about their children by the 10th week of pregnancy (Beutal, Deckardt, von Rad, & Weiner, 1995) and second is research indicating a lack of a relationship between ultrasound viewing and distress after a miscarriage (Ritsher & Neugebauer, as cited by Klier, Geller, &

Ritsher, 2002). It seems that from the early days of pregnancy, women typically feel that they are carrying a known and already cherished child, not just a nebulous and unknown fetus. At present, then, the only conclusion that can justifiably be made is that no matter how long she had been pregnant or whether or not she had viewed the child by ultrasound technology, a woman feels significant grief after having miscarried a desired pregnancy.

Little research has examined the effects of miscarriage on the father, but some research finds that men are deeply affected, although they may display less obvious signs of grief. Men whose children have been miscarried feel despair and report having difficulty in coping with the situation, especially if the miscarriage occurred later in the pregnancy and the men had seen the child in an ultrasound scan. In fact, these men may experience even more distress than the women who miscarried, but it is typically not displayed or recognized because the men feel that they must appear strong for their female partners (Puddifoot & Johnson, 1999).

The conclusion that must be reached is that parents who have a miscarriage generally feel that they have lost a child, although the grief may not be as intense or as long lasting as if the child had been born and lived. The grief, however, is as intense as it is in parents, like Davina and Ned, who choose to terminate a pregnancy because of a fetal abnormality (Keefe-Cooperman, 2004–2005).

THE TERMINALLY ILL ADULT

About 47 000 adults between the ages of 20 and 64 years died in Canada in 2003 (Statistics Canada, 2006), and many of them had experiences like the case of Richard Cartwright in Box 7.6, finally succumbing after lingering illnesses. For many of these people, the end of life begins at the moment of their diagnosis, and thus starts their journey through the ultimate challenge of life: facing their own death. Levine and Karger (2004) outline the trajectory of this journey:

1. *The initial jolt.* In today's world of medical miracles, most people assume that if something goes wrong with their health, treatment—and most likely cure—will be available. With the diagnosis of a terminal or potentially terminal illness, the individual's whole life changes irrevocably. Such questions as "Why?" and "How long?" abound, and

---

BOX 7.6 Richard Cartwright

Richard Cartwright is 47 years old. He has been coughing quite a bit lately, and at his wife's insistence, he finally consulted a physician. After much testing, the physician returned with the diagnosis of advanced lung cancer. Treatment could help Richard's symptoms and prolong his life somewhat, but the measures would be palliative. Richard is going to die. He can't understand how this can be happening—he and his wife never smoked and he never worked in any location that involved the possibility of inhaling carcinogenic fumes. They must have made a mistake! But his doctor assures him that the tests are conclusive, and although the probability of lung cancer is greater for some people, anyone can get it. When Richard asks how long he has left to live, the doctor equivocates, noting that different people respond differently to the disease. When Richard presses the doctor, though, he admits that Richard probably has less than six months left.

Richard's mind is reeling. How can he tell his wife, Sheryl, and their sons? Sheryl is 44 years old, a teacher who loves her work, and the boys are both in college. The boys will be OK, he tells himself; they're almost grown and they have enough money in their college funds to see them through their education. Sheryl has a great job and job security, and she'll have the insurance money, so she probably won't need to worry about finances. *But she's so young,* he agonizes, *how will she manage without me there to listen to her and comfort her when she's down, and have fun with her, and make love to her, and hold her when she has a bad dream, and. . . . Maybe she'll remarry. I want her to. I don't want her to go through life alone.*

Then Richard's mind goes to the immediate future. What will happen? Will I have pain? Will Sheryl have to take care of me for a long time while I die? I can't stand the thought of doing that to her! But I want to die at home. I want to be aware of what's going on every step of the way. I have to tell Sheryl not to let anyone use heroic measures to prolong my life. I have to tell her to make sure I don't suffer, if she can. I have to tell her what to say to the boys for me when they graduate, when they marry, when they have kids. Oh God, I have to tell her how much I love her. Damn it! This is wrong. It shouldn't be happening. We never did anything to deserve this. Oh please, let this just be a horrible nightmare.

---

at a time when the individual is most reeling from the shock of the diagnosis, decisions often must be made: should treatment be given? Which treatment? Will the treatment be disfiguring? Is this an important consideration? In the midst of this, the rest of life goes on. Plans must be made for practical matters: child-care must be arranged, financial provision must be made, the decision of whether to involve family members and friends must be made, and so on. Richard Cartwright, the case study in Box 7.6, has a wife to rely on to help with these problems, but many people do not. In some cases, people even refuse treatment that might save or prolong their lives because of the responsibilities they have in taking care of family members.

2. *Treatment.* People enter treatment with a variety of expectations. For most, the possibility of saving their lives, prolonging their lives, or at least making them more comfortable in their illnesses provides positive feelings and motivations for complying with medical directives. These feelings are often balanced against the negative feelings that some people have about the treatment itself. Medical treatments can be very disruptive of normal life, invasive of privacy and control in life, physically debilitating, and even extremely painful. They may result in disfigurement, which may cause an individual to question his or her identity. For example, a hysterectomy, the removal of the uterus, can be very traumatic for a woman who values her childbearing capabilities and equates this with her femininity. Similarly, treatment for some medical conditions may render a man impotent, a huge blow for men who identify themselves with their sexuality. Some people are concerned about whether they "can take it" in terms of maintaining control, strength, and dignity in the face of a difficult treatment program.

Even greater than these concerns, however, is the anxiety of wondering whether the treatment will actually work. They may make an implicit bargain with the universe: "If I go through the treatment, then I will get better/have a longer life/feel better." Hope is derived from the possibilities that treatment can bring, but it is balanced with the fear that the hope will be dashed and the hardships endured during treatment will be for nothing. For some people, this provides a real ambivalence about treatment, even leading them to reject treatment in order to avoid the disappointment that might follow if the treatment is unsuccessful. At the same time as the individual is contending with the emotions surrounding treatment, he or she is also usually experiencing anger, depression, and

resignation, with these emotions swinging back and forth in what often seems to be an erratic manner (see Chapter 5).

3. *Post-treatment.* If treatment successfully saves or prolongs the individual's life, he or she has a period of readjustment to normal life. In point of fact, nothing will ever be the same for the individual. In the first place, life often has new meaning and new appreciation for the individual who has undergone such great trauma. People in the individual's environment often have the expectation that the individual will be happy and want to celebrate his or her successful completion of treatment and resumption of normal life. This is frequently not the case, however; the individual may still have anxiety that the disease will recur, that the remission will be short-lived, with the symptoms reappearing. Additionally, life has gone on for others while it has been put in a holding pattern for the person who has been undergoing treatment. The individual must catch up with the changes that have occurred, and people around him or her may be less than understanding of the adjustments the individual must make. If the treatment has only prolonged the person's life somewhat, or made him or her more comfortable, he or she has the added concern of what is to come in the process of dying and what is to come for the family who must now undertake the role ("burden") of being caregivers. The individual also worries about the suffering the family will have when he or she eventually dies. Although each day may be greatly appreciated, the individual may also be depressed and angry that so little time is left. The future is known to be limited, and people must decide, within their physical, financial, and social limitations, how to spend the days that are left. Hope remains for people at this point in their lives, but now the hope is no longer for a cure. Hope is for reaching goals, such as seeing a family member again, or for achieving a remission of pain and discomfort, or for dying with grace and dignity.

Most people with terminal illnesses have a variety of choices for their physical care in their final days, which we will review in Chapter 11. Their desires are often very modest. Quill et al. (2006) examined the answers that people undergoing palliative care consultations gave to the question "What is most important for you to achieve?" They found that 95 percent of the answers fell within four categories:

1. *Improving the quality and meaning of their lives.* More than half of the people in this study wanted to be able to go home or leave the hospital, to be

able to support family and friends, or to regain functions, such as eating or walking. Overall, the most common answer concerned the poor quality of their lives at present and their desire to make their final days more comfortable and meaningful with their loved ones without becoming a caretaking burden to them.

2. *Achieving relief or comfort.* The second category reflected the need to relieve distress. Pain control and physical comfort were important to these people, but so was emotional comfort.

3. *Altering the course of the illness.* For some people, the greatest desire was for them to be cured of their disease or disorder or to at least live until certain milestone events in their lives had been reached. This included searching for alternative treatments that might hold the possibility for a cure or an improvement in their conditions. For others, the importance of making medical decisions on the course of their treatments was paramount. For a very few people, the main desire was to accelerate the progress of their illness so that death might come sooner.

4. *Preparing for dying.* Some people wanted to finish family affairs or prepare themselves emotionally and spiritually for death. For some, the only desire was to achieve a peaceful and comfortable death, free of all or most symptoms of their illnesses.

These answers are very much in accord with a brief informal survey that the author undertook in a university course on dying and bereavement that she taught to upper-year nursing and social work students in 2005. None of the students (to the author's knowledge) had been diagnosed with a terminal illness, so all were speculating on their final desires. No student gave an answer indicating that he or she might want to partake of activities never attempted before or to travel to unseen places. Rather, their desires were uniformly modest; to be pain free and to be with their family and friends. One upper-year nursing student, Julia Bevilacqua, called this "Porch Duty": her family home had a large porch on which she and her family and friends would gather in all seasons to talk, reminisce, and simply enjoy each other's company. Julia expressed only the wish to be able to die while so engaged.

As a terminal illness progresses, Hinton (1999) found that awareness and acceptance of the certain imminent end of life increased progressively over the eight weeks of the study in both terminally ill patients and their families. More than 50 percent of the patients became fully or nearly accepting of their deaths, as did 69 percent of the relatives. Hinton also found that 81 percent of the relatives became more aware of the inevitability of their loved one's death. That means that 12 percent of the family members were aware of the imminent death but did not accept it. Relatives of these patients showed more depression in their certainty that the death was coming shortly, but patients did not. For patients, not being certain that death was coming was more anxiety inducing than knowing that death was inevitable.

The presence of pain had no effect on the acceptance of death; rather, acceptance was described "in terms of death's inevitability, faith and spiritual values, life's diminishing rewards, completing life, final benefits, humour, sharing, etc." (p. 19). The grief and sometimes lack of acceptance on the part of the terminal patient's loved ones are perhaps reflected in an earlier study done by Hinton (1996) in which he compared the recollections of family members regarding the symptoms of the now-deceased person with their reports of symptoms in the person's final months and the dying person's self-reports. In retrospect, the family of the deceased person remembered the person as having had more pain, depression, weakness, and lack of appetite than they or the patient had reported at the time. The reality of bereavement, it seems, negatively influences mourners' memories of the final days.

Awareness and acceptance of death is clearly influenced by the culture of the terminally ill patient. In such cultures as Native Canadian or Chinese, talking about death is thought to hasten it (see Chapter 3), so the ill person is generally not told of the terminal nature of the illness. It is likely that the ill person becomes aware of this as the illness progresses, but it is not mentioned aloud. Under these conditions, it is difficult to determine whether the ill person has accepted the inevitability of death or not because he or she cannot be questioned about this.

Richard Cartwright, the terminally ill man in Box 7.6, has a difficult journey ahead of him. He has decisions to make about his treatment and care, including what kind of treatment he wants, whether he will pursue any means possible to prolong his life, and where he wants to die; he will want to make sure his financial affairs are in order and that his family is provided for; he will want to resolve any family problems he may have, and he will want to take leave of those he loves. Whether he will reach an acceptance of his death remains to be seen, but his wife and children will grieve: no amount of preparation will be enough to eliminate their pain and they will probably remember Richard's last days as being worse than they really were. Many of us will take this journey too, and each of us will, if given the choice, make choices that reflect our beliefs and our lives up to that point.

SUMMARY

- The death of a child causes perhaps the greatest grief that adults experience. This is compounded by the many roles the child plays in the parents' life and the perceived violation of the parental role of protector.

- Bereaved parents often experience despair, confusion, guilt, anger, stress reactions, and marital problems in the aftermath of their children's deaths.

- Fathers often appear to grieve less than mothers do because of the societally prescribed male role of being strong and unemotional. Mothers are freer to express their grief, although they may feel unable to function when their societally prescribed role of nurturer and centre of the family is shattered.

- The differences each parent shows in expressions of grief are often misinterpreted by the other parent, leading to marital problems.

- The death of a life partner brings both the emotional pain of losing a loved one and the practical problems of assuming the roles and responsibilities of the deceased partner.

- Men suffer more distress from losing a life partner than women do. This may be explained by the traditional male gender role, which mandates that a man not openly express or confront his emotions.

- The death of a parent brings with it the disruption of the longest-lasting bond in most people's lives, leaving them feeling like orphans with no secure, unconditionally loving base.

- The death of a parent often brings reexamination of our life and priorities.

- When one parent dies, adult children often mask their own grief out of concern for the surviving parent. The grief at the first parent's death is often released at the time of the surviving parent's death.

- Loss of a sibling brings a great deal of grief, with men showing more physical complaints and women showing more psychological upset.

- The emotions of parents whose child is stillborn resembles most closely the grief of parents whose child has lived for a significant time and then died. They experience a shattering disappointment at the death of plans and dreams for the child and entire family, and feel a loss of meaning in life.

- Mothers of stillborn children tend to feel guilt and inadequacy at their abilities to carry and give birth to a live baby.

- Several reports indicate that after an elective abortion in the first trimester of pregnancy, women generally experience few negative emotions. But between 7 percent and 14 percent of women who undergo an abortion report having significant emotional distress after the procedure: guilt, doubt, anger, regret, depression, and fear of disapproval.

- If the abortion was performed because of the deformity or nonviability of the fetus, the woman generally feels a grief that has the potential to become pathological in anxiety and depression.

- Fathers feel intense grief when a child dies before birth, often reporting that their entire view of life is challenged by the tragedy. The death of the child is generally perceived as a waste of life and a violation of the natural order of life.

- Following a miscarriage, a woman is likely to experience depression, anxiety, and a yearning for the lost child. In addition, she often feels the need to find a meaning in the experience and a desire to talk to others about what happened. She may also question her adequacy, given the "failure" she has just experienced, particularly if this was not her first miscarriage and she has no other children. She may also use the experience as a trigger for reexamining her life and her priorities.

- Men whose children have been miscarried feel despair and report having difficulty in coping with the situation, especially if the miscarriage occurred later in the pregnancy and the men had seen the child in an ultrasound scan.

- When given the diagnosis of a terminal illness, shock is generally the first response. Decisions about medical care must be made, and the possibilities for treatment bring both positive and negative elements. Hope remains, for a cure, for a miracle, or for reaching important goals.

- Most people with terminal illnesses want to (1) improve the quality and meaning of their lives in the time remaining, (2) achieve physical and emotional relief or comfort, (3) alter the course of their illnesses, and (4) prepare themselves interpersonally, emotionally, and spiritually for their deaths.

- Acceptance of death seems to come to about half of terminally ill patients, but their loved ones may find this difficult in their bereavement, remembering the last days as being worse than they really were.

KEY TERMS

abortion
elective abortion

miscarriage

stillbirth

INDIVIDUAL ACTIVITIES

1. If you have lost a child, spouse, parent, or sibling, reflect on your own reactions. Do you have different feelings from those described in this chapter? Were there special circumstances in your life that may account for this?

2. Go to the websites of some of the bereavement support groups that are listed in the Appendix. Why are these groups needed? By whom? What functions does each seem to serve? Is the support group potentially adequate in helping those who have been bereaved? Why or why not?

3. What similarities and differences do you think would be found in bereavement because of the loss of a friend as opposed to the loss of a family member?

4. How do you think you would answer the question "What is most important for you to achieve?" if you were terminally ill? Write your own obituary as if you had died today. Then write it again, reflecting the person you hope to be in five or ten years.

GROUP ACTIVITIES

1. In class or in small groups, compare your experiences as adults with the death of family members. Are there cultural differences? What role did religion or spirituality play in your feelings about the death?

2. In class or in groups, watch a movie in which an adult has experienced the death of a child, spouse, parent, or sibling (e.g., *Braveheart*, *Hamlet*, *Mystic River*) and discuss how the bereaved characters reacted to the deaths. Or discuss how the death

of a main character has been presented in a television series (e.g., *CSI: Miami, 8 Simple Rules*). Are the depictions of the survivors' reactions realistic? How would you rewrite the scripts to enhance the realism?

3. In class or in groups, watch a movie, such as *Beaches* or *One True Thing*, that deals with terminal illness. Are the depictions of the terminally ill people realistic? How would you rewrite the script to enhance the realism?

4. In groups of four or five, have each member contact a bereavement support group (see the Appendix or your school's counselling centre for information on how to contact some of these groups) and ask what particular types of problems are encountered by the support group's members. Share the information with the rest of the group.

5. In groups of four or five, compare the answers you gave to question 4 in the individual activities. What similarities and differences are there in your group's answers?

Death and the Senior Adult

What Is Old, Anyway?

They grew up without computers or Internet services. Their entertainment came from listening to the radio and going to the movies, as well as the entertainment the community provided for itself. They did not have microwave ovens, and refrigeration of food was done in small iceboxes, if they were lucky enough to have them. The iceman might have delivered the ice on a regular basis if they lived in urban areas, and milk and bread were often delivered this way too. They remember World War II because they lived through it and some even fought in it. Perhaps their fathers or brothers or other family members died in the war. The men may have seen action in the Korean conflict as well. The women stayed at home and looked after the house, in some cases, or became the war icon "Rosie the Riveter," a poster image representing the women who were taking on jobs they had never touched before, all for the war effort.

After the war, they married and had children—many, many children. Enough children to cause what occurred to be called a baby boom. Raising kids has always been tough, but in some ways these women had it tougher. They tried to teach their children what they had been taught: that men and women had distinctly different skills and talents, and each had a proper domain to stay within; that society had rules about what constituted a "proper" way of living, and these rules could not be broken without risking ostracism from the group for the individual and the whole family; that the government knew what was best for society and would never, never deceive the people. But their children questioned and, in many cases, rejected these teachings. The world their children lived in was very different from the one the parents had grown up in. And it was sometimes confusing as the changes came so quickly that they scarcely had time to apprehend them. Yet they managed. They themselves made many of the discoveries that changed the world, and they adapted and raised children who were strong enough and confident enough to question. They have much to be proud of.

Now they are old. Maybe. Certainly when their parents and grandparents were their age, they were considered old. But maybe they do not feel so old. In fact, inside many of them feel pretty darn young! People seem to be living much longer now too. When Dad retired at age 65 years, he hoped he would have 5 or 10 years left to him. Dad's son, however, can usually plan for 10 or 15 more years at least. What is "old," anyway? And what will happen to them as they grow older? They remember their grandparents living with them in the family home, and Mom took care of the older relatives. Of course she did; that was part of her job as a housewife. And they may have cared for their own parents in their senior years, though hospitals and seniors' homes helped as well. But many of their daughters have full-time careers now, and their sons are maintaining the masculine tradition of working full time. So who will care for them? Many of them see their friends moving into seniors' residences, and some seem very nice, with lots of activities and camaraderie. Should they make the move too? Should they be preparing for their end in ways that their ancestors did not have to? One thing they know for sure: more and more of their friends and family members are dead and gone. It seems now that they are becoming the last survivors. How much longer will they survive? Is anything left but memories? And was it all worthwhile? Did their lives make a difference?

According to Statistics Canada (2004), the 2003 population of Canada was 31 629 677. Of these people, 4 060 147, or 12.8 percent, were over the age of 65 years. Denton, Feaver, and Spencer (2002), analyzing fertility rates, longevity, and immigration patterns, predicted that by the year 2021, the percentage of the Canadian population over the age of 65 will rise to 17 percent to 18 percent, and by 2051, to possibly more than 21 percent. But is a person "old" at age 65? What is "old" in today's society? How is "senior" defined? It is difficult to classify and varies among researchers, cultures, and even individuals. When the Canadian government issues an "Old Age Security pension," the generally accepted age is 65 years although, in some instances, a younger age is acceptable. This cutoff was the same as the mandatory age of retirement, but the mandatory retirement age was abolished by the Government of Canada in 2006. The reasoning that people over the age of 65 could not and should not work the way they had a few years earlier is no longer supportable. In an age of great advances in medicine and nutrition, when the expected life span is 75 years for males and 81 years for females born since 1990–1992 in Canada (Statistics Canada, 2004), 65 years old seems quite young.

As the oldest baby boomers (those people born between 1946 and 1964 in the post–World War II population explosion) reached the age of 60 in 2006, the concept of "elderly" in North America has changed. In fact, the use of the word "elderly" has fallen out of favour. People now prefer to be called "seniors" or "older adults," reflecting the fact that many of them are still active and vibrant people who do not fit the stereotype of an "elderly person." We will use those preferred terms, despite the fact that many of the studies cited do use the word "elderly" to refer to those over the age of 65. In this chapter, the ages of the people examined will vary; some are as young as 55 years and others are in extreme old age at 90 to 100 years.

ATTITUDES TOWARD DEATH

In examining the cognitive functions of older people, many people expect a lessened ability to think or reason and a greater rigidity in thinking. This myth of old age has been debunked by several researchers who found that, apart from those experiencing dementia, seniors simply think differently from younger people. Specifically, older people are more capable of thinking in terms of multiple viewpoints and they can more easily encompass ambiguity and contradiction than younger people can (Commons, Demick, & Goldberg, 1996; Sinnott, 1998). Such flexibility in thinking may be born of their

many years' experience, which has taught them that little in life is black and white; therefore, they are more likely to make judgments based on the context and the pragmatic implications of a situation rather than by following hard and fast rules. It is thereby reasonable to suppose that this type of thinking will be reflected in the attitudes seniors hold about end-of-life issues.

How do seniors feel about their own deaths? Do they fear it because it is (presumably) relatively close, feeling that it is a grim state to be avoided at all costs? Or do they feel more sanguine about it, even welcoming it, given their years of experience with loss of all types? A cogent argument can be made for either position, as well as for the position that age has no effect on attitudes toward death. In fact, seniors show wide diversity in their attitudes, depending on their cultural background, their patterns of socialization, their experiences with death, and their own personal characteristics (Abengózar, Bueno, & Vega, 1999; DePaola, Griffin, Young, & Neimeyer, 2003; Lockhart et al., 2001).

Some researchers, such as Abengózar, Bueno, and Vega (1999), find more despair, fear, loneliness, and depression in 60- to 75-year-olds than in younger people, a finding that is heightened when people are asked to consider their own deaths. But other researchers consider this to be too sweeping a statement. Rather, they regard attitudes toward death as having several components, and their research indicates that having a high anxiety on one component does not necessarily indicate a higher anxiety on other components (DePaola et al., 2003). For example, DePaola et al. (2003), studying Caucasian Americans and African Americans, found that senior Caucasian Americans fear the process of dying more than do African Americans, whereas African Americans had more fear related to the state of death (e.g., fear for the body after death). The researchers suggested that these results are related to the receptivity of each group to hospice or palliative care. Caucasian Americans are more likely to avail themselves of hospice or palliative care, but this leads them to the fear that in an impersonal setting, they may not have responsive caretakers who will see to their comfort and rid them of pain. African Americans, conversely, who are more likely to die in the care of their families, are confident that they will be supported and taken care of in the process of dying, but afterward, when others are involved in the care of the body, the results may be different. These results suggest that in cultures in which nuclear and extended families traditionally care for seniors and the dying, the process of dying itself is not as much of a concern as is the disposal of the body and the fear of the unknown, whereas in cultures that delegate care of the sick and dying to professional caretakers, concern for the process of dying itself is of major concern.

These differences have important implications for giving comfort and support to the dying in a multicultural society, such as Canada; clearly, one form of comfort will not be sufficient, and attention must be paid to the cultural background of the individual as well as to his or her particular needs. For example, Rosenbaum (1991) surveyed senior Greek-Canadian widows and found that because of cultural norms that discouraged the expression of negative emotions, support groups are not helpful to first-generation Canadian women or those who maintained Greek traditions. For these women, talking to their religious leader or a culturally sensitive bereavement worker on a one-to-one basis would be more helpful (see Chapter 12 for more on helping).

Do attitudes toward death inevitably include fear and anxiety? It seems clear that anxiety about death does appear in some older people. Who are these people? What characteristics set them apart from those who do not have any anxiety about death? A review of the literature (Fortner & Neimeyer, 1999) indicated that seniors who have anxiety about death have low **ego integrity.** Ego integrity is a term used by Erik Erikson (1963) to describe the positive state in old age of feeling satisfied and proud of what has been accomplished with the person's life. If the person sees only the missed opportunities and all that was not accomplished, the person has *despair* and, not surprisingly, according to literature review, an anxiety about death. It seems that in old age if we feel that we have lived a good life, filled with meaning, then death is not fearful, as can be seen by Mr. Foxworth's comments in Box 8.1. Conversely, if our lives are judged to have been a failure, as Mr. Greener in Box 8.1 seems to feel about his life, death becomes fearful.

Seniors who have physical or psychological problems also show a greater anxiety about death (Fortner & Neimeyer, 1999). The studies reviewed, however, provide little detail about the kinds of problems that specifically relate to death anxiety. For example, if an older person has an anxiety disorder (e.g., phobia, panic disorder, etc.) or depression, then it seems logical that his or her general tendency to these feelings will manifest in the attitude toward death as well. The relationship to physical problems is illuminated somewhat by research done by Lockhart et al. (2001). They found that American adults aged 65 years and older did not regard death as primarily a fearful experience, but rather as an escape from life or the entryway to a better existence. This is especially, and understandably, the case for those seniors who perceive their physical or mental health to be poor.

An important point to note is that these researchers found that the *perceptions* of the seniors they examined were the predictors of their attitudes toward death, not necessarily the reality of their physical or mental condition, although the two are mainly congruent. Thus, the presence of pain did not predict viewing death as a welcome escape; this may be because the particular sample of subjects in this study had relatively little pain, or it may be because if a person is able to cope with the pain, it is not perceived as an indication of poor physical health. That is, some people may in essence be saying, "Yes, I have pain, that comes with age, but I can handle it and I'm in pretty good physical health for my age." If this is the case, then pain in and of itself may not necessarily be related to the perception of ill health, and therefore death is not seen as a welcome respite. Conversely, some individuals may have less pain, but if they find even a little pain difficult to cope with, their perception of their health may be that it is poor and death is welcome escape from the suffering. Lockhart and her colleagues also found that among seniors who fear death or welcome it as an escape are strong concerns about whether they will be able to make their own decisions about their end-of-life care.

BOX 8.1   Mr. Foxworth's and Mr. Greener's Discussion

Mr. Foxworth: I'm getting pretty old now, but I look back on my life with a lot of satisfaction. My kids turned out well and the business I started is thriving. When I started the business in making baby foods, I hoped it would turn into such an enterprise for the kids to take over. We never made millions, but the baby food we made was good for babies and it was priced right, and the kids have started an organic foods line that people want too.

Mr. Greener: You're lucky. I never seemed to be able to catch a break. The business I started went bust when the buyers decided they didn't want

handheld fans anymore. My kids think I'm just an old idiot who never could make a decent living. I don't even know where my son is now.

Mr. Foxworth: Now that's a real shame. I *am* lucky, and I'm grateful. I don't particularly want to die, but I'm ready to meet my maker and I'll have some fine things to tell him about how our family has developed.

Mr. Greener: Well, I definitely don't want to die. I don't even want to think about it. The Lord probably won't have any more use for me than my family does.

It has been assumed that women are more fearful (or admit to more fear) about death than men, but this seems not to be the case among seniors (Fortner & Neimeyer, 1999); both older men and older women report equal amounts of anxiety when contemplating death. It may be that this reflects different concerns that men and women may have. For example, Cicirelli (1999) found that women have more fear of dying than men do, but less fear of the unknown (a major component of a more general fear of death), while men have greater fear of the unknown, but less fear of dying. This may be related to the general finding that women tend to be more religious than men are, thereby feeling greater assurance that what follows death is not an unpleasant unknown.

In keeping with the speculated reasons for the gender difference in fear of death is another common assumption: those who are religious, faithfully attending religious services as part of their affiliation with an organized religion, with beliefs about an afterlife and faith in a caring and compassionate divinity, fear death less. This idea is *not* borne out by the evidence, although the situation here may be more complex. Fortner and Neimeyer (1999) reported that a review of the literature indicated that, among older people, higher religiosity is not related to lower fear of death. When examining seniors, however, it must be taken into account that, in general, they were born and raised in a societal period in which religion played a larger part in day-to-day life than it did for those born later. It may be that most of the seniors studied were high in religiosity as compared with younger people, so no meaningful relationship between religiosity and death anxiety was manifested in this group. That is, researchers cannot tell whether being religious mitigates fear of death if all those studied are religious. Certainly other research indicates that high religiosity predicts a lower fear of death and the unknown (e.g., Cicirelli, 1999). In essence, then, research has shown that being religious may or may not reduce the fear of death. It is difficult to tell whether a causal relationship exists because of the generational differences in being involved in day-to-day religion.

Another part of the problem in determining the role of religiosity seems to lie in the confusion between **intrinsic religious motivation** and **extrinsic religious motivation** (Clements, 1998). Intrinsic religious motivation refers to the internal aspects of a person's religious belief: the nature, complexity, and reasons for the beliefs. Extrinsic religious motivation refers to their external religious behaviours and affiliations. Thus, it is perfectly possible for someone to score high on measures of religiosity because he or she faithfully attends religious services, participating in and conforming to religious rites, while having very little internal belief in a deity. It is equally possible to have strong and deep sustaining beliefs in a deity while not showing outward behaviours, such as church attendance. Not unexpectedly, then, seniors with strong intrinsic religious motivation are found to have less anxiety about death than do those with only extrinsic religious motivation (Clements, 1998).

Consistent with the finding that intrinsic religious motivation is related to lower anxiety about death is the research on spirituality in seniors. Spirituality is related to intrinsic religious motivation but may not rest on a belief in the divine; rather, spirituality is concerned with the search for meaning and desire for self-completion that may or may not be part of a religious belief system. In general, older people tend to think in more spiritual terms (Commons, Demick, & Goldberg, 1996; Sinnott, 1998). Moremen (2004–2005) found that women explore their spirituality and belief systems more as they get older, and part of their questioning revolves around issues of death and dying. Moremen's subjects who felt inner peace, and connected to others and to something larger than themselves, had less fear of death than did those women who felt alone in their environments and in the universe. A major part of spirituality is **self-transcendence,** which Decker and Reed (2005) defined as follows:

> the expansion of personal boundaries inwardly (as through soul-searching and self-enlightenment), outwardly (in terms of entrusting oneself in relationships with others and the surrounding environment), transpersonally (toward God or Higher Process), and temporally (by integrating insights of one's past and future in a way that enhances the present. (p. 830)

Reed (1991) found that seniors facing death have a greater sense of well-being if they, like Mrs. Constantine in Box 8.2, have achieved this self-transcendence. This seems to have little regard for cultural boundaries, as indicated by Mrs. Constantine's neighbour, Mrs. Parmar, and as seen in the example of the Taiwanese in Box 8.3.

END-OF-LIFE NEEDS AND SENIORS' WISHES

Many of the wishes and frustrations of seniors can be seen in the case of Mrs. Felder in Box 8.4. If death cannot be avoided, she, like virtually everyone else, wants a "good death." But what is a good death? Cameron (2002) states:

> A good death is not a single act, but a series of events accompanied by pain and symptom management, clear decision making, openness or an awareness of dying, completion

My husband and son are both dead, dead for 45 years now, and not one day goes by without me thinking about them and missing them. But I had to survive, even though I thought I never would. The new priest at church helped a lot. He told me that we're all part of a bigger network of life, that God's hand spreads everywhere, and just because you're dead, it doesn't mean you're not still just as much a part of the network. I never thought of that before, but Father Kotsopoulos told me to meditate about it and pray on it. And you know, after I did that for a while, I saw what he meant. I started to really feel connected to something larger than I am. I realized that my griefs were less hurtful when I saw my husband and son as part of that bigger something, just the way they were when they were alive. I started to feel closer to people around me too, as if we were all in this big network together, sometimes doing well and sometimes messing up, but all part of the same thing. Now I see my life, and the lives of everyone else, as part of a huge embroidery pattern, like my mother used to make, all the threads weaving together and each one having a part to play and a relationship to every other one. Death doesn't end that, but every baby that's born adds another thread. I still miss my husband and son, but I can see their threads still working, having an effect on me, and through me, on everybody I speak to, and through them, to so many others. Funny thing, I told my new neighbour, Mrs. Parmar, about how I felt, and she said that was a lot like what her grandmother, who was a Hindu, used to say. It's good. Death doesn't seem frightening to me now—it's only a change and the thread still keeps going.

Lin (2003) questioned older adults living in some of the urban centres of Ohio in the United States, and in Taipei, Taiwan. In both the American and the Chinese samples, as the level of spirituality increased, the fear of death decreased. Feeling a sense of meaning and connectedness is dependent neither on religious affiliation, be it Catholic, Protestant, Buddhist, Taoist, or Confucian, nor on racial identity. Spirituality allows for transcendence from the fear of death. This is not to say that no differences exist among cultures; Lin also found that in the Chinese sample was more **death avoidance**, that is, a lack of talking or thinking about death, but she noted that this is part of Chinese culture and not necessarily reflective of a fear of death as it might be among Americans. Older American adults seem to accept death because of their particular religious views of a satisfying afterlife. Older Chinese adults, however, base their belief in a good afterlife, or next life when they have a belief in reincarnation, on whether a person has currently lived a moral life. Thus, moral values inform the Chinese viewpoint while religious values inform the American viewpoint. This difference is reasonable because, from the American religious standpoint, the afterlife provides an escape from the travails of this life, while to the Chinese, no escape exists because death in this life leads to reincarnation back into life with its attendant suffering.

and saying good-bye, helping others, resolving conflict, control or autonomy, optimism and hope, readiness or preparing for departure, location or living with one's choice about where to die, and affirmation of the whole person. Each component involves interconnected ethical, spiritual, physical, emotional and social issues. (p. 539)

The wish for this kind of death is clearly apparent from the responses of the seniors who were interviewed or surveyed in the research that follows. How older adults view the end of their lives and their needs at that time can be discovered by examining those people who are actually in the terminal phase of their lives, and those who are planning for the end, but may be some time away from it.

It is important to note that the senior years and the end of life require decisions to be made about how the dying process and the death itself should be handled. When dying is sudden or the dying person is a child or is incapacitated or not competent, the decisions are typically made by legally designated others (e.g., family, friends, court system). For older people who have no dementia and are conscious, the decisions are theirs, unless they choose to pass them to another (which in itself is another decision).

BOX 8.4 Mrs. Felder Speaks

I'm dying. I know it. It's not unreasonable because I'm 82 years old. I've outlasted almost everyone I grew up with. I survived my husband and my baby son. But now it's my turn, and that's all right. I lived a good life and I did a lot of things, some bad, but mostly good. I raised four strong healthy children who brought up their own children and are now grandparents themselves. I gave them the basis for living and learning and loving—they all say that. I tried to help people outside my family as much as I could too, and when they needed a volunteer for some charity work at the church, they knew they could count on me. Yes, it's been a pretty good life. I keep thinking more and more about the past, reliving so many of the little moments, not just the big events. I try to tell my kids about them, but they've heard the stories before and don't really want to hear them again. But it seems important to me—it seems to help me put my life in perspective and besides, my memories are my main source of comfort.

I wish I didn't have to be in this hospital to die. I wish I could be in my own home, but they say that my care is too complicated to be at home, and goodness knows the kids and grandkids can't take time out of their careers and their own child-raising to take care of an old woman like me. The doctors and nurses here try to be as nice as they can, but they're overworked and don't have much time to spend with me. That one nurse who comes in at night is driving me crazy though! He keeps waking me up to take my blood pressure (as if that matters now!) and he says in a chirpy voice, "Hey, Molly, time to take our blood pressure!" "Our" blood pressure indeed! And when did it become all right to call your elders by their given name without permission? I feel like a patronized child when he calls me Molly—that's a liberty for me to give, not a licence for him to take. Ah, but I guess things are different from when I was young. Still, I don't feel like I'm getting much respect here. My doctor spends as little time as he can with me, and when I ask about my treatment, he chucks me under the chin and says, "Now you let me worry about that, young lady." Then, sometimes, he talks to the kids about me, and between them, I suppose they make the decisions. When did I become incompetent? Do they really think they're sparing me? I know I should get tougher with them, but they mean well, and with the end near, there doesn't seem to be much point.

All I hope is that my oldest, Roger, isn't the one to decide about whether I should be kept alive on machines. I don't want that and I've told him so, but he's scared to let Mommy go, I think. Poor lad, I don't want to push him, but I wish I could have a chance to talk to my doctor about this myself, without him saying, "Now, young lady, don't you go talking about that!"

How a person feels and what a person wants when he or she knows that death is coming very soon affect the decision-making process on end-of-life issues, whether these are formalized in an advance directive or not. Not surprisingly under these circumstances, people usually focus on the quality of their lives for whatever time they have left. Senior American men whose deaths were a few months away and who knew they were dying centred on three issues in particular (Vig & Pearlman, 2003):

1. *Living while dying.* They partook of activities and hobbies for as long as they could, and they thoroughly enjoyed them, seeing themselves as *living* people rather than as *dying* people. The sense of normalcy that this imparted in their lives was important to them. Even though they knew that adherence to the diet regimen prescribed by the medical team made them feel better, sometimes they indulged themselves in the forbidden (e.g., salt) because the quality of the moment improved for them in the better-tasting food. Their attitude was that to not live as fully as they could meant moving into an active dying phase, a phase they were not yet ready for, although they were actively preparing for it.

2. *Anticipating the actual dying process.* Especially when new symptoms arose, these men thought about what their actual dying process would be like for them and their loved ones. This enhanced their desire to put their affairs in order and to attain goals they had set for themselves, such as making videotapes for their grandchildren. By preparing as much as they could, they believed that they were maximizing their chances of having a good death, without fears or regrets. They felt the need to make sure that they were "right" with themselves, their families, and their religious/spiritual beliefs.

3. *Receiving good health care.* These men valued their independence and worried about losing that in the dying process. They wanted to feel that health-care personnel respected them and their wishes. They

wanted health-care workers who would answer their questions and communicate honestly with them. Pain control was important to them, but not as important as their independence and the time they would spend with family and friends.

It seems clear that the concerns of the end of life for seniors revolve around the quality of their lives and their independent participation in activities, which includes preparing themselves and their families for the end of life while avoiding being a burden or source of conflict (see, as well, Cicirelli, 2002; Decker & Reed, 2005; Young, Ofori-Boateng, Rodriguez, & Plowman, 2003). Consistent and additional issues were found by Coppola et al. (1999): the seniors they interviewed indicated that their preference for life-sustaining measures depended on the situation they were in. These people did not want their lives prolonged if they were in pain, if they were cognitively impaired, or when no real chance of recovery remained.

The issues that are important to older adults who are contemplating their deaths are also revealed in research that interviewed older Americans about their directives for their end-of-life care (Rosenfeld, Wenger, & Kagawa-Singer, 2000). These people asked for medical interventions to be applied to them *only* if these interventions would return the quality of their lives to them. If such procedures as cardiopulmonary resuscitation would allow them to engage in their most favoured activities again, they wanted these interventions to be applied. But if the interventions could only keep them alive, while physically or cognitively impaired, ending their independence and productivity, and leaving them a caretaking burden, they found these interventions to be undesirable. In making these decisions, the individuals indicated that their advanced age (72–92 years) was a major factor to consider. Having lived a long and full life, they saw little reason to prolong it unless they could be restored to independent functioning. In this regard, they also indicated the importance of "caring" at the end of life in their decision making. To them, caring usually meant not burdening their families with having to nurse them in their infirmities and pain, although caring to their families usually meant gladly providing and taking responsibility for the welfare of the older loved one.

The seniors interviewed did not want their families to bear the emotional and financial burden of their care, and they did not want this care if it meant being a burden or being kept alive without a good quality of life. These older adults hoped that their final end-of-life decisions would be made by using a combination of their wishes, the expertise of medical personnel, and the interpersonal compassion and love of their families. These results led the researchers to suggest that perhaps asking for end-of-care directives regarding such interventions as cardiopulmonary resuscitation is incorrect and insensitive: it is not the procedures that are important to the seniors, it is the outcome. The goal for the seniors in this study was to function independently in their favourite activities. The researchers suggested that asking what their goal is informs the medical personnel and the family more fully than asking about specific interventions and must be in itself the main factor of the decision making, a suggestion heartily endorsed by other medical personnel dealing with terminally ill patients (e.g., Quill et al., 2006). Note that older people may change their minds over time regarding the degree of life-sustaining intervention they want (Ditto et al., 2003), so it should not be taken for granted that goals and desires remain unchanged. Even formal advance directives and living wills need periodic updating.

In the senior years, most individuals experience their own ill health and the ill health of others. They may have seen what sometimes appears to be torturous aggressive measures made to prolong life in others; they may have seen families torn apart by the burden of caring for ill and aging relatives; they may have been preceded in death by many of the people they cared about. It is to be expected that these sorts of experiences will affect their decisions concerning their own end-of-life care. With a history of these types of experiences, seniors are understandably less likely to desire aggressive measures to prolong their lives (Cicirelli, 1999, 2002; Decker & Reed, 2005; Rein et al., 1996).

The person's individual characteristics and his or her situation also affect decision making at the end of life. Feeling that they have unfinished business, for example, increases fear of death in older adults and makes them more likely to desire aggressive life-sustaining measures (Mutran, Danis, Bratton, Sudha, & Hanson, 1997). If a person has close family contact and support, however, he or she is less likely to have unfinished business in these relationships at the end of life, and so fear of death is less, as is the desire to prolong life. This is not to suggest that people with a close supportive family want to die sooner, only that they are able to achieve peace and an acceptance of an inevitable death that may be lacking in others.

Another individual factor that has an impact on whether seniors want aggressive life-sustaining measures is their **locus of control,** that is, whether they feel that control over their lives lies within themselves or without. Those people who believe that their fates are controlled by outside forces (external locus of control) have a greater fear of death and more desire to prolong life, along with less ability to deal with stress in general (Maddux, 1999), than do those with an internal locus of control (Cicirelli, 1999). Consistent with this is the finding that as the number of years of education increases, fear of death and desire to prolong life decrease (Cicirelli, 1999; Mutran et al., 1997), perhaps because higher education is positively correlated with internal locus of control (Burger, 1999).

Box 8.5 examines the experiences of seniors at the end of their lives in some European countries, and Box 8.6 discusses the myths surrounding the treatment of senior Inuit.

BOX 8.5 A Cross-Cultural View: The European Experience

Laakkonen, Pitkala, and Strandberg (2004) talked to senior Finnish patients in acute care facilities. Although the sample size was small (only 11), these researchers found that their subjects did not accept or realize that they were, in fact, in the terminal phase of their lives; they believed that they still had more time left and perhaps more treatments to try. They expressed a desire for more contact and conversation with their medical caregivers, but they were extremely kind and modest in stating that the caregivers were very overworked and stressed, doing as much as they could. These patients were not very concerned about autonomy of decision making; rather, they were content to allow their physicians to make the decisions regarding their care.

In Belgium, Denmark, Italy, the Netherlands, Sweden, and Switzerland, seniors actively make decisions about their end-of-life care to a great extent (between 23 percent for Italy and 51 percent for Switzerland), according to van der Heide et al. (2003). Some of these decisions revolve around physician assistance in suicide, with the lowest numbers requesting this in Italy, Denmark,

Sweden, and Switzerland, a high number in Belgium, and the highest number in the Netherlands, but in general, few requests for physician-assisted suicide were made in any country. A more common request was for the administration of medications to alleviate pain, even if it hastened death. The lowest numbers requesting this were in Italy (19 percent) and the highest were in Denmark (26 percent). The request that no treatment be given or that potentially life-sustaining treatment be withheld or withdrawn was found in all six countries but with variability: in Italy, only 4 percent of those who died had made this request, while the percentages rose to 14 percent in Belgium, Denmark, and Sweden; 20 percent in the Netherlands; and 28 percent in Switzerland. In most cases, the decisions are discussed with the family and physician, but, remarkably, in Sweden and Italy, more than 50 percent of all end-of-life decisions were made by physicians or the medical team without consultation with the patient or the family, whether or not the patient was competent to make his or her own decisions.

BOX 8.6 A Cross-Cultural View: The Myth of the Inuit

A belief persists that Inuit in the north put their seniors on ice floes to die when they are no longer productive. In fact, an article in the prestigious *Journal of the American Medical Association* (*JAMA*) even described in great detail the voluntary suicide of a senior Inuit man in Alaska who was now "useless" (Shah, 2000). But the event never happened! *JAMA* editors exposed the fiction when it was discovered. In reality, Inuit have a longstanding tradition of valuing their seniors simply because they are old and so have much wisdom to impart. In times of terrible famine, to conserve food for the survival of the group, a very few Inuit tribes, with much grief in their desperation, did allow their seniors to choose to be

directly killed (not set adrift on an ice floe) by a younger relative or abandoned, sometimes when the whole village moved without them. But this was more akin to an assisted suicide (although it may be that some elders were coerced into asking for death). It was much more likely that under these extreme conditions, infants would be sacrificed instead because their worth was less than that of the elders. If the famine ended and it was possible, the elders who had been abandoned were often rescued, to the great relief and joy of the group.

Sources: Crystal (n.d.); Hamilton (2001); Straight Dope Science Advisory Board (2004).

SENIOR BEREAVED SPOUSES

When a spouse is lost after many years of marriage, it is expected that the remaining spouse will have deep grief and loneliness. Some people have assumed that senior widows or widowers have a more difficult time in coping with bereavement than younger spouses because of the general lack of resiliency in later life. Others have assumed that the adjustment to spousal bereavement is easier for seniors because of their own proximity to death and their experience with bereavement. The research literature on this subject is mixed, but even seniors see some positive outcomes of spousal bereavement, just as younger adults do (see Chapter 7).

How do senior spouses respond to the death of their partner of many years? Their responses coincide greatly with younger people who have lost a spouse: they feel sadness, depression, anger, guilt, and loneliness (Costello & Kendrick, 2000). In addition, both their perceived physical health and their actual physical health deteriorate after a bereavement (Charlton, Sheahan, Smith, & Campbell, 2001; Fry, 2001). Sometimes, among older bereaved adults, the physical symptoms are surrogates for emotional symptoms; that is, seniors may show their distress through their bodies rather than through their psychological functioning (Williams, Baker, & Allman, 2005). Older bereaved people also indicate that they have not broken their attachment to their dead spouses; rather they have developed a new connection, an inner representation. They often say that they feel that the spouse is in some way still with them and will always be with them. This connection is perceived as a comfort to them; their long years of association with their spouses do not disappear simply because the spouse was now dead. This can be seen in Mr. Warwick's continuing conversation with his dead wife, Irma, in Box 8.7.

In a Canadian study, Fry (1998) interviewed a number of senior widows and widowers shortly after their bereavement and then again one year later. Deep grief and suffering were experienced by almost 85 percent of these people shortly after the death of their spouses, but one year later, although they still had "waves" of deep grief and loneliness, many of the bereaved reported some positive changes as well. These changes were in four major areas:

1. *Renewed sense of self-discovery.* Many of the widows and widowers reported finding new aspects of themselves that they had not explored before. For example, a woman whose husband had always taken care of all the family's financial matters found, to her surprise and pleasure, that she could manage finances, including doing her income tax. Similarly, a man whose wife had been the caring and demonstrative one in the family found that, in his regret for not having been more affectionate

---

BOX 8.7   Mr. Warwick Speaks

I can't believe she's gone. Irma died last week and she was only 72 years old. I never said goodbye or I love you, I never told her how much I valued the way she took care of me. I don't even know how to warm up a can of soup for myself. I don't suppose I have to worry much about that though; the kids and grandchildren are swarming around me, and so is everybody from the church. I don't know those people very well—Irma took care of the religion for both of us. She's in Heaven, I bet. Hey, Irma, I hope you can pull a few strings to get me there when the time comes. Everybody wants me to talk about how I'm feeling, cry a little. I do cry, but not when people are around. My father taught me that grown men don't cry. I guess I let Irma do the crying for both of us too. Are you crying for me now, my darling?

ONE YEAR LATER
It's been a terrible year. Lonely. I've felt very depressed and I'm getting achy in the joints, more than I was, and my digestion has taken a bad turn. I guess this old warhorse hasn't too long left either. Irma, maybe I'll see you soon. There have been some bright spots, I suppose. I did survive and I hadn't bet that I would. I did learn how to make a few simple meals, and I swear when I do, I feel like that TV chef, what's his name? Emeril? Elizabeth, that widowed lady down the block, has been a big help. I'm thinking about doing a little courting. You'd understand, wouldn't you, Irma? I'm getting old and I don't think I can take proper care of myself. Maybe getting married again would be a good thing. Maybe Elizabeth would feel a little less lonely too if she married me. But then, Elizabeth seems to have a lot of other widows for friends, so maybe she's not so lonely. She said it was hard for her to learn how to manage money after her husband died because she'd never done it before. I could do that for her, and she could cook. Would she go for that? Or am I being an old fool, Irma?

---

with his wife, he too could communicate his love to other family members.

2. *Renewed sense of resilience.* In the first few months of bereavement, many widows and widowers thought that they would never survive without their spouses, that their lives were over in every meaningful way. One year later, they found to their astonishment that they were, in fact, stronger and more competent than they had given themselves credit for. They felt a new determination to get on with their lives with self-sufficiency and independence.

3. *Renewed meaning in life.* For some of the seniors, their spouses had been the focal points of their lives. With the death of the spouse, their lives had no purpose anymore. After a year, however, they found new purpose and new enjoyments in their lives, often in relating to others more than they had before their bereavement.

4. *Self-transcendence.* The death of someone close often precipitates an examination of people's values and beliefs about the meaning of their lives. This was the case for several of the people Fry talked to. One year after the death of their spouses, they began to look outward more, feeling themselves to be part of something bigger than the couple they had been. For some, this meant a greater feeling of connection with God; for others it meant more involvement in charity work and service to others.

That positive outcomes can result from losing a spouse is confirmed by Carr (2004) who found that widows aged 65 years and older who had been emotionally dependent on their husbands had an increase in self-esteem following their bereavement. Similarly, widowers aged 65 years and older who had been dependent on their wives for home and financial management experienced personal growth after their bereavement. Carr learned that as they discovered that they could manage life on their own, both senior men and women found a psychological reward from their pain.

Positive outcomes are an unexpected and welcome side effect of bereavement, but they do not preclude the social and emotional loneliness that seniors feel when their spouses die (van Baarsen, van Duijn, Smit, Snijders, & Knipscheer, 2001–2002). This loneliness may not decrease, but wax and wane, or even increase as time goes on. Those who were lonely before their spouse died are particularly vulnerable because, for them, the bereavement places stress on top of a pre-existing stress. For example, people who had felt lonely because of a personal characteristic or because of situational forces, such as children living far away, before their spouses died found their loneliness intensified. The loneliness that is experienced may not be relieved by social contacts or by receiving social and emotional support.

Older men and women have some different reactions to their bereavements, as do younger men and women (see Chapter 7). Specifically, in the senior years, men are more likely to want to remarry because of their concerns about facing old age and ill health alone, while women are less likely to desire remarriage because they enjoy their newfound freedom (Davidson, 2001). This refutes the stereotype of women being more eager to find a mate and men considering a wife to be "the ball and chain." Also refuting gender stereotyping is evidence regarding other differences between the sexes in their reactions to bereavement. For example, older British men and women say that women cope with bereavement better than men do because of men's inhibitions about revealing their emotions and their inability to handle domestic chores. Women, they felt, have domestic abilities and greater social support, making bereavement easier for them to cope with. In actuality, many men are highly socially engaged and are also domestically facile. Men do, however, receive more social support in their bereavement than women, despite their perceived inability to talk about their feelings (Bennett, Hughes, & Smith, 2003, 2005), yet they report feeling more depressed after their spouses' deaths than women do (Bennett, Hughes, & Smith, 2003; Bennett, Smith, & Hughes, 2005). Certainly evidence shows greater increases in poor health and higher death rates in the first years following a spouse's death in bereaved men than women, which may relate to the depression and general stress that they feel (Stroebe, Stroebe, & Schut, 2001).

Fry (2001) conducted a study of seniors in Canada and found that older men and women had feelings of self-efficacy in different domains, which later affected their adaptation to widowhood. **Self-efficacy** refers to the extent to which an individual feels competent and able in a specific domain of functioning. Men tend to feel more self-efficacy in financial, instrumental (practical day-to-day living), and physical health domains. Women feel more self-efficacy in the emotional, social, and spiritual domains. After their wives died, widowers reported a lower quality of life in terms of their emotional, social, and spiritual welfare (i.e., the female-strong domains), while widows reported that after their husbands died, the quality of their lives in terms of dealing with day-to-day matters, financial matters, and their physical health decreased. Where people are strong to begin with, contends Fry, they feel confident and continue to feel strong after bereavement, but where people feel weaker to begin with, they experience more problems in adjusting. Thus, it is not so much a question of who feels the grief more deeply, men or women, but in which domain their adaptation problems lie.

Other gender differences among seniors in their reactions to bereavement include the finding that widowed men are more likely to express resignation and acceptance that their spouses had died, while widowed women were more likely to express stoicism and the need to "soldier on" in spite of their husbands' deaths. In addition, not surprisingly, older men who are coping well with their grief are more likely to talk about their loss. Those men who cope well call themselves "selfish" for their enjoyment of being free to please themselves instead of having to worry about the needs and wants of a partner. For older women, those who are comfortable being alone cope better than those who are not. Friendship patterns change more for senior women than for senior men who are bereaved: these women report that their married friends often drop them from their social circle, but they gain support from other widows and they volunteer to help others more (Bennett, Hughes, & Smith, 2005).

SENIOR BEREAVED PARENTS

In Box 8.8, Mrs. Schrammer speaks of her continuing grief many years after the death of her daughter. Ruth Malkinson and Liora Bar-Tur (1999, 2004–2005) talked extensively with a group of people often overlooked by both the bereavement literature and the literature on aging: people who are now seniors but lost a child many years previously. Specifically, in one study (2004–2005), they talked to 47 Israeli parents between the ages of 61 and 92 years whose sons had been killed in war or in military service 26 to 35 years previously. It is usually assumed that after this length of time, the pain of loss has dulled, leaving only sweet and poignant memories. This is not the case, as found by Malkinson and Bar-Tur. The parents they interviewed remembered hearing the news of their son's death in vivid detail, as if it had just occurred, and they often experienced the same emotional and physical reactions when recounting the story as they experienced at the time. Over time, the pain of the bereavement became somewhat less intense but not markedly so. It did, however, become more familiar and was regarded as an expected part of the parents' lives. The researchers quote one mother as saying, "One can get used to it, but one can't get over it" (Malkinson & Bar-Tur, 2004–2005, p. 112.). This sentiment was shared by the vast majority of the interviewees.

Although they had diverse and individual reactions to the deaths of their sons, the great majority of the parents reported that the deceased son continued to play a major role in their lives, one that was often exacerbated as the parents aged. From the time their son died, they made the deceased the centrepiece of their lives, often reporting that they had neglected their other children in their grief. As time passed, the deceased remained at the centre of their personal lives. But now, their other children were grown up and moving out; in many cases, the parents were retired from their work; friends may have

---

BOX 8.8   Mrs. Schrammer Speaks

It's been 27 years since my beautiful Karin was killed by that drunk. She was only 18 and she had her whole life in front of her. She was so popular, everyone loved her, and she was smart—she always got A's in school and she wanted to be a lawyer. She would have been a great one too—so talented. And sports! She played tennis like a professional. I still talk to her in my head. I have so many things of hers around that it feels like she's still here. I miss her more and more as I get old. I think of the grandchildren she would have given me. I think of sharing the raising of them. I think of her holding my hand as my own end comes. But I've been robbed. Everything was taken from me the day that the drunk decided he could drive a car. I can still feel the cold in my stomach when I think of the police officers coming to the door that day. I feel it every time the doorbell rings. I guess that will never stop. The agony never ends, but you get used to living with agony.

I have two other children, younger than Karin, and I feel bad about them. I wasn't much of a mother after my Karin died. I couldn't be there for them. My 10-year-old daughter, Camilla, did her best to take Karin's place, but how could she? The kids are grown now, with their own kids. I love them to pieces, but I can't help but think about how empty life still is without my Karin. My husband and I got through some bad times. I thought for a while he wasn't as devastated by Karin's death as I was, but I came to realize that he was grieving in his own way. Different from mine, but just as deep.

Now that I'm a senior, I think about how it won't be too long before I'm with Karin again. I tell my grandchildren all about her over and over again because I don't want her to be forgotten after I die.

died or moved. In general, these parents reported that their interpersonal world shrank, and their homes were empty save for the presence of their deceased son in their thoughts, which then had room to expand. In some cases, the parents imagined the child growing older as the years passed, and they carried on interactions with the deceased son. In some ways the deceased son became closer to them and more real to them than their living children and grandchildren. The dead son became more and more the main presence in the live of these parents, especially in their often-idealized thoughts of what might have been if the son had lived, how they might feel differently, how the circumstances of their lives would be changed, what they missed in not having their son.

The suffering of their bereavement did not diminish as these parents grew older; rather it was a central component of their day-to-day lives and, in fact, in some ways became more onerous to bear as their need for support from their children increased. Although the need for family relationships was strong in these parents, and their love for their remaining children and grandchildren was unquestionable, the void left by the deceased son was never filled, and the family never felt complete to them. Many of these parents had ambivalent feelings about their own deaths: on one hand, they felt a desire to end the pain and rejoin the deceased child, but on the other hand, they feared that, as their deceased son had lived within them, their deaths would lead to the second, and final, death of their son.

SENIORS AND OTHER BEREAVEMENTS

As people grow older, their family and friends grow older too and become more prone to terminal illnesses and death. Thus, in old age, seniors have more bereavements to cope with and less time between bereavements, as Mr. Carter relates in Box 8.9. For example, Williams et al. (2005) found that in a sample of almost one thousand people over the age of 65 years who were living in the community (i.e., not in residential placements) in the American South, a full 23 percent reported a nonspousal family death within the previous six months. They also found that these nonspousally bereaved people had greater depression and anxiety, although not necessarily enough to be detected through standard psychological tests. Women who were also widows, however, were particularly vulnerable, a finding that is consistent with the literature indicating that stress is cumulative: stresses add up, and each subsequent stress is more difficult to deal with (Weiten & Lloyd, 2003). Why widowers were not equally vulnerable is unclear.

> **BOX 8.9   Mr. Carter Speaks**
>
> My old school friend Bert died last week. It seems incredible. We were friends for 70 years. He and I were the last of the old crowd. I think about him more and more, and sometimes I feel that I'm closer to him now than I was before. Before he died, we didn't see much of each other, neither one of us was up to doing a lot of gadding about and socializing. But we thought about each other. It feels lonely just knowing that the world is without Bert now. I wish I had my old digestion back. I'd get a bottle of Bert's favourite beer and I'd toast him in a right formal way. I would say what we always said when we parted: "Don't be your worst enemy!" It would be our little ceremony of goodbye.

These people, even when they have the physical ability to be mobile and functional, may not function adequately; that is, although they possess the physical ability to go out, they do not. This reaction may be tied to their feelings of depression, which is often associated with lethargy and decreased physicality (Davison, Neale, Blankstein, & Flett, 2002).

Most of the studies that have looked at the effects of bereavement on seniors have used a very broad definition of senior, in some cases regarding the senior years as starting at 50 or 55! What of the very senior people though? Do people over the age of 80 have the same reactions to the death of a significant person in their lives? Johnson and Barer (as cited by Lalive d'Epinay, Cavalli, & Spini, 2003) say that the very senior people cope well with sad events. They have many opportunities to both experience and cope with tragic events because, as Lalive d'Epinay et al. (2003) found, over five years, 61 percent of a sample of 295 Swiss people over the age of 80 experienced the death of a close relative, a dear friend, or both. Among very senior people, they found, no clear indication exists that bereavement is bringing about a decline in health or depressive symptoms. It may be, then, that these people, far from being too fragile to deal with the death of a significant person in their lives, deal with it in a very adaptive but less emotional manner. When very senior people experience the death of a close family member, the amount of interaction with remaining family tends to increase; but when a close friend dies, no ritual, no marker, occurs. Very senior people report feeling lonelier after the death of a friend, but interactions with others who might lend support neither increase nor decrease. In extreme old age, the number of interactions the individual has with friends tends to decline in any case; the individual is less able to physically maintain a relationship with friends as he or she ages, so the physical loss of the deceased is not missed, as in a bereavement pattern seen among younger mourners. Instead, very senior people, as they age, compensate for their physical infirmities by strengthening their mental representations of their friends. The death of a loved person, then, impinges more on their realizations of themselves as being survivors ("I'm the last one left"), deepening their feelings of loneliness.

In conclusion, no single pattern or trajectory of mourning exists for seniors any more than it does for younger people. Grief is an individual process and is coped with in a multitude of ways. Only a few very general trends have been identified, reminding us that grief is no respecter of age or gender or culture or any other factor.

SUMMARY

- What ages constitute the "senior years" is debatable, but it is not debatable that the percentage of seniors in the population is growing and will continue to do so for some time.

- Older people think a little differently from younger people, using more flexibility and less black-and-white reasoning.

- People experience a heightened feeling of depression in old age as they contemplate their own death, but the makeup of that depression varies as people concentrate on different facets of death (e.g., the process of dying, the disposal of the body), depending on their own backgrounds and personalities.

- Seniors with high ego integrity feel less fear of death than do those with low ego integrity. Also, seniors who perceive themselves as having poor health or psychological problems have more death anxiety than those who perceive themselves as having better physical and mental health.

- Senior men and women have equal amounts of death anxiety, but men fear the unknown more than women do, and women fear the process of dying more than men do.

- Older people with high intrinsic religious motivation and spirituality fear death less than those who have high extrinsic religious motivation. Those who attained self-transcendence also have little death anxiety.

- Older people want the end of their lives to be of good quality and as pain free as possible, leaving them with as much control and decision making as possible. They want to continue participating in enjoyable activities and being with their friends and family for as long as they can, and they want to avoid becoming a caretaking burden to their families. Seniors want life-sustaining medical interventions to be applied to them only if these interventions would return the quality of their lives to them, but not if they would live on with physical or cognitive impairments. This is especially the case if they have had experience with severe illnesses or have witnessed others being sustained in a poor quality of life through extreme medical intervention.

- Seniors who feel that they have unfinished business are more likely to want to avoid death through extreme medical interventions than are those who feel more closure in their lives.

- Those older adults who have an internal locus of control have less desire to employ extreme means to prolong life than do those with an external locus of control.

- As the number of years of education increases, fear of death and desire to prolong life decrease.

- When a spouse dies, seniors feel sadness, depression, anger, guilt, and loneliness, and, in addition, both their perceived physical health and their actual physical health deteriorate. Older bereaved people also indicate that they have not broken their attachment to their dead spouses; rather they have developed a new connection, an inner representation. Some positive outcomes may occur in terms of a heightened sense of self-discovery and resilience following the loss of a spouse, as well as a renewed meaning in life and, for some, self-transcendence.

- Senior widowers are more likely to want to remarry because of their concerns about facing old age and ill health alone while senior widows are less likely to desire remarriage because they enjoy their newfound freedom. Men receive more social support in their bereavement than women do, yet they report feeling more depressed after their spouses' deaths than women do. Evidence suggests that bereaved men have more increases in poor health and death than women do, which may relate to the depression and general stress that they feel.

- After their wives died, widowers reported a lower quality of life in terms of their emotional, social, and spiritual welfare (i.e., the female-strong domains), while widows reported that after their husbands died, the quality of their lives in terms of dealing with day-to-day matters, financial matters, and their physical health (i.e., male-strong domains) decreased.

- Widowed men are more likely to express resignation and acceptance that their spouses have died, while widowed women were more likely to express stoicism and the need to "soldier on" in spite of their husbands' deaths. Older men who are coping well with their grief are more likely to talk about their loss. Those men who cope well enjoy the freedom to please themselves without having to consider a partner. For older women, those who are comfortable being alone cope better than those who are not. Women report that their married friends often drop them from their social circle, but they gain support from other widows and they volunteer to help others more.

- Senior bereaved parents remember hearing the news of their child's death as if it had just occurred, with the same emotional and physical reactions. Over time, the pain of the bereavement becomes somewhat less intense but not markedly so. It does, however, become an expected part of their lives.

- The deceased child continues to play a major role in older parents' lives, increasingly so as the parents age. Their memories are often idealized thoughts of what might have been if the child had lived, how they might feel differently, how the circumstances of their lives would be changed, and what they had missed in not having their child.

- The bereaved parents often report that they had neglected their other children in their grief, and they feel a desire to join the deceased child in death. However, they fear that, as their deceased child lives within them, their deaths will lead to the second, and final, death of their child.

- Senior nonspousally bereaved people have greater depression and anxiety, although not necessarily enough to be detected through standard psychological tests. Widows are particularly vulnerable.

- Among very senior people, no clear indication exists that bereavement brings about a decline in health or depressive symptoms, but they feel lonelier after a death of a significant person. Very senior people strengthen their mental representations of their loved ones, which impinges more on their realizations of themselves as being survivors, deepening their feelings of loneliness.

KEY TERMS

death avoidance

ego integrity

extrinsic religious motivation

intrinsic religious motivation

locus of control

self-efficacy

self-transcendence

INDIVIDUAL ACTIVITIES

1. Talk to a senior who has been bereaved. Ask the individual to describe his or her feelings about the bereavement. Have the person's feelings changed over time since the bereavement? Are the feelings expressed very different from those that you have felt or believe that you might feel in a bereavement?

2. If possible, visit a palliative care facility and talk to someone who works in that area. What do workers in the area perceive as their greatest challenges in dealing with seniors who are dying?

3. Imagine yourself as a very senior person. What do you want to look back on in your life? What kind of life would you live to make your death an emotionally peaceful one?

4. If you have not read it already, read Canadian author Margaret Laurence's book *The Stone Angel* (McClelland and Stewart, 1995). This book's narrator, 90-year-old Hagar Shipley, poignantly recounts the events of her life in Manitoba, including the bereavements she has experienced and her own views of aging. Do Hagar's reactions surprise you? Do you feel that Laurence accurately portrayed the experiences of a bereaved senior, as presented in this chapter?

GROUP ACTIVITIES

1. In a group of four or five compare your findings from the first individual activity above with those of your classmates. Are there differences that might be attributed to gender, type of bereavement, or cultural/religious background?

2. As a group, watch the movie *Driving Miss Daisy*. What features do you see in the main characters that are consistent with the attitudes toward death and the desires at the end of life that have been described in this chapter?

3. Many of the reactions to bereavement show gender differences based on the traditional upbringing that seniors have had in the past. What do you think the differences (if any) will be in the future as men's and women's roles continue to change? In a group of four or five, discuss what these changes might be, paying attention to the role of culture in defining the expectations placed on men and women.

Suicide

Two Tragedies

▶ John Parmenter Robarts was a Canadian lawyer and premier of Ontario from 1961 to 1971. He was a strong promoter of education and he paved the way for French instruction in Ontario schools. He was responsible for the construction of York University in Toronto and the Ontario Science Centre, and he launched the Ontario Scholarship fund. The John P. Robarts library at the University of Toronto was named for him, as was the Robarts Research Institute at the University of Western Ontario and several other schools. He was given the honour of being made a Companion of the Order of Canada in 1972. After a series of severe strokes, he committed suicide with a shotgun on October 18, 1982, at the age of 65.

Ernest Hemingway was a vital, much-loved (and much-hated) writer. His boisterous ways were well known among the Hollywood set and the media. He loved women, whiskey, and bullfights. Among his many works are *The Sun Also Rises* and *The Snows of Kilimanjaro*. He won the Pulitzer Prize in 1953 for *The Old Man and the Sea*, and he was awarded the Nobel Prize in Literature in 1954. His life was full of dramatic ups and downs, and he served as a model for many on how to live life to the fullest. He was also treated for depression on more than one occasion. On July 2, 1961, just shy of the age of 62 years, Ernest Hemingway killed himself with a shotgun blast to his head.

The two men described in the opening vignette made great contributions to society and were, by any external measures, highly successful. Yet both found life to be unendurable enough to take their own lives. The question of suicide is troubling to society because there is such an expressed desire to preserve lives, our own especially. That some people choose not to live is perplexing to many and shocking to others. The families and friends of those who have committed suicide are typically left with extreme guilt, usually unrealistic, that they could have prevented the suicide, or that they did not repair problematic relationships when the suicide victim was still alive. They are also left with an increased possibility that they, too, will choose death over life (Westefeld et al., 2000). Greater understanding of suicide is clearly necessary.

THE DEFINITION OF SUICIDE

The *Oxford English Reference Dictionary* (Pearsall & Trumble, 1996) defines **suicide** as "the intentional killing of oneself" (p. 1443). This definition fits with the common conceptions of suicide and seems straightforward; however, closer examination indicates that it may be overencompassing in some regards and underencompassing in others.

Regarding the problem of being too inclusive, the example of what happened on 9/11 serves well. It is estimated that perhaps two hundred people jumped from the World Trade Center on that terrible day of September 11, 2001, when the towers were destroyed by terrorists. Presumably, they did this to avoid the more agonizing death that awaited them as the towers burned and collapsed. Their behaviour accords to the dictionary definition of suicide, but most people would not classify their action as suicide. Indeed, legally, by the medical examiner's determination, all these deaths were categorized as homicides, a categorization which intuitively seems more appropriate to most people. Many of the terrorists themselves died as well at this time, yet it is unlikely that they would have said that they were going to commit suicide. On the contrary, they viewed themselves as martyrs, as have many people through the ages who have died for their beliefs (Joiner, 2005). Other examples are those of the mass deaths of members of the Solar Temple in Canada, France, and Switzerland; the Heaven's Gate cult in the United States; and the Peoples Temple group led by Jim Jones in Jonestown, Guyana. Hundreds of people in total, led by highly charismatic leaders, were induced to take their lives in anticipation of either receiving great post-death rewards or avoiding an untenable outcome of living. Many would argue that these deaths were not suicides either but homicides by

the manipulative cult leaders. Also, it is unlikely that the individual who habitually engages in known potentially life-threatening behaviour (e.g., the breathing-impaired person who smokes, the war correspondent who volunteers to cover combat in areas that are under attack) has the end of his or her life as a goal.

Another problem with the dictionary definition of suicide is that "the intentional killing of oneself" suggests an active component in the victim's methodology. This seems to overlook cases in which people have refrained from action in order to bring about their own deaths: the case of the person who refuses proven effective medical treatment for a potentially terminal disease or the vastly different case of the person who stands on a train track without moving as the train bears down, for example. These cases are typically referred to as **passive suicide** because minimal action is taken by these people, who simply initiate a series of events that result in their deaths.

Taking these and other considerations into account, the World Health Organization's (WHO) European Centre's study on suicide, the *WHO/EURO Multicentre Study on Suicidal Behaviour*, defines suicide as the following:

> Suicide is an act with a fatal outcome which the deceased, knowing or expecting a potentially fatal outcome, has initiated and carried out with the purpose of bringing about wanted changes. (De Leo, Burgis, Bertolote, Kerkhof, & Bille-Brahe, 2004, p. 33)

This definition is not problem free. For instance, it is not always possible to determine that the individual knew and expected that his or her action would result in death. The example of the death of Marilyn Monroe is a case in point: in 1962, Ms. Monroe, who had a history of depression and substance abuse, died by ingesting a fatal mixture of drugs and alcohol. Even today, more than 40 years later, many people question whether or not she realized the potentially fatal results of her actions. No one can know what she was thinking at that time, so it is possibly incorrect to label her death, which may have been accidental, as a suicide. Nonetheless, the WHO's definition of suicide probably comes closer to accurately reflecting the realities of suicide and will be used in this chapter.

DEMOGRAPHICS

Ascertaining how many people commit suicide is difficult, first because of the problems in defining suicide, and second because often suicides are hidden. In some cases, this is done by the family and sometimes it is done by officials who know the family and want to spare them the grief and the stigma of having their loved one identified as having taken his or her own life. The problem is even more complex when unsuccessful suicide attempts are considered: we have no way to know how many of these are never reported. However, while recognizing that suicide incidence is underreported, the WHO (2005) revealed the following numbers for Canada in 2001:

- Three thousand six hundred ninety Canadians took their own lives, a rate of 11.9 per 100 000 of the total population. (The rate was about the same in 2003; BC Partners for Mental Health and Addictions Information, 2006.)
- Of these individuals, 2870 were males and 820 were females. Thus, male suicides outnumber female suicides by 3.5 to 1.
- Twenty-seven of these suicides were committed by children between the ages of 5 and 14 years, with equal numbers of males and females.
- Five hundred three of these suicides were committed by young people between the ages of 15 and 24 years. In this age range, the gender difference first appears and remains for the rest of the life span.
- Seniors (people over the age of 65) account for 399 of the total number of suicides.
- That leaves middle adulthood, the years from 25 to 64 as the years in which the greatest number of suicides occur, with ages between 25 and 54 being the years of highest occurrence, especially for males.
- Canada's suicide rate has remained relatively consistent since 1980.

Further, when looking at suicide rates globally, the WHO (2005) reported that the available data indicate the following:

- Industrialized countries have higher suicide rates than do nonindustrialized countries.
- The highest rate is in Lithuania (88.2 per 100 000 population in 2003).
- Canada's suicide rate is about in the middle of industrialized nations, above that of the United Kingdom and slightly above that of the United States.
- Male suicides outnumber female suicides in all countries except for selected parts of China.
- Approximately one million people committed suicide globally in 2000; this is a rate of 16 per 100 000, or 1 death every 40 seconds.
- Since 1960, suicide rates have increased by 60 percent worldwide; suicide is now among the three leading causes of death for those aged 15 to 44 years for both males and females.
- Suicide rates have increased among young people, to the extent that they are now the group at highest risk

in one-third of all countries, including both developed and developing nations.

(Reprinted with permission of the WHO.)

In addition, it was found that women attempt suicide three times more often than men, but men complete suicide three and one-half to four times more often than women. This is the case in all countries for which statistics are recorded, except for China, where the rate of female suicides equals that of males (Joiner, 2005; WHO, 2005). Part of the reason is that women are more likely to ask for help when in a crisis and that women tend to use less lethal means of killing themselves (e.g., poisoning); men use more violent means, such as guns, that are more likely to be fatal (Westefeld et al., 2000).

The suicide of one person is estimated to deeply affect at least six other people, leaving them with more guilt than in the case of other forms of death and a greater possibility of complicated grief (discussed in Chapter 10; Rando, 1993; Westefeld et al., 2000). That means roughly 15 percent of the Canadian population is personally affected by the suicide of someone in a given year. In addition, the suicide rate among Canada's First Nations is three to four times higher than in the general population (Weir, 2001). Among First Nations youth, it is five to seven times higher than the Canadian average (Health Canada, 2006; Royal Commission on Aboriginal People, 1995) and among Inuit youth, it is 11 times higher than the Canadian average (Health Canada, 2006). These phenomena and tragedies are discussed more fully later in the chapter.

WHAT CAUSES A PERSON TO COMMIT SUICIDE?

Risk Factors

In determining what causes a person to commit suicide, studies have compared suicidal people with nonsuicidal people. In an extensive review of the literature, Westefeld et al. (2000) determined that no single factor can be isolated, but some of the following aspects tend to be present in suicidal people. The more aspects that are present, the higher the risk for suicide is thought to be.

1. *Psychological problems.* Certain psychological problems and disorders are highly correlated with suicidality. These problems include depression, schizophrenia and other disorders involving psychosis, personality disorders (borderline personality disorder in particular), neuroticism, and panic disorders.
2. *Personality factors.* Suicidal persons tend to be more submissive, generally unpleasant, and easily agitated than nonsuicidal people. In addition,

suicidal persons seem to have more difficulty in controlling and regulating their emotions than others. They are generally more anxious and depressed as well, although not enough to be classified as having a psychological disorder.

3. *Cognitive factors*. The thinking patterns of suicidal persons show more perfectionism and irrationality in their beliefs than do the thinking patterns of nonsuicidal persons. Their approach to problem solving is less effective as well: they show less ability to generate alternative solutions to problems and less skill at anticipating the possible negative outcomes of these alternatives. Their solutions to problems are more likely to be inappropriate, partly because the experiential basis for dealing with problems is more likely to be biased toward a better memory for negative events than for positive events. They view their lives as being controlled mainly by forces outside of themselves, and their attitudes toward the future are mainly negative. Overall, their thinking is characterized by hopelessness and helplessness, with the belief that nothing will ever change for them and they are powerless to change their life circumstances.

4. *Environmental stress*. People who are suicidal often have or have had more stressful life circumstances than their nonsuicidal peers. They are more likely to have been physically or sexually abused, or both, and to come from highly dysfunctional families; their personal relationships are more likely to have changed for the worse and they typically have less social support than others, sometimes even being socially isolated. In addition, they may have experienced or are experiencing events in their lives that are overwhelmingly stressful or they may have lives of chronic stress.

5. *Alcohol and drug use*. Compared with nonsuicidal people, people who are suicidal use more alcohol and drugs. It may be that the use of these substances is to alleviate the depression and anxiety that many suicidal people feel, but their effects are often even more detrimental to the individual, lowering inhibitions, impairing rational thinking, alienating people who are potential sources of social support, and causing further problems.

6. *Physical illness*. People with chronic physical illnesses, especially those that involve pain, are more likely to be suicidal than other people.

7. *Behavioural indicators*. People who have attempted suicide previously are at higher risk for subsequent attempts than are other people. As well, the more recent the suicide attempt and the more lethal the attempt, the higher the risk of a subsequent attempt. A critical behavioural indicator is a verbalization that the individual is contemplating harm to himself or herself. In fact, from the psychological counsellor's perspective, one of the best indicators of a possible suicide attempt is how the client answers the question "Have you been feeling so bad lately that you have thought about harming yourself?" (p. 453).

In most countries, such as the United States, married people are less likely to commit suicide than are unmarried people, perhaps because of the enhanced possibility for social support and the increased feeling of responsibility that marriage can bring. Curiously though, being married does not seem to serve as a protection against suicide in Canada, where the rates of married and nonmarried people committing suicide are roughly equal (Leenaars, Yang, & Lester, 1993).

Models of Suicide
Émile Durkheim's Classification

French sociologist Émile Durkheim was one of the first social scientists to investigate suicide. His research led him to the belief that suicide was highly related to social factors. Noting that societies provide individuals with a sense of belongingness; structure, regulation, and stability to help govern their lives; and many other things, Durkheim (1966/1897) posited that suicide was greatly affected by how strongly the individual felt connected to the rest of society, that is, his or her **social integration,** and by how well the society regulated its members. He demonstrated this by classifying suicide into types:

1. **Egoistic suicide** occurs when people do not feel connected with the rest of society. These suicides take place among those who feel that they cannot relate to society or take part in society as a normal person because they have particular qualities that set them apart from others. For example, the person with a genius intellect or the amazingly talented musician may feel that other people do not understand or relate to them, and they cannot understand and identify with others. They may feel quite alone and disconnected from the lives that others lead and the interests others have.

2. **Altruistic suicide** is the name given to the act of a person taking his or her life for the benefit of others. These individuals may be overly connected to a society that exerts a great deal of control over the individual, and they may see it as their duty to die for the group. Examples of this may be seen in those who take their lives to make a political point, such as suicide bombers or self-immolating Buddhists monks who take their own lives to

protest violence. Leming and Dickinson (2002) also note a type of altruistic suicide that is sadly on the rise in Japan. This type of suicide, *karoshi*, is found mainly in middle-aged men who are so integrated into the work group that they work themselves to the point of exhaustion, and subsequently to death, to demonstrate their loyalty to the work group. They regard their extreme overwork as "for the good of the company."

3. **Anomic suicide** occurs in people who once felt connected to society but now feel let down by the social institutions that had sustained them. An example of this might be the individual who has faithfully worked for an institution for many years, taking a large part of his or her identity and self-worth from the work, and who is suddenly left without a job because of institutional restructuring or downsizing. The connection to his or her immediate society is broken and new connections are not readily available, leaving the person rudderless in a changed environment.

4. **Fatalistic suicide** is said to occur mainly in highly regulating, controlling, and restrictive societies that demand social integration from citizens but allow for very little personal fulfillment. The despair felt by people under totalitarian regimes, or by women in some cultures, may lead to this form of suicide, as might the frustration and hopelessness felt by workers compelled to work for companies with unreasonable and inflexible rules.

Durkheim's formulation was not aimed at finding the cause of suicide but at understanding more clearly society's role in suicide. The supporting evidence of risk factors notwithstanding, many people feel disengaged from society or overly engaged in it, but they do not take their own lives. Social factors, then, are part of the understanding of suicide but not the whole explanation.

Edwin Shneidman's Cubic Model

After many years of studying people who attempted suicide, as well as the histories and, when present, the notes of those who have completed suicide, Edwin Shneidman wrote a classic book entitled *Definition of Suicide* (1985). In this book, he suggested that commonalities exist among suicides, while recognizing the many individual differences that exist as well. Shneidman formulated the cubic model, a model comprising three factors, which he believed interact to predict suicidal behaviour. Each factor represents one dimension of a cube. The first factor is what Shneidman termed **press**, or the events to which the individual reacts. These events might be positive or negative, but only the ones interpreted by the individual as negative move him or her toward suicidal behaviour.

Such events might include rejection, humiliation, or failure, which the individual perceives as a further indication that life is intolerable. The second factor is pain, or what he has termed **psychache.** Shneidman believed that the greatest commonality among suicidal people is the presence of unendurable psychological pain (e.g., depression, sadness, anguish, despair) resulting from frustrated psychological needs (e.g., lack of belonging or feeling valued, lack of intimate companionship). The third factor is **perturbation,** or the state of being upset. This state may derive from any number of possible sources, but once suicidal people are upset, they become increasingly more so. Their thinking becomes more constricted and irrational, leading them to the conclusion that suicide is the only answer to their seemingly hopeless situation.

Clearly, the three factors postulated by Shneidman (1985) interact with one another. Thus, an event may occur, press (e.g., loss of a meaningful relationship), resulting in deep upset (perturbation) and increased psychache. When press, psychache, and perturbation reach extreme levels, suicidal behaviour in a vulnerable individual is often the result, claimed Shneidman.

Thomas Joiner's Additional Factor

While recognizing the roles of the factors noted by Shneidman (1985)—such as the importance of a perception of lack of belongingness and the sense of being worthless, incompetent, ineffective, or a burden to others—Joiner (2005) pointed out that another factor is also critical as a precursor to suicide. He stated that human beings have a strong instinct for self-preservation and will, in the vast majority of cases, take extreme measures to avoid pain or death. Those who take their own lives, however, seek what others avoid. He asked how this was possible. His answer was that those who commit suicide build up to it gradually, providing a trajectory leading to the suicide. The trajectory can be traversed by many possible means. Given that the individual possesses the other two factors crucial in the decision to commit suicide (lack of belongingness and lack of a sense of worth or effectiveness), he or she also has the ability to overcome the strong urge for self-preservation. This ability could be attained by having a history of exposure to death, violence, or pain, or through prolonged and intense rumination about suicide and the details surrounding the action itself. Thus, he said, suicide is more common among those who have been physically or sexually abused as children, those who have terminal illnesses, and those who have lived in violent surroundings, such as prisons. He also suggested that this is the reason that having attempted suicide previously is a warning sign for further attempts: having once tried (and failed), the individual is more accustomed to the action and less sensitive toward the discomfort involved in it. That is, the individual becomes used to the idea of taking his or her own life and less sensitive to the pain and discomfort attendant on it.

Many think that the violent and suicidal themes of some music, such as alternative rock and heavy metal, may also decrease sensitivity to the thought of suicide. Research on this idea is discussed in Box 9.1. Box 9.2 indicates the warning signs that someone may be contemplating suicide or is ready to commit the act.

ATTITUDES TOWARD SUICIDE

It is not surprising that the research data indicate a generally negative view about suicide (see, for example, Beautrais, Horwood, & Fergusson, 2004; Dahlen & Canetto, 2002; Parker, Cantrell, & Demi, 1997; Smyth & MacLachlan, 2004; Wastell & Shaw, 1999). Although both Canadians and Americans see suicide as undesirable, Canadians are somewhat less negative in their views than are Americans (Domino & Leenaars, 1989; Leenaars & Domino, 1993). Specifically, Canadians are less likely to see suicide as a moral transgression and more likely to accept suicide as an answer to problems. In addition, Canadians are less likely to attribute suicide to mental illness than are Americans. In a survey of 196 widely diverse English-speaking urban Canadian adults, Domino and Leenaars (1995) found the following:

- Sixty-three percent of Canadians surveyed felt that suicide is a serious moral transgression.
- Fifty-two percent believed that almost everyone has thought about suicide at one time or another, and 49 percent felt that anyone is a potential suicide victim.

BOX 9.1   The Effects of Music on Suicide

The emergence of some styles of music among young fans has alarmed many because of the death and, particularly, suicidal content of some of the music. The question has been asked, "Does listening to such music increase the tendency toward suicide?" Studies can merely look at the relationship between music preferences and attitudes or thoughts about suicide because, methodologically, determining causality could only be done by procedures that would expose some people to a heightened risk of suicide, an unethical situation at best. Consequently, we do not know whether a preference for a particular type of music influences the tendency to suicide acceptance or suicidal thought, whether having the propensity to accept suicide and thoughts about it inclines someone to prefer a particular type of music, or whether other factors are involved that might lead to both music preference and tendency to suicidal behaviour.

Parental fears of their children's preferences for heavy metal, alternative, and punk rock and the possible association with suicidal tendencies receive mixed support. On one hand, Scheel and Westefeld (1999) found that adolescents who liked heavy metal music scored higher on measures of suicidal ideation than did adolescents who preferred another type of music, and Lester and Whipple (1996) found that adolescents who preferred heavy metal and alternative music had thought more about suicide in the past than had adolescents with different musical preferences. On the other hand, Burge, Goldblat, and Lester (2002) found that although no relationship between music preference and suicidal ideation was present among adolescent females, adolescent males who preferred country music and pop rock had higher scores on a measure of suicidal thinking than did adolescent males who preferred other types of music.

Steven Stack has done a great deal of research in this area with adults (1998, 2000, 2002) and found that adults who like blues music are no different in their acceptance of suicide from those who like heavy metal music. But he has found a difference in acceptance of suicide in those who enjoy opera as compared with those who do not. Suicide is present in 20 percent of the 50 most frequently performed operas and in 25 percent of the 306 operas listed in the foremost opera guides (Stack, 2002). In opera, suicide is portrayed most often as a response to an event that has brought dishonour to the individual. A striking example of this is the well-known suicide of Madama Butterfly in the opera of the same name. In this opera, Madama Butterfly marries an American military officer and gives birth to his child. He leaves, promising to return, but when he does, he brings with him an American wife and makes claims on Madama Butterfly's child. Madama Butterfly gives up the child and commits suicide at this dishonour. Stack's findings reveal that opera fans are more accepting of suicide than are nonfans but only when the suicide is a response to dishonour; they are no more accepting of suicide when the cause is physical illness, bankruptcy, or simple fatigue with living.

Although interesting and worthy of further study, no concrete causative role exists between types of music and suicide.

BOX 9.2 Warning Signs That Someone May be Suicidal

The following are some of the warning signs that someone may be contemplating suicide or is ready to commit the act:

1. *Talking about suicide and death.* Someone who does not habitually talk about suicide and death but who begins doing so should be taken seriously and attempts should be made to help this person. This does not include common figures of speech, such as, "I'll kill myself if [fill in the politician of your choice] is elected!"

2. *Withdrawing from friends and family.* Pulling away from people with whom the individual has normally associated and holds a caring relationship is sometimes a sign of depression and suicidal thinking. It is often a signal that the person is pulling away from his or her current state of living, preparing for death. Sometimes this is first recognized when friends and family try to help the individual but are met with anger or increased cheerlessness.

3. *Changing behaviour, attitudes, appearance, or thinking, whether sudden or gradual.* This could include such statements as, "I'd be better off dead" or "Everyone would be better off without me," or increased drug and alcohol consumption. Also, the person may show an uncharacteristic lack of interest in personal appearance, have mood swings or outbursts of anger, lose a sense of humour, or joke excessively.

4. *Giving away possessions, finishing tasks, or planning for the future of others.* When an individual gives away personal possessions, especially those that have been meaningful; takes actions that can be construed as "tying up loose ends"; or initiates steps to protect others, such as children or pets who will be left behind, it strongly suggests that this individual is planning to commit suicide in the very near future.

5. *Demonstrating uncharacteristically reckless behaviour.* Sometimes suicidal people begin to engage in activities that are high risk, such as the overconsumption of alcohol followed by driving, or the taking of illegal and dangerous drugs. This behaviour suggests that they are courting an end to their lives.

6. *Lacking interest in normal activities.* Suicidal people often lack interest in activities, such as work, hobbies, or family recreation, that they previously enjoyed.

7. *Having sudden changes in eating and sleeping behaviours.* Suicidal people often show eating and sleeping disturbances. If someone loses or gains weight rapidly without consciously trying to change his or her weight, or develops insomnia, disturbing dreams, restless sleep, or sleepwalking, the person might have a problem that needs attention.

8. *Showing a sudden elevation of mood.* When a person who has been despondent suddenly seems to be happy, many people assume that the depression has lifted. But it may be that the person has finalized his or her suicide plans and is awaiting the chance to carry them out.

9. *Obtaining access to lethal means of self-harm.* The individual who is contemplating suicide may have to acquire the means with which to commit the act, such as stockpiling drugs or acquiring a firearm.

10. *Experiencing a recent loss or serious disappointment.* Suicides often follow on the heels of losing something or someone that the person has treasured, such as the loss of a job or a meaningful relationship.

Children and adolescents show many of the same warning signs when they are contemplating suicide. In addition, they may also show other behaviours:

- running away from home
- acting in disruptive ways
- showing an uncharacteristic lack of attentiveness, attendance, or performance at school, with a drop in academic performance
- avoiding touch, reward, or praise
- being accident prone
- self-mutilating
- displaying impulsivity
- showing extreme dependency
- increasing compulsive behaviour
- having unrealistically high self-expectations

- Eighty-one percent do not believe that suicide is normal behaviour.
- Eighty percent do not think that suicide is sometimes the only answer to a problem, but only 51 percent disagreed with the statement "there may be situations where the only reasonable solution is suicide."
- Seventy-seven percent believed that it is acceptable to intervene in someone's decision to take his or her own life.
- Thirty-one percent agreed with the idea that suicide is acceptable when a person has an incurable illness, with 33 percent disagreeing and 36 percent undecided.

- Eight-three percent believed that suicide is a cry for help, with 67 percent believing that people who attempt suicide do not really want to die and 58 percent believing that those whose suicide attempt was unsuccessful were not serious in their wish to die in the first place.
- Forty-eight percent believed that people who threaten to commit suicide rarely do so and that these people are trying to get sympathy from others.
- Only 31 percent of those surveyed believe that people who commit suicide are mentally ill, but more than 80 percent believe that suicide victims are depressed and lonely.
- Between 50 percent and 60 percent of the respondents to the survey believed that people who commit suicide had poor family relations in their younger years.
- Fifty-two percent believed that suicides are typically impulsive, and 65 percent felt that the suicide victim's family had no idea of what was about to happen.
- Thirty-five percent agreed with the statement "Once a person is suicidal, he/she is suicidal forever."

Beyond these findings are the other factors that influence attitudes toward suicide. One large factor is the motivation behind the suicidal behaviour. If the suicidal behaviour is the result of an incurable or debilitating illness, acceptance and understanding of the behaviour increase (Dahlen & Canetto, 2002; Rogers, Gueulette, Abbey-Hines, Carney, & Werth, 2001; Smyth & MacLachlan, 2004; Westefeld, Sikes, Ansley, & Yi, 2004). Note that this refers only to acceptance and understanding, not to approval; respondents to the questions asked by researchers examining attitudes about suicide consistently reported a negative view toward suicide, but under some conditions, predominantly physical illness, they indicated that they understood the suicide behaviour even if they did not condone it.

Another factor that makes suicidal behaviour more understandable, though not acceptable, revolves around the theme of loss (Smyth & McLachlan, 2004). Among postsecondary students in particular, the loss of intimate bonds with another, loss of physical abilities even if not the result of a life-threatening illness, and loss of a job or money are examples of situations that make suicidal behaviour more understandable. The theme of loss undoubtedly involves what Shneidman (1985) referred to as psychache in the suicide victim. Thus, when suicidal behaviour is seen as the result of emotional pain, it is more understandable.

The effects of age of the respondent are confusing. On one hand, Segal, Mincic, Coolidge, and O'Riley (2004) found that older adults tend to be more understanding and accepting of suicidal behaviour than are younger adults, under some circumstances. As opposed to adults under the age of 26, they found that people over the age of 60 are more likely to regard suicide as normal in some situations. Moreover, the older adults these researchers questioned were less likely to characterize the suicide victim as depressed or lonely, or to regard the suicide victim as crying for help. Consistent with this is research by Parker, Cantrell, and Demi (1997), who found that older adults, particularly, empathize with suicide victims who are ill, especially with cancer, but again, their view of suicide is negative overall. On the other hand, Domino and Groth (1997) and Neeleman, Halpern, Leon, and Lewis (1997) found that younger adults are more accepting of suicide than are older adults, while Sorjonen (2002, 2002–2003) found no effects of age on attitudes toward suicide. The reasons for these discrepancies are unknown, but clearly further research is needed; the differences have implications for suicide-prevention programs: if seniors are more accepting and empathic about suicidal behaviour, they may be more prone to suicidal behaviour themselves, and perhaps they should constitute a more critical target group for suicide intervention.

A similarly confusing situation exists in determining the effects of the respondents' gender on their attitudes toward suicide. Some researchers, such as Domino and Leenaars (1989), Beautrais et al. (2004), Smyth and MacLachlan (2004), and Parker et al. (1997), found no gender differences; other researchers found males to be more accepting of suicide than females are (e.g., Dahlen & Canetto, 2002; Stack, 1996–1997); and still others have found females to be less critical of suicidal persons than are males (Norton, Durlak, & Richards, 1989; Overholser, Hemstreet, Spirito, & Vyse, 1989).

A more consistent result is found when the relationship between the respondent and the suicide victim is examined. In a survey of mental health counsellors, Rogers et al. (2001) found that acceptance of the decision to commit suicide was least accepted when the suicide victim was a client, became progressively more acceptable when the victim was a friend, and became even more so when the victim was proposed to be the counsellor himself or herself. Similar findings were obtained when people were asked about their attitudes about suicide (Jenner & Niesling, 2000; Mueller & Waas, 2002). It appears, then, that suicide may be seen as a rational answer to a life situation regarding the self, less so for a friend, and even less so for a mental health client. The attitude seems to be "If *I* choose suicide, I'm making a rational, acceptable choice, but my friend, making the same decision, is not so likely to be making a rational, acceptable choice, and my client is definitely not making a rational, acceptable choice."

A further research finding concerning attitudes about suicide is somewhat troubling. Wastell and

Shaw (1999) asked Australian college students who were training to be teachers about their attitudes toward suicidal behaviour in adolescents. Their responses indicated that they believed that suicidal behaviour was a cry for help; however, they saw those who exhibited this behaviour as being manipulative. If behaviour is considered to be manipulative, the response is likely to be less supportive and caring than if the behaviour is seen to be a genuine communication about distress. Teachers who are in contact with children and adolescents for long periods each day are in the unique position of being able to observe them and potentially detect behaviour that might predict a suicide attempt. If these teachers regard the behaviour as manipulative, though, they are more likely to overlook or ignore the message of distress the child or adolescent is sending. Intervention that could have helped the child or adolescent may not, then, be forthcoming.

SUICIDE AND CHILDREN AND ADOLESCENTS

It seems impossible that children and adolescents, who should have their lives ahead of them, could choose to take their own lives. Yet in 2001 in Canada, 27 children

between the ages of 5 years and 14 years, and 503 young people between the ages of 15 and 24, committed suicide. In the 5- to 14-years-old group, no gender difference is seen, but in the 15- to 24-years-old group, the ratio of males to females takes on the ratio seen in adults, almost four to one. The rates of suicide for young people have remained relatively constant in Canada over the past three decades (WHO, 2005), but in the United States, a dramatic increase has occurred, from 4.5 per 100 000 in 1950 to 12.9 per 100 000 in the 1990s (Leming & Dickinson, 2002).

Little is known about suicide in young children, but the suspicion exists that the rates may be higher because some supposedly accidental deaths may have been intentional on the part of the child. For example, in many cases it cannot be definitively determined whether a young child who runs into traffic or who puts a plastic bag over his or her head is acting with intent or has merely shown a typical childhood lack of understanding of the possible consequences of the act. It is known, however, that many young children have thoughts about suicide, and these children, although lacking access to lethal means, are at a higher risk for suicide later in their lives (DeSpelder & Strickland, 2005).

For adolescents, such as Meghan in Box 9.3, many of the same risk factors that apply to adults are relevant.

BOX 9.3 Meghan

Meghan, aged 15 years, is eying her mother's bottle of anti-depressants and wondering whether it has enough pills left to kill her. Her first boyfriend, James, just broke up with her. This is always a hard situation for a teenager, but for Meghan, it is profoundly tragic because James was her only friend, the only person who listened to her and supported her in her troubled life with her family and school. Her family has moved seven times in the last 10 years, and Meghan has attended five different schools. She is always behind in school because of the relocations, and the teachers sometimes seem impatient with her. Her grades are low and she has little hope of ever being accepted into a college or university, even if she could find a way to pay for it. It matters little to her, since she has no particular dreams of a future or a career, especially now that James is gone.

By high school, she had given up trying to make friends because of the pain she knew would ensue when the family moved again, a move she felt certain would come, as it had in the past when her father lost his job because of his alcohol addiction. Her mother is sunk in a depression, and her

medication seems to help her very little, certainly not enough for her to pay attention to Meghan. Her older brother has become immersed in the drug world himself and is unavailable to the family because of this. Meghan feels completely alone; she is certain that this will never change, that she has nothing in her life to plan for or dream about. She remembers when her uncle committed suicide and how she secretly wondered whether his choice had not been the only one available in his circumstances.

One year ago, before she met James, she took 10 Aspirins in an attempt to end her life, but she vomited immediately and lacked the courage to try again. She has only told James about her attempt and he seemed to understand, even saying that maybe one day they would commit suicide together. But he still left her. She picks up the telephone to call the local suicide hotline; maybe they will have an answer for her. The line is busy. Her feeling now is that she is just a loser who will never be able to escape her tortured existence except through death.

On April 8, 1994, 27-year-old musician and pop icon Kurt Cobain of the musical group Nirvana was found dead of a self-inflicted gunshot wound in the garage of his home in Seattle, Washington. He had led a troubled life, with substance abuse and other suicide attempts. Despite the adulation of many fans and the interventions of his friends and family, Cobain rejected life (see his suicide note in Box 9.5).

A great deal of evidence indicates that suicide rates increase in young adults and adolescents (though not adults) after media coverage of a suicide (Gould, Wallenstein, & Davidson, 1989), and certainly media attention was given to Cobain's suicide. It was greatly feared that this would cause a multitude of suicides of other young people in response; suicides among young people are often found in clusters, with one suicide triggering more (Gould et al., 1989). These suicides may occur by prearrangement, with several young people agreeing to commit suicide at the same time, or by the effect of imitation, with one suicide lowering the inhibitions others might have of committing suicide and glamorizing suicide as a solution to problems. It is important to note that the young people in these suicide clusters have typically already shown characteristics that indicate the possibility of suicide.

After Cobain's suicide, the clustering effect in Seattle did not emerge however. Much credit for this is given to the way the Seattle media handled this event and the role played by the Seattle Crisis Clinic and Cobain's wife, Courtney Love. A candle-light vigil was held in which a tape made by Courtney Love reading excerpts from Cobain's suicide note, interspersed with her raging in evident anger and pain, was played. The director of the Seattle Crisis Clinic also attended and spoke to the seven thousand or more fans to educate them about suicide and to ask them to reach out to one another with comfort and compassion. The telephone number of the Crisis Clinic was given, and the media, in their reporting of Cobain's suicide, included this telephone number in all their coverage. In addition, the Crisis Clinic held a press conference for the media to further educate them about suicide, to publicize its availability to help, and to emphasize the tragedy of not only Cobain's suicide but of all suicide cases. In this incidence, suicide was portrayed by the media as a tragedy, not as a glamorous solution to problems.

In the following seven weeks, only one suicide that could be linked to Cobain took place in the Seattle area (Jobes, Berman, O'Carroll, Eastgard, & Knickmeyer, 1996). However, the Crisis Clinic registered a significant increase in the number of calls for help made to them. Cobain's tragic death may have served to provide an opportunity for people to become more informed about suicide, and the Crisis Clinic and the Seattle media's handling of the event may have saved several lives.

One factor that has been found to be particularly relevant to adolescent suicide is social disruption and discord. Adolescents who have experienced separation from their families in early life, family dissolution, family conflict, or social isolation are at a higher risk for suicide than other adolescents. These young people often have little social support, with families that may be unresponsive to their needs and emotional concerns. If other members of the family have committed suicide, or have psychological disorders, including substance abuse, the risk for suicide in the adolescent is heightened. In addition, problems with school or work, or the adolescent's sense of "drifting" through life rather than being actively engaged in activities or goal-oriented behaviours (such as attending college or university) may also increase the tendency to suicide. Box 9.4 discusses the phenomenon of copycat suicides, a rise in suicide rate of adolescents and young adults that is often found after a publicized suicide. For further discussion of adolescent suicide, see Brent and Mann (2003); Gould, Shaffer, and Greenberg (2003); and Wagner and Zimmerman (2006).

SUICIDE AND SENIORS

As medicine has progressed in its ability to prolong life, more people are reaching an old age. In the United States, seniors have the highest suicide rate of all age groups (Westefeld et al., 2000); in Canada, people in middle adulthood account for the highest number of suicides. However, seniors do make up a substantial percentage—more than 9 percent—of all suicide deaths (WHO, 2005). This rate of suicides among the older adults in Canada may be an underestimation; the usual problems of defining suicide exist in these cases, along with additional problems. For example, determining whether or not an overdose of medication is deliberate when the individual in question is somewhat cognitively impaired

BOX 9.5   Suicide Notes

Frances and Courtney, I'll be at your
altar. Please keep going Courtney,

for Frances for her life will be so much
happier without me. I LOVE YOU.

I LOVE YOU.
Suicide note of Kurt Cobain, musician, died April 5,
1994

Dear World, I am leaving you because I
am bored. I feel I have lived long enough.
I am leaving you with your worries in this
sweet cesspool—good luck.

Suicide note of George Sanders, actor, died April
25, 1972

I must end it. There's no hope left. I'll be
at peace. No one had anything to do
with this.
My decision totally.

Suicide note of Freddie Prinze, comedian, died
January 29, 1977

To my friends: My work is done. Why wait?

Suicide note of George Eastman, inventor, died
March 14, 1932

What is in the minds of those people who are
about to commit suicide? One of the best indictors
of this might be thought to be the notes left by
those who take their own lives. However, the
majority of people who commit suicide do not
leave a suicide note behind; in fact, it is estimated
that only about one-quarter to one-third leave
notes (Salib, Cawley, & Healy, 2002; Shiori et al.,
2005). Evidence regarding who leaves notes and

who does not is inconsistent and highly diverse.
Some studies found that women leave notes more
often than men do, but other studies found that
men are more likely to leave notes than women,
for example (see Salib & Maximous, 2002, for a
review). The contents of suicide notes, however,
bear more similarity: most are very brief, many are
often banal and disorganized, and most indicate
the themes of unbearable emotional pain (sometimes because of physical causes) and disrupted or
problematic interpersonal relationships (O'Connor
& Leenaars, 2004). Although popular stereotypes
suggest that women kill themselves for love while
men kill themselves for money, an examination of
suicide notes suggests that this is not the case.

Canetto and Lester (2002) examined the suicide notes of 56 American men and women and
found that love and relationships comprised the
predominant theme of the notes for both men and
women. The same results were found in Germany
(Linn & Lester, 1997), Hong Kong (Ho, Yip, Chiu, &
Halliday, 1998), Hungary (Leenaars, Fekete,
Wenckstern, & Osvath, 1998), Northern Ireland
(O'Connor & Leenaars, 2004), and in the United
Kingdom (McClelland, Reicher, & Booth, 2000). No
gender differences are found in Canadian suicide
notes either, but unlike American suicide notes,
notes written by Canadians are more likely to
include statements indicating their desire to leave
a distressing situation (Leenaars, 1992).

The results of leaving a note behind are profound: the recipients of the notes are left with
even more guilt and distress than the families of
those who commit suicide without leaving a note,
especially if the note is self-blaming (Rudestam &
Agnelli, 1987).

because of age and is taking a multitude of drugs for age-
related physical conditions is difficult. Another example
can be found in cases in which the individual dies simply
because he or she has stopped taking appropriate life-
sustaining measures, such as taking medications consistently or ingesting proper food and drink. This form of
passive suicide may be especially prevalent among seniors
who have basically lost the will and desire to live.

Particular attention is paid to cases of seniors
because so many of the possible predictors of suicide are
often present as a function of aging. For example, it is
more likely that chronic illnesses and pain are present in
seniors than in other age groups and that a significant
attrition of social support for seniors has occurred
through deaths and infirmities of older friends and family members. Younger friends and family members are

often so occupied with their own responsibilities that
they may have little time for providing support to seniors. Because of age and infirmities, seniors are more
likely to need assistance in living, which may be difficult
to obtain. Sometimes, when assistance is obtained, seniors, having lived lives of assisting others, find it difficult
to accept the assistance and feel they are a burden on
their families and society.

Older adults come from a generation in which
expressing personal distress and reaching out for help
were not as acceptable as they are today; as a result they
indicate their distress less and communicate suicidal
intent less than younger people. Additionally, Western
society places a premium on youth and vitality, qualities
that may be sorely missed by seniors. However, such
factors as living alone, financial problems, and a death or

illness in the family have not been consistently found to affect the suicide rate of seniors (Steffens & Blazer, 1999). It is likely, then, that many of the conventional predictors of suicide, while often present, are not as useful when determining the risk level for older adults as when examining younger people. This is troubling as well because, besides possibly being more tolerant of suicide, seniors are increasingly likely to use more violent and lethal means of committing suicide, and they use suicide attempts as a means of communicating their distress less often than younger people (DeLeo & Spathonis, 2004; Steffens & Blazer, 1999). Intervention programs to prevent suicide among seniors become more difficult to develop and deliver when the highest-risk people cannot be more readily identified. This is a critical situation because the number of suicides among seniors has increased globally, especially in Asian and Latin countries, and as the baby-boom generation ages, the number of people aged 60 years or older will represent about 14 percent of the total population of the world (DeLeo & Spathonis, 2004).

SUICIDE AND NATIVE PEOPLES

In January 1993, people in Canada and around the world saw a video of six 12- to 14-year-old Innu children in Davis Inlet, Newfoundland and Labrador, inhaling noxious gasoline fumes from plastic bags. The children fought their rescuers and screamed that they wanted to die. This horrifying and tragic video made formerly complacent or uninformed people aware of the desperate situation of some Indigenous Peoples in Canada. As mentioned earlier, the suicide rate for Aboriginal Peoples in Canada is three to four times higher than the rate for non-Indigenous Peoples; for First Nations youth, it is five to seven times higher; and for Inuit youth, it is eleven times higher.

After the televising of the tragedy at Davis Inlet, attention was finally focused on the problems of Aboriginal Peoples in Canada, a focus long overdue. In 1995 a Royal Commission on Aboriginal Peoples focusing on suicide was published. It estimated that approximately 25 percent of the accidental deaths among Canadian Aboriginals were, in fact, suicides. A great deal of variability exists across groups of Aboriginal Peoples, with some groups, such as those in Davis Inlet, showing much higher suicide rates than other groups. The Royal Commission highlighted the continuing disruption of cultural identity as being a major factor behind the suicides, although noting that many other complex factors play a part, as is the case in all suicides.

Canada has a long history of the dominant culture (white, Anglo) devaluing and disrupting Native culture through dislocating Aboriginal groups to progressively marginalized and inappropriate areas. Even today, in northwestern Ontario, 60 percent of Native communities have no potable fresh water (Webster, 2006). This situation is particularly difficult because the culture of Native Peoples relies heavily on geographical location. Vine Deloria (1994, 1999) makes the case that the land serves as the basis for the identity of Native Peoples. He feels that the European mode of understanding life is through time, placing historical events in a clear chronology. But for Aboriginal Peoples of North America, life is understood through space—not *when* it happened, but *where* it happened.

In addition to the removal of the Indigenous Peoples from their traditional homes, Canada's policy beginning in the 1960s and lasting for nearly three decades was to acculturate Native children by removing them from their family homes and placing them in residential schools. They were required to abandon their cultural norms and even their languages to better assimilate into the dominant white Anglo culture. Many Native children were even taken away from their families and communities and placed in foster homes. On returning to their family homes, many children felt that they did not belong anywhere anymore, undoubtedly resulting in a feeling of dislocation, loss of identity, lowered self-esteem, and understandably, great anger (Kirmayer, Brass, & Tait, 2000; Kirmayer, Simpson, & Cargo, 2003).

In an examination of completed suicides in 80 bands of Native Peoples in British Columbia, Chandler and Lalonde (1998) found that bands that had self-government; involvement in land claims; and band control of education, health services, cultural facilities, and police and fire service had no suicides, while bands lacking these factors had extremely high rates. These data, being correlative, cannot be used to establish a causal link between any factors and suicide rates. However, it is difficult not to conclude that people who live in bands that have none of the amenities that are typically taken for granted in non-Indigenous communities feel less connected to the wider society and feel more despair in general, factors that are highly related to suicide.

Higher rates of suicide are also found in the Indigenous Peoples of New Zealand and Australia, as well as the United States, where governmental policies have disrupted Aboriginal culture. None of these rates are as high as those of Canada (Hunter & Harvey, 2002; Lester, 2001).

In concluding this section, it is perhaps most fitting to quote the words of Chief Jean-Charles Piétacho of the Mingan First Nation:

Collective despair, or collective lack of hope, will lead us to collective suicide. This type of suicide can take many forms, foreshadowed by many possible signs: identity crisis, loss of pride, every kind of dependence, denial of our customs and traditions, degradation of our environment, weakening of our language, abandonment of our struggle for our Aboriginal rights, our autonomy and our culture, uncaring acceptance of violence, passive acknowledgement of lack of work and unemployment, corruption of our morals, tolerance of drugs and idleness, parental surrendering of responsibilities, lack of respect for elders, envy of those who try to keep their heads up and who might succeed, and so on. (Royal Commission on Aboriginal Peoples, 1995, p. 38)

SUICIDE PREVENTION

Suicide will never be completely eradicated as long as people experience unhappiness in the world, and eliminating everyone's unhappiness is not possible. But measures can and have been put in place to reduce the numbers of suicides. In Canada, almost every community has suicide prevention centres and hotlines. A major goal has been to educate people about suicide and the warning signs that someone may be about to engage in suicidal behaviour and to provide information about where help can be obtained. Such strategies as counselling for psychological problems, addictions, and domestic violence aim to reduce the despair that so often engenders suicidal behaviour. Professional counsellors, peer counsellors, teachers, nurses, and volunteers have been instrumental in these efforts.

Because youth suicide is of particular concern, programs for suicide prevention have been placed in many schools, yet when examining the efficacy of these programs, the results are conflicting, with no clear effectiveness in preventing suicidal behaviour (Hayden & Lauer, 2000; Stuart, Waalen, & Haelstromm, 2003). Aseltine and DeMartino (2004) reported on one successful program that reduced suicide attempts among young people, although not suicidal thinking. The Signs of Suicide Prevention Program combined education about suicide with individual self-evaluation for depression. Young people were taught to recognize warning signs of suicide in themselves and others, to acknowledge the signs, and to seek help for themselves or to tell a responsible adult about the concerns for another person. It was stressed that suicide is a not a normal response to distress but is a sign of depression. The researchers believed that the reduced number of suicide attempts after the program reflected the participants' change in knowledge and attitudes, and that the program increased the chance of peer intervention. Peer intervention has been demonstrated to be effective in many areas, such as conflict resolution, because of the tendency of young people to turn to each other rather than to adults for help when a problem arises. Moreover, adolescents can be trained effectively to detect and report the warning signs of suicide (Stuart et al., 2003). King (2001) advocated the following steps to develop a comprehensive school suicide prevention program:

- Each school district needs to have a policy concerning student suicide in place before suicides occur. This policy should describe the steps that faculty and staff will take when the threat of suicidal behaviour is detected, as well as the response of the school should a suicide occur.
- School staff should all be educated about risk factors and warning signs for suicide.
- All school staff should collaborate in their efforts to detect and prevent suicidal behaviour in students.
- Suicide prevention should be included in the school's curriculum.
- Peer counsellors should be trained to detect and report suicidal thinking and behaviour.
- School staff should make special efforts to promote each student's feeling of being an integral part of the school community.
- School–family relationships should be promoted and be supportive in nature.
- A school crisis team should be established with a team leader present in the school at all times. This team should have the responsibility for determining the school's response to a suicide as well as for conducting educational sessions at regular intervals.

King also counselled teachers confronting suicidal students to listen to them carefully, asking direct questions (e.g., "Are you thinking of harming yourself?"), rather than denying their feelings (e.g., "Oh come on, things aren't that bad") and to stay with them while alerting an intervention team or a mental health professional.

King (1999) also discussed the school's response to a suicide (**postvention**). He advocated having a postvention plan prepared before a suicide occurs so that the school is ready to respond in an organized fashion. A postvention team should be created to handle the postvention and to educate students and staff about suicide, as well as to establish and maintain close ties to the larger community. A postvention plan, he continued, should be implemented within 24 hours of the suicide. Teachers should be informed immediately and they should inform their students in the first class. Counselling sites throughout the school should be made available for students, faculty, and staff, and the general emotional environment of the school should be monitored for a much longer time. King suggests avoiding large public displays or meetings after a suicide as this might serve to glorify the event, but indications of concern and sadness, such as a minute of silence in the classroom or a fundraiser for suicide prevention might be considered. A designated media liaison should inform parents and handle media inquiries. Following the postvention, the postvention team should meet to evaluate the school's response and the postvention plan for the future should be modified if necessary.

Seniors are more likely to consult religious leaders than physicians or mental health professionals (Leming & Dickinson, 2002). Therefore, religious leaders, and physicians, must be aware of the warning signs and risk factors of suicide in older adults and take the time to question seniors about their feelings and their life situation.

When considering suicide prevention among Native Canadians, the same factors influencing non-Aboriginal individuals apply, of course, but additional factors must be considered. The high rate of suicide among Native Canadians is affected by wider social issues than the person's relationship network. For Aboriginal Canadians, the broad historical framework in which they have lived is one of disempowerment and social inequity. This framework affects the individual by decreasing his or her sense of identity and self-worth.

Without collective pride and self-esteem, it will be difficult to imbue Native young people with a strong sense of their own worth to combat the despair they often feel. Psychologically speaking, at least part of the answer to this problem is to discontinue the customary surveillance mode of governing the Native population and to empower Native communities to govern themselves. As has been discussed, suicide rates are very low in Native communities that determine their own needs and have the resources to provide for these needs (Chandler & Lalonde, 1998). As Kirmayer et al. (2003) said:

> Mental health promotion with Aboriginal peoples must go beyond the focus on individuals to engage and empower communities. Aboriginal identity itself can be a unique resource for mental health promotion and intervention. Knowledge of living on the land, community, connectedness, and historical consciousness all provide sources of resilience. At the same time, the knowledge and values held by Aboriginal peoples can contribute an essential strand to the efforts of other peoples to find their way in a world threatened by environmental depredation, exhaustion and depletion from the ravages of consumer capitalism. (p. S21)

One promising program for suicide prevention is the Helping Hands project in the Ojibwa/Cree

---

BOX 9.6 Gun Control

In Canada and the United States, the preferred method of suicide is by gunshot. Unlike the United States, where gun control is controversial, Canada has had a policy of regulating firearms for many years, in part because of the belief that this would reduce the number of suicides in the population. This belief is supported by American research that indicates that the presence of a firearm in the home increases the risk for suicide (Brent et al., 1991; Kellerman et al., 1992). The *Criminal Law Amendment Act* of 1977 (Bill C-15) put strict limitations on the availability of firearms to some people and required permits for those selling firearms. In addition, sentences for firearm offences were increased. This bill was enforced from 1978 on. Not surprisingly, the number of suicides in which firearms were used decreased after the passage of Bill C-15, but the overall rate of suicides decreased only slightly (Lester & Leenaars, 1993). Further research indicated that gun control was related to decreases in suicides only in people under the age

of 55 (Leenaars & Lester, 1997). In a more recent study of the effect of Bill C-15, Leenaars, Moksony, Lester, and Wenckstern (2003) demonstrated that even when such variables as high unemployment rates and the proportion of young males in the population (a high-risk group for suicide) are present, the suicide rate decreased after gun control was implemented. They also found that men, denied access to firearms, often switched to another method, but women did not.

This beneficial effect will have to be studied to determine whether or not the decreasing rates of suicide continued after the passage of Bill C-68 in 1995, which further restricted access to guns. As Leenaars and his colleagues have noted, guns are just one means of committing suicide, and although they have found that restriction of access to lethal means, such as poison, has provided a decrease in suicide in many countries (Leenaars et al., 2000), a person determined to commit suicide will find a way.

community of Muskrat Dam in Ontario (Minore, Boone, Katt, & Kinch, 1991). Based on traditional Native values, the Nishnawbe-Aski Nation developed this program to improve the mental health of the community and, in particular, to reduce the incidence of youth suicide by

(1) instilling a sense of value within the general community population; (2) rebuilding the lives of disturbed youth, thereby enabling them to proceed with direction and purpose; (3) restoring pride and a sense of well-being to members of the community; (4) motivating young people to lead constructive and productive lives; (5) providing life-skills training that can be applied within the family and community; and (6) helping individuals develop good mechanisms for coping with mental health problems. (DeSpelder & Strickland, 2005, pp. 441–442)

More information about this ongoing project, and many others like it, can be found at the website for the journal *In the Spirit of Healing & Wellness*, produced by the Aboriginal Healing & Wellness Strategy: http://www.ahwsontario.ca.

Prevention of suicide is clearly a large concern in Canada. Box 9.6 discusses the effect that gun control has had on suicide rates. In Box 9.7 are suggestions for what you can do, as an individual, to prevent someone from taking his or her own life.

BOX 9.7 What an Individual Can Do to Help Prevent a Suicide

Preventing a suicide isn't always possible, but the following are suggestions for how to try to prevent someone from taking his or her own life.

- Be aware of the warning signs of suicide. Any mention of suicide should be taken seriously.
- Listen calmly to the person and ask direct questions, such as, "Are you thinking about suicide?" and "Do you have any definite plans for killing yourself?" (Note that the question is phrased positively, not negatively as in, "You're not thinking about suicide, are you?" as this suggests that the listener is not open to hearing an admission of suicidal plans.)
- Positive, accepting statements may include "I can see how distressed you are. Maybe I can help you find other ways of coping with this difficult situation," or "You're important to me and I don't want you to die." Do not be judgmental or try to solve the individual's problems.
- Make sure the individual is not left alone. Keep him or her talking.
- If possible, suggest reasons to continue living, such as love for children or pets, the possibility of a failed suicide attempt, or hope that counselling can help the individual resolve problems and change feelings.
- Encourage the individual to get counselling. If the idea of seeing a mental health professional is aversive to the individual, stress that therapy today is not just for "crazy people" but also for normal people who are in crisis situations or who want to grow. Offer to help the individual find the appropriate help or even to accompany the individual to a counselling session.
- If the suicide seems imminent, call for help (911) or take the person to a crisis centre or mental health facility.
- Make sure to pay attention to your own feelings afterward. Even if you have been successful in intervening, you will be feeling the stress and talking with someone who understands will be helpful. If you have not been successful in intervening, resist blaming yourself; you did what you could.

SUMMARY

- Suicide is an act with a fatal outcome that the deceased, knowing or expecting a potentially fatal outcome, has initiated and carried out with the purpose of bringing about wanted changes.

- In Canada, about 12 people per 100 000 take their own lives each year, with about 3.5 times more males than females.

- Since 1960, suicide rates have increased by 60 percent worldwide. Suicide is now among the three leading causes of death among those aged 15 to 44 years for both males and females.

- The suicide rate among Canada's Native Peoples is three to four times higher than in the general population; among First Nations youth, it is five to seven times higher than the Canadian average. Among Inuit youth, the rate is 11 times higher than the Canadian average.
- Risk factors for suicide include psychological disorders, personality characteristics, cognitive factors, environmental stress, alcohol and drug use, physical illness, and behavioural indicators, such as previous suicide attempts and verbalizing an intent to commit suicide.
- The categorization of suicide by Durkheim (1966/1897) highlighted the role of social integration in society as a factor in suicide, with both overintegration and underintegration playing an important part in the decision to commit suicide.
- Shneidman (1985) conceived of suicide as being determined by press (an immediate negative event that acts as a trigger), psychache (the despair and misery felt by the individual), and perturbation (the general upset state of the individual).
- Joiner (2005) added that having become accustomed to the idea of causing harm to oneself or having experienced harm decreases the suicidal individual's will to live or need for self-preservation.
- Canadians are inclined to believe that although suicide is not a good answer to problems, it is often understandable and not necessarily the result of disordered thinking.
- Suicide among young people is influenced by many of the same factors that affect adult suicide, but the role of social disruption through insufficient family support, school problems, and interpersonal stresses is particularly highlighted.
- Suicide among seniors is often a result of the infirmities of age and the need for assistance in living, with its resultant loss of independence and sense of self-worth.
- Suicide among Canada's Native Peoples is affected by the disruption of their Aboriginal cultural identity, as well as other individual factors.
- Suicide-prevention programs aim to educate people about suicide and identify those people who are most at risk for suicidal behaviour. Among young people, in particular, providing peers with information to understand suicidal behaviour seems most promising.

KEY TERMS

altruistic suicide	passive suicide	psychache
anomic suicide	perturbation	social integration
egoistic suicide	postvention	suicide
fatalistic suicide	press	

INDIVIDUAL ACTIVITIES

1. Have you been affected by the suicide of someone? How did it make you feel?
2. Did you ever contemplate suicide yourself? What stopped you? Do you still feel that suicide is an option for you?
3. If you know someone who seems depressed who might contemplate suicide, what can you do to help?
4. Take some action. Consider visiting or calling an older relative or friend on a regular basis. Consider volunteering some time per week to a suicide hotline.

GROUP ACTIVITIES

1. In groups of four or five, explore the resources available in your community to prevent suicide. Discuss these with the group and decide whether you think they are adequate.

2. Rent a movie, such as *'night, Mother; The Virgin Suicides;* or *Leaving Las Vegas,* and discuss the way suicide is portrayed in the movie. What interventions were applied? What interventions might have been applied successfully?

3. In groups of four or five, find out whether your school or workplace has a suicide prevention or postvention plan in place. If so, is it an adequate program? Devise a suicide prevention and postvention program for a school or institution. What elements should be included? How could the program be delivered most effectively?

Death and Trauma: When Mourning Is More Difficult

Ripped from the Headlines

- **Is Canada's burden in Afghanistan too heavy? Canada's death rate higher than U.S.**
  Six more Canadian soldiers died in Afghanistan Sunday. . . . With 51 soldiers and one diplomat dead, and 2,545 troops currently deployed in Afghanistan, Canada's loss rate is 2 per cent.
  The Toronto Star, Ontario, April 10, 2007

- **Gang murder sparks retaliation shooting: Police chief fears violence will escalate**
  The battle between two warring Calgary gangs erupted after an eight-month lull with the fatal shooting of a well-known criminal—followed by a linked attack less than 24 hours later.
  Calgary Herald, Alberta, March 10, 2006

- **Swissair plane crashes off coast of Nova Scotia; no survivors**
  Blandford, Nova Scotia (CNN)—A Swissair jetliner, with 229 people on board bound from New York to Geneva, Switzerland, crashed off the coast of Nova Scotia Wednesday evening. Swissair said Thursday there are no survivors.
  CNN webpage, http://www.cnn.com, September 3, 1998

- **Hurricane Katrina: The overview; hurricane slams into gulf coast; dozens are dead**
  Hurricane Katrina pounded the Gulf Coast with devastating force at daybreak on Monday, sparing New Orleans the catastrophic hit that had been feared but inundating parts of the city and heaping damage on neighboring Mississippi, where it killed dozens, ripped away roofs and left coastal roads impassable.
  The New York Times, National Desk, New York, August 30, 2005

- **Militants kill 87 in Iraq**
  Baghdad—Iraqi police found the bodies of at least 87 men killed in execution-style shootings in the previous 24 hours in a wave of apparent sectarian killing, the Interior Ministry said Tuesday. They include at least 29 bodies in a mass grave in an eastern Shiite Muslim neighbourhood.
  The Globe and Mail, Toronto, Ontario, March 14, 2006

- **Teen killed, 6 wounded in Toronto shooting**

  Toronto—A Boxing Day excursion turned tragic for a teenage girl out shopping with her family after gunmen sprayed a crowded downtown street with bullets Monday, killing the teen and injuring six other people, including an off-duty police officer.

  The Globe and Mail, Toronto, Ontario, December 27, 2005

- **Counting terror's toll; Grim task begins; New York orders 6,000 body bags**

  Rudolph Giuliani said the best estimate is "a few thousand" victims would be left in each building, potentially including 250 missing firefighters and police officers.

  The Record, Kitchener, Ontario, September 13, 2001

- **Montreal Massacre: Railing Against Feminists**

  A Gunman Kills 14 Women on a Montreal Campus, Then Shoots Himself

  Maclean's Magazine, December 18, 1989

The headlines in the opening vignette clearly illustrate the horrors that society is confronted with every day. Death is reported in small or great numbers on a daily basis, and sometimes the manner of death is particularly devastating. While reading the headlines, many people become, to a greater or lesser extent, disengaged from the pain depicted, but it must always be remembered that many people cannot so easily disengage; they have been witnesses to these dreadful occurrences, or their friends and family members have been victims of the event. What of their grief? Is their mourning more profound or qualitatively different from the mourning of those whose loss has been more anticipated or less horrific? In this chapter, we will examine the effects of what has been termed *traumatic death*.

WHAT IS TRAUMATIC DEATH?

In the psychological sense, **trauma** is loosely defined as an event that creates intense fear, horror, or sense of helplessness in the experiencer or observer (Davison, Neale, Blankstein, & Flett, 2002). The death of a loved one is often, if not usually, traumatic; however in some cases of bereavement, the death is sudden, unexpected, or violent, leaving the survivors not only with grief but also with a shock to their entire sense of reality and world view. This is termed **traumatic death**. Rando (1993) has stipulated that a death can be considered traumatic when any of the following elements are present:

(a) suddenness and lack of anticipation;
(b) violence, mutilation, and destruction;
(c) preventability and/or randomness;
(d) multiple death; and (e) the mourner's personal encounter with death, where there is either a significant threat to personal survival or a massive and/or shocking confrontation with the death and mutilation of others. (pp. 568–569)

In these cases, the mourning is more complex for the survivors because they have to deal with their loss and with the trauma. Although it was once assumed that such situations simply intensified the grieving process (Rando, 1993), today it is known that traumatic death may produce two overlapping problems: that of dealing with the loss and that of dealing with the trauma. In some cases, it may even be that the survivor develops **posttraumatic stress disorder (PTSD),** a disorder formally classified in the psychological and psychiatric diagnostic system, which impairs the individual's functioning in all aspects of his or her life for sometimes several years. PTSD is "an extreme response to a severe stressor, including increased anxiety, avoidance of stimuli associated with the trauma, and a numbing of emotional responses" (Davison et al., 2002, p. 194). Symptoms of PTSD include re-experiencing the traumatic event, through flashbacks, nightmares, or highly intrusive and vivid memories, and the phenomenon of alternating attempts to avoid thinking about the event and the numbing of the emotions. Also found in PTSD is the common symptom of extreme stress, that of hyperarousal, in which the individual is overly alert, startles very easily, has difficulty concentrating, and typically has problems sleeping. Suicidal thoughts are common as the individual experiences depression and anxiety, as well as anger and guilt regarding the event.

It is not uncommon, then, for survivors of traumatic deaths to have increased problems in their grieving and find the trajectory of mourning that was discussed in Chapter 5 to be disrupted, lengthened, or stalled. Just as nontraumatic bereavement has been shown to increase physical and psychological problems for the survivors (Ott, 2002; Parkes, 1996), traumatic bereavement is noted to cause even more physical and psychological problems for the survivors, which, cyclically, increase the overall stress caused by the bereavement in the first place. To illustrate some of the reactions of those whose bereavement has been traumatic, it is instructive to examine the case of those who have survived the homicide of a loved one.

THE BEREAVED OF HOMICIDE VICTIMS

In 2005 in Canada, 658 people were victims of homicide (Statistics Canada, 2006). This represents a very small percentage of a population of almost 31 million, but consider that when one person dies, around 10 other people are affected (including family, friends, coworkers). This means that at least 6220 people in Canada were affected by homicide in 2004. In the United States, the numbers are much higher because of the larger population and because of a higher homicide rate: a conservative estimate is that at least 240 000 Americans may be affected by homicide every year (Bucholz, 2002) with at least 50 000 considered to be the bereaved of homicide victims (Hatton, 2003). Consider the implications for such countries as those in the Middle East, which are war torn and whose citizens live in constant danger of some sort of homicidal death. It seems clear that worldwide hundreds of thousands of people have to cope with the sudden, unexpected loss of a loved one through homicide. If we include those bereaved by disasters created by human beings, such as the gas leak in Bhopal, India, which is widely attributed to the irresponsibility of Union Carbide, or the tragedy known as 9/11 in which thousands were killed in the World Trade Center in New York City in 2001 by acts of terrorism, the numbers of people worldwide who might consider themselves as the bereaved of homicide victims climbs.

Research tells us that stress that is caused by human activity (agency) or action produces more negative effects than stress caused by natural disasters (Weiten & Lloyd, 2003); this reflects the difference between attributing a death to an unavoidable "act of God" and dealing with the pain of a death inflicted because of a decision made by another human being. So it is reasonable to view those bereaved by disasters of human agency as being similar to the mourners of homicide victims; in both cases, loved ones died because of the deliberate or careless act or omission of another. Someone bears responsibility for a death that did not have to occur.

The death of someone we love is hard enough to take when it comes after a long life or an illness and perhaps suffering. But how much harder might it be when we know that the person we loved did not have to die, that his or her life was taken by someone else, suddenly, unexpectedly, and maybe arbitrarily? Although not a great deal of research examines the reactions of those bereaved by homicide as compared with those bereaved by other forms of traumatic death, some does indicates quite clearly the extra problems that arise in these cases (Murphy, Johnson, & Lohan, 2002; Murphy, Johnson, Chung, & Beaton, 2003; see also Parents of Murdered Children, 1995).

One problem that is confirmed by both empirical and anecdotal research is the mourners' feelings of isolation and helplessness in a world that now appears hostile, malevolent, uncaring, and insensitive (Bucholz, 2002). We all view the world through filters that we develop over time, from our experiences with the world. These filters are essentially assumptions we make about the way the world works and the way people are. For example, this **assumptive world** for many individuals may indicate that the world is generally a good place, although bad things may happen and bad people do exist. This world view may further suggest that people are responsible for their own fates, with the presumption that if a person behaves well, life will treat him or her well. The murder of a loved one cruelly challenges the view that the world is generally a good place with kind and loving people in it (Matthews & Marwit, 2004). A greater sense of meaninglessness may permeate the mourner's thinking about life when, for no apparent reason, a loved one's life is snatched away by another person. The adjustment that must be faced by the bereaved of a homicide victim, then, is not only an adjustment to the loss of the deceased and the social network that had existed but also an adjustment to seeing the world and other people with new eyes and a different perspective (Hatton, 2003).

Anger is heightened in those bereaved by homicide; not only has their loved one been taken away deliberately by someone who believed that he or she had some right to do so, but the system of justice that is meant to find and punish the perpetrator is often insensitive and sometimes ineffective. Some of these survivors may even be considered possible perpetrators themselves until (or unless) the real murderer is found (see Bucholz, 2002), thus adding insult to the already almost unbearable injury. When the perpetrator is found, the mourners may be outraged at the time it takes to bring the accused to trial, at delays within the trial, of appeal processes, and at perceived leniency of sentencing or plea bargains. Again, the assumptive world view may have included ideas about the fairness of the justice system and the sensitivity that would be shown to those bereaved by a homicide (Thompson, Norris, & Ruback, 1998). Once more, the world view may be challenged and even shattered by the realities of the situation. It should be noted that the anger is often kept alive for a longer time for those bereaved by homicide than for other bereaved people because of the processes of the justice system; trials, appeals, parole hearings, and so on, mean that the mourner's immediate experience of the homicide is stretched to years. This is one reason that many of those bereaved by homicide favour capital punishment for the perpetrator: not only do they want the perpetrator punished, but they also want the whole legal process to be over (Bucholz, 2002). As an example of the delays that can occur, see the case in Box 10.1.

BOX 10.1 In the News

On the night of December 3, 1984, in Bhopal, India, 40 tonnes of toxic gas leaked from a pesticide plant run by the former Union Carbide. Thousands died that night, and many claim that thousands more have died from related illnesses since then. The death toll to date is more than 15 000. On March 29, 2006, more than 22 years after the tragedy, the Indian government agreed to push for a cleanup of the area and compensation for victims from Dow Chemical Co., which took over Union Carbide in 2001. To date, no one has been charged with any liability for the leakage, and survivors of the disaster contend that the water in the area is contaminated, leading to further health problems in a new generation. After 22 years of nonaction, survivors and mourners feel angry and cynical that they will ever obtain justice.

Anger may also be directed at the media, whose publicizing of the homicide and the trial may be sensationalized or may portray the victim in unflattering and inaccurate ways. Sometimes the perpetrator is portrayed in sympathetic ways, which often comes at the expense of the victim, as does the justice system's concern for the rights of the perpetrator. In addition, survivors may be angry at society, which seems to find the situation entertaining or at least has a prurient interest in the event, thus feeding the sensationalized media accounts, and at the general indifference and inattentiveness that is often given to the survivors of the victim. This is the case in the examples given in Box 10.2.

The bereaved of a homicide victim are also faced with uncertainty. They endure the frustration of not knowing exactly what happened to the loved one ("Who did it?" "Did he suffer?" "Was she afraid?" "Did he have any idea what was coming?") and the lack of information from the criminal justice system as the search for the perpetrator is carried out. This is in addition to the continuing question of "Why?" which is most particularly painful in the case of a random murder, such as a drive-by shooting, or of an "accidental" murder, such as cases in which a bystander is caught in crossfire. Read the poignant words of a bereaved woman whose partner died in Afghanistan in Box 10.3.

Parents of murdered children have the added pain in experiencing feelings of guilt (Hatton, 2003; Murphy, Tapper, Johnson, & Lohan, 2003). The duty of a parent is to protect the child, yet when a child is murdered, the protection has failed. Even in cases in which no parent could have protected the child or the child was an adult, the parent feels guilt and a sense of decreased self-worth because of it.

In keeping with the effects of trauma, the bereaved of homicide victims report having intrusive thoughts of the loved one's death, even five years later, along with increased anxiety, depression, suicidal ideation, and more general stress reactions (Hatton, 2003; Murphy, Tapper, et al., 2003).

As has been noted from the demographics, mercifully, most people in Western society will not be bereaved by homicide. Yet a sizable number of people, depending on the country and location within the country, are faced with this experience. This means that many people are dealing with such an incident while the experience is removed from the commonplace for the majority, leaving that majority unsure of how to relate to those who have experienced or are experiencing the double load of intense grief and trauma. In fact, controversy exists in the professional bereavement counselling community as to whether it is better to treat the trauma first and then attempt grief counselling, or whether the grief and the trauma can even be separated at all for treatment (see Hatton, 2003, for further discussion of this).

Bereavement by homicide or by human agency clearly provides additional problems in coping with grief, and it is not surprising that this kind of bereavement does not follow the usual trajectory. Bereavement by homicide sometimes leads to what has been termed *complicated grief*. We shall now turn to a discussion of what complicated grief is and what else can lead to it.

COMPLICATED GRIEF

"She has to pull herself together. It's been almost two years since her husband died and she won't even consider dating. She must need psychiatric help." These words were spoken by a highly educated and sensitive professional woman about a friend of hers. The woman is clearly concerned and wants very much to help her friend, but her ideas about what is "normal" in mourning and what calls for the help of a mental health professional indicate a lack of understanding of the experience of grief. Her words are not uncommon, though. It is often assumed that mourning has a time limit, after which showing signs of grief is in some way pathological. Mourning for "too long" or "too much" is often regarded as inappropriate and indicating a need for mental health intervention. As has been pointed out in previous chapters, however, no fixed limit or precise formulation constitutes "normal" mourning. This does not suggest that all mourning and all experiences of grief can be considered as normal, with no need for professional help. In some cases, as in homicide, grief does not follow the general trajectory that has been described in previous chapters. Sometimes the difficult process of mourning is made even more difficult by a variety of factors, such as the personality of the mourner or the circumstances of the loved one's death. In these cases, what may result is what is called *complicated grief* (Rando, 1993).

Complicated grief is not easy to define. It is highly individual, and each case must be examined on its own merits to decide whether the grief falls under the category of complicated, but in general, this term is used when the mourning process is not proceeding to the point at which the mourner can re-establish a new relationship with the deceased, re-engage in life-affirming activities that bring pleasure, and re-invest in new relationships. The process of mourning has, for any number of reasons, become distorted, is incapable of completion, and provides a trajectory of continued and even increased distress and suffering for the mourner over time.

The symptoms of complicated mourning include the following:

- Overreaction to experiences of loss and separation. This is sometimes seen as a heightened sensitivity or vulnerability to issues surrounding the possibility of loss.
- Psychological and behavioural "busyness," including heightened activity, arousal, and restlessness. The individual often feels that he or she must keep busy in order to function or to avoid thinking about the loss.
- A high anxiety about death of the self or loved ones. This may be manifested in overconcern for others (e.g., the "smother-mother" who hovers over her children unnecessarily, checking their temperatures when they are not sick), or in concern about the person's own health even in the absence of symptoms.
- Inaccurate memories of the deceased that seem to canonize the departed loved one and idealize the relationship. Memories of human flaws or snags in relationships tend to be denied.
- Impairment of day-to-day functioning because of rigid patterns of behaviour. For example, a man may be fired from his job because of his compelling need to visit his wife's grave for hours each day.
- Continual rumination and obsession with thoughts about the deceased and the death. These thoughts impede daily functioning and persist for long periods.
- Lack of some or all emotional reactions that are normally found in those who have been bereaved. For example, the individual may show no sign of grief or that anything untoward has happened, although the relationship with the deceased was one of strong attachment.
- Inability to talk about the deceased and about feelings of loss.
- Withdrawal from relationships and an inability to imbue relationships with intimacy. It is usually clear that the individual avoids intimate relationships out of fear of future loss.
- Self-destructive relationships that may take several forms, such as overinvolvement and caregiving, and replacement or rebound relationships.
- Self-destructive and acting-out behaviour, such as substance abuse, gambling, or promiscuity.
- Chronic feelings of depersonalization, numbness, or isolation and alienation from the rest of society.

- Chronic and very long-lasting anger or anger/depression symptoms. These may include belligerence, annoyance, intolerance, and so on.

Some symptoms of grief not listed here may trouble others who are concerned and watch the mourner; in fact, these symptoms do not automatically mean that anything other than normal grieving is occurring. For example, feeling sorry for ourselves or feeling that part of ourselves has died along with the deceased is not necessarily abnormal or indicative of complicated mourning, and neither is resenting that others live and the world goes on as if nothing happened. Emotions other than sadness are to be expected, as are some behaviours that are not usually part of the mourner's repertoire. These may include continuing a relationship with the deceased, perhaps by maintaining the bedroom as the deceased left it, for example, by continuing to celebrate the deceased's birthday, or by having conversations with the deceased at the graveside.

Perhaps the most common reason that some people assume a complicated grief is occurring is that the mourner seems to mourn for "too long." The question is, what exactly does "too long" mean? Is there a time limit on mourning beyond which the mourning has become complicated or even pathological? The descriptions of normal mourning in Chapter 5 indicate that grief has no magical time limit. How long mourning continues depends on the individual and the situation, and, in some ways, the mourning may go on forever. Certainly, new situations arise in life that remind the mourner of the absence of the deceased and require new adaptation to the loss. Whether a sudden temporary upsurge of grief (STUG, see Chapter 5) occurs at this time or not, a feeling of bereavement and loss is normal and reasonable.

Complicated grief, then, is not easy to diagnose. Each case must be examined on its own merits. Concerned individuals often assume that mourners are showing complicated grief because of their own lack of understanding about what constitutes normal grieving and because of their own discomfort in dealing with grief-stricken people. In general, complicated grief requires the aid of experienced professional help.

TYPES OF COMPLICATED MOURNING

Although several theorists have discussed complicated grief (e.g., Bowlby, 1980–1981; Parkes, 1996; Worden, 1991), Thérèse Rando (1993) has perhaps been most complete in describing several kinds of complicated mourning, each providing unique problems for the mourner. Her categorization follows.

BOX 10.4   Absent Mourning

Tabitha's husband of 22 years died four years ago, but Tabitha insists that he is on an extended trip abroad and will return shortly. She continues to buy gifts for his birthday and their anniversary, wrapping them extravagantly and insisting that he will be delighted with them on his return. When questioned, she may become vague about the details of her husband's "trip" or she weaves an elaborate story about why he can't call her or write to her. Evidence of her husband's death is denied by her, to the extent that she accuses those who would have her face the reality of his death of being in collusion against her and wanting to "drive her mad."

Absent Mourning

Box 10.4 illustrates a case of one type of complicated mourning. **Absent mourning** refers to a state in which the bereaved individual either completely denies that a death has occurred, or remains in a state of complete shock. Clearly, both conditions are extremely difficult to sustain, and so true absent mourning is extremely rare. Often, it is assumed that absent mourning is present because the mourner is inhibiting grief reactions, perhaps because of societal or cultural prescriptions as to what reactions are appropriate, or perhaps because of what the mourner perceives as an overriding need to postpone grief reactions. For example, the father whose child has died may not be socially allowed to show the anguish he feels because of a gender-role stereotype that demands that men not cry. Or a mourner may feel that the demands of arranging a funeral and taking care of other mourners are of higher priority than his or her own expressions of grief, which can be released when these demands become less onerous. These behaviours do not necessarily indicate a complicated mourning, and they are not examples of absent mourning. Absent mourning can be demonstrated only by an individual who has a powerful ability to block out reality, and as such, it is rarely seen.

Delayed Mourning

As illustrated in Box 10.5, **delayed mourning** can only be ascertained retrospectively. In this manifestation of complicated mourning, the individual may be perceived to be in partial or even absent mourning, until later (perhaps much later), when something triggers a full or partial mourning response. For example, a mourner may

BOX 10.5   Delayed Mourning

Daniel was strong and stoical in arranging the funeral of his only son and in supporting his wife's sorrow. He returned to work five days after the death and performed his professional duties as he always had: competently and efficiently. Most of those who knew him remarked on how "well" he was taking his son's death. His wife thought him cold and uncaring, however, and three years later, filed for divorce. When served with the divorce papers, Daniel fell apart. His life was over, he claimed, and he had no desire to live. On examination by a health-care professional, it became apparent that Daniel, while clearly upset about the marital breakdown, was even more distraught at the grief he now experienced for the loss of his son three years earlier.

BOX 10.6   Inhibited Mourning

Fayyaz had a troubled relationship with his father, whom he regarded as old-fashioned and disapproving of his son's more modern beliefs. After his father's death, however, Fayyaz mourned deeply, talking loudly and often of how wonderful his father had been, how supportive, how understanding, how loving. Most people believed that this was an indication that Fayyaz regretted not having been closer to his father, but as time went on, it became apparent that he was recalling only the good times with his father. When his sister reminded him that their father was often difficult and obstinate, Fayyaz reacted angrily, telling her that she had been an unappreciative daughter. Within a few months, Fayyaz developed tension headaches, which debilitated him with their attendant pain.

show some or no mourning for the loss of a loved one, but years later, when another loss occurs, a full mourning response is observed, not only in response to the new loss but also, and more pointedly, to the old loss. Note that delaying mourning for conscious, practical purposes (e.g., until after the funeral, or to concentrate on healing injuries sustained in the accident that killed the loved one) is not considered to be complicated delayed mourning. But when the delay occurs because the individual wants to avoid the pain and stress of bereavement and the implications of the loss, or when the individual has fears surrounding the issues of dying and bereavement, the delay may indicate a complication of mourning.

Complicated delayed mourning is more likely to be observed when the mourner (1) has no social support, (2) has experienced multiple losses simultaneously, or (3) doubts the death is real because, perhaps, the body has not been found or the mourner has not viewed the body. This complication of mourning is sometimes confused with the mourning delay that is often found during the time of shock and denial that may follow a death. This delay is short-lasting, until the shock wears off, and in some cases may be conscious, as the mourner puts his or her emotions on hold until he or she feels ready to experience the pain.

Inhibited Mourning

Like Fayyaz in Box 10.6, in **inhibited mourning,** the mourner concentrates on part of the deceased individual's personality or a part of the relationship that the mourner had with the deceased. The mourner often blocks out the negative elements, mourning only the positive aspects to the point that the deceased and the relationship become idealized. Without acknowledgment of the less positive elements of the individual and the relationship, mourning is incomplete and much of the grief reaction is deeply buried. Often, physical or psychological symptoms occur, which appear to the mourner to be unrelated to the grief but which have been hypothesized to take the place of the inhibited aspects (e.g., Fayyaz's tension headaches; Rando, 1993; Worden, 1991).

This form of complicated mourning is more likely to be found in individuals who have had a conflicted relationship with the deceased that leaves them with a feeling of guilt that is difficult to bear. These individuals are also more likely in general to shy away from negative or conflicted emotions. Inhibited mourning is more likely to occur in cases in which the grief has been disenfranchised or not given significance by societal norms that suggest that a high level mourning is not appropriate (e.g., in the cases of suicide, stillbirth, the death of someone very old, as discussed later in the chapter).

Distorted Mourning

Although all complicated mourning encompasses some distortion, the syndrome of **distorted mourning** refers to situations in which (usually) anger or guilt predominate other manifestations of the grief response to the extent that the individual's functioning in life and relationships is impaired. This can be seen in the case of Pablo in Box 10.7. When anger is the predominant emotion, it is usually directed against the deceased, as if the death were more indicative of abandonment than of a forced severing of the relationship. In some cases, it seems as if the mourner wants to punish the deceased for this abandonment, and he or she experiences a loss of

BOX 10.7   Distorted Mourning

Pablo's wife died when her car was hit by a drunk driver as she was on her way to the grocery store for milk. Pablo is very, very angry. He talks continually about how his wife should not have been driving at that time, about how she insisted on going out when she "should have known" that drunk drivers might be on the road. His anger spreads from the specific incident in which his wife went out to the store, to an anger that she did not have enough milk in the house for the next morning's breakfast, to her general housekeeping skills, an issue that Pablo had never seemed concerned with before. Shortly after his wife's death, Pablo's anger seemed understandable, if not justifiable, to his friends and family who supported him in the belief that the anger against his wife was actually an anger against the whole situation and was therefore a normal manifestation of his grief. But Pablo has become increasingly isolated from friends and family as he continues to rage against his wife, a woman beloved by them. His employer has warned him that his hostility is being seen in his work and has suggested that he consider taking another job. In fact, Pablo's anger has made his life narrow, endangering his livelihood and driving away people who care about him and want to support him. Pablo shows no signs of sadness or depression in missing his wife, whom he had loved dearly, only anger.

had fantasies of the deceased's death (Raphael, 1983). Rando (1993) also observed distorted mourning to be more likely in cases in which the mourner has actually played a part in the deceased's death (e.g., having driven the car in a car accident), when the deceased is a child, and when the mourner has a tendency toward perfectionism and an unrealistic sense of responsibility, which gives the feeling that somehow the mourner could have prevented the death.

Conflicted Mourning

Wojtek, in Box 10.8, is showing conflicted mourning. **Conflicted mourning,** like distorted mourning, is hallmarked by a sense of guilt and remorse. In the case of conflicted mourning, however, the remorse is for what had been an ambivalent relationship. This type of relationship is marked by a strong attachment but also a great deal of conflict and trouble. The mourner's grief is twofold: he or she mourns the deceased individual, and the relationship that never was and now can never be. Often the conflicted mourner perceives himself or herself as defective, inadequate, hypocritical, and blameworthy. With this lowered self-esteem, he or she has great difficulty working through the grief, which becomes chronic.

BOX 10.8   Conflicted Mourning

When Wojtek's brother died, Wojtek seemed to experience very little grief. Most people thought it was because Wojtek's brother had been severely competitive with him when they were children, and their relationship had been strained and competitive in adulthood. But after several months, to his surprise, Wojtek began to experience acute grief, missing his brother terribly. He wished that they could be together again and that he had had a chance to patch up their relationship. Wojtek started to reproach himself for the needless competition they had shown, even to the point of telling himself that it had been his own fault, that he had provoked his brother into a constant rivalry. Wojtek continued to berate himself and felt great remorse for the unhappiness he was convinced he had caused both himself and his brother. He had only one brother, he told himself, how could he have missed the only opportunity that he would ever have for a strong sibling relationship? Family members tried to console Wojtek, but, in fact, he had few memories of happy times with his brother or of times when they supported each other. "If only I had it to do over," he mourned. "I must be a truly defective human being. And now I'll never have another chance."

security that may mirror the loss of security felt in earlier losses (e.g., of a parent in childhood).

A second pattern of distorted mourning is that of guilt, with exaggerated feelings of self-loathing and remorse. Again, hostility is present, but now the anger is directed toward the self as deserving of punishment. For example, in this manifestation, Pablo might believe that his wife's death was his fault because he did not go the store instead of her. He might feel that his life is now meaningless and that he is a contemptible human being because of his great "sin." In extreme cases, this pattern leads to suicidal rumination and even suicide attempts.

Whether the predominant emotion is anger or guilt, other expected emotions, such as sadness or sorrow, are absent as the exaggerated emotion of anger or guilt takes up all the emotional energy. In normal mourning, anger and guilt often coexist with other emotions: the absence of other emotions is what makes this complicated mourning.

Distorted mourning is more likely to occur in cases in which the deceased and the mourner had a strong but conflicted relationship, often with the mourner having

Chronic Mourning

Chronic mourning is perhaps the best-known form of complicated mourning. In this condition, the mourner never seems to progress in the trajectory of working with grief, like Antonetta in Box 10.9. On the contrary, the grief seems to be as fresh as if the death had occurred only days before, even though years may have gone by. The mourner may be chronically depressed or chronically angry, or show the disorganization of thought and emotion that is characteristic of shock.

Chronic mourning is more often seen in individuals who have little self-confidence in their abilities to function alone and who had established a highly dependent relationship with the deceased. The loss of the dependent relationship throws the mourner into a fear of not being able to live without the deceased, and this exacerbates the grief that the mourner would normally feel, thus trapping him or her in this highly emotional state. In some cases, it may be that this emotional state has the secondary gain of maintaining social support for a longer period. The chronic mourner may try (consciously or unconsciously) to re-create the dependent relationship with someone else in the social network. The social network may respond to the mourner's distress by inadvertently fostering this dependency. The chronic mourner may therefore be highly reinforced for chronic grief, making it even less desirable to change.

It is important to note that many people assume that chronic mourning is present when normal mourning is occurring. As discussed in Chapter 2, societies have expectations about the manifestations of mourning and the duration of mourning. If the mourner deviates from these expectations, especially in terms of the intensity of grief and the duration of grief, people all too often assume that he or she is showing a complicated chronic mourning. The error lies in the expectations of a society with little understanding of the mourning process in its many manifestations.

Unanticipated Mourning

Box 10.10 illustrates a case in which someone died suddenly and violently. **Unanticipated mourning** incorporates reactions to a great deal of shock and trauma. Although no one is ever truly prepared for the death of a loved one, when a loved one dies as a result of a long, terminal illness, the death comes as an expected, and sometimes even welcome, outcome of a long time of debilitation. But when a death occurs with no advance warning, the shock engendered by the death may persist long past the usual time and may lead to further emotional, cognitive, and behavioural problems for the mourner. Especially in situations in which no body is available for the mourner to view, he or she has an increased sense of unreality about the event that may be very difficult to overcome. The transition to a new reality is abrupt and the world view of the mourner is suddenly challenged and perhaps destroyed. The insecurity created by discovering that the whole world can change instantly produces an anxiety that makes dealing with the bereavement process even more difficult. The mourner may feel a lack of trust in everything he or she had ever counted on. The idea of committing to relationships may become untenable, given how quickly and arbitrarily these relationships may be shattered. Conversely, the mourner may cling even more tenaciously to existing relationships, feeling that unless he or she exerts iron control over these relationships, they too may be shattered.

Clearly, in an unanticipated death, a person has no chance to say goodbye, correct mistakes, or complete any unfinished business in the relationship with the deceased. The mourner may be left with a discomforting lack of closure, which produces more stress for him or her. Unanticipated mourning can occur even when the deceased had a terminal illness and the time left was

---

BOX 10.9	Chronic Mourning

Antonetta's husband died 10 years ago, but people meeting her assume that he died only days ago. She seems to be a woman in the early stages of grief, vacillating between disbelief that he can really be dead and acutely missing her husband, yearning for his presence, and angrily protesting the terrible event. Her family has urged her to move on in life, but she is horrified by such a suggestion: to her, her strong grief is an indication of her attachment and connection to her dead husband. She cannot even conceive of enjoying life without him. After years of giving her sympathetic attention, many of Antonetta's friends have abandoned her, feeling that her unrelenting grief is either a ploy to gain attention and sympathy or too intractable and unremitting for them to handle. Antonetta functions only marginally in her day-to-day life; she is too grief-stricken to concentrate on her previous job as an accountant; her appetite is poor and she does not cook for herself because this reminds her too much of cooking for her husband; her once immaculate house is often dusty because she sees no point in keeping a house without her husband. In addition, her children are uneasy having her around the grandchildren who have been born since the death of Antonetta's husband; Antonetta frightens the children with her crying and wailing that her husband cannot see his grandchildren and they will never know him.

BOX 10.10   Unanticipated Mourning

The airplane that Ian's father was in went down in flames over the Indian Ocean. No one survived and only a few body parts were recovered. The investigation into the cause of the explosion is ongoing, and no conclusion has been made so far. Ian can't seem to get his head around what has happened, even though two years have gone by. He still can't believe that his father is dead. He can't understand how such a terrible explosion could happen. *But Dad was fine,* he thinks sometimes, in a daze. *There wasn't a body. Maybe Dad survived or didn't even board the plane and is wandering around somewhere with amnesia. Maybe I could have stopped him from travelling. Maybe . . .* Ian is haunted by doubts and confusion. The world looks very unpredictable, uncontrollable, and frightening to him. He wonders constantly whether the explosion was an accident or whether it was the result of sabotage. Somehow he feels that he could tolerate knowing an accident caused the explosion better than knowing a deliberate act ended his father's life. He feels rage at having been cheated of saying goodbye.

known to be limited. For example, take the following case: Georgia's father had a serious heart condition that the physicians felt would end his life in the near future. One morning three days before Christmas, Georgia, aged 21 years, checked on her father, who seemed to be fine and who told her to follow her plans to go shopping that day. When Georgia returned home a few hours later, she found her father dead on the floor.

In this case, Georgia knew her father's days were limited, but she surely did not anticipate his dying that day. Sadly, the support system in cases like this may not adequately recognize the shock of this situation and may have expectations for the course of mourning that is more appropriate for an anticipated death than for an unanticipated death. The mourner, then, may be treated to a social reaction that places even more unrealistic expectations on him or her than normally occurs.

Many unanticipated deaths can be classified as traumatic because of their very nature. For example, as we have seen earlier in this chapter, if the death has been caused by the actions of another person, the mourner is left with additional problems.

DISENFRANCHISED GRIEF

Doka (2002) defined **disenfranchised grief** as a grief in which society or the cultural milieu does not officially recognize the bereavement as being major or the right of the individual to mourn. Because of this, disenfranchised grief is hallmarked by a distinct lack of social support and empathy for the mourner. In Doka's words, "Survivors are not accorded a 'right to grieve'" (p. 5). Attig (2004) stated that disenfranchisement occurs when the social order responds to societal expectations rather than to the depth of attachment and the feelings of the bereaved individual. This, he rightly pointed out, is nothing but disrespect for the grieving individual. Not surprisingly, disenfranchised grief often results in complicated mourning.

Disenfranchisement of grief can occur under a number of conditions, all embedded in society's cultural norms regarding what is or is not acceptable. The following are conditions that Doka (2002) and Corr, Nabe, and Corr (2006) have suggested may be situations in which the very real grief felt by survivors may be disenfranchised:

1. *Diverse relationships.* Society sanctions many relationships, especially those based on marriage or kinship. But these are not the only relationships in which individuals feel deep attachment and, subsequently, grief at the loss of the relationship. For example, although Canadian law has recently allowed same-sex marriage, many parts of the world have not; indeed, to many Canadians, the idea of same-sex marriage is still unacceptable. In these situations, a bereaved same-sex spouse may not be accorded the same "right" to grieve as an opposite-sex spouse. In many areas and in many individuals, the idea of cohabitation as partners, either heterosexual or homosexual, may not be seen as legitimate; therefore, the bereaved cohabiting partner may find his or her grief disenfranchised. Similarly, in cases of extramarital or secret relationships, the grief felt by a surviving partner is likely to be unacknowledged and unsupported.

2. *Underestimation of the depth of the relationship.* Disenfranchisement may occur when an ex-spouse or lover dies, when a business colleague with whom one has worked, perhaps for years, dies, or even when a close friend dies. Society develops clear ideas of what degree of grief is acceptable and what "doesn't count." Strangely, although it is common to say that people who look very downcast look as if they have "lost their best friend," support and sympathy is very limited when it actually occurs. A worker is rarely given the day off even for the funeral of a best friend and is expected to get back to work immediately after the funeral, with no sign of grief, even though the individual may have just lost the most important relationship in his or her life. Likewise, although a relationship may be over (e.g., through divorce),

the surviving individual may still experience the pain of bereavement but again is given little or no support in bearing the loss. Other disenfranchised bereavements occur in the cases of miscarriages, abortions, and stillbirths. Society's reasoning seems to be that if the dead individual did not truly "live," the survivor should have little or no grief. This is of no comfort to the parents who feel the loss of their child.

The death of a pet or companion animal is also often disenfranchised. The lack of empathy for the pain that is felt at this death is seen in the common occurrence of other people (e.g., parents) quickly buying a replacement animal. Because an animal can be "replaced," the reasoning seems to go, the grief felt at the death of an animal should not be great.

The individual need not be technically dead for grief to occur, so unsurprisingly such grief is often of the disenfranchised variety once more. For example, the grief felt by the family of an Alzheimer's patient who no longer recognizes them may be profound, but society holds no funeral or commemorative ritual to mark and support the family's suffering.

3. *Characteristics of the bereaved person.* Society may sometimes suggest that some individuals intrinsically are less capable of grief than others and, therefore, less attention needs to be paid to their grief. Into this category fall children, who are often assumed to be unaware of or to lack understanding of death; seniors, who are sometimes assumed to be able to cope with death more easily because they are near the end of their lives as well; and people with mental disabilities, who also are assumed to be like children, unaware and lacking in comprehension. As has been discussed in Chapters 6 and 8, this is not the case, and grief may be profound in all these individuals.

4. *Conditions of the death.* The circumstances of the death may clash with the expectations of society or clash with the forms of death that are found to be "acceptable" by society. In this case, bereaved people are often not given the support and sanctioning of their grief that they need. For example, the families of people who commit suicide report that their support group fades away quite quickly (see Chapter 9). Similarly, the families of people who have been murdered may find their grief disenfranchised, perhaps with the spoken or unspoken societal belief that a person who is murdered in some way "deserved" it (Bucholz, 2002). The grief of families whose loved one has been executed by the criminal justice system is also disenfranchised;

the assumption is that the execution is merited and rids the world of a dangerous element. If the death occurred as a result of a stigmatized disease, such as AIDS, or a substance addiction or accidental overdose, or if the death resulted in severe mutilation of the body, disenfranchisement may also occur. In general, disenfranchisement of grief is more likely to occur in cases in which society judges that the person who died is not reflective of what that society considers to be "a nice person."

In addition, the death of a very senior person is not expected by some people to occasion intense grief. If the senior person died of natural causes, in particular, mourners may be expected to view the death as little more than the usual course of life and to refrain from displaying signs of sorrow.

5. *Grieving style.* Even if the death of a loved one is socially recognized and supported, the mourner's style of grieving may be unacceptable to that society and so result in disenfranchisement. For example, in most of Canada and the United States, bereaved people are expected to show quiet and controlled emotions, with perhaps a small bit of weeping, at a funeral. Loud wailing, beating of the breast, and throwing yourself on the casket is not seen as acceptable behaviour in this part of the world, and the bereaved individual who performs these behaviours may find his or her social support decreased or even removed. Paradoxically, the same disenfranchisement may occur if the bereaved person shows too little emotion. The particular society the bereaved person is in dictates what is acceptable behaviour in mourning, and deviation from this acceptability often results in disenfranchised grief; however, no single culturally expected grieving style encompasses the wide diversity in Canada or can be assumed to be right for everyone. Closely related to this is the disenfranchisement that bereaved individuals may be exposed to because of others' disapproval of their feelings and thoughts. For example, the mourner who states, "I wish I were dead too," may be met with shocked disapproval and responses of "Don't talk that way." Other examples include a mourner being told not to dwell on the bereavement, or to think about other things, or even being discouraged from performing rituals, such as visiting a graveside. All too often a bereaved parent is met with the comment, "You can have other children," or the bereaved spouse hears, "You're young; you'll find someone else." The lack of support, sensitivity, and respect for the bereaved person's very real and, indeed, common feelings constitute disenfranchisement.

That disenfranchisement may lead to complicated grief highlights the need for social support and empathy in dealing with bereavement. Greater understanding of the emotions of grief and the processes through which cultures and individuals deal with grief can be of great help in reducing instances of complicated grief and certainly will increase levels of compassion so that disenfranchisement of grief does not occur. The next three chapters of this book will discuss practical ways of helping in the last stages of life and with the bereavement of survivors.

SUMMARY

- When death occurs in the context of a traumatic event, grief reactions may become more difficult, because both the effects of the shock of the trauma and the grief combine in the mourner. In some cases, posttraumatic stress disorder may even result.

- The particular problems of people bereaved by homicide are noted because the deaths resulting from homicide or from the agency of other people's deliberate or irresponsible acts are particularly hard to cope with and may be misunderstood by society.

- Among the particular problems of those bereaved by homicide are the loss of an assumptive world and increased anger, guilt, and uncertainty. In these cases, as in others, complicated grief may arise.

- Complicated grief does not follow the general trajectory of grief processes, and the mourning process is compromised, distorted, or fails, given the time since the death.

- Complicated grief is often assumed in cases in which grieving seems to be continuing for "too long" or is "too intense." In most cases, the grieving described is not complicated but reflects society's lack of understanding of and discomfort with the normal grieving process.

- Forms of complicated grief include absent mourning, delayed mourning, inhibited mourning, distorted mourning, conflicted mourning, chronic mourning, and unanticipated mourning.

- Disenfranchised grief is a grief in which society or the cultural milieu does not officially recognize the bereavement as being major or the right of the individual to mourn. Because of this, disenfranchised grief is hallmarked by a distinct lack of social support and empathy for the mourner and is more likely to lead to complicated grief than is the case when ample social support is given.

- Disenfranchisement of grief is more likely to occur in diverse relationships, when the depth of the relationship is underestimated, when characteristics of the bereaved person are assumed to mean that the individual does not feel much grief, under certain conditions of the death, and when the grieving style of the mourner is not considered to be socially acceptable.

KEY TERMS

absent mourning
assumptive world
chronic mourning
complicated grief
conflicted mourning

delayed mourning
disenfranchised grief
distorted mourning
inhibited mourning

posttraumatic stress disorder (PTSD)
trauma
traumatic death
unanticipated mourning

INDIVIDUAL ACTIVITIES

1. Have you ever experienced a trauma? What was it like? How did you feel? How does the memory of it make you feel today? Ask family members if they have experienced trauma that they are willing to describe to you.

2. Check your local newspapers. Are there reports of homicides or traumatic deaths occurring in your area? Consider writing a brief condolence note to the survivors who may already be feeling isolated.

3. Have you read books or seen movies in which one or more of the characters were exhibiting complicated grief? What forms of complicated grief occurred in these situations?

4. In your society/culture/religion/community, what types of grief do you think are most likely to be disenfranchised? Have you ever felt the disenfranchisement of grief yourself? Have you ever unwittingly disenfranchised the grief of another person?

GROUP ACTIVITIES

1. In groups of four or five, consider the following cases and decide whether they represent complicated grief or not.

   a. Queen Victoria's husband, Prince Albert, died suddenly after a short illness at the age of 42. She never remarried, wore "widow's weeds" for the rest of her life, and for several years following the death, maintained his private rooms with fresh clothes, towels, and hot water laid out each day. However, beside his bed was a picture of his corpse. The Queen continued to reign over what was then the British Empire for many years.

   b. Mackenzie King, 10th prime minister of Canada during several periods from the 1920s to the 1940s, had a close relationship with his mother. After her death, he continued his relationship with her by means of séances and mediums. He continued as prime minister, with more than 21 years in total in office.

   c. Thousands of people visit Graceland, the home of Elvis Presley, each year. Presley, a rock-and-roll icon, died of what were presumed to be drug-related problems in 1977. Visitors to Graceland are often observed crying uncontrollably, even though they never met Presley or, in fact, may not even have been born until after his death.

2. As a class or a small group, watch the movie *Ordinary People* and discuss the forms of grief that the various characters are exhibiting. Would you classify these forms as complicated grief or not?

3. In groups of four or five, discuss instances in which you believe there has been insufficient support for someone's loss (through death or otherwise). How could such disenfranchisement be prevented in the future?

End-of-Life Care

"That's Too Bad"

▶ Reba Bryan had just celebrated her 70th birthday when she received the diagnosis of an inoperable cancerous tumour in her sinus cavity. Within a month, the tumour had grown to such proportions that she was unable to swallow food. She was admitted to hospital to have a feeding tube implanted in her stomach. Within a day, she developed an infection behind the tumour, one that did not respond to antibiotics. She became irrational and delusional, accusing the medical staff of mistreating her, but she made the accusations pleasantly and with a smile. Her only family was a middle-aged daughter, Madeleine, who had a professional career.

Madeleine had cared for her mother for several years, because of unrelated medical conditions, and had maintained her career with difficulty. She spent every day that her mother was hospitalized at her mother's bedside, and during the final 38 hours, when her mother lost consciousness, she never left the room. During that time, nurses entered infrequently, giving Reba a cursory look and not speaking to Madeleine. Breakfast—pancakes—was brought to her mother on the last morning of Reba's life, the staff apparently unaware that Reba could not swallow. Physicians briefly entered twice, the last time to inform Madeleine that death was imminent, a fact Madeleine already recognized by her mother's condition. When death occurred, Madeleine informed the nursing staff, who told her she could stay with her mother for as long as she wanted and gave her a green garbage bag to put her mother's personal belongings in. No one offered to talk with Madeleine, no one had suggested she leave the room to get something to eat or even a coffee for herself while they remained with Reba. Madeleine remained alone and unsupported during that final time. She had no other family and friends were unavailable—after all, it was a weekend and they had their own families and concerns. But when Madeleine left, one nurse did say, "That's too bad."

The sad story in the opening vignette is, unfortunately, a true one (the names have been changed). It occurred in 1997 in a major hospital in a large Canadian city. The story reflects what most of us do not want for our own final days and certainly not for our loved ones.

Of course, everyone will die; for about 10 percent of people in Western society, the death will come suddenly, but the remaining 90 percent of people will need medical terminal care at the end of their lives (Plonk & Arnold, 2005). How long this care will be needed is vague; even physicians are inaccurate in determining when death is imminent, typically overestimating the time left. The common terminal symptoms include the following:

- severe fatigue
- severe pain (although this tends to decrease as death approaches)
- respiratory problems
- lack of appetite and refusal to eat
- anxiety
- constipation
- nausea/vomiting
- incontinence
- pressure sores
- insomnia
- delirium

Dying people also have reduced ability to communicate in their last days, making it difficult for family and medical personnel to know exactly what their needs and wishes are. For this reason, as well as because of misinterpreted behavioural grimaces and movements caused by delirium, the level of pain that the person is experiencing is often overestimated. Nutritional support by feeding tubes does not usually benefit the person at this time and may, in fact, cause additional distress. The body is stressed in the process of dying, and neither the delirium of the dying person nor treatment with painkillers or sedatives changes this (Plonk & Arnold, 2005).

As difficult as this process is outside a hospital, the Dorothy Ley Hospice Organization (2006) reports that more than 86 percent of Canadians would like to die in their homes. But dying at home is not always possible. In the sections that follow, we will examine death in various settings.

DEATH IN HOSPITALS AND NURSING HOMES

Hospitals are geared toward saving lives more than toward helping people leave life. In some hospitals, certain beds are designated as palliative care beds and are reserved for people who are dying. The hospital may have a special palliative care team who tends to the needs of the dying person and, sometimes, the family. In nursing homes, care is generally provided for people whose physical conditions do not allow them to care for themselves. When death is imminent, it is not uncommon for a person in a nursing home to be transferred to a hospital. In most cases, especially when the hospital does not have a specially designated palliative care section or a palliative care team available, the usually overworked medical staff has little time to meet the needs of the dying patient and his or her family. This was undoubtedly the case of Reba Bryan and her daughter. Additionally, the rules and regulations of hospitals often mean that some of the dying person's wishes cannot be fulfilled and the family is relegated to waiting rooms and corridors instead of having complete access to their dying loved one.

Hospitals, known for their cutting-edge technology and their interest in understanding disease, sometimes promote a more scientific than humane approach to the care of patients and sometimes neglect the families entirely. About half of the families of people who die in hospital complain that they had little communication with the medical staff and little contact with physicians. About 80 percent of the families felt that their dying relatives were not always treated with respect (Teno et al., 2004). Sadly, people who have serious illnesses with poor prognoses spend, on average, more than 18 hours a day alone (Sulmasy & Rahn, 2001), although nurses did spend more time with patients who had do-not-resuscitate orders (Sulmasy & Sood, 2003).

In many cases, although death at home is preferred, and death in a nursing home preferred over a death in a hospital, death does occur in a hospital because of the fears of both the family and the patient that providing the necessary care and easing terminal symptoms will not be possible elsewhere. Patients also express concern that terminal care and a death at home would be too much of a burden for their families (Fried, van Doom, O'Leary, Tinetti, & Drickamer, 1999).

Today, hospitals have become more involved in the care of terminally ill patients. Many have palliative care programs in place in which the individual receives home care with sporadic visits to the hospital.

DEATH IN A HOSPICE

Hospice, as discussed in Chapter 1, refers to both a fixed place or setting and a program of care for the terminally ill. The setting reflects the philosophy of palliative care, life, and death that governs the treatment of patients and the people who are important to them, whether the palliative care is given in a hospital, in a nursing home, in a hospice, or at home. The Canadian Hospice Palliative Care Association states part of its mission statement as "the pursuit of excellence in care for persons approaching death so that the burdens of suffering, loneliness and grief are lessened" (1999). The definition of palliative care given by the World Health Organization (WHO) is as follows:

> Palliative care is an approach that improves the quality of life of patients and their families facing the problem associated with life-threatening illness, through the prevention and relief of suffering by means of early identification and impeccable assessment and treatment of pain and other problems, physical, psychosocial and spiritual. (2006; Reprinted with Permission of the WHO.)

Palliative care does not strive to postpone the death of an individual and regards death as a natural process. It works alongside medical treatments designed to prolong life and later, when medical treatments have been deemed no longer useful. It supports the family of a terminally ill person throughout the illness and in the bereavement after the death. The principles and requirements of palliative care are reflected in the case described in Box 11.1 and are elucidated in Boxes 11.2 and 11.3.

As a setting, a hospice is a place that may be attached to a hospital or to a nursing home, or it may stand alone. It is a place where dying patients can spend their last days being cared for and making those last days as full of life as they want. Bedrooms are fitted for privacy and comfort, much as a bedroom at home, with patients allowed and encouraged to bring personal items for use and display. Living rooms, kitchens, patios, and gardens may all be available to the patient and the patient's family members, who are permitted to visit whenever and for as long as they want.

Staffing in a hospice includes medical personnel (physicians, nurses, pharmacists) who tend to the physical care of the patient, and mental health workers and social workers who attend to the social and emotional needs of the patient and family and help with practical matters, such as insurance forms, medical coverage, and so on. The hospice may also have physiotherapists, whose aid can be invaluable in increasing the patient's comfort, and occupational therapists who provide the opportunity for the patient and family to work together in enjoyable projects and activities. Art therapists, music therapists, and therapeutic recreation specialists, if available, can provide both enjoyment for the patients and families and an atmosphere and a medium in which communication between the dying person and his or her family is facilitated. Clergy from a wide variety of religions often visit and work with the rest of the staff to provide as much as they can for the spiritual needs of the patient and family. This is particularly important in providing the patient and family with comfort and reinforcing the support of their religious community. Usually, a number of trained volunteers work at the hospice and give their time and labour to do whatever work is needed, or to simply sit with the patient and family. Sometimes, staffing also includes one or two dogs, cats, birds, or fish. Although each staff member has particular roles that reflect his or her training and skill, hospices encourage teamwork. It is well recognized, for example, that the emotional needs of the dying individual can have an impact on his or her physical condition, just as worry over insurance claims, for example, may distract the family from spending quality time with their dying relative.

The goals of hospice palliative care are to reduce the suffering and loss of dignity that often attend death, and to ease the burden of the family at this critical time. The needs and desires of the dying individual and his or her family often change as the terminal illness progresses, and the hospice palliative care philosophy includes flexibility to keep abreast and meet, as far as possible, these changing needs. The aim is to help provide the dying individual with a "good death." What constitutes a good death is dependent on each individual, his or her personality, culture, religion, and social and financial circumstances, and the nature of the terminal illness. Some elements are common for many people (see Box 11.4).

DEATH AT HOME

Making the Decision for Home Care

The families of people who have terminal illness often opt to care for their loved one in the home, as did the Lionel family in the case in Box 11.5. More than one in eight Canadians over the age of 15 years provide health care in the home for people with chronic or life-threatening illnesses (Stajduhar & Davies, 2005). The reasons for this decision are many: for one thing, many people perceive dying in the home as part of a good death. Indeed, most Canadians would like to die at home, and terminally ill people may request home care by their families. For some people, caring for family in the home is a cultural norm and the decision may be made with little forethought as to how home care will be accomplished. But adequate home care for a terminally ill person depends on the availability of more than one

BOX 11.1   The DeAngelis Family

Danny DeAngelis was 45 years old when he had a heart attack so severe that his heart was irreparably damaged. He and his family hoped for a heart transplant, but no matching donor was found. Finally, Danny's condition worsened to the point that a transplant was no longer feasible, and hospital personnel suggested transfer to a hospice for the final days. Although Danny's family wanted to care for him at home, they recognized that he needed attention they could not provide and no time was left for them to learn the requisite skills that would be needed for his terminal care. Reluctantly, Danny and his family agreed to the transfer.

On arrival at the hospice, they were pleasantly surprised to find what seemed more like a large home than an institution. Danny was settled in his room by one staff member, while another took the family on a tour of the hospice. They found lounge areas, a kitchen, and gardens. People in bathrobes and in wheelchairs mingled among others in all these areas, laughing and talking. In the kitchen, the DeAngelis family felt quite at home as they smelled the lasagna in the oven—the wife of one of the residents was cooking his (and Danny's) favourite dinner. The staff member told the DeAngelis family that they were welcome to avail themselves of any of the facilities at any time they wanted; they could visit when they wanted and even bring Danny's dog, Bozo, to visit as well. Returning to Danny's room, they found him settled in an easy chair by a large window overlooking the garden.

The family left soon because it was apparent that Danny was tired by the transfer and wanted to sleep. A nurse told them that she would be there all night, only a few steps away, listening for his call. She would be available to talk with him or read to him or listen to music with him if he couldn't sleep. She suggested that the family bring some of Danny's personal possessions, such as pictures, music, books, blankets, and so on, whatever might make Danny feel more comfortable and at ease. The next day, when they returned, they brought Bozo with them. Danny

was in a wheelchair with a hospice worker in the garden, so they let Bozo off his leash. Soon, several other people, some residents of the hospice, their family and friends, and some hospice workers, joined them to watch the dog's antics. Maria, Danny's wife, brought her homemade lasagna, heated it in the hospice kitchen, and the family shared a meal together.

During the next three weeks, Danny's family visited every day and when they were not there, a hospice worker, Michelle, sat with him if he wanted company. Danny talked with Michelle about many things, some of which he was reluctant to discuss with his family, such as his worry that Maria would spend her life in mourning. He wanted her to move on, marry again. With Michelle's facilitation, he finally told Maria this, adding that he wanted another man to have a wonderful life with Maria, just as he had. Danny, Maria, and Michelle all cried, and they smiled as Maria began to reminisce about all the love she and Danny had had in their marriage and what great times they had had.

A few days later, Danny was so weak that it was apparent that death was near. The family priest, a frequent visitor, joined the family and Michelle at Danny's bedside for prayers. The hospice workers moved a cot into Danny's room at Maria's request. She dozed in the cot beside him, holding his hand throughout the night, and early the next morning, Danny died. Maria called the family and was immediately swept into Michelle's arms as they cried together. After the funeral, which Michelle attended, Maria and her family were offered individual counselling and the services of an ongoing bereavement support group. They gratefully declined, but Michelle called Maria every week for the next few months, asking how the family was coping with their bereavement and giving Maria advice and support. Now, 18 months later, Maria still hears from Michelle occasionally and calls her when she needs to talk. Maria is mourning deeply, but she feels consoled by knowing that Danny died a good death. Her gratitude and admiration for the hospice staff is unending.

caregiver, the financial ability of the family to shoulder the responsibility, whether the patient can function without continual support from professional caregivers (e.g., self-feeding, enough movement to allow bed sheets to be changed or to use a bedpan), and whether the patient's physical symptoms can be controlled in the home. Clearly, effective home care relies on the

availability of skilled palliative caregivers along with the family, as the Lionel family discovered (Stajduhar & Davies, 2005).

The decision to care for a terminally ill person in the home is sometimes made against the family members' preferences. A report compiled for Health Canada by Decima Research Incorporated (2002) found that

BOX 11.2 Principles and Requirements of Palliative Care

The principles of palliative care were elucidated by Dame Cicely Saunders (1995), the British physician who opened St. Christopher's Hospice in 1967, the first hospice of the modern age. Dr. Saunders's work made these principles the basis for hospice care throughout the world:

1. Dying people have the right to be enabled to live until they die.
2. Dying people must be recognized as unique individuals with differing needs and wants.
3. Dying people must be allowed to have control of their lives and be independent for as long as possible.
4. Dying people should be given information about the seriousness of their diseases to help them make informed decisions regarding their care and how to spend their final days.
5. Dying people are part of larger social networks and must be helped to continue their relationships.
6. Dying people must be given the opportunity to reach out to their hopes and dreams of whatever is most meaningful to them, allowing them to feel a sense of completion at the end of their lives.
7. The families of dying people must be allowed to participate in the final days of their loved one, to resolve issues, engage in activities together, and fulfill the possibilities for personal and family growth that can occur in these days.
8. The staff involved in the care of a dying person must become aware of their own feelings about death so that they can support the dying individual, the family, and one another. In doing this, they should come to recognize the beauty that can exist in even the most adverse circumstances.

BOX 11.3 Palliative Care for Children

Bruce Himelstein (2006), a physician in the palliative care unit of Children's Hospital of Wisconsin, expanded on the principles of palliative care put forth by Dame Cicely Saunders (see Box 11.2), feeling that even more conditions must be met when the terminally ill patient is a child. The principles he suggested are as follows:

1. Care is child focused, family oriented, and relationship centred.
2. Care focuses on relief of suffering and enhancing quality of life for the child and family.
3. All children suffering from chronic, life-threatening, and terminal illnesses are eligible.
4. Care is provided for the child as a unique individual and the family as a functional unit.
5. Palliative care is incorporated into the mainstream of medical care regardless of the curative intent of therapy.
6. Care is not directed at shortening life.
7. Care is coordinated across all sites of care delivery.
8. Care is goal directed and is consistent with the beliefs and values of the child and his or her caregivers.
9. A multidisciplinary team is always available to families to provide continuity.
10. Advocacy for participation of the child and caregivers in decision making is paramount.
11. Facilitation and documentation of communication are critical tasks of the team.
12. Respite care and support are essential for families and caregivers.
13. Bereavement care should be provided for as long as needed.
14. Do-not-resuscitate orders should not be required.
15. Prognosis for short-term survival is not required.

Source: Adapted from Himelstein (2006, p. 163).

more than half of family caregivers perceived no choice in caring for their ill relatives, and other studies have found that 80 percent of family caregivers believed that better care for their relatives would be found in inpatient palliative care facilities (Stajduhar & Davies, 2005). In attempting to understand the reasons that families opt for home care of a dying loved one, Stajduar and Davies (2005) interviewed both active and bereaved family

BOX 11.4   What Constitutes a "Good Death"?

Studies have examined what people believe constitutes a "good death." These studies have included interviews with dying people, their families, medical personnel, social workers, chaplains, and volunteer hospice workers (Masson, 2002; Payne, Langley-Evans, & Hillier, 1996; Steinhauser et al., 2000). Although, of course, wide individual differences and differences among groups of people interviewed exist, the following common elements of a good death can be extrapolated:

- *Pain and symptom management.* No one wants to die or to see other people die with a great deal of pain and discomfort. Dying people and their families in particular want to know that their pain and discomfort, both now and in the future, will receive attention. This alleviates distress in the present and worry about the possibility of distress at a future time.

- *Clear communication.* A good death requires that the dying person and the family receive comprehensive and comprehensible information about options and what to expect during the dying process. This aids in informed decision making, which should lie in the hands of the dying person for as long as possible. Many people feel that a good death includes enough information about what to expect physically, emotionally, and socially so that they can make plans for their death. For example, some people want the opportunity to plan their own funerals or write their own obituaries. The family needs information about what to expect as well, so that they will not be caught by surprise and possibly misunderstand the symptoms that their dying loved one may show. They too need to make decisions and plans before they experience the death, when their emotionality is intense.

- *Affirmation of the whole person.* With a good death, a person is treated with an understanding of the context of the person's whole life and his or her values, beliefs, and perspectives. The good death involves the understanding that a unique individual is dying and that he or she is not defined by a disease or by a physical condition at the end of life. This affirmation includes respect for the person's religion, culture, and social milieu.

- *Completion.* To have a good death, people need opportunities to partake of culturally or religiously prescribed rituals, to finish unfinished business, to resolve conflicts, to prepare spiritually, to review their lives, to spend time with friends and family, and to say goodbye.

- *Contributions to other people's lives and welfare.* The good death includes an opportunity for dying people to make gifts of their possessions to loved ones, to pass on what they have learned in life, even to bring a smile to someone's face. This final giving can bring purpose and meaning to the closing days and make death seem like more of an appropriate ending to life.

The differences among the groups of people interviewed are noteworthy. Physicians, for example, focused on the medical and biological issues of death and rarely if ever mentioned "completion" (Steinhauser et al., 2000). Dying people are more likely to mention the wish for a sudden death (i.e., without lapsing into a coma) than are hospice workers (Payne, Langley-Evans, & Hillier, 1996), and are less likely than their families to indicate that a good death is one that comes after a long life and occurs in a pleasant environment of care (Masson, 2002). Masson (2002) noted that sometimes what constitutes a good death for the patient is not what constitutes a good death for the family and that the dying individual is more focused on the immediate concerns of death and the realistic expectations of what will occur.

caregivers, and found that their decisions fell into three categories:

1. *Uninformed decisions.* A little more than one-third of the caregivers interviewed indicated that they had given little or no thought to the decision to care for a dying loved one at home, that it had been a spontaneous decision based on the requests of the ill person or on the dissatisfaction with institutional care, or that they believed that the caregiving time would be short because death was imminent. They revealed that they had unrealistic expectations of the dying process or what to expect of their relative's physical condition. They consequently had no idea of the stresses that caring for a terminally ill person would have on them and their families. Even when given information about these areas by palliative care counsellors, they sometimes did not comprehend the reality of the situation they were facing, instead romanticizing the idea

BOX 11.5   The Lionel Family

Jamal Lionel was only seven years old and he was dying. He had spent his short life going back and forth to hospitals for treatment of leukemia, but finally the physicians told his family that no potentially curative treatments were left. Rosalie, his mother, immediately asked if she could take Jamal home to die. She knew how much he hated the hospital, and she wanted him to have the comfort of his own room in his own home for as long as possible. Rosalie, a daycare worker, had already been informed by her employer that she could take as much time off work as she needed and her job would be waiting for her whenever she returned. This would be a financial burden for the Lionel family—without Rosalie's full income, money would be tight, especially if Jamal's condition remained the same for several weeks. But Serge, Rosalie's husband, reassured her that his income would get them through the short term, and he wanted Jamal home as much as she did. Before taking Jamal home, a palliative care nurse and a social worker called Rosalie and Serge to a conference in which they taught the parents about what to expect of Jamal's condition as his health further deteriorated, and they all made plans for visits by a home-care nurse every few days to help Rosalie in administering and monitoring Jamal's medications. The nurse would also be present when Jamal's physician dropped by to check on her patient's condition and he would see to it that a physician's help would be available in case of a medical emergency. A palliative care home worker would also visit every day to help with domestic chores that Rosalie would not have the time and energy for. The nurse then trained the Lionels in the proper administration of Jamal's medications and how to care for him themselves.

The nurse and social worker arranged for a hospital bed to be moved into Jamal's bedroom at home, and they accompanied the family when Jamal was transferred home. Assuring himself that Jamal's family understood and could manage his physical care, the nurse left, saying that he would call the family every week to find out how they were doing. The social worker stayed a little longer, talking to each family member individually about how they felt and what they could expect. She then gathered the family together for a group discussion about how Jamal's dying at home and his eventual death would affect them, even discussing with them what funeral arrangements they would like to make. This was a difficult discussion. When everyone seemed comfortable and decisions had been made, the social worker said she would call them every few days and left

them her telephone number so that they could call her whenever they wanted.

During the next few weeks, Rosalie, who had initially been reluctant to have a nurse and a home-care worker come into her home every day, found how much she needed them. Thankfully, she knew what to expect of Jamal's health in these weeks because of the information she had been given before the transfer, and now she knew for sure how right the palliative care nurse and social worker had been in insisting that she receive extra help daily. She had had visions of being able to cook and clean while Jamal slept, but the reality was that she had neither the time nor the energy to do either. With the home-care worker's help, though, she had no worries about accomplishing anything other than being with Jamal and her two other children.

Jamal's friends came to visit him, accompanied by a nurse who explained to them what was happening to Jamal. This removed their fear of the tubes in Jamal's arms and allowed them to talk and play quietly with him. Jamal enjoyed these brief visits and felt "normal," he said. A highlight for Jamal came when his family's church pastor, another frequent visitor, sent the choir to sing on the lawn outside his bedroom window. Jamal had always loved their jubilant hymns and clapped his hands along with them.

As death came near, Jamal's physician was summoned by the nurse. He suggested that Jamal, who was now experiencing enough pain to be medicated to the point of semi-consciousness, be given more sedation. This might hasten his death somewhat, said the physician, but not appreciably, and everyone would know that Jamal would die comfortably. Rosalie burst into tears and protested that she wanted Jamal to be with her for as long as possible, but Serge, choking back his own tears, told her that the decision had to be based on Jamal's welfare now. Gradually, Rosalie calmed down and agreed, remembering the talks she had with the social worker. The physician administered the extra sedation, and Jamal seemed to sleep more easily. Eight hours later, the child died without awakening.

Rosalie and Serge thought they were prepared for Jamal's death, but they quickly found that no one is prepared to lose their child. They called the social worker, who put the funeral arrangements they had decided on into action, arriving at the Lionel home to oversee the transfer of Jamal's body to the funeral home. She also called the pastor of the family church, who quickly arrived as well. All of them, together, talked of Jamal and wept.

that a home death would come soon and be quiet and peaceful. Often, they found themselves overwhelmed by the reality.

2. *Indifferent decisions.* In this category fell almost half of the caregivers interviewed. They also felt unprepared for the situation they were facing but felt that they had little choice but to care for their dying relatives at home. They gave precedence to the wishes of their terminally ill relatives to die in the home, with little consideration for their own desires and best interests, often indicating that they would feel too guilty if they opted to have their relatives die elsewhere. Most of these caregivers tried to maintain a positive attitude, especially in front of the patient lest he or she feel like a burden.

3. *Negotiated decisions.* A minority of the interviewed caregivers had histories of openness about the topic of dying and discussed the option of home palliative care with the dying relative. The decision was made jointly, as had many other decisions before the onset of the illness. These caregivers were the best prepared and most knowledgeable about home palliative care, and they coped best with the situation.

Stajduhar and Davies (2005) also found that, regardless of the type of decision made, three prominent factors affected their decision to care for their terminally ill relatives in the home:

1. *Making promises to care.* Many people indicate their desire to die at home to their loved ones. This request can occur a long time before the onset of the illness, or anywhere in the progress of the illness. Many relatives make the promise to care for the individual when and if the time comes. Consequently, they often feel obligated to fulfill their promises even when they know how difficult the situation will be. For some caregivers, the fulfillment of the promise gave them a sense of accomplishment and pride as well as the satisfaction that they gave their loved one what he or she had wanted. For others, however, regret that they had made the promise seemed predominant. If the time came in the progress of the illness or for other reasons that the caregiver felt that he or she ~ould no longer maintain home care, he or she ~n felt great guilt and a sense of failure at the ~ing of the promise.

   ~ning normalcy. For many home caregivers, ~ force behind their decision to care for ~ relatives at home was the need to be ~ situation and to regain some ~mily life for themselves and

their relatives. In the home, they could determine when and what meals could be served; the family could eat, participate in activities, and talk together in privacy. In short, the dying relative could participate in the life of the family in natural surroundings as long as possible. This also allowed the caregivers to feel less helpless and more effectual in the last days of their loved one's life. For many of these caregivers, the next factor played a large part in their need for control.

3. *Disliking institutionalized health-care practices.* Most of the caregivers interviewed found institutional care to be impersonal and paternalistic. Negative experiences of feeling as if they were a nuisance in their requests of medical staff or were in the way left them feeling humiliated and mistrustful of the quality of care that their terminally ill relatives were receiving. Although many caregivers were appreciative of the care and advice that medical personnel gave them, they felt that medical personnel are generally overworked, with little time to provide the attention and care to their loved ones that they could give them at home. Additionally, they found acute care settings in hospitals to be overly governed by rules and policies that were not conducive to a good death, and the scarcity of palliative care beds in hospitals and in hospices, where rules are more flexible, gave them little choice but to take their relatives home.

Care in the Home

It is clear that home care for the terminally ill requires the assistance of a multidisciplinary team. Home visits by nurses and home-care workers are imperative if the caregivers are not to become overwhelmed by the magnitude of their tasks. Furthermore, the palliative care team must be aware of and respect cultural and religious norms that operate in the family's home. For example, as was discussed in Chapter 3, some cultures do not want death to be discussed or the patient informed of the seriousness of the illness. Just as with palliative care in a hospital or hospice, the assistance given the family must be in accordance with their desires and not violate their values and beliefs. In all cases, the control and wishes of the patient are paramount and should be maintained for as long as possible. This needs to be discussed and understood before any decisions about care are made (Kemp, 2005).

Before home care is attempted, the patient and the caregivers must be given adequate information about what to expect of the physical condition and what the medications will do. In a study done in Quebec, for example, information about pain medication was found to significantly improve the effective use of pain medication in the home and consequently reduce the amount of pain the patient experiences (Aubin et al., 2006). Professionals in the appropriate areas are needed to perform ongoing evaluations of the ill person's medical and psychological conditions as well. For example, without professional assessment, family caregivers may assume that the ill person's depression is a normal part of the illness and impending death. Yet in some cases, the depression may be severe enough to be pathological and can be effectively treated, thereby decreasing the person's distress (Block, 2006).

As we will discuss later, the stresses on the at-home caregivers are extreme and sometimes continue for long periods. In these cases, it is highly advantageous for a palliative care program to include such services as **respite care,** in which the terminally ill person is cared for temporarily by someone else. This may mean that the ill person is transferred to an institution or hospice, or that other professional caregivers move into the home for a brief time. Respite care can be very helpful in providing a much-needed reprieve for the caregivers, who can be relieved of immediate responsibilities while knowing that their loved one is comfortable and well-attended. It would be beneficial for Rosalie and Serge Lionel, for example, to be able to go out for dinner and a movie, or away for the weekend, to have a short distraction from their great grief, knowing that the respite caregiver is trained to handle any of their ill child's needs. More normalcy is also provided for all members of the household by such a respite.

Assistance during the final days is not enough; palliative care principles demand that families, in their bereavement, also receive support and empathy. When the practical jobs of caring for the terminally ill person are over, the job of caring for the family continues, and although palliative care programs differ from place to place, depending on resources and priorities, the best of them include after-death contact and support of the family for a lengthy period (Himelstein, 2006).

Transfer Back to Institutional Care

Most terminally ill patients who are cared for in the home die there, but in some cases terminally ill patients are transferred to other facilities. Evans, Cutson, Steinhauser, and Tulsky (2006) explored the reasons for the transfer:

1. *An acute medical event.* In some cases, a new disorder is diagnosed, an injury occurs, or a chronic condition unrelated to the terminal illness deteriorates to the point at which home care is unfeasible.
2. *An uncontrolled symptom.* In other cases, a physical symptom of the terminal illness that had been controlled in home care changes or becomes more severe. Extra measures that are not possible in the home are required, precipitating the transfer to another facility.
3. *Imminent death.* In some cases, when death became imminent, the dying person is transferred to another facility for the actual death. Sometimes an intensification in pain or an increase in dementia make a death at home undesirable. In other cases, the caregiver simply does not want the death to occur in the home because of the possibility of a future filled with reminders of the occurrence. In general, family caregivers are more likely than terminally ill patients to prefer that the actual death occur in a facility other than the home, as found in a study done in southcentral and western Ontario (Brazil, Howell, Bedard, Krueger, & Heidebrecht, 2005).
4. *Inability to provide needed care at home.* Sometimes the dying patient experiences problems, such as a fall, or a progressively debilitated condition that compromises their safety. In these cases, the home caregiver does not have the physical ability to assist the patient (e.g., is not capable of assisting the patient in getting up). Home care is then deemed unfeasible and transfer to another facility is mandatory.

In these cases under study (Evans et al., 2006), caregivers wanted to continue to care for their loved ones at home, but this was not possible, or continued home care would have shortened whatever time was left to the patient or made the time left unreasonably uncomfortable. The caregivers had little regret, as they knew they had done the best they could to care for their loved ones at home, but they were more satisfied when the patient was transferred to a hospice than to a hospital. This preference seemed to revolve around the cleanliness of the facility, the homelike feeling of the hospice, and the proximity to nature. When transfer was to an acute care setting (a hospital), the caregivers' satisfaction depended on how well the medical personnel communicated with them about the goals of care and followed treatment preferences, and how personalized the care given to their loved ones was.

The Lionel family, in Box 11.5, felt that they had made the right decision for their son, but they also realized that without the education and the assistance of home-care nurses and workers, they could not have done it. According to an old saying, it takes a village to raise a child. The Lionels discovered that it also takes a village to give a person a good death at home.

CAREGIVER STRESS

The Family

A very positive picture has been painted of hospice palliative care in this chapter. But the reality is sometimes far from this. Consider the case of George and Glenda in Box 11.6.

As has been discussed, giving home care to a terminally ill person is extremely difficult, if not often impossible, without aid from visiting palliative care workers. But not everyone knows these services are available and not everyone has access to them; as reported in Chapter 1, only 53 percent of Canadians have heard of palliative care and fewer than 15 percent of the people who die in Canada each year have access to these services (Dorothy Ley Foundation, 2006). People living in some rural communities, like George and Glenda, or on reserves may have only a visiting physician or nurse come to their areas and then sporadically. Nurses, social workers, and so on, who are involved in palliative care are very rarely seen. In such cases as these, the family may have no choice but to hospitalize a dying relative in a centre far away or to try to manage as best as they can at home. The stresses of trying to visit a far-off hospital or take time off work (if possible) to stay in the area of the hospital (with the attendant costs and inconvenience) are clear. Yet if the family does neither of these, they have the stress of additional guilt and pain of not being able to be at their loved one's side. If they try to manage home care on their own, they are undertaking an enormous task and one that may not be accomplished without

---

BOX 11.6   George and Glenda

George, a conservation officer, and his wife, Glenda, a waitress, lived in a small, remote, rural community—so small that their only medical service came from a visiting nurse practitioner who arrived once a week to care for the people. They had no children or family living close by, but their friends and neighbours were kind and supportive. On one of the nurse's visits, she arranged for George to be examined for his persistent cough by a medical specialist in the nearest small city. George and Glenda both took time off work to go to the city, paying for their transportation and their stay in a hotel with money they could ill afford. George was diagnosed with lung cancer. With many costly trips to the city hospital and much time off work, he received treatment for the cancer, with Glenda at his side. Sadly, the treatment was unsuccessful, and it was suggested that he receive palliative care until his death.

George and Glenda had always lived in the country and found city living uncomfortable and lonely. But their community had no hospices and no palliative care team to facilitate George's care at home. Glenda was particularly miserable: not only was her beloved husband dying, but she also knew he wanted to die at home and she didn't know how she could manage it. The alternative was for George to stay in the palliative care section of the hospital. Only a few beds were set aside for palliative care, and the palliative care team was very small, consisting mainly of volunteers. The unavailability of people trained in pal-liative care took its toll in this city, as it does in all others. But Glenda felt she couldn't leave George to die alone in a strange city, even though he might be given excellent care. She had already taken so much time off work that the couple's financial situation was precarious. She knew she was eligible for compassionate care leave, but this was only for eight weeks. What if George lasted longer than eight weeks? Glenda felt terrible about even thinking that it might be best if George died quickly, but the truth was, if he didn't, she would have no money and no job to go back to.

George and Glenda finally made the decision that George would spend his last days in his own home for as long as possible. The medical personnel at the hospital trained Glenda to handle many situations that might come up in George's condition, but she was scared. What if a medical emergency occurred that she was untrained for? How would she get help for them? The horrible vision of George in pain and dying because he had no one with the skills to help him haunted her. Then again, the spectre of George dying away from the home where he grew up and that he loved was equally distasteful. She hadn't even considered how burdensome and exhausting caring for George on her own would be; she hoped that some people in the community would drop by and help sometimes, but she knew how busy they were with their own lives, and she didn't count on much.

---

undue discomfort to both the caretakers and the dying person.

Financial considerations also play a part in the stress of the family. In Canada, medical care and hospitalization are covered by a governmentally administered medical insurance plan, so unless the family of a terminally ill person wants specialized care (e.g., a private nurse) or a special setting (e.g., a private or semi-private room), no cost is attached to death in an institution. Other countries, such as the United States, do not have universal medical coverage, and the family of a terminally ill person may have no choice but to care for the loved one in the home because of the prohibitive costs of institutional care. However, the family may have to pay extreme additional costs to fit the home for care of a seriously ill person and endure costs in terms of wages lost if one person must quit a job to become a caregiver. Costs to refit a home are often borne by families in Canada as well if home care is chosen, although some financial help is available for the home care. For example, Canadian employment insurance gives benefits for up to six weeks over a six-month period to eligible workers who take time for the caretaking of terminally ill family members (Service Canada, (2007). Most employees under federal jurisdiction are permitted eight weeks of compassionate care leave for caregiving with no jeopardy to their job (Human Resources and Social Development Canada [HRSDC], 2007).

But not all employees can count on this: many workplaces, such as the corner grocery store, are not covered by Canada's *Labour Code*. Most workers are covered by provincial and territorial labour legislation, which includes compassionate care leave in all jurisdictions except Alberta and the Northwest Territories (HRSDC, 2007). Thus, in choosing to give care at home, a family may bear a financial burden as well as the possibility of job loss, especially if the final illness is lengthy. Such considerations often militate against the possibility of giving home care.

Even if the family has ready access to palliative care services from a local medical or social welfare centre, the stresses of caring for a terminally ill loved one in the home are still very great. Obviously, unless they have several trained helpers, the family's freedom is severely curtailed; for example, if Serge Lionel, the father in Box 11.5, is working and the mother, Rosalie Lionel, is caring for Jamal, the dying child, what happens when the school calls to say that one of Jamal's siblings is feeling ill and needs to be picked up and brought home? Rosalie cannot leave Jamal unattended to fetch one of her other children, but clearly the sibling cannot be left at school while he or she is sick. Without helpers to pick up the sibling or to stay with Jamal, Rosalie is left in an untenable position. Glenda, in Box 11.6, may have even more

problems when no helpers are available at all to help her. In case of an emergency situation for George, the nearest emergency medical centre is a three-hour drive away, and Glenda may not be able to even get George into the car.

The progressively demanding physical work of caring for a terminally ill person may leave caretakers overwhelmed as well. Medications need to be administered at regular intervals throughout the day and night, feeding may need to be done for each meal, bathing or washing the ill person requires physical strength in lifting, as does changing bedding or diapers in cases of incontinence. Also, the role formerly enacted by the terminally ill person within the family must be taken on by others (e.g., child-care, meal preparation, bill paying, household maintenance). Again the need for more than one person to care for the ill loved one becomes apparent. The caregiver often increasingly becomes the decision maker for the ill person; as the ill person becomes sicker, he or she may no longer be able to make decisions about care, and medical personnel rely on the caregiver for information, such as the level of pain the ill person is experiencing. Pearlin and Aneshensel (1994) conceptualized the caregiving role as threefold:

1. *Role acquisition.* As the terminally ill person becomes progressively sicker, the role of the caregiver changes to encompass more responsibilities. For example, at the onset of the illness, the ill person may need little help in eating or going to the bathroom. This changes as the illness progresses and the person becomes more and more debilitated. After a while, the terminally ill person needs assistance in performing these and other tasks. The caregiver needs to be trained in how to help in the most effective way, as well as being trained in administering medications, preventing bedsores, changing dressings, and so on.
2. *Role enactment.* This encompasses carrying out the tasks demanded by the role of caregiver.
3. *Role disengagement.* When the terminally ill loved one dies, the role of caregiver is over, and the caregiver must relinquish the role and what has become a large part of his or her life. Being bereaved, the caregiver may find himself or herself at a loss to know what to do because the accustomed role is over. Simply resuming the previous life is extremely difficult at this time because of grief and because of the sudden loss of the role.

Managing change can be one of the stresses the caregiver also faces: the terminally ill person's condition may change rapidly, requiring new tasks to be mastered without delay. The caregiver is also usually the person responsible for communication within the terminally ill person's social network. It is the caregiver who is typically contacted or who contacts friends and family to report the ill person's condition and to monitor visiting in a way that the ill person will appreciate but that will not unduly tax him or her. As well, the caregiver is usually the person on whom the ill person depends to fulfill his or her wishes, such as the distribution of possessions, the funeral arrangements, and so on.

For most caregivers, however, one of the greatest stresses lies in watching a person they love become progressively sicker and debilitated until death occurs. This is particularly difficult when the ill person's personality and physical condition change in unpredictable ways or when dementia sets in. For the caregiver, the job has no happy ending, a fact that may only gradually become real to the caregiver who, as is common when facing the terminal illness of a loved one, may not be emotionally aware or prepared even though he or she has the intellectual knowledge that the end is near (Waldrop, Kramer, Skretny, Milch, & Finn, 2005; see also Chapter 5). The only rewards for the caregiver come from personal satisfaction and pride in caregiving and the knowledge that he or she has done everything possible to give the loved one a good death. These rewards are not inconsequential, and many caregivers report after the death that they are glad and even grateful for having had the opportunity to care for their loved ones, an experience that they found to be profoundly meaningful (Cohen, Colantonio, & Vernich, 2002).

The degree of stress experienced by a family caregiver depends on several factors. A group of researchers studied family caregivers in the Quebec City area who were taking care of loved ones with advanced cancer (Dumont et al., 2006). They, along with other Canadian researchers (Grunfeld et al., 2004), found that the caregiver's distress increased as the ill loved one's condition worsened. Along with other studies, they also found that the closeness of the relationship with the ill loved one, the age of the ill person, the age and gender of the caregiver, and the degree of perceived social support all played a part in the caregiver's stress (see also Fried, Bradley, O'Leary, & Byers, 2005; Given et al., 2004; Vachon, 1998):

- Young caregivers experienced more distress than did older caregivers. More distress was experienced when the ill person was young, when the ill person was completely bedridden, or death came closer.
- Women experienced more distress than men did.
- Feeling little social or emotional support was related to higher levels of distress.
- Caregivers who felt a financial burden through loss of income reported more distress than other caregivers.

- Caregivers with poor health themselves felt more distress than do healthy caregivers.

These researchers reported on other studies that indicated that as the caregiver's level of distress increases, so does the ill person's, and vice versa, but less distress is experienced by caregivers who feel a high degree of self-competence.

Caregiving may have long-term effects as well. In studies that examined the effects of caregiving on spouses, both positive and negative effects were found. On one hand, if the term of caregiving has been long and arduous, the bereaved spouse may feel relief at the death, obtain more social support, and feel purpose and efficacy (Bennett & Vidal-Hall, 2000). On the other hand, physical well-being may be decreased by demanding caregiving situations (Navaie-Waliser et al., 2002). Additionally, one study found that levels of depression and loneliness were higher among spousal caregivers for as long as three years, as compared with noncaregivers (Robinson-Whelan, Yuri Tada, MacCallum, & Kicolt-Glaser, 2001), although at four years after the end of caregiving, the effects of having been a caregiver seem to be mainly positive (Prokos & Keene, 2005).

Interventions to help caregivers cope with the stress they are undergoing are needed, but very few studies have been done to examine the effects of such interventions. One well-conducted study, however, found that when hospice nurses gave support to caregivers of cancer patients and taught them about how to cope with specific symptoms during three visits, caregiver quality of life increased while their distress about the symptoms of the ill person and their feeling of burden decreased (McMillan, 2005). But for most Canadians, services and trained personnel are not available to help them care for someone during their last days. Glenda, from Box 11.6, speaks again in Box 11.7.

End-of-Life Care Personnel

The effects of stress of end-of-life care felt by end-of-life care personnel are often overlooked. People often assume that medical personnel react little to watching a patient in the process of dying because they are used to it or because their unemotional personality has drawn them to this type of work. This is emphatically not the case for most physicians, nurses, psychologists, social workers, and others involved in palliative care. On the contrary, physicians are trained to save lives, and many regard a patient's death as a personal failure. Most physicians have no training and little experience in dealing with terminal illnesses, let alone the social and emotional needs of the patient and family. It is not uncommon for patients and families to report that when

BOX 11.7   Glenda Speaks

George died two days ago. The funeral is tomor-row. I hate myself for saying this, but I'm relieved. I know he suffered, and I know it caused him pain to see what the last four months have been like for me. When I brought him home to die, I wanted him to live for as long as possible, but I was afraid that it would go on too long. I think four months was too long.

I'm so tired. I haven't had a day off in all this time and I haven't had one night when I could sleep right through. George needed constant attention, and of course I couldn't even think of leaving him. A couple of the neighbours offered to stay with him for a few hours so that I could at least get in groceries and supplies, but I always got home as fast as I could. I was so afraid that something would happen that the neighbours couldn't handle while I was gone. And once it did—I got home just in time to clear George's breathing tube. Poor Peggy who was staying with him was in a panic; she had no idea what to do. If I hadn't come in at that moment, George would have died right then and there. After that, some-body else always got the groceries for me while I stayed home. Rosie, the nurse, brought me

medical supplies on her weekly visits and some-times she came twice a week when she could, just to check in and to do some of the things for George that I couldn't do. Near the end, he could-n't move much, and she helped me bathe him. I thought I was strong, but George was a big man, and it wasn't easy for me to move him as much as I would have liked. He got a bedsore because I couldn't move him too much. I feel so guilty for that. Rosie said that it was time to move him back to the hospital when he got the bedsore, but be-fore she could arrange it, he died.

I'm not sorry I brought him home. I loved him so much. Caring for him at the end was all there was left that I could do for him, and I feel good about doing it. But now what am I going to do? They had to hire somebody to replace me at work. I understand that—four months is a long time to be off. George's insurance money isn't going to last me for long and jobs are scarce around here. I may have to sell the house and move to some other place to get work. I can't think about that now. Even though I'm relieved that he's gone, I want my husband back.

---

a terminal illness is diagnosed, visits from the physician are rare and brief. This can be remedied, at least in part, by giving physicians further education that palliative care is not just a service provided by nurses and that their participation is both needed and wanted (Hanratty et al., 2006).

Nurses, perhaps, witness more of the sadness and pain of the terminally ill patient and his or her family because they are on the frontline, intimately involved in the day-to-day care of the patient in hospitals. Nurses working in hospitals are faced with trying to maintain high-level quality of care while often being overworked, with responsibilities for many patients at the same time. They have little opportunity to spend time simply talk-ing to the patient and family despite their oft-expressed desires to do so and despite their lack of training in how to help and support terminally ill patients and their fam-ilies. Sometimes, as well, nurses have ethical misgivings about the treatment the physicians are giving the patient, treatments that they feel are futile and decrease the patient's chances of having a good death (Cronqvist, Theorell, Burns, & Lützén, 2004; Ferrell, 2006; Morita, Miyashita, Kimura, Adachi, & Shima, 2004). Their dis-tress at the death of a patient, whom they have been car-ing for on a regular basis, is compounded by the feeling that they had no chance to become well acquainted with

the patient on a more personal level, something they often feel guilty for. Consider the reports that two nurses made to the author:

I had been taking care of him for three weeks. Every day I tried to spend as much time as I could with him. He was so cool, always upbeat, even when he could hardly talk or even breathe. He called me his ray of sunshine. I wasn't even on duty when he died. I came back to work after the weekend, and somebody told me that he had died on Sunday. I found another patient in his bed already. And I was supposed to go on as if nothing had happened. I'm supposed to be a strong man and a professional, but I just couldn't. I ducked into the washroom and closed myself in a stall and just cried for about ten minutes. Then I had to get to work. It felt even worse later when the wife called me and thanked me for being so nice to him and to them. What could I say? I could have done so much more! I should have found a way to spend more time with all of them. I could have stayed later after work instead of rushing home. All I could do was say how sorry I was that I wasn't there at the end and how much I'd miss him. Some help I was.

The mother was late in her sixth month of pregnancy when a crisis made immediate delivery mandatory. We induced labour and after eight hours, she gave birth to twin boys. They were born within five minutes of each other and they were beautiful, perfect—except neither one lived. We couldn't even get them to breathe. People think that we can always do this, but we can't. We tried, oh God, how we tried! We went on trying for I don't know how long, but it was no use. And the parents were watching and, I guess, praying, looking for us to perform a miracle. We all felt like we had failed in the worst possible way. We didn't want to even look at the mother. How could she stand it? We have kids too, and the thought of a dead baby, let alone two, was too much for any of us to bear. We tried to keep it together until we got outside the delivery room, but then we just cried. A couple of us managed to get back to work with other patients, we had to, our hospital has financial problems, I guess they all do today, and we were badly understaffed. But every time we looked at each other, we could see it in each others' eyes that we were suffering.

Another nurse couldn't get back to work at all. She was just totaled. Even today, seven months later, we still talk about it, and we still feel so sad.

If nurses work in palliative care settings, they have more opportunity to interact with patients and families. In fact, their goals are to form relationships of trust with the patient and family, becoming more like a friend and part of the family. This relationship is one that they find meaningful and enriching (Mok & Chiu, 2004), but then their distress at the time of death often encompasses the fact that they feel they have lost a friend; they, with specialized training, often feel they must strive to put their own grief aside in order to be a support and comfort for the family.

In some cases, more than the illnesses and deaths of patients are troublesome to the staff. Rushton and colleagues (2006) reported that the staff of a children's hospital felt that sometimes communication was lacking and even conflict existed between the families and the staff or among the staff themselves. This provided the extra burden of trying to ameliorate these problems; for example, nurses often felt they had to step outside their roles of following physicians' orders to advocate for the family's needs. They were then open to the charge that they were acting unprofessionally and were insubordinate, yet they felt their professional integrity and their moral imperative made speaking up vital. This role conflict increased their own distress over the patient's and family's circumstances and made them unsure of what their roles really were and how to balance competing professional and ethical obligations. One survey found that nearly half of medical personnel had acted against their consciences in giving care to terminally ill people, especially when futile life-sustaining measures were used and resulted in greater distress for the patient (Solomon et al., 1993).

Most palliative care facilities and many hospitals have support groups where end-of-life care personnel can share their experiences and become more educated about end-of-life issues and how to deal with them. One such program has been put in place at the Johns Hopkins Children's Center in Baltimore, Maryland, where the cumulative distress of dealing with the life-threatening illnesses and the deaths of children tax the personnel greatly (Rushton et al., 2006). In this program, a network was made of all the units in the hospital in which patients had a great likelihood of having life-threatening illnesses. The network was interdisciplinary, including physicians, nurses, social workers, child-life specialists, and others. The network sponsored training sessions on palliative care issues, presenting perspectives from all the disciplines involved. Palliative care rounds and conferences were also initiated in which the treatment plans and the social and emotional needs of individual palliative care patients and their families were discussed, as were emotional needs of the health-care team. By these means, information from different perspectives was shared. The morale and feeling of competence of the health-care workers increased, and the mutual support decreased feelings of distress. Finally, bereavement debriefing sessions were held after the death of a patient, giving staff members an opportunity to explore and manage their own grief responses. Included in these sessions were informal rituals of remembrance for the child who had died, such as signing sympathy cards for the family or sharing a poem. These sessions helped in dealing with grief by supplying grief management strategies and decreasing the feeling of isolation through the team participation.

Such approaches as the Johns Hopkins program are promising, but the existing programs in most terminal-care facilities are far less comprehensive. In many cases, no help at all is available for medical personnel. Consider the case of the nurse practitioner Rosie,

George died this morning. Glenda called me on my cell phone when I was travelling to another community. I turned around and went to her right away, but I couldn't stay for long—I have six communities that rely on me for their medical care. I'm completely overworked, and it isn't fair that these people have no one else but me. I try to do what I can, but in a case like George's, properly trained people should come and help Glenda. No money for it. No people trained in palliative care. What few people there are mainly stay in the cities in hospitals. That's fine, especially since I understand that there aren't enough for the city hospitals either. But it still makes me mad. Not everybody lives in a city, and they have the right to care in their homes as much as everybody else does. It's going to get worse, too. The people I see are getting older. What happens to them? Who takes care of them? The government talks about helping people care for their dying relatives at home, but I don't see much happening in the communities I visit.

I'm going to miss George. I've known him and Glenda for 15 years. Good people, people I count as friends. They both deserved better than they got. I want to go to George's funeral, and I'm going to try, but I'm so busy, I don't know if I'll be able to take the time. I don't know how much longer I can stay in this job. I feel like I'm getting burned out with all the work and the sadness. I try to remember all the times I made a positive difference, even saving some people's lives. But cases like George and Glenda's discourage me.

who visited George and Glenda (Box 11.7). In Box 11.8, she speaks about her feelings.

The Dying Person

The stress of dying is very great, as discussed in Chapter 5, but when receiving home care, in particular, the stress of feeling like a burden to caregivers, family, and friends may become an additional debilitating problem to dying people, substantially decreasing their quality of life. Wilson, Curran, and McPherson (2005) found that three-quarters of the terminally ill cancer patients they interviewed were concerned with being a burden, with 38 percent rating this as a moderate to extreme concern. This is particularly true of those people who are in pain and are anxious about death, but it is most predominantly the case for people who felt that their illnesses had resulted in a loss of dignity. In Chapter 9, the relationship between feeling like a burden to others and the connection to suicide was discussed: those people who have attempted suicide or have left suicide notes very often indicate that they have felt worthless, ineffectual, and a burden to other people, and that others would be better off without them. If this is the case, the stress of feeling like a burden to others may be a large factor in the suicide or suicide attempts of some terminally ill people. Similarly, it may play a role in some terminally ill patients' requests for euthanasia. Clearly, more research needs to be done to explore the relationship between terminally ill people's feeling of being a burden and a wish to die, so that interventions can be designed and implemented.

The challenges of caring for a person who is in the final days of a terminal illness or disorder are very great, yet those who have taken on the challenges, whether professionally or as informal caregivers, often find it rewarding, especially if adequate education and assistance are provided. In Chapter 15, we will discuss the proposed future of palliative care and look at the problems associated with implementing these proposals.

SUMMARY

- Common terminal symptoms include severe fatigue, severe pain, respiratory problems, lack of appetite and refusal to eat, anxiety, constipation, nausea/vomiting, incontinence, pressure sores, insomnia, delirium, and a reduced ability to communicate.

- More than 86 percent of Canadians would like to die in their homes.

- In regular units in a hospital, the usually overworked medical staff has little time to meet the needs of the dying patient and his or her family.

- Families of people who die in hospital complain about a lack of communication between the medical staff and the patient and family, and about the little contact with physicians. About 80 percent of the families felt that their dying relatives were not always treated with respect.

- *Hospice* refers both to a fixed place or setting and to a program of care for the terminally ill.

- Palliative care is an approach in a hospital, in a hospice, or at home that improves the quality of life of patients and their families who are facing the problems associated with life-threatening illness. It does so through the prevention and relief of suffering by means of early identification and assessment and treatment of pain and other physical, psychosocial, and spiritual problems. The goals of hospice palliative care are to reduce the suffering and loss of dignity that often accompany dying and to ease the burden of the family at this critical time.

- Staffing in a hospice includes a multidisciplinary team who tends to the physical care of the patient and to the social, emotional, and spiritual needs of the patient and family.

- Adequate home care for a terminally ill person depends on the availability of more than one caregiver, the financial ability of the family to shoulder the responsibility, whether the patient can function without continual support from professional caregivers, and whether the patient's physical symptoms can be controlled in the home. Clearly, effective home care relies on the availability of skilled palliative caregivers along with the family.

- Families opt for home care of a dying loved one because of cultural norms, personal preferences, promises made to the dying person, a desire to maintain some semblance of normalcy in life, or dissatisfaction with institutional care.

- Before home care is attempted, the patient and the caregivers must be given adequate information about what to expect of the physical condition and what the medications will do.

- Palliative care in the home requires frequent visits to the home by home-care nurses and, usually, daily visits from people who provide help with domestic chores.

- Palliative care principles demand that the family, in their bereavement, also receive support and empathy.

- In some cases terminally ill patients are transferred to other facilities because of an acute medical event, an uncontrolled symptom, or imminent death, or the caregiver's inability to continue to provide care in the home.

- The stresses of caring for a terminally ill loved one in the home are many and great. Along with financial problems, both the progressively demanding physical work of caring for a terminally ill person and the emotional pain can leave caretakers overwhelmed.

- Many home caregivers report after the death that they are glad and even grateful for having had the opportunity to care for their loved ones, an experience that they found to be profoundly meaningful.

- Home caregivers' distress increases as the ill loved one's condition worsens, and the closeness of the relationship with the ill loved one, the age of the ill person, the age and gender of the caregiver, and the degree of perceived social support all play a part in the caregiver's stress.

- Nurses in hospitals feel distress at the death of a patient whom they have been caring for on a regular basis. This is compounded by the feeling that they had no chance to become well acquainted with the patient on a more personal level. Role conflict increases their distress and makes them unsure of what their roles really are and how to balance competing professional and ethical obligations.

- If nurses work in palliative care settings, their goals are to form relationships of trust with the patient and family, becoming more like a friend and part of the family. This relationship is one that they find meaningful and enriching, but their distress at the time of death often encompasses the fact that they feel they have lost a friend. They, with specialized training, often feel they must strive to put their own grief aside in order to support and comfort the family.

- The stress of feeling like a burden to caregivers, family, and friends may become an additional debilitating problem to dying people, substantially decreasing their quality of life.

KEY TERM

respite care

INDIVIDUAL ACTIVITIES

1. How does the description of the last symptoms of death compare with what you expected? Are they the same, or were you surprised?

2. If you had a terminal illness, where would you want to die? What would you consider a good death?

3. If you have experienced the death of a loved one through a terminal illness or know someone who has, where did that person die? What were the last days like? Were you or the family satisfied with the care the person received? Why or why not?

4. If you had a terminal illness, what assistance would you want a palliative care team to give to you and your family?

GROUP ACTIVITIES

1. In groups of four or five, compare your ideas of a good death. Are there cultural or religious differences among you? Are the only differences simply individual preferences?

2. If possible, ask a palliative care worker to visit your group or class to discuss the kind of program that he or she works in and what stresses are experienced.

3. In groups of four or five, design a palliative care program that could be administered from a local hospital. What problems might be encountered in implementing this program?

4. In groups of four or five, think of ways in which palliative care workers might reduce the stress they feel on their jobs.

How to Help

After a Death

▶ Arne's best friend since childhood, Roy, was 44 years old yesterday, and this morning he died of an unknown and unexpected aneurism while he was jogging. Roy left his wife, Hannah, and their three children, Brad, aged 15 years, Lois, aged 8 years, and Moira, aged 2 years, as well as his 70-year-old mother, Bridget. Arne, grieving himself, desperately wants to help his friend and his friend's family. But what can he do? What can he say? Nothing in his life has prepared him for this, but he knows that he needs and wants to do everything he can for Roy's family. As a single man with no family of his own, he has the time to spend with them.

Learning about death, dying, and bereavement often sensitizes people to the needs and emotions of those who are at the end of their lives and those who are grieving for loved ones they have lost. But simple knowledge is not enough. "What can I do to help?" is a worthwhile and meaningful question. Putting the information gained into practice is not always easy, but it is almost always the most valuable endeavour. In this chapter, we will see how we, as individuals, and like Arne in the opening vignette, can be of the greatest help, and how institutions and services that deal with the bereaved and those at the end of life could be more useful. We must remember that as members of society and as citizens of the world, we have input into societal views and practices regarding the dying and the bereaved. If we want society to change, it must start with us.

HOW AN INDIVIDUAL CAN HELP THE BEREAVED

Helping Bereaved Infants and Toddlers

What can be done to help pre-verbal children? Infants do feel the pain of bereavement (see Chapter 6), so strategies for helping must be developed on pre-verbal levels. Infants, said Hames (2003), are best soothed and comforted by human touch. Cuddling, rocking, and holding the baby for long periods will help the most. This is not the time to worry that too much physical stimulation will "spoil the child"! Because the baby's task is to learn trust in the world, it is imperative that the child have a caretaker who consistently meets his or her needs. Hames suggested that one person be designated as the infant's caretaker at the time of bereavement so that the child meets with a reliable, loving caretaker who adheres to a predictable schedule. In this way, the disruption to the child at the family's time of deep distress may be minimized and the child can learn to trust again.

Hames (2003) further suggested that a predictable routine with a consistent, reliable, preferably familiar, caretaker will help toddlers cope with bereavement and the family distress and disruption that the death has caused. The toddler has limited verbal skills but enough to enable adults to explain to the child what has happened. By using simple words and no euphemisms that may be misunderstood (e.g., "gone to sleep"), adults can tell the child about the death and what caused it. Hames stressed that openly discussing the cause of death is important because toddlers often draw the conclusion that they have in some way caused the death. By explaining to the child what has happened, the toddler can be reassured that he or she is not at fault and that he or she will always be taken care of. In addition, the foundations for an adaptive understanding of the concept of death are laid. In doing this, bear in mind that toddlers' cognitive processes are at a very concrete level; discussion of spiritual or religious matters (e.g., "God took him") may not be correctly comprehended by the child and may prove frightening and additionally stressful. Toddlers have short attention spans, so their interest in grief may be very brief, coming and going at unpredictable intervals. Showing adult grief to the child is fine, said Hames, because it provides an acceptable role model for children, but it should be made clear to the child that adults are crying because they are sad or angry at the death, not at something the child has said or done.

Hames (2003) stated that it is also important to note that toddlers may show a regression to babyish behaviours, such as forgetting their toilet training or using baby talk. Such **regressed behaviours** should never be punished, nor should the child be belittled or made to feel ashamed of these lapses. "With a bit of time and an extra dose of loving care, the toddler will return to his former level of development as the insecurity lifts" (Hames, 2003, p. 106). Because toddlers show many of their emotions in their play and drawings, paying attention to their play and engaging them in conversations about what they are playing (e.g., "Why do you think the doll is so mad?") or what they have drawn (e.g., "Why is it raining all over this picture?") may reveal the child's understanding or misunderstanding and his or her feelings and fears. This interaction allows adults to correct misapprehensions and reassure the child. Many excellent books are available for very young children who have been bereaved (see the Appendix for some suggestions), and these can be used to help toddlers process the situation. Some toddlers may want to own some of these books to read them over and over again.

When an infant or a toddler has been bereaved, it is helpful for their future reprocessing of their bereavement if adults provide them with descriptions and photographs of the deceased family member or even, if possible, with gifts, letters, or videos from the deceased for milestone events in the growing child's life (Hames, 2003). Box 12.1 illustrates some of the helping techniques we have discussed.

Helping Older Children

Older children are, of course, more verbally adept and more cognitively sophisticated. In order to help them cope with the death or impending death of a loved one,

BOX 12.1 What Arne Can Do for Moira

Moira, age two, has limited verbal ability but can understand that something very disturbing is going on around her. Because Arne, as Roy's best friend, has been around Moira since her birth, he can take on some of the caretaking role, keeping to her normal routine, while Hannah, her mother, is freed to attend to her own grief and that of her other children. While caring for Moira, he can make sure that he is a consistent presence in her life, someone she can count on. He can be patient when she lapses into babyish behaviours that she has not shown for some time. He can cuddle her and soothe her to sleep; he can draw pictures with her and play with her. He can tell her, in very simple terms, that Daddy died and Mommy is very sad because of this. Arne can be the comforting adult who is ready to take her to the funeral home for short periods and take her out when she feels ready. He can read books about death that are suitable for toddlers and share them with her. He can be available to answer her questions, even when she repeats them again and again. He can let her know how sad he is and how he deals with his sadness by crying, by doing activities, and so on. Arne can help Moira put together a collage or photo album of her father, along with whatever she wants to put into it. Arne can post pictures of himself as well as of the rest of the family in Moira's room to help her remember all the people who love her. Most of all, Arne can listen to her, responding to whatever she wants to talk about. Arne can be prepared to repeat his explanations to Moira and field difficult questions ("Daddy coming home soon?"). As Moira grows, Arne can be ready to answer more mature questions and to frame his answers according to her level of cognitive development. Overall, Arne can be an important person in helping Moira cope with her grief.

it is important to include them in what is happening as much as possible without overwhelming them (Busch & Kimble, 2001). Many of the guidelines that apply to toddlers apply to older children as well: they need a caring, consistent adult available to them, someone who will concentrate on them. As discussed in Chapter 6, children adjust best to a death in the family when the post-death environment provides them with as much stability and social support as possible, including consistent reasonable discipline (Tremblay & Israel, 1998).

Children should receive, as soon as possible, an explanation of what is happening—serious illness or death—in clear, concrete, noneuphemistic language that is at their level, preferably in a quiet and familiar environment. They should be encouraged to ask questions and reveal their feelings and fears, and they should be allowed to see the emotional reactions of adults around them. This, and verbal reassurance, can validate their feelings, letting them know that it is not wrong for them to feel anger or confusion or sadness or fear or indeed, whatever it is that they are feeling. It will also help children to manage any feelings that might be overwhelming to them (Buxbaum & Brant, 2001; Schoen, Burgoyne & Schoen, 2004; Willis, 2002). Preschool- and school-age children also need play time, as many of their feelings will be revealed and managed through their play and other creative endeavours, such as art or music. Drawing pictures or writing letters to the person who has died may be comforting to the child as well (Willis, 2002).

Unlike babies, older children may feel guilt about the illness or death of someone they love. They may feel that their negative thoughts in moments of anger may have actually influenced the fate of the loved one. For example, most children, when thwarted in their desires will have such thoughts as, "I wish you were dead!" They may even say this out loud. When the loved one does then fall ill or suddenly dies, the child may feel that he or she has caused the death by having the wish. Children need to be reassured, often repeatedly, that they did not cause the death, that they bear no responsibility for the illness. If they want to, older children should be allowed to help with the care of an ill person, and they should be part of making arrangements for the funeral or memorial service. Depending on the age of the child, they might take on tasks from fetching a glass of water to reading the newspaper for an ill person. After the death, children might be allowed to pick out poems or music for the post-death service, or help decide on clothing for the deceased. Children over the age of toddlerhood can pick something meaningful to include in the casket. Children should be allowed to attend the funeral or memorial service if they want, after a caring adult has described fully to them what to expect and reassured them that they can leave whenever they want. Being included in pre-death and post-death activities will help children to remember the help they gave the deceased and how glad and grateful the deceased was for their presence when he or she was alive, thereby assisting children in managing any guilt that they feel.

Many useful books about death available for preschoolers and school-age children are listed in the Appendix at the end of this book. Children may be helped by one or several of these books. An adult who knows the children well should preview the books to make sure that they are suitable for the particular children and, if the children want, should read and discuss the book with the child.

Children need to remember the deceased loved one as well. It is helpful to them if adults allow them to talk about the dead person and join in the discussion, using the deceased's name. This kind of talk is usually repeated again and again. The helpful adult will listen and reminisce with the children, not try to distract them or change the subject.

Children over the age of toddlerhood will also be aided in coping with their grief and remembering the deceased if a caring adult helps them form their own **memorial.** Depending on the age and interests of a child, this could take the form of making a collage of pictures of the child and the deceased; making a scrapbook of activities that the deceased did or enjoyed in life; creating a tape or disk of favourite music of the deceased; or planting a plant, tree, or whole garden. Busch and Kimble (2001) suggested such activities as making paper lanterns; putting thoughts, feelings, and regrets on the lanterns; and letting them float away on a body of water to help children deal with feelings. This technique could also be used as a way for children to continue to communicate with the deceased person. Some of the useful techniques for older children are illustrated in Box 12.2.

Helping Bereaved Adolescents

In early adolescence (ages 11 to 15 years), children are concerned with fitting in with the peer group and in not appearing to be different (see Chapter 6). The peer group is not always sympathetic to the bereaved adolescent; not knowing quite how to behave, peers may ignore the fact that their friend has been bereaved or may actually avoid him or her. For this reason, adolescents often do not show emotions publicly because this would be considered "uncool." They usually express a desire to return to their normal lives as soon as possible after a death in the family. Onlookers sometimes believe that early adolescents or preadolescents are not grieving, but they decidedly are, usually in the privacy of their own room.

As with younger children, the early adolescent profits from knowing that he or she has stable caring adults who will be nonjudgmental and supportive. Even if the child does not want to share feelings, he or she needs to know that someone is around with whom it is safe to say anything. Pressing the early adolescent to talk or to mourn openly is not beneficial; it is generally perceived as an intrusion and another instance of adults telling the child what to do at a developmental period in which the child is working on gaining independence. In the adolescent years, children consider self-help to be one of their most beneficial means of coping with death (Rask, Kaunonen, & Paunonen-Ilmonen, 2002). Children do need information, though. Children in these years typically want only the facts of the death or illness (Christ, Siegel, & Christ, 2002), and these facts need to be provided to the child in a factual and age-appropriate manner.

BOX 12.2	What Arne Can Do for Lois

Lois, age eight, is well aware of the sorrow and turmoil around her. Arne can be the consistent, caring person in her life too. He can ask her whether she has any questions or fears about the death, and he can answer her questions as honestly as possible. If he does not know the answer, he can simply admit that. He can watch her play, and from this and her conversation, he can determine whether she is feeling any responsibility for her father's death. He can explain to her that thinking does not make an accident happen and that no one would ever say that she was in any way responsible. He can show her his own sadness and they could talk about all the memories they have of Roy. Arne can explain to her what the funeral will be like, giving her the option of attending or not attending. He can reassure her that he will be with her if she wants to stay at home or he can be with her at the funeral, and they can leave whenever she wants. He can help her to choose what she would like to do for the service, whether it is to ask that a particular piece of music be played, to pick out the socks that Daddy will wear in the casket, or to put one of her small dolls in the casket with him. He can help her create a memorial project for her father, and he can participate in whatever sort of ritual she creates. He can continue to be supportive of her, sharing his own grief with her and listening to her feelings and fears without judgment but with acceptance. He cannot take Roy's place, but he can be one of the people that she can always talk to openly and honestly.

Preadolescents and early adolescents often want to wear the deceased's clothing or take custody of some of the deceased's meaningful possessions. This should be allowed, as the child finds this comforting and helps the child in establishing a new relationship with the deceased (Worden, 1996).

In the preadolescent and early adolescent years, children's thinking is inconsistent, sometimes showing sophisticated abstract reasoning and sometimes showing a marked lack of logic and self-absorption. It is easy for adults to misinterpret the child's behaviour, calling it callous or even morbid. Understanding the child's developmental level is critical in minimizing conflict and supporting the child. For example, the child may vacillate between taking on many new responsibilities after the death of a parent in particular and showing no interest in doing anything for the family. It is important that the adults around the child ensure that the child is neither overburdened with new responsibilities, nor shirks the normal responsibilities, helping to create the balance for the child he or she cannot yet attain alone.

In later adolescence (aged 15 years and older), the child (or almost young adult) is showing almost complete abstract thinking and is less concerned about fitting into the peer group. Peer groups in this age level are more likely to be compassionate and accommodating to the bereaved teenager, and their presence should be encouraged. At this time the individual is more likely to be open about showing grief in an adult manner and is in need of a supportive person, in this case a peer, to talk to and reminisce with, just as adults are.

A problem that often arises with adolescents in this age range is that when the death is in the family, other family members may rely too heavily on the teenager both for emotional support and for the assumption of practical responsibilities (Christ, Siegel, & Christ, 2002). The teenager often responds by taking on others' concerns and duties, but this may impede his or her own mourning. Teenagers may concentrate on others' feelings and try so hard to support others that they neglect themselves. Indeed, some teenagers are of so much help to others that onlookers assume that they have dealt with their own grief in a short time and in a very adaptive manner. This is not necessarily true. Attention needs to be paid to this individual. It is easy for a teenager to be overwhelmed by others' feelings and to decide that his or her own feelings do not matter. In some cases, the teenager even changes plans for the future, such as deciding not to go away to college or university, believing that he or she cannot leave the family ("They need me too much for me to go"). It is important that someone recognizes how much stress is placed on the teenager at the time of a death in the family and moves to reduce it. For example, when a parent or sibling dies, it is common for the surviving parent(s) to use the remaining older adolescent as a confidante, saying that the teenager has become a best friend. The teenager often rises to the occasion admirably, but this child still needs a parent, not another friend. Although it is certainly appropriate for family members to support one another and share their feelings, care must be taken that the developing child is not required to take on the role of an adult.

Both early and later adolescents need to be involved in a terminally ill patient's final days to the extent that they desire it. They should be encouraged to visit a terminally ill person for final goodbyes, but they should not be forced to do so. At this stage of their development, early adolescents, in particular, tend to feel an ambivalence about visiting and even more about saying goodbye, and although they should be encouraged and supported, their wishes should also be respected. This includes their participation in funeral and memorial services. Most adolescents express a desire to attend the post-death service, and early adolescents may find it helpful to be accompanied by a supportive peer. Early adolescents often write letters, stories, or poems to the deceased. If they would like to share this at a post-death service, they should be encouraged to do so, but no one should be surprised or judgmental if they want to keep their thoughts private. Older adolescents may be more willing to share what they have written and may even respond favourably if asked to give a eulogy. This may give them the feeling that they can do one last thing for the deceased, and it may help them deal with the feelings of helplessness that they, as well as adults, feel at the time of a death.

After the death, early adolescents often want to return to school and their normal activities as soon as possible. They should be allowed and encouraged to do so, as should older adolescents, who may feel that they should stay at home to be available to others in their time of bereavement. Many adolescents develop a memorial service or ritual of their own to honour and remember the deceased. This is particularly the case when the death has been that of a friend. In this case, the peer group may join together at school or outside of school to support one another and devise a meaningful remembrance (O'Brien & Goodenow, 1991). Adults should encourage this, and schools should accommodate the adolescents' desires.

As with younger children, and indeed with adults, the bereaved individual should be aware that a supportive and nonjudgmental adult is consistently available for talking, listening, or just sitting quietly together. In Box 12.3 we can see the ways that Arne can help teenager Brad.

Brad, in the early years of adolescence, may not want to interact with adults very much, but Arne can give him factual information about his father's death and answer his questions. He can give Brad space to be alone and can suggest that he contact a friend to talk to or to be with him. Arne can understand that Brad's moods may fluctuate and he may sometimes appear callous; moreover, Arne can make sure that Brad's mother understands this too and does not look to Brad, her oldest child, to take his father's place as her confidant or as parent to his younger siblings. Arne can help Brad pick out something of his father's to keep or wear, and he can encourage Brad to express himself through whatever medium he wants. For Brad, listening to music is the way to deal with emotions, and he plays the same music over and over. The rest of the household is tired of hearing this music, so Arne can make sure that Brad has headphones to use.

Arne can ask Brad what he wants to do regarding his father's funeral: attend all or part of it, or not attend at all. If Brad wants to participate in the planning of the funeral or in the funeral itself, Arne can make sure that Brad has this opportunity. He can also let Brad know that he can have a friend with him at these times if he wants. Arne can encourage Brad to get back to school and resume his activities with his friends if he wants, and he can also make Brad aware that having private downtime is fine too. He can suggest to Brad that if he wants to make a ritual or a memorial to his father, Arne will be happy to help, to just observe, or to stay out of Brad's way. He can make sure that Brad is aware that Arne is consistently available to talk or listen or just hang out with him.

Helping Bereaved Adults

One of the most difficult tasks imaginable is telling someone that a person they have loved is dead. Usually, it is the physician or the police who have this responsibility and usually they will have some training in doing so, but this is not always true. It is hoped that they will impart the news gently and compassionately, in a quiet private place, although this is not always the case.

Bereaved adults often ask, "Why did the death happen?" or more simply "Why?" relating to the entire situation, but unlike children, they do not really expect an answer. Nonetheless, they need and expect full disclosure of what caused the death and whether their loved one suffered. Often, if they have not been present at the death, they want to be with the dead body for a few minutes. Clearly, this should be allowed; as seen in Chapter 10, not being allowed to view the body sometimes produces complicated grief at worst, and at best, it deprives the survivors of saying a final goodbye, exacerbating their pain.

For most people, the question of what to say and how to behave around someone who has been bereaved is troubling and uncomfortable. This is unfortunate because one of the major problems the bereaved have is the feeling of isolation and intense loneliness in their bereavement. As discussed in Chapter 7, the bereaved complain of people who try to comfort them by distracting them (welcome at times but often a technique of avoidance) and saying well-meaning but hurtful things. Box 12.4 lists some of the *least* useful statements that people say to the bereaved. See also WidowNet at http://www.widownet.org/faqs/topten.shtml.

What *should* a person do? The bereaved need caring and compassionate people to be there with them, even if those people say nothing. Sometimes a touch of the hand or a pat on the back can communicate sympathy and solidarity better than any words. The mere presence of someone who also cares and grieves indicates to the survivors that they are not alone in their suffering. The old saying "a grief shared is a grief halved" is not quite true, but it is easier to bear grief in the company of those who also mourn. The most useful thing to say is harder to determine than the least useful, but "I'm so sorry. This must be terrible for you. My thoughts/prayers/best wishes are with you" will probably work best, followed by taking the mourner's lead in listening, reminiscing, and revealing feelings about the death.

Hearing someone else express their feelings about the death, that they too feel pain, reduces the mourner's feelings of isolation. Many times comforters try not to cry and to be "strong" for the bereaved so that they will not cry either. The bereaved are not served well by being forced to withhold their emotions. Another technique that is often used by comforters is to talk about something else in an effort to distract the mourner. Although distraction is sometimes welcome and appropriate, for the most part, especially with the recently bereaved, the death of someone they loved is the only thing they can think about, and efforts to distract them from this often communicates the message that the comforter does not really want to talk about the death. This isolates the mourner even more, with the feeling that he or she has to go through the pain alone. It is more helpful to allow the bereaved person to take the lead: if he or she wants to cry, this must be expected and accepted; if he or she needs to remain stoical, through cultural or milieu-induced prescriptions or through individual personality characteristics, this must also be respected.

BOX 12.4   The Least Helpful Things to Say to the Recently Bereaved

When speaking with the bereaved, use common sense and avoid these least helpful things to say.

1. You need to move ahead/think of the future/get over it/snap out of it/think of the children/take better care of yourself.

   Obviously bereaved people would like to do all of these things—the point is they can't because they are in mourning.

2. You're young, you can find someone else/marry again/have more children.

   People are not coffee mugs that can be replaced.

3. My mother/son/husband/friend died too. So I know how you feel.

   No, you don't. Each individual relationship is different. Your experience with the death of a loved one, even if you had the same affiliation as the bereaved person you're speaking to, was not the same as anyone else's.

4. God must have wanted him/her.

   The obvious reaction to this is "But I wanted him/her too! God has enough and I don't!" At a time when spirituality could have proved a comfort, this might well have the effect of turning someone away from it.

5. At least he/she didn't suffer.

   How do you know? There are many kinds of suffering, not the least of which is the suffering that the bereaved are feeling.

6. Maybe it was for the best.

   Whose best? The mourner certainly doesn't feel that it was best for him or her.

7. He/She looks so natural in the casket, like he/she is sleeping.

   No, he/she doesn't. He/She looks dead.

8. Have you thought about what you're going to do now?

   The only thing the bereaved can think about is how to get through the next hour. Making plans for the future is a long way off.

9. You took care of him/her for so long. Maybe it's a blessing because now you can do all the things you missed.

   The bereaved caregiver would usually be glad to endure more laborious caregiving if it meant having the loved one back.

10. [In the case of suicide] Didn't you see that something was wrong? Couldn't you get him/her help?

    Often the bereaved of a suicide do not know that anything is wrong because the suicide victim hides it. If the bereaved did know that something was wrong, he or she may have tried desperately to get the suicide victim to accept help, but the help was rejected. Any statement that implies that the bereaved might have prevented the suicide is needlessly cruel.

11. He/She lived a good long life.

    In most cases, the bereaved feel that their loved one's life could never be long enough. The deceased's advanced age in no way precludes deep grief at his/her death.

The recently bereaved, in particular, often feel the need to recount the story of the illness and death of their loved ones, including how they were told. It is not uncommon to hear them recount the story again and again. If they do this spontaneously, it is more than likely beneficial to them because this allows them to process what has happened more fully and make it real, helping them to realize that death has actually occurred, a critical part of dealing with grief (see Chapter 5). Patience in this circumstance is often required, and admonitions not to dwell on these events only contribute to feelings of isolation. Reminiscence about the deceased and events that occurred in his or her life is also common, and it is helpful to mourners to have others reminisce along with them, even if it brings fresh tears.

Because the recently bereaved often have problems in thinking clearly and remembering all the tasks that need to be done on a day-to-day basis, and in preparation for a post-death service, it is helpful to have someone nearby who will remind them or actually do the tasks for them. For example, returning books to the library, making sure the car has gas, and picking up dry cleaning are specific tasks that may not occur to the bereaved, but being reminded and having these tasks done may be greatly appreciated. One woman in the author's class reported that on the day of her brother-in-law's funeral, her neighbour quietly and unceremoniously polished the children's shoes, an act that the woman had not thought of in her grief but that was a great relief to her. Some people might find this intrusive, so the sensitive comforter will ask first about what needs to be done by suggesting specific tasks. The specificity of the tasks is important in this context. Often people tell the mourner that they are available for "anything you need." This is a kind and undoubtedly sincere offer, but at this time, the mourner is unlikely to be able to focus on specifics without help and consequently often goes without the needed assistance. Bringing casseroles and cakes to the home of those who have been bereaved is another compassionate act, but it may be more helpful to make sure the home is well-stocked with bread, milk, and cereal. Even in an age of credit and debit cards, it may be useful to the bereaved to have cash on hand as well; a trip to the bank machine at this time may be another hassle for the bereaved to handle.

Keeping in touch with bereaved people is also a compassionate and caring act. Often people tell the bereaved to "just call if you need anything," but the bereaved will be unlikely to do this because, again, they may not think in terms of specifics that need to be taken care of and also because they do not want to be a burden to others. Although comforters indicate that they are available if the mourner "just wants to talk," it is unlikely in most cases that the mourner will call because of the fear of being a nuisance and depressing others. It is better for the comforter to call the bereaved, just to check in and see how the mourner is and if he or she is in need of some service. If the mourner does not wish to talk, the call can be brief and followed by another call the next week. The important point here is for the comforter to stay in touch and not expect the mourner to do so. The comforter must not be dissuaded because the mourner does not make the call; the lack of contact reveals the grief, not that the comforters are not needed or wanted.

Although these guidelines apply to all adults, extra care needs to be applied to seniors who are bereaved. The actual physical health and the perceived physical health of older adults deteriorate after they have a bereavement (Charlton, Sheahan, Smith, & Campbell, 2001; Fry, 2001). Sometimes, among older bereaved adults, the physical symptoms are surrogates for emotional symptoms; that is, seniors may show their distress through their bodies rather than through their psychological functioning (Williams, Baker, & Allman, 2005). Even when they have the physical ability to be mobile and functional, they may not function adequately; that is, although they possess the physical ability to go out, they do not go. This may be tied to their feelings of depression, which are often associated with lethargy and decreased physicality (Davison, Neale, Blankstein, & Flett, 2002). Special care should be taken to recognize that the physical state of seniors who are bereaved may reflect their emotional distress, and they need encouragement to physically do what they can. In addition, many people overlook the grief felt by the very senior when a loved one dies. Because their health may not deteriorate in response to the death, and because they may not show the typical signs of mourning, such as anger, guilt, or pining, it may be thought that they are not grieving. This is not the case; they very much feel the loneliness of living on and on while their family members and friends die (Lalive d'Epinay, Cavalli, & Spini, 2003). Extra support is needed to help them deal with this.

In addition, Fry (2001) found that senior widows and widowers perceive a poorer quality of life following their bereavements in the domains in which they previously experienced lower self-efficacy. If so, the areas of perceived lower self-efficacy should be determined for individuals and modified to help them cope with their new life circumstances. As an example, the domain of spiritual health is one in which a man raised in a traditional gender role in much of Western society tends to feel somewhat inadequate. It is not uncommon for older men to say that their wives take care of the religion/spirituality for the family. When their wives are gone, this is a domain in which men may find themselves at a loss. This is a problem because Fry (2001) reported that self-efficacy in this domain is a strong predictor of life satisfaction and self-esteem for seniors. Similarly, when their husbands die, women who have lived according to a relatively traditional gender role may find themselves despairing over handling the daily practical matters of life, such as paying bills. Training programs can be developed to help teach the skills to men and women in the areas in which they feel a lower self-efficacy. Once they have been trained to be more effective in these areas, their self-esteem is expected to improve, as will their quality of life, making their bereavements a little more bearable.

Bereaved adults are required to return to work after only a brief time. For example, most workplaces allow only one week (five days—including weekends for some) off after the death of a spouse or child. When bereaved people return to work, their efficiency may be diminished, so expectations of them should be adjusted. But most bereaved people want to try to do their jobs as best they can. Letting them know that help is available is useful, but taking over their usual tasks or interrupting their concentration while they are working is often an unwelcome intrusion.

In caregiving institutions, medical personnel may also want to follow some of these guidelines. For example, the nurse or social worker who is meeting with the family of someone who has died might say, "He was such a joy to be with. I remember he talked about how terrific his family was. We're going to miss him." He or she might also pass on ideas to friends and family about how they can be most helpful now, giving them the condolences of the

BOX 12.5   What Arne Can Do to Help Hannah and Bridget

Arne, as Roy's best friend, has undoubtedly been familiar with Roy's home and his family for some time. He can be at Hannah's side as quickly as possible and, if she wants, help her to tell the children of Roy's death and make arrangements for Roy's funeral. He may well feel comfortable enough in his best friend's home to check the refrigerator and pantry to ensure the family has food, or he can ask the oldest children for help in making a grocery list of items that he can then purchase. Arne can ask gently if Hannah has enough cash on hand, and if not, he can provide it (Hannah may well want to repay him, but at this time, he should not ask for a cheque immediately).

By being a consistent and caring person with the children, Arne is helping Hannah immensely; she will probably be worrying that her grief is making her a less attentive mother and she may also be worrying about how to raise the children without her husband. Arne's presence in the children's lives can reduce Hannah's concern to a great extent.

Immediately at the time of the death and as time passes, Arne can also simply sit, cry, and reminisce with Hannah. He can distract her at times to give her that needed momentary break from her pain by taking the family out to dinner (even a fast-food dinner may be a relief to the family) or renting a funny movie for the family to watch with him, and he can make sure that the day-to-day tasks of the household are taken care of, whether, with the family's permission, he does them himself or arranges for someone else to do them (e.g., hiring someone to finish the shed that Roy was building). Arne may also be aware of the fact that Roy and Hannah divided the labour of daily life, and he can be sensitive to the fact that

Hannah must now take over some chores that she does not at present have the skills for. He can help her learn those skills. Arne must be careful in this regard: his help should be in terms of assisting Hannah to learn, not in taking over Roy's tasks. Hannah will be better served by increasing her competency rather than fostering dependency on Arne.

Arne can also be aware of the grief that Roy's mother, Bridget, is feeling. She may be thinking that she should have died instead of her son as no parent should have to bury a child. She may also be worrying about how she will manage without the help that Roy gave her. Arne can sit, listen, and reminisce with Bridget as well as with Hannah, and he can find out what practical needs Bridget has that Roy looked after. For example, perhaps it was Roy who took her grocery shopping each week. Arne can take on this task himself, or he can arrange for someone else to do it. He may not be as close to Bridget as he is to Hannah, but he can still check in with her on a weekly basis to make sure that, as a senior, she is not isolated from her friends and family and that her practical needs are being met. As he does this, Arne should be aware that Bridget's grief may affect her physical condition and he can monitor her health and feelings of physical well-being. As she may become less active as a reaction to her grief, he can encourage her to be more active, even accompanying her on a walk to the park. He does not have to take the place of a son and a husband, nor should he try, but Arne can be a valuable helper to his best friend's family. In doing this, a double benefit is reaped: he will be continuing to be Roy's best friend and he will help himself deal with his own grief at Roy's death.

staff and assuring them that the body of the deceased will be respected and cared for.

It is essential to note that cultural and individual differences exist in how people mourn (see Chapter 3). The responsive comforter will respect these differences and never judge them or try to impose his or her own way of grieving on another. Taking the time to become aware of the differences that cultures and individuals have will increase the sensitivity and the usefulness of the help that can be given at this painful time. Box 12.5 illustrates how Arne can help Roy's adult survivors.

We have presented a very idealistic picture of Arne, the helper, in the boxes above. In reality, many "Arnes" may be needed to help a suddenly bereaved

family. In cultures in which an extended family is close at hand, the situation is eased with the presence of loving family members who help with the many tasks involved following a bereavement. But the norm in Western culture is that a nuclear family lives apart from many of their family members and so must rely on the help of friends and the community. In the case study that has been described, Arne is presumed to be close enough and comfortable enough with the family he is helping to be able to assume many roles. This is not always the case, however. For example, a man with a traditional gender-role background may not feel at ease in handling babies or even older children. Another helper who is more comfortable with these tasks may be of more assistance in this role. As well, a helper, no matter how close a friend, needs to remember that the ultimate control for what happens after a death must lie in the hands of the mourners. So, for instance, Arne should not take on any roles with the children without receiving the mother's full understanding of what Arne will do and her permission to do so.

Cultural sensitivity is also vital in helping bereaved people. The example of Arne and the family he is assisting assumes that they share a common cultural background. When this is not the case, the helper needs to become informed as to what the cultural traditions and expectations are for the people he or she is assisting. The attitude must, of course, be nonjudgmental and caring. Thus, if Hannah, the widow, is from a traditional Italian or Greek background, for example, she may prefer to wear black mourning clothes for a longer time than a widow from a different cultural background. Obviously, this is her right and it may, in fact, provide some comfort to her to adhere to the rituals of her own family history.

As we will see in Chapter 13 on making meaning, the role of religion should not be overlooked. A spiritual leader is often of great assistance to a bereaved family that has a religious or spiritual faith. The comfort and aid of a religious or spiritual community can help the mourners cope with their loss in a very meaningful way that often cannot be provided by anyone else. This may especially be the case for those mourners who are recent immigrants and may feel closer to their religions and their religious communities than to other people in their new environments. Other helpers should never interfere with this but should encourage and support the mourners in seeking this aid, even if their own beliefs differ.

HOW THE INDIVIDUAL CAN HELP THE TERMINALLY ILL

On the individual level, one of the most difficult situations is to find a way to help people who have been diagnosed with a terminal illness. When the individual is a child, the event is heart-breaking for everyone but for the parents most of all.

Helping Terminally Ill Children

As discussed in Chapter 6, terminally ill children usually know how very sick they are, and they feel a need for specific information about their medical condition. But adults have real difficulty in sharing this information with these children. Wanting to "spare" a child from the dire reality is the usual excuse, while others say that telling a

child the truth deprives the child of hope. Nitsche, Meyer, Sexauer, Parkhurst, Foster, and Huszti (2000) rejected this argument, saying that although the child has no hope for a cure, he or she does hope for other things, like taking a trip, going back to school for a while, playing with friends, planning a funeral, distributing possessions, even learning about God. The researchers' work at a cancer centre for children indicated that open discussion is best for children over the age of four.

Kreicbergs, Valdimarsdóttir, Onelöv, Henter, and Steineck (2004) asked 449 Swedish parents whether they had talked with their terminally ill children about death and whether or not they regretted their decision. The parents who had talked with their children about their impending death had no regrets about this, but 27 percent of the parents who had not talked with their children regretted that decision. These parents focused their regret on the fact that they could tell that their children were aware of the terminal nature of their illnesses so they regret not talking honestly with them, not allowing them a chance to explore their feelings or make known their own wishes. Kreicsbergs and her colleagues reported that the parents who had not discussed death with their dying children were more likely to experience higher levels of anxiety following the death, perhaps, they speculated, because the parents felt that they had left their dying child psychologically alone and uncomforted in his or her last days.

But how does a parent tell a child about the seriousness of his or her disease? Ishibashi (2001), in her review of the literature, gave some guidelines for this difficult task as it relates to a diagnosis of cancer, although these suggestions can apply to other illnesses. First, the child needs information about the disease. In the case of cancer, children between the ages of 7 and 13 years often misunderstand the cause of their disease. Information about the disease given in an age-appropriate way (i.e., at a level the child can understand, by using words the child is familiar with) decreases fear and helps the child maintain relationships with peers. When the child knows about the diagnosis and the prognosis, he or she is more likely to realistically hope for the efficacy of a medical treatment. Even being told that death is possible is preferable to children than is being left without information, gleaning information from adults' discussions, or surmising the medical condition through comparisons with other children on a cancer ward. If adults are open with children, it indicates to the children that adults can be trusted to tell the truth. Then, when adults say that a particular treatment may be unpleasant but effective, children are more likely to have hope and to deal with the unpleasantness in an adaptive way. Their anxiety is decreased and their security increased; they know they are not alone and nothing completely unpredictable will happen to them.

Accurate, developmentally appropriate information should be given to children when they are ready for it, said Ishibashi (2001). Children typically indicate their readiness to their parents or medical caretakers by directly asking, "What's wrong with me?" From the initial diagnosis, informing children of their condition and updating them as the condition and interventions change will help children to deal with the diagnosis, feel less fear and anxiety, feel secure, and actively participate in their own treatment regime.

How to tell the child may be a problem when the child is very young. Although older children and adolescents can understand more of the biology of the disease, younger children, with less advanced cognitive development and experience with the world, may need analogies. For example, Ishibashi (2001) reported on one study that used slides of a flower garden and weeds to tell children about leukemia: the weeds are threatening to take over the flowers in the garden and the medical team's job is like that of a gardener, to get rid of the weeds, trying to make sure that they do not come back, and to strengthen the flowers to resist any new weeds. Another technique that may be helpful is to take advantage of some of the excellent books that are available for different age levels of children. The Appendix makes some suggestions for age-appropriate books.

In general, keeping to the child's usual routines as much as possible is best for both the child and the adolescent. Children both need and want the company of their healthy peers, and although some peers may feel awkward around an ill friend, they can be taught to understand their friend's illness. Once the children are more familiar with their friend's disorder, they become more supportive and interact more freely (Ishibashi, 2001). Adolescents, who rely more heavily on their peer group for their identities and for gaining independence from their families, feel this need in particular. Although family is identified as a major source of support for adolescents, the families of these youths also experience increased conflict (Ishibashi, 2001). The main problem seems to be that parents, in their distress over their child's illness, may be overprotective and treat the adolescent in what he or she perceives as a manner more fitting for a much younger child. This, combined with the extra time ill adolescents spend with parents, hinders the process of giving support to the adolescent and may even be perceived as unsupportive. Care must be taken to both look after the child and let the child have as independent a life as possible. But this, of course, can be problematic for parents even when their child is not ill. The central point is that the child's life should be dictated as little as possible by the illness; the child has an

identity apart from that of "sick child" and this identity should be maintained, reinforced, and encouraged.

Support groups for terminally ill children and adolescents have generally been found to be beneficial in that the children report that they can share their feelings and thoughts about their illness, as well as information, with peers who are also facing a serious illness (Ishibashi, 2001). The support, acceptance, and empathy gleaned from each other were found to be very useful but do not take the place of relationships with healthy peers.

Helping Terminally Ill Adults

The same guidelines that apply to helping bereaved people generally apply to helping the terminally ill adult. In most cases, the individual will be the one to tell others of his or her illness. Listening respectfully and asking fact-based questions, such as "What course of treatment have the doctors suggested?" is a good idea. A following question of "How are you feeling about all this?" is acceptable if the relationship is close enough, but if the individual does not want to share his or her deepest thoughts and emotions, this too should be respected and not responded to with obvious relief. Asking the question will be enough for the person to know that he or she has someone who is not reluctant to be a support. Simply being there, holding a hand, and revealing feelings about the individual and the impending loss is a comfort for most terminally ill people.

Just as with the bereaved, distraction has a welcome place as well, and taking an ill person out for dinner and a movie, if possible, is often a caring act. Distraction can be appropriate, provided it is not used for or confused with avoidance of the subject. Taking the cue from the individual is the best course. What does he or she need? Instead of guessing, it is probably better to ask, "What do you want right now? to go out? to watch a football game? to talk? to just sit?" Again, specifying the many options is better than expecting the ill person to make suggestions (although any suggestions the person makes should, of course, be heeded).

If the terminally ill person is bedridden, whether at home or in an institution, gifts of flowers and plants are nice, but it may be that a cheeseburger from a favourite fast-food restaurant, a refill of a favourite cologne, or a manicure is more appreciated. Unless the terminally ill individual is in the very last stages of the illness and is unable or unwilling to expend energy in interacting with others, he or she will most likely welcome news about the events of other people's lives. It is vital to remember that this individual has the same identity with the same interests as before the illness struck. This does not mean that the illness should be ignored; it simply means that this is not "Dying Bob" but "Bob," who wants to live until he dies, which includes hearing about the joys and tribulations of those he cares about, just as he always has. Of course, care should be taken not to overwhelm someone who has limited physical and emotional energy and to be responsive to turning the conversation to something the ill person wants to discuss.

Just as in helping the bereaved, the consistent presence of supportive others is crucial. Although an argument can be made that in the long run everyone dies alone, very few people want to be abandoned in their last days. A visit or a telephone call to a terminally ill person does not have to be long, but it does have to be regular to be maximally helpful. One of the author's students reported that her terminally ill grandmother was delighted when her grandson set up a computer with email for her and showed her how to correspond with her friends easily, without her having to depend on others to fetch paper and a pen, envelopes, and a stamp, and then to mail a letter for her. The speed of her correspondence helped her feel more in touch with the daily events of people she cared about, especially if they were unable to visit her.

HOW THE INSTITUTION CAN HELP THE TERMINALLY ILL

At the institutional level, help for terminally ill people requires the aid of physical and emotional health personnel, who typically do not have a personal relationship with the individual or the individual's family but who now interact with them almost every day. Providing the best possible medical care is, thankfully, obvious to most of the institutional team, but care for terminally ill people requires more than this. It can become a difficult proposition for the often badly overworked personnel in institutions that are understaffed.

Helping Terminally Ill Children

Institutions must be aware that both the physical and the emotional palliative needs of terminally ill children differ from those of adults (Morgan & Murphy, 2000). Faulkner (1997) suggested that insofar as possible, an institution caring for a terminally ill child should follow these guidelines:

- *Be flexible.* Faulkner related her experiences in dealing with a five-year-old who had terminal cancer. When he did not want to be examined by nurses or physicians, who suspected he was in pain, Faulkner suggested they examine his teddy bear to find out what was wrong. In

doing this, Faulkner showed her awareness of the nonverbal means that small children often use to communicate their feelings, both physical and psychological.
- *Give the child respect.* Sometimes children want to share their feelings and sometimes they desire privacy. The caring adult needs to be alert and open to those times when the child wants to discuss his or her feelings, but also needs to know when to grant the child space. (This is also noted by Nitsche et al., 2000.)
- *Be specific and literal in talking about disease and death.* Clearly, discussions should be at the child's cognitive level, but explanations that use euphemisms, such as "passed away" or "went to sleep," can be frightening and confusing to a child. The child can handle the truth if it is presented at his or her level and with compassion and time for questions.
- *Let children know that no one will ever forget them or stop loving them after they die.* It is also important for children to know how much they have accomplished and what they have given in their lives. Children, as well as adults, need to know that their lives have had a purpose. (Nitsche et al., 2000, also noted that children need to know that they will not be alone.)
- *Let children make decisions as much as possible.* Children, like adults, tend to feel powerless when they have serious illnesses. They too feel more secure and in control if they are allowed to have some decision-making power in their day-to-day activities and in their own care.

These recommendations are based on the assumption that the parents have informed the child about his or her illness. They are, in fact, useful suggestions for parents as well as for other caregivers.

On a higher institutional level, Masera and colleagues (1999) and Sahler, Frager, Levetown, Cohn, and Lipson (2000) made recommendations for the caregiving team's care of the child:

1. Develop a consistent policy and approach within the institution regarding the care given to children.
2. As a team, reach a decision about a particular plan of care best for each individual child.
3. Do not keep trying when all hope is gone. What some of these authors call a **"ruthless obstinacy"** approach should be avoided; the health care team must know when to move from cure-oriented therapy to palliative care. This move is made too infrequently, mainly because no one, especially parents, wants to give up hope. The North American norm is to keep fighting, to never give up, and medical personnel do not want to admit that nothing more can be done to save a child.
4. Create open communication at an appropriate developmental level and a good relationship with

the child. Build open communication and a good relationship with the family to eliminate feelings of isolation and abandonment, and to ensure clear and consistent information is provided.

5. Make the child and siblings (if the age and development are far enough advanced), as well as parents and the family physician, part of the final decision-making process.

6. Strive to control both physical and psychological pain as well as other symptoms, such as incontinence and vomiting; again, the importance of listening to the child's complaints and feelings is highlighted.

7. If the child and the family desire it, enable the child to die at home if at all possible. Follow up with the child and family so that no one feels abandoned by the medical team.

8. Recognize that members of the health-care team may also feel the grief of bereavement when a child dies. Have supports in place to help the team members deal with this.

9. Recognize that good health care does not end at the death of the child. Parents and siblings should be allowed post-death follow-up visits with the medical team to reflect on the medical history of the child and to acknowledge the ongoing needs of parents, siblings, and other family members (e.g., grandparents). In this regard, recognize that parents may need to vent anger at health-care personnel and at the health care-system; this is not necessarily unnatural or a sign of ingratitude—it may only reflect the pain and concerns of the family. Further, contacting the family at the anniversary of the child's death for at least two years supports the family in their bereavement and shows the continuing care and remembrance from the health-care team.

Helping Terminally III Adults

Quill et al. (2006) interviewed adults of various ages who were having palliative care consultations. Their results indicated that although physical care cannot be underestimated, caring for the terminally ill person in a psychological and spiritual way should be part of the palliative package. In asking these people "What is most important for you to achieve?" the answers inform the way that care can best be given to each individual. For example, if a person were to respond that the most important thing is to find relief from physical pain, then very aggressive pain relief should be given. But if the individual says that the most important thing is to make amends with family members, pain control might be less aggressive, ensuring that the

individual retains enough consciousness to make reparations before more aggressive pain therapy is given. Similarly, if the person states the most important thing is to just sit on the porch with friends, it may be that advising new treatments is not what the individual needs or wants.

Werth, Gordon, and Johnson (2002) agreed that although physical problems should take top priority at the end of life, the psychosocial needs of the dying person should not be overlooked. They pointed out that the end of life generally requires that decisions be made concerning treatment plans, termination of treatment, and even assisted suicide. A person who is suffering does not often make the best decisions, and suffering can entail more than just physical pain. Some psychosocial issues lead to even more pain, and perhaps the presence of pain is not the greatest form of suffering. For example, they noted that according to the literature, ending the pain is not the foremost reason given by people in Oregon who are requesting assisted suicide (where it is legal, see Chapter 14). Rather, people requesting assisted suicide cite reasons that are of a psychosocial nature, such as, "I don't want to be a burden to my family," or "I don't want to lose more of my dignity/autonomy/control." For both humanitarian reasons and to help individuals make the best possible decisions at the end of life, these researchers advocated the examination of psychosocial factors as part of the full palliative care package. Specifically, they feel that the following factors should be examined:

1. *Diagnosable mental disorders.* Often depression (sometimes because of pain) is present, as is anxiety, delirium, or substance abuse. None of these is a necessary component of the dying process, and all are amenable to treatment. Enhancing the quality of life at the end of life may include treating these problems, with or without medication.

2. *Autonomy/control.* Individual requests for autonomy and the related fear of loss of control are common in the psychosocial needs of dying people; they had independence of thought, movement, and decision making before they were dying, so why would they not fear the loss of it in the final part of their lives? Every effort should be made to give people as much control over their lives as possible.

3. *Dignity.* The issue of dignity is an intensely personal one: what seems dignified and acceptable to one person may not seem so to the next person or to the same person under different circumstances. The individual's definition of dignity, both in personal and in cultural terms, needs to be explored as the individual's condition changes, and every effort should be made to give each human being the dignity that is his or her right.

4. *Existential issues and spiritual beliefs.* A person exploring the meaning of his or her life and feeling complete and satisfied is common at the end of life (see Chapter 13). These issues may or may not intersect with religious/spiritual beliefs, and they may or may not intersect with the decisions that the individual makes at the end of life. The individual's beliefs must be explored and respected, even when they conflict with the beliefs of the health-care team.

5. *Fear.* Fear is not an unreasonable emotion at the end of life, and unlike anxiety, it is not a mental disorder, although it can lead to an anxiety disorder. It is the logical response to a situation fraught with uncertainty. Fear can be greatly alleviated with open and honest communication and information, thereby diminishing the possibility that anxiety of a clinical nature will emerge.

6. *Grief.* It is sometimes forgotten that the dying person is in mourning. The dying person is, after all, losing everything that he or she had in life. Attention must be paid to the grief the individual feels at the loss of life and loss of hope for the future.

7. *Hopelessness.* Although it seems that hopelessness is logical when the end of life approaches (after all, no hope remains for a much longer life), the type of hopelessness that dying people experience is more likely to be a lack of hope for a decent quality of life in whatever time is left. Addressing the need for a better quality of life may go far in decreasing a terminally ill person's feeling of hopelessness.

8. *Feelings of being a burden.* After having lived their lives with autonomy and independence, while often being the one to help others, being the one who requires help can be a very large problem for many terminally ill people. Many indicate that they want to stop life-sustaining treatment or even ask for assisted suicide because of their distaste for being a burden and overtaxing the caretaking capacities of their loved ones. Their loved ones may be overburdened and stressed by caretaking duties, but in many cases, they find that the caretaking can give them a sense of meaning and purpose in an end-of-life situation in which they often feel helpless. Communicating the benefits of caretaking to the dying person, and providing support and relief for caretakers, can reduce the distress of this issue for both the dying person and the caretaker.

9. *Financial variables.* Although the cost of health care in Canada does not touch the individual to the extent that it does in the United States, financial matters are still of concern to the terminally ill. The dying person worries that a loved one must lose pay to be a caretaker, or must pay for daycare for children who would otherwise not need it. It may concern dying people that their extended life is depleting their own savings (which now will not be available to pass on to heirs) and depleting the resources of their caretakers. This may translate into a feeling that it would be better to die sooner rather than later, thus influencing decisions about treatment. It may be useful for both the dying person and the caretaker to have access to a financial planner who can help them work out the least burdensome and most reasonable way of dealing with finances so that economics does not become the prime factor in end-of-life decision making.

10. *Presence/absence of significant others.* For some people, especially seniors who may have outlived their significant others, the lack of meaningful relationships and social support may be a reason to lessen their compliance with treatment or even to terminate treatment. This absence engenders feelings of isolation and depression. Conversely, some terminally ill people may persist in their efforts to live because of the presence of their families. It is not uncommon for dying people to feel that, despite their own desires, they must try a new treatment because their family will be devastated by their deaths. The palliative care team should be alert and provide social support for the dying person who is alone to make sure that the person does not feel that his or her living or dying would be inconsequential. As well, they may need to help the family of a dying person to allow the individual to let go when and if he or she feels the need to do so.

11. *Pressure/coercion.* Although it may seem ghoulish to contemplate, the reality is that many terminally ill people feel or perceive pressure from different sources to end their lives quickly. Thus, the overtaxed caretaker, the harried medical staff, or the inattentive family member may communicate, albeit unknowingly or unwillingly, that they wish the end would come. It is not surprising then that the dying person may elect to terminate treatment or to refuse a new treatment (or to request physician-assisted suicide) on the basis of feeling like a burden. It is of paramount importance that the dying person not feel such coercion; every effort must be made to ensure that the caretaker, whether at home or on the medical team, not feel overburdened and not communicate such an impression to the dying person.

12. *Cultural factors.* All of the above issues are affected by the culture that the individual is part of. Thus, among some cultures, such as some Native Peoples' groups, open communication in terms of telling the dying person the truth about his or her condition is seen as harmful and should be avoided. The individual's culture may also influence how much effort is made to postpone death, with some cultures (e.g., Italian) feeling that every effort must be made, and other cultures (e.g., British) feeling that a treatment that lessens dignity should be avoided even if it may prolong life. Being aware of and respecting the diversity of the dying person's cultural background is essential.

The same principles apply to terminally ill people of all ages, but additional research has been done with seniors, whether they are terminally ill or not. When Kelner (1995) surveyed healthy Canadians over the age of 65 years, she found that overwhelmingly (90 percent) they wanted to hold the control over the timing and circumstances of their deaths themselves. Most of the older, sick individuals she interviewed agreed with this. In fact, only a minority of older ill people and a very small percentage of older healthy people were willing to delegate the responsibility of decision making to someone else in their end-of-life care.

It should also be noted that older people may change their minds over time regarding the degree of life-sustaining intervention they want (Ditto et al., 2003), so it should not be taken for granted that goals and desires remain unchanged. Even formal advance directives and living wills need periodic updating.

DO GRIEF INTERVENTIONS HELP?

Whether **grief interventions** help is unclear. It is often taken for granted that grief therapy or counselling will be helpful to people experiencing grief, especially if it is complicated, but is this true? Although interventions for those people experiencing complicated grief certainly seems indicated, very little methodologically sound research indicates that for the majority of people experiencing normal grief, benefits accrue from interventions.

On an individual level, it seems apparent from the reports of bereaved people that the presence of a supportive, caring listener is comforting and helpful in dealing with grief, and this seems just as true for adults as for children.

On an institutional level, the answer is less concrete. Very often, on the institutional level, help for the bereaved takes the form of counselling or psychotherapy groups, led by a qualified counsellor. In these groups, the participants are typically similar in their losses and stages of their lives. For example, college students who have lost someone significant to them report that bereavement groups of other college students have been helpful to them in feeling supported and understood, an important finding given that college life is not usually conducive to support for those mourning (Janowiak, Mei-Tal, & Drapkin, 1995). Similarly, Tonkins and Lambert (1996) reported on the positive effects of a bereavement group for children aged 7 to 11 years, all of whom had lost a parent or sibling. This study utilized more than self-reports and gave more detail about the contents of the group's discussion, so it merits a closer examination as an exemplar of the kind of intervention that is used.

For eight weeks, once a week, the therapist in Tonkins and Lambert's (1996) study led discussions on various aspects of the losses the children had experienced (see Box 12.6 for a description of each week's discussions). The children were encouraged to talk, draw, and read about grief, and to support each other. After the eight weeks, these children were found to have less sadness, withdrawal, guilt, loneliness, anger, anxiety, and helplessness than they had before the group began, and less than other bereaved children who were waiting to join such a group as this one. By their own reports, the children felt better, and their parents and teachers reported a decrease in behavioural problems. It seems clear that this intervention helped the children. Although this is but one study, and the number of children in the group was small (10), the results suggest that even children who have normal rather than complicated grief and who may have adequate individual social support can benefit from an organized group. While urging more research in this area, Tonkins and Lambert suggested that positive effects arise because of a combination of factors:

1. The children found that their feelings and reactions were common to others.
2. The environment of the group made revealing feelings and exploring emotions nonthreatening and supported.
3. The group used different media to express their feelings.
4. The children were given information about the grief they were experiencing and what they might expect.

The intervention for children described in Box 12.6 certainly was successful in allowing children to

BOX 12.6   Outline of Children's Group Therapy Sessions

Tonkins and Lambert (1996) structured the eight weeks of group therapy for children 7 to 11 years of age in the following manner:

Week 1 The therapist, the children, and the group were introduced, with a discussion of what the children could expect of the group and the rules that would be followed. The children were explicitly told that the information they heard from other children in the group was to remain confidential, and they were encouraged to express their feelings without fear of ridicule or rejection.

Week 2 The second week's discussion revolved mainly around a more factual expression of who the deceased was and how he or she had died, as well as what the child had been doing at the time of the death (e.g., was the child involved in the long-term care of a sick parent or sibling? Was the death sudden, as in a car accident?)

Week 3 The discussion of the third week centred on positive memories of the deceased and activities that said thank you to the deceased for those positive memories. In addition, children talked about how the death had affected their self-image and what support they had received. The therapist also introduced a game to elicit questions the children might have about death in general.

Week 4 In this session, the children took part in art projects that centred on what the children missed most about the deceased, and they discussed sadness and fear in relation to the death.

Week 5 Week 5's discussion was about the feelings of anger and unfairness that the children felt about the death. They also expressed this through using books and an art project.

Week 6 In Week 6, the therapist focused the children's attention on any guilt feelings they might have and on the process of forgiving themselves by using guided imagery (i.e., imagination exercises directed by the therapist). The children also discussed unfinished business that they might feel still existed with the deceased.

Week 7 In this week, the children formed scenarios in which they said goodbye to the deceased. They also learned of the long-term positive and negative impacts that grief would have on them as they grew and developed.

Week 8 Finally, the children were led in a discussion of the importance of support systems and they said goodbye to the group.

voice and understand their feelings following a bereavement. Unfortunately, reviews of studies looking at the effects of grief interventions find that the research consists of small samples of bereaved individuals, it often does not follow their progress over time, and it has other methodological problems (Curtis & Newman, 2001; Jordan & Neimeyer, 2003; Wortman & Silver, 2001). Other explanations, such as the normal effects of time since the bereavement and the presence of social support, can often explain the improved psychological functioning of the participants in the interventions. However, studies that find no beneficial effects may be using measures that are insensitive to the real outcomes. Overall, many studies combine participants who have been bereaved for different lengths of time and differ from one another on such factors as age, race, gender, and previous experience with bereavement. It has also been suggested that because no firm conclusion can be made as to whether interventions actually work, the possibility exists that in the long run, interventions may be harmful to some people. If and when grief intervention is contraindicated remains an area in which research is definitely needed.

Some Canadian educational and support resources are listed in Box 12.7.

HOW SOCIETY CAN HELP THE BEREAVED AND THE TERMINALLY ILL

North American society has already begun to increase its sensitivity to those who are bereaved or terminally ill. That college and university courses now exist in the area of thanatology bears witness to this. But as a society, we all need to become more educated and more aware of what can be done to help those who are dealing with loss. We need to accept that we ourselves have been or will be among the number facing the ultimate challenge. We have seen that palliative care services are not universally available to those with the need, and we can and should petition our governmental representatives to remedy this. More funds need to be allocated to these services and more personnel need to be trained and hired for end-of-life care. Moreover, more services need to be in place to help those working in the field to manage the stress and grief that they feel. The next few decades will see an increase in the need for palliative care as the large segment of the population, the baby boomers, become seniors. It will be too late then to argue for more resources; the resources need to be in place now. As citizens of the world, the responsibility is ours.

BOX 12.7 Some Canadian Resources

The following is a brief list of some of the support and educational agencies available in Canada. Other resources can be located through hospitals, places of worship, and funeral homes.

THE CANADIAN HOSPICE PALLIATIVE CARE ASSOCIATION

The Canadian Hospice Palliative Care Association (CHPCA) provides information about hospice palliative care in Canada and a directory to hospice palliative care services across Canada. The provinces each have hospice palliative care organizations as well, which can be accessed through the CHPCA website. Territorial hospice palliative care associations are not in place in Yukon, the Northwest Territories, or Nunavut.

Canadian Hospice Palliative Care Association
Annex B, Saint-Vincent Hospital
60 Cambridge Street North
Ottawa ON K1R 7A5
613-241-3663 or 1-800-668-2785
Hospice Palliative Care Info Line: 1-877-203-4636
Fax: 613-241-3986
E-mail: info@chpca.net
http://www.chpca.net/home.htm

BEREAVED FAMILIES OF ONTARIO

This bereavement support organization offers programs and services to children, adolescents, and adults in groups or on a one-to-one basis. The programs are based on a mutual support model.

Bereaved Families of Ontario
602-36 Eglinton Avenue West
Toronto ON M4R 1A1
416-440-0290 or 1-800-236-6364
Fax: 416-440-0304
E-mail: info@bfotoronto.ca
http://www.bfotoronto.ca

CANUCK PLACE CHILDREN'S HOSPICE

This program provides respite and end-of-life care to children and their families, with bereavement support and follow-up for two to three years following the child's death. It also has programs for anticipatory grief support for a child or family and support groups for a child's parents and siblings.

Canuck Place Children's Hospice
1690 Matthews Avenue
Vancouver BC V6J 2T2
604-731-4847
Fax: 604-739-4376
http://www.canuckplace.org

THE COMPASSIONATE FRIENDS OF CANADA, INC.

This international, nonprofit, nondenominational, self-help organization offers support groups and grief education to families who have experienced the death of a child. The website offers links to provincial and territorial chapters, as well as resources and links to other useful organizations.

The Compassionate Friends of Canada, Inc.
PO Box 140
RPO Croydon
Winnipeg MB R3M 3S7
Toll Free: 1-866-823-0141
E-mail: NationalOffice@TCFCanada.net
http://www.tcfcanada.net

MOTHERS AGAINST DRUNK DRIVING (MADD)

This organization uses social activism to fight one of the leading causes of accidental deaths in Canada. The website links to other useful resources and has links to 85 provincial and territorial chapters across Canada.

MADD CANADA National Office
2010 Winston Park Drive, Suite 500
Oakville ON L6H 5R7
905-829-8805 or 1-800-665-6233
Fax: 905-829-8860
E-mail: info@madd.ca
http://www.madd.ca

MAKE-A-WISH FOUNDATION INTERNATIONAL

This international organization grants as many wishes as possible to children between the ages of 3 and 17 who have life-threatening illnesses. Since its creation in 1980, more than 144 000 wishes have been granted. Children must be nominated (by anyone, including themselves) and judged medically eligible by the foundation's criteria. Canada has its own chapter.

Make-A-Wish Canada
4211 Yonge Street, Suite 521
Toronto ON M2P 2A9
416-224-9474 or 1-888-822-9474
Fax: 416-224-8795
E-mail: nationaloffice@makeawish.ca
http://www.makeawish.ca

GRIEFSHARE

GriefShare is an organization based on nondenominational religious beliefs that conducts 13-week educational and support groups for anyone who has lost a loved one. The parent organization, Church Initiative, is based in the United States, but chapters of GriefShare are located internationally.

Church Initiative
P.O. Box 1739
Wake Forest NC 27588
919-562-2112 or 800-395-5755
Fax: 919-562-2114
E-mail: info@griefshare.org
http://www.griefshare.org

SUMMARY

- An adult can do much to help a bereaved baby or toddler:
  a. Touch, cuddle, and rock the child.
  b. Be consistent in keeping to the child's normal routine.
  c. Depending on the child's age, explain what has happened in clear, concrete, and noneuphemistic terms.
  d. Answer the child's questions, even when they are repeated over and over.
  e. Reassure the child that he or she is not to blame, is loved, and will always be taken care of.
  f. Allow the child to see adult grief reactions.
  g. Be patient with regressed behaviour such as bedwetting or clinginess.
  h. Allow the child ample playtime and engage the child in conversation about the play because the child's feelings and fears may be revealed in this way.
  i. Provide the child with descriptions and pictures of the deceased.

- An adult can do much to help an older child:
  a. Depending on the child's age, explain what has happened in clear, concrete, and noneuphemistic terms.
  b. Answer the child's questions, even when they are repeated over and over.
  c. Allow the child to see adult grief reactions.
  d. Allow the child ample playtime and engage the child in conversation about the play because the child's feelings and fears may be revealed in this way.
  e. Reassure the child that he or she was not responsible for the death.
  f. Include the child in pre-death tasks for the ill person and in the post-death services.
  g. Tell the child exactly what to expect at the funeral or memorial service, asking whether the child wants to attend, and assure the child that he or she can leave at any point, with the adult accompanying him or her.
  h. Provide suitable books about death to read and discuss with the child.
  i. Allow the child to talk about the deceased, and reminisce with the child.
  j. Help the child find a satisfying memorial tribute to the deceased.

- An adult can do much to help a bereaved adolescent:
  a. Give factual and age-appropriate information to the adolescent about the illness or death.
  b. Allow the younger adolescent or preadolescent to have privacy and even to withdraw if he or she desires it.
  c. Help the early adolescent pick out clothing or mementoes of the deceased to keep.
  d. Understand and accept the volatility of the adolescent's moods and expressions of grief.
  e. Encourage the presence of peers, especially those that the adolescent finds supportive.
  f. Involve the adolescent in the planning of the funeral or memorial service to the extent that he or she wants, and allow the adolescent to participate in the service.
  g. Ensure that the adolescent is not being overwhelmed with adult expressions of grief and is not being overburdened by adult responsibilities and demands.
  h. Encourage the adolescent to return to school and resume normal activities as soon as possible.
  i. Encourage the adolescent to develop a memorial or ritual of his or her own to honour and remember the deceased.

- A person can do much to help a bereaved adult:
  a. Break the news of the death gently and compassionately, in a quiet and private place, allowing the bereaved to be with the body if he or she wants.

b. Avoid making hurtful statements or judging the bereaved person's reactions or emotions. Silence and touch are preferable to an ill-conceived statement or judgment.

c. Simply be with the bereaved person, as a consistent and caring supporter who listens.

d. Reminisce about the deceased with the bereaved and allow the bereaved to see your own feelings.

e. Use distraction sparingly.

f. Suggest specific tasks that need to be done and in some cases do them.

g. Check in frequently and consistently with the bereaved. Do not wait for the bereaved person to initiate the contact.

h. Pay attention to the health and activity level of seniors who have been bereaved.

i. Help the bereaved to learn skills that will be necessary for their roles in the changed family constellation.

j. Be aware of cultural differences among people that may affect their mourning.

- An adult can do much to help a terminally ill child:

a. Give the child clear information at his or her developmental level about the disorder and the treatment plans.

b. Answer questions honestly.

c. Keep the child's routine as normal as possible.

d. Encourage the child to interact with healthy friends as well as those who might be met in a hospital setting.

- A person can do much to help a terminally ill adult:

a. Be a consistent and caring listening presence in the ill person's life.

b. Ask the ill person what he or she needs or wants and, if possible, fulfill the requests.

c. Remember that the individual's identity has not changed and his or her interests remain the same as before the illness struck.

- The staff in caregiving institutions can do much to help a terminally ill child:

a. Be flexible.

b. Give the child respect.

c. Be specific and literal in talking about disease and death.

d. Let the child know that no one will ever forget him or her or stop loving the child after he or she dies.

e. Let the child make decisions as much as possible. Involve siblings and the family physician as well as the parents in decision making.

f. Develop a consistent policy and approach within the institution regarding the care to be given to children.

g. As a team, reach a decision about a particular plan of care best for each individual child.

h. Avoid "ruthless obstinacy."

i. Strive to control the child's physical and psychological pain as well as other symptoms.

j. Enable the child to die at home if at all possible and if desired by the child and family.

k. Allow post-death follow-up visits.

- The staff in caregiving institutions can do much to help a terminally ill adult:

a. Find out what the individual finds most important to achieve in the last days and govern treatment accordingly.

b. Diagnose and treat any mental disorders that may be present.

c. Make sure the individual has as much autonomy and control as possible.

d. Find out what the individual means by dignity and try to ensure that this dignity is maintained.

e. Understand and respect the individual's spiritual/existential beliefs.
f. Recognize whether the individual has fear, grief, or a sense of hopelessness, and treat through communication and medical/psychological interventions.
g. Reduce the individual's concern about being a burden on others.
h. Attend to financial concerns the individual may have.
i. Encourage family and friends to visit and be supportive.
j. Ensure that the individual is under no coercion in making decisions about the instigation or termination of treatment.
k. Be aware and respectful of cultural norms that affect the individual's treatment and sense of well-being.
l. Update the understanding of people's wishes about their treatment at the end of life.

- Because of a lack of sound methodological research, it is unknown whether grief interventions are beneficial to people with normal grief, although the support and empathy found in many support groups have been found useful to many adults and children.
- Society can help people who are bereaved or terminally ill by providing more funds and resources for palliative care and by increasing knowledge and understanding of the bereavement process.

KEY TERMS

grief intervention   regressed behaviour   ruthless obstinacy
memorial

INDIVIDUAL ACTIVITIES

1. If you have been bereaved, what were the most helpful things that other people did for you? What were the least helpful?

2. If a friend of yours died, what would you do to help his or her family?

3. If you were terminally ill, what would help you?

4. As an individual, what can you do to change society's treatment of the bereaved and the terminally ill? Educate others about what you have learned.

GROUP ACTIVITIES

1. In a group of four or five, pick out library books (those listed in the Appendix or others) that deal with bereavement in children. As a group, discuss their merits and shortfalls. Which of the books would the group recommend for different age groups of children?

2. Call some of the bereavement organizations listed in Box 12.7 and ask how the organization helps the bereaved. Discuss the results in the group. Are there other groups in the area that would be helpful? For example, those aimed at particular cultural segments of society?

3. If possible, ask someone who works in the area of palliative care to talk to a group of students, outlining his or her duties and the frustrations and joys of the job.

4. As a group, send a letter to the minister of health, urging more resources be allocated to giving help to the bereaved and the terminally ill.

Making Meaning

Finding Meaning and Purpose

Viktor Frankl was a psychiatrist who was incarcerated for several years in Nazi concentration camps during World War II. He had already been formulating ideas about factors that helped people deal with the difficult situations of their lives, and in the camps, he found more examples that helped to clarify his ideas. He was particularly aware of the way that some of the camp inmates struggled to survive in the face of almost insurmountable odds; many managed to live through the horrors in spite of the best efforts of their Nazi captors. But Frankl also witnessed many people losing all hope and giving up on the struggle. They inevitably died, and their impending deaths were apparent to others. Frankl wondered what accounted for the difference. He found his answer in talking to many of his fellow prisoners and in examining his own survival. The difference, he found, was in the way that some prisoners, he included, were determined to find a meaning and a purpose to go on living. For many, the purpose was to live through the Holocaust and testify to what had happened so that the dead would be remembered and the horror would never happen again. For others, it was to find their families again and help them deal with the terrible experiences they had had. For still others, the attitude that survival was expected of them was enough to make them live up to this expectation. Frankl felt these meanings too, but he realized that in recognizing the role that purpose and meaning gave to people, he could help future patients more effectively and teach other mental health professionals how to be more helpful as well.

At that time, psychiatry was predominantly rooted in the idea that past occurrences were responsible for people's feelings and actions in the present. Frankl realized that although the causal role of the past was important, the role of meaning in the present and purpose for the future was equally important. People are not simply pushed by the past; they are also pulled by the future. In the camps, those who gave up saw no future. To them, they had no reason to continue living, especially in the face of the torture with which their present lives were imbued. Frankl saw that people could make meaning in their lives in three ways: (1) by doing a deed or creating something, (2) by experiencing something or someone with a full appreciation for the uniqueness and growth inherent in people and the overall universe, and (3) by facing inescapable suffering with an attitude of making it count and growing through its challenges.

When the war was over and the prisoners in the camps were finally released, Frankl wrote a book that encompassed both the story of his incarceration and the lessons he learned from it. His book, *Man's Search For Meaning,* published in 1984, remains a stirring testimonial to the Holocaust experience and a deeply respected and highly regarded psychological and philosophical treatise on the makeup of the human being.

We have all had the experience of interpreting a situation differently from others. For example, someone may normally see a party as a welcome release from stress, but when he or she is ill or unhappy or in the midst of examinations, that same party may be perceived as an unwelcome intrusion and something to be avoided. To take another example, a house may be seen as a warm home by the happy family who lives there, a place of fear by the abused child, a source of income to a real estate agent, an obstacle to the city developer, and so on. The same object or event means something different depending on who is regarding it and that person's frame of mind.

In a similar fashion, we have all had the experience of feeling so overwhelmed with events in our daily lives that we have difficulty thinking clearly or accomplishing tasks. Often we make lists of things to do so that we will not forget them. We may go over events several times in our minds or with someone else, making a story of sorts out of the events. In doing these things, we are imposing some structure or coherence on the chaotic elements of our lives and, in fact, making meaning out of disorder and disorganization. Without this structure, life can become extremely stressful.

WHAT IS MAKING MEANING?

To cope with daily life, we impose a structure on it. Life then becomes coherent and organized, and thus more understandable, more predictable, and much easier to deal with (Neimeyer & Levitt, 2001). We can then fit the events of our lives into a meaningful configuration that makes sense to us. This configuration is up to us alone; another person may make a completely different configuration of the same events. This process of **making meaning** is therefore individual to each person. So, one good student may explain the reason for getting an uncustomary poor mark on an essay by thinking, "The instructor gave poor instructions for the essay." This thought explains (perhaps truthfully and perhaps not) why a bad mark was obtained by someone whose life experience consisted of receiving good marks. The poor mark, an incongruous element in this student's life, now fits with the coherent whole of his or her life. An equally bright classmate may explain a poor mark as his or her own responsibility because of a lack of preparation. For this student, who has a history of not attending to schoolwork in a conscientious manner, the poor mark is congruent with his or her previous experience in school life. Still another intelligent student, one who is taking many classes and has a part-time job, may contend that the mark was a result of not having enough time to do a thorough job on the essay, a thought that renders a poor mark understandable in view of the life that this student is leading.

In the cases described above, people are making sense of the events of their lives. They are putting events in a context that fits with what they understand their life conditions to be. In doing this, they gain not only understanding but also predictive ability for the future. Thus, the first student knows that in the future, he or she may need extra clarification of instructions for an assignment; the second student may understand that with his or her present lack of attentiveness to schoolwork, future marks may also be poor; the third student can recognize that in taking several courses at one time and working part time, he or she may be trying to fit too much activity into the day, with the consequence of lower marks.

People are often required to restructure their understanding of what life is about for them. A clear example is the case of first-year university students who received top grades in their high-school classes. In the first semester, these students may find that they are now considered average because all the students in the class were also at the top of their high-school classes. Students then must restructure their understanding of themselves, changing their identification of themselves from someone who gets the highest grade in the class with little effort, to someone who needs to put extra work into class assignments to get the highest marks.

O'Connor (2002–2003) contends that people can make meaning in their lives in several ways:

- They can find a purpose in their present state or experiences. Present suffering or deprivation may be seen as a necessary step toward a goal, as in students who tolerate monetary problems, hard work, lack of time for leisure activities, and frustration because of their desire to obtain an education.
- They can construct stories in which actions and events are transformed from undesirable to desirable, as in the common experience of saying, after a disappointment, "It was really all for the best," or "I hated it at the time, but now I see that it was all for my own good." Similarly, people may find meaning and purpose in their own actions when they convince themselves that their actions were valid and right. For example, the individual who tells a lie ("I'm sorry, I can't go out with you because my mother is visiting me") may then rationalize the action ("I didn't want to hurt his feelings") when the reality of the lie was less than noble ("I want to keep him around in case I have nothing else to do").
- They can construct stories that highlight how to exert control and thereby make the environment more predictable and pleasant. An instance of this might occur when people remember a disappointment and their actions that contributed to it. Knowledge of what led to the disappointment may help individuals avoid a similar disappointment in the future. The memory or

story of what happened becomes transformed from a simple disappointment to a learning experience. For example, the student who does poorly in the first semester of college might remember the disappointment in terms of having learned what *not* to do as well as how to study, write, and manage time at a postsecondary level, leading to a much more successful second semester.

- They can construct stories that focus on how attractive or competent the individual is. For example, after gloating about getting the highest mark in the class, the individual may transform the story into a reflection of other people's jealousy over his or her intelligence rather than a story of how he or she behaved rather badly in the face of success.

Biographies of famous people fill large areas of libraries and bookstores. Many people find the story of someone's life to be fascinating. This may, in part, be because we all construct stories of our lives to impose structure and meaning out of a mass of events. By constructing a story of our lives, we find connections among events and relationships between the past and the present. The stories of our lives even give us some predictions about the future in terms of actions to take and what to expect in many situations (Bosticco & Thompson, 2005).

MAKING MEANING IN BEREAVEMENT

When we experience a loss, making meaning may be more difficult because the structure of our lives often becomes incoherent. Our future plans, our future story, are interrupted and even devastated. The assumptions we made about our lives and the stories we created about our futures seem to be shattered. This is particularly the case when the loss is of someone we have held dear. Our identities seem undercut when someone who has shared and been witness to the important events in our lives is removed (Neimeyer, Prigerson, & Davies, 2002). The shock and denial typically felt when the news of a death is received may reflect the fact that the death is in direct conflict with the tacit world view that life is generally good, orderly, and predictable. Fitting the trauma into a coherent world view and an understanding of life takes time. A natural question when someone dies or when confronting the diagnosis of a potentially terminal disease is "Why?" To make this more concrete, examine the case history in Box 13.1.

The Dupré family is in shock, the customary first part of bereavement, especially when a death is unexpected. For all three of these women, not only have they

---

BOX 13.1 Case History of the Dupré Family

Pierre Dupré was 54 years old when he suddenly died of a heart attack. His wife, Lucille, and his children, Anna, aged 24 years, and Belinda, aged 19 years, are in shock, not believing that such a terrible and unexpected thing could have happened. "But he was well!" they say to each other. "It's not as if he were old and sick. How can this happen?" The physicians can only tell them that sometimes heart attacks just happen with no warning, an explanation they find little comfort in.

Lucille thinks of the way she and Pierre talked about their retirement, the travelling they would do, their plans to buy a sailboat and sail to the Caribbean for holidays. She cannot conceive of how she will spend the rest of her life without him. The children are grown and able to take care of themselves; she can be replaced in her job at the corner store with little difficulty. *Why should I continue to live?* she wonders. What would be the purpose when life is so empty without her beloved husband? And she never even got a chance to say goodbye. *It's not fair!* she thinks.

Anna and her fiancé were about to start planning their wedding, but the thought of having a happy wedding celebration now seems repugnant to them. Anna thought she would walk down the aisle on her father's arm, shining as a new bride, with love and pride on her father's face. Now, will she walk alone? And will she shine, or will she weep at the absence of her father? She dreamed of the day when she would put her first child in her father's arms. What a wonderful grandfather he would have been! She had planned to buy them matching baseball caps, and she could see them watching baseball games on television together. Now the dreams are devastated. *It's not fair!* she thinks.

Belinda simply cannot understand what has happened. Her father was so well! She had been telling him about an assignment she was doing for one of her classes at school just last night. He was so interested! And he asked to read the assignment when she was done. He promised her that when she graduated, he would buy her orchids. She had never had orchids before. *And now,* she thinks, *I never will.* But then, she doesn't want them anymore: if her father can't give them to her, receiving orchids would be like pouring salt in a wound. Besides, what point is there in even attending her graduation if he won't be there to see it? *It isn't fair!* she thinks.

---

lost a person so dear to them, but they have also lost their future plans and dreams. Their view of the world as being mainly good and predictable has been broken. Now life looks dark and threatening, with unexpected tragedies at every turn. Their view of themselves will change as well: Lucille must start to regard herself as a widow, not a wife. The daughters must see themselves as being partially orphaned, without the stability and security of a much-loved father in their lives. What the Dupré family must do now, in fact, is to restructure the meaning in their lives and reconstruct future stories of their lives. These are difficult and painful tasks, but many workers in the field of bereavement feel it is necessary for them to do this in order to deal with their grief.

Neimeyer (2000) contended that meaning restructuring contains many elements, including the following:

1. *The finding or creation of meaning in both the death of a loved one and the life of the survivor.* The death of a loved one is not necessarily imbued with a sense of purpose, such as "dying so that others might live," but it is possible to find meaning in terms of how one grows and changes in the wake of a death. For example, about one-third of bereaved people surveyed reported that in the year following the death of someone they loved, they had become more mature and independent. Many also noted that they had become more compassionate and expressive, and were living more fully in the present (Frantz, Farrell, & Trolley, 2000). In these changes, bereaved people can find that not only do they discover a new structure and meaning to their lives, but they can also make some good of their personal tragedies, thus imbuing the loved one's death with meaning and purpose.

2. *Integration and construction of meaning within a larger context of life.* After a bereavement, the reconstruction of meaning may be incorporated into an individual's framework of life beyond the grief of the death. For example, the partners and caregivers of men who died of AIDS found spirituality to be important in providing them with meaning and structure in their initial grief, but over time, this spirituality came to pervade the rest of their lives, enhancing their own sense of purpose and their relationships with others.

3. *An interpersonal process.* The reconstruction of meaning does not occur in a vacuum; for example, in the Dupré family the family constellation had consisted of a mother, a father, and two daughters. After Pierre's death, the whole constellation has changed with the removal of a central element. By sharing their feelings, the Dupré family may glean new understandings of their identities after Pierre's death. Thus, Lucille can recognize Belinda's pain at having no father at her graduation and can help in reformulating a strategy whereby Dad can be included. Perhaps the family can take a picture of Belinda in her graduation robes to the graveside, leaving it there as a symbolic and ritualistic inclusion of Pierre, an acknowledgment of his pride in his daughter, and their continuing tribute to him in their accomplishments. In this, Lucille may also see the continuing importance of her presence in her daughters' lives, as the living reminder and conduit to the memory of their father.

4. *A cultural process.* As each culture, society, and religion envelops death with rituals and tradition, so the grieving of the bereaved becomes imbued with cultural significance. Grieving people become an intrinsic part of the cultural meaning of death and the role of the survivors. Thus, saying Kaddish, for example, in the Jewish tradition, makes the mourners an integral part of the customs that have sustained the culture for millennia. Their place and their purpose within their cultural tradition become even more concrete and significant in their reconstructed meaning framework.

Over time, the content of meaning making may shift. In the beginning, the emphasis is on making sense of the tragedy, finding a personal explanation of why the death occurred. Such meanings may include, "It's part of the cycle of life," "He was suffering," or "It was the will of God." Later, and separately, however, the emphasis may be on finding a benefit to survivors, a silver lining, although an undesired one. So, for example, the mourner may focus on the way the death of a loved one has enhanced family closeness, or how, since the death, the mourner has had a broader perspective and greater appreciation of life (Davis, Nolen-Hoeksema, & Larson, 1998; Neimeyer, 2000). The content of the meaning is unimportant; the only important factor is whether it satisfies the mourner (Davis et al., 1998).

THE ROLE OF STORYTELLING

Making sense of a tragedy is more easily done when the events surrounding the tragedy can be put in narrative form. For illustration, recollect the example of the Dupré family in Box 13.1. When Pierre was killed, Lucille was informed of his death by the police who advised simply that he had been found dead on the street. The autopsy said he had died of a heart attack. This information provided her with an incomplete picture of what had happened to her husband. Over time, however, she learned from her daughter Belinda that Pierre had gone to the drug store that morning and died before returning. Anna, Lucille's older daughter, added the information that Pierre had earlier complained of having indigestion and felt that he needed an antacid. Lucille could then piece together a story that Pierre had probably felt a discomfort in his chest that he interpreted as being indigestion. He then went to the drug store to purchase an antacid but died of a heart attack, the real reason for the chest pains, before getting there. Lucille and her daughters now had a complete story that fulfilled their need to make sense of how Pierre died, one that provided a reason and some predictive value, giving more meaning to the death. As Bosticco and Thompson (2005) said, "Story telling maintains the association of things that happen in any given situation and produces an account that condenses a complicated set of events and perceptions into a single comprehensive unit" (p. 10).

A further function of storytelling is to keep memories alive. This is particularly important in the case of the bereaved. Keeping the memory of the deceased alive is a vital part of forming a new relationship with the deceased and honouring the past relationship. Bosticco and Thompson (2005) quoted a parent whose son has died to illustrate this:

> We celebrate the holiday and celebrate [him] because he was kind of freaky about Christmas, so we celebrate [my son] in that moment when we have breakfast, . . . and tell stories [about him]. Everybody's got stories [about him], but we all, you know, we all shed a tear who can be there. (p. 4)

Another function of storytelling is to provide a **catharsis,** or a release of emotional tension, for the narrator. By forming a story of an event, and telling it repeatedly, people are able to confront their emotional reactions to the event more readily. With repeated telling of the story, they gain a measure of control over those emotions, further relieving emotional tension. Barney Downs (1993) quoted one of his students who had just recounted his tale of loss as saying, "Each time I tell my story it occupies less space and grief in my soul" (p. 303).

The Healing Alliance is a special interest group of the National Storytellers Network that has the goal of exploring and promoting the use of storytelling in healing many kinds of grief. Their website is http://www.healingstory.org/home.html.

HOW MEANING IS MADE

To construct a story about events, people must make meaning of those events. Storytelling helps in this process and the storytelling and making meaning usually merge, with meaning made from one fragment of an event, which is then woven into the story. The story then helps the narrator make meaning of another fragment, which in turn is woven into the story, and so on.

To make meaning, people must examine the relevance and significance of events in their lives by examining both the positive and the negative effects the events have had on them. For many mourners, the process of making meaning of the death of a loved one comes through verbalizing what has occurred. With repetition of the story of what happened to their loved one, people not only impose order and coherence on the event and become more aware of their own feelings about the event, but they also recognize the impact it had on them. Discussing the event with others seems to be a need for many people, especially in milieus in which formal mourning rituals are weakened or deemed unimportant (Klass & Walter, 2001). It is not uncommon to find someone who has been bereaved telling and retelling the story of the event, even though the listener has heard the story before or was present when the event happened (see Chapter 5).

Often, however, discussing the event is not permitted in social interactions. When a bereaved person is met with a response of "Don't be morbid" or "You have to move on," the message is very clear that the listener does not want to hear the story, and naturally the mourner feels constrained to end the discussion. This is unfortunate because perceived social constraint against discussing the tragedy and the resultant feelings it has engendered is associated with greater feelings of depression in the mourner (O'Connor, 2002–2003). When a story of loss and broken dreams is not heard or accepted, disenfranchised grief (as discussed in Chapter 10) may result (Bowman, 1999). Presumably, then, not being allowed to verbalize events and feelings impairs the mourner's ability to make meaning of the event and leads to greater future distress. The presence of a supportive and empathic listener facilitates the meaning-making process and demonstrates to mourners that they are not as completely alone as they often feel and that someone still values and respects them in a world that is not totally devoid of comfort (O'Connor, 2002–2003).

When family members share meaning making with one another, adjustment to the death can be facilitated (Nadeau, 2001). Without knowing the feelings of other family members, it is all too easy for each to assume that the others are feeling the same emotions and wonder why their reactions seem so different. This may lead to misunderstandings and even resentment among the family, rather than the support that each member needs and wants to give to the others. Thus, Lucille Dupré may not realize that her daughters feel very specific losses with their father's death, and the daughters may not realize that their mother is questioning the very possibility of going on with her own life. But if they share their grief with each other, they may be able to provide some solace in their bereavement. For example, consider the conversation among the three women in Box 13.2.

BOX 13.2   Family Meaning Making

Belinda: I can't stand the fact that Daddy won't be at my graduation.

Anna: Yeah, I can see the problem, but at least you'll have us there. What about me? Daddy won't walk me down the aisle. How am I even supposed to be happy about getting married when Daddy isn't here? And how do you think it will feel when I have kids who won't even know Daddy?

Lucille: It's sad, but you girls have your whole lives in front of you. You'll have a life, but mine feels like it's over.

Anna: Mom, don't you see how much more we need you now? My kids will know Daddy through you more than through me.

Belinda: Yeah, Mom. And if you're at my graduation, I'll feel like part of Daddy is there as well.

Lucille: I can do my best to represent him. I know he would want that. But why did he have to die so suddenly? I never even got a chance to say goodbye!

Anna: I've been thinking about that too, and I think that maybe that's the way Daddy would have wanted it. He was never big on goodbyes and maybe he wouldn't have been able to bear saying goodbye to us.

Belinda: I never thought of that. Yeah, saying goodbye would have been awful for him, and he was so proud he never would have wanted to let us see him suffer through a long illness.

Lucille: Your father's main concern was always to protect us from pain. This isn't the way I wished death would come, but then I guess somehow I thought death would never come until we were both very old.

Belinda: I never thought about life without either one of you. As far as I was concerned, you guys would never age and die.

Anna: It sure makes you appreciate what you've got, doesn't it? Maybe you could walk me down the aisle, Mom?

Lucille: Of course I will. And you need to know that your father will be right beside you in spirit. And I'll be sure your children know all about their grandfather. I want you girls to know how proud he was of you and how proud I am. Maybe we'll make it.

This conversation is, of course, imagined. The points made by each woman would be more likely to come out in several conversations rather than just one, but it is clear that in the course of such a discussion, the women came to understand the grief that each was feeling and were able to offer some support and comfort to one another. They helped one another find meaning in Pierre's death and the hope that there would be a future for each of them, even without him. Lucille finds a satisfying explanation for the suddenness of her husband's death and a purpose in her life in representing her husband. In the future she may find more purpose, especially if she keeps sharing her grief with her daughters. Her daughters, in turn, recognize their mother's need for a reason to go on living and try to provide it in their need for her to represent their father and to be a parent to them. With the assurance of their mother's presence and feeling that she stands for their father, their momentous occasions, a graduation, a wedding, the birth of children, will be less painful for them. The three women have also taken a large step in growing from the agony of their experience by learning to appreciate the moment more than they ever had. They all know that life will never be the same for them, but they have taken the first steps in creating a new future story for themselves, one that will include the pain of their grief and a new relationship with the memory of Pierre.

Sometimes individuals find meaning and purpose on a larger level. Families sometimes commemorate the lives and deaths of their loved ones by public service means, such as through donating money to charity, founding a scholarship, or establishing a foundation. One poignant example is the AIDS quilt. Sponsored by the NAMES Project-Canada, this quilt strives to preserve the memories of those who have died of AIDS and HIV-related diseases. The website is http://www.quilt.ca/e_home.html.

At times the examples of such memorials affect society at large. See Box 13.3 for examples of how two bereaved parents found meaning in working to prevent others from experiencing the grief they had felt.

In some cases, groups of people have joined together to combat the problems of coping with crises, such as suicides and family violence. For example, the Aboriginal Healing & Wellness Strategy (AHWS) is a policy and service initiative formed by many Native Canadian bands and government agencies in Ontario to promote health and healing within Aboriginal communities. This strategy uses traditional Aboriginal approaches and values in their endeavours with community programs and services provided throughout the life span and for a wide variety of problems. For more information about AHWS, see their website at http://www.ahwsontario.ca.

BOX 13.3   John Walsh and Candy Lightner

John Walsh was a partner in a successful hotel-management company when his world changed tragically in July 1981: his six-year old son, Adam, was abducted from a shopping mall. Adam's body was found 16 days later more than 160 kilometres from his home. The prime suspect in the case died without confessing his guilt, leaving the Walsh family with no chance to ever know the complete truth of their child's death. John and his wife, Revé, became advocates for missing children and victims' rights, and they were instrumental in the passage of the *American Missing Children Act of 1982* and the *Missing Children's Assistance Act of 1984*. The latter bill created the Center for Missing and Exploited Children, which is now the central information centre for missing children in the United States and for the prevention of child victimization. John Walsh has written three books about his ordeal and the state of the law concerning children in America, and he has been honoured many times by law enforcement agencies and American presidents. He may be best known for his television program, *America's Most Wanted,* which has publicized crimes and alerted the citizenry to report any suspects of crime to the local authorities. Many crimes have been solved and many missing children returned to their homes because of this program.

Candy Lightner's 13-year-old daughter, Cari, was killed by a drunk hit-and-run driver while walking to a church carnival in May 1980. Devastated by this loss, she made a pledge to herself in her dead daughter's bedroom that she would work to end drunk driving. Many other mothers, also bereaved, banded with her and one of the most influential grassroots organizations was formed. Mothers Against Drunk Driving (MADD) has made the public in many countries aware of the heinous nature of drunk driving by showing the faces of the victims. By successfully personalizing the potential dangers of drunk driving, this organization has sensitized people to the preventable tragedies in a manner that dry statistics can never do. Legislation has been passed in the United States and Canada, as well as in other countries, that makes drunk driving a serious offence and promotes safety and victims' rights. This is in no small part due to the tireless work of MADD. Alcohol-related traffic fatalities have been dramatically decreased. Because of the publicity the group has received, especially with their campaigns to have supporters wear red ribbons, many people in the general public feel a personal responsibility to stop others from drinking and driving.

Societies also find ways to make meaning of death. For example, on December 6 each year, several memorial services are held across Canada, especially on university campuses, to commemorate the deaths of women that occurred at Montreal's École Polytechnique on December 6, 1989. These services typically include a protest against violence against women. In some cases parks, universities, roads, halls, and so on, are named for individuals whose lives have affected their community. Ryerson University in Toronto, Kruger Park in South Africa, and the John F. Kennedy Center in the United States are only three examples of memorials honouring individuals for their contributions to society. Memorials are especially prominent for those deaths that occurred tragically and in service to their country. In Canada, Remembrance Day on November 11 of each year commemorates these deaths with the motto "Lest We Forget." Yearly observations of Memorial Day in the United States also serves this purpose on the Monday closest to May 30, as do the National Day of Commemoration in Ireland on the Sunday nearest July 11, and Anzac Day in Australia on April 25. In addition, war

memorials are present throughout the world in the form of museums, parks, and statues. Box 13.4 lists some of the most famous war memorials in many countries of the world. In all cases, cross-culturally, these memorials indicate the determination of survivors to honour the war dead and to never forget the sacrifices they made, giving additional meaning to the lives and deaths of these people. These memorials also serve to provide a lasting tribute to the dead that many of the families of the deceased find comforting and significant.

Those who fought for their countries during wartime are not the only wartime dead whose lives and deaths are given meaning by society. The United States Holocaust Memorial Museum in Washington, D.C., and the Hiroshima Peace Memorial Museum in Japan pay tribute to the innocent lives lost in World War II. In the United States in August 2006, the World Trade Center Memorial Foundation and the Port Authority of New York and New Jersey began construction on the World Trade Center Memorial and Museum on the site of the twin towers, which were destroyed on September 11, 2001, killing thousands of people.

IN CANADA AND FOR CANADIANS
National War Memorial (Ottawa)

National War Memorial (Newfoundland and Labrador)

Saint Julien Memorial (a Canadian memorial in Belgium)

Canadian Tomb of the Unknown Soldier (Ottawa)

Canadian National Vimy Memorial (a Canadian memorial in France)

Beaumont-Hamel Newfoundland Memorial (France)

Groesbeek Memorial (a Canadian memorial in the Netherlands)

Gapyeong Canada Monument (a Canadian memorial in South Korea)

IN THE UNITED STATES AND FOR AMERICANS
Korean War Veterans Memorial (Washington, D.C.)

Arlington National Cemetery (Virginia)

Tomb of the Unknowns (Virginia)

Marine Corps War Memorial (Virginia)

Vietnam Veterans Memorial (Washington, D.C.)

Vietnam Women's Memorial (Washington, D.C.)

National World War II Memorial (Washington, D.C.)

Normandy American Cemetery and Memorial (an American cemetery in Normandy, France)

IN THE UNITED KINGDOM
Tomb of the Unknown Warrior (Westminster Abbey, London)

The Cenotaph (Whitehall, London)

Moreton in Marsh & Batsford War Memorial, Gloucestershire (southwest England)

IN FRANCE
Douaumont Ossuary (Verdun)

Notre Dame de Lorette (Arras)

Verdun Memorial

IN GERMANY
Völkerschlachtdenkmal ("Monument of the Battle of the Nations," in Leipzig)

Befreiungshalle ("Hall of Liberation," on Mount Michelsberg)

Hermannsdenkmal ("Hermann Monument," in North Rhine Westphalia)

IN INDIA
India Gate (National Monument of India, in New Delhi)

IN IRELAND
Garden of Remembrance (Dublin)

National War Memorial (Islandbridge, Dublin)

IN JAPAN
Yasukuni Shrine (Tokyo)

IN RUSSIA
Tomb of the Unknown Soldier (Moscow)

Piskarevskoye Memorial Cemetery (St. Petersburg)

Poklonnaya Gora (Moscow)

Mamayev Kurgan (Volgograd, formerly Stalingrad)

IN SINGAPORE
Kranji War Memorial

IN SOUTH KOREA
War Memorial of Korea (Seoul)

IN CHINA
Monument to the People's Heroes (Beijing and Shanghai)

IS MEANING MAKING AN INEVITABLE PART OF BEREAVEMENT?

The short answer to the question of whether meaning making is an inevitable part of bereavement is no. Not everyone who is bereaved searches for meaning in the death of the loved one or in their own continuing life. In a study of 124 parents who had lost their children to SIDS (sudden infant death syndrome), it was found that although these deaths were sudden and unexplained, 14 percent of the parents reported that they had never searched for the meaning of this tragedy in their lives, and most of them indicated that it was not at all important for them to make sense of their children's deaths. These parents also had higher scores on measures of general well-being than did other parents who were actively searching for meaning. A further study of people who had lost a spouse or a child in a motor vehicle accident found that an even higher percentage of mourners reported never having searched for meaning in these deaths (30 percent of those who lost a spouse and 21 percent of those who lost a child). Again, these individuals showed better adjustment to the death than mourners who had or were searching for meaning (Davis, Wortman, Lehman, & Silver, 2000).

Although this research indicated that most people who are bereaved suddenly do search for meaning, it is clear that for a sizable number of people, this search is not a necessary component of the grieving process. The question becomes why do some people need to search for meaning and others do not? For some people—some of the ones who do not search for meaning—it may be that the bond they shared with the deceased was weaker than the bond shared between the deceased and those who do search for meaning. For example, the death of a spouse may come as a relief if the marriage had been stressful and unhappy. Similarly, relief might be felt if death brought about an end to onerous caregiving responsibilities. In each of these circumstances, the mourner's feeling of well-being might be improved through the death, making a search for meaning less likely in these cases. It has also been suggested that people who grow up in environments where emotional bonds were not valued or reinforced might subsequently not form close emotional bonds with others. These people, having never experienced normal attachment to their caregivers and having effectively shut down their emotions, may not feel deep grief at the loss of someone close. In this case, the mourner has not organized his or her identity with the deceased as a focal point, misses the deceased very little, and so feels little need for a search for meaning (Davis et al., 2000; Fraley & Shaver, 1999). In other cases, it may be that people who do not search for a meaning after a death are simply not introspective; highly introspective people may be more likely to search for meaning in the wake of the death of a loved one because of their general tendency to reflect on events and the meaning of events to them and their world view.

In many cases, though, the basic assumptions about the world and life in general, the world view that an individual has, are incongruent with the brutal fact of a death. For instance, it is common to believe that children are safe when tucked in bed in the home and that the children will be fine if parents take good care of them. How can parents whose child has died of SIDS continue to believe this? Some very basic and widespread assumptions and securities about the way life works are drastically violated. The need to make sense of what has happened may be increased in these parents. That is, the more the world view has been shattered, the greater the need to find meaning may be. Certain kinds of deaths are more likely to devastate the world views of mourners and

hence are more likely to necessitate a search for meaning. Sudden death, as in the cases of SIDS and motor vehicle accidents, have been found to cause this, as do deaths by the intentional acts of an individual (e.g., homicides, suicides) and deaths that occur in an untimely fashion (e.g., the death of a child or young person). Deaths involving violence, suffering, or mutilation may also provoke an enhanced need for the survivors to find a meaning in the deaths and in their ongoing lives. In summary, according to Davis et al. (2000), those people who are thought to be the highest risk for difficulty in dealing with grief and most in need of finding a meaning are the following:

- highly distressed individuals who are striving to find meaning shortly after the death of a loved one
- those who have lost a loved one in circumstances that are highly traumatic, such as through violence, or when the death has been sudden or untimely
- bereaved spouses who experienced disordered attachment in childhood and who found stability in their relationship with the deceased
- bereaved spouses who were highly dependent on their partners
- those who used their relationship with the deceased as part of their identities
- parents who lose a child

THE ROLE OF RELIGION

As discussed in Chapter 3, religion typically imposes meaning on life and death. Religion attempts to answer the major questions of what life and death are about, what makes life meaningful and worthwhile, and thus, what makes death meaningful. The meaning given by religions to death may include "God's will," "making the survivor a stronger person" or "being in a better place," with the idea that the deceased and the survivors will one day be reunited. Some religions regard death as part of the cycle of life, reminding the dying and the bereaved that they are part of something far greater and vaster than is immediately apparent to them. Religion also provides rituals for the experiences surrounding death, a formula in many cases for what to do and how to proceed at the very time that the bereaved are most confused and unable to plan effectively. A religious community's shared beliefs and the commonality of values and rituals provide strong social ties that terminally ill people and mourners may cling to at the time of their greatest isolation. It is clear that religious communities are often invaluable in supporting the bereaved, reducing their feelings of isolation, and helping them find their place and their contributions within the community (DeSpelder & Strickland, 2005).

Logically, then, people who are more religious should have less difficulty in finding the meaning of the death of a loved one because their religious commitment gives them a ready world view within which to incorporate their loss and a community with which to share it. Their subsequent distress would be lessened with a religious mitigation for the death and their co-believers' presence, support, and reassurance. Indeed, such a result is often found (Davis et al., 2000; McIntosh, Silver, & Wortman, 1993), but sometimes a religious faith may be severely challenged in the face of the death of a loved one, and individuals may find their beliefs shaken and of little comfort, even compounding their distress. Davis et al. (2000) quoted Margaret, a devout Catholic whose husband died of pancreatic cancer, as saying, "Every day I would say the rosary asking God to keep my husband safe. . . . I feel as though God has betrayed me" (p. 515). Faith in a divinity whom the person trusted to protect and care for the individual may become impossible as the divinity is seen as having broken the covenant. The mourner then has extra loss: loss of the loved one, loss of a coherent world view and identity, and loss of the comfort and joy found within the religion. At present it is not clear which characteristics in people will lead them to find solace in their religion and help in making meaning of the death of a loved one, and which will lead to finding their religious faith shattered by the death.

AIDING THE SEARCH FOR MEANING

Saying goodbye to someone who is dying is painful, but if the leave taking is significant and satisfying, the mourner may find that this process has helped in making meaning of the death. People who have had a satisfying leave-taking experience fewer posttraumatic stress symptoms, perhaps because of the meaning making that occurs at this time (Schut, DeKeijser, Vanden Bout, & Dijkhuis, 1991). This may be important for mourners who have been highly dependent on the relationship with the deceased for their own identities and security because these are people who may not have prepared themselves for the death. The meaningful leave taking then may prepare them more adequately for their loss and render their subsequent distress easier to bear.

The use of ritual is also helpful in making meaning: rituals, such as memorial services held regularly, charity work in the name of the deceased, or letter writing to the deceased, may help mourners find a purpose in their lives and a commemoration of their loved ones.

People usually see their lives as an ongoing narrative or story, one that has been sadly disrupted by the death of someone central in their lives and thus central to their narrative. Often, writing a narrative of life, with the inclusion of the death of the loved one and its effect on the mourner, will help in putting the death within a larger context and aid in making sense of the confused and incoherent jumble that his or her life seems to be without the deceased.

When the bereavement has been the loss of a child at birth or shortly thereafter, it is particularly difficult for many parents to make a story of their loss because they were denied the opportunity of knowing the child and sharing experiences with him or her. In fact, this grief is often disenfranchised, denied the support of society because of the belief in the minds of many that a stillborn child was never really alive and therefore no real cause of grief to the parents. For this reason, many hospitals have instituted programs to help these parents create memories, commemorate their child, and thus create meaning. Parents are often encouraged to see or hold their deceased child, to name him or her, and they may be given a picture of the child, a lock of hair, or a hospital bracelet to further reinforce the child's existence. Worden (2002) also suggested that drawing, writing, and role-playing may also help these bereaved parents create a family history that includes the dead child. These strategies may also help the parents reflect on the meaning of their child's death to their lives and identities (Neimeyer, 2002).

Most important to bereaved people striving to make meaning is a supportive and empathetic individual to listen to their stories. To be this kind of listener, it is essential that people use **active listening.** Active listening involves more than the passive reception of what another person is saying; it involves the direct questioning and clarifying of information. Active listening probes into the speaker's meanings and feelings, and it rephrases what has been said to make sure that the correct message has been transmitted and understood. Box 13.5 outlines the keys to active listening.

Making meaning is a critical part of handling life crises for many people. The reflection that they give to these events in their lives may actually have effects beyond this, though: it may lead to their own personal growth and increase their capacity for dealing with other events in their lives.

BOX 13.5   Active Listening

1. *Ask for clarification.* Friendly and gentle questions, such as "Can you tell me more about this?" or "What happened then?" encourage the speaker and make him or her feel that attention is focused on what is being said and the listener is interested. In some cases, the narrator may indicate a lack of awareness of contradiction. An example of this may be found in the following case: For many years after the death of her husband, a mother expressed resentment toward her only child for leaving home to go to university less than a year later. When a supportive listener gently pointed out that the mother had stated that the husband had died *two* years before the daughter left, the mother came to understand that her resentment against her daughter was not really about the short time after the death but about the daughter leaving her at all. The mother gained insight into the main focus of her grief: her being left by her husband and her fear of being left by her daughter as well.

2. *Paraphrase.* Put what the speaker has said into your own words. This allows the speaker to correct any misapprehensions and to affirm that the correct message has been received. It may also convey a perspective that the listener had not considered, aiding in the meaning-making process.

3. *Listen to the tone of voice as well as the content.* Look at the body language of the speaker. Try to understand the feelings of the speaker and reflect what is ascertained. For example, such statements as, "You seem shocked by what happened," or "It seems hard for you to tell me this," lets the narrator know that both the content of the story and the emotions aroused by the story are being heard.

4. *Summarize and reflect meaning.* Paraphrasing what has been heard, both in content and in emotion, and then interpreting what has been said in a larger context also aid the meaning-making process. For example, on hearing the story of Pierre's death, a listener might say to Lucille, "You feel totally bereft and rudderless in a world in which your beloved husband has so suddenly died, especially when you can't understand exactly what happened or how it happened." This helps the listener gain understanding and insight, and assures the narrator that his or her message has been understood with sensitivity. It may also help the narrator summarize the larger meaning of the story.

Source: Hadad and Reed (2007); Knippen and Green (1994); Schafer (1996).

SUMMARY

- Making meaning is the imposition of structure, coherence, and significance on events of our lives.

- People make meaning in their lives by (1) finding a purpose in their present state or experiences, (2) constructing stories in which actions and events are transformed from undesirable to desirable, (3) constructing stories that highlight how to exert control and thereby make the environment more predictable and pleasant, and (4) constructing stories that focus on how attractive or competent the individual is.

- By constructing a story of our lives, we find connections among events and relationships between the past and the present, which help us make some predictions about the future in terms of actions to take and what to expect in many situations.

- Making meaning of a loss is particularly difficult because the structure of the lives involved often becomes incoherent, assumptions made about people's lives are shattered, and their future story is interrupted and even devastated. Additionally, their identities seem undercut when someone who has shared and been witness to the important events in their lives is removed.

- When meaning and future stories are disrupted because of a loss, meaning must be reconstructed. This includes (1) the finding or creation of meaning in both the death of a loved one and the life of the survivor, (2) integration and construction of meaning within a larger context of life, (3) an interpersonal process, and (4) a cultural process.

- Over time, the content of meaning making may shift. In the beginning, the emphasis is on making sense of the tragedy, finding a personal explanation of why the death occurred. Later the emphasis may be on finding a benefit to survivors, although an undesired one.

- The content of the meaning is unimportant; the only important factor is whether it satisfies the mourner.

- Making sense of a tragedy is more easily done when the events surrounding the tragedy can be put in a narrative form. Storytelling reduces a complicated set of events and perceptions into a single inclusive entity, keeps memories alive, and provides emotional catharsis for the narrator.

- To make meaning, people must examine the relevance and significance of events in their lives by examining both the positive and the negative effects the events have had on them.

- Perceived social constraints against discussing the tragedy and the resulting feelings they engender is associated with greater feelings of depression in the mourner, and disenfranchised grief may result.

- When family members share meaning making with one another, adjustment to the death can be facilitated.

- Not everyone who is bereaved searches for meaning in the death of the loved one or in their own continuing life.

- Those who do not search for meaning may have had a weaker bond with the deceased or they may have grown up in environments where emotional bonds were not valued or reinforced. This would lead them to lack close emotional bonds with others and not organize their identities with the deceased as a focal point; therefore, they miss the deceased very little, and so feel little need for a search for meaning.

- Highly introspective people may be more likely to search for meaning in the wake of the death of a loved one than are less introspective people because of their general tendency to reflect on events and the meaning of events to them and their world view.

- Certain kinds of deaths are more likely to devastate the world views of mourners and hence are more likely to necessitate a search for meaning. Sudden death, deaths by the intentional acts of an individual, and deaths that occur in an untimely fashion have been found to do this. Deaths involving violence, suffering, or mutilation may also provoke an enhanced need for the survivors to find a meaning in the deaths and in their ongoing lives.

- Many religious people can have less difficulty in finding the meaning of the death of a loved one because their religious commitment gives them a ready world view within which to incorporate their loss; however, sometimes a religious faith may be severely challenged in the face of the death of a loved one, and individuals may find their beliefs shaken and of little comfort, compounding their distress.

- At present it is not clear which people will find solace in their religion and help in making meaning of the death of a loved one and which will find their religious faith shattered by the death.

- If the leave taking of a dying loved one is significant and satisfying, the mourner may find that this process has helped in making meaning of the death.

- The use of ritual is also helpful in making meaning.
- Often, writing a narrative of life, with the inclusion of the death of the loved one and its effect on the mourner, will help in putting the death within a larger context and making sense of the confused and incoherent jumble that his or her life seems to be without the deceased.
- When the bereavement has been the loss of a child at birth or shortly thereafter, it is particularly difficult for many parents to make a story of their loss because they were denied the opportunity of knowing the child and sharing experiences with him or her.
- Most important to bereaved people striving to make meaning is a supportive and empathic individual to actively listen to their stories.

KEY TERMS

active listening   catharsis   making meaning

INDIVIDUAL ACTIVITIES

1. What meaning do you place on the following events?
    a. The announcement that your next test will be multiple choice format
    b. Your friend's uncharacteristic silence during lunch
    c. Your or your partner's possible pregnancy
    d. The unexpected death of your closest friend

2. Go back to the first exercise and construct at least two possible alternative meanings for each event.

3. Write the story of your life or your hoped-for future life. What disrupted your life the most, or what would disrupt your future life the most?

4. Ask someone (a parent or grandparent, a friend) to tell you the story of the most meaningful experience in his or her life. What meaning does this person attach to the event? Is this the same meaning you would attach to it if it had happened to you?

GROUP ACTIVITIES

1. In groups of four or five, compare your answers to the first exercise in individual activities. Do you all find the same meanings in these events?

2. In groups of four or five, compare the most meaningful events of your lives. Practise active listening as each member of the group recounts his or her story. Do all of you find the same meaning in these events?

3. Contact different hospitals in your area to find out how they deal with stillbirths and in a group of four or five, compare the different strategies used.

4. Find out what memorials to the dead exist in your area. Start with your own school to see whether any scholarships or bursaries have been established in the name of a deceased student or staff member. Bring the information to a group or to your class and discuss which memorials you find most personally meaningful.

CHAPTER 14

Ethical and Legal Issues at the End of Life

LEARNING OUTCOMES

In this chapter, we will discuss

- the ethics and legalities surrounding the end-of-life issues of

  ◆ the definition of death
  ◆ organ donation
  ◆ advance directives/living wills
  ◆ euthanasia
  ◆ physician-assisted suicide

Case Study: Jeff

▶ **J**eff was riding his motorcycle without a helmet. He crashed, smashed his skull to bits, and was rushed to the emergency room of a local hospital. The emergency response team did what they could, but even though only his head was injured, it was apparent that he could not survive the accident. He was put on a ventilator and an external heart pump until his family could be notified. When his family arrived at the hospital, they were apprised of Jeff's prognosis and asked if they would like to donate Jeff's viable organs. Jeff's brother became belligerent and accused the doctors of not doing all they could to save his brother's life because they wanted the organs for other people. He called the retrieval team "cannibals." Jeff's mother, crying, protested that her son was still breathing and might revive, even if it took years. Jeff's father, equally distraught, said that he could not stand to see his physically active, life-loving son in such a state and demanded that life-support be discontinued immediately. "If he doesn't die right away, I want you to give him something that will let him pass on," said Dad. "If you won't, I will."

The case in the opening vignette brings up several issues that trouble society, especially the medical community, in terms of the ethical problems they demonstrate. The last half of the twentieth century brought scientific medical marvels. Hearts can be restarted after stopping for a few minutes, paralyzed people can be kept alive with machines to breathe for them, medications can cure diseases that were hitherto fatal and terrifying (e.g., leprosy), other medications can maintain good functioning in people with potentially fatal diseases (e.g., HIV/AIDS), organs can be transplanted from a donor to a recipient who would otherwise die. But, as is always the case with any innovation, our new miracles come at a price. One of the major prices involves the ethical issues that surround the innovations. In this chapter, we will examine some of the ethical and legal controversies that encircle end-of-life issues because of new discoveries and age-old questions. We will look at arguments on all sides of these issues and see examples of how these questions affect people. We will not cover all the possible ethical and legal issues that exist, and we will not resolve any questions. The only hope for the eventual resolution of some of these issues (and some may never be fully resolved) is for the public to become informed about the arguments.

THE ISSUE: THE DEFINITION OF DEATH

Birth, life, death. Three one-syllable, easy-to-spell words that sum up existence. And yet these words contain the thorniest problems of humankind. People are not necessarily clear about what constitutes birth; for example, is the term *born* to be reserved for those who enter the world through a traditional vaginal birth? This question was raised when cesarean sections became possible to aid mothers who could not deliver their children vaginally. The commonality of cesarean sections, however, seemed to put the question to rest as it became tacitly accepted that birth consisted of removal from the mother's womb. But what happens when (and if) medical science reaches the point at which fetuses can be brought to gestation in an artificial womb? Can we still say that the resulting person has been "born"? Opinions differ on this, to the point of debating whether such a child is, in fact, human and has a soul.

The term *life* has been debated in both academic and lay circles. "This isn't living," moans the unhappy person. "It's only existence." Does "life" imply quality? or simply organic functioning? This seems to be the issue that troubles Jeff's father in the opening vignette the most: his position is that even if his son's body is functioning, his son is dead. The quality of life is a more important matter than is biological function to him.

The question of what constitutes life cannot be answered without also examining what constitutes death. Until the middle part of the twentieth century, death was defined as the cessation of heartbeat and breathing. Movies and television programs showed people being shot or stabbed or dying in some other way, and someone (usually the hero) put a finger to the individual's neck or wrist and within two seconds, looked up and said, "He's dead." Actually, many movies and television programs still show this scenario. But the issue of declaring death has never been that straightforward.

Until fairly recently, it was not always easy to detect when the heart had stopped beating or when breathing had completely ceased. This difficulty was the cause of the premature interments discussed in Chapter 1. Another major problem with the idea of cessation of heartbeat and breathing signifying death is that sometimes hearts begin beating again spontaneously and sometimes breathing begins again after a brief stoppage. Consider the victim who has almost drowned: he or she may experience just such an occurrence. Heartbeat and breathing have stopped, but on arrival on dry land, these functions may suddenly resume. Was this individual "dead" for a short time? Or was this just a brief organ malfunction until the victim could rally? To make this situation even more complicated, what if heartbeat and breathing stopped until some artificial means, such as cardiopulmonary resuscitation (CPR), could be administered? Can it be said that the victim was literally brought back from the dead? Or did CPR only jumpstart the organism? In the 1950s, people who had contracted poliomyelitis and became paralyzed were often artificially supported on a heart-lung machine. These large tanklike structures did the breathing and kept blood circulating for the polio victim. If a mechanism substitutes for natural heartbeat and breathing, can the individual whose heart and lungs have stopped functioning truly be said to be dead? In the case study at the beginning of this chapter, Jeff's mother does not believe that her son is really dead; she is hoping for that spontaneous resumption of cardiopulmonary functioning, which, to her, is the ultimate measure of life and death.

To jump into the world of the future, cryonics, the freezing of the body, may become perfected so that it is possible to maintain the body until a means is found to cure the person of whatever caused his or her death. This individual's heartbeat and breathing have stopped. Is this individual dead? The cryonics scenario provides several other ethical dilemmas, as well as serious theological problems, such as where the soul is during the period between freezing and resuscitation.

The advent of organ transplantation brought a more immediate need for a definition of what constitutes death. In the opening case study, Jeff has been quickly hooked up to a ventilator and an external heart pump while the critical response team evaluates his injuries and determines that his brain is too damaged to function. An electroencephalogram (EEG) reveals virtually no brain activity. His brother fears that the medical team will not put forth a maximum effort to save his brother and will prematurely call his brother dead in order to retrieve his organs. This is not an uncommon fear. Rightly or wrongly, many people report wariness about organ donation because of this and a general lack of agreement in the medical community about what constitutes death (see, for example, van Norman, 1999). If Jeff's grieving family does agree to donate his organs, at what point can the transplant team begin to remove his organs? That is, at what point can it be said that he is dead? One logical test is to remove the artificial means of life support to see if Jeff's body can sustain itself. If it cannot, if the heart and lungs stop functioning, most people would have no trouble in declaring the man dead. But what if his heart and lungs begin to function on their own (Jeff's mother's hope)? In this case, it may be that Jeff's whole brain has not stopped operating: the brainstem, responsible for autonomic functioning, may be able to continue keeping his body oxygenated, but the parts of his brain that keep him awake, alert, thinking, planning, and dreaming are destroyed and will never regenerate. Is he alive or dead? This type of permanent vegetative state has provided the arena of biomedical ethics with some of its stickiest dilemmas, and shortly we will discuss this further.

Bioethicists and, indeed, most medical personnel, fear the possibility of retrieving organs from a donor who is not really dead. This is not simply an abstract issue. What many people do not know is that anesthetists give "dead" donors painkillers and sedation while their organs are being retrieved because sometimes the donor's blood pressure and pulse increase from their artificially sustained level when the first incision is made. They may even move on the operating table (Keep, 1998; Young & Matta, 2000). These reactions indicate to many that some live functioning of the nervous system remains. It is very difficult for many people watching this to believe that the donor is really dead. Retrieval of organs seems more like murder. But is it? Or is what is seen only autonomic response of an artificially sustained body? Is the *donor* feeling pain? Or are the *donor's remains* reacting reflexively?

Today, what is considered at least part of the definition of death is brain death. Yet this concept itself is not without controversy. In the 1960s, various groups attempted to determine what constitutes brain death, a necessary step because it was clear that a determination of death could not be made by looking at the functioning of the heart and lungs. The most notable of these groups was the Ad Hoc Committee of the Harvard Medical School to Examine the Definition of Brain Death. This committee issued a report in 1968 indicating that death could be inferred with the permanent loss of all brain functions, from brainstem to higher cortical functioning. The individual cannot be considered dead (and organs cannot be retrieved) until the entire brain ceases to function. Implicit in this is the notion that the condition of the individual is irreversible.

The Harvard group's standards seem clear-cut and reasonable at first glance; however, the controversy is still not over. Sundin-Huard and Fahy (2004) stated that established practices in medicine cannot, in fact, reliably diagnose brain death. In fact, in some cases, people who have been diagnosed as being brain dead have recovered and, in some cases, even done well for a significant time afterward. Halevy (2001) indicated that several studies show that residual brain functioning may be present in individuals who have been determined to be brain dead by conventional medical standards. Is this brain functioning that matters in determining life and death? Who determines what amount or area of brain functioning matters? Many (e.g., see arguments reported by Veatch, 2004) contend that once the higher cortical areas of the brain no longer function, the individual is no longer aware or conscious. Thinking, planning, dreaming, and, in general, being part of society are over. The individual's quality of life has been termed "vegetative." By this definition, an individual in a permanent vegetative state is, in fact, dead.

The concept of *irreversibility* is also problematic (e.g., Cole, 1992; Shewmon, 1997). Given the miracles of medical science, it is, some contend, absurd to assume that any medical condition, including what has been termed brain death, is truly irreversible: if cardiopulmonary functioning can be restored, why is it not possible that some day brain functioning, at the higher cortical level or at the brainstem level, may be restored as well (Hershenov, 2003)?

The issue of determining what constitutes death has often centred on the ethical problems surrounding organ donation and when organs can be retrieved. But other issues remain, even if organ donation has been rejected or is not a possibility. At what point is it reasonable to discontinue artificial means of life support? If the individual is considered alive, clearly discontinuation of life support is a different dilemma from the situation in which the individual is considered dead. That is, continuation of life support when brain functioning is still apparent involves an ethical dilemma that will be discussed later. But if the individual is deemed dead, continuance of life support is at best an expensive and labour-intensive futility and, at worst, a needless cruelty to the deceased's loved ones. At what point is it permissible to assume that the individual is dead and so feels no

BOX 14.1   Definitions of Death

1. *Death is defined by the cessation of heart and lung functioning; that is, the individual's cardiopulmonary system ceases to operate.* This is a traditional definition used historically because these were the only measures that could be readily made and the condition was, in most cases, irreversible.
2. *Death is defined as the cessation of functioning of both the brainstem and the higher cortical areas.* This is the **whole brain definition of death.** It recognizes that heart and lung functioning can be sustained artificially, but it mandates that both higher cortical functioning, responsible for consciousness, alertness, thinking, and so on, as well as brainstem functioning, responsible for autonomic responses, such as breathing, have ceased.
3. *Death is defined as cessation of higher cortical functioning.* This definition allows for brainstem functioning to keep the biological organism alive but suggests that without higher cortical functioning, the human being's true life, in terms of consciousness and awareness has ceased, and death can be declared.

pain? At what point can pain medication and sedation be discontinued? Because the amount of sensation that is experienced by patients in permanent vegetative states and comas is unclear, people would want to be sure that pain management is undertaken until the patient can obviously no longer feel pain (i.e., until the patient is "truly" dead).

The arguments surrounding what constitutes death have been simplified in this chapter; philosophers, bioethicists, and theologians raise complexities that cannot be covered here (for further discussion, see Dagi & Kaufman, 2001; Lizza, 2005; Lustig, 2001). But it is plain that the issue is not as simple as it first appears. Surely a better answer than "Death, like beauty, is in the eye of the beholder" will be found.

Box 14.1 summarizes the various definitions of death, with an indication of the arguments used to sustain these definitions.

What Does the Law Say?

In general, the law in most countries is equivocal. Local community standards and judgments of hospital ethics boards tend to govern the definition of death in their venues for the most part. The Law Reform Commission of Canada made the following recommendation regarding the definition of death in 1981: "For all purposes within the jurisdiction of the Parliament of Canada, a person is dead when an irreversible cessation of all that person's brain functions has occurred." This is the "whole brain" definition of death: death occurs when no functioning occurs in either the brainstem or the higher cortical areas. Although this recommendation of the Law Reform Commission has not as yet been enacted into law, it is a standard that is used in most situations in Canada.

The whole brain definition of brain death is the definition used in the United States and in the United Kingdom, although in some areas, more emphasis is put on higher brain functioning. In the United States, the *Uniform Determination of Death Act* in 1981 did not legislate criteria for determining death but allowed states to establish guidelines "in accordance with medical standards" (Capron, 2001, p. 1246). Other European countries all have guidelines governing the determination of death following the concept of brain death, but wide variation exists in the tests used and the amount of time needed to make the determination of brain death. Japan, although technologically advanced, has only recently accepted the concept of brain death as the legal definition of death, while most African countries have no legal criteria for death at all. In all, only about two-thirds of the world's countries have guidelines for determining death, and even those vary widely (Wijdicks, 2002).

Interestingly, no evidence suggests that any grounds exist to expand the definition of death to the nonfunctioning of higher cortical areas, even if brainstem functioning is still occurring. Siminoff, Burant, and Youngner (2004) gave three scenarios to a sample of more than 1300 people in Ohio and asked them if the people in the scenarios were legally alive or dead. In the first scenario, the person described was whole brain dead, but his heartbeat and breathing were being artificially sustained. In this case, 86.2 percent said that the individual was legally dead. In the second scenario, the individual was described as severely brain damaged to the point that consciousness would never be possible and respiration was being artificially sustained. In this case, 57.2 percent of the respondents identified this patient as dead. In the third scenario, the patient was breathing on his own but was in a permanent vegetative state, indicating that higher cortical areas were not functioning but

Jeff had signed an organ donor card, indicating that he wanted his organs to be donated in the event of his death. Jeff's family has been approached about this, and his mother is horrified. Even if she can accept that her son is dead, she has a further problem in donating her son's organs. Her first thought is, "No, no, don't touch him any more, don't carve him up. Let me bury my son whole, just as I bore him." Jeff's father has thought about reincarnation and wonders if his son will be reborn whole and well if some of his organs have been taken in this life. Jeff's brother is still uncomfortable that his brother might be declared dead prematurely simply because the retrieval team is ready and waiting, as are the potential recipients of Jeff's organs. A nurse says to the family, "You don't have any choice—Jeff signed the donor card."

the brainstem was. This patient was identified as dead by 34.1 percent of the respondents. Although it is unclear whether the respondents were knowledgeable about the definition of brain death, it is clear that a substantial number of them regarded some individuals as dead that the law would say are alive. Because law is supposed to reflect the will of the people in a democracy, this study opens the possibility that public standards may not be in line with legal definitions.

Because the definition of death is so closely tied to the issue of organ donation, this ethical issue will be discussed next (see Box 14.2).

THE ISSUE: ORGAN DONATION

Organ donation is regarded by many, including many religious institutions, such as the Catholic Church, to be a wonderful, ethical, and moral gift that should be encouraged. Certainly, it is seen by most as a gift, that is, something that is freely given, without coercion or thought of personal gain. This, in itself, is providing an ethical dilemma for many, because in Western society, organ donation is widely encouraged and many potential recipients are in danger of dying before receiving a transplant. For example, in Canada in 2002, nearly 4000 Canadians waited for donor organs; during this same year, 237 Canadian potential recipients died while waiting (Knoll & Mahoney, 2003). Is society coercing the individual to become an organ donor? Did Jeff really want to donate his organs? Or did he feel that he "should" do it, to be a good person? Imagine a scenario in which

Jeff was asked by friends if he had signed his donor card, and when he said no, they asked him why, in essence, shaming him into signing. It is entirely conceivable that Jeff (and others) had serious reservations about donating his organs after death but did not feel that he could reasonably deny others the chance for life. As possibly noble as organ donation may be, donating simply to avoid feeling guilty about not donating implies coercion by society that most ethicists would agree is unacceptable.

Another ethical concern arises when the wishes of the potential donor are not known and the family or surrogate decision maker is asked to make the choice regarding donation. No matter how sensitively and gently the family is asked, the reality is that no time is worse for them to make a major decision, especially one that has not been discussed previously. In most cases, the death of a loved one who is a potential donor comes as a shock to the family. That is, if the death has been long anticipated, as in the case of metastasized cancer or a very senior person, the organs may not be suitable for donation, so no ethical dilemma exists. But when the case is like that of Jeff, in which only the head of a young person has been injured but the rest of the organs are healthy, the death may well be traumatic (see Chapter 10). The family is under extreme stress and in shock. Ethically, it is questionable whether the family should be asked to make any major decisions at this time. And yet, to wait would mean losing the chance to retrieve viable organs. The only way out of this dilemma is to prevent its occurrence by having open and frank discussions about organ donation among family members so that everyone knows and can respect the wishes of everyone else. For a further discussion of these problems, see Melvin and Heater (2001) and Youngner (2003).

Jeff's brother's concerns should not be overlooked, either. Guest and Devitt (2000) suggested that he may have a point; they propose that, especially in a climate of urgency, with a somewhat nebulous definition of death, physicians may rush the declaration of death in a manner that would not be used if retrieving organs were not a possibility. And Jeff's brother is not the first to refer to the practice of organ retrieval as "cannibalism" (see Fox, 1993, for further discussion), indicating that some find the practice extremely distasteful.

Other ethical dilemmas surround the transplantation of organs that do not directly involve end-of-life issues: Is organ donation itself ethical or is it an immoral attempt to escape destiny? If it is ethical, who should receive the donated organs? What criteria should be used in this determination, given that waiting lists have more potential recipients than donors? Should high-risk people, such as those with existing and unrelated disorders, those with risky lifestyles, those who are over 65, be removed from the recipient list? Should individuals or

In April 2006, newspapers reported the first Canadian case of live donation of kidneys within two families, called a paired kidney exchange. Joe Leung's kidneys had failed and he required a transplant urgently to live. His wife, Heidi, volunteered to donate a kidney, but her tissues were not a match for Joe's. At the same time, Tom McCabe's wife, Antoinette, urgently required a new kidney, and Tom was not a match. The transplant physicians of both families devised a trade plan in which Tom McCabe gave a kidney to Joe Leung, and Heidi Leung gave a kidney to Antoinette McCabe. Although the story seems like a wonderful miracle, ethicists are concerned that this will lead to the selling of organs and the elimination of appropriate, objectively determined criteria for receipt of an organ. Did someone even more desperate miss a chance of a matching kidney because these two families decided to exchange their organs? One argument says that need counts for more than private arrangements and that such a swap suggests that the donors have been compensated for the donation by being given a transplant organ for a loved one in need (i.e., the transplant organ has been "sold," not "donated.") But another argument says that individuals have the right to give their organs to whomever they please, that perhaps the donors would not donate an organ at all if their partners were not exchange recipients, and that such an exchange then removes two people from the transplant waiting list, thereby moving the remaining people up a little higher on the list.

The physicians who managed this swap see the arrangement as highly beneficial if it is made into a national program, linked to a computer registry. The British Columbia Transplant Society started a paired kidney exchange program in June 2006 (see the British Columbia Transplant Society at http://www.transplant.bc.ca/index.asp).

their families be allowed to sell their organs? Is the case discussed in Box 14.3 ethically acceptable?

What Does the Law Say?

All countries that have the facilities to perform organ transplantation abide by the **dead donor rule,** which stipulates that removal of organs must not result in the donor's death. The donor must be clearly dead before certain organs (e.g., heart, lungs) are retrieved or else, clearly, the removal of these organs will remove the possibility of life for the donor and be equivalent to homicide. Laws regarding transplantation revolve around the country's or community's definition of death.

In Canada, the *Human Tissue Gift Act* of 1996 stipulates that a donor must be brain dead (whole brain death is implied in this law) and may not be reimbursed for the donation. Further, the law stipulates that a potential donor's signature on a donor card is binding and the family's or surrogate decision maker's objections cannot supersede the expressed wishes of the donor. Essentially the same legislation has been passed in the United States as the *Uniform Anatomical Gift Act of 1987.* In both countries though, most retrieval teams do consider the wishes of the family. When an individual wished to donate organs and the family objects, efforts are typically made to change the minds of the family, reminding them of the potential donor's wishes, but if the family remains adamant, most hospitals will acquiesce to their requests, even though they are not legally bound to do so. The same situation is in effect in most other transplant countries, whether actual legislation is in effect or not.

The strength of society's desire to increase organ donation can be seen in the campaign being led by the Ontario government. On January 9, 2006, the Ontario government enacted a law requiring the 13 major hospitals in the province to report every death to the Trillium Gift of Life Network (TGLN) in order to identify potential donors. In January 2007, the program was expanded to include 21 hospitals and TGLN is seeking to have this requirement expanded to all Ontario hospitals (Trillium Gift of Life Network, 2007). In addition, legislation has been proposed in Ontario that would presume consent; that is, unless a person has signed a card opting out, it will be presumed that the person consented to donating his or her organs in the event of death. The law has not yet been written, so it may or may not specify that the retrieval of the organs will require the explicit consent of the individual or the family.

Additionally, in the study done by Siminoff et al. (2004) discussed previously, the researchers continued their questioning of their sample of Ohioans by asking them under which of the three presented scenarios the respondents felt that organ retrieval was acceptable. They found that one-third of the respondents believed that organ retrieval was acceptable in patients that they had classified as legally alive in at least one scenario. Specifically, in the first scenario, of a brain dead patient, 66.8 percent of the respondents who said that the patient was alive were also willing to retrieve the patient's organs for donation. In the second scenario of a patient with severe brain injuries on mechanical support, 45.7 percent of respondents who regarded the patient as alive found organ retrieval to be acceptable. In the third scenario of a patient in a permanent vegetative state (i.e., no functioning of higher cortical areas but brainstem functioning),

In November 2004, CBC News reported on the rec-ommendations of the Quebec Science and Tech-nology Ethics Committee regarding when organs can be ethically retrieved. The committee recom-mended that the definition of death be expanded to increase the number of potential donors. Presently, in Canada, only whole brain dead indi-viduals are considered to be ethically appropriate donors. The committee suggested that people whose hearts have stopped beating and cannot survive without artificial means could also be con-sidered as donors. Brain functioning is not neces-sarily examined in this case. This would imply that medical personnel might well be placed in the dif-ficult ethical dilemma of having to decide whether to resuscitate patients or consider them to be organ donors. The chair of the committee, François Pothier, a professor at Laval University, noted that some American hospitals are already acting on this expansion of the definition of death and suggested that Quebec should institute some limited trials of the practice.

After several days of watching Jeff being sus-tained by life support technology, Jeff's brother discovered a letter in Jeff's home that was entitled "Living Will." In this letter, signed by Jeff and two witnesses, Jeff stated that in the event of his inca-pacitation and inability to give directions for his care, he wanted physicians to exert no undue effort to save his life by artificial means and that if he showed no chance of recovering conscious-ness, he wanted all life support to be suspended to let him die as naturally and with as much dig-nity as possible. He asked that pain management procedures be followed, if appropriate, but no other treatment be given if he showed no higher cortical functioning. He named his father as his decision maker in the event of his inability to indi-cate his further preferences for treatment. Jeff's brother showed the letter to his family. His father nodded sadly in agreement, but his mother vio-lently opposed what she saw as "giving up" on life. "I'm his mother and I should have the right to make the determination of what happens to my son. He wrote that letter when he didn't know what the future held. I know my son and I believe his decision may well be different if he could speak to us right now. My wishes should override his letter."

34.3 percent of respondents who classified the patient as alive were willing to retrieve organs for donation. Once more, perception of quality of life seemed to be a deter-mining factor in respondents' decisions of whether or not organ retrieval was acceptable. The researchers wisely noted that their study is only suggestive, needing replica-tion among many more samples of individuals, but they also noted that such results as these highlight the need for more education and more public dialogue regarding the issues surrounding the definition of death and organ donation. Again, the possible mismatch of the law and the public will may be in evidence. See Box 14.4 for further evidence of the controversial nature of organ donation and the definition of death.

THE ISSUE: ADVANCE DIRECTIVES OR LIVING WILLS

A growing number of people are following Jeff's lead as seen in Box 14.5, and writing a **living will** or giving **advance directives** regarding what course of action they want physicians and family to follow in the case of their being injured so badly that they have no chance of their returning to full consciousness and functioning. A living will, a more formal written document than advance directives, which may be oral, may also nominate a substi-tute decision maker in the event of the individual's

incapacitation, including a durable power of attorney for health-care decisions. These procedures typically specify the individual's wishes regarding what measures should be taken to save or prolong his or her life and what measures to forgo, and under what conditions life-saving or life-sustaining measures may be undertaken and under what conditions they should be discontinued. Medical person-nel may be grateful for such directives because it often removes the necessity of making ethical treatment deci-sions for someone else. In other cases, however, the advance directives may stipulate a treatment (or lack of treatment) that violates medical ethics and thus provides a greater problem for medical personnel. For example, what if Jeff's brain injuries had been less severe but still severe enough to render him mentally or physically impaired? And what if his living will had requested that physicians end his life under these circumstances? Can physicians comply with the wishes of a quadriplegic patient, say, who wants to die? This lands the physicians in the area of either committing euthanasia or assisting in a patient's suicide, both issues we will discuss later.

The families of those who have made a living will are also sometimes divided on the contents of the direc-tives, as Jeff's family seems to be. On one hand, Jeff left little ambiguity about his wishes, but if a family member disagrees, the situation can become even more painful than it already is. Jeff's mother does not want to lose her son under any conditions, even though she is confronted with what he stated he wanted. Her only recourse is to deny that the living will truly reflects what his decision would be at that moment. This is perhaps a valid argument because which one of us really knows how we will feel if put into such an extreme situation? Thus, ethically, the problem of inflicting pain arises: not following Jeff's instructions will cause pain to family members who want his desires to be paramount and, perhaps in an ethical sense, cause pain to Jeff. But following Jeff's instructions will cause pain to Jeff's mother and perhaps to Jeff if he would have changed his mind, given the changed situation since the writing of his living will.

This ethical dilemma has no clear-cut answer (see Palazzani, 2004, for a more in-depth discussion).

What Does the Law Say?

As in the case of organ donation, Canadian law supports honouring the individual's wishes in his or her medical treatment. Most provinces and one territory have passed statutes to allow people to issue binding advance directives and living wills (only New Brunswick, the Northwest Territories, and Nunavut do not have this legislation as of 2006). Similarly, most states in the United States uphold living wills, as does the United Kingdom, France, and most countries in Europe. This is also the case in New Zealand, Australia, Poland, Germany, and, more recently, it is being discussed in India (Mendelson & Jost, 2003; Rao, 2005). The federal *Patient Self-Determination Act of 1991* in the United States was, in fact, an attempt to encourage people to use living wills and advance directives.

When family objects to the instructions in a living will, it is usually much easier for the medical team to follow the patient's directives than it is in the case of organ donation alone, because the living will typically names an advocate with durable power of attorney for the health care for the patient. Thus, medical personnel are not placed in the extremely uncomfortable position of having to argue for a patient's rights against a grieving family; the designated decision maker (often a family member) has the obligation to follow the directives set out by the patient, including convincing or even overriding the family members who object to the living will directives. It can clearly be seen that it is preferable to discuss the contents of a living will or advance directives with family members before the need to act on these directives arises.

It is important to note that except for some cases discussed below, requests in living wills to terminate treatment or life support in the case of irreversible brain death are the common extent of legal directives. Requests to terminate life deliberately (as in euthanasia and physician-assisted suicide) provide extra issues that are much more controversial. Several different forms for living wills and advance medical directives exist, specifically applicable to each country, province or territory, or state, which are readily available in many book and stationery stores and on the Internet. One source is the Living Will Registry Canada (http://www.livingwills.com), which provides information and forms (for a small charge) for living wills, power of attorney for personal care, a personal values statement, and an organ donation statement. Also, the Health Law Institute of Dalhousie University has instituted the End of Life Project, which gives valuable information on issues of living wills, potentially life-shortening palliative interventions, and withdrawal of potentially life-sustaining treatments. You can visit their website at http://as01.ucis.dal.ca/dhli/cmp_welcome/default.cfm. The need for advance directives is illustrated in the Terri Schiavo case, discussed in Box 14.6.

THE ISSUE: EUTHANASIA

What Jeff's father and brother are asking for in Box 14.7 is **euthanasia** or a *mercy killing* for Jeff. Although the definition of euthanasia can include such cases as that of Terri Schiavo in which nutrition and hydration tubes are removed from a patient in a persistent vegetative state (e.g., see Snelling, 2004), or cases in which palliative treatment measures, such as giving high doses of morphine, may hasten death, for the purpose of this chapter we will define euthanasia as deliberate treatment designed to end the life of a patient in a terminal medical state or a patient who is suffering intractable pain. For this discussion, we will limit the discussion of euthanasia to those cases in which someone other than the patient (usually medical personnel) actively administers a treatment that will bring about the end of life.

The ethical arguments surrounding euthanasia are both simple and complex. On one hand, deliberately ending the life of another person is considered unacceptable by virtually every society, except in the special cases of self-defence, defence of others, execution (in some societies), or wartime. Most societies consider the value of a single human life to be a cornerstone of their principles. These societies maintain that life must be preserved at all costs. On the other hand, allowing someone to continue experiencing agonizing pain and suffering with no hope of respite until death seems cruel and heartless. Intuitively, as individuals watch patients suffer, the desire to end this suffering is often seen as more immediate than a nebulous and abstract principle of preservation of life. In this situation, many would argue, as Jeff's father does, that the state the patient is in is not "life," and to preserve this state is morally wrong.

BOX 14.6   The Terri Schiavo Case

In February 1990, Terri Schiavo, 26 years old, collapsed in the hall of her apartment and experienced a lack of oxygen to her brain for several minutes. She was placed on a feeding tube because she could not swallow. By late 1990, she was determined to be in a persistent vegetative state and in the absence of a living will or advance medical directive, Terri's husband, Michael, was named her legal guardian. Her parents raised no objection to this, and Terri's husband, with their help, made sure that regular and aggressive physical, occupational, and speech therapies were instituted in the hopes that Terri might recover. But no patient has ever recovered after a year of being in a permanent vegetative state (Perry, Churchill, & Kirshner, 2005), and definitely after 15 years of being in this condition, any hope for Terri's recovery was medically determined to be gone. Michael, Terri's husband, came to believe that his wife was, in effect, gone, and he firmly believed that she would not have wanted to have her body kept alive in this state. Terri's parents, however, disagreed.

The media brought this tragic situation to the attention of much of the world, showing pictures of Terri with her eyes open and moving, sometimes even appearing to smile. These actions are fairly common for patients in persistent vegetative states; intuitively, it may seem that the patient has some awareness of the environment, but medical personnel report that this is, in fact, not the case. These actions are simply autonomic nervous system responses. Michael Schiavo decided that Terri's artificial nutrition and hydration should be discontinued. Terri's parents vehemently opposed this, leading to court action in Florida. The court's task was to determine what Terri would have wanted. Because she left no written instructions, both her husband and her parents presented witnesses and made arguments, one side contending that she would have wanted life support discontinued and the other side contending that she would have wanted every effort made to keep her alive. The court decided that Terri would not want to live in a permanent vegetative state and ordered her nutrition and hydration discontinued. Terri Schiavo died on March 31, 2005.

The court's decisions will always cause agreement and disagreement in such situations as this, but these situations highlight the magnitude and importance of making known wishes for treatment in the case of severe incapacitation. This would preferably be in writing through, perhaps, a living will, although even this will not cover all contingencies (see Mathes, 2005).

BOX 14.7   Euthanasia

Jeff has been removed from artificial means of sustaining breathing and heart beat, and remarkably to his physicians, he has resumed cardiopulmonary functioning on his own, although at a low rate. The physicians now say that with artificial feeding and hydrating, they have no way of knowing how long Jeff's body will remain functioning. They stress, however, that he has sustained too much damage to the higher cortical areas of his brain to ever regain consciousness or any awareness. Jeff's mother maintains hope, but after one month, Jeff's father and brother feel that Jeff is already gone and that maintaining his body, the "shell," Jeff's father calls it, is a needless cruelty, especially because he doesn't know whether Jeff's body is in pain on some level. Jeff's father and brother now beg the physicians to end what they see as a "travesty." "Give him an overdose of morphine, do something," they plead. "You're doctors—you're supposed to end suffering, so end his. If you don't do it, then we will, and since we aren't medical people, we may not know how to do it as humanely as you do."

From the medical perspective, the physician's oath of "first, do no harm" would appear to indicate that under no circumstances should a life be taken. But many interpret this oath in a different sense: some see the oath as being broken if intractable suffering is allowed to continue. Is it not "doing harm" to allow someone to continue in pain until their inevitable death? This issue revolves around the ethical **principle of double effect.** In this principle, ethicists generally agree that if an action, such as giving high dosages of morphine, is intended to bring about a good effect but it can achieve this effect only at the risk of producing a harmful effect, such as a hastened death, the action is ethically acceptable.

In reality, it is a common procedure in many countries (including Canada, the United States, the United Kingdom, the Netherlands, Belgium, Denmark, Sweden, Switzerland, Australia; see ten Have, 2001; van der Heide et al., 2003) to administer drugs to reduce pain and hasten death. Thus, under the ethical intent of pain management, many physicians are administering doses of painkillers that they know will lead to the death of the patient. Such cases as these rarely make news, the actions are not prosecuted, and few people protest that the medical personnel's actions have been in any way immoral (Cohen et al., 2005). In most cases, the family and the medical personnel who have been intimately involved in the care of a terminally ill and suffering patient are grateful that the end of the suffering has come and the death of the patient is registered as being the result of the patient's presenting illness.

Other implications of the deliberate killing of someone judged to be suffering exist, however. The first is, "Who makes the decision that the individual is suffering to such an extent that he or she would wish to terminate life?" To illustrate this, we examine the case of the death of Tracy Latimer in Box 14.8.

Many groups, especially those made up of people with chronic illnesses, argued that Tracy had the right to live for as long as she could and certainly for as long as she appeared to be getting enjoyment from her life. Their argument was that the suffering that Robert Latimer wanted to end was his own; that *he* could not stand what Tracy was going through, not that *she* could not stand it. An additional ethical problem is raised: how much does an individual have to be suffering before someone (a decision maker?) judges that the suffering is too great? For example, in condoning Robert Latimer's actions—and clearly as a father of a minor he was the decision maker—would this suggest that people with cognitive impairments and cerebral palsy should be considered for euthanasia? What about those whose intellectual impairments leave them with almost no independent functioning? If the person has a mental disorder, such as schizophrenia, that is not responsive to medication or therapy, shall society consider this person to be suffering too much to live? What of the very senior people who can no longer take care of themselves and may be experiencing dementia? Shall they too be given a "merciful death"? Opponents of euthanasia point to the slippery slope that must exist when a society says that it is justifiable to hasten the death of some people who have not specifically requested it. As one death becomes justifiable, the argument is that it becomes easier to justify other deaths. "People who have not specifically requested it": those are, perhaps, the key words in the argument concerning euthanasia. But what about those patients who *have* requested that their lives be terminated? These cases will be discussed later.

What Does the Law Say?

The law in most countries (e.g., Canada, United States, United Kingdom, Australia, Poland, Germany, France) is unequivocal: no one may hasten the death of another person without his or her consent. But cases in which physicians hasten the death of their terminally ill and suffering patients while administering pain-reducing medications, such as morphine, are virtually never brought to the attention of the legal system. This is not necessarily the case when other means of bringing about death are used, however. The following Canadian examples illustrate this (Lemmens & Dickens, 2001).

- In Timmins Ontario, in 1991, Dr. Alberto de la Rocha administered an injection of morphine and potassium chloride to his 70-year-old patient Mrs. Mary Graham, who was suffering from terminal cancer of the cheek, mouth, and lung. The doctor's motives were to save his patient further pain and suffering, and the patient's family supported him. Initially, the doctor was charged with second-degree murder, but the charge was later reduced and he pleaded guilty to the lesser charge of administering a noxious substance. He received a three-year suspended sentence and was not banned from practising medicine.
- In 1994, a couple named Myers smothered Mrs. Myers's father who was dying of cancer. They were initially charged with second-degree murder but were allowed to plead guilty to the lesser charge of manslaughter. They were sentenced to three years' probation and 150 hours of community service.
- Mrs. Bush was an 81-year-old woman who had been happily married for 58 years. She and her husband,

---

BOX 14.8	In the News: The Case of Robert Latimer

On October 24, 1993, a farmer in Saskatchewan named Robert Latimer killed his 12-year-old daughter, Tracy. Tracy was a quadriplegic with severe cognitive impairments and cerebral palsy who had had several surgeries, including one pending, and who experienced pain. Latimer admitted to placing her in the cab of his truck, running a hose from the exhaust into the cab, turning on the motor, and watching Tracy die of carbon monoxide poisoning. He claimed this was a mercy killing because she was in constant chronic pain that would only become worse.

After two trials and appeals, including one to the Supreme Court of Canada, Latimer, to his surprise and to the surprise of many, was convicted of second-degree murder and was sentenced to 25 years' incarceration, with no chance of parole before 10 years. The Saskatchewan juries and courts stated their belief that Latimer had acted with love and concern for his child, but felt that he had made serious errors in judgment. Questions still surround whether Tracy would have agreed with her father's decision to end her life. Witnesses testified to Tracy's enjoyment of life, and pictures and videos of Tracy show a laughing, smiling child who did not seem to be in great pain. Yet that she also had periods of intense pain was irrefutable. Latimer made the decision that Tracy's continued life was untenable, and the courts had no way of determining whether this was the case or not, from Tracy's viewpoint.

whose health was failing, entered into a joint suicide pact. When the joint suicide failed, she stabbed her husband (whether he consented to this is unclear), killing him, and attempted suicide herself, but was again unsuccessful. She was charged with murder, but this was reduced to a charge of manslaughter for which she was convicted. Her sentence was suspended, with 18 months on probation.

These examples indicate that the law in Canada (as in many other countries) recognizes the deliberate killing of a dying person as a legal wrong, but the leniency of the sentencing indicates that certain moral and ethical understanding mitigates the act. Hence, sentencing is extremely light in the case of some mercy killings.

But then why was sentencing not light in the case of Robert Latimer? The answer seems to be in the ambiguity of his daughter's condition. In the above examples, the people who were killed were, without question, dying anyway. In the case of Tracy Latimer, however, this is not clear, and the Canadian courts, while noting the father's love for his child, ruled that killing when death is not imminent is not viewed with as much sympathy, and no legal mitigation is seen. On the contrary, the courts believed that Tracy's pain could have been managed by means that Robert Latimer had not sufficiently explored.

Not all societies agree with the laws of most Western countries, however. Japan, for example, is more open to the legitimacy of euthanasia than most other countries but is less likely to countenance the withdrawal of treatment in terminal cases. In Japan, the courts have stated that euthanasia is appropriate if "(1) the physical pain is difficult to bear (mental suffering does not suffice); (2) the time of unavoidable death is near; (3) methods of eliminating the pain are exhausted; and (4) there is a clear expression of intent to accept death" (Mendelson & Jost, 2003, p. 137).

Thus, Western society gives a certain understanding to cases in which the death of dying persons is hastened to end their suffering. The cases that have been discussed are those in which it appears that the dying individual did not specifically give end-of-life directives. What of cases in which the individual clearly asks for termination of life from his or her physician? This brings us to the next issue, illustrated in Box 14.9: physician-assisted suicide.

THE ISSUE: PHYSICIAN-ASSISTED SUICIDE

It is difficult for physicians to face a situation in which they recognize that they can do no more to help a patient to live or to relieve a patient's suffering. When the patient asks that the physician help to terminate his or her life, the situation is often even more difficult for the physician. Many ethical and theological arguments exist

---

BOX 14.9   The Case of Margo

Margo had thought very hard about having genetic testing. Her father had died of the effects of Huntington's disease, a genetically carried disease that brings about the degeneration of the central nervous system, leading to both severe physical and cognitive impairment as well as emotional disturbances. She recalled vividly how her dynamic, intelligent, fun-loving father turned into someone who could not control his movements, who could not understand the words in the newspaper, and who had outbursts of violent temper tantrums interspersed with deep depression. She deeply regretted that she was not present when he choked to death while eating because his swallowing was so badly impaired. Perhaps she could have saved him, she thought. Knowing that she had a 50 percent chance of carrying the genetic material for this disorder, she decided to be tested before symptoms began so that she could plan her life accordingly.

The results of testing indicated that Margo had inherited her father's disorder. She could not come to terms with the fact that she would lose her physical, cognitive, and emotional control and become much like her father. She viewed suicide as the only way for her to avoid the ravages of the disease, but she wanted to live for as long as her life had a good quality. Her fear was that by the time her life was untenable to her, she would not have the physical or cognitive ability to kill herself. She therefore wanted to make a living will that stipulated that her mother, who has her power of attorney for heath care, would arrange for a physician-assisted suicide for her.

---

against suicide itself on the grounds of the sanctity of life, but many arguments support the idea that the individual has the right to choose his or her life or death. As a society, in Canada, most people regard suicide as tragic and believe that means should be taken to prevent suicide (see Chapter 9), but an understanding generally exists that a person with intractable suffering may choose death over life. Many might feel sad, but few, perhaps, would be unforgiving of the person with untreatable pain and a terminal medical condition committing suicide. The issue of involving another person in this suicide, however, becomes much more controversial.

Physician-assisted suicide is suicide in which a physician has provided the patient with the means to end his or her own life. Assisting in the suicide of another person is considered to be morally and legally wrong by most societies, and the physicians' code of "do no harm" would seem to be unequivocal in condemning a physician who aids a patient in actively taking his or her own life.

CHAPTER 14 Ethical and Legal Issues at the End of Life

Yet, many would argue that because physicians are already ending the lives of suffering, terminally ill patients by overdoses of pain medication or by the removal of life support, it is hypocritical to then consider these physicians to have committed a criminal offence if they provide patients who request it with the means of taking their own lives. On the contrary, goes part of the argument, patients who are terminally ill and suffering may not have the physical means to arrange for their suicides by themselves and so may be either condemned to a continuation of life that they do not want, a painful and degrading death by their terminal disease, or a botched or unpleasant suicide attempt unless they have help. Physicians, says this point of view, have the responsibility of helping or else they will, in fact, be doing their patient harm by their inaction (for a more complete discussion, see Grosswald, 2002; Meisel & Cerminara, 2004).

Conversely, opponents of physician-assisted suicide point out that other moral implications must be considered. For example, if suicide comes to be seen as a reasonable means of dealing with the prospect of a difficult and painful death, will this not detract from the need to fund alternatives, such as hospice care? Will this not militate against finding new and better ways of pain management? Will this not decrease the desire to find more compassionate means of dealing with the terminally ill in society? And will this provide coercion for those who are terminally ill? That is, if physician-assisted suicide becomes legally available and ethically condoned, will people with terminal illnesses feel coerced into requesting suicide rather than putting their families and friends through the experience, and perhaps expense, of watching them die difficult deaths, even if that is their preference? The possibility of the slippery slope problem arises again: at first, physician-assisted suicide may be seen as reasonable and acceptable for those whose death is imminent. But then, perhaps it will become acceptable for those whose death is a little further off, and then for those whose death may not be completely certain, and so on. Will society reach a point, for example, at which seniors feel that they must request suicide simply because of their age? Or a point at which parents of children with cognitive impairments are made to feel that these children are a drain on society and so their lives should be terminated? These possibilities may or may not be far-fetched.

What Does the Law Say?

As can be seen by the case of Sue Rodriguez in Box 14.10, the law in Canada prohibits physician-assisted suicide, although the closeness of the Supreme Court decision suggests that discussion will continue on this topic. On June 15, 2005, Francine Lalonde introduced a private member's bill, Bill C-407, to the Canadian Parliament, which would permit physician-assisted suicide. Parliament was dissolved shortly after the debate on second

---

BOX 14.10   In the News: The Case of Sue Rodriguez

The most dramatic and high-profile court case in Canada with respect to the issue of physician-assisted suicide involved Sue Rodriguez in 1992–1993. Sue Rodriguez was 40 years old when she was first diagnosed with amyotrophic lateral sclerosis, also known as Lou Gehrig's disease. Mrs. Rodriguez was an intelligent woman who knew the final outcome of her disease: she would gradually become unable to walk, move her body, eat, or breathe without technological assistance. Her mind would remain unaffected, though, so she would be aware of and suffer through every change and debilitation in her body. Mrs. Rodriguez had a small child and wanted to spend as much time as possible with her child, but she also wanted to avoid the kind of death that she knew awaited her. To that end, she formally requested physician-assisted suicide; she would determine the time and manner of her death. She decided that she would like to activate a machine that would bring about her death, but she would also like to have a physician present, in case something went wrong and she needed further help in dying.

The Supreme Court of British Columbia denied her request, as did the British Columbia Court of Appeal. The issue was then taken to the Supreme Court of Canada, which also dismissed her appeal by a narrow five-to-four decision on September 30, 1993. The controversial nature of this decision is seen within the Supreme Court itself, in which four dissenting judges concluded that the prohibition against assisted suicide violates rights protected by the *Canadian Charter of Rights and Freedoms:* the right to security of the person, which protects the dignity and privacy of individuals with respect to decisions concerning their own body; and the right to equal treatment under the law, because the prohibition prevents persons physically unable to end their lives without assistance from choosing an option that is available to other members of the public (Seguin, 1994).

Sue Rodriguez may have lost her legal battle but she did obtain a physician-assisted suicide, with an unidentified physician, her family, and Member of Parliament Svend Robinson (who had championed her cause) at her side.

reading of the bill. Lalonde plans to fine-tune the bill and resubmit it, so the issue in Canada is pending.

Physician-assisted suicide is also prohibited in most states in the United States. The most famous (or infamous) proponent of physician-assisted suicide in the United States is Dr. Jack Kevorkian, who, after practising physician-assisted suicide for at least 130 people and having been tried and acquitted several times, was convicted of second-degree murder and illegal delivery of a controlled substance in March 1999 after he gave a consenting adult a lethal injection. He was released on June 1, 2007, is terminally ill himself, and is no longer practising medicine in any form (CBS News, 2006). Although he had been supported by many people who regard his actions as humane if not legal, Dr. Kevorkian has been regarded as an overzealous proponent of physician-assisted suicide by others (e.g., see Roscoe, Malphurs, Dragovic, & Cohen, 2001), and they have suggested that his work has, in fact, strengthened the arguments of those opposed to physician-assisted suicide (Lemmens & Dickens, 2001) by highlighting the vulnerability of those who might request assistance in ending their own lives.

Oregon, however, is an exception to the general American avoidance of physician-assisted suicide. Oregon has had a physician-assisted suicide law since 1994 that was implemented in 1997, the *Death With Dignity Act*. Interestingly, by 2005, only 208 terminally ill people had taken advantage of it (Carlson, Simopolous, Goy, Jackson, & Ganzini, 2005).

The United Kingdom is discussing a bill before Parliament that would make physician-assisted suicide acceptable under some conditions (Hanks, 2005). As in other Western countries, support for this initiative is mixed.

In other European countries, Switzerland, Belgium, and the Netherlands today legally permit physician-assisted suicide of dying patients. Sweden, Norway, Finland, and Denmark do not permit it, but penalties may be light. The same situation exists in New Zealand and Australia, although the Northern Territory of Australia permitted voluntary euthanasia and assisted suicide for nine months in 1997 until the law was repealed (only four people availed themselves of the law in that time). Japan approved voluntary euthanasia in 1962 but instances are extremely rare because of cultural proscriptions on suicide, dying, and death in that country. In Colombia, voluntary euthanasia was approved by its Constitutional Court in 1997, but Colombia's parliament has never ratified the law. Assisted suicide is a crime, though. Uruguay's penal code stipulates that a person who has lived an "honourable" life should not be punished if he or she kills another person on compassionate grounds and if the person has repeatedly requested it. It appears, then, that in this country the act of euthanasia or assisted suicide is considered a criminal offence, but one that may or may not be punished, depending on the situation. In fact, no one in Uruguay has ever been punished for euthanasia or assisted suicide. Box 14.11 discusses the Dutch experience with physician-assisted suicide.

BOX 14.11   The Dutch Experience With Physician-Assisted Suicide

The Social and Cultural Planning Office of the Netherlands reports that the proportion of Dutch people who support physician-assisted suicide had risen from 50 percent to almost 90 percent by 1998 (Rurup, Onwuteaka-Philipsen, & van der Wal, 2005). Similarly, the number of opponents had decreased from 50 percent to 10 percent. The numbers of those requesting physician-assisted suicide are not small: 2000 people of a population of 16 million are euthanized each year, and the number of unreported cases may be higher ("Dutch government intends," 2005). Still, it is clear that the majority of Dutch citizens believe that the individual should have the right to govern his or her own death, with many even advocating the development of a "suicide pill" for seniors to end their lives whenever they choose (Rurup et al., 2005). Yet many have labelled euthanasia "a disaster" and the World Medical Association has adopted a resolution condemning the practice as unethical (Sheldon, 2002). Claims have been made of physicians euthanizing patients without following the

guidelines of Dutch law to the extent of forcing seniors in nursing homes to carry certificates indicating their wish *not* to have their lives terminated by artificial means. Others claim that the Dutch laws governing euthanasia are not enforced consistently ("Involuntary euthanasia," 1999).

Doctors at the Groningen University Medical Center have devised guidelines known as the Groningen Protocol that state that euthanasia would be permissible "when a child is terminally ill with no prospect of recovery and suffering great pain, when two sets of doctors agree the situation is hopeless and when parents give their consent" (Canadian Press, 2005). The prospect of killing babies has raised the ire of many in the international community, some even likening it to the Nazi eugenics policies of terminating infants and older people with disabilities or those labelled as "undesirable" (Smith, 2006). The Dutch government remains firm, however, and is forming commissions to investigate how the laws and guidelines may be applied justly and compassionately.

CHAPTER 14 Ethical and Legal Issues at the End of Life

Leming and Dickinson (2002) report that public acceptance of euthanasia and physician-assisted suicide is growing and so we may expect that legal challenges to laws forbidding these practices will continue, as will greater testing of new laws that make these practices legal. In the author's class of almost one hundred nursing and social work students, all of whom had experience working in their fields, physician-assisted suicide was considered as the most important medico-ethical dilemma to be faced in the next 10 years. Note that making physician-assisted suicide legal does not mean that physicians are compelled to assist in their terminal patients' suicide requests if they choose not to. What is legal is not necessarily ethical in many people's minds, just as what is ethical is not necessarily legal.

SUMMARY

- The issues discussed in this chapter have no definite right or wrong answers to them; they are presented to stimulate thought and discussions because it is only by informed opinion that laws can be formed and justice can be at least approximated.

- The definition of death is controversial, ranging from a traditional reliance on failure of cardiopulmonary functioning to brain death. Even the definition of brain death is open to question, with brainstem death and the cessation of higher cortical functioning both signifying death of the individual to some.

- Organ donation is socially encouraged, but exactly when organs may be retrieved depends on an adequate definition of death, as well as on individuals' and their families' wishes. How such decisions should be made provides another area of ethical dilemma for society.

- Advance directives and living wills are often regarded as being the appropriate means of indicating what an individual wants in terms of medical treatment in cases in which he or she cannot indicate any preferences. These too come under fire for providing some dilemmas for medical personnel and family who are, or at least feel, obligated to fulfill the wishes of the individual.

- The issue of euthanasia—or the taking of life when all medical treatment is futile, death is imminent and the patient is suffering—provides a medical, legal, ethical, and theological problem. Is it right to preserve a life that will soon end and is unbearable in the meantime? Or is it right to take responsibility for the ending of a human life before the medical or "natural" end has truly come?

- Physician-assisted suicide is widely disputed in many countries of the world, and laws are in the process of change in many areas as public attitudes support the idea that it is acceptable for the physician to assist in a dying patient's request to be given a means of committing suicide.

KEY TERMS

advance directives
dead donor rule
euthanasia

living will
physician-assisted suicide

principle of double effect
whole brain definition of death

INDIVIDUAL ACTIVITIES

1. Try to determine what your definition of death is. Under what conditions would you consider yourself to be dead? Under what conditions would you consider a loved one to be dead? Are there differences in these conditions?

2. Decide whether you want to be an organ donor. If so, sign a donor card and make your wishes known to your family. If not, communicate this as well to your family.

3. Check out the Internet for living will forms for your area. Consider what directives you want followed in case of your incapacitation. At this time, you may want to make out a living will, or at least discuss advance directives with your family and physician.

4. What is your position on euthanasia and physician-assisted suicide? Make up a scenario in which you feel that euthanasia might be justified, and one in which it would not be justified. Do the same for physician-assisted suicide.

GROUP ACTIVITIES

1. In a group of three or four, discuss definitions of death. Are there disagreements among members of the group? Are these based on philosophical, cultural, or religious differences?

2. Designate class members to obtain information from different foundations, such as the Heart and Stroke Foundation of Canada and the Kidney Foundation of Canada, regarding transplants and bring the information back to share with the group.

3. In groups of three or four, discuss whether blood transfusions, bone marrow donations, or skin grafts can be counted as transplants. If so, by using what criteria? If not, why not?

4. Share the scenarios from the fourth exercise in the individual activities with the group. To what extent does the larger group agree on which scenarios justify or do not justify euthanasia and physician-assisted suicide?

**In this chapter, we will
discuss**

- future issues in the area of
  thanatology

- the future of palliative care

- the need for more
  education in thanatology

The Future

What Is Important to You?

► Consider the following issues surrounding the end of life. Which of the following issues (if any) do you find most pressing to resolve in Canada in the next 10 years? Do you know of other issues which are more pressing? Rank order them in terms of what you feel Canada's priorities should be.

- *Suicide prevention:* The rate of suicide, especially among young people and Aboriginal Peoples, is high, and the number of people adversely affected by someone's suicide is much higher. How can we prevent the feelings of hopelessness and despair that engender suicidal behaviours? How can we comfort the mourners of those who have been so bereaved?

- *Advance directives:* Should it be mandatory for Canadians of legal age to have a living will or advance directives to prevent controversy in the event of their inability to direct their medical treatment? Would this infringe on the rights of individuals? That is, should it be mandatory for people to contemplate the possibility of their own serious and/or terminal illnesses and eventual deaths? Or does the individual have the right *not* to think about such painful issues and trust that families and medical personnel will make decisions that they will agree with?

- *Organ donation:* The number of organs needed for transplantation is far greater than the number of organs available. Should organ donation be mandatory, except when individuals specify that they do not want to be donors? How can ethical and just decisions be made concerning who receives donated organs? Should organ donation and transplantation research be abandoned to increase funding for research in alternative life-saving and life-sustaining treatments?

- *Accessibility of palliative care in rural and remote areas:* Between 85 percent and 95 percent of Canadians do not have access to hospice palliative care services. What can be done to make these services more accessible to everyone?

- *Physician-assisted suicide:* When a person with no hope of recovery is unable to take his or her own life, should a physician be allowed to assist, if the patient wants it? Does this violate an ethical or moral code?

Are there particular people who should or should not have this option of ending their lives? What are implications of making physician-assisted suicide available? Will some people feel coerced to ask for it?

- *Euthanasia:* In cases of suffering with no hope of recovery, euthanasia has been practised in Canada with few or no legal ramifications. Should mercy killing be a crime? Who should make the decisions about the mercy killing of individuals: the patient, family, physician, a panel?

- *Cultural sensitivity about views of death and dying:* A multicultural country, such as Canada, encompasses a wide variety of views about end-of-life issues. Should everyone in Canada be required to follow the same rules and practices for the end of life to make the country more homogenous? If so, which practices will be considered the "norm"? If not, how can respect and sensitivity for differing cultural and religious views be increased?

- *Unrealistic portrayals of death in the media:* The media present portrayals of death and dying in a variety of ways that often seem to minimize, glorify, or distort the reality of death and the suffering of the survivors. Should the media be forced to be more realistic? Should the media be subjected to more censorship? Should the public be asked to boycott these portrayals (in books, movies, television programming, music, and so on) to induce change in the media depictions?

- *Disposal of bodies:* Cemeteries in large cities in particular are becoming overcrowded, with some cemeteries already burying people on top of one another. The land that is used is sometimes thought to be "wasted" and better land use has been suggested. Should cremation as an alternative be made mandatory except in cases of religious prohibitions?

Although many other issues face Canadians (e.g., environmental conservation, homelessness, Aboriginal rights), these issues pertain specifically to the topic of this book. In the author's thanatology class of upper-year student nurses and social workers, the majority of the class felt that physician-assisted suicide was the issue that most needs to be resolved and quickly. Do you agree?

In 2005, a group of bioethicists at the University of Toronto published a list of what they considered to be the top 10 challenges in health care facing the public. They concluded that the top challenge was disagreement between patients/families and health-care personnel about treatment decisions. Ranking second was waiting times for medical tests and treatment, and third was access to needed resources for chronically ill and senior people, and those with mental illnesses (Breslin, MacRae, Bell, & Singer, 2005). Do you agree with the bioethicists' ranking?

Canada is a huge country, embracing many cultural, religious, and regional differences. Managing and governing this giant is difficult to say the least. Many issues crowd the landscape, pushing to be made a top priority. But of course, not all can go to the head of the list. Each of the issues listed in the opening vignette are important, but programs for each are expensive. Additionally, many require trained and skilled workers who are not readily available. If the personnel were available, the required ongoing training would be expensive as well. How to provide services for those people in need of them in the outlying regions of this country is a problem that seems insurmountable. Communities, with or without trained helpers, have developed programs to deal with some of these issues based on volunteers helping their neighbours. For example, one grassroots project, funded by Canada Council for the Arts, is ongoing at the time of this writing (April 2007): Karen Haffey and Esther Kalaba have organized a project called *Collecting Loss: Weaving Threads of Memory* (http://www.collectingloss.com/home.html) in which bereaved people can donate a piece of clothing and the stories of their deceased loved ones to be compiled into a memorial tapestry. Also, the mental health initiatives for suicide prevention in many Aboriginal communities stand as a testament to what people can do to help each other. But forming such grassroots community projects takes the time, determination, and willingness of many dedicated hands, and money is usually needed, even when volunteers carry the workload.

As we saw in Chapter 14, debates are ongoing in governmental circles regarding physician-assisted suicide and organ donation. Those who govern, however, know that whatever decisions they reach will be rejected as immoral and unethical by many of their voting constituents. Task forces are formed to explore the will of the people, but frequently these task forces take a great deal of time to prepare and present a report. Often this final report remains on a shelf, unimplemented. The majority of Canadians are living lives that are, at present, untouched by many end-of-life issues, and so they display little concern for the implementation of plans to deal with these issues. They, as a majority, do not lobby the government to make decisions and put programs in place. Their lack of concern is understandable for their present lives. But issues surrounding death, dying, and bereavement will concern everyone at some points in their lives. It will be too late to insist that organ donation be made mandatory, for example, when a person learns that his or her loved one needs an organ transplant immediately.

Nonetheless, many groups do lobby for programs to be put in place immediately, and the valuable work that these groups do should not be underestimated. As a prime example, we will examine the future of palliative care in Canada.

THE FUTURE OF PALLIATIVE CARE

Foley (2005) noted that more attention is being paid to the need for end-of-life care than has been the case in the past. With an aging population and medical technology that prolongs life to a point far past what used to be expected, the media have given more attention to ethical, moral, and legal issues, such as physician-assisted suicide and patients' rights of self-determination. Palliative care programs in particular are receiving more attention from medical personnel and from an increasingly affected stakeholding public. The demand for expansion of these services is becoming greater. But barriers to implementation of expanded palliative care programs are coming from economic realities and especially the lack of adequate education and training for personnel to work in this area. Another area of concern that might provide a barrier to expanded palliative care is the notion that if more medical personnel are trained in this area, there is a possibility that palliative care might be seen as the domain of medicine entirely. This is wholly in opposition to the principles of palliative care which regards death as a natural part of life which should be in the hands of the wider community of the dying person. Foley noted that in the United States, one-third of the patients admitted to hospices die within seven days of admission. "This means that hospices often provide 'brink of death' care rather than having the opportunity over several months to prepare patients and families for death" (p. S45). Again, this is essentially antagonistic to the principles of palliative care and Foley urged expansion of palliative care programs, with more education and information about palliative care given to the public in order to make the available services more accessible for patients at an earlier point in their illnesses.

Gillick (2005) advocated a somewhat different approach to palliative care. She suggested that palliative care should be a multidisciplinary approach that is concerned with advance planning, the psychosocial issues of the patient and family, and the treatment of illness and management of symptoms for *every* patient, not simply those who have been designated as terminal. The principles of palliative care, then, would apply to each patient, regardless of the prognosis of their physical complaint, not postponed until an individual is deemed to be at the end of life. In this way, the goals of palliative care would be accomplished over an individual's lifetime, changing with the person's changed physical conditions. For Gillick, the role of personnel specifically trained in palliative care would be as consultants on especially challenging cases because the primary-care physicians and hospital staff (including nonmedical personnel) would be trained and equipped to deal with such issues as decision making, advance planning, and the emotional needs of any patient and family. This idea is interesting and appealing to anyone who has experienced an impersonal attitude on the part of medical staff. For example, it is common for patients to be discharged after day surgery without being asked if they have someone at home to care for them as they recuperate. With Gillick's idea, every patient, even those with minor complaints, would be given full information about his or her condition, with discussions surrounding the feelings and needs of the patient and his or her family. Family physicians would enter into discussions about advance planning long before a patient had a life-threatening illness. Implementing Gillick's ideas would require a large change in attitude among many medical personnel, with accompanying changes in educational curricula. The Canadian Hospice Palliative Care Association (2006) reports that as of 2004, only 12 of the 142 nursing schools in Canada offered palliative care as part of their curricula. At Ryerson University in Toronto, for instance, a course on death, dying, and bereavement is offered to students in nursing, but it is not mandatory. This would have to change, along with the curricula at many other institutions.

A common objection to calls for expanded palliative care programs comes from those concerned with the economics of expansion. "We don't have enough money!" is a response that the Canadian public has heard often in its requests for expansion of many social welfare programs, but this need not be an impediment to the development of increased and improved end-of-life care. In the next section, we will describe a study that demonstrated this.

PALLIATIVE CARE FOR THE HOMELESS

Hwang (2000) discovered that the mortality rate for homeless men in the city of Toronto was significantly higher than for men in the general population, although lower than the mortality rate for homeless men in the American cities of New York, Boston, and Philadelphia. The mean age of death for these men was 46 years. Some of these men die on the street or in the emergency rooms of hospitals because the presence of a mental illness or their behaviours (e.g., smoking, drinking alcohol to excess, dementia-induced disruptive behaviours) preclude their admission to hospices. Some of these men refuse to leave homeless shelters even though they know they are terminally ill because the shelters are familiar to them and permit them to leave long enough to acquire illicit drugs, alcohol, and tobacco (Podymow, Turnbull, & Coyle, 2006).

Podymow et al. (2006) reported on a pilot project, the Ottawa Inner City Health Project, designed in part to provide shelter-based palliative care to 28 homeless terminally ill men in Ottawa. The men were housed in a section of a shelter designated as The Hospice and were provided with beds and meals. In addition, the men had special care:

- Registered nurses worked full time seven days a week.
- Registered practical nurses worked evenings and overnight five days a week.
- Client care workers worked 24 hours a day, seven days a week. These workers provided supervision for the patients, assistance in daily living tasks and in applications for financial assistance, and help attending to medical appointments.
- One of two physicians supervised the medical care of the patients 24 hours a day, seven days a week, and saw patients on rounds in the shelter weekly. Symptom management, including pain management, was accomplished on site with the aid of a specialist physician.
- Patients were transported and accompanied to hospital appointments.
- Patients were given physical and occupational therapy, chiropody, and nutritional support in The Hospice.
- Psychological disorders were monitored and treated on site.
- Clean needles and safe syringe disposal were provided for the patients who were intravenous drug users. An area for smoking outside the shelter was provided for those patients who were nicotine addicted. As well, standard 14 gram drinks of alcohol were dispensed on demand to patients addicted to alcohol.
- Nonmedicinal treatments were also provided, including the use of a hot tub, chiropractic services, and traditional healing techniques, such as "smudging" for Aboriginal patients.
- The patients received religious counselling and discussions of their preferences for end-of-life care. Most wanted do-not-resuscitate orders so that they could die in The Hospice (82 percent of the men actually died there).
- The Hospice staff contacted patients' families, with the patients' permission.

This comprehensive program continued until the men died, a span that ranged from 3 to 523 days (the average was 120 days). Although some men attempted to sell the medically approved narcotics given for pain control in order to procure additional illicit drugs or alcohol, this was controlled effectively with a policy of barring the patient from The Hospice services for 24 hours and the subsequent signing of a contract. Illicit intravenous drug use was found to decrease substantially when the addicted patients' pain was controlled.

The results were highly noteworthy: patients reported a sense of trust, well-being, and gratitude during their stay in The Hospice, indicating that The Hospice was their preferred place of death. Most patients were visited by their families, some of whom had had infrequent or no contact with them for several years. A panel of experts calculated the costs of these men spending their final days and ultimately dying in probable alternative locations (dying on the street was not considered). Their conclusion was that care in The Hospice provided a savings of $1.39 million to taxpayers for these patients alone. This demonstrates that with the will to implement such programs, a workable, compassionate palliative care system for the homeless does not need to entail a financial burden assumed by the government and the taxpayer.

THE STRATEGIC PLAN OF THE CANADIAN HOSPICE PALLIATIVE CARE ASSOCIATION

The Canadian Hospice Palliative Care Association (2006) has joined with the GlaxoSmithKline Foundation in a project called the Living Lessons, designed to encourage open dialogue on issues pertaining to death and dying, particularly in furthering the hospice palliative care movement in Canada. To this end, one of their efforts has produced a Bill of Rights for patients with terminal conditions:

As a person facing the end of my life, I have the right to:

- Be treated as a living human being until I die.
- Live free of pain.
- Participate in the decisions that affect me and my quality of life.
- Have my decisions and choices respected and followed, even though they may be contrary to the wishes of others.
- Be treated with openness and honesty without deception or half-truths.
- Receive ongoing medical and nursing care even though the goals must be changed from cure to comfort.
- Express my feelings and emotions about my approaching death in my own way.

- Maintain a sense of hopefulness, however changing its focus might be.
- Be cared for by those who can maintain a sense of hopefulness, however changing its focus might be.
- Discuss and enlarge my spiritual and religious experiences, regardless of what they mean to others.
- Be cared for by compassionate, sensitive and knowledgeable people who will attempt to understand my needs and try to meet them.
- Receive support from and for my loved ones in learning how to accept my death.
- Die in peace and with dignity.

(Source: Living Lessons®, www.living-lessons.org)

To put these rights into effect, the Canadian Hospice Palliative Care Association (2006) outlined in its *Strategic Plan and Process Report* the key issues it will address for 2006 to 2009:

- greater access to programs of palliative care, delivering such services across Canada
- the further development of public policy that supports this care and these programs across Canada
- development of a strategy to increase the awareness of the general public and other professionals about what hospice palliative care entails

FINALLY

In this book, we have discussed only some of the issues surrounding end-of-life care and the aftermath of death. More issues will occur to all of us as we face our own deaths and the deaths of others. In some cases, the requirement on us will be to vote, making decisions affecting our own lives and the lives of others. In some cases, we will need to make the decisions on an individual level regarding what is best for us and our loved ones. In still other cases, we will be required to respond to and support those people who are making the decisions for themselves or others. All of us will need to know what to expect and how to respond to grief sensitively. Only through education can this good will and sensitivity be increased and informed decisions made. Such books as this one aim to provide people with at least some of the knowledge that they will need. The rest is up to all of us.

INDIVIDUAL ACTIVITIES

1. Which of the issues listed in the opening vignette do you think is the most important? Which is the least important? Rank order the issues in terms of the importance you see.

2. Where do you stand on the issues in the opening vignette? If you find you need more information before deciding on an issue, research it. There are many references listed in the other chapters of this book (especially in Chapter 14), in the Appendix, and in this chapter.

3. Ask people you know what their thoughts are about the issues listed in the opening vignette. (You may want to avoid debate at this time while you focus on the arguments that other people have on the various sides of the issues.)

4. What action can you take to make your views known on these issues? For example, you might consider starting your own grassroots project, as Karen Haffey and Esther Kalaba did in their *Collecting Loss* project. Or you might volunteer as a support worker at a palliative care centre, a group for the bereaved, or a local suicide prevention centre. You might also write a letter to your local member of Parliament, outlining your feelings and giving him or her guidance about what programs might be pursued and the way to vote if some of these issues are presented in a bill before Parliament.

5. Go back to Chapter 1 and take the Leming Fear of Death Scale again. Then take the Attitudes toward Death Survey in Chapter 2 again. Have your feelings about death, dying, and bereavement changed after reading this book?

GROUP ACTIVITIES

1. Stage a group or class debate on one or more of the issues presented in the opening vignette. Allow the audience to vote on the issue debated. Do the results surprise your group?

2. Invite people who work with the dying and their families to speak to your group or class about what they see as challenges for the future. For example, palliative care physicians, nurses, social workers, funeral directors, and so on, can provide interesting and cogent views on the problems they face and how they feel these problems might be solved.

3. Consider how, as a group, you might start a grassroots project, such as the *Collecting Loss* project conducted by Karen Haffey and Esther Kalaba. Explore the possibilities of local funding for this project, as well as funding by governmental agencies, such as the Canada Council for the Arts.

4. Write a group letter or a petition to send to your local member of Parliament, outlining your views and what solutions you endorse to some of the problems in the area of death, dying, and bereavement.

5. In groups of five or six, discuss how, if at all, your views on death, dying, and bereavement have changed after reading this book.

The books, videos, movies, and resources listed in this appendix were all available in Canada at the time of writing.

BOOKS

For Adults

Boone, P., & Headington, B. (2003). *Our walk with elephants: Surviving the death of adult children.* Frederick, MD: PublishAmerica.

Buckman, R. (2005). *I don't know what to say: How to help and support someone who is dying.* Toronto, ON: Key Porter Books.

Carmack, B. J. (2002). *Grieving the death of a pet.* Minneapolis, MN: Augsburg Fortress.

Doka, K. J. (1998). *Living with grief: Who we are, how we grieve.* London: Routledge.

Esposito, J. L., Fasching, D., & Lewis, T. (2005). *World religions today.* New York: Oxford University Press.

Finkbeiner, A. K. (1998). *After the death of a child: Living with loss through the years.* Baltimore: Johns Hopkins University Press.

Fox, S., & Byrne, R. (2000). *I have no intention of saying good-bye: Parents share their stories of hope and healing after a child's death.* Lincoln, NB: Writers Club Press.

Foxall, R. E. (2003). *Before their time: The death of a child.* New York: Writers Advantage.

Goldberg, N. (2005). *The great failure: My unexpected path to truth.* San Francisco: Harper.

Ilibagiza, I. (2006). *Left to tell: Discovering God amidst the Rwandan holocaust.* Carlsbad, CA: Hay House.

Jeffreys, J. S. (2004). *Helping grieving people—When tears are not enough: A handbook for care providers.* London: Routledge.

Jeffreys, J. S. (2005). *Coping with workplace grief: Dealing with loss, trauma, and change* (Rev. ed.). Boston: Thomson Nelson.

Johnson, C. (2007). *Crucial decisions for your critically ill child: Life and death choices parents must face.* Far Hills, NJ: New Horizon Press.

Kelly, L. (2000). *Don't ask for the dead man's golf clubs: What to do and say (and what not to) when a friend loses a loved one.* New York: Workman.

Kirkwood, N. A. (2001). *Pastoral care to Muslims: Building bridges.* Binghamton, NY: Haworth Press.

Kolf, J. C. (1999). *Comfort and care in a final illness: Support for the caregiver.* Tucson, AZ: Fisher Books.

Kübler-Ross, E. (1997). *On children and death.* New York: Simon & Schuster.

Kumar, S. M. (2005). *Grieving mindfully: A compassionate and spiritual guide to coping with loss.* Oakland, CA: New Harbinger.

Levang, E. (1998). *When men grieve: Why men grieve differently and how you can help.* Minneapolis, MN: Fairview Press.

Levy, A. (1999). *The orphaned adult: Understanding and coping with grief and change after the death of our parents.* New York: Perseus.

Lewis, S. (2006). *Race against time: Searching for hope in AIDS-ravaged Africa* (2nd ed.). Toronto, ON: House of Anansi.

Lief, J. L. (2001). *Making friends with death: A Buddhist guide to encountering mortality.* Boston: Shambhala.

Lothrop, H. (2004). *Help, comfort, and hope after losing your baby in the pregnancy or first year.* New York: Da Capo.

Marx, R. J. (2004). *Facing the ultimate loss: Coping with the death of a child.* Belgium, WI: Champion Press.

Mathes, C. (2005). *And a sword shall pierce your heart: Moving from despair to meaning after the death of a child.* New York: Chiron.

Neeld, E. H. (2003). *Seven choices: Finding daylight after loss shatters your world.* New York: Warner Books.

Obershaw, R. J. (2004). *Cry until you laugh: Comforting guidance for coping with grief.* Edina, MN: Beaver's Pond Press.

Rando, T. A. (1991). *How to go on living when someone you love dies.* New York: Bantam.

Rank, M. (2004). *Free to grieve: Healing and encouragement for those who have suffered miscarriage and stillbirth.* Minneapolis, MN: Bethany House.

Rosenblatt, P. C. (2000). *Help your marriage survive the death of a child.* Philadelphia: Temple University Press.

Ross, E. B. (2001). *After suicide.* New York: Perseus Books.

Snyder, R. (2005). *Take your time, go slowly: After The tragic and sudden death of a child. For the parents and siblings with no time to say good-bye.* Bloomington, IN: Authorhouse.

Swanson, J. (2005). *Physician's guide to coping with death and dying.* Montreal, QC: McGill-Queen's University Press.

Talbot, K. (2002). *What forever means after the death of a child; Transcending the trauma, living with the loss: transformed by the death of a child.* London: Routledge.

Wolfelt, A. D. (2001). *Healing a friend's grieving heart: 100 practical ideas for helping someone you love through loss.* Ft. Collins, CO: Companion Press.

Wolfelt, A. D. (2003). *Creating meaningful funeral experiences: A guide for caregivers.* Ft. Collins, CO: Companion Press.

Wolfelt, A. D. (2004). *When your pet dies: A guide to mourning, remembering and healing.* Ft. Collins, CO: Companion Press.

Wolfelt, A. D. (2005a). *Healing the adult child's grieving heart: 100 practical ideas after your parent dies.* Chicago: Independent Publishers Group.

Wolfelt, A. D. (2005b). *Healing your holiday grief: 100 practical ideas for blending mourning and celebration during the holiday season.* Ft. Collins, CO: Companion Press.

Wolfelt, A. D. (2005c). *Companioning the bereaved: A soulful guide for counselors & caregivers.* Ft. Collins, CO: Companion Press.

York, S. (2000). *Remembering well: Rituals for celebrating life and mourning death.* Mississauga, ON: John Wiley & Sons.

For Adults Helping Children

Christ, G. H. (1999). *Healing children's grief.* New York: Oxford University Press.

Dodds, B. (2001). *Your grieving child: Answers to questions on death and dying.* Huntington, NY: Our Sunday Visitor.

Goldman, L. (2005). *Children also grieve: Talking about death and healing.* London: Jessica Kingsley.

James, J. W. (2002). *When children grieve: For adults to help children deal with death, divorce, pet loss, moving, and other losses.* New York: Harper Collins.

Lewis, P. G., & Lippman, J. G. (2004). *Helping children cope with the death of a parent: Guide for the first year.* Westport, CT: Praeger.

Marta, S. Y. (2003). *Healing the hurt, restoring the hope: How to guide children and teens through times of divorce, death.* Emmaus, PA: Rodale Books.

O'Connor, J. (2004). *Children and grief: Helping your child understand death.* Grand Rapids, MI: Revell.

Rae, T., & Weymont, D. (2006). *Supporting young people coping with grief, loss and death.* London: Paul Chapman.

Seibert, D. (2003). *Helping children live with death and loss* [with CD]. Carbondale: Southern Illinois University Press.

Stickney, D. (2004). *Water bugs & dragonflies: Explaining death to young children.* Cleveland, OH: Pilgrim Press.

Turner, M. (2006). *Talking with children and young people about death and dying: A resource book.* London: Jessica Kingsley.

Vander Wyden, P. W. (2002). *Butterflies: Talking with children about death and life eternal.* Allen, TX: Thomas More.

Wolfelt, A. D. (2001a). *Healing a child's grieving heart: 100 Practical ideas for families, friends and caregivers.* Ft. Collins, CO: Companion Press.

Wolfelt, A. D. (2001b). *Healing a teen's grieving heart: 100 practical ideas for families, friends and caregivers.* Ft. Collins, CO: Companion Press.

For Younger Children (Six Years and Younger)

Anaya, R. (1999). *Farolitos for Abuela.* Los Angeles: Disney Publishing Worldwide.

Bahr, M. (2002). *If Nathan were here.* Grand Rapids, MI: Eerdmans.

Britain, L. (2002). *My grandma died: A child's story about death and loss.* Seattle, WA: Parenting Press.

Brown, L. K. (1998). *When dinosaurs die.* New York: Little Brown.

Burrowes, A. J. (2000). *Grandma's purple flowers.* New York: Lee & Low Books.

Buscaglia, L. (2002). *The fall of Freddie the Leaf: A story of life for all ages.* New York: Henry Holt.

Demas, C. (2004). *Saying goodbye to Lulu.* New York: Little Brown.

Depaola, T. (2002). *Nana upstairs Nana downstairs:* Toronto, ON: Penguin Young Readers.

Durant, A. (2004). *Always and forever.* San Diego, CA: Harcourt.

Fox, M. (2001). *Tough Boris.* San Diego, CA: Harcourt.

Kübler-Ross, E. (1998). *Remember the secret.* Berkeley, CA: Tricycle Press.

Lemieux, J. (2004). *Toby's very important question*. Halifax, NS: Formac.

Pellegrino, V. (1998). *I don't have an Uncle Phil anymore*. Washington, DC: Magination Press.

Perkins, G. (1996). *Remembering Mum*. Markham, ON: Fitzhenry & Whiteside.

Rogers, F. (2002). *When a pet dies*. New York: Puffin.

Silverman, J. (1999). *Help me say goodbye: Activities for helping kids cope when a special person dies*. Minneapolis, MN: Fairview Press.

Thomas, P. (2001). *I miss you: A first look at death*. Hauppauge, NY: Barron's Educational Series.

Varley, S. (1992). *Badger's parting gifts*. New York: HarperCollins.

Viorst, J. (1987). *The tenth good thing about Barney*. North Richland Hills, TX: Aladdin.

Williams, L. E. (2000). *Long silk strand*. Honesdale, PA: Boyds Mills Press.

Wolfelt, A. D. (2001). *Healing your grieving heart for kids: 100 practical ideas*. Ft. Collins, CO: Companion Press.

Wood, N. (2004). *Old Coyote*. Cambridge, MA: Candlewick Press.

For Children in Middle Childhood (Seven to Eleven Years)

Brisson, P. (2006). *I remember Miss Perry*. New York: Dial Books for Young Readers.

Clifford, E. (1985). *The remembering box*. Boston: Houghton Mifflin.

Coerr, E. (1999). *Sadako and the thousand paper cranes*. New York: Puffin.

Greenlee, S. (2003). *When someone dies*. Atlanta, GA: Peachtree.

Heegaard, M. (1988). *When someone very special dies: Children can learn to cope with grief*. Chapmanville, WV: Woodland Press.

Heegaard, M. (1992). *When something terrible happens: Children can learn to cope with grief*. Chapmanville, WV: Woodland Press.

Hest, A. (2006). *Remembering Mrs. Rossi*. Cambridge, MA: Candlewick Press.

Jordan, M. K. (1993). *Losing Uncle Tim*. Morton Grove, IL: Albert Whitman.

Kwalwasser, E. I. (2006). *Beyond the tears: Helping kids cope with death*. Jerusalem, Israel: Pitspopany Press.

Levine, K. (2003). *Hana's suitcase: A true story*. Morton Grove, IL: Albert Whitman.

Liss-Levinson, N. (1995). *When a grandparent dies*. Woodstock, VT: Jewish Lights.

Liss-Levinson, N., & Baskette, M. P. (2006). *Remembering my grandparent: A kid's own grief workbook in the Christian tradition*. Woodstock, VT: SkyLight Paths.

Lowry, L. (2007). *A summer to die*. New York: Delacorte Books for Young Readers.

Maple, M. (2002). *On the wings of a butterfly: A story about life and death*. Seattle, WA: Parenting Press.

McKeever, S. (2006). *Why is Keiko sick? A conversation with your child about why bad things happen*. Green Forest, AR: Master Books.

Moser, A. (1996). *Don't despair on Thursdays! The children's grief-management book*. Kansas City, KS: Landmark.

Paterson, K. (2004). *Bridge to Terabithia*. New York: Trophy.

Romain, T. (1996). *What on earth do you do when someone dies?* Minneapolis, MN: Free Spirit.

Rosen, M. (2005). *Michael Rosen's sad book.* Cambridge, MA: Candlewick Press.

Ruiz, R. A. (2001). *Coping with the death of a brother or sister.* New York: Rosen.

Shriver, M. (1999). *What's heaven?* New York: St. Martin's Press.

Smith, C. (2001). *Rain is not my Indian name.* Toronto, ON: HarperCollins.

Spelman, C. (1996). *After Charlotte's mom died.* Morton Grove, IL: Albert Whitman.

Stalfelt, P. (2002). *The death book.* Toronto, ON: Groundwood Books.

For Adolescents and Teenagers

Grollman, E. A. (1993). *Straight talk about death for teenagers.* Boston: Beacon Press.

Hughes, L. B. (2005). *You are not alone: Teens talk about life after the loss of a parent.* New York: Scholastic Press.

McGhee, A. (2005). *All rivers flow to the sea.* Cambridge, MA: Candlewick Press.

Murphy, B. B. (2005). *Life! How I love you!* Sante Fe: Museum of New Mexico.

Rabb, M. (2007). *Cures for heartbreak.* New York: Delacorte Books for Young Readers.

Thornhill, J. (2006). *I found a dead bird: The kids' guide to life & death.* Toronto, ON: Maple Tree Press.

FILMS AND VIDEOS

The following are available from Visual Education Centre Limited, 41 Horner Avenue, Suite 3, Toronto, ON M8Z 4X4; http://www.visualed.com/search.htm.

Cinema Guild. (Producer). (2003). *View from the inside: You're never over love* [Motion picture]. Friends and relatives mourn a cancer victim.

Condon Productions. (Producer). (1995). *Vigil of hope* [Motion picture]. Unresolved grief.

TVOntario. (Producer). (2000). *Bereavement* [Motion picture]. Speaking with caregivers who have lost a spouse or parent.

The following are available from National Film Board of Canada, P.O. Box 6100, Station Centre-ville, Montreal, QC H3C 3H5; http://www.nfb.ca.

Bochnar, S., & Hénaut, D. T. (Producers). (1996). *You won't need running shoes, darling* [Motion picture]. Final illness of parents.

Elliott, F. (Producer). (1991). *"Just one big mess": The Halifax explosion 1917* [Motion picture]. Description of the explosion and the aftermath.

Gryphon Productions Ltd. (Producer). (1993). *Beyond the shadows* [Motion picture]. The effects of residential schools on Native Canadians.

Hubert, N. (Producer). (1990). *After the Montreal massacre* [Motion picture]. Description of the massacre, with interviews.

Kawamura, A., Kibe, N., & Verrall, D. (1994). *The Tibetan book of the dead: The great liberation* [Motion picture]. Death rituals of Tibetan Buddhism and conversations with the Dalai Lama.

Kawamura, A., & McLean, B. (1994). *The Tibetan book of the dead: A way of life* [Motion picture]. Death rituals of Tibetan Buddhism and conversations with the Dalai Lama.

Kovanic, G. D. (Producer). (1998). *Surviving death: Stories of grief* [Motion picture]. Interviews with people from different cultures experiencing grief.

Lamothe, N. (Producer). (2000). *Let me die* [Motion picture]. Explores assisted suicide and euthanasia in Canada.

Leany, C., Silver, M., & Torrance, J. (Producer). (1995). *Unsung lullabies* [Motion picture]. The grief of miscarriage.

Ménard, J. (Producer). (2001). *Aftermath: The legacy of suicide* [Motion picture]. Reactions to a parent's suicide.

National Film Board of Canada. (Producer). (1996). *Across generations* [Motion picture]. Aging and death.

Obomsawin, A. (Producer). (2003). *For John* [Motion picture]. Reactions to a suicide.

Philips, D. (Producer). (1991). *Living with dying* [Motion picture]. Terminal illness, palliative home care.

Robertson, B., & Holmes, M. (Producers). (1993). *The events leading up to my death* [Motion picture]. A family after their dog dies.

Roth, L., & Johnson, G. (Producers). (2002). *When every moment counts* [Motion picture]. Palliative care staff dealing with a dying child and the family.

Symansky, A. (Producer). (1997a). *Caregivers. Episode one: Madeline and Rose* [Motion picture]. Stories of caretakers and those they care for.

Symansky, A. (Producer). (1997b). *Caregivers. Episode two: Doris and Tom* [Motion picture]. Stories of caretakers and those they care for.

Symansky, A. (Producer). (1997c). *Caregivers. Episode three: Kurt and Elizabeth* [Motion picture]. Stories of caretakers and those they care for.

Symansky, A. (Producer). (1997d). *Caregivers. Episode four: Pat and Molly* [Motion picture]. Stories of caretakers and those they care for.

Symansky, A., & Lapointe, P. (Producers). (2003). *Bearing witness: Jocelyn Morton* [Motion picture]. The last months of a 44-year-old woman with cancer.

This film is available from Public Affairs Television, Inc., http://www.shoppbs.org.

Moyers, B. (Producer.). (2000). *Our own terms, Moyers on dying* [Motion picture].

The following are theatre-release movies dealing with dying and bereavement. All are available for rent or purchase in Canada.

Andruc, M., & Zsigmond, V. (Producers). (2001). *Life as a house.*

Bailey, J. (Producer). (1980). *Ordinary people.*

Costanzo, J., Halsted, D., Hanley, C., & Lachman, E. (Producers). (1999). *The virgin suicides.*

Galluzzo, V., & Lanci, G. (Producers). (2001). *The son's room.*

Midler, B. (Producer). (1988). *Beaches.*

Nicholson, W., & Pratt, R. (Producers). (1993). *Shadowlands.*

Paulsson, E., Tam, S., & Bolduc, N. (Producers). (2005). *Eve and the fire horse.*

Spelling, A., & Katz, S. M. (Producers). (1986). *'Night, Mother.*

Stewart, A., & Quinn, D. (Producers). (1995). *Leaving Las Vegas.*

Walker, P. (Producer). (2003). *Dying at grace*.

Ufland, H. J., & Quinn, D. (Producers). (1998). *One true thing*.

Zanuck, R. D., & James, P. (Producers). (1989). *Driving Miss Daisy*.

DYING AND BEREAVEMENT SUPPORT AND INFORMATION RESOURCES

The Canadian Hospice Palliative Care Association

The Canadian Hospice Palliative Care Association (CHPCA) provides information about hospice palliative care in Canada and a directory to hospice palliative care services across Canada. The provinces each have hospice palliative care organizations as well, which can be accessed through the CHPCA website. Territorial hospice palliative care associations are not in place in Yukon, the Northwest Territories, or Nunavut.

Canadian Hospice Palliative Care Association
Annex B, Saint-Vincent Hospital
60 Cambridge Street North
Ottawa ON K1R 7A5
613-241-3663 or 1-800-668-2785
Hospice Palliative Care Info Line: 1-877-203-4636
Fax: 613-241-3986
E-mail: info@chpca.net
http://www.chpca.net/home.htm

Bereaved Families of Ontario

This bereavement support organization offers programs and services to children, adolescents, and adults in groups or on a one-to-one basis. The programs are based on a mutual support model.

Bereaved Families of Ontario
602-36 Eglinton Avenue West
Toronto ON M4R 1A1
416-440-0290 or 1-800-236-6364
Fax: 416-440-0304
E-mail: info@bfotoronto.ca
http://www.bfotoronto.ca

Canuck Place Children's Hospice

This program provides respite and end-of-life care to children and their families, with bereavement support and follow-up for two to three years following the child's death. It also has programs for anticipatory grief support for a child or family and support groups for a child's parents and siblings.

Canuck Place Children's Hospice
1690 Matthews Avenue
Vancouver BC V6J 2T2
604-731-4847
Fax: 604-739-4376
http://www.canuckplace.org

The Dorothy Ley Hospice Organization

This organization runs a hospice and provides an informational website for patients, families, and health-care providers concerned with end-of-life care.

The Dorothy Ley Hospice Organization
170 Sherway Drive, Suite 3

Etobicoke ON M9C 1A6
416-626-0116
Fax: 416-626-7285
http://www.dlhospice.org/

The Compassionate Friends of Canada, Inc.

This international, nonprofit, nondenominational, self-help organization offers support groups and grief education to families who have experienced the death of a child. The website offers links to provincial and territorial chapters, as well as resources and links to other useful organizations.

The Compassionate Friends of Canada, Inc.
PO Box 140
RPO Croydon
Winnipeg MB R3M 3S7
Toll Free: 1-866-823-0141
E-mail: NationalOffice@TCFCanada.net
http://www.tcfcanada.net

Mothers Against Drunk Driving (MADD)

This organization uses social activism to fight one of the leading causes of accidental deaths in Canada. The website links to other useful resources and has links to 85 provincial and territorial chapters across Canada.

MADD CANADA National Office
2010 Winston Park Drive, Suite 500
Oakville ON L6H 5R7
905-829-8805 or 1-800-665-6233
Fax: 905-829-8860
E-mail: info@madd.ca
http://www.madd.ca

Make-A-Wish Foundation

This international organization grants as many wishes as possible to children between the ages of 3 and 17 who have life-threatening illnesses. Since its creation in 1980, more than 144 000 wishes have been granted. Children must be nominated (by anyone, including themselves) and judged medically eligible by the foundation's criteria. Canada has its own chapter.

Make-A-Wish Canada
4211 Yonge Street, Suite 521
Toronto ON M2P 2A9
416-224-9474 or 1-888-822-9474
Fax: 416-224-8795
E-mail: nationaloffice@makeawish.ca
http://www.makeawish.ca

GriefShare

GriefShare is an organization based on nondenominational religious beliefs that conducts 13-week educational and support groups for anyone who has lost a loved one. The parent organization, Church Initiative, is based in the United States, but chapters of GriefShare are located internationally.

Church Initiative
P.O. Box 1739
Wake Forest NC 27588

919-562-2112 or 800-395-5755
Fax: 919-562-2114
E-mail: info@griefshare.org
http://www.griefshare.org

WidowNet

This online information and self-help site is run for and by widows and widowers. It is helpful to people of all religious backgrounds and sexual orientations, providing information and related weblinks on topics including bereavement and recovery.
http://www.widownet.org

National Organization of Parents of Murdered Children, Inc.

This site provides information and support for families and friends of people who have died through acts of violence.
http://www.pomc.com

The Healing Alliance of National Storytellers Network

This site explores and promotes the use of storytelling in making meaning and healing emotional suffering.
http://www.healingstory.org

The Names Project—Canada: The Canadian AIDS Memorial Quilt

This site memorializes the names of those people who have died of HIV- or AIDS-related illnesses by making a quilt with each section dedicated to one person.
http://www.quilt.ca/e_home.html

The Aboriginal Healing & Wellness Strategy

This site provides resources to anyone interested in the promotion of Native Canadian physical and mental wellness and the reduction of violence.
http://www.ahwsontario.ca/

Buddhist Hospice Care in the Greater Toronto Area

This University of Toronto website provides information about Buddhist beliefs and Buddhist hospice care in Toronto, Ontario. It also provides web links to a variety of Canadian palliative care resources.
http://chass.utoronto.ca/~fgarrett/hospice/

HereToHelp

This website, based in British Columbia, provides information and weblinks to a number of resources for people who are feeling distressed.
http://www.heretohelp.bc.ca/

Living Lessons

This Canadian website provides resources and information for patients, caregivers, and health-care personnel who are involved with care at the end of life.
http://www.living-lessons.org/

End-of-Life Project

This website is conducted by the Health Law Institute of Dalhousie University and gives valuable information on issues of living wills, potentially life-shortening palliative interventions, and withdrawal of potentially life-sustaining treatments.
http://as01.ucis.dal.ca/dhli/cmp_welcome/default.cfm

The Living Will Registry (Canada)

This is a privately operated website that registers living wills and provides information about living wills, advance directives, and organ donation. Forms for living wills can be obtained through this site.
http://www.livingwills.com/

Health Canada

This government site provides information on palliative care in Canada.
http://www.hc-sc.gc.ca/hcs-sss/palliat/index_e.html

Canada's Office of Consumer Affairs: Canadian Consumer Handbook 2006

This government site provides consumer information and tips about funerals.
http://consumer.ic.gc.ca/epic/site/oca-bc.nsf/en/ca01492e.html

The Canadian Child Care Federation

This organization's website provides information and weblinks regarding a variety of issues surrounding the care of children.
http://www.cccf-fcsge.ca/home_en.html

World Health Organization

This organization's website provides information regarding health around the world. Included are demographics on illnesses and deaths.
http://www.who.int

GLOSSARY

abortion the termination of a pregnancy before the fetus is viable

absent mourning a state in which the bereaved individual either completely denies that a death has occurred, or remains in a state of complete shock, showing no grief reactions at all

active listening a listening technique that probes into the speaker's meanings and feelings and rephrases what has been said to make sure that the correct message has been transmitted and understood

advance directives less formal, sometimes oral, instructions regarding end-of-life care for the individual

affective denial an inhibition of an appropriate emotional response, even though the death is cognitively recognized and accepted

altruistic suicide suicide committed for the benefit of others; indicates an overconnectedness to society

anomic suicide suicide committed because of a feeling of being let down by a society to which the person was connected

anticipatory grief a time before an expected death in which people prepare themselves for the loss to come

assumptive world the views that people develop about the way the world and people operate in general

attachment the bonds that tie children to their primary caretakers early in life

attitude a belief or feeling that gives people the tendency to respond in particular ways to certain objects, events, and people

bardos Buddhist stages that the soul experiences after death on the way to the next incarnation or to Nirvana

bereavement the state of being deprived or having lost something meaningful in life

catharsis the release of emotions, relieving emotional tension

causality the reasons that death occurs

chronic mourning mourning that does not proceed on a normal course but remains stuck in the early reactions to a death

complicated grief the term used when the mourning process is compromised, is distorted, or fails, given the amount of time since the death

complicated mourning the problematic responses following some losses

conflicted mourning mourning in which the mourner predominantly feels a sense of remorse and grief for a poor relationship and yearns for a reconnection with the deceased

cremains the ashes left from cremation

cultural sensitivity an awareness and a willingness to acknowledge that people of different cultures act in different ways and have different norms and values

dead donor rule removal of organs must not result in the donor's death

death anxiety a fear of death, often demonstrated by a refusal to talk about death and an avoidance of anything related to it

death avoidance lack of talking or thinking about death

defensive exclusion the cognitive tendency to block the processing of information that is perceived to be threatening or painful

delayed mourning mourning that is minimized or denied at the time of the loss, only to be manifested later, usually triggered by another loss

disenfranchised grief grief that people experience that is not socially supported or sanctioned

distorted mourning mourning that typically exaggerates either any anger or the guilt that may be present, to the exclusion of other facets of the normal grief response

ego integrity a term used by Erik Erikson (1963) to describe the positive state of old age in which people feel satisfied and proud of what they have accomplished in life

egoistic suicide suicide committed because people do not feel connected to the rest of society

elective abortion the termination of a pregnancy at the request of the mother, done before the fetus is viable

euphemisms substitutions for actual terms, often to serve the function, in this context, of distancing people from the harsh reality of the real term or communicating deeper beliefs about the meaning of death

euthanasia deliberate treatment designed to end the life of a patient in a terminal medical state or a patient who is suffering intractable pain

extrinsic religious motivation people's external religious behaviours and affiliations

fatalistic suicide suicide committed because highly regulating, controlling, and restrictive societies that demand social integration allow for very little personal fulfillment

feng shui the Chinese practice of optimally positioning objects in a space to balance the influences of earth, water, and air

grief the reactions to the loss of something meaningful in life

grief intervention psychological services designed to help mourners cope with their grief

hajj the pilgrimage undertaken by Muslims

hospice a setting devoted to the care of terminally ill patients

inhibited mourning mourning only parts of the deceased individual and parts of the relationship, rather than the whole

intrinsic religious motivation the internal aspects of a person's religious belief; the nature, complexity, and reasons for the beliefs

irreversibility once death has occurred, it cannot be reversed

Kaddish Judaic prayer for the dead

karma the moral law of cause and effect that is inherent in everything; all actions have consequences

keeping of the soul Lakota Sioux rituals for purification of the soul so that it may move on to the afterlife

Koran (Qur'an) the Islamic holy book containing the words and teachings of Muhammad, discussing both spiritual devotion and the way to live a virtuous life

liminality the state of being in transition

living will a formal written document that typically specifies the individual's wishes regarding what measures can be taken to save or prolong his or her life and what should not be undertaken; it may also nominate a decision maker in the event of the individual's incapacitation, including a power of attorney for health-care decisions

locus of control whether people feel that control over their lives lies within them or without

loss the removal of something meaningful from a person's life

magical thinking thinking that immutable facts of living can be changed

making meaning the imposition of structure, coherence, and significance on events in our lives

Mass a Catholic religious service

māyā a human perception of reality; illusion

memorial an action or a ritual done in remembrance of a deceased person

merit transference a Buddhist ceremony to send positive energy and goodwill to the deceased for his or her next incarnation

minyan a Jewish group of at least 10 males above the age of 13

miscarriage the spontaneous abortion of a fetus before 16 to 20 weeks of gestation

mourning the way in which grief is expressed by an individual

Nirvana literally, blowing out; the end of the cycle of karma in which the soul is absorbed into the All

nonfunctionality when death occurs, all life-sustaining functions cease

palliative care care for the dying that is aimed at symptom relief to improve the quality of time remaining but not directly intended to prolong life or to bring about a cure

passive suicide suicide committed because minimal action is taken by people who initiate a series of events that results in their deaths

personal mortality an understanding that the individual himself or herself will die

perturbation the state of being upset

physician-assisted suicide suicide in which a physician has provided the patient with the means to end his or her own life

posttraumatic stress disorder (PTSD) an extreme response to a severe stressor that includes increased anxiety, avoidance of stimuli associated with the trauma, and a numbing of emotional responses

postvention the helping response following a suicide

potlatch a ceremony of gift giving practised by Native Peoples of the Pacific Northwest Coast to honour the dead

press the events to which a person reacts

principle of double effect if an action is intended to bring about a good effect but can achieve this effect only at the risk of producing a harmful effect, the action is ethically acceptable

psychache unendurable psychological pain engendered by frustrated psychological needs

rabbis teachers; often leaders of Jewish religious groups

regressed behaviour behaviour in response to grief that returns to an earlier developmental level of the child

respite care care for the terminally ill person that is carried out by someone other than the usual caregiver in order to give the caregiver some temporary relief from the caregiving responsibilities

rites of incorporation or integration rituals to signify that a transition has been made from one state to another, with the individual assimilated into the final state

rites of passage rituals or ceremonies that mark the change from one state to another

rites of separation rituals separating the dying individual from the society and mourners from the presence and the roles of the deceased

rites of transition rituals marking the time between one state and another, such as a dead spirit still inhabiting this world and moving to being a spirit inhabiting the afterlife

rituals patterned responses to a situation that are usually symbolic and give expression to the emotions of the individual or group

ruthless obstinacy persistence in giving medical treatment when hope of saving a life is gone

self-efficacy the extent to which an individual feels competent and able in a specific domain of functioning

self-transcendence an aspect of spirituality concerned with an expansion of an individual's humanistic and theological boundaries

separation anxiety the fear and trepidation experienced with the real or potential loss of an attachment figure

shivah primary Judaic mourning period

social integration the extent to which an individual feels connected or tied to society

stillbirth the birth of a child who never takes a breath

subsequent temporary upsurges of grief (STUGs) brief periods of acute grief usually precipitated by a memory trigger that emphasizes the absence of the deceased loved one

suicide an act with a fatal outcome that the deceased, knowing or expecting a potentially fatal outcome, has initiated and carried out with the purpose of bringing about wanted changes

sutras Buddhist prayers taken from sacred writings

suttee the cremation of living wives on the funeral pyre of the dead husband

Talmud a collection of writings expounding and interpreting the Torah; often referred to as the Oral Torah

thanatology the study of the area of death, dying, and bereavement

Torah the first five books of Moses: Genesis, Exodus, Leviticus, Numbers, and Deuteronomy

transitional or linking objects objects belonging to the deceased that a bereaved person may use to keep a connection with the deceased

trauma an event that creates intense fear, horror, or a sense of helplessness in the experiencer or observer

traumatic death a death that is sudden, unexpected, and often violent and arbitrary, leaving survivors with the experience of both grief and traumatic stress

unanticipated mourning the complicated mourning that follows an unexpected death

universality death comes to every living thing

wake a celebration of the life of the deceased, held before or just after the funeral

whole brain definition of death both higher cortical functioning and brainstem functioning have ceased

REFERENCES

CHAPTER 1

Ariès, P. (2004). The hour of our death. In A. C. G. M. Robben (Ed.), *Death, mourning, and burial: A cross-cultural reader* (pp. 40–48). Oxford, England: Blackwell.

Auger, J. A. (2003). Canadian perspectives on death and dying. In J. D. Morgan & P. Laungani (Eds.), *Death and bereavement around the world: Vol. 2: Death and bereavement in the Americas* (pp. 13–35). Amityville, NY: Baywood.

Bhagavad Gita. (J. Mascaró, Trans.). (1962). Harmondsworth, England: Penguin Books.

Bunyan, J. (1678/2005). *The pilgrim's progress*. Retrieved June 27, 2007, from http://www.ccel.org/ccel/bunyan/pilgrim.html

Canadian Hospice Palliative Care Association. (2006). *A history*. Retrieved August 14, 2006, from http://www.chpca. net

Corr, C. A., Nabe, C. M., & Corr, D. M. (2006). *Death and dying: Life and living* (5th ed.). Toronto: Thomson Nelson.

Davies, D. J. (2005). *A brief history of death*. Oxford, England: Blackwell.

Dorothy Ley Hospice. (2006). *Hospice palliative care in Canada*. Retrieved August 14, 2006, from http://www.dlhospice.org/pages/m7/HospiceCareCanada

Eastman, A. M. (Ed.). (1970). *The Norton anthology of poetry* (shorter ed.). New York: Norton.

Eliade, M. (1969). *Yoga: Immortality and freedom*. Princeton, NJ: Princeton University Press.

Frager, R., & Fadiman, J. (1998). *Personality and personal growth* (4th ed.). New York: Longman.

Gilley, G. E. (2000). *The afterlife: Part 1*. Retrieved August 12, 2006, from http://www.svchapel.org/Resources/Articles/read_articles.asp?id=76

History of Halloween. (n.d.). Retrieved August 12, 2006, from http://www.historychannel.com/exhibits/halloween/?page=origins

Homer. (1967). *The odyssey of Homer* (R. Lattimore, Trans.). New York: Harper & Row.

Kübler-Ross, E. (1969). *On death and dying*. New York: Macmillan.

Kübler-Ross, E. (1974). *Questions and answers on death and dying*. New York: Macmillan.

Mabbott, T. O. (Ed.). (1951). *Selected poetry and prose of Poe*. New York: The Modern Library.

Ortiz, A., & Erdoes, R. (1996). Woman chooses death. In W. S. Penn (Ed.), *The telling of the world: Native American stories and art* (p. 203). New York: Stewart, Tabori, & Chang.

Plato. (2003). *Republic* (R. Waterfield, Trans.). London, England: The Folio Society.

Robinson, B. A. (2004). *Teachings in the Hebrew scriptures about the afterlife: A liberal interpretation*. Retrieved August 12, 2006, from http://www.religioustolerance.org/aft_bibl1.htm

Solzhenitsyn, A. (1969). *Cancer ward*. New York: Bantam Books.

Taylor, T. (2002). *The buried soul: How humans invented death*. Boston: Beacon Press.

CHAPTER 2

Altheide, D. (2002). *Creating fear: News and the construction of crisis*. Hawthorne, NY: Aldine deGruyter.

Ariès, P. (2004). The hour of our death. In A. C. G. M. Robben (Ed.), *Death, mourning, and burial: A cross-cultural reader* (pp. 40–48). Oxford, England: Blackwell.

Clarke, J. N. (2005–2006). Death under control: The portrayal of death in mass print English language literature in Canada. *Omega, 52*(2), 153–167.

Comstock, G., & Strasberger, V. C. (1993). Media violence: Q & A. *Adolescent Medicine, 4*(3), 495–509.

Corr, C. A., Nabe, C. M., & Corr, D. M. (2006). *Death and dying: Life and living* (5th ed.). Toronto: Thomson Nelson.

DePaola, S. J., Griffin, M., Young, J. R., & Neimeyer, R. A. (2003). Death anxiety and attitudes toward the elderly among older adults: The role of gender and ethnicity. *Death Studies, 27*, 335–354.

DeSpelder, L. A., & Strickland, A. L. (2005). *The last dance: Encountering death and dying* (7th ed.). New York: McGraw-Hill.

Doka, K. J. (2002). Introduction. In K. J. Doka (Ed.), *Disenfranchised grief: New directions, challenges, and strategies for practice* (pp. 5–22). Champaign, IL: Research Press.

Eyetsemitan, F. (1998). Stifled grief in the workplace. *Death Studies, 22*(5), 469–479.

Harding, S. R., Flannelly, K. J., Weaver, A. J., & Costa, K. G. (2005). The influence of religion on death anxiety and death acceptance. *Mental Health, Religion & Culture, 8*(4), 253–261.

Human Resources and Social Development Canada. (2005). *Compassionate Care Leave, Canada Labour Code, Part III, Division VII*. Retrieved July 16, 2007, from http://www.hrsdc.gc.ca/en/lp/lo/opd-ipg/ipg/063.shtml

Jung, C. G. (1967). *Collected works of C.G. Jung (Vol. 9, Part I: The archetypes and the collective unconscious)*. Princeton, NJ: Princeton University Press.

King, J., & Hayslip, B. (2001–2002). The media's influence on college students' views of death. *Omega, 44*(1), 37–56.

Lattanzi-Licht, M. (2002). Grief and the workplace: Positive approaches. In K. J. Doka (Ed.), *Disenfranchised grief: New directions, challenges, and strategies for practice* (pp. 167–180). Champaign, IL: Research Press.

Rando, T. A. (1993). *Treatment of complicated mourning*. Champaign, IL: Research Press.

Schiappa, E., Gregg, P. B., & Hewes, D. E. (2004). Can a television series change attitudes about death? A study of college students and *Six Feet Under*. *Death Studies, 28,* 459–474.

Stroebe, M., & Schut, H. A. W. (1999). The dual-process model of coping with bereavement: Rationale and description. *Death Studies, 23*(3), 197–224.

Walter, T., Littlewood, J., & Pickering, M. (1995). Death in the news: The public invigilation of private emotion. *Sociology, 29*(4), 576–596.

Worden, J. W. (2002). *Grief counseling and grief therapy* (3rd ed.). New York: Springer.

CHAPTER 3

Braun, K. L., & Nichols, R. (1997). Death and dying in four Asian American cultures: A descriptive study. *Death Studies, 21,* 327–359.

Catlin, G. (1993). The role of culture in grief. *Journal of Social Psychology, 133*(2), 173–184.

Chödrön, P. (2005). *When things fall apart: Heart advice for difficult times.* Boston: Shambhala.

Conklin, B. A. (1995). Thus are our bodies, thus was our custom: Mortuary cannibalism in an Amazonian society. *American Ethnologist, 22,* 75–101.

Deloria, V., Jr. (1994). *God is red: A native view of religion.* Golden, CO: Fulcrum.

Deloria, V., Jr. (1999). *For this land: Writings on religion in America.* New York: Routledge.

Evans-Pritchard, E. E. (1968). *Witchcraft, oracles and magic among the Azande.* Oxford, England: Clarendon.

Frager, R., & Fadiman, J. (1998). *Personality and personal growth* (4th ed.). New York: Longman.

Goss, R. E., & Klass, D. (1997). Tibetan Buddhism and the resolution of grief: The *Bardo-Thodol* for the dying and the grieving. *Death Studies, 21,* 377–395.

Grabowsky, J. A., & Frantz, T. (1992). Latinos and Anglos: Cultural experiences of grief intensity. *Omega, 26,* 273–275.

Hadad, M., & Reed, M. J. (2007). *The post-secondary learning experience.* Toronto: Thomson Nelson.

Hirschfelder, A., & Molin, P. (1992). *The encyclopedia of Native American religions.* New York: MJF Books.

Jayaram, V. (2006). *Hinduism and death.* Retrieved October 27, 2006, from http://www.hinduwebsite.com/hinduism/h_death.asp

Lamm, M. (1969). *The Jewish way in death and mourning.* New York: Jonathan David.

Lawson, L. V. (1990). Culturally sensitive support for grieving parents. *Maternal Child Nursing, 15,* 76–79.

Lobar, S. L., Youngblut, J. M., & Brooten, D. (2006). Cross-cultural beliefs, ceremonies, and rituals surrounding death of a loved one. *Pediatric Nursing, 32*(1), 44–50.

McGaa, E. (Eagle Man). (1990). *Mother Earth spirituality: Native American paths to healing ourselves and our world.* New York: HarperCollins.

Mechon Mamre. (2002). *The Hebrew Bible in English, according to the Jewish Publication Society's 1917 edition.* Jerusalem: Author.

National Spiritual Assembly of the Bahá'i of the United States. (2007). *Bahá'i core beliefs.* Retrieved June 13, 2007, from http://www.bahai.us/bahai-beliefs

Oltjenbruns, K. A. (1998). Ethnicity and the grief response: Mexican American versus Anglo American college students. *Death Studies, 22,* 141–155.

Palgi, P., & Abramovitch, H. (1984). Death: A cross-cultural perspective. *Annual Review of Anthropology, 13,* 385–417.

Radcliffe-Brown, A. R. (1964). *The Andaman islanders.* New York: Free Press.

Renault, D. (Wa'na'nee'che'), & Freke, T. (1996). *Native American spirituality.* London: Thorsons.

Robinson, B. A. (2005). *Description of Judaism.* Retrieved June 12, 2007, from the Ontario Consultants on Religious Tolerance website: http://www.religioustolerance.org/jud_desc.htm

Rosenblatt, P. C., Walsh, R., & Jackson, A. (1976). *Grief and mourning in cross-cultural perspective.* New Haven, CT: Human Relations Area Files Press.

Smith, H. (1986). *The religions of man.* New York: Harper-Perennial.

Sogyal Rinpoche. (1993). *The Tibetan book of living and dying.* San Francisco: HarperCollins.

Statistics Canada. (2003). *Religions in Canada, 2001 census* (Catalogue No. 96F0030XIE2001015). Retrieved June 13, 2007, from http://www12.statcan.ca/english/census01/Products/Analytic/companion/rel/contents.cfm

Straus, A. S. (1978). The meaning of death in Northern Cheyenne culture. *Plains Anthropologist, 23,* 1–6.

Thomas, N. D. (2001). The importance of culture throughout all of life and beyond. *Holistic Nursing Practice, 15*(2), 40–46.

Yick, A. G., & Gupta, R. (2002). Chinese cultural dimensions of death, dying, and bereavement: Focus group findings. *Journal of Cultural Diversity, 9*(2), 32–42.

CHAPTER 4

Beck, M. G. (1993). *Potlatch: Native ceremony and myth on the northwest coast.* Anchorage, AL: Alaska Northwest Books.

Bopp, J., Bopp, M., Brown, L., & Lane, P., Jr. (1984). *The sacred tree: Reflections on Native American spirituality.* Twin Lakes, WI: Lotus Light.

Brown, J. E. (1989). *The sacred pipe: Black Elk's account of seven rites of the Oglala Sioux.* Norman: University of Oklahoma Press.

Carmody, D. L., & Carmody, J. T. (1993). *Native American religions: An introduction.* New York: Paulist Press.

Emke, I. (2002). Why the sad face? Secularization and the changing function of funerals in Newfoundland. *Mortality, 7*(3), 269–284.

Froggatt, K. (1997). Rites of passage and the hospice culture. *Mortality, 2*(2), 123–136.

Funeral pyre runs afoul of British law. (2006, July 22). *Toronto Star*, L11.

Grimes, R. L. (2000). *Deeply into the bone: Re-inventing rites of passage*. Berkeley: University of California Press.

Hertz, R. (2004). A contribution to the study of the collective representation of death. In A. C. G. M. Robben (Ed.), *Death, mourning, and burial: A cross-cultural reader* (pp. 197–212). Malden, MA: Blackwell.

Hopwood, A. (2003). Jamaican dead yard cultures and customs through the years. In J. D. Morgan & P. Laungani (Eds.), *Death and bereavement around the world: Vol. 2. Death and bereavement in the Americas* (pp. 77–94). Amityville, NY: Baywood.

Irion, P. E. (1990–1991). Changing patterns of ritual response to death. *Omega, 22*(3), 153–171.

Kastenbaum, R. (2004, Summer). Why funerals? *Generations*, 5–10.

Kawano, S. (2004). Pre-funerals in contemporary Japan: The making of a new ceremony of later life among aging Japanese. *Ethnology, 43*(2), 155–165.

Lamm, M. (1969). *The Jewish way in death and mourning*. New York: Jonathan David.

Laungani, P. (2005). Cultural considerations in Hindu funerals in India and England. In J. D. Morgan & P. Laungani (Eds.), *Death and bereavement around the world: Vol. 4. Death and bereavement in Asia, Australia, and New Zealand* (pp. 39–63). Amityville, NY: Baywood.

Martinson, I., Chao, C. C., & Chung, L. (2005). Dying, death, and grief: Glimpses in Hong Kong and Taiwan. In J. D. Morgan & P. Laungani (Eds.), *Death and bereavement around the world: Vol. 4. Death and bereavement in Asia, Australia, and New Zealand* (pp. 123–134). Amityville, NY: Baywood.

Mitford, J. (1963). *The American way of death*. New York: Simon & Schuster.

Parsons, B. (2003). Conflict in the context of care: An examination of role conflict between the bereaved and the funeral director in the UK. *Mortality, 8*(1), 67–87.

Patch, C. (2006, May 27). How to build your own "fancy" coffin. *Toronto Star*, M5.

Prothero, S. (2001). *Purified by fire: A history of cremation in America*. Berkeley: University of California Press.

Quartier, T., Hermans, C. A. M., & Scheer, A. H. M. (2004). Remembrance and hope in Roman Catholic funeral rites: Attitudes of participants towards past and future of the deceased. *Journal of Empirical Theology, 17*(2), 252–280.

Rando, T. A. (1985). Creating therapeutic rituals in the psychotherapy of the bereaved. *Psychotherapy, 22*, 236–240.

Rando, T. A. (1993). *Treatment of complicated mourning*. Champaign, IL: Research Press.

Recommended. (2006, May 1). Green exit. *Macleans, 119*(18), 71.

Romanoff, B. D., & Terenzio, M. (1998). Rituals and the grieving process. *Death Studies, 22*(8), 697–711.

Ross, R. (1992). *Dancing with a ghost: Exploring Indian reality*. Toronto: Reed Books.

Ross, R. (1996). *Returning to the teachings: Exploring Aboriginal justice*. Toronto: Penguin Books.

Salvador, R. J. (2003). What do Mexicans celebrate on the Day of the Dead? In J. D. Morgan & P. Laungani (Eds.), *Death and bereavement around the world: Vol. 2. Death and bereavement in the Americas* (pp. 75–76). Amityville, NY: Baywood.

Sheehy, G. (1976). *Passages: Predictable crises of adult life*. New York: Dutton.

Sofka, C. J. (2004, Summer). What kind of funeral? Identifying and resolving family conflicts. *Generations*, 21–25.

Turner, V. W. (1969). *The ritual process: Structure and anti-structure*. Chicago: Aldine.

Vandendorpe, F. (2000). Funerals in Belgium: The hidden complexity of contemporary practices. *Mortality, 5*(1), 18–33.

van Gennep, A. (1960). *The rites of passage*. Chicago: University of Chicago Press.

Wu, J. (2005). Death and bereavement among the Chinese in Asia. In J. D. Morgan & P. Laungani (Eds.), *Death and bereavement around the world: Volume 4. Death and bereavement in Asia, Australia, and New Zealand* (pp. 135–139). Amityville, NY: Baywood.

CHAPTER 5

Bowlby, J. (1980). *Attachment and loss: Loss, sadness and depression* (Vol. 3). New York: Basic Books.

Doka, K. J. (2005–2006). Fulfillment as Sanders' sixth phase of bereavement: The unfinished work of Catherine Sanders. *Omega, 52*(2), 143–151.

Freud, S. (1984). Mourning and melancholia. In A. Richards (Ed.), *The Pelican Freud library: Vol. II* (pp. 251–268). Hammondsworth, England: Penguin Books.

Gamino, L. A., Sewell, K. W., & Easterling, L. W. (2000). Scott and White grief study – Phase 2: Toward an adaptive model of grief. *Death Studies, 24*(7), 633–660.

Klass, D. (1996). Grief in an Eastern culture: Japanese ancestor worship. In D. Klass, P. R. Silverman, & S. L. Nickman (Eds.), *Continuing bonds: New understandings of grief* (pp. 59–70). Washington, DC: Taylor & Francis.

Klass, D. (1999). Developing a cross-cultural model of grief: The state of the field. *Omega, 39*(3), 153–178.

Klass, D., & Goss, R. (1999). Spiritual bonds to the dead in cross-cultural and historical perspective: Comparative religion and modern grief. *Death Studies, 23*, 547–567.

Klass, D., & Goss, R. (2002). Politics, religions, and grief: The cases of American spiritualism and the Deuteronomic reform in Israel. *Death Studies, 26*, 709–729.

Klass, D., & Goss, R. (2003). The politics of grief and continuing bonds with the dead: The cases of Maoist China and Wahhabi Islam. *Death Studies, 27*, 787–811.

Kübler-Ross, E. (1969). *On death and dying*. New York: Macmillan.

Kübler-Ross, E. (1974). *Questions and answers on death and dying*. New York: Macmillan.

Kübler-Ross, E. (1981). *Living with death and dying*. New York: Macmillan.

Moos, N. L. (1995). An integrative model of grief. *Death Studies, 19*, 337–364.

Parkes, C. M. (1996). *Bereavement: Studies in grief in adult life* (3rd ed.). Philadelphia: Taylor & Francis.

Prigerson, H. G., Frank, E., Kasel, S., Reynolds, C. F., Anderson, B., Zubenko, G. S. et al. (1995). Complicated grief and bereavement-related depression as distinct disorders: Preliminary empirical validation in elderly bereaved spouses. *American Journal of Psychiatry, 152*, 22–30.

Rando, T. A. (1992–1993). The increasing prevalence of complicated mourning: The onslaught is just beginning. *Omega, 26*(1), 43–59.

Rando, T. A. (1993). *Treatment of complicated mourning.* Champaign, IL: Research Press.

Rosenblatt, P. C. (1983). *Bitter, bitter tears: Nineteenth century diarists and twentieth century grief theories.* Minneapolis, MN: University of Minnesota Press.

Rubin, S. S. (1999). The two-track model of bereavement: Overview, retrospect, and prospect. *Death Studies, 23*, 681–714.

Rubin, S. S., Malkinson, R., & Witztum, E. (2003). Trauma and bereavement: Conceptual and clinical issues revolving around relationships. *Death Studies, 27*, 667–690.

Sanders, C. (1999). *Grief: The mourning after* (2nd ed.). New York: Wiley.

Selye, H. (1976). *The stress of life.* New York: McGraw-Hill.

Shapiro, E. R. (1994). *Grief as a family process.* New York: Guilford Press.

Shapiro, E. R. (1996). Family bereavement and cultural diversity: A social developmental perspective. *Family Process, 35*(3), 313–332.

Stroebe, M., & Schut, H. A. W. (1998). Culture and grief. *Bereavement Care, 17*, 7–10.

Stroebe, M., & Schut, H. A. W. (1999). The dual-process model of coping with bereavement: Rationale and description. *Death Studies, 23*(3), 197–224.

Stroebe, M., & Stroebe, W. (1987). *Breavement and health. The psychological and physical consequences of partner loss.* Cambridge, England: Cambridge University Press.

Wikan, U. (1988). Bereavement and loss in two Muslim communities: Egypt and Bali compared. *Social Science and Medicine, 27*, 451–460.

Wikan, U. (1990). *Managing turbulent hearts: A Balinese formula for living.* Chicago: University of Chicago Press.

Worden, J. W. (2002). *Grief counseling and grief therapy* (3rd ed.). New York: Springer.

CHAPTER 6

Baker, J., Sedney, M., & Gross, E. (1992). Psychological tasks for bereaved children. *American Journal of Orthopsychiatry, 62*(1), 105–116.

Balk, D. E. (1996). Models for understanding adolescent coping with bereavement. *Death Studies, 20*, 367–387.

Bluebond-Langner, M. (1977). Meanings of death to children. In H. Feifel (Ed.), *New meanings of death* (pp. 47–56). New York: McGraw-Hill.

Bowlby, J. (1960). Grief and mourning in infancy. *Psychoanalytic Study of the Child, 15*, 9–52.

Bowlby, J. (1980). *Attachment and loss: Loss, sadness and depression* (Vol. 3). New York: Basic Books.

Busch, T., & Kimble, C. S. (2001). Grieving children: Are we meeting the challenge? *Pediatric Nursing, 27*(4), 414–418.

Buxbaum, L., & Brant, J. M. (2001). When a parent dies from cancer. *Clinical Journal of Oncology Nursing, 5*(4), 1–6.

Christ, G. H. (2000). Impact of development on children's mourning. *Cancer Practice, 8*(2), 72–81.

Christ, G. H., Siegel, K., & Christ, A. E. (2002). Adolescent grief. *Journal of the American Medical Association, 288*(10), 1269–1278.

Davies, B. (1999). *Shadows in the sun: The experiences of sibling bereavement in childhood.* Philadelphia: Brunner/Mazel.

Dickinson, G. E. (1992). First childhood death experiences. *Omega, 25*(3), 169–182.

Dowdney, L., Wilson, R., Maughan, B., Allerton, M., Scofield, P., & Skuse, D. (1999). Psychological disturbance and service provision in parentally bereaved children: Prospective case-control study. *British Medical Journal, 319*(7206), 354–357.

Elliott, M. P. (1981). Parent care: Total involvement in the care of a dying child. In E. Kübler-Ross (Ed.), *Living with death and dying* (pp. 95–159). New York: Macmillan.

Ens, C., & Bond, J. B., Jr. (2005). Death anxiety and personal growth in adolescents experiencing the death of a grandparent. *Death Studies, 29*, 171–178.

Erikson, E. H. (1963). *Childhood and society* (Rev. ed.). New York: Norton.

Faulkner, K. W. (1997). Talking about death with a dying child. *American Journal of Nursing, 97*(6), 64–69.

Freeman, K., O'Dell, C., & Meola, C. (2003). Childhood brain tumors: Children's and siblings' concerns regarding the diagnosis and phase of illness. *Journal of Pediatric Oncology Nursing, 20*(3), 133–140.

Furth, G. M. (1981). The use of drawings made at significant times in one's life. In E. Kübler-Ross (Ed.), *Living with death and dying* (pp. 63–94). New York: Macmillan.

Geis, H., Whittlesey, S., McDonald, N. B., Smith, K., & Pfefferbaum, B. (1998). Bereavement and loss in childhood. *Child and Adolescent Psychiatric Clinics of North America, 7*(1), 73–85.

Hames, C. C. (2003). Helping infants and toddlers when a family member dies. *Journal of Hospice and Palliative Nursing, 5*(2), 103–110.

Hinds, P. S., Schum, L., Baker, J. N., & Wolfe, J. (2005). Key factors affecting dying children and their families. *Journal of Palliative Medicine, 8*(S1), S70–S78.

Holland, J. (2004, March). Should children attend their parent's funerals? *Pastoral Care*, 10–14.

Ishibashi, A. (2001). The needs of children and adolescents with cancer for information and social support. *Cancer Nursing, 24*, 61–67.

Kemp, H. (1999). Grieving the death of a sibling or the death of a friend. *Journal of Psychology and Christianity, 18*, 354–366.

Kenyon, B. L. (2001). Current research in children's conceptions of death: A critical review. *Omega, 43*(1), 63–91.

Kirwin, K. M., & Hamrin, V. (2005). Decreasing the risk of complicated bereavement and future psychiatric disorders in children. *Journal of Child and Adolescent Psychiatric Nursing, 18*(1), 62–78.

Kramer, K. (2004–2005). You cannot die alone: Dr. Elisabeth Kübler-Ross (July 8, 1926–August 24, 2004). *Omega, 50*(2), 83–101.

Kübler-Ross, E. (1983). *On children and death.* New York: Macmillan.

Kwok, O., Haine, R. A., Sandler, I. N., Ayers, T. S., Wolchik, S. A., & Tein, J-Y. (2005). Positive parenting as a mediator of the relations between parental psychological distress and mental health problems of parentally bereaved children. *Journal of Clinical Child and Adolescent Psychology, 34*(2), 260–271.

Lazar, A., & Torney-Purta, J. (1991). The development of subconcepts of death in young children: A short-term longitudinal study. *Child Development, 62*(6), 1321–1333.

Lenhardt, A. M. C., & McCourt, B. (2000). Adolescent unresolved grief in response to the death of a mother. *Professional School Counseling, 3*(3), 189–196.

Lin, K. K., Sandler, I. N., Ayers, T. S., Wolchik, S. A., & Luecken, L. J. (2004). Resilience in parentally bereaved children and adolescents seeking preventive services. *Journal of Clinical Child and Adolescent Psychology, 33*(4), 673–683.

Macdonald, A. M. (2002). Bereavement in twin relationships: An exploration of themes from a study of twinship. *Twin Research, 5*, 218–226.

Nagy, M. (1948). The child's theories concerning death. *Journal of Genetic Psychology, 73*, 3–27.

Nitsche, R., Meyer, W. H., Sexauer, C. L., Parkhurst, J. B., Foster, P., & Huszti, H. (2000). Care of terminally ill children with cancer. *Medical and Pediatric Oncology, 34*, 268–270.

Noppe, I. C., & Noppe, L. D. (2004). Adolescent experiences with death: Letting go of immortality. *Journal of Mental Health Counseling, 26*(2), 146–167.

Normand, C. L., Silverman, P. R., & Nickman, S. L. (1996). Bereaved children's changing relationships with the deceased. In D. Klass, P. R. Silverman, & S. L. Nickman (Eds.), *Continuing bonds: New understandings of grief* (pp. 87–111). Washington, DC: Taylor & Francis.

Norris-Shortle, C., Young, P. A., & Williams, M. A. (1993). Understanding death and grief for children three and younger. *Social Work, 38*(6), 736–742.

O'Halloran, C. M., & Altmaier, E. M. (1996). Awareness of death among children: Does a life-threatening illness alter the process of discovery? *Journal of Counseling & Development, 74*(3), 259–262.

Orbach, I., Gross, Y., Glaubman, H., & Berman, D. (1985). Children's perception of death in humans and animals as a function of age, anxiety and cognitive ability. *Journal of Child Psychology and Psychiatry, 26*, 453–463.

Pantke, R., & Slade, P. (2006). Remembered parenting style and psychological well-being in young adults whose parents had experienced early child loss. *Psychology and Psychotherapy: Theory, Research and Practice, 79*, 69–81.

Rowling, L. (2002). Youth and disenfranchised grief. In K. J. Doka (Ed.), *Disenfranchised grief: New directions and strategies for practice* (pp. 275–292). Champaign, IL: Research Press.

Sahler, O. J. Z., Frager, G., Levetown, M., Cohn, F. G., & Lipson, M. A. (2000). Medical education about end-of-life care in the pediatric setting: Principles, challenges, and opportunities. *Pediatrics, 105*(3), 575–584.

Schaefer, D. J. (2004). Communication among children, parents, and funeral directors. *Annual Editions: Dying, Death, and Bereavement, 04/05*, 32–36.

Schoen, A. A., Burgoyne, M., & Schoen, S. F. (2004). Are the developmental needs of children in America adequately addressed during the grieving process? *Journal of Instructional Psychology, 31*(2), 143–148.

Schwab, R. (1997). Parental mourning and children's behavior. *Journal of Counseling & Development, 75*, 258–265.

Shapiro, E. R. (1994). *Grief as a family process.* New York: Guilford Press.

Silverman, P. R. (2000). *Never too young to know: Death in children's lives.* New York: Oxford University Press.

Silverman, P. R. (2002). Living with grief, rebuilding a world. *Journal of Palliative Medicine, 5*(3), 449–454.

Speece, M. W., & Brent, S. B. (1984). Children's understanding of death: A review of three components of a death concept. *Child Development, 55*, 1671–1686.

Speece, M. W., & Brent, S. B. (1992). The acquisition of a mature understanding of three components of the concept of death. *Death Studies, 16*(3), 211–229.

Stambrook, M., & Parker, K. C. H. (1987, April). The development of the concept of death in childhood: A review of the literature. *Merrill-Palmer Quarterly, 33*, 133–157.

Stillion, J. M., & Papadatou, D. (2002). Suffer the children. *American Behavioral Scientist, 46*(2), 299–315.

Statistics Canada. (2006). *Deaths, by age group and sex, Canada, provinces and territories, annual* (CANSIM Table 102–0503). Retrieved July 17, 2007, from http://cansim2.statcan.ca/cgi-win/CNSMCGI.EXE

Tamm, M. E., & Granqvist, A. (1995). The meaning of death for children and adolescents: A phenomenographic study of drawings. *Death Studies, 19*, 203–222.

Thompson, F., & Payne, S. (2000). Bereaved children's questions to a doctor. *Mortality, 5*(1), 74–96.

Tremblay, G. C., & Israel, A. C. (1998). Children's adjustment to parental death. *Clinical Psychology: Science and Practice, 5*(4), 424–438.

Wilson, L. R. (1995). Differences between identical twin and singleton adjustment to sibling death in adolescence. *Journal of Psychological Practice, 1*, 100–104.

Withrow, R., & Schwiebert, V. L. (2005). Twin loss: Implications for counselors working with surviving twins. *Journal of Counseling & Development, 83*, 21–28.

Worden, J. W. (1996). *Children and grief: When a parent dies.* New York: Guilford Press.

CHAPTER 7

Adler, N. E., David, H. P., Major, B. N., Roth, S. H., Russo, N. F., & Wyatt, G. E. (1990). Psychological responses after abortion. *Science, 248*, 41–44.

Adler, N. E., David, H. P., Major, B. N., Roth, S. H., Russo, N. F., & Wyatt, G. E. (1992). Psychological responses in abortion: A review. *American Psychologist, 47*, 769–790.

Beutal, M., Deckardt, R., von Rad, M., & Weiner, H. (1995). Grief and depression after miscarriage: Their separation, antecedents, and course. *Psychosomatic Medicine, 57*, 517–526.

Brier, N. (2004). Anxiety after miscarriage: A review of the empirical literature and implications for clinical practice. *Birth, 31*(2), 138–142.

Cleiren, M. (1991). *A comparative study of the aftermath of death from suicide, traffic accident and illness for next of kin.* Leiden, Netherlands: DSWO Press.

Cramer, D. (1993). Living alone, marital status, gender and health. *Journal of Applied and Community Social Psychology, 3*, 1–15.

Eaves, Y. D., McQuiston, C., & Miles, M. S. (2005). Coming to terms with adult sibling grief: When a brother dies from AIDS. *Journal of Hospice and Palliative Nursing, 7(3),* 139–149.

Forrest, L. M., & Austin, A. E. (2002). Death of a partner: Perspectives of heterosexual and gay men. *Journal of Health Psychology, 7*(3), 317–328.

Hays, J. C., Gold, D. T., & Peiper, C. F. (1997). Sibling bereavement in late life. *Omega, 35*(1), 25–42.

Hinton, J. (1996). How reliable are relatives' retrospective reports of terminal illness? Patients' and relatives' accounts compared. *Social Science & Medicine, 43*(8), 1229–1236.

Hinton, J. (1999). The progress of awareness and acceptance of dying assessed in cancer patients and their caring relatives. *Palliative Medicine, 13*, 19–35.

Hsu, M., Tseng, Y., Banks, J. M., & Kuo, L. (2004). Interpretations of stillbirth. *Journal of Advanced Nursing, 47*(4), 408–416.

Hughes, P., Turton, P., Hopper, E., & Evans, C. D. H. (2002). Assessment of guidelines for good practice in psychosocial care of mothers after stillbirth: A cohort study. *Lancet, 360*, 114–118.

Keefe-Cooperman, K. (2004–2005). A comparison of grief as related to miscarriage and termination for fetal abnormality. *Omega, 50*(4), 281–299.

Kersting, A., Reutmann, M., Ohrmann, P., Baez, E., Klockenbusch, W., Lanczik, M. et al. (2004). Grief after termination of pregnancy due to fetal malformation. *Journal of Psychosomatic Obstetrical Gynecology, 25*, 163–169.

Klier, C. M., Geller, P. A., & Ritsher, J. B. (2002). Affective disorders in the aftermath of miscarriage: A comprehensive review. *Archives of Women's Mental Health, 5*, 129–149.

Levine, A., & Karger, W. (2004). The trajectory of illness. In J. Berzoff & P. R. Silverman (Eds.), *Living with dying: A handbook for end-of-life healthcare practitioners* (pp. 273–296). New York: Columbia University Press.

Maker, C., & Ogden, J. (2003). The miscarriage experience: More than just a trigger to psychological morbidity? *Psychology and Health, 18*(3), 403–415.

Marshall, H. (2004). Midlife loss of parents: The transition from adult child to orphan. *Ageing International, 29*(4), 351–367.

Moss, M., Resch, N., & Moss, S. (1997). The role of gender in middle-aged children's responses to parent death. *Omega, 35*(1), 43–65.

Murphy, S. A., Johnson, L. C., & Lohan, J. (2003). Challenging the myths about parents' adjustment after the sudden, violent death of a child. *Journal of Nursing Scholarship, 35*(4), 359–364.

Pantke, R., & Slade, P. (2006). Remembered parenting style and psychological well-being in young adults whose parents had experienced early child loss. *Psychology and Psychotherapy: Research and Practice, 79*, 69–81.

Parkes, C. M. (1996). *Bereavement: Studies in grief in adult life* (3rd ed.). Philadelphia: Taylor & Francis.

Petersen, S., & Rafuls, S. E. (1998). Receiving the scepter: The generational transition and impact of parent death on adults. *Death Studies, 22*, 493–524.

Pope, A. (2005). Personal transformation in midlife orphanhood: An empirical phenomenological study. *Omega, 51*(2), 107–123.

Puddifoot, J. E., & Johnson, M. P. (1999). Active grief, despair, and difficulty coping: Some measured characteristics of male response following their partner's miscarriage. *Journal of Reproductive and Infant Psychology, 17*(1), 89–93.

Quill, T., Norton, S., Shah, M., Lam, Y., Fridd, C., & Buckley, M. (2006). What is most important for you to achieve? An analysis of patient responses when receiving palliative care consultation. *Journal of Palliative Medicine, 9*(2), 382–388.

Renner, C., Verdekal, S., Brier, S., & Falucca, G. (2000). The meaning of miscarriage to others: Is it an unrecognized loss? *Journal of Personal and Interpersonal Loss, 5*, 65–76.

Robinson, L., & Mahon, M. M. (1997). Sibling bereavement: A concept analysis. *Death Studies, 21*, 477–499.

Samuelsson, M., Rådestad, I., & Segesten, K. (2001). A waste of life: Fathers' experience of losing a child before birth. *Birth, 28*(2), 124–130.

Sanders, C. M. (1999). *Grief, the mourning after: Dealing with adult bereavement* (2nd ed.). New York: Wiley.

Schwab, R. (1997). Parental mourning and children's behaviour. *Journal of Counseling & Development, 75*, 258–265.

Statistics Canada. (2005a, July 12). Stillbirths. *The Daily.* Retrieved August 14, 2006, from http://www.statcan.ca/Daily/English/050712/d050712d.htm

Statistics Canada. (2005b, February 11). Induced abortions. *The Daily.* Retrieved August 14, 2006, from http://www.statcan.ca/Daily/English/050211/d050211a.htm

Statistics Canada. (2006). *Deaths, by age group and sex, Canada, provinces and territories, annual* (CANSIM Table 102–0504). Ottawa, ON: Author.

Stroebe, M., & Stroebe, W. (1983). Who suffers more? Sex differences in health risks of the widowed. *Psychological Bulletin, 93,* 297–301.

Stroebe, M., Stroebe, W., & Schut, H. (2001). Gender differences in adjustment to bereavement: An empirical and theoretical review. *Review of General Psychology, 5*(1), 62–83.

Tentoni, S. C. (1995). A therapeutic approach to reduce postabortion grief in university women. *Journal of American College Health, 44*(1), 35–37.

CHAPTER 8

Abengózar, M. C., Bueno, B., & Vega, J. L. (1999). Intervention on attitudes toward death along the life span. *Educational Gerontology, 25,* 435–447.

Bennett, K. M., Hughes, G. M., & Smith, P. T. (2003). I think a woman can take it: Widowed men's views and experiences of gender differences in bereavement. *Ageing International, 28*(4), 408–424.

Bennett, K. M., Hughes, G. M., & Smith, P. T. (2005). Psychological response to later life widowhood: Coping and the effects of gender. *Omega, 51*(1), 33–52.

Bennett, K. M., Smith, P. T., & Hughes, G. M. (2005). Coping, depressive feelings and gender differences in late life widowhood. *Aging & Mental Health, 9*(4), 348–353.

Burger, J. M. (1999). Personality and control. In V. J. Derlega, B. A. Winstead, & W. H. Jones (Eds.), *Personality: Contemporary theory and research* (2nd ed.) (pp. 282–306). Belmont, CA: Wadsworth.

Cameron, M. E. (2002). Older persons' ethical problems involving their health. *Nursing Ethics, 9*(5), 537–556.

Carr, D. (2004). Gender, preloss marital dependence, and older adults' adjustment to widowhood. *Journal of Marriage and Family, 66*(1), 220–235.

Charlton, R., Sheahan, K., Smith, G., & Campbell, I. (2001). Spousal bereavement: Implications for health. *Family Practice, 18,* 614–618.

Cicirelli, V. (1999). Personality and demographic factors in older adults' fear of death. *The Gerontologist, 39*(5), 569–579.

Cicirelli, V. (2002). *Older adults' views on death.* New York: Springer.

Clements, R. (1998). Intrinsic religious motivation and attitudes toward death among the elderly. *Current Psychology, 17*(2/3), 237–248.

Commons, D. L., Demick, J., & Goldberg, C. (1996). *Clinical approaches to adult development.* Norwood, NJ: Ablex.

Coppola, K. M., Bookwala, J., Ditto, P. H., Lockhart, L. K., Danks, J. H., & Smucker, W. D. (1999). Elderly adults' preferences for life-sustaining treatments: The role of impairment, prognosis, and pain. *Death Studies, 23,* 617–634.

Costello, J., & Kendrick, K. (2000). Grief and older people: The making or breaking of emotional bonds following partner loss in later life. *Journal of Advanced Nursing, 32*(6), 1374–1382.

Crystal, E. (n.d.). *Inuit Indians.* Retrieved June 23, 2007, from http://www.crystalinks.com/inuit.html

Davidson, K. (2001). Late life widowhood, selfishness and new partnership choices: A gendered perspective. *Ageing and Society, 21,* 297–317.

Davison, G. C., Neale, J. M., Blankstein, K. R., & Flett, G. L. (2002). *Abnormal psychology* (Canadian ed.). Toronto: John Wiley & Sons.

Decker, I. M., & Reed, P. G. (2005). Developmental and contextual correlates of elders' anticipated end-of-life treatment decisions. *Death Studies, 29,* 827–846.

Denton, F. T., Feaver, C. H., & Spencer, B. G. (2002). Alternative pasts, possible futures: A what if study of the effects of fertility on the Canadian population and labour force. *Canadian Public Policy, 28*(3), 443–459.

DePaola, S. J., Griffin, M., Young, J. R., & Neimeyer, R. A. (2003). Death anxiety and attitudes toward the elderly among older adults: The role of gender and ethnicity. *Death Studies, 27,* 335–354.

Ditto, P. H., Smucker, W. D., Danks, J. H., Jacobson, J. A., Houts, R. M., Fagerlin, A. et al. (2003). Stability of older adults' preferences for life-sustaining medical treatment. *Health Psychology, 22*(6), 605–615.

Erikson, E. H. (1963). *Childhood and society.* New York: Norton.

Fortner, B. V., & Neimeyer, R. A. (1999). Death anxiety in older adults: A quantitative review. *Death Studies, 23,* 387–411.

Fry, P. S. (1998). Spousal loss in later life: A 1-year follow-up of perceived changes in life meaning and psychosocial functioning following bereavement. *Journal of Personal & Interpersonal Loss, 3*(4), 369–391.

Fry, P. S. (2001). Predictors of health-related quality of life perspectives, self-esteem, and life satisfactions of older adults following spousal loss: An 18-month follow-up study of widows and widowers. *The Gerontologist, 41*(6), 787–798.

Hamilton, N. G. (2001). *JAMA right-to-die piece was a fake.* Retrieved August 12, 2006, from the Hospice Patients Alliance website: http://www.hospicepatients.org/jamaarticlewasfake.html

Laakkonen, M. L., Pitkala, K. H., & Strandberg, T. E. (2004). Terminally ill elderly patient's [sic] experiences, attitudes, and needs: A qualitative study. *Omega, 49*(2), 117–129.

Lalive d'Epinay, C. J., Cavalli, S., & Spini, D. (2003). The death of a loved one: Impact on health and relationships in very old age. *Omega, 47*(3), 265–284.

Lin, A. H. H. (2003). Factors related to attitudes toward death among American and Chinese older adults. *Omega, 47*(1), 3–23.

Lockhart, L. K., Bookwala, J., Fagerlin, A., Coppola, K. M., Ditto, P. H., Danks, J. H. et al. (2001). Older adults' attitudes toward death: Links to perceptions of health and concerns about end-of-life issues. *Omega, 43*(4), 331–347.

Maddux, J. E. (1999). Personal efficacy. In V. J. Derlega, B. A. Winstead, & W. H. Jones (Eds.), *Personality: Contemporary theory and research* (2nd ed.) (pp. 229–256). Belmont, CA: Wadsworth.

Malkinson, R., & Bar-Tur, L. (1999). The aging of grief in Israel: A perspective of bereaved parents. *Death Studies, 23*(5), 413–431.

Malkinson, R., & Bar-Tur, L. (2004–2005). Long term bereavement processes of older parents: The three phases of grief. *Omega, 50*(2), 103–129.

Moremen, R. D. (2004–2005). What is the meaning of life? Women's spirituality at the end of the life span. *Omega, 50*(4), 309–330.

Mutran, E. J., Danis, M., Bratton, K. A., Sudha, S., & Hanson, L. (1997). Attitudes of the critically ill toward prolonging life: The role of social support. *The Geronotologist, 37*(2), 192–199.

Quill, T., Norton, S., Shah, M., Lam, Y., Fridd, C., & Buckley, M. (2006). What is most important for you to achieve? An analysis of patient responses when receiving palliative care consultation. *Journal of Palliative Medicine, 9*(2), 382–388.

Reed, P. (1991). Self-transcendence and mental health in the oldest-old adults. *Nursing Research, 40*, 5–11.

Rein, A. J., Harshman, D. L., Frick, T., Phillips, J. M., Lewis, S., & Nolan, M. T. (1996). Advance directive decision making among medical inpatients. *Journal of Professional Nursing, 12*, 39–46.

Rosenbaum, J. N. (1991). Widowhood grief: A cultural perspective. *The Canadian Journal of Nursing Research, 23*(2), 61–76.

Rosenfeld, K. E., Wenger, N. S., & Kagawa-Singer, M. (2000). End-of-life decision-making: A qualitative study of elderly individuals. *Journal of General Internal Medicine, 15*, 620–625.

Shah, S. (2000). Five miles from tomorrow. *Journal of the American Medical Association, 284*, 1897–1898.

Sinnott, J. D. (1998). *The development of logic in adulthood: Postformal thought and its applications.* New York: Plenum.

Statistics Canada. (2004). *Annual demographic statistics, 2003.* Retrieved August 12, 2006, from http://www.statcan.ca

Straight Dope Science Advisory Board. (2004). *Did Eskimos put their elderly on ice floes to die?* Retrieved August 12, 2006, from http://www.straightdope.com/mailbag/meskimoicefloe.html

Stroebe, M., Stroebe, W., & Schut, H. (2001). Gender differences in adjustment to bereavement: An empirical and theoretical review. *Review of General Psychology, 5*(1), 62–83.

van Baarsen, B., van Duijn, M. A. J., Smit, J. H., Snijders, T. A. B., & Knipscheer, K. P. M. (2001–2002). Patterns of adjustment to partner loss in old age: The widowhood adaptation longitudinal study. *Omega, 44*(1), 5–36.

van der Heide, A., Deliens, L., Faisst, K., Nilstun, T., Norup, M., Paci, E. et al. (2003). End-of-life decision-making in six European countries: Descriptive study. *The Lancet, 361*, 345–350.

Vig, E. K., & Pearlman, R. A. (2003). Quality of life while dying: A qualitative study of terminally ill older men. *Journal of the American Geriatrics Society, 51*(11), 1595–1601.

Weiten, W., & Lloyd, M. A. (2003). *Psychology applied to modern life: Adjustment in the 21st century* (7th ed.). Toronto: Wadsworth.

Williams, B. R., Baker, P. S., & Allman, R. M. (2005). Non-spousal family loss among community-dwelling older adults. *Omega, 51*(2), 125–142.

Young, A. J., Ofori-Boateng, T., Rodriguez, K. L., & Plowman, J. L. (2003). Meaning and agency in discussing end-of-life care: A study of elderly veterans' values and interpretations. *Qualitative Health Research, 13*(8), 1039–1062.

CHAPTER 9

Aseltine, R. H., Jr., & DeMartino, R. (2004). An outcome evaluation of the SOS Suicide Prevention Program. *American Journal of Public Health, 94*(3), 446–451.

BC Partners for Mental Health and Addictions Information. (2006). *Suicide: Following the warning signs.* Retrieved June 23, 2007, from http://www.heretohelp.bc.ca/publications/factsheets/suicide.shtml

Beautrais, A. L., Horwood, L. J., & Fergusson, D. M. (2004). Knowledge and attitudes about suicide in 25-year-olds. *Australian and New Zealand Journal of Psychiatry, 38*, 260–265.

Brent, D., Perper, J., Allmen, C., Moritz, G., Wartella, M., & Zelenah, J. (1991). The presence and accessibility of firearms in the homes of adolescent suicides: A case control study. *Journal of the American Medical Association, 266*, 2989–2995.

Brent, D. A., & Mann, J. J. (2003). Familial factors in adolescent suicidal behavior. In R. A. King & A. Apter (Eds.), *Suicide in children and adolescents* (pp. 86–117). Cambridge, England: Cambridge University Press.

Burge, M., Goldblat, C., & Lester, D. (2002). Music preferences and suicidality: A comment on Stack. *Death Studies, 26*, 501–504.

Canetto, S. S., & Lester, D. (2002). Love and achievement motives in women's and men's suicide notes. *The Journal of Psychology, 136*(5), 573–576.

Chandler, M. J., & Lalonde, C. (1998). Cultural continuity as a hedge against suicide in Canada's First Nations. *Transcultural Psychiatry, 35*, 191–219.

Dahlen, E. R., & Canetto, S. S. (2002). The role of gender and suicide precipitant in attitudes toward nonfatal suicide behavior. *Death Studies, 26*, 99–116.

De Leo, D., Burgis, S., Bertolote, J. M., Kerkhof, A., & Bille-Brahe, U. (2004). Definitions of suicidal behaviour. In D. De Leo, U. Bille-Brahe, A. Kerkhof, & A. Schmidtke (Eds.), *Suicidal behaviour: Theories and research findings* (pp. 17–39). Göttengin, Germany: Hogrefe & Huber.

De Leo, D., & Spathonis, K. (2004). Suicide and suicidal behaviour in late-life. In D. De Leo, U. Bille-Brahe, A. Kerkhof, & A. Schmidtke (Eds.), *Suicidal behaviour: Theories and research findings* (pp. 253–286). Göttengin, Germany: Hogrefe & Huber.

Deloria, V., Jr. (1994). *God is red: A native view of religion.* Golden, CO: Fulcrum.

Deloria, V., Jr. (1999). *For this land: Writings on religion in America.* New York: Routledge.

DeSpelder, L. A., & Strickland, A. L. (2005). *The last dance: Encountering death and dying* (7th ed.). New York: McGraw-Hill.

Domino, G., & Groth, M. (1997). Attitudes toward suicide: German and U. S. nationals. *Omega, 35*, 309–319.

Domino, G., & Leenaars, A. A. (1989). Attitudes toward suicide: A comparison of Canadian and United States college students. *Suicide & Life-Threatening Behavior, 19*, 160–172.

Domino, G., & Leenaars, A. A. (1995). Attitudes toward suicide among English-speaking urban Canadians. *Death Studies, 19*, 489–500.

Durkheim, E. (1966). *Suicide: A study in sociology. Translated by J. A. Spalding & G. Simpson*, New York: The Free Press. (Original work published in 1897)

Gould, M. S., Shaffer, D., & Greenberg, T. (2003). The epidemiology of youth suicide. In R. A. King & A. Apter (Eds.), *Suicide in children and adolescents* (pp. 1–40). Cambridge, England: Cambridge University Press.

Gould, M. S., Wallenstein, S., & Davidson, L. (1989). Suicide clusters: A critical review. *Suicide and Life-Threatening Behaviors, 19*, 17–29.

Hayden, D. D., & Lauer, P. (2000). Prevalence of suicide programs in schools and roadblocks to implementation. *Suicide & Life-Threatening Behavior, 30*, 239–251.

Health Canada. (2006). *First Nations and Inuit health: Suicide prevention*. Retrieved July 10, 2007, from http://www.hc-sc.gc.ca/fnih-spni/promotion/suicide/index_e.html

Ho, T. P., Yip, P. S., Chiu, C. W. F., & Halliday, P. (1998). Suicide notes: What do they tell us? *Acta Psychiatrica Scandinavica, 98*, 467–473.

Hunter, E., & Harvey, D. (2002). Indigenous suicide in Australia, New Zealand, Canada and the United States. *Emergency Medicine, 14*, 14–23.

Jenner, J. A., & Niesling, J. (2000). The construction of SEDAS: A new suicide-attitude questionnaire. *Acta Psychiatrica Scandinavica, 102*, 139–146.

Jobes, D. A., Berman, A. L., O'Carroll, P. W., Eastgard, S., & Knickmeyer, S. (1996). The Kurt Cobain suicide crisis: Perspectives from research, public health, and the news media. *Suicide and Life-Threatening Behavior, 26*(3), 260–264.

Joiner, T. (2005). *Why people die by suicide*. Cambridge, MA: Harvard University Press.

Kellerman, A., Rivara, F., Somes, G., Reay, D., Francisco, J., & Banton, J. G. et al. (1992). Suicide in the home in relation to gun ownership. *New England Journal of Medicine, 327*, 146–147.

King, A. (1999). High school suicide postvention: Recommendations for an effective program. *American Journal of Health Studies, 15*(4), 217–222.

King, K. A. (2001). Developing a comprehensive school suicide prevention program. *Journal of School Health, 71*(4), 132–137.

Kirmayer, L. J., Brass, G. M., & Tait, C. L. (2000). The mental health of Aboriginal peoples: Transformations of identity and community. *Canadian Journal of Psychiatry, 45*(7), 607–616.

Kirmayer, L. J., Simpson, C., & Cargo, M. (2003). Healing traditions: Culture, community and mental health promotion with Canadian Aboriginal peoples. *Australasian Psychiatry, 11*, S15–S23.

Leenaars, A. A. (1992). Suicide notes from Canada and the United States. *Perceptual and Motor Skills, 74*, 278.

Leenaars, A. A., Cantor, C., Connolly, J., EchoHawk, M., Gailiene, D., He, Z. et al. (2000). Controlling the environment to prevent suicide: International perspectives. *Canadian Journal of Psychiatry, 45*, 639–644.

Leenaars, A. A., & Domino, G. (1993). A comparison of community attitudes towards suicide in Windsor and Los Angeles. *Canadian Journal of Behavioral Science, 25*, 253–266.

Leenaars, A. A., Fekete, S., Wenckstern, S., & Osvath, P. (1998). Suicide notes from Hungary and the United States. *Psychiatrica Hungarica, 13*, 146–159.

Leenaars, A. A., & Lester, D. (1997). The impact of gun control on suicide and homicide across the life span. *Canadian Journal of Behavioural Science, 29*, 1–6.

Leenaars, A. A., Moksony, F., Lester, D., & Wenckstern, S. (2003). The impact of gun control (Bill C-51) on suicide in Canada. *Death Studies, 27*, 103–124.

Leenaars, A. A., Yang, B., & Lester, D. (1993). The effect of domestic and economic stress on suicide rates in the United States and Canada. *Journal of Clinical Psychology, 49*(6), 918–921.

Leming, M. R., & Dickinson, G. E. (2002). *Understanding dying, death, and bereavement*. Toronto: Wadsworth.

Lester, D. (2001). *Suicide in American Indians*. New York: Nova Science.

Lester, D., & Leenaars, A. A. (1993). Suicide rates in Canada before and after tightening firearm control laws. *Psychological Reports, 72*, 787–790.

Lester, D., & Whipple, M. (1996). Music preference, depression, suicidal preoccupation, and personality. *Suicide & Life-Threatening Behavior, 26*, 68–70.

Linn, M., & Lester, D. (1997). Content differences in suicide notes by gender and age: Serendipitous findings. *Psychological Reports, 78*, 370.

McClelland, L., Reicher, S., & Booth, N. (2000). A last defence: The negotiation of blame within suicide notes. *Journal of Community and Applied Social Psychology, 10*, 225–240.

Minore, B., Boone, M., Katt, M., & Kinch, R. (1991). Looking in, looking out: Coping with adolescent suicide in the Cree and Ojibway communities of Northern Ontario. *The Canadian Journal of Native Studies, 9*(1), 1–24.

Mueller, M. A., & Waas, G. A. (2002). College students' perceptions of suicide: The role of empathy on attitudes, evaluation, and responsiveness. *Death Studies, 26*, 325–341.

Neeleman, J., Halpern, D., Leon, D., & Lewis, G. (1997). Tolerance of suicide, religion and suicide rates: An ecological and individual study in 19 Western countries. *Psychological Medicine, 27*, 1165–1171.

Norton, E. M., Durlak, J. A., & Richards, M. H. (1989). Peer knowledge of and reactions to adolescent suicide. *Journal of Youth and Adolescence, 18*, 427–437.

O'Connor, R. C., & Leenaars, A. A. (2004). A thematic comparison of suicide notes drawn from Northern Ireland and the United States. *Current Psychology: Developmental, Learning, Personality, Social, 22*(4), 339–347.

Overholser, J. C., Hemstreet, A. H., Spirito, A., & Vyse, S. (1989). Suicide awareness programs in the schools: Effects of gender and personal experience. *Journal of the American Academy of Child and Adolescent Psychiatry, 28*, 925–930.

Parker, L. D., Cantrell, C., & Demi, A. S. (1997). Older adults' attitudes toward suicide: Are there race and gender differences? *Death Studies, 21*, 289–298.

Pearsall, J., & Trumble, B. (Eds.). (1996). *Oxford English reference dictionary* (2nd ed.). Oxford, England: Oxford University Press.

Rando, T. A. (1993). *Treatment of complicated mourning*. Champaign, IL: Research Press.

Rogers, J. R., Gueulette, C. M., Abbey-Hines, J., Carney, J. V., & Werth, J. L. (2001). Rational suicide: An empirical investigation of counselor attitudes. *Journal of Counseling & Development, 79*, 365–372.

Royal Commission on Aboriginal People. (1995). *Choosing life: Special report on suicide among Aboriginal people*. Ottawa, ON: Canada Communication Group.

Rudestam, K. E., & Agnelli, P. (1987). The effect of the content of suicide notes on grief reactions. *Journal of Clinical Psychology, 43*(2), 211–218.

Slaib, E., & Maximous, J. (2002). Intimation of intent in elderly fatal self-harm: Do the elderly who leave suicide notes differ from those who do not? *International Journal of Psychiatry in Clinical Practice, 6*, 155–161.

Salib, E., Cawley, S., & Healy, R. (2002). The significance of suicide notes in the elderly. *Aging & Mental Health, 6*(2), 186–190.

Scheel, K. R., & Westefeld, J. S. (1999). Heavy metal music and adolescent suicidality. *Adolescence, 34*, 252–273.

Segal, D. L., Mincic, M. S., Coolidge, F. L., & O'Riley, A. (2004). Attitudes toward suicide and suicidal risk among younger and older persons. *Death Studies, 28*, 671–678.

Shiori, T., Nishimura, A., Akazawa, K., Abe, R., Nushida, H., Ueno, Y. et al. (2005). Incidence of note-leaving remains constant despite increasing suicide rates. *Psychiatry and Clinical Neurosciences, 59*, 226–228.

Smyth, C. L., & MacLachlan, M. (2004). The context of suicide: An examination of life circumstances thought to be understandable precursors to youth suicide. *Journal of Mental Health, 13*(1), 83–92.

Shneidman, E. (1985). *The definition of suicide*. New York: John Wiley & Sons.

Sorjonen, K. (2002). For whom is suicide accepted: The utility effect. *Omega, 45*(4), 349–359.

Sorjonen, K. (2002–2003). For whom is suicide accepted: The dependency effect. *Omega, 46*(2), 137–149.

Stack, S. (1996–1997). Does being a parent affect suicide ideology? *Omega, 34*, 71–80.

Stack, S. (1998). Heavy metal, religiosity, and suicide acceptability. *Suicide & Life-Threatening Behavior, 28*, 388–394.

Stack, S. (2000). Blues fans and suicide acceptability. *Death Studies, 24*, 223–231.

Stack, S. (2002). Opera subculture and suicide for honor. *Death Studies, 26*, 431–437.

Steffens, D., & Blazer, D. (1999). Suicide in the elderly. In D. Jacobs (Ed.), *The Harvard Medical School guide to assessment and intervention* (pp. 443–461). San Francisco: Jossey-Bass.

Stuart, C., Waalen, J. K., & Haelstromm, E. (2003). Many helping hearts: An evaluation of peer gatekeeper training in suicide risk assessment. *Death Studies, 27*, 321–333.

Wagner, B. M., & Zimmerman, J. H. (2006). Developmental influences on suicidality among adolescents: Cognitive, emotional, and neuroscience aspects. In T. E. Ellis (Ed.), *Cognition and suicide: Theory, research, and therapy* (pp. 287–308). Washington, DC: American Psychological Association.

Wastell, C. A., & Shaw, T. A. (1999). Trainee teachers' opinions about suicide. *British Journal of Guidance & Counselling, 27*(4), 555–565.

Webster, P. (2006, July 22). Canadian Aboriginal people's health and the Kelowna deal [Electronic version]. *Lancet, 368*(9532), 275–276.

Weir, E. (2001). Suicide: The hidden epidemic [Electronic version]. *Canadian Medical Association Journal, 165*(5), 634–636.

Westefeld, J. S., Range, L. M., Rogers, J. R., Maples, M. R., Bromley, J. L., & Alcorn, J. (2000). Suicide: An overview. *The Counseling Psychologist, 28*(4), 445–510.

Westefeld, J. S., Sikes, C., Ansley, T., & Yi, H-S. (2004). Attitudes toward rational suicide. *Journal of Loss and Trauma, 9*, 359–370.

World Health Organization. (2005). *Mental health*. Retrieved June 23, 2007, from http://www.who.int/mental_health

CHAPTER 10

Attig, T. (2004). Disenfranchised grief revisited: Discounting hope and love. *Omega, 49*(3), 197–215.

Bowlby, J. (1980–1981). *Attachment and loss: Loss, sadness, and depression* (Vol. 3). New York: Basic Books.

Bucholz, J. A. (2002). *Homicide survivors: Misunderstood grievers*. Amityville, NY: Baywood.

CBC News. (2006). *Steven Truscott: The search for justice*. Retrieved July 2, 2007, from http://www.cbc.ca/news/background/truscott/

Corr, C. A., Nabe, C. M., & Corr, D. M. (2006). *Death and dying, life and living* (5th ed.). Toronto: Thomson Nelson.

Davison, G. C., Neale, J. M., Blankstein, K. R., & Flett, G. L. (2002). *Abnormal psychology* (Canadian ed.). Toronto: John Wiley & Sons.

Doka, K. J. (2002). Introduction. In K. J. Doka (Ed.), *Disenfranchised grief: New directions, challenges, and strategies for practice* (pp. 5–22). Champaign, IL: Research Press.

Harper, T. (2006, November 21). O. J. book, Fox show cancelled. *Toronto Star*, p. A2.

Hatton, R. (2003). Homicide bereavement counseling: A survey of providers. *Death Studies, 27*, 427–448.

Lam, R. (2006, April 7). Your heart just wants to know something. *Toronto Star*, p. A12.

Matthews, L. T., & Marwit, S. J. (2004). Examining the assumptive world views of parents bereaved by accident, murder, and illness. *Omega, 48*(2), 115–136.

Murphy, S. A., Johnson, L. C., Chung, I-J., & Beaton, R. D. (2003). *Journal of Traumatic Stress, 16*(1), 17–25.

Murphy, S. A., Johnson, L. C., & Lohan, J. (2002). The aftermath of the violent death of a child: An integration of the assessment of parents' mental distress and PTSD during the first 5 years of bereavement. *Journal of Loss and Trauma, 7*, 203–222.

Murphy, S. A., Tapper, V. J., Johnson, L. C., & Lohan, J. (2003). Suicide ideation among parents bereaved by the violent deaths of their children. *Issues in Mental Health Nursing, 24*, 5–25.

Ott, C. H. (2002). The impact of complicated grief on mental and physical health at various points in the bereavement process. *Death Studies, 27*, 249–272.

Parkes, C. M. (1996). *Bereavement: Studies of grief in adult life* (3rd ed.). Philadelphia: Routledge.

Parents of Murdered Children. (1995). *Problems of survivors.* Retrieved July 2, 1007, from http://www.pomc.com/problems.cfm

Rando, T. A. (1993). *Treatment of complicated mourning.* Champaign, IL: Research Press.

Raphael, B. (1983). *The anatomy of bereavement.* New York: Basic Books.

Statistics Canada. (2006). *Homicide offences, number and rate, by province and territory* (CANSIM Table 253-0001). Retrieved July 2, 2007, from http://www40.statcan.ca/l01/cst01/legal12a

Thompson, M. P., Norris, F. H., & Ruback, R. B. (1998). Comparative distress levels of inner-city family members of homicide victims. *Journal of Traumatic Stress, 11*, 223–242.

Weiten, W., & Lloyd, M. A. (2003). *Psychology applied to modern life: Adjustment in the 21st century* (7th ed.). Toronto: Wadsworth.

Worden, J. W. (1991). *Grief counseling and grief therapy: A handbook for the mental health practitioner.* New York: Springer.

CHAPTER 11

Aubin, M., Vézina, L., Parent, R., Fillion, L., Allard, P., Bergeron, R. et al. (2006). Impact of an educational program on pain management in patients with cancer living at home. *Oncology Nursing Forum, 33*(6), 1183–1188.

Bennett, K. M., & Vidal-Hall, S. (2000). Narratives of death: A qualitative study of widowhood in later life. *Ageing and Society, 20*, 413–428.

Block, S. D. (2006). Psychological issues in end-of-life care. *Journal of Palliative Medicine, 9*(3), 751–772.

Brazil, K., Howell, D., Bedard, M., Krueger, P., & Heidebrecht, C. (2005). Preferences for place of care and place of death among informal caregivers of the terminally ill. *Palliative Medicine, 19*, 492–499.

Canadian Hospice Palliative Care Association. (2003). *Mission statement.* Retrieved August 14, 2006, from http://www.chpca.net/about_us/mission_statement.htm

Cohen, C. A., Colantonio, A., & Vernich, L. (2002). Positive aspects of caregiving: Rounding out the caregiver experience. *International Journal of Geriatric Psychiatry, 17*, 184–188.

Cronqvist, A., Theorell, T., Burns, T., & Lützén, K. (2004). Caring about–caring for: Moral obligations and work responsibilities in intensive care nursing. *Nursing Ethics, 11*(1), 63–76.

Decima Research Incorporated. (2002). *National profile of family caretakers in Canada—2002: Final report.* Retrieved July 1, 2007, from http://www.hc-sc.gc.ca/hcs-sss/alt_formats/hpb-dgps/pdf/pubs/2002-caregiv-interven/2002-caregiv-interven_e.pdf

Dorothy Ley Hospice Organization. (2006). *Hospice palliative care in Canada.* Retrieved August 14, 2006, from http://www.dlhospice.org/pages/m7/HospiceCareCanada.htm

Dumont, S., Turgeon, J., Allard, P., Gagnon, P., Charbonneau, C., & Vézina, L. (2006). Caring for a loved one with advanced cancer: Determinants of psychological distress in family caregivers. *Journal of Palliative Medicine, 9*(4), 912–921.

Evans, W. G., Cutson, T. M., Steinhauser, K. E., & Tulsky, J. A. (2006). Is there no place like home? Caregivers recall reasons for and experience upon transfer from home hospice to inpatient facilities. *Journal of Palliative Medicine, 9*(1), 100–110.

Ferrell, B. R. (2006). Understanding the moral distress of nurses witnessing medically futile care. *Oncology Nursing Forum, 33*(5), 922–930.

Fried, T. R., Bradley, E. H., O'Leary, J. R., & Byers, A. L. (2005). Unmet desire for caregiver-patient communication and increased caregiver burden. *Journal of the American Geriatric Society, 53*, 59–65.

Fried, T. R., van Doom, C., O'Leary, J. R., Tinetti, M. E., & Drickamer, M. A. (1999). Older persons' preferences for site of terminal care. *Annals of Internal Medicine, 131*, 109–112.

Given, B., Wyatt, G., Given, C., Sherwood, P., Gift, A., DeVoss, D. et al. (2004). Burden and depression among caregivers of patients with cancer at the end of life. *Oncology Nursing Forum, 31*, 1105–1117.

Grunfeld, E., Coyle, D., Whelan, T., Clinch, J., Reyno, L., Earle, C. C. et al. (2004). Family caregiver burden: Results of a longitudinal study of breast cancer patients and their principal caregivers. *Canadian Medical Association Journal, 170*(2), 1795–1801.

Hanratty, B., Hibbert, D., Mair, F., May, C., Ward, C., Corcoran, G. et al. (2006). Doctors' understanding of palliative care. *Palliative Medicine, 20*, 493–497.

Human Resources and Social Development Canada. (2007). *Compassionate care leave provisions in employment standards legislation in Canada.* Retrieved July 10, 2007, from http://www.hrsdc.gc.ca/en/lp/spila/clli/eslc/01Employment_Standards_Legislation_in_Canada.shtml

Himelstein, B. P. (2006). Palliative care for infants, children, adolescents, and their families. *Journal of Palliative Medicine, 9*(1), 163–181.

Kemp, C. (2005). Cultural issues in palliative care. *Seminars in Oncology Nursing, 21*(1), 44–52.

Masson, J. M. (2002). Non-professional perceptions of good death: A study of the views of hospice care patients and relatives of deceased hospice care patients. *Mortality, 7*(2), 191–209.

McMillan, S. C. (2005). Interventions to facilitate family caregiving at the end of life. *Journal of Palliative Medicine, 8*(Suppl. 1), S132–S139.

Mok, E., & Chiu, P. C. (2004). Nurse-patient relationships in palliative care. *Journal of Advanced Nursing, 48*(5), 475–483.

Morita, T., Miyashita, M., Kimura, R., Adachi, I., & Shima, Y. (2004). Emotional burden of nurses in palliative sedation therapy. *Palliative Medicine, 18,* 550–557.

Navaie-Waliser, M., Feldman, P. H., Gould, D. A., Levine, C., Kuerbis, A. N., & Donelan, K. (2002). When the caregiver needs care: The plight of vulnerable caregivers. *American Journal of Public Health, 92,* 409–413.

Payne, S., Langley-Evans, A., & Hillier, R. (1996). Perceptions of a good death: A comparative study of the views of hospice staff and patients. *Palliative Medicine, 10,* 307–312.

Pearlin, L. I., & Aneshensel, C. S. (1994). Caregiving: The unexpected career. *Social Justice Research, 7,* 373–390.

Plonk, W. M., & Arnold, R. M. (2005). Terminal care: The last weeks of life. *Journal of Palliative Medicine, 8*(5), 1042–1054.

Prokos, A. H., & Keene, J. R. (2005). The long-term effects of spousal care giving on survivors' well-being in widowhood. *Social Science Quarterly, 86*(3), 664–682.

Robinson-Whelan, S., Yuri Tada, R. C., MacCallum, L. M., & Kicolt-Glaser, J. K. (2001). Long-term caregiving: What happens when it ends? *Journal of Abnormal Psychology, 110,* 573–584.

Rushton, C. H., Reder, E., Hall, B., Comello, K., Sellers, D. E., & Hutton, N. (2006). Interdisciplinary interventions to improve pediatric palliative care and reduce health care professional suffering. *Journal of Palliative Medicine, 9*(4), 922–933.

Saunders, C. (1995). Preface. In D. Doyle, W. C. Hanks, & N. Macdonald (Eds.), *Oxford textbook of palliative medicine.* Oxford, England: Oxford University Press.

Service Canada. (2007). *Employment insurance (EI) compassionate care benefits.* Retrieved July 10, 2007, from http://www.hrsdc.gc.ca/en/ei/types/compassionate_care.shtml

Solomon, M. Z., O'Donnell, L., Guilfoy, V., Wolf, S. M., Nolan, K., Jackson, R. et al. (1993). Decisions near the end of life: Professional views on life-sustaining treatments. *American Journal of Public Health, 83,* 1–14.

Stajduhar, K. I., & Davies, B. (2005). Variations in and factors influencing family members' decisions for palliative home care. *Palliative Medicine, 19,* 21–32.

Steinhauser, K. E., Clipp, E. C., McNeilly, M., Christakis, N. A., McIntyre, L. M., & Tulsky, J. A. (2000). In search of a good death: Observations of patients, families, and providers. *Annals of Internal Medicine, 132*(10), 825–832.

Sulmasy, D. P., & Rahn, M. (2001). I was sick and you came to visit me: Time spent at the bedsides of seriously ill patients with poor prognoses. *American Journal of Medicine, 111,* 385–389.

Sulmasy, D. P., & Sood, J. R. (2003). Factors associated with time spent at the bedsides of seriously ill patients with poor prognoses. *Medical Care, 41,* 458–466.

Teno, J. M., Clarridge, B. R., Casey, V., Welch, L. C., Wetle, L. C., Shield, R. et al. (2004). Family perspectives on end-of-life care at the last place of care. *Journal of the American Medical Association, 291,* 88–93.

Vachon, M. L. S. (1998). Psychosocial needs of patients and families. *Journal of Palliative Care, 14,* 49–56.

Waldrop, D. P., Kramer, B. J., Skretny, J. A., Milch, R. A., & Finn, W. (2005). Final transitions: Family caregiving at the end of life. *Journal of Palliative Medicine, 8*(3), 623–638.

Wilson, K. G., Curran, D., & McPherson, C. J. (2005). A burden to others: A common source of distress for the terminally ill. *Cognitive Behaviour Therapy, 34*(2), 115–123.

World Health Organization. (2006). WHO definition of palliative care. Retrieved August 14, 2006, from http://www.who.int/cancer/palliative/definition/en/

CHAPTER 12

Busch, T., & Kimble, C. S. (2001). Grieving children: Are we meeting the challenge? *Pediatric Nursing, 27*(4), 414–418.

Buxbaum, L., & Brant, J. M. (2001). When a parent dies from cancer. *Clinical Journal of Oncology Nursing, 5*(4), 1–6.

Charlton, R., Sheahan, K., Smith, G., & Campbell, I. (2001). Spousal bereavement: Implications for health. *Family Practice, 18,* 614–618.

Christ, G. H., Siegel, K., & Christ, A. E. (2002). Adolescent grief. *Journal of the American Medical Association, 288*(10), 1269–1278.

Curtis, K., & Newman, T. (2001). Do community-based support services benefit bereaved children? A review of empirical evidence. *Child Care, Health and Development, 27*(6), 487–495.

Davison, G. C., Neale, J. M., Blankstein, K. R., & Flett, G. L. (2002). *Abnormal psychology* (Canadian ed.). Toronto: John Wiley & Sons.

Ditto, P. H., Smucker, W. D., Danks, J. H., Jacobson, J. A., Houts, R. M., Fagerlin, A. et al. (2003). Stability of older adults' preferences for life-sustaining medical treatment. *Health Psychology, 22*(6), 605–615.

Faulkner, K. W. (1997). Talking about death with a dying child. *American Journal of Nursing, 97*(6), 64–69.

Fry, P. S. (2001). Predictors of health-related quality of life perspectives, self-esteem, and life satisfactions of older adults following spousal loss: An 18-month follow-up study of widows and widowers. *The Gerontologist, 41*(6), 787–798.

Hames, C. C. (2003). Helping infants and toddlers when a family member dies. *Journal of Hospice and Palliative Nursing, 5*(2), 103–110.

Ishibashi, A. (2001). The needs of children and adolescents with cancer for information and social support. *Cancer Nursing, 24*, 61–67.

Janowiak, S. M., Mei-Tal, R., & Drapkin, R. G. (1995). Living with loss: A group for bereaved college students. *Death Studies, 19*, 55–63.

Jordan, J. R., & Neimeyer, R. A. (2003). Does grief counseling work? *Death Studies, 27*, 765–786.

Kelner, M. (1995). Activists and delegators: Elderly patients' perspectives about control at the end of life. *Social Science Medicine, 41*, 537–545.

Kreicbergs, U., Valdimarsdóttir, U., Onelöv, E., Henter, J-I., & Steineck, G. (2004). Talking about death with children who have severe malignant disease. *The New England Journal of Medicine, 351*(12), 1175–1186.

Lalive d'Epinay, C. J., Cavalli, S., & Spini, D. (2003). The death of a loved one: Impact on health and relationships in very old age. *Omega, 47*(3), 265–284.

Masera, G., Spinetta, J. J., Jankovic, M., Ablin, A. R., D'Angio, G. J., Van Dongen-Melman, J. et al. (1999). Guidelines for assistance to terminally ill children with cancer: A report of the SIOP working committee on psychosocial issues in pediatric oncology. *Medical and Pediatric Oncology, 32*, 44–48.

Morgan, E., & Murphy, S. B. (2000). Editorial: Care of children who are dying of cancer. *The New England Journal of Medicine, 342*(5), 347–348.

Nitsche, R., Meyer, W. H., Sexauer, C. L., Parkhurst, J. B., Foster, P., & Huszti, H. (2000). Care of terminally ill children with cancer. *Medical and Pediatric Oncology, 34*, 268–270.

O'Brien, J. M., & Goodenow, C. (1991). Adolescents' reactions to the death of a peer. *Adolescence, 26*(102), 431–440.

Quill, T., Norton, S., Shah, M., Lam, Y., Fridd, C., & Buckley, M. (2006). What is most important for you to achieve? An analysis of patient responses when receiving palliative care consultation. *Journal of Palliative Medicine, 9*(2), 382–388.

Rask, K., Kaunonen, M., & Paunonen-Ilmonen, M. (2002). Adolescent coping with grief after the death of a loved one. *International Journal of Nursing Practice, 8*, 137–142.

Sahler, O. J. Z., Frager, G., Levetown, M., Cohn, F. G., & Lipson, M. A. (2000). Medical education about end-of-life care in the pediatric setting: Principles, challenges, and opportunities. *Pediatrics, 105*(3), 575–584.

Schoen, A. A., Burgoyne, M., & Schoen, S. F. (2004). Are the developmental needs of children in America adequately addressed during the grieving process? *Journal of Instructional Psychology, 31*(2), 143–148.

Tonkins, S. A. M., & Lambert, M. J. (1996). A treatment outcome study of bereavement groups for children. *Child and Adolescent Social Work Journal, 13*(1), 3–21.

Tremblay, G. C., & Israel, A. C. (1998). Children's adjustment to parental death. *Clinical Psychology: Science and Practice, 5*(4), 424–438.

Werth, J. L., Gordon, J. R., & Johnson, R. R. (2002). Psychosocial issues near the end of life. *Aging & Mental Health, 6*(4), 402–412.

WidowNet. (2006). *WidowNet top ten or whatever.* Retrieved August 14, 2006, from http://www.widownet.org/faqs/topten.shtml

Williams, B. R., Baker, P. S., & Allman, R. M. (2005). Nonspousal family loss among community-dwelling older adults. *Omega, 51*(2), 125–142.

Willis, C. A. (2002). The grieving process in children: Strategies for understanding, educating, and reconciling children's perceptions of death. *Early Childhood Education Journal, 29*(4), 221–226.

Worden, J. W. (1996). *Children and grief: When a parent dies.* New York: Guilford Press.

Wortman, C. B., & Silver, R. C. (2001). The myths of coping with loss revisited. In M. S. Stroebe, R. O. Hansson, W. Stroebe, & H. Schut (Eds.), *Handbook of bereavement research* (pp. 405–429). Washington, DC: American Psychological Association.

CHAPTER 13

Bosticco, C., & Thompson, T. L. (2005). Narratives and story telling in coping with grief and bereavement. *Omega, 51*(1), 1–16.

Bowman, T. (1999). Shattered dreams, resiliency, and hope: Restorying after loss. *Journal of Personal and Interpersonal Loss, 4*, 179–192.

Davis, C. G., Nolen-Hoeksema, S., & Larson, J. (1998). Making sense of loss and benefiting from the experience: Two construals of meaning. *Journal of Personality and Social Psychology, 75*, 561–574.

Davis, C. G., Wortman, C. B., Lehman, D. R., & Silver, R. C. (2000). Searching for meaning: Are clinical assumptions correct? *Death Studies, 24*, 497–540.

DeSpelder, L. A., & Strickland, A. L. (2005). *The last dance* (7th ed.). New York: McGraw-Hill.

Downs, B. (1993). Lessons in loss and grief. *Communication Education, 42*, 300–303.

Fraley, R. C., & Shaver, P. R. (1999). Loss and bereavement: Bowlby's theory and recent controversies concerning grief work and the nature of detachment. In J. Cassidy & P. R. Shaver (Eds.), *Handbook of attachment theory and research: Theory, research, and clinical applications* (pp. 735–759). New York: Guilford.

Frankl, V. E. (1984). *Man's search for meaning.* New York: Washington Square Press.

Frantz, T. T., Farrell, M. M., & Trolley, B. C. (2000). Positive outcomes of losing a loved one. In R. A. Neimeyer (Ed.), *Meaning reconstruction and the experience of loss* (pp. 191–209). Washington, DC: American Psychological Association.

Hadad, M., & Reed, M. J. (2007). *The post-secondary learning experience.* Toronto: Thomson Nelson.

Klass, D., & Walter, T. (2001). Processes of grieving: How bonds are continued. In M. S. Stroebe, R. O. Hansson, W. Stroebe, & H. Schut (Eds.), *Handbook of bereavement research: Consequences, coping and care* (pp. 431–448). Washington DC: American Psychological Association.

Knippen, J. T., & Green, T. B. (1994). How the manager can use active listening. *Public Personnel Management, 23*(2), 357–359.

McIntosh, D. N., Silver, R. C., & Wortman, C. B. (1993). Religion's role in trauma: A systematic review of the literature. *Journal of Traumatic Stress, 11*, 697–710.

Nadeau, J. W. (2001). Meaning-making in family bereavement: A family systems approach. In M. S. Stroebe, R. O. Hansson, W. Stroebe, & H. Schut (Eds.), *Handbook of bereavement research: Consequences, coping and care* (pp. 329–348). Washington, DC: American Psychological Association.

Neimeyer, R. A. (2000). Searching for the meaning of meaning: Grief therapy and the process of reconstruction. *Death Studies, 24*, 541–557.

Neimeyer, R. A. (2002). Traumatic loss and the reconstruction of meaning. *Journal of Palliative Medicine, 5*(6), 935–942.

Neimeyer, R. A., & Levitt, H. (2001). Coping and coherence: A narrative perspective on resilience. In E. Snyder (Ed.), *Coping with stress* (pp. 47–67). New York: Oxford Press.

Neimeyer, R. A., Prigerson, H. G., & Davies, B. (2002). Mourning and meaning. *American Behavioral Scientist, 46*(2), 235–251.

O'Connor, M. (2002–2003). Making meaning of life events: Theory, evidence, and research directions for an alternative model. *Omega, 46*(1), 51–75.

Schafer, W. (1996). *Stress management for wellness* (3rd ed.). Toronto: Harcourt Brace.

Schut, H. A. W., DeKeijser, J., Vanden Bout, J., & Dijkhuis, J. H. (1991). Post-traumatic stress symptoms in the first years of conjugal bereavement. *Anxiety Research, 4*, 225–234.

Worden, J. W. (2002). *Grief counseling and grief therapy: A handbook for the mental health practitioner* (3rd ed.). New York: Springer.

CHAPTER 14

Ad Hoc Committee of the Harvard Medical School. (1968). A definition of irreversible coma: Report of the Ad Hoc Committee of the Harvard Medical School to examine the definition of brain-death. *Journal of the American Medical Association, 205*, 337–340.

Canadian Press. (2005, August 28). *Dutch government intends to endorse new guidelines on child euthanasia.* Retrieved August 14, 2006, from the CBC News website: http://www.cbc.ca/cp/world/050929/w092978.html

Capron, A. M. (2001). Brain death – Well settled yet unresolved. *New England Journal of Medicine, 344*, 1244–1246.

Carlson, B., Simopolous, N., Goy, E. R., Jackson, A., & Ganzini, L. (2005). Oregon hospice chaplains' experiences with patients requesting physician-assisted suicide. *Journal of Palliative Medicine, 8*(6), 1160–1166.

CBC News. (2004, November 4). *Broader definition of death debated to boost organ donors.* Retrieved June 14, 2007, from http://www.cbc.ca/health/story/2004/11/22/organ-donors041122.html

CBS News. (2006, December 13). Jack Kevorkian granted parole. Retrieved July 17, 2007, from http://www.cbsnews.com/stories/2006/12/13/national/main2257569.shtml

Cohen, L., Ganzini, L., Mitchell, C., Arons, S., Goy, E., & Cleary, J. (2005). Accusations of murder and euthanasia in end-of-life care. *Journal of Palliative Medicine, 8*(6), 1096–1104.

Cole, D. J. (1992). The reversibility of death. *Journal of Medical Ethics, 21*(5), 26–30.

Dagi, T. F., & Kaufman, R. (2001). Clarifying the discussion on brain death. *Journal of Medicine and Philosophy, 26*(5), 503–525.

Fox, R. C. (1993). An ignoble form of cannibalism: Reflections on the Pittsburgh Protocol for procuring organs from non-heart-beating cadavers. *Kennedy Institute of Ethics Journal, 3*, 231–239.

Grosswald, B. (2002). The right to physician-assisted suicide on demand. *Law and Policy, 24*(2), 175–198.

Guest, C. B., & Devitt, J. H. (2000). Non-heart-beating organ donation. *Canadian Medical Association Journal, 162*(2), 194.

Halevy, A. (2001). Beyond brain death? *The Journal of Medicine and Philosophy, 26*, 493–501.

Hanks, G. (2005). The proposed Assisted Dying Bill in the UK. *Palliative Medicine, 19*, 441.

Hershenov, D. (2003). The problematic role of irreversibility in the definition of death. *Bioethics, 17*(1), 89–100.

Involuntary euthanasia is out of control in Holland. (1999, February 16). *The Times* (UK).

Keep, P. (1998). Dead reckoning. *Today's Anaesthetist, 13*(5), 7–11.

Knoll, G. A., & Mahoney, J. E. (2003). Non-heart-beating organ donation in Canada: Time to proceed? *Canadian Medical Association Journal, 169*(4), 302–303.

Law Reform Commission of Canada. (1981, March). *Criteria for the determination of death.* Ottawa, ON: Author.

Leming, M. R., & Dickinson, G. E. (2002). *Understanding dying, death, and bereavement* (5th ed.). Toronto: Wadsworth.

Lemmens, T., & Dickens, B. (2001). Canadian law on euthanasia: Contrasts and comparisons. *European Journal of Health Law, 8*, 135–155.

Lizza, J. P. (2005). Potentiality, irreversibility, and death. *Journal of Medicine and Philosophy, 30*, 45–64.

Lustig, B. A. (2001). Theoretical and clinical concerns about brain death: The debate continues. *Journal of Medicine and Philosophy, 26*(5), 447–455.

Mathes, M. (2005). Terri Schiavo and end-of-life decisions: Can law help us out? *MEDSURG Nursing, 14*(3), 200–202.

Meisel, A., & Cerminara, K. L. (2004). *The right to die* (3rd ed.). New York: Aspen.

Melvin, C. S., & Heater, B. S. (2001). Organ donation: Moral imperative or outrage? *Nursing Forum, 36*(4), 5–14.

Mendelson, D., & Jost, T. S. (2003). A comparative study of the law of palliative care and end-of-life treatment. *Journal of Law, Medicine & Ethics, 31*, 130–143.

Palazzani, L. (2004). Advance directives and living wills. *NeuroRehabilitation, 19*, 305–313.

Perry, J. E., Churchill, L. R., & Kirshner, H. S. (2005). The Terri Schiavo case: Legal, ethical, and medical perspectives. *Annals of Internal Medicine, 143*(10), 744–748.

Rao, M. J. (2005). Legal issues relating to the limitation of life support – a review of the international legal position. *Indian Journal of Critical Care Medicine, 9*(2), 115–119.

Roscoe, L. A., Malphurs, J. E., Dragovic, L. K., & Cohen, D. (2001). A comparison of characteristics of Kevorkian euthanasia cases and physician-assisted suicides in Oregon. *The Gerontologist, 41*(4), 439–446.

Rurup, M. L., Onwuteaka-Philipsen, B. D., & van der Wal, G. (2005). A suicide pill for older people: Attitudes of physicians, the general population, and relatives of patients who died after euthanasia or physician-assisted suicide in the Netherlands. *Death Studies, 29*, 519–534.

Seguin, M. (1994). *A gentle death.* Toronto: Key Porter Books.

Sheldon, T. (2002). World Medical Association isolates Netherlands on euthanasia. *British Medical Journal, 325*, 675.

Shewmon, D. A. (1997). Recovery from brain death: A neurologist's apologia. *Linacre Quarterly, 64*(1), 31–96.

Siminoff, L. A., Burant, C., & Youngner, S. J. (2004). Death and organ procurement: Public beliefs and attitudes. *Social Science & Medicine, 59*, 2325–2334.

Smith, W. J. (2006, March 27). Killing babies, compassionately: The Netherlands follows in Germany's footsteps. *The Daily Standard.* Retrieved August 14, 2006, from http://www.weeklystandard.com/Content/Public/Articles/000/000/012/003dncoj.asp

Snelling, P. C. (2004). Consequences count: Against absolutism at the end of life. *Journal of Advanced Nursing, 46*(4), 350–357.

Sundin-Huard, D., & Fahy, K. (2004). The problems with the validity of the diagnosis of brain death. *Nursing in Critical Care, 9*(2), 64–71.

ten Have, H. (2001). Euthanasia: Moral paradoxes. *Palliative Medicine, 15*, 505–511.

Trillium Gift of Life Network. (2007). Ontario's tissue and organ donation agency. Retrieved June 14, 2007, from http://www.giftoflife.on.ca

van der Heide, A., Deliens, L., Faisst, K., Nilstun, T., Norup, M., Paci, E. et al. (2003). End-of-life decision-making in six European countries: Descriptive study. *The Lancet, 361*, 345–350.

Van Norman, G. A. (1999). A matter of life and death: What every anesthesiologist should know about the medical, legal, and ethical aspects of declaring brain death. *Anesthesiology, 91*, 275–287.

Veatch, R. M. (2004). Abandon the dead donor rule or change the definition of death? *Kennedy Institute of Ethics Journal, 14*(3), 261–276.

Wijdicks, E. F. M. (2002). Brain death worldwide: Accepted fact but no global consensus in diagnostic criteria. *Neurology, 58*, 20–25.

Young, P. J., & Matta, B. F. (2000). Anaesthesia for organ donation in the brainstem dead – Why bother? *Anaesthesia, 55*(2), 105.

Youngner, S. J. (2003). Some must die. *Zygon, 38*(3), 705–724.

CHAPTER 15

Breslin, J. M., MacRae, S. K., Bell, J., & Singer, P. A. (2005). Top 10 health care ethics challenges facing the public: Views of Toronto bioethicists. *BMC Medical Ethics 6*(5). Retrieved August 14, 2006, from http://www.biomedcentral.com/1472–6939/6/5

Canadian Hospice Palliative Care Association. (2006, April). *Strategic plan and process report 2006–2009.* Retrieved August 14, 2006, from http://www.chpca.net

Foley, K. M. (2005, November-December). The past and future of palliative care. *Hastings Center Report Special Report 35*(6), S42-S46.

Gillick, M. R. (2005). Rethinking the central dogma of palliative care. *Journal of Palliative Medicine, 8*(5), 909–913.

Hwang, S. W. (2000). Mortality among men using homeless shelters in Toronto, Ontario. *Journal of the American Medical Association, 283*(16), 2152–2157.

Living Lessons. (2006). *Patient bill of rights.* Retrieved August 14, 2006, from http://www.living-lessons.org/cando/patient.asp

Podymow, T., Turnbull, J., & Coyle, D. (2006). Shelter-based palliative care for the homeless terminally ill. *Palliative Medicine, 20*, 81–86.

SUBJECT INDEX

The page locators for definitions of key terms are indicated by boldface.

A

Aboriginal Healing & Wellness Strategy (AHWS), 207
abortion
    elective, 107
    grief, 107–108
    mothers and reactions, 107–108
absent mourning, **155**
acceptance, stage of dying, 62
active listening, **211**, 212
    clarification, 212
    paraphrasing, 212
    summarizing, 212
    and tone of voice, 212
adolescent(s)
    and affective denial, 86
    bereaved-, helping, 184–86
    bereavement, developmental issues and, 185
    death, denial and risky behaviour, 87
    and grieving process, behaviour of, 86–87
    long-term parental loss reactions, 92
    sibling death, and social relationships, 90–91
    suicide prevention and, 143, 144–45
    terminally ill, 96
    view of death, 83
    and withdrawal re sibling death, 90–91
adult(s), *see also* bereaved adults
    bereaved, helping, 186–90
    literature, death attitudes and, 18
    psychosocial needs of, 193–95
adults, terminally ill, 109–112
    cultural factors, 195
    dying at home, 165–71
    helping, 191–92, 193–95
    psychological needs, 193–95
    significant others, 194
    treatment, 109–110
affective denial, **86**–87
afterlife
    and Bahá'í faith, 34–35
    belief in, 3
    Buddhism and, 33
    Christianity and, 27–28
    Day of Judgement, and Christians, 28
    development and children's death concept of, 84
    Hindu views of, 30–31
    Islam and, 29–30
    Gehanna (sheol) and, 27
    Judaism and, 27
    Messianic age and, 27
    Native peoples and, 36

    Nirvana, 33
    Roman Catholic *see* Christianity
Algonquin People of the Great Lakes
    end-of-life ritual, 52
    Land of Souls, 52
altruistic suicide, **134**
anger
    bereavement, mourners and suicide, 152–54
    children and bereavement/grief, 85
    media and bereavement, 153
    parental, re child's death, 100
Anglicanism, 36
anomic suicide, **135**
anxiety
    death, **14**
    death and seniors, 119
    separation, **86**
Ariès history of Western culture's view of death, 3–6
    death of the other, 6
    death of the self, 4–5
    invisible death, 5–6
    public attitudes re death, 19
    remote and imminent death, 5
    tame death, 5
arts *see also* literature
    and death attitudes, 13–16
    literature and, re death, 17–18
    music styles and death, 18
assumptive world, **152**
attachment, 63
attitude, **14**
attitude(s), about death (death attitudes)
    Canadian, 14
    catharsis, and horror, 20–21
    college students and media and, 20
    contemporary, psychology and media, 21
    and cultural background, 16–17
    and Disney films, 17
    and entertainment media, 19
    euphemisms, 17
    family and, 14
    language and, 17
    literature and arts and, 17–18
    media and, 18–21
    peers and, 16
    public, and media influence, 20
    school policies and studies and, 16
    sources of, 15–18
    televised trials and, 18–19
    workplace grief and, 21–23

B

Bahá'í
  basic beliefs, 34
  Body preparation, 51
  clergy, 34
  end-of-life ritual, 51–52
  mourning, 52
  Prayer of the Dead, 51
  social principles, 35
bardos
  and Buddhism after-life views, **33**
belief systems (religions)
  children and death concept and, 84
  Christianity, 27
  Hinduism, 30–31
  Islam, 29
  Judaism, 26
  Native Peoples, 35–36
  Sikhism, 33–34
bereaved
  adolescents, helping, 184–86
  adults, helping, 186–90
  assisting/helping, 182–90
  children, explaining death to, 183
  infants/toddlers, helping, 182
  older children, helping, 182–84
  society and helping, 196
bereaved adult(s)
  cautions re helping, 187
  cultural sensitivity, and helping, 189, 190
  guidelines re helping, 186–87
  maintaining contact with, 188
  medical personnel and helping, 188–89
  reminiscence, 187
  seniors, helping, 188
bereavement, *see also* grief
  in adolescence, 86–89, 184–86
  assumptive world and homicide, 152
  and bond with deceased, 65
  Bowlby attachment model of, 63–64
  and catharsis, and storytelling, 206
  children, *see* bereaved children
  cultural sensitivity and helping adults, 190
  and cultures, 37–39
  defined, **59**
  employees/employers and, 21, 22
  and employment, 21–23
  and funeral's effectiveness, 52–54
  and gender, on child's death, 101
  helping adults and, 186–90
  helping children/adolescents, 182–86
  helping senior widows/widowers, 188
  and homicide, 151–54, 164–65
  Islamic mourning ritual and, 49
  Japanese shrine custom, 63
  Judaism believers and, 27
  Klass's model of continuing bonds of, 64–65

and lack of meaning, 209–210
  leave, 21
  and loss, **59**, 65
  meaning and, *see* meaning
  media, victim, issues and, 153–54
  mourners and homicide, 152–54
  mourner's trauma, 68
  and Native Peoples, 52
  parental reactions, child's death and, 100–101
  Parke's phase model of, 63
  psychological illness and children, 85
  psychological models/theories of, 61–76
  public attitudes re, and media, 20
  Rando's six R's model, 70–73
  Sander's integrative phase model of, 65–66
  among seniors, *see* seniors
  separation, and attachment theory, 64
  sibling death, and parental coping, 90
  Sikh end-of life ritual and, 51
  society and, and reality of death, 45–46
  storytelling, catharsis and meaning, 205, 206
  and stress in, 63
  summary of models of, 76
  task theories of, 76
  re unnecessary death, 152–54
  and withdrawal, 66
  Worden's task model of, 68–69
  workplace and, 21–23
Bhagavad Ghita, 30
Bowlby's attachment model of bereavement, 63–64, 76
  defensive exclusion, 63–64
  as a stage/phase theory, 76
Brahman, 30
brain death, 218, 219
  dead donor rule, **220**
  and organ donation, 219–20
Buddha, life of, 31, 32, 33
  and Siddhartha, 32
Buddhism
  and bardos (stages of) after-life, 33
  beliefs and death views, 31–33
  Four Noble Truths, 31–32
Buddhism end-of-life rituals, 49–51
  and merit transference, 51
  sutras, 50

C

Canada, cultural diversity and death views, 37
Canada Labour Code
  bereavement leave and employees, 21
Caregivers, families as
  home care, 165–68, 170
  reprieve time, 171
  stress, 172–74
Child Bereavement Study, 85
childhood
  early views of death, 82

death *see also* dying (*Continued*)
    euphemisms for, 17
    the "good death, " 168
    Hispanics and grief expression re, 37
    historical portrayal, 2–4
    and imagery and children, 17
    Inuit views, 36
    irreversibility concept, 217
    Judaism and, 26, 27
    legal definition, 218
    "meaning" of, 206–208, 209
    mercy killing *see* euthanasia
    movies and graphic portrayal of, 19
    native groups and beliefs re, 37
    organ donation and, 219–20
    post treatment of terminal illness, 110
    pre-birth-, *see* abortion; miscarriage; stillbirth
    religion and meaning of, 26–34, 210–11
    and senior adults, 117–128
    society and death observance days, 208
    of a spouse/life partner, 102–104
    sudden, 158–59
    terminally ill adult, 109–112
    as a transition, 45
    traumatic-, 151
    of a twin, and sibling reaction, 90
    unanticipated death *see infra* sudden death
    unnecessary-, and bereavement/grief, 152–54
death anxiety, **14**
death myths
    Adam and Eve, 2
    banana tree myth and, 2
    Frazer's classification, 2
    and Halloween, and origins, 4
    Hindu beliefs and, 2
    serpent myth re, 2
death of a parent, consequences, 104–106
death, portrayal of
    afterlife, 3
    ancient Greek view, 3
    ancient Israeli view, 3
    Egyptian belief systems, 3
    first-century Christianity, 3
    Gilgamesh, Babylonian epic of, 2–3
    and Homer and *The Odyssey*, 3
    Israelite underworld(Sheol) belief, 3
    and Phillipe Ariès' classification, 3–6
    and Plato and *The Republic*, 3
death practices, and cultures, 37
defensive exclusion, **63**
delayed mourning, **155–56**
    and lack of social support, 156
depression
    dying, stage of, 62
    and home care, 171
    and miscarriage, 108
    and Parke's bereavement model, 63
    seniors and, 117
    seniors' bereavement and, 127–28

disenfranchised grief, **159–61**
    bereaved person's characteristics, 160
    death conditions and, 160
    grieving style and, 160
    relationships and, 159–60
distorted mourning, **156–57**
    anger and grief response, 156–57
    and hostility, 157
    and victim-mourner relationship, 157
dying *see also* death; end-of-life rituals
    acceptance stage, 62
    anger stage, 61
    bargaining stage, 61–62
    Bowlby attachment model re bereavement, 63–64
    burial and end-of-life rituals, 45
    burying (funeral) practices, 38
    and death at home, 165–71
    decision making, 173–74
    denial and isolation stage, 61
    depression stage, 62
    dying person and, 177
    family acceptance stage, 62
    family and caregiver stress, 172–74
    family and homecare, 166–68, 170
    and home care, 170–71
    home care to institutional care, 171–72
    hospitals and nursing homes and, 164
    imminent death and institutional care, 171
    institutional care, reasons for, 171–72
    Kübler-Ross stages model, 61–63
    nurses and end-of-life stress/issues, 175, 176
    and palliative care, 167
    -process, and seniors, 121–23
    types of home care decisions, 168, 170
dying child, *see* children, terminally ill
dying practices *see* end-of-life rituals

E

education, *see also* thanatology
    in death, dying and bereavement, review, 8–9
ego integrity, 118
    employee leave, 173
end-of-life care, 164–77
    and the dying person, 177
    home care, 165–71
    hospices, 164–65
    institutional care, 171–72
    personnel, 174–77
    seniors' needs and wishes, 119–23
    and support groups, 176
end-of-life issues
    advance directives, **221–22**
    definition of death, 216–19
    ethics and, 216–28
    euthanasia, **222–25**
    law and, 218–19, 220–21, 222, 224–25, 226–28
    mercy killing *see* euthanasia
    organ donation, 219–221

passive suicide, **132**

peers, and death attitudes, 16

physician-assisted suicide, 225–28
    Dutch experience re, 227
    Jack Kevorkian case and, 227
    Sue Rodriguez case, 226, 227

Poe, Edgar Allan, and death theme literature, 5

post-traumatic stress disorder (PTSD), **151**

postvention, **143–44**

potlatch, 52

press, and Shneidman cubic model of suicide, **135**

pre-funeral(s), 46
    "seizenso" in Japan, **50**

pregnancy, miscarriage and grief, 109

Protestant churches, afterlife views, 28

psychache, **135**

psychological illness, and children's bereavement, 85

public, media shaping attitudes of, 19–21

R

Rando's Six R's bereavement model, 70–72
    accommodation phase, 70–71
    avoidance phase, 70, 71
    complicated mourning, **70**
    confrontation phase, 70
    mourning process and re-experience, 72
    recollecting/re-experiencing the deceased, 71–72

regressed behaviour, 182

reincarnation, and Native Peoples, 36

religion(s) *see also* belief systems
    communities and meaning, 210–11
    and culture, and death attitudes, 16–17
    faith and death of a loved one, 211
    and pre-death rituals, 46

religious motivation
    extrinsic/intrinsic, and seniors, 119

Remembrance Day, 208

replacement child, 89–90

respite care, **171**

rites, *see also* end-of-life rituals
    of incorporation, or integration, 44–45
    of passage, 44–45
    of separation, 44
    of transition, 44

rituals, end-of life *see also* end-of-life rituals
    as rites of passage, 44

Roman Catholic Church *see also* Christianity
    and afterlife view, 27–28

Roman Catholic end-of-life rituals *see* Christian
    end-of-life rituals

Rossetti, Christina, and poem" Remember," 6–7

Rubin's bereavement model, 66–68
    depression symptoms and, 67
    and extreme stress, 67
    first track, 67
    memories and, re deceased, 67
    second track, 67
    SIDS children and, 67
    and sudden/violent death, 67–68
    summary of 77
    as a task theory, 76, 77

S

Sander's integrative model of bereavement
    healing phase, 66
    renewal phase, 66
    as stage/phase theory, 76, 77
    withdrawal phase, 66

self-efficacy, 125

senior adults (seniors)
    anxiety/fear re death, and illness, 118
    attitudes about death, 117–19
    baby boomers, 117
    as bereaved parents, 126–27
    bereaved spouses, 124–26
    bereavement of, re family/friends, 127–28
    bereavement and depression, 127
    bereavement and health decline, 127–28
    burden of family/independence issues, 122
    bereavement and loneliness, 127–28
    and cultural diversity, 118
    and death, 117–128
    death anxiety, 118, 120
    depression, 117
    dying process issues and, 121–23
    ego integrity, death views, 118
    end-of-life needs/wishes, 119–23
    European acute care centres and, 123
    fear and gender issues, 119
    gender differences re spousal loss, 125–26
    gender and health issues, 125
    and the "good death,"119–20
    and good health care/dying, 121–22
    grief and spousal death, 124
    helping bereaved, 188
    helping widows/widowers, 118
    idealization of lost child, 127
    independence and, 122
    intrinsic/extrinsic religious motivation and, 119
    Inuit ice floe myth re death of, 123
    and living, 121
    locus of control and, **122**–23
    loneliness and spousal death, 125
    major changes and spousal death, 124–25
    medical intervention and, 122
    personal characteristics and dying and, 122
    prolongation of life and, 122
    quality of life, and, 122, 125
    religiosity and role re death, 119
    role of perceptions and, 118
    self-transcendence and anxiety re death, 119
    spousal death and self-efficacy, 125
    stoicism and spousal death, 126
    Statistics Canada and demographics re, 117
    suicide and, 138, 140–42, 144
    thinking flexibility, 117

separation anxiety, and infant loss of parent, **86**
Seventh Day Adventists, afterlife views, 28
shivah, 47
sibling, death of,
    and adolescent sense of identity, 90–91
    adult reaction to, 106–107
    children's reactions, 89–91
    and senior's reactions, 106
SIDS death *see* sudden infant death syndrome
Sikh end-of-life ritual, 51
    cremation and body preparation, 51
    prayers and funeral, 51
    mourning, 51
Sikhism
    afterlife views, 34
    beliefs, 33–34
    Five Evils and, 33
    Five K's of, 34
    Heaven/Hell views, 34
    karma, and reincarnation, 34
    kirpan, 34
    mourning, 34
    and Nanak, 34
social integration, **134**
society(ies)
    and bereaved and terminally ill, 196
    and grieving style, 160–61
    rites of passage and, 44
Solzhenitsyn, Alexander, and *Cancer Ward*, 7
soul *see also* afterlife
    Bahá'í, 34–35
    Buddhism, karma, 33
    Christian, 28
    Hinduism, 30–31
    Inuit and, 36
    Islam and, 29–30
    Judaic, 27
    Sikh afterlife, 34
Spirit house, 36
Spouse/life partner, death of, 102–104, 124–26
    family consequences, 102–103
    health problems of survivor, 103
    and stress of survivor, 102
    and survivor's loneliness, 104
    seniors and, 124–26
stillbirth, 107
    adult reaction to, 107
    mothers and, 107
storytelling
    catharsis, **206**
    re memories, function of, 206
    role of in meaning, 205–206
stress
    bereaved, re homicide victims, 152–54
    caregiver-, 172–77
    and death of a child, 100
    and end-of-life care, personnel/nurses and, 174–77
    on family as caregiver, 172–74
    and suicide, 134

Stroebe's bereavement model, 73–75
    dual process model, 74–75, 77
    and familial discord, 75
    grief work and, 73, 74
    loss orientation and, 74
    mourners and coping and, 74–75
    restoration-orientation and, 74–75
sudden death *see* death
sudden infant death syndrome (SIDS)
    and bereavement, 67
    and mourning issues, 209–210
suicide
    adolescent risk factors, 137–40
    age and, 138
    alcohol/drug abuse and, 134
    altruistic, **134**
    anomic, **135**
    and attitudes, 136–37
    behavioural indicators, 134
    Canadian rates, 133
    Canadian vs. American attitudes, 136–37
    causes, 133–34
    children/adolescent, 139–40
    cognitive factors, 134
    copycat, 140
    defined, **132**
    demographics of, 132–33
    Durkheim model of, 135–36
    egoistic, **134**
    emotional pain/loss and, 138
    fatalistic, **135**
    and gender, attitudes, 138
    and gender, rates, 133
    global rates, 133
    gun control and, 144
    incurable illness and, 138
    Indigenous peoples, dislocation and, 142
    individuals preventing, 145
    Joiner's trajectory factor and, 135–36
    "karoshi" and work groups, Japan, 135
    models of, 134
    music effects, 136
    Native Peoples and, 142
    Native Peoples, Canadian vs international rates, 142–43
    Native Peoples and Davis Inlet, 142
    -notes, 141
    in older adults, 140–42
    older adults and Western society, 141–42
    perception and manipulative behaviour, 139
    personality/psychological factors, 133–34
    persons affected by, 133
    perturbation and, 135
    and physical illness, 134
    physician-assisted-, 225–28
    postvention, 143–44
    risk factors, 133–34
    and sexual/physical abuse, 134
    Shneidman cubic model of, 135
    social institutions and, 135

NAME INDEX

Abengózar, M.C., 117
Adler, N.E., 107
Althcide, D., 21
Altmaier, E.M., 95
Ariès, Philippe, 3–7, 14
Aseltine, R.H., Jr., 143
Aubin, M., 171
Auger, J.A., 8
Austin, A.E., 104
Ayers, T.S., 93

Baker, J., 91, 95
Balk, D.E., 86
Beautrais, A.L., 136, 138
Beck, M.G., 52
Bennett, K. M., 125, 126, 174
Berman, D., 83
Beutal, M., 108
Block, S.D., 171
Bluebond-Langner, M., 95
Bond, J.B., Jr., 81
Bopp, J., 45
Bosticco, C., 204, 206
Bowlby, J., 63–64, 92, 155
Bowman, T., 206
Brant, J.M., 88
Braun, K.L., 38
Brazil, K., 171
Brent, S.B., 82, 140, 144
Brier, N., 108
Brooten, D., 37
Brown, J.E., 52
Brown, L., 45
Brown, Nicole, 153
Bryan, Reba, 163
Bucholz, J.A., 151, 152, 160
Bunyan, John, 5
Burge, M., 136
Burger, J. M., 123
Burgoyne, M., 86, 87
Busch, T., 87, 183, 184
Buxbaum, L., 88

Cameron, M.E., 119
Canetto, S.S., 141
Capron, A.M., 218
Carlson, B., 227
Carmody, D.L., 50
Carmody, J.T., 50
Carr, D., 125
Cartwright, Richard, 109, 111
Chandler, M.J., 142, 144
Chao, C.C., 49
Charlton, R., 124, 188
Chodron, Pema, 33

Christ, G., 82, 85, 184
Chung, L., 49
Cicirelli, V., 119, 122, 123
Clarke, J.N., 20
Cleiren, M., 106
Cobain, Kurt, 141
Cohen, L., 174, 223
Cohn, F.G., 93
Cole, D.J., 217
Commons, D.L., 117, 119
Comstock, G., 19
Conklin, B.A., 37
Corr, C.A., 19, 159
Costello, J., 124
Cramer, 103
Curtis, D., 196

Dagi, T.F., 218
Dahlen, E.R., 136, 138
Davies, B., 92
Davies, D.J., 3
Davis, C.G., 205, 210, 211
Davison, G.C., 151, 188
Decker, I.M., 122
de la Rocha, Dr. Alberto, 224
De Leo, D., 132, 142
Deloria, V., Jr., 35, 142
Denton, F.T., 117
DePaola, S.J., 14, 117
De Sousa, Anastasia, 1

DeSpelder, L.A., 18, 139, 145
Dickinson, G.E., 81
Ditto, P.H., 122, 195
Doka, K.J., 21, 159
Domino, G., 136, 138
Dowdney, L., 92
Downs, Barney, 206
Dumont, S., 174
Durkheim, Emile, 134, 135

Eastman, A.M., 6
Eaves, Y.D., 106
Elliott, M.P., 95
Emke, I., 46, 53, 54
Ens, C., 81
Erdoes, R., 3
Erikson, E., 92
Evans, W.G., 171
Evans-Pritchard, E.E., 37
Eyetsemitan, F., 21. 22

Faulkner, K.W., 95, 192
Foley, K.M., 233
Forrest, L.M., 104

Fortner, B.V., 118, 119
Frager, G., 93
Frankl, V., 201–202
Frantz, T., 37, 205
Frazer, Sir James, 2
Freeman, K., 95
Freke, T., 35
Fried, T.R., 164, 175
Froggat, K., 44
Fry, P.S., 124, 125, 188
Furth, G.M., 95

Gamino, L.A., 75
Geis, H., 86
Gill, Kimveer, 1
Gillick, M.R., 233, 234
Glaubman, H., 83
Gold, D.T., 106
Goldman, Ron, 153
Goss, R., 33, 65
Gould, M.S., 140
Grabowsky, J.A., 37
Granqvist, A., 83
Grimes, R.L., 45
Gross, Y., 83, 91
Grosswald, B., 226
Grunfeld, E., 174
Guest, C.B., 219
Gupta, R., 38

Hadad, M., 37, 212
Haffey, Karen, 233
Hames, C.C., 85, 87, 182
Hamrin, V., 87
Hanks, G., 227
Hanratty, B., 175
Harding, S.R., 14
Harper, Lynne, 153
Hatton, R., 152, 153, 154
Hayden, D.D., 143
Hays, J.C., 106
Hemingway, Ernest, 5, 131
Hertz, R., 44
Himelstein, B.P., 171
Himmelstein, Bruce, 167, 171
Hinds, P.S., 95
Hinton, J., 111
Hirschfelder, A., 36
Ho, T.P., 141
Holland, J., 94
Hsu, M., 107
Hughes, P., 107
Hunter, E., 142
Hwang, S.W., 234